THE ENGLISH-LANGUAGE PRESS
NETWORKS OF EAST ASIA, 1918–1945

THE ENGLISH-LANGUAGE PRESS NETWORKS OF EAST ASIA, 1918–1945

PETER O'CONNOR
Musashino University

GLOBAL
ORIENTAL

THE ENGLISH-LANGUAGE PRESS NETWORKS
OF EAST ASIA, 1918–1945

First published 2010 by
GLOBAL ORIENTAL
PO Box 219
Folkestone
Kent CT20 2WP
UK

www.globaloriental.co.uk

Global Oriental is an imprint of Koninklijke Brill NV, Leiden,
The Netherlands.
Koninklijke Brill NV incorporates the imprints BRILL, Global Oriental,
Hotei Publishing, IDC Publishers, Martinus Nijhoff Publishers, and VSP.

© Peter O'Connor 2010

ISBN   978-1-905246-67-0

British Library Cataloguing in Publication Data
A CIP catalogue entry for this book is available
from the British Library

Set in Stone Serif 9.0 on 10.5 by Mark Heslington, Scarborough, North Yorkshire
Printed and bound in England by CPI Antony Rowe, Chippenham, Wilts.

Contents

Plate section facing page 174

Acknowledgements

This study has benefited enormously from the interest and encouragement of friends and colleagues, especially Aaron Cohen, Okuyama Yasuharu, John Oliphant, Adrian Pinnington, Graham Law and Gaye Rowley. To them and to Nori Morita, Ric Powell, James Raeside and all the members of the NoCoTs reading group at Waseda University I am most grateful for the companionship and learning that have informed this study and helped keep it going. At Musashino University, Saitō Eiri gave unstinting advice and wisdom, Kyotani Miyuki provided considerable technical assistance, and our librarian Niii Kumiko supplied me with essential materials at record speed.

Among media historians, the late Uchikawa Yoshimi of Tokyo University, Kakegawa Tomiko, now retired from Kansai University, Ōsaka, the indefatigable Ariyama Teruo of Tokyo Keizai University, Matsumura Masayoshi of Keio and Teikyo Universities, Barak Kushner of Cambridge University, and, again, Graham Law, have all provided invaluable help and advice. The pointed questioning and criticism of Hayashi Tomohiko has sharpened and illuminated my approach. I am particularly grateful to Barak Kushner, Hamish Ion, Joseph Cronin and Hugh Cortazzi for giving detailed critical attention to this manuscript.

Outside Japan, this book owes more to Albert A. Altman, retired from the Hebrew University of Jerusalem, Jim Huffman, now retired from Wittenberg University, Robert Angel, now retired from the University of North Carolina, Ian Nish of STICERD, LSE, Ayako Hotta-Lister and Richard Arthur than I can account for here. Late in the course of this study, Richard Benefer of Staffordshire University, scholar of the history of the idea of 'the war to end war', became a serendipitous source of information.

I am especially grateful to Jim Hoare for allowing me to use and adapt the chronological tables of the English-language press of Japan from his landmark study of Japan's Treaty Ports (Hoare 1994: 181–8).

Pure luck brought me into contact with relatives of two of the people under study: Deborah Takahashi, paternal grand-daughter of the journalist George Gorman, and Sue Larkin, great-grand-daughter of Robert Young, founding editor of the *Japan Chronicle*. Both shared their research with me and came up with the sort of understandings that can only be bred in the bone. A former *Japan Chronicle* reporter, the late Theodore Van Doorn, generously shared with me his recollections of the times and the lives discussed here and offered invaluable insights.

In the last months of this project, Dr. Lizzie Falvey of Emmanuel College, Boston, provided considerable assistance both in the preparation of this manuscript and in evaluating the surveys in my concluding chapter.

My greatest intellectual debt has been to Richard Sims, who accepted me as a research student at SOAS, University of London, and saw me through the thesis that became the basis of this book. Paul Norbury has been equally steadfast in holding to his commitment to publish in the face of numerous delays and reconsiderations.

This account was written, in Seamus Heaney's phrase, 'between the day job and the night feed'. Without the sustained encouragement of my wife, Hideko, and the cheerful indifference of my children, Emi and Nao, it would not have been finished. I dedicate it to them with love and gratitude.

Graiguenagreana, Blackwater, Co. Kerry
September 2009

Notes on Conventions

TITLES, ABBREVIATIONS, ITALICIZATION, ROMANIZATION

Titles of newspapers are given in full in the main text, and as abbreviations in footnotes and in notes to the tables in the Appendices. INS, UP and AP are often used for the news agencies International News Service, United Press and Associated Press in the main text, as these abbreviations were in common use at the time. The titles of the newspapers and periodicals least frequently cited in this study are given in full both in the main text and in footnotes. Apart from *The Times* and the *Manchester Guardian*, the most frequently cited newspaper titles are abbreviated in endnotes as follows:

China Press: CP
China Weekly Review: CWR
Christian Science Monitor: CSM
Far Eastern Review: FER
Japan Advertiser: JA
Japan Chronicle: JC
Japan News-Week: JN-W
Japan Times: JT
Japan Times & Advertiser: JT&A
*Japan Times & Advertiser Incorporating The Japan Chronicle and The
    Japan Mail*: JT&AJCJM (this abbreviation is also used in the main
    text)
Nippon Times: NT
Manchuria Daily News: MDN
New York Times: NYT
North-China Daily News: NCDN
North-China Herald: NCH
Peking & Tientsin Times: P&TT
Seoul Press: SP
Shanghai Evening Post and Mercury: SEPM
Wall Street Journal: WSJ
Washington Post: WP

ABBREVIATIONS FOR OFFICIAL INSTITUTIONS

CCP: Chinese Communist Party
FO: Foreign Office, London

FM: Ministry of Foreign Affairs (*Gaimushō*)
SMR: South Manchurian Railway (*Minami Manshū Tetsudō Kabushiki-gaisha*)
USDS: United States Department of State

ITALICIZATION AND TITLES

All newspaper titles are given in italics. The definite article that comes before the titles of both Western newspapers and the English-language newspapers of East Asia is not italicized: i.e. 'the *Manchester Guardian'*, 'the *Japan Times'*, with the exception of *The Times* of London. The titles of all vernacular Japanese and Chinese newspapers are italicized, for example, *Nihon oyobi Nihonjin*, and macrons used where necessary, i.e. *Chūgai Shōgyō*. I have not used macrons for Japanese words, usually place names, in the titles of English-language newspapers as macrons were not used in the original title as it appeared in English on the masthead. Thus: *Kobe Herald*, not *Kōbe Herald*. The title of Japanese and Chinese news agencies is italicized when the full title is given, e.g. *Shadanhōjin Dōmei Tsūshinsha*, *Kokusai Tsūshinsha*, and when it is given in the abbreviated form that is commonly used thereafter, for example: *Dōmei*, *Kokusai*. The Japanese title of an organization is usually given in italics in brackets following the English title, e.g. Cabinet Information Committee (*Naikaku Jōhōiinkai*), unless the organization is best known by its Japanese title, for example: *Shōwa Kenkyū Kai* (Shōwa Research Group). To avoid repetition, once given, this bilingual approach has not been repeated.

ROMANIZATION OF CHINESE NAMES AND PLACE NAMES

Romanization of Chinese names and places follows the Wade-Giles usage of the day for Chiang Kai-shek (pinyin Jiang Jieshi), Eugene Chen (Chen Jouren), Wellington Koo (Gu Weizhun), T.V. Soong (Song Ziwen) and Hollington Tong (Deng Chuankai). Otherwise, wherever I have been able to find the correct Romanisation, place names, names of people and newspapers are given in pinyin. The first use of Wade-Giles is followed by the pinyin Romanisation in brackets and the first use of pinyin by the Wade-Giles Romanisation in brackets.

ROMANIZATION OF JAPANESE NAMES AND PLACE NAMES

I have followed the convention with Japanese names of giving the family name first, given name second, as in Yamagata Aritomo. However, although they do not follow standard conventions, the Romanization of their own name favoured by some Japanese writers and contributors to the English-language press has been respected here, for example: Honda Masujiroh, Henry Satoh, Yamagata Isoh. Because he worked so publicly in English-language media and perhaps developed a taste for 'international' mannerisms, the name of the *Japan Times* editor Gō Toshi was consistently given in the Western order in English-language material and he is Toshi Gō throughout this account.

Foreword

Scholars, diplomats and journalists with an adequate knowledge of the vernacular are generally scornful of the English-language press in foreign countries. They think that the English-language papers with their small circulations and limited resources cater only for the expatriate community and are hardly worth bothering about. As Peter O'Connor's book shows, this view is certainly wrong in the case of the English-language press in East Asia in 1918–45. The number of foreigners capable of reading Japanese and Chinese in the years covered in this book was very small. As a result the foreign community had to rely on the English-language press for information on Japan and in China. Articles in the English-language press were also read in capitals around the world. In London and Washington, where officials received despatches from British and American missions in East Asia, these reports were compared with those of the vernacular press and with other information.

English-language newspapers appeared in Japan before there were any significant Japanese newspapers. As early as the 1880s, the Japanese government recognized the importance of the foreign press as a means of ensuring that the Japanese case for revision of 'the unequal treaties' was duly heard. They accordingly cultivated and subsidised foreign journalists such as Edward H. House of the *Tokio Times* and Frank Brinkley of the *Japan Mail*, who also became Japan correspondent of *The Times*.

O'Connor divides the English-language press of East Asia into three main groups. One group can be described as promoting the Japanese point of view, another as more or less reflecting American interests and a third as closer to British interests. But there was considerable fluidity in these groupings and his account extends to a fourth group run by the Chinese Nationalists.

Recognizing their cultural and linguistic limitations in getting their views across in international forums, the Japanese employed foreign journalists up to the outbreak of war in 1941. These experts were not traitors or Quislings. The greatest challenges for them and their employers were, of course, the facts of Japanese aggression in Manchuria and China. Their task was also complicated by statements emanating from their own leaders in government.

As O'Connor points out, the Japanese did not have a master plan to win foreign acceptance for their aims in China and Manchuria. Competing groups among the elites often produced contradictory propaganda. However, with the establishment of an Information Bureau in the Ministry of Foreign Affairs in 1921 Japanese news management and propaganda became systematic and polished.

The most difficult question that O'Connor tries to answer is the extent to which the press networks gained access to and thereby influenced public opinion and foreign policies in the United States and Britain. Undoubtedly public opinion was swayed by press reports but it was not so much what the various papers wrote as what was happening in China that counted. No amount of exculpatory comment could cover up the reality.

Did the Japanese come to believe their own propaganda? Did propaganda come to dictate Japanese or US foreign policy? O'Connor draws attention to some provocative articles which were carried in the *Japan Times & Advertiser* in October and November 1941 and argues that these articles may have been a contributory factor to the outbreak of war.

Unlike their counterparts in Whitehall, to whom such understandings came tragically late, succeeding Japanese governments recognized and utilised the power of the English-language press throughout the first half of the twentieth century. Peter O'Connor's study fills an important gap in the international history of East Asia in these years and refreshes our understanding of Japanese efforts to be better understood and liked abroad.

Sir Hugh Cortazzi
British Ambassador to Japan, 1980–84

List of Figures

List of Plates

The opinions of individuals are not necessarily direct functions of the information they receive.

Ernest May, 1973

Introduction

This book argues that the English-language press of East Asia played a significant role in the shaping of international perceptions of Japan and East Asia and that this role can only be fully understood if it is realized that there existed within the East Asian media world three informal networks of the English-language press and that a similar editorial line was generally taken by those newspapers, magazines and news agencies that belonged to each network.

These three networks I have termed the Foreign Ministry network, the *Japan Advertiser* network and the *Japan Chronicle* network. The newspapers at the centre of these three networks were the *Japan Times*, the *Japan Advertiser* and the *Japan Chronicle*, each based in Japan but with a variety of connections to opinion leaders and official bodies in China, Britain and the United States. These three newspapers, their affiliated media institutions in East Asia, the US and UK and the local and international reports and other writings of their staff, stand at the core of this account.

Although the *Japan Times* was the flagship of Japan's semi-official press network in East Asia, which I refer to as the Foreign Ministry network, this network is the only one of the three discussed here to be named after an official institution rather than the newspaper which most consistently represented it. With senior management drawn from a series of Foreign Ministry bureaucrats and political figures with media experience or interests, the *Japan Times* did not have to go to the Foreign Ministry for detailed copy approval, but the Ministry nevertheless guided the editorial line of the *Japan Times*, as it guided the rest of the Foreign Ministry media network.

The purpose of the Foreign Ministry network was to make Japan better understood and to have it held in greater respect by the English-speaking world. To this end it nurtured personal links with media institutions in the US and set up its own press bureaux and journalists there. In East Asia the Foreign Ministry network set up newspapers and news agencies or rearranged the management of existing institutions in order to promote a more favourable understanding of Japan. It arranged tours of East Asia by sympathetic Western observers who published articles and sometimes books describing their experiences in positive terms. The Foreign Ministry network also contracted with individual Western and Japanese journalists to present and explain Japan in the Foreign Ministry network media in East Asia and in otherwise independent newspapers based in the West. Some of the Western journalists who promoted the case for Japan in the English-language newspapers of East Asia and in the West were entrusted with the task of acting as spokesmen and publicists for Japan on the sidelines of international conferences: in Paris in 1919, in Washington in 1921–22, and at the League of Nations in Geneva in 1931–33, where some also helped present the case for the state of Manchukuo.

The second network, the *Japan Advertiser* network, resembled the Foreign Ministry network in consisting of a group of media institutions and media professionals in East Asia with strong links to the US media. Like the Foreign Ministry network, it enjoyed access to State officials and US consuls and ministers in East Asia of the American equivalent, the United States Department of State. And yet, despite these links, the *Japan Advertiser* network was the result of private, not official US initiatives. Thus, the *Japan Advertiser* network has been named after a Tokyo-based newspaper which, while it did not lead this network throughout the period under study, was one of its most durable participants and its most consistently managed representative, although its version of the editorial line expressed by the other organs in its network was comparatively mild. The *Japan Advertiser's* owner from 1908 to 1940, B.W. Fleisher, also had a commercial interest in key organs in the network. Thus the name *Japan Advertiser* network was chosen because it was the most consistently representative of the organs in the *Japan Advertiser* network.

The *Japan Advertiser* network might have been called the *China Weekly Review* network, as that journal came a close second to the *Advertiser* in terms of consistency of editorial line and ownership, had not the *China Weekly Review*, which was based in Shanghai, been less focused on Japan as such, and more on Japan in relation to events in China. Both publications overlapped in terms of ownership, interests, editorial line and access to official interests in Washington, but the *China Weekly Review* had no access to official or business interests in Tokyo, while the *Japan Advertiser* was a Tokyo newspaper with access to supportive connections there, in the US and, indirectly, in China.

For similar reasons, the third network, the *Japan Chronicle* network, has been named after the British-owned newspaper, based in Kōbe, which most consistently represented its line on Japan. Like the Foreign Ministry and *Japan Advertiser* networks, the *Japan Chronicle* network consisted of a group of media institutions and media professionals in Japan and China linked by editorial line, as well as the nationality of its ownership.

Again, like the *Japan Advertiser* network, the *Japan Chronicle* network might have been given another name, in this case the *North-China Daily News* network. The *North-China Daily News* was the leading British-owned newspaper in China and sometimes had more in common with the other key organs in the *Chronicle's* network in China, the *Peking & Tientsin Times* and the *Central China Post*, than did the *Japan Chronicle*.

The *North-China Daily News* may also have been closer, through a lengthy association with officials in Whitehall and a series of China correspondents for national newspapers in Britain, to some institutions in another, broader network, the news system of what has become known as the 'British world' (see below). It was also a more conservative paper than the *Chronicle*, which espoused liberal and sometimes socialist principles, celebrated the Russian Revolution of 1917, and seldom beat the drum for the British or any other empire or any wars waged on its behalf. Thus within the *Japan Chronicle* network there were undeniable differences of outlook between the two most important newspapers in the network, but as shown in Chapter 3, these were gaps that would narrow in the 1930s. The *Japan Chronicle* network of British-owned media in China and Japan has been so named not only because the *Chronicle* was based in Japan, but because it, rather than the *North-China Daily News*, most consistently and clearly represented the network's overall editorial line on Japan, rather than on Japan in relation to China, and seems therefore to best exemplify this network's role in shaping international perceptions of Japan.

All three networks had commonalities and distinctions. The *Chronicle* itself was not geographically or socially close to the *Japan Advertiser* in Japan, although the editors Morgan Young and Hugh Byas were on good terms. In China, some members of the *Chronicle* network saw some members of the *Advertiser* network there as competitors and undermined them commercially. Overall, the media institutions and journalists in the *Japan Advertiser* network and those in the *Japan Chronicle* network were wary of those in the Foreign Ministry network.

The chapters that follow, by examining official comments made in East Asia, Whitehall and Washington on these newspapers and their reports, attempt to demonstrate that these newspapers occupied some intellectual space in the deliberations that contributed to the shaping of international official perceptions and, by extension, international policy on Japan. Although a small group of newspapers, most notably the *Japan Times*, consistently received more Western attention than the rest in the period under review, this book does not maintain that any one of the English-language newspapers of East Asia was the most consistent influence on international perceptions of Japan held by British or American readers or foreign policy-makers on East Asia. However, it does argue that the English-language press networks of East Asia as a whole were a factor in the formulation of international perceptions of Japan and East Asia. Discussing official sentiment and policy formation, I also show that the media in these networks were not ignored by officials concerned with foreign policy in Whitehall, Washington, Tokyo and the series of capitals housing the Nationalist government of China, although the editors and newspapers in the *Chronicle* network were often seen, in Whitehall as in Tokyo, Nanjing (Nanking) and Chongqing (Chungking), as a nuisance and a hindrance to diplomacy.

The importance of international perceptions in general and of international perceptions of Japan in particular, has certainly been acknowledged by historians. The work of Iriye Akira and Christopher Thorne has put understanding and accounting for the way people and governments perceive the people, the political conditions and the economic and military capacity of other nations among the first tasks of international history. In both the US and Japan, there is a demonstrable history of concern with national character and experience and consequently with the way each country has been seen by others, especially with the ways in which America and Japan perceived each other in the 1930s, when the direction of both nations' foreign policy was far from settled.

The historiography of the image approach indicates that the practice of accounting for international perceptions as just that, as little more than impressions backed by prejudice and information gaps, was less common until Harold Isaacs' groundbreaking study of images of China in the US, *Scratches on our Minds* (1958 [1965]). This was followed by Storry's short but sharp (1975) analysis, by Lehmann's (1978) study of images of Japan in Britain in the second half of the nineteenth century, and by Endymion Wilkinson's widely-read *Japan Versus the West* (1980), which became a best-seller in Japan and inspired further studies in the West, particularly in the US (Yokoyama 1987; Johnson 1988; Schodt 1994; Littlewood 1996; Hammond 1997; Henning 2000).

Some elements of the Image of Japan fit the paradigm of 'Orientalism', as developed by the writer and historian Edward Said. That is, 'the absolute and systematic difference between the West, which is rational, developed, humane, superior, and the Orient, which is aberrant, undeveloped, inferior'.[1] However, the distinctions are far from clear: in the West, Japan seems to fall between the status of radical Other to the West and sometimes as a sort of receptacle of the best and worst of both East and West. As an approach to a subject that often falls outside the lines of clear definition, the image approach often yields unsatisfactory results. This is reflected in some of the shorthand used for these images: Lotus Land, the Exotic, the Friend, and Aliens and Aesthetes for the early modern period; the Menace, or the Ghastly Menace, and the Foe, for the years c.1910–45; and the Post-War Phoenix, the Busy Bee, and the Model and Mirror here and there in the post-war years. Post-Bubble Japan seems to be more or less uncharted territory. In Chapter 9, while acknowledging that these images are indistinct, I refer to the images outlined by Storry (1975) and suggest another.

A central concern of this book is the role played by the English-language newspapers of East Asia in shaping perceptions of Japan and East Asia, primarily at the official level, but also in the fourth estate and among opinion leaders and ordinary citizens in the US and Britain, as well as among Anglophone settlers in East Asia during the period under study. Here the focus is on the English-language newspapers of East Asia, but the Western press and its correspondents in East Asia, as well as other English-language writings on Japan, are also discussed.

'Shaping perceptions' needs to be distinguished from 'influence' which, like 'public opinion', is a slippery factor in any history. On the whole, this study has taken a similar approach to that adopted by the American scholar Warren Cohen in qualifying his assessment of the role of press, business and diplomatic groups in the formulation of US policy on China, namely: 'My aim is not to measure the elusive quality of *influence* but rather to chart lines of access to decision-makers and to the public.'[2] This discussion of the networks of the English-language newspapers of East Asia has tried to assess their role in shaping international *perceptions*, as opposed to knowledge, of Japan. To this end, I have endeavoured to survey as broad a range of sources, case studies and issues as possible.

This study examines instances in which Japanese officials in the Foreign Ministry and elsewhere suspected the connivance of the English-language press networks of East Asia in press campaigns which reflected badly on Japan and its role in East Asia. It tries to show how and why the networks of the independent, English-language newspapers of East Asia appeared powerful and sometimes even overpowering to the managers of Japan's Foreign Ministry network, either as a result of these networks' shared assumptions and cultural codes or through the sheer quality of their writing. It therefore traces the development of Japanese responses, in Foreign Ministry reports and as reported in British and American diplomatic correspondence, to such challenges.

In attempting to provide a rounded picture of the struggle between the three networks, this study only touches on Japan's network of Chinese-language newspapers and on China's Chinese-language and Japanese-language propaganda counter-offensives. However, it does include some discussion of Nationalist China's involvement with the English-language press there, and with China newspapers in the *Advertiser* network, although I should acknowledge that the China case studies are more selectively representative than comprehensive.

READERSHIP AND CIRCULATION

Who read the English-language newspapers of East Asia? Obviously, their first audience was the settler communities that first gave rise to them in the treaty ports in the Meiji era, but there were others: readers who bought them as exercises in language learning or in the hope of discovering news and opinions that they might not find in the vernacular press.

The main papers were all scrutinized by officialdom in East Asia and the Western capitals, either by officials who might be curious about the interpretation of their doings by foreign observers or those who wished to keep an eye out for subversive thinking and critical commentary. We can see from the correspondence that most British and American consulates and embassies in China and Japan scanned both the local and further-flung English-language newspapers of East Asia. The US embassy in Tokyo had subscriptions to most of the English-language papers of Japan and China, as well as to the vernacular press which they had translated every day, as USDS correspondence and diaries like those of Joseph Grew, who was particularly sensitive to the effect of press commentary on Japan-US relations, attest.

In December 1930, officials at the British embassy in Tokyo and the Foreign Office considered cancelling the *Japan Chronicle* subscription following an embarrassing *Chronicle* report on a cheque-bouncing case involving the son of the ambassador, Sir John Tilley.[3] In 1935, when the Foreign Office suggested the subscription be cancelled and be replaced by monthly bulletins from the embassy, Tokyo argued against such a move on the grounds that the paper was essential reading as it was 'completely independent' and made 'no endeavour to keep in with the Japanese or with the British official view'.[4] Only in December 1940, following the *Chronicle*'s unexpected sale to the *Japan Times* did the British ambassador in Tokyo, Robert Craigie, successfully advocate cancelling both the embassy and the Foreign Office library subscriptions to it.[5] The question of cancelling the *Advertiser* subscription never even came up at the US embassy in Tokyo, where the Fleishers, father and son, were both neighbours and frequent visitors. As for the *Japan Times*, as the creation and often the voice of the Foreign Ministry network, its existence was too central to the expression of Foreign Ministry programmes and its administration too close to their formulation for it to be left out of the picture.

Circulation figures are hard to come by. All the English-language newspapers in Japan and China claimed large circulations in their advertising, but only the *Japan Times* published its figures, although these were inflated by subsidized purchases. In 1893, when the combined Anglophone populations of Yokohama, Tokyo, Kōbe and Nagasaki numbered around 2,000, a visitor maintained that 'probably no foreign paper in Japan has a circulation of more than 1,000'.[6] In 1916, the British journalist John Robertson-Scott, probably influenced by the need to promote his own plans for the *New East*, put the combined daily circulation of all the English-language papers published in Japan at 5,000, though he only gave figures for the *Japan Times* (500).[7]

There were seldom more than half-a-dozen going concerns at any one time in Japan, all of them with circulations small enough to be significantly affected by seasonal factors such as the number of foreign visitors. In 1926–7, Harry Wildes, the first Western scholar to research the English-language press of Japan, estimated that 'Perhaps in all Japan there are not more than 10,000 foreign inhabitants at the outer limit able to read an English periodical.'[8]

Compare these figures to one Chinese city, Shanghai, in the early 1920s, where the Anglophone population was between 8,000–10,000, and where the *China Weekly Review* inherited its predecessor's circulation of around 4,000 to 5,000 weekly, not including a growing subscription base in the US and Britain. The *Review* also had readers in the outports, and was read and studied by Chinese in Shanghai and elsewhere.[9] Again in Shanghai, by 1937 the *China Press* had a healthy circulation of around 5,000 copies on weekdays and 8,000 on Saturdays, of which about 60% of the readership were Chinese, a record for English-language papers in China.[10] As the city's only evening daily in Shanghai, the newly amalgamated *Shanghai Evening Post and Mercury* saw its circulation grow from 4,800 in 1931 to over 7,000 in 1938, giving it over 23% of the total English-language newspaper sales in Shanghai and 10% of the total in China, and putting it about 3,000 copies behind the *North-China Daily News*, the acknowledged leader of China's English-language press in 1931, with a total daily circulation that February of 7,817. This leadership was not just a matter of circulation figures but of geographical reach: of those 7,817 copies, 6,663 were sold in Shanghai, 1,154 elsewhere in the 'outports' and elsewhere in China.[11]

Regarding circulation among Japanese readers, although in 1916 Robertson-Scott was convinced that none but Anglophone readers took the English-language papers in Japan,[12] the editor of the *Japan Times* told Wildes in 1925 that 75% of his subscribers were Japanese, while the editor of the English-language edition of the *Ōsaka Mainichi shinbun* put his Japanese readership at 50%.[13] In the late 1930s, Joseph Grew, who was on close terms with its proprietor and his editor, reported that the *Advertiser* had a daily circulation of 4,000, of whom 60% were Japanese readers.[14] In the spring of 1925, Wildes asked the 'rival editors' of all the main English-language newspapers in Japan, Korea and Manchuria, and 'other informants' for the circulation figures of these organs and compiled this table:[15]

Osaka Mainichi	26,000
Tokyo Nichi-nichi	20,000
Japan Times	6,300
Japan Chronicle	3,000
Seoul Press	1,000
Japan Advertiser	10,000
Kobe Herald, Nagasaki Press, Manchuria Daily News	3,000

If we discount the *Seoul Press* and take Wildes's informants at their word, in 1925 the combined circulations of the three Japan-based newspapers at the centre of this study, the *Japan Times, Japan Chronicle* and *Japan Advertiser*, would have come to between 19,300 and 10,900. This is a considerable variation, and Wildes's more conservative estimate of 10,000 readers (above) was probably closer to the truth. By the late 1930s, if Grew's circulation figures for the *Japan Advertiser* can be trusted and the figures for the *Japan Times* and *Japan Chronicle* remained about the same (which seems unlikely) the variation for the three newspapers' combined circulation is smaller and seems more reliable at between roughly 13,300 and roughly 10,900.

There was stiff competition between the *Japan Times*, the *Japan Advertiser* and the *Japan Chronicle*, but the semi-official nature of the

Japan Times, as with the other organs in the Foreign Ministry network, gained it subsidies through official subscriptions that the foreign-owned English-language newspapers could not match. Competition for readers between the *Advertiser* and *Chronicle* was to some extent blunted by simple geography: with their locations in Tokyo and Kōbe separated by a twelve-hour train journey, Kōbe readers tended to subscribe to the *Chronicle* as the earliest source of morning news, while, for the same reason, the real competition in Tokyo was between the *Japan Times* and the *Advertiser*.

In a period lasting over two decades, the situation and reputation of all three papers changed as their readers and their opinions changed. Like influence, public opinion is another slippery quantity that demands acknowledgement and discussion but defies measurement – at least in the years before widespread market research and opinion polls. As indicators of public opinion, the circulation figures of these newspapers should tell us a great deal about their readership; however, subsidies, uneven distribution, and the unwillingness of their management to give accurate figures mean that they cannot provide a basis for reliable judgements.

Before and during the period under study, the rise of the mass media and the proportionate increase in the coverage of international issues led to the rise of that intrepid figure, the foreign correspondent, in the popular imagination. British journalists would be sent to hotspots in Europe, and American journalists to South America and Cuba. In points further afield that were seen to merit attention, such as Tokyo, Peking and Shanghai, a bureau might be opened and a correspondent sent out to man it or, more often, a journalist on one of the local English-language newspapers would be appointed, either as a 'stringer' or as a fully-accredited correspondent.

Both the full-time foreign correspondents and the local stringer would gain for the newspaper the cachet of having a 'man on the spot'. Gradually, Western newspaper readers may have come to regard the journalistic credentials of the 'man on the spot' as superior to those of the man (and they were invariably men) who stayed in the metropolis. Having a journalist on the spot seems to have become a sign of authenticity and reliability. This in itself constituted a trend in public opinion that is relevant to the reputation of the English-language press networks of East Asia and it is therefore examined in more detail in Chapter 2.

CONCEPT AND HISTORIOGRAPHY

To date, no historical scholarship has focused on the history of the English-language press in East Asia as a whole, although limited runs of the English-language newspapers of Japan, China and Korea have long been available to researchers. A particularly useful contemporary guide in English to China's English-language press has been Thomas Ming-Heng Chao's *The Foreign Press in China* (Shanghai, 1931). For background, Frank King and Prescott Clarke's *Research Guide to China-*

coast Newspapers 1822–1911 gives an essential overview of the early
modern field (King and Clarke 1965). C.S. Chong's Ph.D. dissertation on
Ernest Bethell's *Korea Daily News* provides valuable evidence of Anglo-
Japanese cooperation in gagging independent English-language and
Korean-language newspapers in 1900–10 (Chong 1987).
    A number of scholars have worked on the English-language press of
Japan, though the only book-length history of the English-language
newspapers published in Japanese remains Ebihara Hachirō's *Nihon ōji
shinbun zasshi shi* (History of Western-Language Newspapers and
Magazines in Japan) (1934).[16] Other Japanese scholars, notably
Uchikawa Yoshimi, Kakegawa Tomiko and Haruhara Akihiko, have
referred to the English-language newspapers in other historical contexts
in Japanese (Uchikawa 1967; Kakegawa 1983; Haruhara 1985). More
recent studies by Japanese media historians have included articles on
aspects of the foreign papers in English (Fujita 1991; Haruhara 1994;
Kakegawa 2001).
    Western scholarship on the English-language newspapers of Japan
began with Harry Emerson Wildes's landmark *Social Currents in Japan*
(1927). Wildes's scholarship is erratic but his book has been a rich source
for this study. Robert M. Spaulding's unpublished *Bibliography of
Western-language Dailies and Weeklies in Japan, 1861–1961* provided a
rough chronology of English-language newspapers published in Japan
(Spaulding 1961). The Finnish scholar Olavi Fält has used editions of the
Japan Times and *Osaka Mainichi* for an analysis of nationalism in the
1930s (Fält 1985), and of a broader range of English-language newspapers for a study of the impact on Japan of Western influences in the
treaty ports in the Meiji era (Fält 1990). The American scholar of the
Meiji press, James Huffman, published a thoughtful account of the life
and work of the American journalist E.H. House (1836–1901), editor of
the *Tokio Times* in the 1880s, and compiled and introduced a collection
of his writings (Huffman 2003, 2004). James Hoare surveyed the history
of the English-language newspapers of Japan in the context of Japan's
treaty ports (Hoare 1994).
    Three more recent studies (Young 1998; Matsusaka 2001; Wilson
2002) have combined analysis of domestic trends within Japan with the
history of the 1931–33 crisis and the establishment of Manchukuo,
breaking away, first, from a tendency in Western scholarship to see the
Manchurian crisis more as a consequence of international tensions in
China than as an extension of domestic political developments in Japan
and China, and, secondly, from a general tendency to utilize a narrow
range of vernacular newspaper sources that usually includes the *Yomiuri
Shinbun* and the *Asahi Shinbun*, but overlooks equally valuable provincial organs. Wilson (2002) not only draws extensively on Japanese-
language newspaper archives, but also cites 1930s articles in the *Japan
Chronicle*, *Mainichi Daily News* and *Trans-Pacific* and examines some of
the presentations of Japan's case in China published by the Japan Times
Press.

Of the newspapers under study, only the *Japan Times* has published its own histories. Of these, the *Jyapan Taimuzu Shōshi* (*Short History of the Japan Times*) (Okamura, ed., 1941) is less than candid in its discussion of events close to the experience of one of the founders of the *Japan Times*, Zumoto Motosada. The bilingual *Jyapan Taimuzu monogatari: bunkyū gan'nen kara gendai made / The Japan Times Story: from 1861 to the present* (Hasegawa, ed., 1966), presents a partial version of events. *The Japan Times: Front Page 1897–1997* (1997), offers a selective range of reproductions of front pages. The press magnate Hanazono Kanesada's two English-language histories, *The Development of Japanese Journalism* (1924) and *Journalism in Japan and its early Pioneers* (1926) provide useful information on the early English-language newspapers but tend to concentrate on the history of the *Ōsaka Asahi Shinbun*, with a surprisingly frank account of the watershed 'White Rainbow' Incident (*hakkō jiken*) of 1918 (Hanazono 1924, 1926). The *Kodansha Encyclopaedia of Japan* (1999) retrospectively upgrades the significance of the *Japan Times* at the expense of Japan's other English-language newspapers, an error neither Kodansha nor the *Japan Times* has hastened to correct. Louis Frédéric's *Japan Encyclopedia* (2002) not only describes the pre-war *Japan Times* as 'pro-government' but also gives an account of its takeover of the *Japan Chronicle* and the *Japan Advertiser* in 1940.[17]

A number of scholars have referred to the English-language press of East Asia in the course of studies focused on broader topics. Until the 1970s and 1980s, where historians of Japan and the international history of East Asia made use of contemporary newspapers, they most often cited reports in British or American newspapers filed by correspondents or news agencies operating in East Asia (Bassett 1952; Nish 1966, 1972; Lowe 1977; Thorne 1978, 1985). However Thorne (1985) also draws on a broad selection of reports from the press of Australia, France, India, and the Netherlands and even cites an English-language newspaper dating from the Japanese occupation of Singapore, the *Syonan Shimbun*.[18]

Since the 1980s, scholarship on East Asian history has increasingly cited newspapers published in the nations under study, with an emphasis on vernacular Japanese, Chinese or Korean newspapers rather than, as in this study, the English-language newspapers. Those making the greatest use of the vernacular press have tended to be media historians (Huffman 1980, 1997; Mitchell 1983; Kasza 1988; Hung 1994; Mittler 2004; Goodman 2004; Kushner 2006), or scholars of Japan's cultural or intellectual history (Gluck 1985; Sato 2003; Wilson 2002). Scholars writing the international history of East Asia with an eye on Japan's imperial project in East Asia (Beasley 1987; Best 1995, 2002) have made less use of newspaper archives. However, in her account of Japan's campaign for racial equality at the Paris Peace Conference (1919), Shimazu draws extensively on Japanese, French, Italian and American newspaper archives, confining her use of East Asia's English-language press to the reports of the *North-China Daily News* of Shanghai.[19]

The term 'press network' has been problematic. I have yet to find any contemporary use of this term in English sources in connection with the English-language newspapers of East Asia, let alone the names given to the networks outlined above. However, although I found no exact contemporary references, the concept was implied by numerous tangential and anecdotal references and media gossip in contemporary sources: most conspicuously in the English-language newspapers of East Asia themselves and in the contemporary memoirs of their staff.[20]

In Japanese, contemporary private sources such as Ugaki (1923) have also demonstrated sufficient suspicions regarding the purpose and grouping of the English-language newspapers in China and Japan to sustain its viability as a research project. Official sources such as the reports of the North China Army Information Department (*Hokushigun hōdōbu*) perceived patterns of collusive anti-Japanese sentiment among the English-language newspapers and news agencies operating in China, and minutes and memoranda in British, American and Japanese diplomatic correspondence also showed patterns of interest and affiliation between the English-language media both in the early treaty ports and in the more mature settler communities and present a fragmented picture of the workings of the English-language press networks of East Asia.

These readings have been augmented by secondary sources on the history of the foreign presence in East Asia, and, in a broader context, more recent scholarship on the role of the press in British imperial history and the British world. These sources, which I discuss below, contributed to the essential task of relating my findings to the work of other scholars on press networks.

It has been necessary to develop a definition of the term 'press network'. Basing a historical study on the concept of press networks in a period marked by a series of international crises and by dynamic upheavals in every sphere is difficult unless one defines these press networks fairly loosely. The binding interests have to be strong enough to ride the waves of change and yet loose enough to survive numerous departures and schisms, much apathy, frequent disloyalty and the multitude of personnel and institutional developments that occur within any media organization or, as often occurs in this study, were brought about by the actions of other interests in other networks and other agencies. The definition of press network also needed to bear some relation to the historiographical approaches to press networks taken in the imperial,[21] transnational[22] and British world[23] studies discussed below, although some of these titles are themselves ambiguous and might, like those of the English-language press networks of East Asia, have gone by other names. Thus the working definition of press network used in this study reads as follows:

A press network is a group of independent media institutions linked by common, more or less binding, interests. A press network can be linked by concrete commercial, political or national interests, or by less specific but, in times of crisis, just as binding factors such as outlook, prejudice or even fear: all that is necessary is that these elements be held in common by all the members of the network. These interests and outlooks need not be pursued with a common zeal or held with the same degree of conviction, and they can hold different degrees of significance for each member and appear more or less significant to different members at different times, but they should be held in common to the extent that they distinguish one network from another.

This understanding of East Asian English-language press networks was initially brought to one of the approaches mentioned above: the transnational. In this encounter, the transnational approach added complex new dimensions to the links that seemed to bind the English-language press networks of East Asia. This book does, after all, deal with the networks of the *English-language* newspapers of East Asia. Adopting a transnational approach meant enmeshing the English-language press networks in new pluralities and complex interactions: between Western settlers in East Asia and the 'native' Chinese, Japanese and Koreans living there, and between a variety of other settlers whose interests often transcended their origins or identity as Asian Americans, Jews, Parsees, Indians, Eurasians, diasporic Chinese, White Russians, Irish, Scots, Welsh and other groups.

Wildes's contemporary (1927) study and more recent readings incorporating transnational approaches to the history of the treaty ports and settler communities of East Asia (Ion 1996; Bickers 1999; Bickers and Henriot 2000) provided useful background on the role of Western, Japanese and Chinese journalists working for the English-language newspapers of Japan and China. The two latter readings also showed that because the treaty port system did not formally incorporate either China or Japan in the British or any other empire, historians had, by default, tended to reach for the expression 'informal empire' with regard to China, an uneasy compromise that either left a significant interest, Japan, unqualified by even this unsatisfactory term or tended to treat Japan's as the only truly imperial project in China.

In particular, Bickers and Henriot (2000), complementing Henriot (1993) and Bickers (1999), augmented by readings in Henriot and Yeh (2004), demonstrated that the absence of 'real' imperialism, as in India or Africa, either clouded the historiography of East Asia in ambiguity or invited histories of East Asia to frame imperialism within cut-and-dried East Asian nationalist narratives of victimhood, resistance, struggle and liberation or the more drawn-out but equally familiar bounds of Britain's national narrative. Such default approaches failed to engage with the ambiguities of transnational life in East Asia: the collusive processes by which even the most, or perhaps especially the most 'informal' imperialism was managed, and the participation of 'subject' races and settler interests in that collusion. With the exception of the above authors and Auslin (2004), few scholars have counted the history of the treaty ports, and by association the history of the English-language press of East Asia, as more than discrete elements in the history of East Asia. A transnational approach would show both the ports and their press as institutions and communities as relevant to the history of East Asia as they were to the history of the nations that populated them.

Having posited the existence of press networks about four years into this study, I was encouraged to find that it was utilized in Bryna Goodman's paper on transnational networks in the Shanghai press in the 1920s (Goodman 2004). Following a reference in Goodman, I turned to C.A. Bayly's (1996) study of the way the British administration of eighteenth- and nineteenth-century India developed networks of information and intelligence in an attempt to keep abreast and if possible ahead of political developments in a nation in which they were only a powerful minority and where information was a source of power, at a time when knowledge itself was a scarce commodity and a badge of privilege. By now I was beginning to realize that, as a concept, networks, whether of the press, of intelligence, of news, of power and control, or all of these, were attracting scholarly attention.

However, although the existence of Goodman and Bayly's scholarship seemed to support the validity of the concept of the English-language press networks of East Asia, Goodman's work showed that the networks in East Asia could be comfortably situated in a transnational context, at least as far as Shanghai, arguably the media centre of East Asia, was concerned. In naming two of my three networks the *Japan Chronicle* network and *Japan Advertiser* network, I had already steered them away from a nationalist narrative that would require them to be known, for example, as the British or the American press network. However, in using 'Foreign Ministry network' to describe a media group run by an official national institution, I had not hesitated to frame Japanese interests in a national, even a nationalist, narrative.

Goodman's 2004 paper showed a complex variety of interests overlapping in Shanghai and transcending specific national interests, largely because political expedience at a time and in an arena of significant change required that various actors of various nationalities combine their connections and abilities in pursuit of shared interests and ideals. In Goodman's study, Shanghai reflected in microcosm the disintegration of Yuan Shikai's post-revolutionary Republic and the growing strength of a broader Chinese Nationalism aided and abetted by a mixed group of non-Chinese and diasporic Chinese personalities and institutions working through the press: a transnational press network.

An article by Su Lin Lewis in Kaul (2006 ed.) locates a study of the English-language press closer to East Asia, in Penang, in an examination of press networks in the Straits Settlements. In a variation on the transnational approach, Lewis usefully sets the range of language choices confronting 'indigenous' Malay, Chinese and Tamil communities in Penang's English-language press, most notably the *Straits Echo*,

Chinese-owned and edited by a Ceylonese, which became 'the antithesis of a colonial mouthpiece'[24] in the context of 'cosmopolitanism', and was used by the non-white communities to 'advance their interests and engage with the democratic ideals of empire'.[25]

In discussing another aspect of Penang's press, the vernacular press, Lewis brings the transnational aspect of the press networks to bear on a concept that still cannot be overlooked in any debate on the press which touches on national identity: Benedict Anderson's classic notion of the role of 'print-language' in the creation of 'imagined communities' (Anderson 1991 [1983]). Most of the scholars cited here, especially those who have studied transnational communities, agree that Anderson's contentions do not always stand up. Lewis's article closely supports arguments made in Potter[26] and Goodman[27] (Kaul is ambivalent) that Anderson's claim that 'print-language invents nationalism' fails to encompass the actualities of national identity in the Dominions or in transnational realities prevailing among the inhabitants of most Asian port cities.[28] In the multi-racial reality of Malay society (which, as Lewis points out, is ignored in Anderson's study) each community used its own language in its own periodicals. The 'imagined communities' of these diasporas transcended their location, solidified links to 'home' and helped segregate their exiled communities: as such, the vernacular press in Malaya was not a unifying but a divisive force.[29]

My readings in Bickers, Bickers and Henriot, and Goodman and others helped to situate the networks of the English-language press networks among the transnational realities developing further east in the treaty ports and later the main cities of China and Japan, in what Bickers and Henriot aptly describe as 'a network of multiple overlapping imperialisms, in the interstices of which opportunistic groups carved out new livelihoods and new roles'.[30] The ways in which these and other scholars have been re-examining the foreign presence in East Asia seem to embrace far more realistically than hitherto the interactions of interest, race and profession operating in interwar-treaty-port China, in post-treaty-port Japan and in Japan's colonies in Taiwan and Korea. Consequently, rather than approach the English-language press networks of East Asia through the binaries of imperial/informally imperial states, communities and subjects, I have tried to reconsider them in transnational terms, and to embrace such related concepts as Brian Martin's 'compradors of violence' and 'compradors of social control'.[31] Where they seem most relevant, such terms and the transnational viewpoint in general have broadened the conceptual grasp of this book: it would not stretch logic to describe the English-language press networks of East Asia as 'compradors of opinion'.

Two groups of readings covering events outside the East Asian sphere have had particularly close relevance to the development of the concept of press networks here: those of Chandrikar Kaul (2003, and 2006 ed.) and Simon Potter (2003, and 2004 ed.). These studies all deal with press networks in contexts outside East Asia. Kaul's earlier book analyses

'networks of information and communication' in the reporting of political issues in India and the Empire by the British or metropolitan press
in Fleet Street and to a lesser extent by India's English-language press. In
his earlier work, discussed below, Potter studied press networks on one
level as an 'Imperial press system' operating between Fleet Street and the
press in the Dominions, that is, in Canada, Australia, South Africa and
New Zealand, and through a broader, and more recently developed
approach, the British world, in which he discusses in collective terms
the increasingly independent Dominions press and its interdependence
and exchange with the Imperial press system.

In tandem with Bayly's (1996) work on India, Kaul's conceptual
approach to press networks (2003) raises new questions. How did the
English-language press networks of East Asia sit within or alongside
Kaul's networks of information and communication in the broader
context of Empire? Could, for example, the *Japan Chronicle* network
have served as an extension of Britain's imperial news system, given its
anti-Imperial tradition and the gaps between its editorial line and the
principles espoused by the *North-China Daily News*? Did the *Chronicle*
writers fully comprehend the dilemma faced by most of its China affiliates, given the divisions, that became most overt in the late 1920s,
between those member newspapers in China confronting, without
much success or finesse, let alone the support of Whitehall, the onward
march of Chinese nationalism, and those papers, like the *Chronicle*, that
did not stand directly in the path of this confrontation and viewed it
with greater detachment?

To extend these questions, how do the East Asian press networks fit
Kaul and Bayly's shared understanding of an 'all-India information
order'?[32] Given the development, described in Bayly, of the Indian information order from its early incarnation as an instrument of imperial
control to an information revolution that ultimately threatened British
rule, were there parallels or exceptions in the history of the English-
language press networks of East Asia? Could Bayly's 'all-India
information order' and its successors in Kaul be compared to the *Japan
Advertiser* network's early nurturing of post-revolutionary Chinese
nationalism (designed to further American interests in China and
combat Japanese influence), the Nationalist press restrictions that took
hold in the late 1920s, and the even more successful information revolution commandeered by the Chinese Communists against, in tandem,
the Guomindang and their American helpers, against the Japanese, and
later against the British and Americans who lingered in post-1945
China?

Could the penetration and closure of the foreign-owned English-
language press networks of East Asia by the Guomindang and Japan be
read as an exception to the rule, developed in Potter (2003), that Britain
and its commercial news interests were able to stretch the imperial news
system to absorb the requirements of the Dominions and thereby retain
a dominant position in global media? The networks described in Bayly,

Kaul, and Potter all raise questions about the networks described in this book, just as this book raises questions about them.

Kaul built on Bayly's (1996) study of information networks in eighteenth- and nineteenth-century India in her (2003) examination of the British press reporting of India and its role in imperial policy. Her book only slightly overlaps with the early years of this study, but it has clear conceptual and historical implications not only for the English-language press networks of East Asia but also for their role in shaping international perceptions of Japan.

Some of these implications are to be found in Kaul's approach to ground that is covered, at different stages of its development, both in her study and here. Kaul's assessment of the contemporary British press on India is far more comprehensive than mine is on its coverage of East Asia, yet there are useful personal and institutional continuities between the two studies. For example, in Kaul we can see Edwin Haward as correspondent for *The Times* in Lahore, Delhi and Simla (1914–26) and at the India Office from 1928, a journalistic-cum-bureaucratic career both disrupted and raised to new heights of responsibility by his appointment to the editorship of the *North-China Daily News* in 1930, replacing O.M. Green, as discussed below.[33] Haward's relocation demonstrates the length of Britain's imperial reach in the appointment of important actors between the Empire in India and the international settlements in China, even though they were not part of the Empire. Haward's move east helped establish channels of administration, information and experience between the Empire and the non-Empire in China. It may also have served to obscure China's relatively low importance in Whitehall's purview of the Empire and raised false hopes in Shanghai of a greater imperial commitment to their outpost of the British world.

Kaul also discusses the contemporary advantages and risks associated with official press management of the visits of the Duke of Connaught and, later, Edward, Prince of Wales, to India in 1921.[34] Connaught went on to visit Japan and to bestow the Order of the Garter on the Emperor of Japan, an event that was made much of by official Japan and encouraged the campaign waged by the Foreign Ministry network to bring about a renewal of the Anglo-Japanese Alliance, a topic discussed here.

Kaul also discusses Lord Northcliffe's role as a supporter of Empire, as a power in the fourth estate and as a shrewd exploiter of colonial conflict as an issue that sold newspapers, at precisely the conjunction of two trends: the huge growth of the modern press as a factor in political life (the 'fourth estate') and the development of the Empire and colonies as 'a major concern'.[35] Kaul describes Northcliffe's friendship with Lloyd George and Northcliffe's appointment as Director of Enemy Propaganda in the wartime Department of Information, the schism with Lloyd George that resulted in Northcliffe's exclusion from the Paris Conference in 1919 and the effect this may have had on Northcliffe's press coverage of Indian political affairs in *The Times*. She also describes the Viceroy's cultivation of Northcliffe during his visit to India in January 1922.[36]

As discussed in Chapter 5 of this study, Northcliffe's Indian visit was the next leg of his 1921–22 world tour following a controversial circuit of East Asia where he took soundings from his employees and other contacts, many of them in the *Japan Chronicle* network, and resisted attempts by the early Foreign Ministry network to manage and influence his views and the impact of statements he made in Kōbe, Tokyo, Seoul, Shanghai and Hong Kong casting doubt on the viability of the Anglo-Japanese Alliance. Echoing their British counterparts, the Japanese authorities seemed convinced that what Northcliffe said inside and outside his newspapers influenced public opinion. As Kaul points out, the source of Northcliffe's power may have lain more in this conviction than in his actual influence on public opinion.[37]

Northcliffe's visits to East Asia and India preceded and coincided with the Washington Conference held over the winter of 1921–22. Before and during the Conference, as is demonstrated in Chapter 4, members of the *Japan Advertiser* network were lobbying in Washington, London and the Dominions in an unofficial campaign to prevent the renewal of the Anglo-Japanese Alliance. In the spring of 1922, Northcliffe followed up the statements he had made in East Asia with a personally written and orchestrated press campaign headlined 'Watch Japan!' which he ran simultaneously in *The Daily Mail* and *The Times*, in *The Englishman* of Calcutta, and in newspapers in the Dominions, the US and even Japan.

Another important common topic is Kaul's analysis of the role of two other Fleet Street figures, John St. Loe Strachey, editor of *The Spectator* and Lord Burnham, proprietor of *The Daily Telegraph*, both of whom were to sit on the London committee supervising the agreement between the Foreign Office and business and British interest groups in Japan to supervise publication of the British propaganda vehicle, the *New East*, by John Robertson-Scott, in 1916–18.[38]

Finally, Kaul devotes an entire chapter to the official management of British press commentary on the political crisis in India affairs and the Empire precipitated by the Jallianwallah Bagh (Amritsar) Massacre of 1919–20.[39] In Japan, organs in the Foreign Ministry network portrayed the Massacre as a stern necessity comparable to Japan's own dilemma in suppressing the Korean independence movement and the 'Mansei' uprising of 1919–20. Factors that include Britain's active collusion with Japan in removing critical voices from Korea's English- and Korean-language press in 1907–10, the impending renewal or otherwise of the Anglo-Japanese Alliance, the cross-currents between the *Chronicle* and *Advertiser* networks' support of the Korean movement and the *Chronicle*'s critical commentary on Amritsar, the uproar Amritsar evoked in the British press, and consequent reforms in the management of both Korea and India, all serve to illustrate and define the relationships between the networks of information and communication established between Fleet Street and India in Kaul's study, and the English-language press networks of East Asia discussed here.

The English-language press networks of East Asia also bear comparison with the Imperial press system as described by Potter (2003). As in the two books by Kaul discussed here and his own later (2004) collection, Potter's focus is on the Empire and news, but he brings in a further dimension. First, in his 2003 book, he shows how the Imperial press system served the British world. Second, in his edited collection of essays on newspapers and journalists in Britain and Ireland (2004), Potter shows how they and their journalists either participated in or took leave of the British world, either in a conscious rejection of Empire or as an assertion of Irish nationalism.

But where was the Empire and what were the boundaries of the British world and how could either of these overlapping contexts inform the concept of the English-language press networks of East Asia? Kaul (2003) traced the 'networks of information and communication' along which Britain's metropolitan press reported Indian politics and the politics of Empire, which for her, as for the British press, occupied the accepted geographical boundaries of the day. Potter (2003) simultaneously illustrates the workings of the Imperial press system as a sort of multi-channelled system of news and information exchange between Fleet Street and the contemporary geographical reality of the Dominions (Canada, South Africa, New Zealand and Australia), but he broadens the conceptual base of his argument and, for East Asia, makes it possibly even more transnational, by situating the Dominions in the context of recent scholastic developments in the study of the British world. With an eye to developments in Asia, he points to similar patterns of exchange 'where local white settler populations set up their own newspapers in tropical colonies, British models and Fleet Street journalists were imported in exactly the same way as in the Dominions' and local expatriate journalists wrote the correspondence for Fleet Street newspapers just as their colleagues did in the Dominions.[40] Potter's example in this instance is the *Straits Times* but he could have just as easily instanced the *North-China Daily News*, the *Peking & Tientsin Times*, the *Japan Times* and the *Japan Chronicle*, and he could have gone on to show the parallel development of this pattern for the American world in the operations of the *Japan Advertiser* network in China and Japan.

Just as Kaul does with the British press on India, Potter examines the workings of the imperial press in systematic terms. Both accounts of the British and imperial press are descriptions of press networks. However, taking the further step of situating the English-language press networks of East Asia in relation to these networks shows that they are not a perfect fit. In the *Japan Chronicle* network, the *Chronicle* was not a natural subscriber to the ideals reinforcing Britain's imperial news system, whereas the *North-China Daily News* tended to see itself and be seen by many Chinese observers as an official mouthpiece for British policy on China. However, the *Chronicle* network was at one with its affiliates in reinforcing the British world, perhaps because it could embrace a broader church: its members could feel at home with one another without necessarily agreeing, a situation itself nicely encapsulated by the Japanese expression, 'Same bed, different dreams' (*dōshō imu*).

In the *Advertiser* network, the anti-imperialistic or, more specifically, ingrained anti-British Empire views of Thomas Millard, his protégé John B. Powell, Carl Crow, their main investor, Charles R. Crane, and their Chinese associate and Guomindang liaison, the journalist-bureaucrat Hollington Tong, and the more mildly expressed but no less strongly-held views of B.W. Fleisher, and their promotion in its organs, most notably the *China Weekly Review*, the *China Press* and the *Japan Advertiser*, were of a piece in opposing any extension of imperial power to China and promoting American influence there and throughout East Asia. There was no question of the *Advertiser* network promoting any extension of the British world: its business was the promotion of Nationalist China and through that promotion the extension of the American world. Even in 1902–22, (some said *particularly* in 1902–22), the lifespan of the Anglo-Japanese Alliance, the Foreign Ministry press network was devoted to presenting the case for extending the Japanese empire in East Asia, and protecting the rights and interests of the Japanese communities in Shanghai, Formosa, Korea, South America and the United States which could be described as the Japanese world.

These notions of a British, an American and a Japanese world spring partly from the different contexts in which Kaul and Potter place their notions of press network. While Kaul considers the British press and the Imperial press system in relation to Indian politics and the Empire at large, Potter considers the British press in relation to an Imperial press system which allows for a looser, broader exchange between the British metropolitan press and the English-language press operating in the Dominions. This approach to the Imperial press system connects the British press as a network to the English-language publications operating within the potentially less restrictive, (and even potentially less British), dimension of the British world.

Reading Kaul and Potter situates the English-language press networks of East Asia outside the Empire but shows that there are individual and institutional links, as personified by Edwin Haward, to the Imperial press system. The English-language press networks of East Asia can be placed within the British world, even in transnational Shanghai, insofar as that world transcended the geographical bounds of Empire and the Dominions. Kaul and Potter examine their press networks in virtually the same period, Kaul's in 1880–1922, Potter's in 1876–1922. However, while it would be possible to read the history of the English-language press networks of East Asia given in this book as the continued story of some developments explored in Potter, it would be more difficult to see it as a further volume of Kaul's narrative. While there are institutional and individual links between the press networks examined in both of their studies and in the English-language press networks of East Asia, Potter's press networks are more dispersed among the Dominions, less tied to the dominance of Empire, and therefore more potentially inclusive.

The commonalities are worth registering here. Many of the institutions and people common to the networks discussed here and by Kaul are amplified by Potter: the proprietors Northcliffe and Burnham, the outlook and influence of the editor St. Loe Strachey, the Reuters news agency and its eventual manager Roderick Jones,[41] and larger areas of discussion such as the role of the British press and the Imperial news system and of Lloyd George, Beaverbrook and Northcliffe in developing its potential for propaganda in the Imperial Press Conferences inaugurated in 1909.[42]

One aspect of Potter's study that brings his imperial news system closer to the English-language press networks of East Asia is the way he shows journalists in the Dominions working the system in search of employment, like roving players performing before any audience that could 'understand the language and respond to the play'.[43] Kaul brought up one such example in the Indian context, Edwin Haward, discussed here as editor of the *North-China Daily News*. In common with Kaul, Potter mentions a number of media professionals, such as Roderick Jones, whose roots in the Dominions were no hindrance to a career in Fleet Street.[44] Like Kaul, he examines the Fleet Street career of one of Japan's most consistent champions, the *Morning Post* editor, H.A. Gwynne,[45] but ignores locally significant, but in most cases externally less commanding, figures such as the London *Times* correspondents G.E. Morrison, Hugh Byas and W.H. Donald and local English-language newspaper editors such as Thomas Millard, E.A. Kennard, H.G.W. Woodhead, Robert Young and others, although all of these had a background of employment in either the metropolitan or Dominions sectors of the imperial news system as well as in the English-language press networks of East Asia. Except for Byas and Morrison, all the locally significant journalists mentioned above had newspaper experience in Shanghai, which could be described both as an outpost of the British world and as the key transnational meeting point of the British, American and Japanese worlds and their press networks.

Morrison sold his earliest writings to *The Melbourne Age* and *The Melbourne Leader* in the early 1880s.[46] Early, unsuccessful attempts to break into journalism in London led to adventures in Philadelphia, Tangiers and finally China. His published account of his Chinese travels brought him to the attention of *The Times* and an invitation in 1895 from Moberly Bell, its then Manager, to report incognito from Vietnam and Thailand. In Thailand he was met by Valentine Chirol, the foreign news editor, who appointed him Peking correspondent of *The Times* in May 1907.[47]

In May 1903, another Dominions journalist, W.H. Donald, was lured from Melbourne's *Daily Argus* to Hong Kong's *China Mail* following a conversation with one Petrie Watson, a journalist on the *Kobe Chronicle*, who instilled in him a distrust of the Japanese that he never lost.[48] Donald, whose career, like his compatriot Morrison's, reads like a manual on serendipity, was subsequently appointed the *New York*

Tribune correspondent in Peking by its owner, James Gordon Bennett, then visiting Hong Kong in his yacht.

Thomas Millard was another Bennett appointment, sent in 1899 to South Africa to cover the Boer War for the *Tribune*. Millard's bitterly anti-British reports for the *Tribune, The Daily Mail* and *Scribner's* magazine led to his ejection from South Africa on the personal orders of Lord Kitchener. The experience left Millard with a lifelong animus for the British Empire, the British and their news system, which he saw as a ruthless Empire-serving monopoly run in concert by Reuters and the British government and which he blamed for withholding truthful accounts of the Boer War from US readers.[49] When Bennett sent Millard to cover the lifting of the Boxer Siege in 1900–1, he reported the bayoneting of unarmed Chinese soldiers by British and European troops. Covering the Russo-Japanese War in 1904–5, Millard reported the barbarous treatment of Russian prisoners by Japanese forces.[50]

Thus Millard's life as a foreign correspondent began within the Imperial press system reporting from South Africa. There he became disenchanted with the Empire and continued to report its faults in China, alongside those of the Japanese, for American press interests alone. We can contrast his career with that of the Scotsman Hugh Byas, whose first job was on the newly-founded *Rand Daily Mail* (1902–9), then on *The Times* in London, where in 1911 he took on the correspondence of Millard, B.W. Fleisher and Charles C. Crane's first joint venture, the *China Press*. From 1914–22, Byas edited the *Japan Advertiser* in Tokyo (with a patriotic spell on the *New East*), returning to London and *The Times* until 1926, when he was appointed *The Times* correspondent in Tokyo and combined that position with editing the *Advertiser*. In 1927, he also became Tokyo correspondent for the *New York Times*, and finally left the *Advertiser* in 1930 to concentrate on his despatches to London and New York.[51]

In 1922, E.A. Kennard left a reporting job on the *Leamington Courier and Warwickshire Standard* for a post on the *Peking & Tientsin Times* under H.G.W. Woodhead. In 1927, he became assistant editor of the *Japan Chronicle*, assuming the editorship in 1936 when Morgan Young was banned from Japan. In 1938, Kennard became one of a *coterie* on the *Japan Chronicle* to benefit from a substantial Foreign Ministry stipend and, following the sale of the *Chronicle* to the *Japan Times*, a substantial 'retirement fee'. In December 1940, he departed for Singapore and an illustrious wartime career on All-India Radio. After the war Kennard retraced his steps, occupying editorial posts on the *Malaya Tribune*, the *Singapore Free Press* and, finally, the *Straits Times*, (in wartime the *Syonan Times*) where under the byline 'Cynicus' he contributed a column until his retirement in 1975.[52]

Even for those journalists who did not work within the Imperial press system, Potter's account has resonances for the *Advertiser* network and its espousal of American interests in China. As he shows, Northcliffe and other Fleet Street figures gave generous financial support to the Imperial

Press Conferences, which ran from 1909 to 1946.[53] Again in Potter, Roderick Jones and others set up the Imperial Overseas Press Association at the inaugural Imperial Press Conference.[54] As I show, the Missourian Walter Williams promoted the Pan-Pacific Press Congresses and the less frequent Press Congresses of the World, and peopled the *Japan Advertiser* network with mid-Western journalists. As will be seen, the most influential foreign adviser to the Foreign Ministry network in 1908, John Russell Kennedy, became involved in the inaugural committee for the International Press Association (*Kokusai Shinbun Kyōkai*), membership of which was essential for journalists' accreditation and the right to file despatches abroad.

Setting East Asia's English-language press networks in the contexts, however ambiguous and thinly-populated in East Asia, of the British world, begs some obvious questions. In the early 1920s, the *Japan Chronicle* network shared the *Advertiser* network's opposition to the Anglo-Japanese Alliance and its stance on other issues such as the Shaw Affair, but it was also steadily being overtaken by the commercial reach and influence of the *Japan Advertiser* network. Was the *Advertiser* network a harbinger of what might well be called the American world, or the American Pacific world? And were not the two foreign-owned English-language press networks discussed here, both in their confrontation with the Foreign Ministry network and as outposts of the British and American worlds, at least temporarily eclipsed by the explosive emergence of the Japanese World in East Asia? If, to quote Potter, 'it could be argued that, for several reasons, the press was *the* single most important institution acting to define the limits for the acceptable integration of the British world in the late nineteenth and early twentieth centuries',[55] were not the English-language press networks of East Asia, at least as discussed here, part of that process of integration not only for the British world but, by extension, the Japanese world from c.1921–45 and the American world in East Asia after c.1911?

Finally, no discussion of international perceptions of Japan can ignore the history of attempts to influence those perceptions. Therefore this study pursues the closely related subject of the English-language press networks of East Asia as vehicles of propaganda and counter-propaganda. Mordechai Rozanski's dissertation on US journalists in China has illuminated the journalistic, commercial and diplomatic interests involved in the development of pro-Chinese sentiment in the US before 1925 (Rozanski 1974). Roger Purdy's dissertation on the development of the *Dōmei* News Agency provides essential guidance to trends in the Japanese media and media bureaucracy in the 1930s (Purdy 1987). Jon Pardoe's (1989) dissertation on the journalist Malcolm Kennedy has provided useful insights into the social and political encounters of this pivotal figure in the international correspondence of Japan in 1925–34. Pardoe's more recently published review of British writing on contemporary Japan between the wars offers an analytical survey of British writing on Japan in 1924–41, although it does not mention the English-language newspapers of Japan (Pardoe 2002).

Of the contemporary literature in English on the role of propaganda in Japanese foreign policy, my use begins with A.M. Pooley's three critical accounts (1915, 1917 and 1920) and ends with Peter de Mendelssohn's critical wartime study (de Mendelssohn 1944). Matsumura Masayoshi's account of the founding of the Foreign Ministry Information Bureau (*Gaimushō Jōhōbu*) in 1921 is one of only a few studies by a Japanese scholar to illuminate the thinking behind Japan's first institutionalized essay in informal diplomacy. It also shows how the project expanded and became more skilfully realized over time, but eventually lost sight of its original purpose (Matsumura 1971, 2002).[56]

In 2001, I edited, introduced and contributed to a collection of essays on Japanese propaganda in a special issue of the British journal *Japan Forum*.[57] In that collection, material from my introduction and my essay, *Endgame: the English-language press networks of East Asia in the run-up to war, 1936–41*, not only laid the groundwork for the notion of press networks explored in this study, but provided material which has been used extensively here.[58] The following year, I published a potted history of the *Japan Chronicle* and its editors that was an outgrowth of this study and has also been used here. In 2005, I published a portrait of the media entrepreneur and journalist, John Russell Kennedy, (1861–1928), which like my other published papers drew on research carried out for this book and has also been used extensively herein.

In 2004, I also edited and, with the media historians Ariyama Teruo, William Hoover, James Huffman, Adrian Pinnington, and Matsumura Masayoshi, introduced a collection of English-language propaganda books presenting Japanese viewpoints. A second series in this collection of readings introduced Japanese propaganda in English-language pamphlets.[59] This book cites the work of most of the scholars involved in the first of these projects and many of the writings collected in both series.

Apart from the theses mentioned above, and John Dower's much-cited study of wartime Japanese and American propaganda and racial attitudes (Dower 1986), few Western accounts view Japan's propaganda efforts in a purely informative spirit, but Richard Storry's short essay on Japan's English-language presentation of its case in the late 1930s and Barak Kushner's study of Japan's wartime propaganda are refreshing exceptions (Storry 1979, Kushner 2006). Kushner's extensive work in Japanese and Chinese archives and propaganda collections found that Japanese propaganda after 1931 was less focused on disseminating emperor-centred belief systems than on promoting Japan's image as a new, modern leader in Asia. Kushner ranges widely, with studies of propaganda messages in film and in live performances. His main focus with regard to print culture is on messages carried in leaflets and posters and his account therefore provides only passing reference to the propaganda functions performed by the English-language newspapers of East Asia (Kushner 2006).

THE ORGANIZATION OF THIS STUDY

The introduction to this book discusses the English-language press networks of East Asia and their readership. It goes on to examine the historiography of press networks and their role in East Asia and to situate the concept of press networks in the broader contexts of the British Empire and the Imperial press system, the Dominions and their press and the more recent notion of the British world, and finally to survey the historiography of propaganda in East Asia.

Chapter 1, *The Background, 1822–1918,* surveys the early history of the English-language newspapers in Japan, China and Korea up to 1918, the year in which my study begins. It also gives an account of a series of related incidents that occurred during the formative period of the English-language press networks of East Asia: the formation of the *Kokusai* News Agency (*Kokusai Tsūshinsha*), the Siemens Scandal, the Twenty-one Demands, the Lansing-Ishii Agreement, the *Outlook* affair, and the 'White Rainbow' and *Kobe Herald* incidents.

Chapters 2, *The Foreign Ministry network, 1904–1937*, 3, *Britain in East Asia and the Japan Chronicle network, 1891–1936* and 4, *The United States in East Asia and the Japan Advertiser network, 1911–1936*, trace the accretion of commonalities of interest among East Asia's English-language newspapers, policy makers and institutions in Japan, Britain and the United States, and the coalescence from around the turn of the century until the late 1930s of the three English-language press networks that were introduced in this chapter: Japan's Foreign Ministry network, the *Japan Chronicle* network, and the *Japan Advertiser* network. Chapters 3, 4 and 5 take the history of the networks to the late 1930s, at which point, armed with the *Dōmei* news agency, (*Shadanhōjin Dōmei Tsūshinsha*), the Foreign Ministry network became more overtly hostile to the other two networks and journalistic activity in East Asia began to operate in the harsher climate that culminated in the events examined in Chapter 7.

Chapter 5, *Reporting Japan, 1918–1930*, is the first of two chapters showing the networks of the English-language newspapers of East Asia in action, reporting, debating and campaigning on the key issues and topics of the day in Japan and China. Chapter 5 focuses on reports and feature articles in Japan's three main English-language newspapers on domestic and international issues and trends running from the post-war years to 1930. The four linked issues are: Japan's colonial management of Korea, the Shaw case, the US Immigration Act of 1924, and the 1930 London Naval Conference. This chapter also examines the reporting of domestic trends with important consequences for international perceptions of Japan: the socialist and labour movements, and the growth of nationalism and patriotic movements.

Chapter 6, *Reporting Japan in China, 1927–1937*, also shows the English-language press networks of East Asia in action, but with an emphasis on Japan's role in China. The first three sections of this chapter cover the networks' competing and sometimes contradictory interpretations of the Manchurian Incident and the occupation of Manchuria in the autumn of 1931, the Sino-Japanese hostilities in Shanghai in January 1932 and the founding of Manchukuo. In a fourth section, the discussion moves to the rejection of Japan's presentation of these events at Geneva in 1932–33 by the League's acceptance of the findings of the Lytton Report, followed by Japan's withdrawal from the League. In a fifth section, I illustrate the success of the Foreign Ministry network in gaining acceptance of Manchukuo as a *fait accompli*. In subsequent sections, I show the involvement of Japan's English-language press in presenting the world with the Amō Statement of April 1934 and move on to the way the English-language press networks of East Asia reported the outbreak of full-scale war between Japan and China in July 1937. Chapter 6 also examines the development of an important trend in the history of the networks, the disenchantment some English-language newspaper journalists and Western correspondents, mostly in the *Advertiser* network, experienced over the nature of the Guomindang, partly due to its increasing control of their despatches, and their increased sympathy for and interest in the Chinese Communists in Yan'an (Yenan).

Chapter 7, *Endgame, 1936–1941*, provides an account of the suppression, coercion subornment and effective nationalization of the foreign-owned organs in the English-language press networks in Japan and China until Pearl Harbor and the outbreak of the Pacific War. The third section of this chapter focuses on the forces and interests involved in the acquisition by the *Japan Times* of the *Japan Advertiser* and *Japan Chronicle*. The fourth section then shows how the Foreign Ministry network utilized the virtual monopoly on news and opinion it had finally gained in Japan, Korea and in swathes of China, with a focus on the months before Pearl Harbor.

Chapter 8, *Publicity warriors: the Japan network, 1941–1945*, takes this history from the attack on Pearl Harbor to the defeat of Japan in August 1945 and a little way into the Occupation, and as far as the retreat of the Guomindang and the accession to power of the Communist Party of China in October 1949. In China, the focus is on the Japanese occupation of the International Settlements of Shanghai and the closing down of independent English-language commentary there and elsewhere in the months after Pearl Harbor. The discussion moves between the rapid advance in 1941–42 and slower retreat of Japan's English-language press network in East and Greater East Asia and the dramatic collapse and hard-won but temporary restoration of Western influence there.

Chapter 9, *Conclusions*, surveys the history of the English-language press networks of East Asia discussed in the main body of this study. It then looks at their history in the light of the arguments and the broader contexts of the press networks presented in the preceding chapters, and looks at exceptions to general patterns. It also provides a comparative survey of the influence of the English-language press and its networks in East Asia on reports of East Asia appearing in Western newspapers.

The *Appendices* provide additional information on the membership of the 'Missouri Mafia' and a selective chronology of the English-language press of Japan, China and Korea in three tables.

A NOTE ON SOURCES

In this account, substantial runs of the English-language newspapers, particularly those of the *Japan Times, Japan Chronicle, Japan Advertiser, China Weekly Review* and, though less frequently consulted, the *North China Daily News*, have often provided vital information not only on the issues of the day, but on propaganda in other English-language newspapers and other media in East Asia and on the history of the English-language newspapers themselves. I use the words 'runs' advisedly, as many of the newspapers I refer to have not been preserved in hard copy or in microfilm. Both in referring to the newspapers listed above and those which come up less frequently in this study, many of my citations are to material found in the archives of correspondence with China and Japan of the British Foreign Office, the US Department of State and the Foreign Ministry of Japan. In all these archives, these materials have usually consisted of single clippings accompanying and illustrating despatches sent from diplomats stationed in East Asia for discussion and written commentary in Whitehall, Washington and Tokyo.

This book has also benefited from research in the archives of Japan's Foreign Ministry (*Gaimushō gaikō shiryōkan*) in Tokyo, which have helped to clarify contemporary official Japanese attitudes to newspapers and journalists, the links between some foreign journalists and the Foreign Ministry Information Bureau (*Gaimushō Jōhōbu*) and its propaganda programmes. My research in the Foreign Ministry archives has focused on correspondence on the English-language newspapers, news agencies (*tsūshinsha*), local English-language journalists and foreign correspondents (*Gaikokujin shinbun kisha*) and propaganda planning in East Asia and on the attitudes and intentions of Foreign Ministry officials towards the English-language press of East Asia, where I could find them, but I have not used Foreign Ministry files for general background on the history of the era.

NOTES

1 Said 1991: 300.
2 See Cohen 1978: 4, and n.1 regarding the terms 'opinion leader' and opinion maker'.
3 FO 395/44/ [P 2303/2303/150] Snow in Tokyo to A. Willert at FO, 18 November 1930. The case had already been briefly reported in the *Evening Standard* and *The Times*.
4 FO 371/19349 [F 55/55/23], Robert Clive, Tokyo, to C.W. Orde at FO, 30 November 1934.
5 FO 371/24728 [F 5646/53/23] Minutes to Telegram from Craigie in Tokyo to

FO, 17 December 1940. According to the last of these the subscription for the Foreign Office library's Weekly edition of the *Chronicle* was paid for by the embassy in Tokyo.

6   Raper 1893: 149.
7   FO 395/17 [F 133472]: July 1916, Memorandum, Annex A by Robertson-Scott, July 1916.
8   Wildes 1927: 373.
9   Chao 1931: 76.
10 Ch'en 1937: 12.
11 Chao 1931: 53. Chao contrasts the NCDN's circulation with that of the official vernacular paper published by Nanjing, the *Central China Daily News*, whose circulation was 10,000.
12 FO 395/17 [F 133472]: July 1916, Memorandum, Annex A by Robertson-Scott, July 1916.
13 Wildes 1927: 373.
14 USDS 894.911/60: Grew to State Dept., 2 March 1938.
15 From Wildes's footnotes for these figures: both the *Osaka Mainichi* and *Tokyo Nichi-Nichi* 'undoubtedly contain a large free list'. The figure given to Wildes for the 'actual pressroom run January 31 1925' of the JT was 6,300. The JC figure is not annotated: the new Managing Director, Eric Young, may have ignored Wildes's enquiry. On the SP: 'The editor [Sheba Sometarō] says, "Well below 1,000"'. On the JA: 'The daily pressroom run in June, 1925, of the *Advertiser* was unofficially, and perhaps unreliably, stated to the writer as about 1,900 copies'. Wildes considered the *Kobe Herald*, *Nagasaki Press*, and *Manchuria Daily News* figures to be 'A very generous estimate' (Wildes 1927: 374, footnotes).
16 Ebihara is prone to errors, among them the notion that the founding editor of the *Japan Chronicle*, Robert Young, was an American (173 and ff.).
17 Frédéric 2002: 415.
18 The *Straits Times* was taken over during the Japanese occupation of Malaya and Singapore and renamed the *Syonan Times*, although it remained an English-language newspaper. The occupiers established a new organ in Singapore, the *Shonan Shimbun* (not *'Shinbun'*), whose title expressed a desire to distance their English-language media from its predecessors by using an inconsistent combination of the new 'Nipponese' Romanization system and Hepburn (Purdy 1987: 408, n.34).
19 Shimazu 1998: 235–6
20 Some journalists have left diaries and papers, of which the most useful have been the Malcolm Kennedy diaries and papers at Sheffield University and the Hugh Byas papers at Yale University. The papers of the media academics Walter and Sarah Williams at the University of Missouri have thrown valuable light on Walter Williams's relationships with journalists, many of them his own alumni, and with media entrepreneurs in East Asia, most notably the JA's B.W. Fleisher.
21 Kaul emphasizes that the problem in 'Imperial studies is to produce integrated media history as well as to integrate media history itself into more mainstream history' and specifically acknowledges that 'it is impossible to talk about the British Empire as a single entity, even less to posit a single theory to explain its rise and fall' (Kaul 2006: 3).

22 For an acknowledgement of the 'eloquent' ambiguity of transnationalism and the possibility that it might often be interchangeable with such terms as 'multinationalism' or 'internationalism', and the 'possibility that its very fashionableness may be destined for … incoherence and obsolescence', see Dirlik 2004: 12–13.

23 Potter highlights Lord Burnham's use of the term 'British world' in 1920 but points out that the term was seldom used 'with any precision' at the time (Potter May 2003: 190).

24 Kaul 2006: 12.

25 Lewis 2006, in Kaul 2006: 203–249.

26 Potter 2003: 67, refers to Anderson's 'now somewhat hackneyed' notion of 'imagined communities'. See also 69, 214, and 215 where he describes Anderson's argument that the press encouraged readers to 'imagine' themselves primarily as members of national communities as 'overly simplistic' and goes on to show that Anderson 'ignored the impact on the press of forces that transcended the boundaries of modern nations', i.e. the impact of British news from the imperial system that helped them to see themselves as Britons first.

27 Goodman claims that 'recent discussions of Chinese nationalism have disputed the analytic relevance for China of several aspects of Benedict Anderson's influential account of the development of nationalism … and argued against Anderson's overriding emphasis on print capitalism and the spread of newspapers in particular, as facilitating the new imagined community of the modern nation' (Goodman 2004 Introduction: 3).

28 Lewis 2006: 235.

29 Op. cit.

30 Bickers and Henriot 2000: 2.

31 In Wakeman and Yeh 1992: 7, 266.

32 Kaul 2003: 29, 23; Bayly 1996: ix.

33 Kaul 2003: 154 and below.

34 Kaul 2003: 232–7.

35 Kaul 2003: 6–7; 'major concern': J.M. MacKenzie's Introduction: xii.

36 Kaul 2003: 122–3, 146, 149–150.

37 Kaul 2003: 19, citing Inwood 1971: 25.

38 Kaul 2003: 6, 17, 55, 149, 263–4, and see Chapter 1, below.

39 Kaul 2003: 199–229.

40 Potter 2003: 10.

41 Roderick Jones's professional life began on the *Pretoria Press*, a paper close to the obviously anti-Imperial government of the Transvaal (Potter 2003: 19, 44).

42 Kaul 2006: 1, and 125–144.

43 Potter 2003: 17, citing Morrison, E. in Cryle, D. (ed.) 1997, 74.

44 Potter 2003: 20, 44, 89, 105–9.

45 Potter 2003: 5, 23, 44–5; Kaul 2003: 6, 19, 55, 61.

46 Pearl 1967: 11, 14, 24, 35.

47 Pearl 1967: 79, 82.

48 Selle 1948: 4–6.

49 Rozanski 1974: 38 and 98, n.7; Rand 1995: 21–25.

50 Rozanski 1974: 40–42.

51 Obituary, Hugh Fulton Byas: NYT, 7 March 1945.
52 'Cynicus': Turnbull 1995: 155. Other details: Obituary, Edwin Allington
    Kennard: *The Times*, 30 June 1977.
53 Potter 2003: 137–38.
54 Potter 2003: 105.
55 Potter May 2003: 191.
56 Matsumura Masayoshi, '*Gaimushō Jōhōbu no sōsetsu to Ijūin shōdai buchō*' (the
    founding of the Foreign Office Information Bureau and its first head, Ijūin
    [Hikokichi])', *Kokusai hō gaikō zasshi*, vol.70 (2), 1971. Revised and expanded
    as 'Japan Calling: the Origins of the Ministry of Foreign Affairs Information
    Department in the early 1920s', (Trans. Matsumura Masayoshi and Peter
    O'Connor), *Transactions of the Asiatic Society of Japan*, Series 4, Vol. 16, pp.51–
    70, December 2002.
57 O'Connor 2001 (ed.)
58 O'Connor April 2001 (ed.): 1–14, 56–76.
59 O'Connor 2005 (ed.)

1

The Background, 1822–1918

THE ENGLISH-LANGUAGE PRESS IN JAPAN, CHINA AND KOREA, 1822–1918

In Somerset Maugham's short story, *The Outstation* (1926), Warburton, a British administrator in an outlying district of Malaysia, receives his copies of *The Times* by sea mail, three or four month's worth at a time:

> It gave him the illusion of living at home. Every Monday morning he read the Monday *Times* of six weeks back, and so went through the week. On Sunday he read the *Observer*. Like his habit of dressing for dinner it was a tie to civilization.[1]

Fiction dwelling on the blinkered isolation of the British in East Asia has occupied a distinct niche since the 1900s, but Maugham may have been stretching a point in *The Outstation*.[2] By the 1920s, when Maugham was preoccupied with writing on the British in Asia, even the most isolated of Malaya's settlers subscribed to one or more local English-language newspapers, such as the *Malay Mail*, and usually only caught up with *The Times* when they visited their club in town.

English-language newspapers have been published in Asia since the eighteenth century. In East Asia, with the exception of enclaves such as Macao, the roots of the English-language press lie in the treaty ports, beginning in Canton in 1827 and in Nagasaki in 1861.[3] Following the end of extraterritoriality in Japan in 1899, some English-language newspapers moved to the capital, but most English-language newspapers in China continued to enjoy the protection of extraterritoriality and this certainly contributed to their comparative outspokenness. Korea's independent, commercial English-language press put up a brief struggle in Seoul from the 1890s until 1911, when a portfolio of semi-official English- Japanese- and Korean-language newspapers was established.*

Japan

The first newspaper in Japan, the foreign-owned *Nagasaki Shipping List and Advertiser*, was founded by a British printer and auctioneer, A.W. Hansard, in June 1861 and was, like most early treaty port newspapers, a shipping list with news items and advertising. During the next forty

---

* As a supplement to what follows, see the chronological tables of the English-language press in Japan, China and Korea in Appendices 7, 8 and 9.

years, over forty foreign-language newspapers and over thirty foreign-language periodicals and magazines appeared in Japan. Of these, among the best managed and most professionally written were the *Japan Mail*, owned and edited by Captain Francis Brinkley (1841–1912), the *Tokio Times*, owned and run by E.H. House from 1877 to 1880, and the *Japan Times*, founded in March 1897 and still going strong, all of them subsidized by the Japanese government. There were also two independent foreign-owned newspapers, the *Japan Advertiser*, established by a Scots-born American, Robert Meiklejohn, in 1891 and owned and run from 1908 to 1940 by an American, B.W. Fleisher, and his son Wilfrid, and the *Japan Chronicle* of Kōbe, founded in 1891 by a Briton, Robert Young, and run by his descendants and their successors until its sale to the *Japan Times* in December 1940, although it continued to publish a Kōbe edition under its own name until the end of January 1942.

There were six English-language newspapers in business in Yokohama, Nagasaki, Kōbe and Tokyo in 1918. These included the *Japan Gazette* (edited by J.R. Black from October 1867 to 1880 and by Douglas Adams from 1906 to 1923), the *Rising Sun and Nagasaki Express*, edited by W.L. Lewis,[4] and the *Japan Times & Mail*, an amalgamation of the *Japan Times* and Brinkley's old newspaper. Besides these three, the *Japan Advertiser* had moved to Tokyo by 1918, and both the *Japan Chronicle* and the *Kobe Herald*, founded and run by Alfred W. Curtis from 1888 until 1926, were established in Kōbe. In 1926, the *Kobe Herald* was acquired by Douglas M. Young, manager of the Far Eastern Advertising Agency (*Tōyō Kōkoku*) of Kōbe and a distant cousin of Robert Young of the *Japan Chronicle*.[5] Either Douglas M. Young or Morgan Young, since November 1922 editor of the *Chronicle*, ran the *Kobe Herald* until 1934.[6] In June 1936, Douglas M. Young was listed as the owner of the *Kobe Herald and Osaka Gazette*, presumably having amalgamated it with the *Osaka Gazette*.[7] By 1939, only a single issue of the *Kobe Herald* was being printed, annually, 'retaining for its owners the right to keep its name'.[8]

The *Japan Times*, *Japan Advertiser* and *Japan Chronicle* all published daily and weekly editions. The *Japan Advertiser Weekly* changed its title to the *Trans-Pacific* in September 1919. The *Trans-Pacific* continued to be published until October 1940 when it was acquired by the *Japan Times Weekly* edition, whose masthead then changed to the *Japan Times Weekly & Trans-Pacific* until June 1942, then the *Japan Times Weekly* until January 1943, when it became the *Nippon Times Weekly*.

Besides these six newspapers, three English-language periodicals are worth noting for their connections to the English-language press. The *Far East*, a fortnightly established by John N. Penlington in March 1912, was published in Tokyo until the 1923 earthquake. Zumoto Motosada, founder of the *Japan Times* and a noted journalist and English-language publicist, founded the weekly *Herald of Asia* in March 1916 and edited it until the earthquake also put it out of business, but revived it from September 1937 until December 1938. Finally, in November 1938, an American, W.R. Wills, founded *Japan News-Week* in Tokyo and ran it until it was closed on 8 December 1941, the last of Japan's independent English-language publications to be shut down.

The vernacular *Ōsaka Mainichi Shinbun* began to publish an English-language edition in April 1922 as a Japanese-owned English-language alternative to the *Japan Times*, which was seen by many as being too close to the Foreign Ministry. The English edition, consisting largely of translations from the *Ōsaka Mainichi* vernacular edition, had the backing of a large commercial publisher, its Japanese parent having achieved a circulation of over a million in 1922.[9] In March 1925, the English-language *Osaka Mainichi* merged with the English-language edition of the *Tokyo Nichi-nichi Shinbun*, which had been founded in 1923 but proved a financial failure. The masthead continued as the *Osaka Mainichi & Tokyo Nichi-nichi* until January 1943 when it changed to the *Mainichi*.

China

The first foreign newspaper in China was a Portuguese paper, published in Macao in 1822. China's first English-language newspaper was the *Canton Register*, established in 1827. Over the next ninety years, hundreds of newspapers, about a hundred of them in English, came and went or amalgamated with others in China.

The *North-China Herald* was founded in 1850 as a four-page weekly carrying news from Britain and news of Britons staying in or leaving Shanghai, with a supplement, the *Daily Shipping List and Commercial News*. In 1864, the supplement became the *North-China Daily News*, and the *North-China Herald* continued as a weekly edition.

By 1918–19, about thirty-five English-language newspapers, half a dozen English-language weeklies, magazines and journals, two or three yearbooks, and a handful of English-language news agencies were in business in China. Of these, the *Shanghai Mercury*, *Shanghai Times*, *North-China Daily News* and its weekly edition the *North China Herald*, half-a-dozen Hong Kong dailies and weeklies, and the weekly *Finance & Commerce*, were controlled by British interests and mostly staffed by Britons. In 1918, the largest news agency in China was Reuters, a British concern with enduring official connections.

In 1918–19, American interests or Chinese interests registered in the US controlled the *Shanghai Evening News*, the *Peking Leader*, the *North China Star*, the *China Press* and two weeklies, *Millard's Review of the Far East* and the *China Digest*. In partnership with *Dentsū*, the United Press had opened an office in Shanghai but posed little threat to Reuters. In 1918, the Chun Mei news agency was set up by Carl Crow and other Americans in Shanghai and Peking (Beijing) and began successfully building a nationwide network. Between 1919 and 1923, the *Japan Advertiser*'s B.W. Fleisher and other Americans ran the Trans-Pacific News Service in an unsuccessful effort to counter the influence of Reuters and the Japanese *Shin-Tōhō Tsūshinsha* (New Eastern News Agency).[10]

In 1908, the South Manchurian Railway Company (*Minami Manshū*

Tetsudō Kabushiki-gaisha) (SMR) set up the *Manchuria Daily News*, an organ which would survive, with breaks, until 1945. In 1918, the SMR established the *China Advertiser* in Peking. In 1919, Japan's emerging Foreign Ministry network founded the *North China Standard* in Peking.

Korea

The independent English-language press of Korea began in the 1890s with the *Seoul Press*, founded by an Englishman, J.W. Hodge. In 1904, a British foreign correspondent, Ernest T. Bethell, founded the *Korea Daily News* as a bilingual daily and in 1905 began publishing the Korean section of the paper separately as the *Taehan Maeil Sinbo*. Both newspapers published critical articles and reports on Japan's growing presence in Korea.

In November 1905, following Japan's victory against Russia and the Treaty of Portsmouth, Korea became a Japanese protectorate with the agreement of Japan's ally, Great Britain. As Resident-General (*tōkan*) of Japan's Korean protectorate from December 1905 to June 1909, Itō Hirobumi, alongside his Anglo-Irish 'confidant', John Russell Kennedy (1861–1928), and their financier, Shibusawa Eiichi, guided many of those working in Japan's semi-official English-language media. Itō took a keen interest in using Korea's English-language press to prepare international opinion for the full annexation of Korea, although he himself was not convinced of the benefits of such a change. Itō's office instituted strong controls on the Korean-language press and set up new Japanese- and English-language newspapers to strengthen Japan's grip on the protectorate.[11] From his office in Seoul, Itō gave opportunities in news management to some of the most capable journalists and media entrepreneurs of the day including Russell Kennedy, Zumoto Motosada, Honda Masujiroh, Baba Tsunego and Yamagata Isoh, all of whom became part of a media triangle of English-, Japanese- and Korean-language publications in Tokyo, Seoul and New York.

In August 1905, following negotiations between Hodge and the Japanese ambassador to Seoul, the Foreign Ministry entered into an arrangement with the *Seoul Press* whereby Hodge would publish material putting Japan's role in Korea in a more positive light than that shed by E.T. Bethell's *Korea Daily News* and *Taehan Maeil Sinbo*, and began paying Hodge ¥350 per month.[12]

In January 1906, Zumoto Motosada organized the acquisition of the *Seoul Press* by the office of the Korea Resident General. Zumoto edited the *Seoul Press* until late 1908 or 1909, when he moved to New York to found the Oriental Information Bureau, an early hub of the Foreign Ministry network on the East coast of the United States.

During the Japanese protectorate, the legal foundations of Japanese publication policy in Korea were set out in the Newspaper Law (*Shimbunshi hō*) of 1907 and the Publication Law (*Shuppan hō*) of 1909. In 1907, the principal targets of the Newspaper Law were the *Korea Daily News* and *Daihan Maeil Shinbo*, whose editor, Ernest T. Bethell, was briefly imprisoned and fined, but whose newspapers continued to be published because their owner's nationality put them outside Japanese jurisdiction.[13] However, in 1908, both of Bethell's newspapers, whose headquarters had become a focus of Korean resistance to Japanese power, were closed down following a legal action instigated by the British consul, Cockburn, at Japan's request. In June 1908, the owner-ship and editorship of the *Korea Daily News* were removed from Bethell and transferred to one of his staff, a move that the most durable semi-official English-language daily in Korea, the *Seoul Press*, applauded, although it felt the action still left the way open to further 'seditious journalism' by foreign newspapers.[14] On 12 June 1908, Britain's Consul-General in Seoul announced new regulations for the control of British newspapers in Korea, drawn up by the British Consul and signed by Edward Grey, the Foreign Secretary.[15]

The Bethell case is significant, first as a litmus test of Anglo-Japanese relations in East Asia in the early years of the Anglo-Japanese Alliance, secondly because the controls applied to the *Korea Daily News* and *Taehan Maeil Sinbo* case were in some respects a dry run for press controls in Japan (although the powers enjoyed by the Governor-General after Korea's annexation in 1910 were far greater than those of the government on the Japanese mainland).[16] The Bethell case matters to this study because it shows the networks of the English-language newspapers of East Asia assuming the positions they would hold for most of the inter-war period, with the *Seoul Press* standing behind Japan, backed by the *Japan Mail*, *Kobe Herald* and *Kokumin Shinbun*, while Bethell, his newspapers, and his stand against Japanese power in Korea, were championed by the *Japan Chronicle* (in whose columns he gave a graphic account of his imprisonment),[17] though without much support from its future affiliates and, in this instance, signs of connivance between the Foreign Ministry network by the *North-China Herald*. In 1908, the Korea correspondent of this newspaper reported that Bethell and one of his staff had confessed to embezzlement. Bethell later brought a successful libel suit against the *North-China Herald* and its parent company, the *North-China Daily News*.[18]

Itō Hirobumi was assassinated in Harbin in October 1909 and Japan formally annexed Korea the following year. Thereafter, until its closure in 1937, the *Seoul Press* operated as an organ of the office of the Korean Governor-General (*sōtoku*), an official answerable to the Emperor alone, not to the Diet. New editors came and went through the revolving door of Japan's semi-official English-language journalism. In 1909, Honda Masujiroh became editor for a year, until he followed Zumoto to New York, replacing Baba Tsunego at the Oriental Information Bureau and *Oriental Review*.

In a parallel development, Terauchi Masatake, Governor-General of the new colony from 1910 to 1916, hired the founding editor of the *Kokumin Shinbun*, Tokutomi Sohō, as a consultant on Korean- and Japanese-language media. Tokutomi brought all Korean-language publications under central control and ensured that they followed the lead of the Japanese-language *Keijō Nippō* by installing trusted employees from the *Kokumin Shinbun* to run these newspapers, travelling to Korea three or four times a year to supervise operations.[19]

Around 1917, Yamagata Isoh, in earlier days one of a radical group of journalists on the *Yorozu Chōhō*, took over as editor of the *Seoul Press*, where he remained until 1925. By 1918, the *Korea Daily News* had folded and the *Seoul Press* was the only English-language newspaper in Korea. Throughout the 'Mansei' Independence protests of 1919–22, the *Seoul Press* held the official line, but under the softer rule of Saitō Makoto, Governor-General 1919–27, it published tempered criticisms of some of Japan's military excesses and bureaucratic errors. In the absence of independent rivals, the *Seoul Press* and its Japanese-language equivalent, *Keijō Nippō*, dominated the Korean media until 1937 and 1945, respectively.

Thus, despite the Independence Movement, the English-language press of Korea ceased to develop as an open forum beyond 1911 and the Foreign Ministry network dominated the public sphere, such as it was. Japan did not achieve the political domination of Korea by repression and press control alone. On the Korean side, the recognition by the independence movement that the support it had received from sympathetic English-language newspapers in East Asia, the press in Britain and the US, and its propaganda campaigns at Paris and Washington, may well have induced changes in international sentiment, but had signally failed to bring about any loosening of Japan's grip on their nation, was another important factor. Observing in April 1922 that the situation in Korea was outwardly calm, Maruyama Tsurukichi, head of the Japanese police in Korea, argued that the agitators had become disillusioned with violence and had probably realized 'that independence will not be easy … All diplomatic and foreign aid efforts have failed, and the realization of this has sunk deeply into the Korean psyche.'[20] Maruyama's judgement was tough but prescient: the English-language newspapers of East Asia continued to bring international attention to bear on the subjugation of the Korean people, but their situation remained substantially unchanged until Japan's defeat in 1945.

EARLY DEVELOPMENTS AND KEY ISSUES

In 1913–18, seven related events occurred which influenced the direction of the networks of the English-language press of East Asia and the overall purpose of Japan's international propaganda programme. These were: the establishment in 1913 of the *Kokusai Tsūshinsha* (International News Agency) by John Russell Kennedy;[21] the Siemens Scandal (*Shiimensu jiken*) of January 1914, and the involvement of the Reuters correspondent in Tokyo, Andrew Pooley, in exposing it; the furore that broke out in 1915 over the Twenty-one Demands (*Taika Nijūikkajō Yōkyū*) made on China by Japan; the Lansing-Ishii Agreement of November 1917; the May 1918 *Outlook* interview with the Japanese

Prime Minister, Terauchi Masatake; the *Ōsaka Asahi Shinbun* 'White Rainbow' affair of late August 1918; the *Kobe Herald* affair of September 1918, and the failure of the British propaganda organ, the *New East* in 1916–18.

These incidents and experiences all contributed to a sense of *malaise* in Anglo-Japanese relations, but they were catalysts rather than causes. They showed the Anglophone communities that their interests were probably better served in friendly competition than in partnership. They taught them and their local collaborators that the delivery of news and opinion required some informal cooperation – with anyone, from anywhere, as long as they had some finance or journalistic skill, or both, and knew their way around – if commercial interests were not to founder on the rocks of national sentiment. In the springtime of propaganda, these incidents taught some highly-placed Japanese and Chinese the importance of public opinion and convinced them that news had a power that could be harnessed in much the same way as military and economic power. Finally, most of those involved in these early incidents realized that, because national power was at stake, there were bound to be similar clashes in future and that they had better arm themselves with as much skill and experience and gather as many friends and connections as they could afford.

The common theme in all these events was the management of Japan's news. The common foreign personality was an Irish-born journalist and businessman, John Russell Kennedy. The Foreign Office bureaucrat and novelist Frank Ashton-Gwatkin once described Russell Kennedy as 'a tempestuous Irishman' [who] 'loves a grievance and a fight'.[22] It could simply be said of these early years that, after some nasty infighting among foreign journalists in Japan, Russell Kennedy found himself at the top of the heap and never looked back. But before the rucks described below, Russell Kennedy was already the chosen one: the anointed foreign architect of the Foreign Ministry's early English-language press network, working with his future partners (and rivals) to lay the foundations of the Foreign Ministry press network in East Asia.

In 1913, Russell Kennedy became President of the *Japan Times*[23] and set up the *Kokusai* news agency with funds gathered by Shibusawa Eiichi and his main contact at the Foreign Ministry, Makino Nobuaki. In February 1914, he negotiated an agreement with the Reuters agency to handle its Japan correspondence and became the Reuters correspondent in Tokyo. In April 1918, Russell Kennedy amalgamated the *Japan Mail* with the *Japan Times*, creating the *Japan Times & Mail*. In the 1920s, the Foreign Ministry Information Bureau hired Russell Kennedy to set up new publications and realign established publications in an extensive network of semi-official European and English-language newspapers, magazines and news agencies in Europe, Japan, China, the US, Britain and most English-speaking countries, with the flagship *Japan Times* and the *Kokusai* and *Shin-Tōhō* news agencies at its headquarters in the Foreign Ministry in Tokyo.

Russell Kennedy had first come to Japan in the early 1900s as a correspondent for the New York based Associated Press. In 1908, he became involved in committee work for the International Press Association (*Kokusai Shinbun Kyōkai*), organized by Zumoto Motosada. The Association provided Russell Kennedy with a vital introduction to Japan's media bureaucracy, as membership of the Association became essential for journalists' accreditation and their ability to file despatches abroad. Helped by introductions from Zumoto and from his mentor at the Associated Press (AP), Melville E. Stone, Russell Kennedy went on to mingle with Shibusawa Eiichi (1841–1931), and elite politicians such as Itō Hirobumi, who, Russell Kennedy claimed, 'made me his confidant'.[24] Russell Kennedy went on to meet Saionji Kinmochi (1849–1940), Hayashi Tadasu (1850–1913), Foreign Minister, Yamagata Aritomo (1838–1922), and Katsura Tarō (1848–1913).[25] All of these figures, with the exception of Yamagata and Katsura, had experience of living, travelling or studying in the West and spoke or read some English, and all of them were keenly interested in improving Japan's foreign relations.[26]

Among these figures, the businessman Shibusawa Eiichi, the president of Nippon Steel, Kabayama Aisuke, and Makino Nobuaki (1861–1949), Foreign Minister in 1913–14 and an important figure in Japan's delegation to the Paris Conference in 1919, became key promoters of the idea of a national news agency for Japan.[27]

During visits to both the US and Europe in 1909–10, Shibusawa Eiichi had been deeply impressed by the strength of anti-Japanese sentiment and the ignorance of his country and its cultural traditions shown by the Americans he met. In California, Shibusawa learned more about the treatment meted out to Japanese immigrants. In 1909, a movement began in California to ban Japanese from owning land in that state. In an attempt to turn the tide of American opinion, a group of Japanese journalists with English-language skills relocated to New York: Honda Masujiroh and Zumoto Motosada from Seoul; Baba Tsunego (1875–1956) and Akimoto ('Shin') Shunkichi, a future *Japan Advertiser* contributor, from Tokyo. In New York, besides preparing press releases and handouts, these journalists produced a 100-page monthly, *The Oriental Review*, aimed at East coast readers with an interest in Japan and East Asia.[28]

On his return to Japan, Shibusawa met with Makino Nobuaki and Russell Kennedy to discuss the idea of a Japanese news agency. Other enthusiasts were Furuno Inosuke, then in his first job in journalism as Russell Kennedy's assistant at AP, and Zumoto Motosada, one of the founders of the *Japan Times*. In 1913, the anti-Japanese movement in California resulted in the passing of the Alien Land Law barring Japanese from owning land in California, and confirming, as far as Shibusawa, Makino, Kabayama, Russell Kennedy, Furuno, Zumoto and others were concerned, the urgent need for a national news agency to present the world with a more sympathetic image of the Japanese as a people and a more convincing case for their policies in East Asia.[29]

Shibusawa Eiichi began soliciting funds from his business contacts, and Makino, as Foreign Minister, began to develop Foreign Ministry support for the new agency.

At the same time, the New York operation was revamped. The Oriental Information Bureau closed down and its successor, the East and West News Bureau, opened an office in the recently completed Woolworth Building in Manhattan in 1913. Iyenaga Toyokichi became Director of the new body; Baba Tsunego and 'Shin' Akimoto stayed on to strengthen the editorial team. The biochemist Takamine Jōkichi (1854–1922), Japan's most prominent unofficial envoy in New York, the journalist and publicist Joseph I.C. Clarke, and the manager of the New York branch of the Yokohama Specie Bank, also served on the board. Takamine discussed with John Russell Kennedy the need for Japan's case to be presented more effectively in the US and arranged with Makino Nobuaki for Clarke to visit Japan and Korea in 1914.[30]

Shibusawa, Makino and Russell Kennedy were also keen to gain greater control of the way Japan was reported by the Reuters correspondent in Tokyo. In 1912, this post was filled by Henry Satoh.[31] However, Satoh had come under the strong influence of Russell Kennedy, then the AP correspondent, and in 1912 Reuters sent Andrew M. Pooley to replace Satoh. Pooley remained in Tokyo only until his reporting of the 1914 Siemens Scandal in January 1914 brought him to trial on a charge of blackmail. When Pooley was ejected from Japan, Russell Kennedy, who had just negotiated a fresh agreement with Reuters, replaced him. Russell Kennedy represented Reuters from 1914 until 1925, when Malcolm Kennedy was appointed as the new Reuters correspondent in Tokyo, a position he held until he resigned in 1934.

Japanese dissatisfaction with Reuters' reporting of Japanese news was another factor that lent impetus to the notion of starting a single national Japanese agency. As Harry Wildes put it in 1927, 'working along a great stretch of British-owned cable, Reuters delivered to Japan only that news for which there was a general demand by all the papers of the chain' – that is, all the newspapers served with Reuters despatches at points along the line – making little effort to seek out and wire Japanese news back up the line for distribution in the West. Reuters was slow to send Europe positive, informational reports on Japan that were lacking in obvious news value, but seemed less hesitant in wiring messages, whatever their news value, whose publication some Japanese would have preferred to hinder. Not without reason, some in Tokyo saw Reuters as an adjunct of the British Foreign Office, just as the Havas, Wolff and Stefani agencies were held to be partial to the French, German and Italian foreign secretariats.[32]

In 1912, Baron Herbert de Reuter and his aides in London had become unhappy with the situation in Tokyo whereby Russell Kennedy had become the *de facto* Reuters correspondent by contributing the most important despatches to both Reuters and the Associated Press. The questions this raised about the integrity of both Satoh and Kennedy led to Russell Kennedy's dismissal as AP's Tokyo correspondent and Satoh's replacement by Andrew M. Pooley as Reuters correspondent in 1912. However, the critical content of Pooley's despatches caused dissatisfaction in Japanese government circles,[33] and Russell Kennedy's more flexible outlook ('I conceived the idea that the duty of a correspondent was, not to send unpleasant news of petty quarrels, nor of trifling corruptions, but to weld together East and West') [34] helped to maintain official interest in the Russell Kennedy group's national news agency scheme.

Early in 1913, Russell Kennedy visited London in an effort to persuade Baron de Reuter to transfer the Reuters business in Japan to his projected Japanese news agency. Initially, de Reuter showed little interest but Russell Kennedy, according to Hugh Byas, 'forced Baron Reuter to sell out by showing Kokusai had government support'.[35] As Byas recalled, '… a ripe moment came for him [Russell Kennedy] to represent to Baron de Reuter that his scheme of a new Japanese news agency was a big one, supported by influential interests, financial and otherwise, in Japan and that it would be wise for the baron to accept the inevitable'.[36] Baron de Reuter came to the pragmatic conclusion that if a powerful new agency were to be established in Japan, Reuters' interests would be best served by a cooperative relationship. When Japan's ambassador to London, Inoue Katsunosuke, assured de Reuter that Russell Kennedy had official backing, the matter was settled and in November 1913, de Reuter and Russell Kennedy finally signed a contract transferring Reuters' interests in Japan to Russell Kennedy's new agency for a period of ten years.[37]

However, the terms agreed between Russell Kennedy and Reuters were far from generous to Japan. Although Reuters granted *Kokusai* sole distribution rights in Japan to Reuters world news, *Kokusai* was not allowed to sell any news, its own or Reuters', to any other news organization, and all news supplied by Reuters had to carry only the Reuters byline, 'Hatsu Roitaa denpō' in vernacular newspapers, and 'From Reuters Telegraph Company' in the English-language newspapers. Furthermore, Russell Kennedy agreed a crippling fee of two thousand yen (£200) a month for Reuters news and five hundred yen (£50) a month for the Reuters telegraph service.[38] Finally, *Kokusai* undertook to refrain from entering the China market, in which Reuters was the dominant agency.[39]

Few of these terms were satisfactory to the group backing *Kokusai*. The financial agreement was a drain on *Kokusai* and meant that it had to be subsidized by the Foreign Ministry. The clause by which *Kokusai* agreed to stay out of China was considered particularly restrictive and in October 1914 the Foreign Ministry network set up the *Tōhō Tsūshinsha* (Eastern News Agency) in Shanghai to circumvent it.[40] In the years following the First World War, *Kokusai* wanted to continue to take Reuters world news but increasingly resented having to publish it under the Reuters byline. In November 1923, when Iwanaga Yūkichi replaced Russell Kennedy as general manager of *Kokusai*, he was able to renegotiate this part of the agreement after paying Reuters £20,000, so that Reuters no longer took sole credit for *Kokusai*'s world news.[41] Although *Kokusai* world news now carried the credit 'Hatsu Kokusai Roitaa' in the vernacular press, and 'From Kokusai-Reuters' in the English-language press in Japan, Kokusai remained at best little more than a favoured Reuters' customer, after a decade of negotiations whose main purpose had been to turn the agency into a credible, acknowledged source of news from Japan. Overall, despite the growing capabilities of *Kokusai*'s rival, the *Dentsū*-UP partnership, East Asia was still Reuters' territory.[42]

Thus, even before *Kokusai* was up and running, some of its original backers were uncertain, not only of the financial wisdom of these arrangements, but of *Kokusai*'s ability to provide Japan with a media institution that would represent its interests and put its case in a way that would command respect and promote a more favourable understanding of Japan.

Nevertheless, preparations moved ahead. Russell Kennedy was appointed *Kokusai*'s general manager as well as the Reuters correspondent for Japan. Branches were opened in Tokyo and Ōsaka, and representative offices in London and Washington. These preparations also necessitated the removal of a likely obstacle to the success of the new venture, namely Andrew Pooley, still formally the Reuters correspondent.

Late in 1913, Pooley paid ¥750 to an ex-clerk from the German armaments firm Siemens Schuckert to obtain papers proving that bribes had passed between Siemens, Vickers in England, Mitsui Bussan and the Japanese Admiralty as inducements to the Admiralty to order equipment for a Japanese cruiser. Admiralty representatives offered Pooley $125,000 for the papers, but he turned them down, proudly declaring, 'I am not selling but publishing.' Siemens met with the same response. Finally a Japanese navy representative gave Pooley a non-negotiable bank order for $125,000. After receiving a further $25,000, Pooley returned the incriminating papers to Siemens.[43] Pooley was then arrested and tried on a charge of blackmail. During the trial, Russell Kennedy sent a letter to the judge incriminating Pooley. Pooley's counsel responded by reading from Russell Kennedy's 1913 correspondence with de Reuter, broadcasting, Hugh Byas noted, 'that Kokusai had government support ... The official nature of [Russell] Kennedy's apparently independent correspondence was thus revealed.'[44]

Pooley was convicted of blackmail but was allowed to leave Japan rather than serve a prison sentence.[45] The Incident enabled Russell Kennedy to remove Pooley as the Reuters representative, but it compromised *Kokusai*'s claims to journalistic integrity even before the new agency was formally established.[46] Kennedy and his backers could no longer ignore the possibility that *Kokusai* might be seen as no more than a propaganda front for Japan. In an attempt to counter this charge, *Kokusai* put in place a new plan whereby it collected news within Japan and then, 'after clarifying and filtering' it, delivered the result to the Reuters representative for transmission to Western newspapers. Thus, *Kokusai* collected but Reuters and, through new agreements, AP, Havas, Wolff, Stefani and other news agencies delivered news from Japan.[47] By the terms of its contract, *Kokusai* was only allowed to broadcast news from Japan in the name of Reuters, AP and the other 'Ring' agencies. This clause was finally removed in January 1924 when the contract was renewed following negotiations in London between Iwanaga Yūkichi and Roderick Jones of Reuters.

However it arranged its affairs, the world did not react positively to *Kokusai*. Strictly speaking, *Kokusai* was not the Reuters or AP correspondent agency, but with Russell Kennedy acting as both the Reuters and the AP correspondent and as the general manager of *Kokusai*, *Kokusai* gained a near-monopoly over the export of Japanese news from its establishment in February or March 1914 until its replacement by the Rengō news cooperative in 1926.

In 1914, the notional exceptions to *Kokusai*'s near-monopoly were the foreign correspondents in Tokyo of *The Times, Morning Post* and *Manchester Guardian,* other Japanese news agencies, most notably *Dentsū* in partnership with UP, and the independent English-language press insofar as it was read outside Japan. Since the *Japan Advertiser* provided, by way of side jobs for its largely young, American editorial staff, practically all the correspondence for American newspapers not signed up to AP or UP, it constituted a considerable exception to the *Kokusai* monopoly. In contrast, *Japan Chronicle* staff wrote no Japan correspondence for Western media until Morgan Young was taken on by the *Manchester Guardian* in 1925.

Despite the existence of these alternative channels, *Kokusai* news, although distributed under other names, became the most widely broadcast influence on foreign views of Japan for the decade 1913–26, a period which saw the Twenty-One Demands, the Peace of Paris, the Ishii-Lansing Agreement, the Yap and Shandong (Shantung) issues, the May 1919 protests in China and the 'Mansei' risings in Korea, the Siberian Expedition, the negotiations for the renewal of the Anglo-Japanese Alliance, the Washington Conference, and the 1924 US Immigration Act cutting Japanese emigration to California. Until May 1925, when he was replaced by Malcolm Kennedy, *Kokusai* reported John Russell Kennedy's versions of Japanese news to the world and Reuters reported the world to Japan, back and forth along thousands of miles of privileged Reuters and AP cable. Many newspapers in the West carried *Kokusai* reports under their home news agency titles. In Japan, they were printed in the *Japan Times* and the vernacular press, and, often with qualifications and misgivings, by the *Japan Chronicle* and the *Japan Advertiser*.

Kokusai had been going for a little over a year when it was suddenly presented with the first major challenge to its ability to manage controversial news. The January 1915 Twenty-One Demands crisis was a watershed in the development of Japan's international image. It is also significant to this study in showing the Western press and the English-language newspapers of East Asia getting into the rough formations that they would occupy for most of the inter-war period.

The Demands were first presented to China's Republican ruler, Yuan Shikai (Yüan Shih-k'ai), by the Japanese Minister, Hioki Masu (Eki), in January 1915. Hioki enjoined Yuan to secrecy but news of the Demands leaked out with the connivance of V.K. Wellington Koo (Gu Weizhun), then an official in Yuan's administration, who informed the American Minister, Paul Reinsch.[48]

In response to the leaks, Russell Kennedy distributed an abbreviated *Kokusai* version comprising '11 Demands' that was accepted by *The Times* correspondent in Tokyo, John N. Penlington, and in Peking, David Fraser, who observed that 'the secrecy enjoined on the Chinese gave rise to many fanciful versions of the demands' and concluded that 'it would be ungracious for Britain to put obstacles in the way of Japan's reasonable enough ambitions in China'.[49]

Such statements were sufficient assurance for most other journalists, and the Demands might have escaped closer scrutiny had it not been for the efforts of Fraser's predecessor as *Times* correspondent, G.E. Morrison, and W.H. Donald, two Australian journalists who had become publicity advisers to the Yuan Shikai administration. Morrison immediately saw the import of the full version of the Demands and arranged for Donald to send a long message to *The Times*. However, in a Leader published the day after Fraser's despatch, *The Times* stuck to its guns, using Donald's information as a platform for a strong attack on the Chinese tendency to cause a 'commotion':

> We must expect that the whole of this Oriental imitation of the 'Reptile Press' will be worked at full pressure for the next few days in order to flood Europe with distorted versions of the Japanese claims ... All news and all views which come from that quarter are tainted at source.[50]

Morrison then sent a copy of the full text to Sir John Jordan, Britain's Minister in Peking (1906–20), commenting that *The Times* Leader clearly conflicted 'with the more correct information cabled home by Donald'.[51] Writing in the *Peking Gazette* and *Peking Daily News*, Eugene Chen (Chen Youren) energetically opposed the Demands and queried the initial judgement of *The Times* in appearing to take the Japanese side. In Japan, the *Chronicle* campaigned against the Demands and reported Russell Kennedy and *Kokusai*'s efforts to suppress news of their true nature. In Britain, the press soon caught up with its East Asian contemporaries and decried the Demands, with the *Daily Telegraph* and *Pall Mall Gazette* in the vanguard with alarming reports from its correspondent, Putnam Weale, under such headlines as 'Dismemberment of China'. These caused Morrison to urge restraint lest the campaign back-fire against China.[52]

Morrison and Donald were not the only foreign journalists who made it their business to expose the nature of the Twenty-One Demands.[53] Nevertheless, in East Asia, much of the opposition of the English-language newspapers and of many Chinese-language newspapers to the Twenty-One Demands was inspired by their campaign. The Twenty-One Demands came as a turning point in Morrison's view of Japan. After 1915, he saw 'Japanese militarism' as 'the counterpart of German militarism' and as the major threat to British interests in East Asia.[54]

The effect of *Kokusai*'s omissions and misstatements over the Twenty-One Demands was in the short term to confuse foreign perceptions of Japan's role in these incidents and cast doubt on the integrity of *Kokusai*, and in the long term to undermine the credibility of news from official sources in Japan. Some sort of foreign policy success was needed, and needed soon, by the group around Kennedy. In November 1917 better days seemed to return, not only for the Kennedy circle and those involved with burnishing international perceptions of Japan, but for foreign policy makers in the area of greatest significance to all their future plans: China.

In November 1917, John Russell Kennedy accompanied Japan's special envoy Ishii Kikujirō to negotiations with US Secretary of State Robert Lansing in Washington. They came back with the Lansing-Ishii Agreement, which recognized Japan's 'special interests' in China. As Lansing's Note to Ishii put it (without closely defining what these 'special interests' were):

> ... the governments of the United States and Japan recognize that territorial propinquity creates special relations between countries, and, consequently, the Government of the United States recognizes that Japan has special interests in China, particularly in the part to which her possessions are contiguous.

Japan had gone to war in 1914–18 alongside the *entente* powers, but the defining issues in Japanese foreign policy lay not in Europe but in China. In 1917, the US attached far narrower significance to the Note than did Japan, and repudiated it in 1923, but while it could, Japan made the most of this apparent encouragement to pursue its interests in China. Russell Kennedy's contribution to the negotiations with Lansing is not clear, although the *Japan Times* trumpeted the centrality of his role in this 'epoch-making Treaty'.[55]

Unfortunately, the triumph implicit in Lansing-Ishii was dampened the following May by a fresh failure in news management: the *Outlook* affair. In an interview published in the May 1918 edition of this New York weekly, Japan's Prime Minister Terauchi Masatake revealed attitudes to the allied cause that many of his officials would have preferred to keep under wraps.

The interview had been conducted by an American, Gregory Mason, in April 1918 shortly before he left his post as editor of the *Japan*

Advertiser, with Tsurumi Yūsuke interpreting as part of an effort to ensure that Terauchi's words were 'on the record'. In Mason's account, Terauchi at first announced that he was not speaking for publication, but then relented, on condition Tsurumi provide an account of the interview in Japanese. After reading the translation, Terauchi showed it to his Foreign Minister, Motono Ichirō, and his Minister of Home Affairs, Gotō Shinpei, and it was returned to Mason and Tsurumi. 'Thus', Mason concluded, Terauchi's words 'are as official as could be'.

The controversy centred on Terauchi's reply to Mason's question, 'What are the chances for an alliance between Japan and Germany?'

> 'That,' he replied, 'will depend entirely on how the present war may end. It is impossible to predict the changes which the conclusion of this war may bring. If the exigencies of international relationships demand it, Japan, being unable to maintain a position of total isolation, may be induced to seek an ally in Germany; but, as far as I can judge from the existing condition of affairs, I see no such danger. In other words, I believe that Japan's relations with the Entente Allies will continue unaltered after the present war.' [56]

Terauchi's words were qualified by their context and by the consequences of events unfolding in Russia, but their effect was to confirm G.E. Morrison's view that Japanese policy in the war was predicated on a belief in German invincibility, particularly in military circles, where Germany had been an influential model since the defeat of France in 1870–71.[57] To observers in the US, Britain and in East Asia, Terauchi's response demonstrated an openly cynical approach to Japan's international obligations.

The *Japan Times* tried to limit the damage by highlighting Terauchi's qualities as a 'bluff, honest soldier', unused to the slippery rules of diplomatic language. The paper even went on the offensive, pointing to 'the international mischief-makers [who] have taken this interview up, and are twisting it into a terrible bludgeon with which to create ill-feeling and arouse distrust'.[58] However, in an obvious swipe at its Tokyo rival, the *Japan Chronicle* also queried the interview: 'The reader may attribute what significance he likes to the fact that the Japanese Press seems almost unanimous in accepting Mr Gregory Mason's account of his interview with Count Terauchi as truthful, while the foreign press (the "Japan Advertiser" for obvious reasons excepted) has its doubts.' [59]

Most Japanese papers felt that Terauchi had committed an indiscretion. Writing in *Shin Nippon*, Nitobe Inazō saw the Terauchi article as part of a tendency to play 'a double faced game when the war situation undergoes any marked change ...'[60] However, the *Chronicle* took comfort from the attitude of the *Yamato*, which he summarized thus: 'It is to the credit of the foreign press that it does not take up the matter as the subject of hostile comment, a fact which shows that foreign journalists are gifted with a larger share of common sense than their Japanese *confrères*.' [61]

No sooner had the reverberations of the *Outlook* affair died, as the stalemate on the Western front broke in Europe and the likelihood of an Allied victory made such issues appear less significant, than two further issues came up. These were more than newsroom squabbles. Both the 'White Rainbow' and *Kobe Herald* Incidents were media reflections of harsh economic realities affecting most ordinary Japanese.

Between July and September 1918 dramatic increases in the price of rice led to rioting (*kome sōdō*) across the nation. The mood was not specifically revolutionary, but the Terauchi government reacted strongly when the *Ōsaka Asahi Shinbun* of 26 August published an article obscurely hinting at the fulfilment of ancient Chinese prophecies of systemic change in which 'the white rainbow would be pierced by the sun'. The ensuing 'White Rainbow' Incident (*hakkō jiken*) saw the *Ōsaka Asahi* shut down and threatened with permanent closure and the fourth estate in Japan considerably cowed and muzzled, with two notable exceptions: the *Japan Chronicle* and the *Kobe Herald*.

In the summer of 1918, in opposing the government's treatment of the *Ōsaka Asahi* and in condemning what it saw as the tendency of Japan's press to lie low and keep its head down, the *Chronicle* staked out its ground as the opposition paper of record. This was a position it would maintain with some consistency into the mid-1930s, as the vernacular press would become increasingly wary and diffident, and the other English-language newspapers of Japan would either tread more carefully or toe the official line.

One recruit to the *Chronicle*'s ranks was the *Kobe Herald*, which, for the first and last time in its existence, found itself branded as a revolutionary organ. Coming just after the offending *Ōsaka Asahi Shinbun* article of 26 August, the republication in the *Kobe Herald* of 3 September 1918 of a week-old article by Putnam Weale in the Chinese nationalist Eugene Chen's recently established *Shanghai Gazette* headlined 'The Revolt in Japan' seemed to constitute a blatant challenge to the authority of the state. Where the *Ōsaka Asahi Shinbun* of the 26 August had contented itself with ominous hints of systemic change, the *Kobe Herald* declared that:

> ... the type of government which governs without being directly responsible to a popularly elected body of men has exhausted its mandate from Heaven and must go ... At the present moment the only means of redress the Japanese people have is what they have just used; they must burn and loot. For in the absence of proper checks upon the executive, they can call attention to glaring wrongs only in this crude manner and force the sovereign to act.[62]

For publishing the article, John Willes, the British editor of the *Kobe Herald*, was imprisoned on a charge of *lèse-majesté*, specifically for the statement that Japan's 'type of government' had 'exhausted its mandate from Heaven', for the notion that the 'sovereign' could be 'forced' to act and for the reference to 'the worship of false gods'.[63] What may have worried the authorities more than these statements was the article's apparent justification of the expression of popular discontent in the form of the Rice Riots, but *lèse-majesté* was still the main charge.

In London, observers at the Foreign Office noted that the charge of *lèse-majesté* was 'based on most insubstantial ground' and British embassy staff in Japan did their best to get Willes off the hook. In the end, he was sentenced to five months imprisonment and a fine of ¥100 as editor, five months imprisonment and another fine of ¥100 as publisher of 'a statement impairing the dignity of the Imperial House, and fined ¥150 as editor and ¥150 as publisher 'on a charge of inserting matters disturbing the public peace and order'.[64]

The *Kobe Herald* affair had an odd postscript. As they had done with Pooley, Willes's jailers allowed him to abscond to Shanghai before he had served his sentence. By early 1920, Willes had replaced Russell Kennedy's old cohort, Henry Satoh, as editor of the Foreign Ministry network's new daily, the *North China Standard*. In the long term, the 'White Rainbow' affair was certainly the more significant of the two issues and an important watershed in Japan's media history, but the *Kobe Herald* affair showed the foreign press community that Japan meant business and that there were limits, although these remained ambiguous in law, to its freedom of comment.

The overall effect of these incidents on the morale of English-language press networks of East Asia is hard to judge. It may be that the ability of an article that originated in an obscure Shanghai newspaper to cause such reverberations and international intercessions upon being reprinted in Japan, rather than acting as a caution, encouraged a sense of its new influence and power in the small world of East Asia's English-language press. If this was so, this sense cannot have been dampened by the failure in 1918 of a new arrival in their ranks: the *New East* of 1916–18.

During its short history, the *New East* and its makers encountered most of the movers and shakers in the networks of the English-language newspapers of East Asia: the Foreign Office, the embassy in Tokyo, the pillars of the foreign community in East Asia, the *Japan Times*, the Japanese press, and, not least, the *Japan Chronicle* and its founding editor, Robert Young.

The Foreign Office set up the bilingual periodical, *New East / Shin Tōyō*, edited by a Briton living in Tokyo, John Robertson-Scott, in 1916. Its self-proclaimed purpose was to express the 'best of the East and West' and so bring together the two 'island empires' of Britain and Japan.[65] Concerned lest the official backing of the *New East* prejudice its chances of success in Japan, Conyngham Greene, the British ambassador, put forward the name of Sir Charles V. Sale, of Sale and Co., a Yokohama firm with inter-ests in the City of London and South America. Greene suggested that Sale would make the *New East* 'a success for both Britain and himself'. Sale was approached and agreed to put up between £8,000 and £9,000 of the total three-year capital of £12,000 suggested by Robertson Scott, and to get the rest from patriotic British residents in Japan. Sale himself suggested that he could put down these costs as 'business expenses' on his Income Tax return, by this arrangement reducing his liabilities so that his actual contribution would be around £2,000.[66]

In order to put some further distance between the *New East* and the Foreign Office,[67] and to disguise Sale's financial role, Robertson Scott suggested a committee be set up to superintend the review, comprising Charles Sale, Lord Burnham of the *Daily Telegraph*, Sir George W. Prothero, editor of the *Quarterly Review*, J. St. Loe Strachey, editor of the *Spectator* and, as secretary, Wilson Crewdson, operating from his home in St. Leonards-on-Sea, near Brighton. With the exception of Crewdson these were all key players in Fleet Street, and Burnham and St. Loe Strachey were stalwarts of the Imperial press system (see Introduction). However, with the exception of Sale, who had twenty-eight years experience of business in Yokohama, none of them had any knowledge or experience of Japan.[68]

Perhaps to make good this defect, a 'New East Sub-committee' was formed in Tokyo under the auspices of the British Association of Japan, and shares of the *New East* invested in it. This consisted of Vivian Bowden, F.H. Bugbird, President of the British Association of Japan, John Struthers, H.B. Higinbotham and others. Charles Sale proposed that the Sub-committee put up the rest of the estimated £12,000 finance needed for three years, but after meeting Robertson Scott, they proved unwilling and Sale agreed to provide the entire cost from the start.[69]

In his proposals to Whitehall, Robertson-Scott was confident that the *New East* would be superior to anything currently provided by the English-language press of Japan. Compared to the estimated 5,000 combined total daily circulation of the *Japan Times*, *Japan Advertiser* and *Japan Chronicle*, Robertson-Scott predicted that the *New East* would achieve 'a basis' of 4,500 copies a month. Less ambitiously, considering the *Advertiser*'s ¥5,000 monthly advertising revenue, he felt the *New East* 'might reckon on at least ¥1,400'. Set against what he saw as the English newspapers' 'almost total lack of influence on Japanese and Japanese government' the *New East*, by addressing the Japanese in Japanese:

> ... with some literary and journalistic skill, authority and firmness, and with due recognition of the character, aspirations, achievement and strength of Japan ... would be, for the first time in Japan, a foreign publication of which the Japanese Government would feel the influence.[70]

Given these claims and aspirations, it is hardly surprising that the new periodical and its editor fell foul of Robert Young. As Robertson-Scott saw it:

> Some of my difficulties have been due to a rather foolish attitude of antagonism on the part of Robert Young on whose intelligent sympathy I had

prematurely counted. He is getting an old man and is easily huffed. He cannot, however, do much harm because his acerbity is notorious.[71]

Robertson-Scott had rented a small house in Tokyo as living quarters for himself and his wife and as the *New East* office. In February 1916, he recruited Hugh Byas from the *Japan Advertiser* as deputy editor and Business Manager.[72] Other staff included Robertson-Scott's sister-in-law, the artist Penelope Keith, and four Japanese journalists and translators, including Nitobe Inazō. Hugh Byas's presence reassured the Sub-committee, who were already becoming wary of Robertson-Scott. Ambassador Greene and other British embassy staff were also involved with preparations for the new journal.

The first issue of the *New East* was published in June 1917. It attracted an ecstatic review from John Russell Kennedy in the *Japan Times*. The *Japan Chronicle* found it 'a compound of *Titbits* and the *Review of Reviews*, with a dash of the *Daily Mail*'.[73] Another reader, at the Foreign Office, also found the review a 'strange hybrid between the Review of Reviews & Tit-Bits', a coincidence of views that showed that the *Chronicle* had at least one subscriber in Whitehall.[74]

The *Chronicle* review tore into statements from the new journal's galaxy of VIP well-wishers, including Prime Minister Terauchi, who interpreted the Anglo-Japanese Alliance as favouring Japan's 1910 annexation of Korea. Following close on Terauchi's gloss on Korea, the *Chronicle* objected to an article by Lord Curzon stating that, 'the mission of the two Island Empires is essentially the same ... Neither is inspired by lust of conquest. Neither desires the exploitation of subject races in its own interest.' The *Chronicle* was underwhelmed: '... it is really diffi-cult to understand the *raison d'être* of this periodical ... There is really nothing of value in the magazine that has not been presented at least as effectively – we venture to say with far less superficiality – in the daily foreign press of this country.' It criticized the choice of Robertson-Scott, for 'in the hands of men without such experience, without even the knowledge of problems and conditions that comes from long residence and study – the project represented by *The New East* is likely to lead to mutual misunderstanding rather than to joint interpretation'.[75]

Next day's *Chronicle*[76] returned to Curzon's piece, 'The Common Ideals of Japan and Britain', laying into the wishful thinking behind his view that the Anglo-Japanese Alliance stemmed from 'common intellec-tual and spiritual aims and on the sympathy of each party in the Alliance with the thoughts, wishes, and hopes of the other'. Robertson-Scott's assertion that the Japanese were ranged with the 'culture group' represented by the Anglo-Saxon nations also got short shrift. 'Japan's culture development has been along lines totally different from the West, and it is doubtful whether many of her intellectual leaders would regard inclusion in an Anglo-Saxon "culture group" even as a compli-ment.'[77]

In January 1918, in a moment of pique, Robertson-Scott suggested that Hugh Byas seek other employment. Byas responded by handing in his notice. Without Byas to protect his flank, Robertson-Scott and the *New East* were harried by the local press in Japan and the relationship with the *New East* Sub-committee came under strain. In March 1918, a British embassy note described the editor of the *New East* as 'notoriously unbusinesslike'.[78] The following May, Charles Sale made continued finance conditional on the Sub-committee gaining 'practically a controlling voice in the conduct of the Review' and on a reduction in Robertson-Scott's salary.[79] In April 1918, Sale gave notice that he did not intend to support the *New East* beyond the end of the year. In its final issue, of December 1918, Robertson-Scott wrote a mawkish farewell headlined 'Sayonara, a Speech before Seppuku'. This marked the effective end of British propaganda in Japan until the deterioration of Anglo-Japanese relations in the late 1930s prompted a review.

☐

The interrelated incidents described in this chapter exhibit many of the patterns of journalistic behaviour, media relationships and official attitudes that shaped the networks of the English-language press of East Asia during the period under review. Even at this early stage, Japanese officialdom was making the moves that would characterize its long-term effort to counter negative images of Japan.

Nothing was simple. Historically, the personal connections between British officials in Tokyo and London and the foreign managers and writers employed by Japan's semi-official propaganda programmes were often better established than the links between British officials and journalists on more independent organs, such as the *Japan Chronicle*. In the 1910s and 1920s, the British embassy was on far better terms with John Russell Kennedy, the master builder of Japan's propaganda network, and with correspondents of *The Times* such as Palmer, Brinkley and John N. Penlington, whose despatches were bought and paid for by the Foreign Ministry, than it was with Robert Young, the editor of the *Japan Chronicle*, or his feisty successor, Morgan Young. In 1918, Conyngham Greene took a hand in replacing the American Gregory Mason as editor of the *Japan Advertiser* with the trusted Scot, Hugh Byas, after the *Outlook* affair exposed Japanese opportunism towards its ally. Would Byas have kept Terauchi's response off the record? Byas, the independent editor who somehow maintained his integrity on a paper dedicated to the promotion of American interests and Russell Kennedy, Japan's hired pen, were sworn enemies, and yet both were regulars at British embassy parties and Karuizawa picnics. H.G.W. Woodhead was awarded a C.B.E. by the British authorities for his wartime services in countering German propaganda in China, just as in Japan Russell Kennedy was decorated for his services to the nation, yet neither was held in particularly high esteem in Whitehall or at the Foreign Ministry in Tokyo.[80]

This frigidity between British officials and East Asia's British-owned newspapers was less consistently reflected by American officials who, beginning with Paul Reinsch, the US Minister to China in 1913–19, cultivated contacts with American journalists and media entrepreneurs in China and Japan, among them George Bronson Rea, Carl Crow, Thomas Millard, John B. Powell, B.W. Fleisher and George Sokolsky.

The warmth of these contacts had its darker side in the shared, almost visceral distaste some well-placed Americans, such as Charles R. Crane, and American journalists associated with the *Japan Advertiser* network, most notably Thomas Millard, felt and expressed towards the Japanese as a people.[81] The willingness of some in Washington to encourage American journalists in East Asia to take a critical editorial line on Japanese ambitions in China and Korea, when compared with the cautious line adopted by British officials, marks an important difference between the two governments and the networks under study. This difference was neither consistent nor long term, but it would become a significant factor, at least in Japanese eyes, during the campaign to renew the Anglo-Japanese Alliance, and would rebound on most foreign journalists in the 1930s, when Japanese suspicions of American collusion in 'anti-Japanese' journalism in China broadened to a view of the English-language press of East Asia and most Western correspondents as the advance guard of Western encirclement.

NOTES

1   Maugham 1926: 64.
2   Hutcheon 1983: 3.
3   Hoare 1994: 141, 142.
4   The editor of the *Rising Sun & Nagasaki Express* from 1897–1900 was William Whitfield Fegen, b.1864 in Devon, a paternal ancestor of Annie Crockett, b. Ōsaka, who married Robert Young, founding editor of the *Japan Chronicle*. In 1900, Fegen left Nagasaki for Bangkok where he edited a local English-language paper for many years until his death aged seventy-two in 1936. I am indebted to Susan Larkin, Robert Young's great-granddaughter, for this information.
5   Young 1933: 160–3.
6   Ibuki 1965: 821–2.
7   *Kokusai Bunka Shinkokai* 1936: 18. Douglas M. Young bought the *Kobe Herald* largely to secure its profitable printing arm, the Kobe and Osaka Press, which published the *Japan Mercantile and Manufacturer's Directory* and enjoyed sole agency rights to *Kelly's Directory of Merchants, Manufacturers and Shippers of the World*.
8   JC Weekly, 12 October 1939, p.390.
9   Wildes 1927: 290–291.
10 The Trans-Pacific News Agency, (1919–23) is discussed in more detail in Chapter 4.
11 Chong (1987) remains the most reliable source for Itō's role in establishing Japanese control of the press in Korea.
12 Hodge was an eager participant in the editorial realignment of his newspaper. In a letter to the Japanese ambassador at Seoul, he reassures him regarding the

strength of his circulation (600 copies a week), future improvements in size
and appearance, and his openness to further cooperation. 'In case the style,
tone and general appearance of our weekly paper does not meet with your
approval, Your Excellency will be at liberty to inform us of the same, and to
make other suggestions, on condition that such alterations or improvements
are reasonable and fall within the limit of the subsidy above mentioned':
Gaimushō gaikō shiryōkan: kankoku seoru pressu (Gaimushō archives: Korea:
Seoul Press) 1/3/1 1/-17. J.W. Hodge to Japanese Minister (*kōshi*) in Seoul, 22
August 1905. See also 'Incendiary Journalism in Korea', (SP: May 1908) and
Wildes 1927: 272.
13 Robinson 1984: 315.
14 'Journalism in Korea': NCH, 13 June 1908, summarizes recent reports by the
Japan Mail (approving the 'extreme care exercised by Great Britain whenever
the cause of justice is concerned'), and the JC of 1 June. JC itself judged that
the concerns about sedition expressed in SP were partial and concluded: 'we
suggest that our contemporary's indignation is a little artificial'.
15 'British newspapers in Korea': NCH, 4 July 1908.
16 Robinson 1984: 316.
17 'My sentence of three weeks' imprisonment' by E.T. Bethell: JC, 3–24
September 1908. Cited in Chong 1987: 340.
18 'Korea's National Fund': NCH, 30 August, reprinted 5 September 1908; 12
December 1908 Court Report and judgement. One witness called was O.M.
Green, then assistant editor of the NCDN. In the course of the trial, Green
was asked why he did not question the original libellous report of Bethell's
'misappropriations' in Korea, which was sent by the NCDN correspondent in
Tokyo, one Shihotsu, since he was on the staff of the *Kokumin Shinbun*, a
Japanese paper that fully supported the campaign against Bethell.
19 Pierson 1980: 298.
20 Maruyama Tsurukichi, *Chōsen chian no genjō oyobi shōrai* (Public Peace and
Order in Korea, Present and Future) (*Keijō: Chōsen Sōtofuku, Jimukan*, 1922), 4–
5. Cited in Robinson 1984: 329.
21 Some of the material on John Russell Kennedy used in this chapter was
published in O'Connor (2005) 'John Russell Kennedy, 1861–1928: Spokesman
for Japan and Media Entrepreneur'. In Hugh Cortazzi (ed.) *Britain & Japan:
Biographical Portraits*, Volume V, (Folkestone: Global Oriental), 383–98.
22 FO 395/334 [F 1242/730/150]: 1920, Frank Ashton-Gwatkin Minute.
23 The *Japan Times* often changed its title: *Japan Times* March 1897-April 1918;
Japan Times & Mail to October 1940; *Japan Times & Advertiser* to January 1942;
*The Japan Times & Advertiser Incorporating the Japan Chronicle and the Japan
Mail* to 1943; *Nippon Times* to July 1956; *Japan Times* to the present. The 1940–
42 changes are explained in Chapter 7 below.
24 Wildes 1927: 169.
25 According to the *Jyapan Taimuzu monogatari*, Kennedy knew these men well
enough to be able to make direct telephone calls to them (Hasegawa 1966:
60), but this was unlikely in the case of Yamagata and Katsura as neither
spoke English and Kennedy's Japanese was rudimentary.
26 Itō and Akita 1981: 395.
27 Haruhara 1985: 315.
28 *Gaimushō gaikō shiryōkan: gaimushō kiroku: senden kankei zakken; shokutaku*

oyobi hojōkin shikyū sonota sendenhi shikyū kankei gaikokujin no bu (Foreign Ministry records, miscellaneous matters relating to propaganda; concerning the payments of commissions, bonuses and other propaganda expenses, foreigner section) 2: 1-3-1, 35–2-2: Takamine Jōkichi to Makino Nobuaki, 26 March 1913; and Lindsay Russell, Japan Society of New York, to Shibusawa Eiichi on the organization of the *Oriental Review* and suggestions for its improvement, 8 January 1912.

29 Hasegawa 1966: 179. JT: 1 July 1956; 12 May 1966.

30 *Gaimushō gaikō shiryōkan: gaimushō kiroku: senden kankei zakken; shokutaku oyobi hojōkin shikyū sonota sendenhi shikyū kankei gaikokujin no bu* (Foreign Ministry records, miscellaneous matters relating to propaganda; concerning the payments of commissions, bonuses and other propaganda expenses, foreigner section) *4, 1–3-1, 3–8-2–287, Taishō-2-nen,* Takamine Jōkichi to Makino Nobuaki, 26 March, 1913. For Clarke's visit and book on Japan see O'Connor 2004, Volume 5, Introduction.

31 Henry Satoh was born Satō Kenri (佐藤顕理) but Romanized his family name as Satoh and adopted the name Henry because his colleagues at the Associated Press and Reuters had problems with 'Kenri' (*Tsūshinsha-shi kankōkai* 1958: 111). Satoh had reported the Russo-Japanese War for Reuters, followed by a spell on the fledgling JT which he combined as Reuters' Tokyo correspondent c.1910–12 (Hasegawa 1966: 62). Satoh was a longstanding member of Kennedy's clique at *Kokusai* and the JT. In December 1919, when the pro-Japanese *North China Standard* was established in Shanghai, he was appointed its first editor.

32 Wildes 1927: 167–8.

33 On his expulsion from Japan, Pooley would publish in Shanghai and London *The Secret Memoirs of Count Hayashi* (1915), with revelations on Hayashi's role in the Anglo-Japanese Alliance and the Twenty-One Demands, *Japan at the Crossroads* (1917) and *Japan's Foreign Policies* (1919), all highly critical of Japan's propaganda programmes. In his 1917 book, Pooley had this to say of J.R. Kennedy: 'This gentleman is now the head of the International News Agency of Japan, [*Kokusai*] a semi-official concern, which controls the Reuter service, the semi-official *Japan Times* and *Japan Mail*, and the correspondence of the *New York Herald*, the *Christian Science Monitor*, and other American papers, besides having alliances with the Havas, Associated Press, and Stefani Agencies' (Pooley 1917: 17).

34 Wildes 1927: 169.

35 Byas 1924: Byas Papers, Yale, Reel 5.

36 Byas c.1914: Byas Papers, Yale, Reel 4.

37 Byas c.1914: Byas Papers, Yale, Reel 5. The JT's explanation for de Reuter's agreement is that he was persuaded by a letter from Kennedy's old boss at AP, Melville E. Stone (JTM 1966: 60).

38 *Tsūshinsha-shi kankōkai* 1958: 106–107.

39 *Tsūshinsha-shi kankōkai* 1958: 90–4.

40 Purdy 1987: 86.

41 Read 1992: 171–2.

42 Iwanaga (Shunkichi) 1980: 24, 28–30.

43 Siemens' involvement was revealed during the trial of a Siemens employee in Berlin in January 1914.

44 Byas c.1924: Byas Papers, Yale, Reel 5.
45 In 1924, Byas gave the amount Pooley received as £5000 (Byas Papers, Yale, Reel 5). In 1939 he put it at $25,000, which was roughly equivalent (Byas 1939: 317–18).
46 Hugh Byas went on to attribute Pooley's downfall as follows: '… it was generally believed at that time that the trio composed of Mr Kennedy, Mr Henry Sato [sic], and Mr Zumoto, or one of the three, gave evidence to Mr Shimada [Saburō], a leader of the Doshikwai and known as one of the best political orators of modern Japan, who mentioned the name of Mr Pooley in the Diet' (c.1914, Byas Papers, Yale, Reel 5). Both JT histories (1941, 1966) trumpet its investigative reporting: 'The Japan Times played a key role in the exposure of the major scandal involving top Navy officials and foreign manufacturers of munitions. A Reuters dispatch carried in the journal touched off the probe …' (1966: 75). That the Reuters dispatch originated with Andrew Pooley, the Reuters correspondent in Tokyo, and that the scandal resulted in Pooley's imprisonment and expulsion from Japan on evidence provided by the President of the JT, John Russell Kennedy, is not mentioned.
47 Wildes 1927: 177.
48 Rozanski 1974: 209–10.
49 *The Times*: despatch from David Fraser, Peking, 12 February 1915.
50 'Japanese Claims on China': Leader, *The Times*, 13 February 1915.
51 Morrison to John Jordan, 15 February 1915. In Lo 1976: 371–2.
52 Morrison to Ts'ai T'ing-kan, 2 March 1915. In Lo 1976: 382–3.
53 Carl Crow, Business Manager of the JA, received the full details in Tokyo eight months before the crisis, courtesy of the Russian ambassador. Crow mailed copies to five UP journalists. One reached its destination, enabling UP to be the first to publish the complete text of the Demands (Crow 1938: 16–20). Frederick Moore, the AP correspondent in Peking, was less fortunate: his report was spiked by Kennedy's mentor at AP New York, Melville E. Stone, following denials by the Japanese ambassador, Chinda Sutemi. Stone sent Moore an admonitory telegram 'for sending [a story of] demands that might start a war' (Abend 1943: 60; Rozanski 1974: 220).
54 Morrison to C. Clementi Smith, 26 May 1915 in Lo 1976: 406–407.
55 JT: 8 November 1917.
56 'Japan, Germany, Russia, and the Allies, An Authorized Interview with Count Masataka [sic] Terauchi, Premier of Japan': The *Outlook*, May 1918, 18.
57 Morrison to Clementi Smith, op. cit., 26 May 1915.
58 JT: 4 June 1918.
59 JC: 6 June 1918, 877.
60 JC: 6 July 1918; JA: 9 July 1918.
61 JC: 6 June 1918, 885.
62 *Shanghai Gazette* 24 August 1918, *Kobe Herald*: 3 September 1918, 4–5.
63 See FO 371/3820 [F 46002] for Procurator Mitsuhashi's copy of the *Revolt in Japan* article.
64 FO 371/3820 [F 46002]: Kawashima Nobukichi, forty-three, printer of the *Kobe Herald*, got three months jail and a fine of ¥70. Kawashima served four years as an apprentice compositor from the age of seventeen on the Chronicle but had been lured to the *Herald*. He returned to the *Chronicle* after serving his time.

65 FO 395/17 [F 133472]: July 1916, Memorandum, Annex A by Robertson-Scott, July 1916.

66 FO 395/17 [F 133472]: Sale quoted by Conyngham Greene in Memorandum, July 1916.

67 Foreign Office interest was close and detailed before and throughout the life of the journal, with, for example, close approval being sought on details such as the appointment and salary of a Japanese journalist, the use of artists and photographs, and liaison between the FO and Japanese journalists in London. FO 395/17 [F 174560], Minutes to telegram from C. Greene in Tokyo, 2 September 1916.

68 FO 395/17 [F 133472]: July 1916, Annex A to Robertson-Scott Memorandum.

69 FO 395/17 [F 174133]: Langley Minute on Conyngham Greene despatch, Tokyo, on the appointment of the *New East* Sub-Committee and Sale's dealings with them, August-September 1916.

70 FO 395/17 [F 133472]: July 1916, Annex A to Robertson-Scott Memorandum.

71 FO 395/91 [F 65]: 1 January 1917. Robertson-Scott to Sale, 3 January 1917.

72 The terms were: Byas to be paid ¥8680 per annum for three years; first class passage to London on termination. Byas's annual income at the *Advertiser* was ¥9880. Byas Papers, Yale, 1916, Reel 4.

73 JC, 5 June 1917, 'The Superlative Magazine'.

74 FO 395/91 [F 147647]: *Newspapers in Japan;* Minute, 26 July 1917.

75 JC: 5 June 1917.

76 JC: 6 June 1917.

77 Op. cit.

78 FO 395/168 [F 75619] 30 April 1918: the *New East.* C. Wingfield, Tokyo, to Gregory Maclesey, FO, 20 March 1918.

79 FO 395/168 [F 92053]: the *New East*: 24 May 1918. Wilson Crewdson to Gasalee, 22 May 1918. Charles V. Sale to Gasalee, 23 May 1918.

80 'It is an unfortunate fact about British journalists in China that the abler they are the more harm do they inflict on British interests': FO 371/11625 [F 1839/1/10]: Vereker in Peking commenting on Woodhead's activities to Wellesley, FO, 5 March 1926. For Far East Dept. on Russell-Kennedy, see the Frank Ashton-Gwatkin Minute in FO 395/334 [F 1242/730/150]: 1920.

81 Rozanski 1974: on Charles Crane's view of America's role in East Asia: 287–8, 301; on Carl Crow, V.S. McClatchy, B.W. Fleisher, J.B. Powell and Japan: 310–11; on Crane and Millard on the Japanese: 312–14.

2
The Foreign Ministry network, 1904–1937

Japan's long campaign to take control of its own news and to manage its own image was hampered by the negative consequences of its earlier forays in that campaign, as outlined above. From the idealized ally of the war with Russia and the new arrival at the top table in Paris, Japan suffered a growing sense of isolation in the 1920s. One consequence of this isolation was the building of the Foreign Ministry English-language media network under whose auspices a number of British-, Chinese- and American-owned newspapers in Japan and China were gradually bought out, suborned or closed down and replaced with new pro-Japanese organs.[1]

Japan's methods of dealing with the representatives of the Western press and the English-language newspapers of East Asia went through five overlapping stages that mixed persuasion and negotiation with tight, well-financed organization, an aggressive 'cold war', and finally, in the run-up to all-out war in China and the Pacific, a no-holds-barred 'endgame'. In the 'endgame' most Western newspaper correspondents and all critical voices on the English-language newspapers of East Asia were silenced and the foreign-owned English-language press networks of East Asia closed, suborned or bought out and effectively nationalized by the Foreign Ministry press network.

In the first stage, Japan started its own English-language newspapers in Japan and China and tried to persuade Western newspaper correspondents and journalists on the English-language newspapers to take a more friendly line towards Japan and Japanese policies. After 1913, Japan's representatives negotiated with Western news agencies in an effort to limit and render more positive the reporting of Japanese news and to filter foreign news coming into Japan.

In the second stage, following embarrassing public relations defeats at the Peace of Paris, Japan took a more considered and organized approach to the problem of making Japan's intentions more favourably understood. In 1920–21, it institutionalized its external propaganda effort in an Information Bureau (*Gaimushō Jōhōbu*) established within the Foreign Ministry,[2] which it followed up with generous and consistent investment in the Bureau's construction of the Foreign Ministry network which focused on East Asia, the United States and Britain, but with branch offices in other parts of Asia, Europe, Africa and South America, fifteen in all.[3]

In the third stage, the Foreign Ministry network enlarged its share of the news market in East Asia by selling its bulletins at prices none of the Western agencies could match. In 1926, it refined its news agency system with the creation of *Rengō*, and began fighting a 'cold war' or a 'thought war' (*shisōsen*) against the independent, foreign-owned *Japan Advertiser* and *Japan Chronicle* and their press networks in East Asia. In this stage, the Foreign Ministry network combined persuasion through subsidies and other inducements with takeovers of critical media in China, usually through a front man or shell company. The Foreign Ministry network also extended its network in the USA, Europe and Britain.

In the fourth stage, following Japan's withdrawal from the League of Nations, Japan's media campaigns heated up as it embarked on the fifteen-year war that would leave Asia in ruins. The Foreign Ministry network abandoned the persuasive tactics of the Shidehara era and adopted a more confrontational tone at its press conferences and in the editorials published in its network. This became more evident after 1936 with the inauguration of *Dōmei*, when the Foreign Ministry network became more proactive, increasingly arguing Japan's case within Japanese terms of reference and continuing to undercut other news agencies in a heavily-subsidized price war.

Finally, during a period of national consolidation, the Foreign Ministry ceded some of its power over the management of news to a series of Cabinet organizations set up in 1936, 1937 and 1940. Working in concert with the Foreign Ministry, these organizations set about amalgamating or simply closing down both the vernacular and the English-language newspapers in Japan, as well as using any means possible to silence critical media in a hard-fought 'endgame' in East Asia. In this final stage before all-out war, Japan served the West with some of its own medicine, establishing its own 'news colonies' in China, Korea and Taiwan.[4]

Given these later efforts to control and eventually close them down, how did the English-language newspapers of East Asia come to be seen as such a threat to Japanese interests? Between c.1890–1941, three contiguous, interconnected developments raised the status and profile of the independent English-language press of Japan and China both among settlers in East Asia and, indirectly, among readers in the West. These developments in turn sharpened and highlighted the challenge the independent English-language newspapers of East Asia presented to Japan's interests there. The first development was a long-term shift in the popularity of writings on East Asia by readers in the West. The second development was a related growth in Western demand for English-language news from and about Japan, especially Japan in East Asia. The third development was an accumulation of mutual interests and affiliations resulting in the formation of three broad networks among the English-language newspapers, magazines and news agencies operating in East Asia.

MOVEMENTS IN THE POPULARITY OF WRITINGS ON JAPAN

The connections between the English language newspapers and writers of Japan books were close. Many English language press journalists wrote books on Japan. Many writers of books on Japan also did bread and butter jobs – book reviews, feature articles – for the English-language press. Most authors of writings setting out Japan's case in East Asia in an explanatory manner were published by presses and newspapers associated with the *Japan Times* and other semi-official organs sponsored by the Foreign Ministry. Authors of critical writings on Japan came to be associated with the *Japan Chronicle* and the *Japan Advertiser* and their networks in China. *Chronicle* journalists sometimes wrote for the *Advertiser* and vice versa but none wrote for the *Japan Times*, whereas some prominent *Advertiser* and *Advertiser* network journalists, such as John N. Penlington, Frank Hedges and Randall Gould, wrote extensively for the *Japan Times* or for other publications sponsored by the Foreign Ministry, or, as in Gould's case, followed a *Japan Times* career by moving to China and adopting a pro-Nationalist stance. Akimoto Shunkichi and Honda Masujiroh's background on the *Oriental Review* did not prevent either from contributing critical analyses of Japanese foreign policy to the *Japan Advertiser*.

These interconnections between the English-language newspapers of East Asia and journalists writing articles and books on East Asia helped to produce a gradual shift in the fashion for writings on Japan and East Asia by readers in East Asia and in the West. The key element in this shift was the increased attention paid by Western newspapers and critical journals and, by extension, their readers, to writings on Japan published in the West by authors based in East Asia. In this shift, the critical tone of Japan's independent English-language press and its journalists' other writings seems to have been more popular than less critical writings by scholars based outside East Asia or by Japanese writers and spokesmen.

At the same time, the tendency of Western critics to praise or view as authentic or authoritative the work of Japanese writers publishing in English may have diminished as authenticity was increasingly attributed to the work of critical, even anti-Japanese, writings by journalists and Western scholars based in Japan and China. This in turn may have increased the *cachet* of all three networks of the English-language press of East Asia, because all of its Western writers were very much 'on the spot' in East Asia, as well as that of the more critical, foreign-owned networks. Thus, over time, alongside the rise of Japan as a power in East Asia, English-language readers there and in the West came to see the critical writings of Western writers based in East Asia as more 'authentic' than writings on these topics by Western authors based in the West and by Japanese writers, irrespective of their location. In this sense, Japanese writers may have been seen as possessing less authority to comment on events in their homeland than critical Western writers who shared the assumptions and background of their readers.

If this was the case, it was not always deserved. As Mordechai Rozanski has shown in the case of Western journalists contracted by the Chinese to lay their case before Western readers, all that was needed were trustworthy, well-connected publicists, not writers possessed of any special sensitivity to Chinese history and culture or even any mastery of the language. Indeed, Rozanski has described these people as:

> ... primarily describers of the superficial, the entertaining, the strange and the 'foreign'. They never approached greatness as expositors of the development of China or even as interpreters of the mass of the people. As publicists and as instruments they communicated pleas and arguments but very little analysis.[5]

This description can be applied to most of the journalists and writers on East Asia in this period. But crass interpretation of East Asia cannot be laid entirely at the journalists' door. Malcolm Kennedy resigned from Reuters in mid-1934 because his carefully balanced analyses of the Japanese political situation kept being spiked in favour of more sensational fare.[6] In any case, despite (and possibly because of) their overall mediocrity, Western writers on East Asia were read with increasing attention in the period under review.

If we examine the reception given to Nitobe Inazō's *Bushido* in the wake of Japan's success in the Russo-Japanese War, we can see that there was a time when Japanese explanations of Japan were at least taken at face value. In an attempt to explain why Nitobe had so much influence on Western, especially British, perceptions of Japan before 1914 and so little influence on them in the 1930s, and to account for the attention Western audiences paid to Western writers based in Japan, the Canadian scholar Hamish Ion has compared the influence of two groups: Western intellectuals and commentators based in Japan, including missionaries and journalists, and their counterparts in the West. Ion maintains that from the turn of the century highs of Sidney Gulick's *The White Peril* and Nitobe's *Bushido* (first published in 1900), Japanese writers on Japan and Western-based foreign writers ceded popularity and readers to writers who adopted a more critical approach to the description of Japan, especially those who did so from 'the spot'.[7]

The interest showed by British and American readers in writings on Japan by critical Western journalists on the spot in Japan and East Asia did not always occur at the expense of Japanese writers: after all, they should have been accepted as natural authorities on the subject. But the evidence that foreign writers on Japan were taken more seriously in these years does not mean that all Japanese writers were taken less seriously. Sugimoto Etsu's *A Daughter of the Samurai* received generous reviews when it was published in Britain and America in the late 1920s, but by the late 1930s, scissors-and paste or even patently fraudulent accounts, such as one by Graham Greene's feckless older brother Herbert, began to cater to a growing market for critical sensation.[8]

The tendency of Japanese writers to present a common, united, positive front on the policies of their nation represented a more balanced approach but it failed to meet this need for sensation, and it may have cost Japan some of the trust that Anglophone readers had previously reposed in writers like Nitobe. Nitobe's fall from fashion did not occur because of any inherent loss of quality in his writing, which was always readable, largely based on Western scholarship on East Asia and seldom fundamentally critical of Western values, but may have had more to do with an increased Western appetite for more critical writings on East Asia by Western authors based there.[9] Reports of political assassinations in Tokyo made the Japanese seem strange and dangerous. The deterioration in Anglo-Japanese relations made the Japanese appear less cordial. As a whole, the work of Japanese writers may have contradicted this hostility and seemed disingenuous, or simply less interesting than more critical writings on Japan: as a term, 'critical' became almost interchangeable with 'analytical', although this was far from the case.

Arthur Morgan Young's three books on Japan all stressed his credentials as a critical on-the-spot observer. Reviewing *Japan Under Taisho Tenno, 1912–1926* (1928), the *Manchester Guardian*, whose correspondent Young had been since 1925, assured its readers, 'Nowhere else than in these pages can the reader get so trustworthy, so comprehensive ... an account of the political, economic and social experiences of Japan.' Reviewing *Imperial Japan, 1926–1938* (1939) the *Contemporary Review* believed that it gave 'A most disturbing and pitiful picture, but it gives a point and a meaning to what we see of Japan abroad ... He writes logically, interestingly and with personal knowledge.' When the December 1937 *Fact* magazine devoted an entire issue to his article, 'Japan's War on China', the introduction by *Fact*'s general editor, Raymond Postgate, stressed Young's long *Chronicle* experience (assistant editor 1912–22, editor 1922–36) as well as his exclusion by the Japanese authorities 'in pursuit of their general line of policy'.[10] Similarly, Carl Crow's *I Speak for the Chinese* (1938) was, according to the jacket, 'a shocking, factual book written from the heart by one who knows the Oriental people as few Westerners do'.[11] Crow was 'brilliantly qualified, by his experience and first-hand knowledge, to present the case for China before the world'.

The popularity of Western writers on Japan was not confined to journalists. We can see early indications of it in the reception granted in the summer of 1921 to the novel *Kimono* by Frank Ashton-Gwatkin (1889–1976). Gwatkin was a Foreign Office official stationed in Kōbe and at the Yokohama consulate in 1913–18, and thereafter at the Far East Department in Whitehall, where he wrote novels of Japanese life under the pseudonym 'John Paris'.[12] *Kimono* offers a well-paced but prurient account of Japan as a nation shot through with venality and hypocrisy. Reviewing it as the product of inside knowledge (the identity of 'John Paris' seems to have been an open secret in Whitehall and in Miyakezaka) one critic professed to see 'a boa-constrictor coiled up outside every Japanese nursery', the better to confine the outlook of those within.[13] Four similar novels followed in 1924, 1927, 1929 and

1932, most of them kindly reviewed in Britain, where their author was treated as an authority on Japan even though he did not return there until the mid-1970s.[14]

One of the most hostile pictures of Japan to emerge in the 1930s was *The Menace of Japan* by 'Professor Taid O'Conroy',[15] who claimed that he was 'considered the "Best Authority, East and West" on anything concerning Japan'.[16] When *The Menace of Japan* was published in 1933, it was sold as the work of a perceptive insider. The back cover emphasized that 'The book is not mere sensationalism; it is a cold, logical thesis compiled by the author during his fifteen years in Nippon', but it went on to advertise its provision of 'authenticated stories of the debauchery of the Buddhist priests, unutterable cruelty, sex orgies, of trafficking in human flesh, of baby brokers'. The introduction stressed the author's 'special credentials and his inside knowledge of Japan'. Not only had he taught at Keio University, 'the Oxford of Japan', but he had married into an 'aristocratic Japanese family' and become 'a 100 per cent Shintoist and Japanese'. Moreover, 'Eamonn de Valera, when he was preparing to act as President of the League during its consideration of the policy of Japan in Manchuria, used parts of this book in manuscript form'.[17] In other words, O'Conroy had alerted the President of the League of Nations to the 'menace' of Japan just when the Council of the League was debating the report of its four-man Commission regarding Japan's behaviour in Manchuria. From a publisher's point of view, the book was well-timed. The Manchurian Crisis was unresolved, British ties to Japan were deteriorating, and Japan's spectacular withdrawal from the League may also have appeared more threatening than capitulation to international consensus, however ineffectual. By May 1938 *The Menace of Japan* was in its seventh British edition and had sold 13,000 copies, according to the Paternoster edition of that year.

O'Conroy (even his name was adopted) may well have sent his manuscript to de Valera, but he was never a professor at Keio and his wife's family was far from 'aristocratic'. Spending most of his spare hours at the bar or in the lobby of the Imperial Hotel cannot have left him much time to live as 'a 100 per cent Shintoist and Japanese', still less to learn the language, but at a time when international attention was focused on the crisis in East Asia the phrase could hardly fail to whet the public appetite for what seemed like 'the inside dope' and O'Conroy could not be ignored by the press. The *Daily Mail*'s Foreign Editor, Douglas Crawford, gave O'Conroy a fulsome introduction to the Foreign Office, where he met and puzzled Sir John Pratt with his complicated theories.[18]

O'Conroy's *The Menace of Japan* was officially published in London in July 1933, but the launch appears to have been postponed to 13 October. On that day Hurst & Blackett brought out both O'Conroy's book and the first English translation of Adolf Hitler's *Mein Kampf*. At the launch party at the Savoy Hotel, George Bernard Shaw told Sidney Campion of the *Daily Dispatch*, 'I don't think the average person in this country realizes how the Japanese are a menace to the peace of the world.' In remarks that would be reproduced on the cover of the 1938 paperback edition, Shaw declared, 'I am saying all this because I want you to tell people to read Professor T. O'Conroy's book on "The Menace of Japan". Professor O'Conroy, who was at Keio University, is one of the most remarkable men in the world. He is married to a Japanese.' Just as the *Express* had done on 26 September, and as Shaw did at the launch party, the press in Britain and the US took their cues from O'Conroy's book and used his bona fides – inside knowledge, Keio, aristocratic Japanese wife – to lend a sort of proxy credibility to their reports and interviews. Fighting back in Japan, the *Tōkyō Asahi Shinbun* ran an article by its London correspondent headlined '*Uso happyaku o narabeta "Nihon no Kyōi" shuppan'* ('Eight hundred Lies published in *"The Menace of Japan"'*).[19]

The Menace of Japan was a scissors-and-paste job, heavily dependent on back numbers of the English-language newspapers of Japan. Citing 'the *Japan Advertiser* (Vernacular Edition)' and 'the *Japan Chronicle* (Vernacular Edition)' cannot have helped his cause in Japan, where the fact that neither paper had a Japanese edition must have been common knowledge. 'Professor Taid O'Conroy' was the joint creation of Tim Conroy, an impoverished autodidact from Co. Cork who died of cirrhosis of the liver in November 1935 (but not before giving dramatic interviews from his deathbed in Hammersmith to the *Evening Standard* and *Sunday Despatch*).[20]

The writers involved in this shift of popularity to critical writers like Morgan Young, Conroy and Crow can be very crudely divided between those associated with the Foreign Ministry network, who fought hard but failed to gain the esteem of Anglophone readers, and the journalists, entrepreneurs, politicians, foreign correspondents and writers associated with the *Japan Chronicle* and *Japan Advertiser* and their networks in East Asia.

As Ion has explained, the rise and fall in the Western public's esteem of pro-Japanese writers was paralleled by a 'reverse fall and rise' in the influence of Western reporters, observers and intellectuals in Japan.[21] Western readers continued to study the work of Foreign Ministry apologists and spokesmen like K.K. Kawakami, John N. Penlington, George Bronson Rea, J.O.P. Bland and Henry Kinney. All of these, save Kawakami, had the authority of being on the spot. But Western readers also consumed the more critical writings of on-the-spot observers working for the foreign-owned English-language press networks of East Asia: Robert Young, Putnam Weale, John B. Powell, Arthur Morgan Young, Frederick Millard, Edgar Snow, H.J. Timperley, H.G.W. Woodhead, Harold Isaacs, George Sokolsky, Rodney Gilbert, Randall Gould and Amleto Vespa, as well that of seasoned observers such as Hugh Byas.

As an established and well-distributed collection of contemporary, on-the-spot serial reportage on Japan and China that employed many of the writers listed above, the independent English-language press of East Asia gained authority, locally and in the West, from this trend. In turn, this higher profile intensified the challenge it appeared to pose to the West's acceptance of Japanese aims and interests in East Asia.

In Japan in July 1937, under the auspices of the Cabinet Information Bureau (*Naikaku Jōhōbu*), where the Home, Army, Naval and Foreign ministries were all represented, a process was set in train by which the vernacular press would be culled and amalgamated from 739 dailies in 1939 to 102 in 1942 and only 54 by 1945.[22] However, to one of the architects of unified press control, J.R. Kennedy's former assistant Furuno Inosuke, 'the real adversary in the Japanese media was the over-powering presence of a strong foreign press in Japan and Asia'.[23]

The English-language press of East Asia and the correspondents of the Western press came to be seen in an increasingly negative and threatening light. In a wartime article, Amō Eiji, successively head of the Foreign Ministry Information Bureau and the Cabinet Information Bureau, declared:

> The Anglo-Americans not only encroached upon East Asia politically and exploited East Asia economically, but also converted East Asia into their 'news colony' ... they misused the right of communication ... Thus, though we all lived in East Asia, our eyes looking at East Asia were kept covered.[24]

Amō, Furuno and Iwanaga devoted themselves to strengthening Japan's ability to make its nature and its activities understood on Japan's terms through a National News Service (*Kokkateki daihyō tsūshinsha*). For these and for other media professionals working within the Foreign Ministry network, what was at stake was the Western world's – especially America's – idea of Japan, and, in particular, of Japan's activities in China. If public opinion and official policy in the West could be brought round to what Foreign Ministry journalists and pamphleteers described as a 'proper understanding' of Japan's mission in East Asia, the likelihood of Western intervention or 'interference' there might be diminished.

THE GROWTH IN DEMAND FOR NEWS OF JAPAN

The threat that English-language newspapers appeared to pose to Japanese interests also stemmed in part from a growth in Western demand for news of Japan, fed by a heightening of international tensions. There were ten full-time Tokyo foreign correspondents for Western English-language newspapers and news agencies in January 1941, compared to five in 1920 and three in 1913. Total foreign correspondents in all languages had gone from three in 1913, to five in 1920, seven or eight in 1926, to twenty in 1933 and thirty-five in 1936. There were forty full-time correspondents in Tokyo in 1937, and thirty in January 1941. Of these thirty, ten represented Western English-language newspapers, and another ten represented newspapers in Asian languages and European languages other than German and Italian. The final ten correspondents represented the primary Axis powers: Germany and Italy. The same period saw an even greater increase in the supply of correspondence by stringers on the local English-language newspapers and in the number of journalists visiting Japan for short investigative tours.[25]

The increased demand for Japan news did not help the sales of Japan's English-language press. In 1925, in an informal survey of claims made by rival editors, Harry Wildes found that the combined circulations of the foreign-owned English-language newspapers of Japan totalled about 13,300: the *Advertiser* had 10,000, the *Chronicle* 3,000, whereas in January of that year the *Japan Times* claimed a pressroom run of 6,300 copies, of which, according to Frank Hedges, then editing the *Advertiser*, a good many went to Japanese embassies abroad and business firms with government connections, some of whom contracted for a hundred copies daily at a cost of ¥100, as a form of subsidy.[26] By 1938, the *Advertiser* had dropped to 4,000 and the *Chronicle* to about 2,600.[27] From 1918 to October 1940 the *Japan Times'* unsubsidized circulation amounted to around 4,000 copies; a considerable advance on John Robertson-Scott's estimate of 500 copies for 1916. In theory, the 4,000 figure should have tripled after the *Japan Times* 'incorporated' its rivals in October and December of that year.[28]

However, the influence of the English-language newspapers did not rest only on circulation but on language, or rather the lack of it. Few non-Japanese learned Japanese between the wars. At SOAS, London University, from 1918 to 1923 the average annual intake of students of Japanese was twenty-seven, and from 1923 to 1941 only eleven.[29] Furthermore, most of these students were studying the language at an elementary level, not for a BA degree. In 1935 in Australia, a survey found only seven people familiar with Japanese: one academic and six persons 'able to read and write imperfectly'.[30] Immediately after Pearl Harbor, Donald Keene heard a radio broadcast to the effect that only fifty Americans knew Japanese.[31]

Some resident English-language journalists spoke Japanese well, among them Thomas Satchell of the *Chronicle*, Frank Brinkley of *The Times* and the *Japan Mail* and, in the early 1930s, the Reuters correspondent and *Japan Advertiser* contributor, Malcolm Kennedy.[32] Apart from Satchell, who was primarily a translator, none of the *Chronicle* writers, including Hearn during his brief tenure as leader writer, had more than a smattering of the language. To most *Chronicle* and *Advertiser* writers, Japanese was a service provided by their translators, not a means of communication, although the *Advertiser* regularly published opinion pieces by Japanese journalists who could write in English. Both Wilfrid Fleisher and Hugh Byas relied on bilingual assistants for translation and interpretation from Japanese. In 1940–41, not one of the ten Anglophone correspondents representing the 'democracies' in Tokyo in 1941 could read Japanese, whereas, of the ten Axis correspondents, all had developed some fluency in speaking and degrees of reading ability in the language.[33] The intriguing exception in Tokyo was the *Frankfurter Zeitung*'s Richard Sorge. Agnes Smedley, Sorge's *Frankfurter Zeitung* stablemate in Shanghai and Yan'an (Yenan) had the same problem with Chinese.[34]

Humorous and not-so-humorous references to language problems were common in readers' letters and among the columnists of the English-language newspapers. However, for most readers the language problem meant the problems experienced by the Japanese in speaking or writing English, seldom the reverse. In 'Language Research Findings' in his weekly *Achi Kochi* column, the *Advertiser*'s O.D. Russell satirized his compatriot's ignorance of Japanese but he also enlivened their leisure moments with such gems as 'Little Led Liding Hood'.[35]

The use of English in the English-language organs of the Foreign Ministry network may have deterred those it was intended to reach. By setting up the news agencies and the newspapers in the Foreign Ministry network, Japan's spokesmen took an increasing share of the English-language news of East Asia and won the freedom to explain Japanese activities, policies and aspirations in Japanese terms. The problem was that their terms were not clear.

Propaganda involves the exercise of rhetorical skills. Propagandists often adopt a worldly, rational tone, but their message does not have to be rational to succeed in its usual purposes: appealing to the emotions and making calls to action. But the vocabulary and style used in most Foreign Ministry English-language publications may have been counterproductive. Describing the war in China and a political assassination equally as an 'Incident' trivialized both, although the distinction was clearer in Japanese, for example, the use of *jihen*, rather than *jiken* for the second Sino-Japanese War. Prime Minister Konoe Fumimaro's announcement in November 1938 of the launching of a 'new order in East Asia' (*Tōa shinchitsujo*) and of a future Great East Asia Co-Prosperity Sphere (*Daitōa kyōeiken*) read like blatant attempts at the sanctification of aggression. The house style that gave the world the headline 'East Hopei Anti-Comintern Autonomous State Is Created Solely Through Desire of 7,000,000 Oppressed People of China' in 1937 reminded readers of similar claims made for Manchuria and Jehol in 1931–33 and is unlikely to have increased their faith in the spontaneity of the changes adopted in East Hopei.[36] Doing their best to tie old-fashioned military aggression and catch-up imperialism to Japan's master narratives of national victimization, isolation and encirclement, the embattled Anglophone journalists and translators of the Foreign Ministry network often stretched meaning to breaking point.[37]

Western journalists with any competence in Chinese were as rare as those with any knowledge of Japanese. One of the best known China journalists, G.E. Morrison, made no attempt to learn Chinese during his years of residence and built his legendary library on English-language accounts of China. In this, he was at one with most 'Shanghailanders', the mostly British settlers for whom learning Chinese was seen as 'a demeaning compromise with indigenous society'.[38] Charles James Fox of the *North China Star* of Tientsin was unusual among foreign newspapermen in his efforts to learn Chinese. The linguistic weakness of foreign journalists in China also tended to box them into a limited, binary East-West interpretation of events.[39] It is worth asking whether the viewpoint of the Chinese nationalist Eugene Chen (Chen Youren), who had been born and educated outside China and did not speak or read Chinese, would have been different had he done so.

Japanese news managers capitalized on the linguistic weakness of foreign journalists, but some in the Chinese media saw it as demeaning. At the Press Congress of the World in October-November 1921 all four Chinese delegates criticized the quality of Western reporting on China, with one of them, Hollington Tong (Deng Chuankai), asking:

> [Would] the powerful Occidental papers ... think of sending to ... France a man who perhaps is not simply ignorant of [French language and history], but who despises them? That is more or less what they do when they send men to China ... The inevitable result is ... that the world is misled, instead of being informed.[40]

Tong was an exception in stressing this ignorance, especially since it was conspicuously displayed by two of his closest associates, Thomas Millard and John B. Powell. Nevertheless, as far as the US was concerned, he had a point: four months after Pearl Harbor, only 60% of a national sample in a poll taken in the US could locate China on an outline map of the world.[41] As Tong later came to appreciate when he was put in charge of censorship and propaganda as Director of the Guomindang (Kuomintang) Ministry of Information in Nanjing and Chongqing, the English-language press of East Asia owed much of its influence to a sort of linguistic default: the fact that as far as Japan and China were concerned, the Western English-language newspapers were represented by illiterates.[42]

Unable to read vernacular newspapers and seldom able to consult the man in the street, most correspondents in Japan took their information from the Foreign Ministry Information Bureau press conferences, and in China from bulletins provided by officials like Eugene Chen and, from the early 1930s, Hollington Tong. They did their best to balance these with whatever they could glean from the local English-language press, which at least provided opinion pieces in English and a range of translations from the vernacular press.

Thus, for journalists, whether Japanese, Chinese and foreign, for diplomats, visiting businessmen and missionaries, the English-language newspapers of China and Japan, foreign-owned and 'independent' and semi-official alike, were required reading. Whatever the linguistic weaknesses and prejudices of their staff, their readers' professional requirements and personal preferences gave the independent English-language press of East Asia a considerable influence on the Western world's idea of Japan in general and, in the period under review, of Japanese policies on and activities in East Asia.

Whether or not it was transferrable, Japan and the Foreign Ministry network, and later China and the Chinese Ministry of Information network, coveted this influence. Indeed, the long endeavour of Japan's Foreign Ministry network, first to counteract, then to suborn and subvert, and finally to destroy or co-opt the influence of the English-language press of East Asia became in itself a factor in the development of the foreign-owned English-language press networks.

THE FORMATION OF NETWORKS IN THE ENGLISH-LANGUAGE PRESS

East Asia's foreign-owned English-language press networks were informal accumulations of commonalities of editorial line, worldview and commercial interest between two groups of journalists and their newspapers and journals in Japan and China, about a dozen in total, clustered around the *Japan Chronicle* of Kōbe (founded in October 1891) discussed in detail in Chapter 3, and the *Japan Advertiser* of Tokyo (founded in November 1890) which I examine in Chapter 4. For the two foreign-owned networks, not the least of their commonalities was their opposition to the editorial line taken by the dozen or so English-language newspapers and agencies supported by the Foreign Ministry Information Bureau, most notably their flagship enterprise, the *Japan Times* of Tokyo, a media group described here as the Foreign Ministry network.

At first glance, these networks were marked by national differences, but the national commonalities of point-of-view, national identity and cultural interest of their owners and journalists were often camouflaged by more complex issues of ownership, registration, investment, translation, readership and subsidy.[43] Most of the journalists and proprietors in the *Chronicle* network were British, but, until very late in the day, they were kept at arm's length by embassy officials in Japan and China, and their reports were seen as creating too many difficulties for the embassy and diplomatic establishment in East Asia for the *Chronicle* to qualify as Britain's network. The most important figures in the *Advertiser* network were American, Frederick S. Millard, Charles R. Crane, Powell and Fleisher. Crane helped Millard gain privileged access to Woodrow Wilson and the network was well represented on George Creel's China Committee on Publicity in 1917–18, through Crane's secretary, Walter Rogers and the journalist Carl Crow.

Finally, the frequent involvement of Western and Chinese nationals in the Japanese press in China should not obscure the fact that the English-language press network supporting Japanese interests in East Asia, Europe and the US can safely be described as the Japan network or the Foreign Ministry network. I have chosen the latter term, although I acknowledge that the 'Japan network' begins to sound more appropriate after the assault on Pearl Harbor.

The networks of the English-language newspapers of East Asia were not cast in stone. A circle of international-minded Japanese at the *Japan*

Times shared some of the principles expressed by their independent contemporaries, but they had to adapt to other ideas whose time had also come. The relationship between the *Japan Times* and the Foreign Ministry fluctuated as different factions dominated the Ministry and different Presidents and editors came and went at the *Japan Times* but it survived the stresses and pressures of the time better than its rivals. Relations between Reuters and the Foreign Ministry became less cordial as those on the Japanese side felt that Reuters was receiving too great a benefit from the agreement of 1913. In the 1920s, they moved into outright competition in China as the *Shin-Tōhō* news agency undercut Reuters at every turn. After the establishment of *Dōmei* in 1936 and the outbreak of long-term Sino-Japanese hostilities in 1937 this competition turned to outright aggression with the harassment of Reuters correspondents in China and Japan.

Although they agreed on many issues, there were clear differences in the way the two foreign-owned network leaders were perceived. Writing in the early 1920s, one H.A. Thompson ascribed rabid anti-Japanese prejudice among expatriates, particularly in Kōbe, to the *Japan Chronicle*: 'Its attitude of condemnation is so extreme that it is no exaggeration to say that it never has a good word for the Japanese'. Thompson had kinder words for the *Japan Advertiser*: 'It is, of course, American owned and American in style, but it endeavours to be neutral, and embittered editorial comment is most notably absent.'[44]

These were differences of perception more than substance, as the *Chronicle* and *Advertiser* networks were agreed (but not united) on many international issues. One bar to the development of a mature understanding was the anti-British, anti-imperialist view held by many American journalists in the *Advertiser* network, most notably Millard and Powell; another was commercial rivalry between British and American interests, especially in China. The *Advertiser* took a more flexible approach to the realities of power in Japan than did the *Chronicle*, undertaking printing work for the Foreign Ministry network, including books and pamphlets for the South Manchuria Railway promoting Japan's build-up in China and the development of Manchukuo, and a number of *Japan Advertiser* network writers and entrepreneurs wrote propaganda for the Foreign Ministry network, among them Henry Kinney, Zoë Kincaid, J.N. Penlington, Vere Redman and Frank Hedges. The *Chronicle*'s *bête-noire* John Russell Kennedy, officially the owner of the *Japan Times*, had been a *Japan Advertiser* shareholder since at least 1908, when B.W. Fleisher first bought the paper in Yokohama.[45] Hugh Byas, the *Advertiser*'s longest-serving editor, maintained cordial relations with the Foreign Ministry and his writings occasionally found their way into its propaganda. At different points in his career, H.G.W. Woodhead had close contacts with all three networks, as did the flexible Putnam Weale and the ubiquitous George Sokolsky.

In the course of the late 1920s and mid-1930s, the *Japan Advertiser* network in China developed into a Sino-American network, where the strongest links were to Nanjing and the Guomindang. In Shanghai, Thomas Millard's *China Press* was established in partnership with the Chinese diplomat Wu Ting-fang in 1911, with finance from the Chinese government and Charles Crane, later US Minister to China (1920–21), and B.W. Fleisher, owner of the *Japan Advertiser*. The *Shanghai Gazette* was founded and financed in the summer of 1918 by a circle around Sun Yatsen (Sun Yat-sen). Sun himself and his editor, Eugene Chen, had spent most of their life outside China. Hired at Sun's behest, the American George Sokolsky (1893–1962) brought considerable energy and a keen nose for news and useful contacts with US officials to the editorial team.

In 1935, Edgar Snow maintained that the *Peking Chronicle* was owned by Chinese nationalist interests for whom Sheldon Ridge, the editor, provided a British front. According to Snow, Ridge received a monthly salary from the Guomindang and ensured that nothing critical of the Party or its members appeared in the newspaper. The *Peking Chronicle* ran severely anti-Japanese editorials from time to time, but kept silent on round-ups and executions of local CCP members. Another *Peking Chronicle* journalist drew two salaries: one from the Guomindang, the other (plus a car) from the German Transocean news agency, then a Nazi propaganda vehicle, for getting as many Transocean stories into the newspaper as possible. Despite its Guomindang connections, the *Peking Chronicle* still had to struggle with the multilayered censorship bureau in Peking (Beijing). This was dominated by the Guomindang but the Mayor's representative took instructions from the Japanese consulate.[46] Obviously, by this time, Ridge was not a member of any particular network but simply working the system and for him, the networks of the English-language newspapers of East Asia were more expressions of *entente* than interest or purpose However, from both Japanese and Chinese perspectives, these newspapers increasingly took on a conspiratorial aspect.

OFFICIAL SUSPICIONS

The idea that the English-language newspapers constituted a hostile network may have occurred to Japanese officials as early as September 1918, when the *Kobe Herald* reprinted Putnam Weale's *Shanghai Gazette* article 'Revolt in Japan' on the politics of the rice riots. A few months later, during preparations for the Paris Peace Conference, Japan's consul general to Shanghai, Ariyoshi Akira, observed:

> It is worth paying attention to the fact that newspapers and magazines funded by Americans, such as the *China Press*, *Millard's Review of the Far East* and others, are printing many anti-Japanese articles. This tends to look as though it may be to some extent an orchestrated campaign.[47]

Ariyoshi's message was based on his reading of these two organs. In late 1918, the links between the *China Press* and *Millard's Review* had been extended to China's delegates to the Peace Conference, from both Peking and Canton (Guangzhou). Of the Canton government delegates to Paris, both Wu Ting-fang and Tang Shaoyi (Tang Shao-yi) had been friendly since at least 1911 with Carl Crow of the *Japan Advertiser* and the China Committee on Public Information. In 1911, Wu was part of the Sino-American consortium that financed Thomas Millard's *China Press*. Tang was close to the 'young China' delegates at the Paris Conference, Wang Cheng-t'ing and V.K. Wellington Koo (Gu Weizhun), both of whom would participate in notable propaganda victories over Japan.[48]

In 1921, the Foreign Ministry took the *Japan Chronicle*'s campaign against the Anglo-Japanese Alliance seriously enough to try to arrange the acquisition of the newspaper by a friendly Kōbe businessman. The term 'propaganda network' (*senden mō*) was often used in discussions for the establishment of the Foreign Ministry Information Bureau in 1919–20.[49] So the notion of a hostile network was gaining currency among Japanese observers when the soldier-politician Ugaki Kazushige (1868–1956), drew the chart shown in Fig. 1 in his diary for 15 July 1923.

SHANGHAI	*The China Press* [American] (Extremely anti-Japanese) (Jewish)
	The Shanghai Mercury [British] (Neutral) (Jewish)
	The North-China Daily News [British] (anti-Japanese) (Jewish)
	The Shanghai Times [American] (Stance unclear) (Jewish)
TIENTSIN	*The Peking & Tientsin Times* [British] (Extremely anti-Japanese)
	The North China Star [American] (Extremely anti-Japanese)
	The Peking Leader [American] (anti-Japanese) (Capitalized by US interests at ¥500,000)
	The North China Standard [Japanese] (Pro-Japanese)
JAPAN	*The Nagasaki Press* [American] (Of no influence)
	The Japan Chronicle [British] (Extremely anti-Japanese)
	The Kobe Herald [British] (Stance unclear)
	The Japan Advertiser [American] (Superficially neutral) (Jewish)
	The Japan Gazette (Yokohama) [British] (Neutral)

Figure 1. *Possible influences on the English-language newspapers of East Asia in 1923.* Source: Ugaki 1971: 434.[50]

In his search for commonalities, Ugaki followed one convention of the day and looked for the 'Jewish connection' (*yudaya kin*), which he found in five newspapers. Of these five, Ugaki found the *China Press*, whose business manager was B.W. Fleisher, 'extremely anti-Japanese' (*kyokutan han-nichi*), the *Shanghai Mercury* 'neutral' (*chūritsu*), the *North-China Daily News*, edited by O.M. Green, 'anti-Japanese' (*han-nichi*), the *Shanghai Times* under 'American' control, and the *Japan Advertiser*, owned and managed by B.W. Fleisher, 'superficially neutral' (*hyō-chū*). Thus Ugaki agreed with those at the Foreign Ministry who did not believe that B.W. Fleisher's attitude to Japanese officialdom was sincere.

However, as his survey indicates, Ugaki was unable to find a workable correlation between Jewish connections and anti-Japanese sentiment. Some newspapers had no Jewish connections but they were also 'anti-Japanese'. Of the seven British-owned newspapers, Ugaki considered two 'extremely anti-Japanese'. Of the three American-owned newspapers, two were 'extremely anti-Japanese'. The one 'American' paper whose stance he found 'unclear', the *Shanghai Times*, was in 1923 under nominal British, not American, management, and furthermore, according to a report from Carl Crow to the US Department of State, the Japanese had 'practically gained control' of it, (as Ugaki might have known, for it had taken a pro-Japanese line since its acquisition in 1911 by the Yokohama Specie Bank).[51] Under the editorship of Alfred Morley, the *Shanghai Times* continued to present Japan's case during the Shanghai Incident.[52] In 1937, the paper was still 'virtually owned by the Japanese but nominally edited by Britishers', according to Hollington Tong, among them the Anglo-Indian journalist R.I. Hope.[53]

Whether Ugaki's chart was inspired guesswork or based on surveillance reports is not known, and it is significant that he drew it up, but by the time he did so, Japanese reports on the Republican press in China were reporting the 'interference' of foreign journalists in Chinese media as a matter of course.[54] In 1939, officials of the North China Army Propaganda Section mapped a similar typology of foreign news agencies in China. See Fig. 2.

To the Foreign Ministry, the *Japan Chronicle* was the most consistently anti-Japanese of Japan's English-language newspapers, and the Kōbe police kept all the Youngs of the *Chronicle* staff – Robert Young and his two sons, Eric and Douglas, and his successor Arthur Morgan Young – under close surveillance. The paper was viewed with even greater suspicion in 1921, when two world figures visited Robert Young in Kōbe: Bertrand Russell in July and Lord Northcliffe in November. Northcliffe's visit to Young's office in Kōbe magnified the *Chronicle*'s reputation as an influence on international perceptions of Japan. When Northcliffe launched his 'Watch Japan!' newspaper campaign the following spring, his meeting with Young gave rise to a number of conspiracy theories, not all of them emanating from the Foreign Ministry.

B.W. Fleisher, the *Advertiser*'s proprietor since 1908, took a far less confrontational stance than any of the *Chronicle* editors, but he was not trusted and was seen as an active impediment to the work of the Foreign Ministry's flagship news agency, *Kokusai*, as a 1921 Foreign Ministry note records:

B.W. Fleisher, the owner and Editor of the *Japan Advertiser* and the *Trans-Pacific*, visited our Ministry. He is trying to set up a correspondence of the *Public Ledger* in the Far East. He asked me to get help from you. But our Ministry and the *Advertiser* and *Trans-Pacific* have no special relationship. Also, it is thought that although he claims to be working for our benefit, Fleisher hides two faces under the same hood and is playing a double game.

Name	Location	Nationality	Character
United Press	Peking, Tientsin	US	Tientsin bureau is anti-Japanese
Associated Press	Peking	US	Anti-Japanese
International News Service	Peking	US	Somewhat anti-Japanese
International News Service	Peking	US	Somewhat anti-Japanese
Reuters	Peking, Tientsin	Britain	Extremely anti-Japanese
DNB	Peking	Germany	Extremely pro-Japanese
Transocean	Peking	German	Moderate
Havas	Peking	France	Somewhat anti-Japanese

Figure 2. *Foreign news agencies and their sympathies in China* in 1939. Source: *Hokushigun hōdōbu, Hokushigun hōdō senden gaiyō* 1939: 15.[55]

> He is at daggers drawn with Mr [John Russell] Kennedy, with whom we enjoy special relations. With this in mind, his presence in Peking on this occasion will probably result in some interruption or hampering of Kokusai News Agency activities. We should bear this in mind, while extending to Mr Fleisher all the usual courtesies during his visit.[56]

Fleisher's association with V.S. McClatchy, editor of California's notoriously anti-Japanese newspaper the *Sacramento Bee*, in a news agency project in 1919–23 confirmed these suspicions, especially in the wake of the 1924 Exclusion Act. In 1908–9 Shibusawa Eiichi had promoted the early Foreign Ministry network to check precisely the sentiments that the Act indulged. Here was Ugaki's 'superficial neutrality' again.

To some officials, Hugh Byas was more convincingly neutral. A 1921 Nagasaki police record noted, '[Byas's] understanding is both pro-Japanese and anti-Japanese. He made a good impression on our staff.'[57] In 1933, Byas was described by the journalist Ukita Heisuke as 'by far the fairest and most temperate of foreign writers on Japan's international political development'.[58] Hugh Byas may have convinced many Japanese of his impartiality because on a number of contentious points he was willing to see the merits of Japan's case. Although he lamented the style of Japanese diplomacy and highlighted what he saw as blind spots in Japanese insensitivities to non-Japanese peoples, Byas gave credence to Japanese accounts of the cause of the Manchurian Incident, for example. Indeed, some of his reports found their way into Japanese propaganda in the late 1930s.[59] However, in November 1941, one of the policemen who interrogated Byas's successor, Otto Tolischus, told him that Byas had always been 'an American spy'.[60] In a later memoir, Tolischus recalled the police accusation, 'You have been doing Intelligence work for the Embassy. Byas, your predecessor, was [Joseph] Grew's outside Intelligence man for years, and you have done the same kind of work.'[61]

In the late 1930s, Byas's long friendship with Makino Nobuaki, Lord Privy Seal, 1925–35, who in conversations over many years helped Byas understand and report the political scene in Japan, may have protected him from arrest.[62] In 1930, when Byas left the *Advertiser* to concentrate on his foreign correspondence, his departure may have left the paper more vulnerable to official pressure, though the move to his foreign correspondence did not endanger his own position and may even have protected it.

NEWS MANAGEMENT AND NATIONAL INTEGRITY: JAPAN AT THE PARIS CONFERENCE

We saw in Chapter 1 how the Siemens Scandal, the Twenty-One Demands incident, the *Outlook* interview, the 'White Rainbow' affair and the *Kobe Herald* incident were each connected to propaganda and news management, and noted that the *Kokusai Tsūshinsha* and the *Jyapan Taimuzu Kabushiki-gaisha* were set up in order to place the management of news of Japan more firmly in Japanese hands. These were important early skirmishes in Japan's long battle for international credibility and national integrity.

None of these incidents redounded to Japan's credit. The Siemens Scandal made Japan look corrupt. The Twenty-One Demands made Japan look like a bully and, just as important for Chinese propaganda, made China look like a victim. The *Outlook* affair made Japanese foreign policy look opportunistic and raised question marks about the strength of Japan's commitment to her ally, Britain. Government handling of the 'White Rainbow' and *Kobe Herald* incidents made Japan look unstable and undemocratic.

These incidents threatened to damage Japan's national integrity just when it was most needed, for in late November 1918 Japanese representatives left Yokohama for Paris, there for the first time to sit at the top table with the victorious powers. In a Conference which did what it could to reshape the world in open diplomacy and according to the principle of self-determination, Japan's early attempts at press management may not have helped the presentation of her case at Paris but, on the other hand, causes that had seemed so explosive to the English-language press networks of East Asia, most notably Japan's handling of Korea's 'Mansei' independence movement and the May 4th Movement were, by agreement, sidelined and not raised in the main deliberations of the Conference.[63]

Japan's publicity team at the Conference was headed by Matsuoka

Yōsuke, with John Russell Kennedy as press manager and a useful team of representatives that included a youthful Toshi Gō (as he would come to style himself), a future editor of the *Japan Times*. One problem for Matsuoka and Kennedy was the unbending formality of the Japanese delegates, not least their 'symbolic'[64] leader, Saionji Kinmochi, who holed up in the Hotel Meurice and only conferred with old Parisian acquaintances, avoiding the press at all costs.[65] Kennedy and Matsuoka were keen to break the ice, but Kennedy's personal involvement in so many controversies made him part of the story, and this may have made him a less credible advocate. As Frank Ashton-Gwatkin of the Foreign Office Far East Department observed:

> He is, I am sure, a perfectly loyal British subject ... but at the same time, it is his professional obligation to champion the Japanese cause and to assist Japanese propaganda. The story of Reuters in Japan, including the Pooley episode, the Naval Bribery scandals, and the Pooley-Kennedy feud has been a very sensational one.

In the same file, Miles Lampson wrote,

> Note that Mr Kennedy accompanied the Japse (*sic*) delegates to Versailles as their chief propagandist. His name is notorious in the F.E. as being practically in Japanese pay. This statement (though I am sure it is true) cannot easily be substantiated. But his paper (?the (*sic*) Japan Mail, in the editorship of which he succeeded Captain Brinkley) can receive valuable support from the Japse (*sic*) govt (*sic*) in devious and indirect ways. Kokusai stinks in the nostrils of the F.E., & as their manager is also Reuters's correspondent, the position is pretty clear.[66]

Japan's performance at the Conference from 1919 to 1920 was undermined by negative publicity on Chinese issues.[67] The consultants to the Chinese delegation – G.E. Morrison, W.H. Donald, Thomas Millard and (in one of his last acts on China's behalf) George Bronson Rea of the *Far Eastern Review* – and prominent onlookers such as Charles R. Crane, worked with the 'Young China' faction among the Chinese delegates, in particular V.K. Wellington Koo, to develop effective propaganda campaigns against the retention of Japanese leases in China.[68] Japan was also conducting a campaign for a racial equality clause to be inserted in the Covenant of the League of Nations. The clause failed to win the unanimous approval that would have made it part of the Covenant, but although this failure had little to do with propaganda campaigns by consultants to the Chinese or other delegations or the influence of critical articles in the English-language newspapers of East Asia, it may have helped energize a new initiative in the management of Japanese propaganda.

In the wake of Japan's publicity failures in Paris a group of younger Foreign Ministry staff, notably Shigemitsu Mamoru, Saitō Hiroshi, Arita

Hachirō and Horinouchi Kensuke, began a campaign for a new, proactive approach to propaganda that led the new Prime Minister, Hara Kei, to establish the Foreign Ministry Information Bureau (*Gaimushō Jōhōbu*) in August 1921.[69] The Bureau marked Japan's first effort in institutionalized propaganda and news management and it continued to operate until 1945. Undeterred by his track record, those planning the new agency charged John Russell Kennedy with the task of opening fifteen branches of the Information Bureau in China, the USA, England, Australia, Russia and elsewhere. Of the ¥5 million secret funding (*kimitsu hi*) set aside for the new agency, about ¥400,000 went through Kennedy's hands in setting up and arranging staff and expenses for these branch offices.[70]

In bringing together Kennedy and Matsuoka, the Paris Conference may also have marked the beginnings of Matsuoka's association with a circle of business and political figures with internationalist inclinations, all of them associated with the *Japan Times*, where Kennedy was a key important player. In a stormy political career marked by abrupt oscillations between rhetorical Japanism and heartfelt internationalism, Matsuoka seems to have kept his lines open both to the internationalist circle around the *Japan Times*, notably to the publicist Toshi Gō, whose career Matsuoka promoted in the Foreign Ministry network and who became editor of the *Japan Times* in 1940, and to journalists writing for the Foreign Ministry network in China and Japan, chief among them George Gorman and the former British M.P. Ernest Pickering. As we shall see in Chapter 7, Matsuoka's enduring relationship with these media figures throws some light on the sale of the *Japan Advertiser* and *Japan Chronicle* to the *Japan Times* late in 1940.

JOHN N. PENLINGTON, *THE TIMES* AND THE FOREIGN MINISTRY INFORMATION BUREAU

Given its substantial resources and relatively open remit, how did the Foreign Ministry Information Bureau operate? The British journalist John N. Penlington makes a good case study. Penlington had worked for the *Daily Telegraph* in London. In Japan, following a pre-war stint as editor of the *Japan Advertiser*, he was the correspondent for the *Daily Mail* from 1905 to 1923, for the *Manchester Guardian* from c.1912 to 1925 and for *The Times* from 1915 to 1923.

Penlington had founded the weekly magazine the *Far East* in Tokyo in 1912. By 1916, the *Far East* was making ¥650 a month, although it 'has hardly any work put into it and is little more than a vehicle for advertising'.[71] In March 1920, Penlington reached an agreement with the Information Bureau to work for the better understanding of Japan in return for between ¥20,000 and ¥50,000 in subsidies to the *Far East*, including ¥5,000 for 500 subscriptions for distribution in Japan and abroad. A year later, with his wife Zöe Kincaid, a *Japan Advertiser* staff writer, Penlington received another ¥30,000 to publicize the Crown Prince's visit to Britain in 1921.

In early March 1923, probably because word of his activities on behalf of the Foreign Ministry Information Bureau had reached the ears of his employers, Penlington received a letter from *The Times* terminating his position as Tokyo correspondent. He sat on this information until the *Japan Advertiser* announced in a 27 May front page news item that it was to be joined by a new staff member, R. Lewis Carton, and that Carton was also to be the new correspondent for *The Times* in Tokyo. This drew a pointed enquiry from the Information Bureau and the termination of its subsidy to the *Far East*.[72] At the end of May, Penlington was dropped as Tokyo correspondent for the *Daily Mail*, another key paper in the Northcliffe stable.

For the Foreign Ministry, Penlington's chief merit lay in his ability to influence international public opinion through his newspaper correspondence. The Ministry had made accommodations with Frank Brinkley and his predecessor as *The Times* correspondent, Major-General H.S. Palmer, and when Penlington succeeded Brinkley, they dealt with him as a matter of course. When *The Times* replaced Penlington with Carton, the Foreign Ministry was unable to come to a similar arrangement with him, but lost no time in ending its subsidy to the *Far East*.

The Information Bureau was pragmatic in its arrangements with foreign journalists, but it was not ruthless, and old hands like Penlington were maintained for long periods for no perceptible return.[73] The *Far East* limped on until its offices were destroyed in the September 1923 earthquake and in 1925 Penlington lost his *Manchester Guardian* correspondence to Arthur Morgan Young of the *Japan Chronicle*. However, in 1932, Penlington made a comeback with a collection of robustly pro-Japanese articles reprinted from the *Far East* and elsewhere.[74] That autumn, he travelled to Geneva to help make the case for Japan at the League of Nations.[75] Six years later, his wife, Zoë Kincaid, joined other Western journalists on a tour of North China arranged by the Cultural Information Board (*Bunka Jōhō Kyōku*) and published her impressions of good works performed by Japanese women in the war zones.[76]

THE FOREIGN MINISTRY NETWORK

From 1900 to 1921, Foreign Ministry archives record numerous initiatives by Japanese based in North America to recruit local opinion leaders to Japan's cause, often on generous terms.[77] News bureaux were established on both coasts, each with an associated journal: the Pacific News Bureau headed by Karl Kiyoshi Kawakami in San Francisco, and the Oriental Information Bureau, then the East-West News Bureau, staffed by a succession of journalists, including Zumoto Motosada, Honda Masujiroh, Yamagata Isoh and Baba Tsunego, producing the *Oriental Review* in New York.[78]

Through the *Kokusai* news agency (1913–26), approved journalists supplied the Japan correspondence of a handful of American local and national newspapers. Friendship societies, such as the Japan Society of

New York and (aided by the *Advertiser*'s B.W. Fleisher) the America-Japan Society and the Japan-America Association were also inaugurated. These beginnings helped the Foreign Ministry Information Bureau hit the ground running when it began operations in 1920–21. Even with little time to prepare, Japan made a far slicker presentation of its case at the Washington Conference than at Paris three years earlier. In 1921–22, the Japanese ambassador to Washington, Shidehara Kijūrō, helped by introducing the Japanese delegates to journalists covering the Conference and the delegates themselves were far more open in their dealings with the press than at Paris. Iwanaga Yūkichi, who observed these improved relations with the press in person, saw them as an encouraging change in official attitudes towards the press.[79]

Initially motivated to counter anti-Japanese feeling in California in 1908–13, then spurred on by publicity failures at the Paris Conference to set up the Information Bureau, the Foreign Ministry network seemed, at least initially, more focused on achieving changes in perceptions of Japan in America than in Europe or Great Britain. The cosy relationship with AP, as well as Kennedy's own correspondence for the *Chicago Daily News* and the *Washington Post*, reflected this early emphasis.

In Japan the network ran the *Japan Times*, periodicals like the *Far East* and the *Herald of Asia*, and the news agencies *Kokusai Tsūshinsha* (*Kokusai*, 1913–26), and its successors *Nihon Shinbun Rengōsha* (*Rengō*, 1926–36) and *Shadanhōjin Dōmei Tsūshinsha* (*Dōmei*, 1936–45). As we saw in Chapter 1, in Korea, the network first established the Japanese-language *Keijō Nippō* and in 1905–9 suborned then bought out the English-language *Seoul Press* to support the protectorate. As Resident-General, Itō Hirobumi brought some of the best and the brightest in Japanese news management to Seoul, including Tokutomi Sohō, John Russell Kennedy, Zumoto Motosada, Honda Masujiroh and Yamagata Isoh. Following the formal annexation of Korea in 1910, Itō's appointees went on to form a central pool of talent to be drawn on by Foreign Ministry network newspapers, magazines, friendship associations and information bureaux in Tokyo, Seoul, New York, Washington, London and even, for a while, Vladivostok.[80]

In China in 1921 the English-language newspapers in the Foreign Ministry network included the *Manchuria Daily News*, the *Far Eastern Review,* the *North China Standard*, the *China Advertiser* and the *Shanghai Times*. The network was well represented by news agencies, first with *Tōhō* in the early 1900s, then with its powerful 1920 relaunch, *Shin-Tōhō*, which supplied all of these newspapers with news sent *gratis* or at extremely competitive rates from Tokyo by *Reuters-Kokusai* until July 1929, when *Rengō* took over its functions. By 1931, *Rengō* had fifteen branch offices in China, a distribution and news collection network unmatched by any of the other agencies in China, including its Japanese rival, *Dentsū* and its partner UP, which had five branches and solo correspondents in six locations.[81] In 1936, *Rengō*'s China network was taken over by *Dōmei*, which opened even more branches and sold its news at prices that undercut other foreign news organizations even more purposefully than its predecessors.

Between the wars, the Foreign Ministry network was characterized by frequent exchanges of senior personnel between the Foreign Ministry Information Bureau and its successors, the Cabinet Information Committee (*Naikaku Jōhōiinkai*) in 1936, the Cabinet Information Bureau (*Naikaku Jōhōbu*) in 1937 and the Cabinet Information Board (*Naikaku Jōhōkyoku*) in 1940, and the President's office at the *Japan Times*.[82] At each of the reviews of news management, policy and historical circumstance that saw *Kokusai* give way to *Rengō* in 1926 and *Rengō* to *Dōmei* in 1936, the new set-up always included past or future top management from the *Japan Times* or the Foreign Ministry Information Bureau.

In 1913 Date Gen'ichirō went from editing the *Kokumin Shinbun* to working under Kennedy at *Kokusai*. In 1919 he accompanied Kennedy to the Conference at Paris to study Western news management, returned to edit the *Yomiuri Shinbun*, helped set up the Foreign Ministry Information Bureau in 1920–21, ran the *Shin-Tōhō* agency from 1921 to 1926, then moved to the Information Bureau until 1932, when he became President of the *Japan Times*. Tanaka Tōkichi headed the Foreign Ministry Information Bureau from 1922 to 1924, moved to the *Japan Times* from 1924 to 1925, left to run the *Chūgai Shōgyō*, became President of *Dōmei* in January 1936 but returned to the *Chūgai Shōgyō* when this proved incompatible with his duties at *Dōmei*. In 1943 Tanaka was chosen to head the *Nihon Shinbunkai* (Japan Press Association) and the *Dai Tōa Shinbun Renmei* (Great Eastern Newspaper Union). Ashida Hitoshi (1887–1959), Date Gen'ichirō's successor as President of the *Japan Times* from 1933 to 1940, was an ex-Foreign Ministry Information Bureau official who simultaneously served in the Diet as a *Seiyūkai* member and joined the Cabinet Information Bureau (*Naikaku Jōhōbu*) from 1937 to 1940. In June 1947 Ashida became Foreign Minister and from March-October 1948 served as Prime Minister in a vigorously anti-Communist coalition cabinet.

From its foundation in 1897 the *Japan Times* was supported and its shares held by a galaxy of big names and companies: Shibusawa Eiichi, Inoue Junnosuke, the Bank of Japan, Mitsui, Mitsubishi, the Yokohama Specie Bank and the Bank of Formosa. These friends in high places ensured the survival of the *Japan Times*, but weakened its credibility among the expatriates it was founded to reach. In 1914, when John Russell Kennedy became President of the *Jyapan Taimuzu Kabushiki-gaisha*, the shares were transferred to his name in an optimistic attempt to dilute the 'semi-official' image of the newspaper.

JOHN RUSSELL KENNEDY AND PROBLEMS AT *KOKUSAI*

As we saw in Chapter 1, John Russell Kennedy became Japan's premier foreign publicity adviser. However, during his second period of office as President of the *Japan Times*, the overlapping nature of Kennedy's official connections and titles began to undermine the credibility of *Kokusai*. As Hugh Byas, editor of the *Japan Advertiser*, put it in 1914:

> Unless the views of Reuters subscribers have changed to a very extraordinary extent, we doubt whether they approve of the interests of Reuters Agency being entrusted to a Japanese news agency financially supported solely by Japanese businessmen, and which is assured of the undivided moral support of the Japanese Foreign Office.[83]

This was the one point that the Foreign Ministry network did not wish to broadcast, but Byas was not the first and would not be the last to do so. In July 1920 the arrangement with Reuters was raised in the House of Commons, when Neil McClean M.P. asked the Under-Secretary for Foreign Affairs, Cecil Harmsworth,

> … whether, in view that the news thus coming from a Japanese source was circulated throughout the world as if it came from a British agency, he would consider the possibility of taking steps which would remove this misunderstanding, which has already caused much dissatisfaction among British and American residents in the Far East.[84]

Kennedy had created a publishing foundation for *Kokusai* by buying a half-share in the *Japan Mail* from the estate of Frank Brinkley in 1912, then, as noted above, acquiring the *Japan Times* in 1914 on behalf of the Foreign Ministry. Put together, the losses on both papers were around ¥10,500 a month when Kennedy bought them. *Kokusai* had been established partly in the hope that it would bring the *Japan Chronicle* and *Japan Advertiser* and other English-language newspapers round to a more positive view of Japan. Thus, 'in order to insure smooth liaison between the news agency and the English-language papers', Kennedy became the General Manager of *Kokusai* in February or March 1914 and President of the *Japan Times* on 2 July 1914, when both bodies became divisions of the newly constituted *Jyapan Taimuzu Kabushiki-gaisha*.[85]

On his appointment, Kennedy displaced the incumbent, Zumoto Motosada. Until now, Zumoto had been an ally. Most of the financial interests assembled by Shibusawa Eiichi to support the *Kokusai* venture had been part of Zumoto and Yamada Sueharu's original 1897 consortium of backers for the *Japan Times*. Moreover, Zumoto had helped Kennedy promote the *Kokusai* agency and backed him up during the Siemens Scandal.

However, Kennedy's appointment as President of the *Japan Times* in 1914 made a lasting enemy of Zumoto.[86] Looking back in 1941, Zumoto commented, 'The management of the Japan Times was left to Mr Kennedy. Thus, Japan's international propaganda lost a chance to detach itself from Reuters.'[87] Zumoto had an axe to grind, but the deal Kennedy made with Reuters undeniably hampered *Kokusai*'s operations, particularly in China. Kennedy tried to refine the arrangement so that

Kokusai collected and synthesized but Reuter delivered the news from Japan, and he negotiated an arrangement along these lines with the Associated Press, but Zumoto was not alone in wishing that Kennedy had made a more advantageous deal with Reuters in 1913.[88]

Zumoto's resentment might not have mattered had he not gone on to set up the *Herald of Asia* in 1916, and through this and other ventures established a small media satellite that would challenge the pre-eminence of *Kokusai* and the *Japan Times* and become a haven for some of those who fell out with Kennedy. In 1921–22 the *Herald of Asia* was the only publication in the Foreign Ministry network to defy the official line and not advocate the renewal of the Anglo-Japanese Alliance, maintaining that Japan had nothing to gain from a continued partnership with Britain.

Apart from financial and geographical limits, the basic problem at *Kokusai* was one of credibility, arising from the fact that Kennedy wore so many hats: President of the *Japan Times,* General Manager of *Kokusai* and the Reuters correspondent. Obviously these positions needed to be occupied by different people if these organizations were to gain any credibility. Besides, concentrating them in Kennedy's person drew attention to *Kokusai*'s closeness to Japanese officialdom or, as a British official in Peking put it in 1917, 'that futile Kokusai Agency, which is nothing more nor less than the Japanese F.O. in a thinly disguised form'.[89]

In 1916 the board of the *Jyapan Taimuzu Kabushiki-gaisha* decided that Kennedy should resign from the *Japan Times* presidency and from the board of directors and that *Kokusai* and the *Japan Times* should become separate companies.[90] Kennedy remained as manager of *Kokusai*, and he would return to the Presidency of the *Japan Times* in 1918, but articles in the vernacular press argued that, under his management, *Kokusai* and the *Japan Times* were not able to win the trust of Anglophone readerships. In an article first published in *Nihon oyobi Nihonjin* in March 1918 and translated in the *Japan Advertiser*, Honda Masujiroh, possibly encouraged by his former colleague Zumoto, urged the creation of a credible successor to *Kokusai* and the *Japan Times*:

> The only newspaper in a foreign language published in Japan by the Japanese is the *Japan Times*. It now has become a possession of the Kokusai News Agency. This newspaper is considered at home and abroad as an organ of the government, yet the government does not seem to be making full use of it, and it does not win the confidence of foreigners as an organ of expression of the voice of the nation. It is a great mistake to leave such an organ under the direction of foreigners ... When conducted by foreign managers, such a newspaper is only overshadowed by its contemporary which is likely to criticize Japan unmercifully. Foreign readers lose their confidence in such an organ and it will be obliged to depend upon the Japanese readers to keep itself alive. An organ of the Japanese nation should be conducted so as to attract the attention of foreigners, even if it may be a financial failure.

Nor could Honda find anything to praise at *Kokusai*:

> We cannot call the work of the Kokusai News Agency a success. As a branch of Reuters it may be necessary to have English managers for it, but when there is so much incoming stuff and so little news is sent out, and when this little of news sent out as Tokyo dispatches is discredited abroad, the undertaking can only enrich the Reuters agency at the expense of Japan. Although it may be necessary now to get so much incoming stuff because of the war, yet all the news which comes from abroad is government news of foreign countries highly censored. This may be due either to the fact that the foreigners connected with the agency are discredited abroad, or that the contract made with the foreign news agency is one-sided.[91]

This article cannot have helped Kennedy's reputation, but it still took the Foreign Ministry three years to address the problems highlighted by Honda.

In February 1921, perhaps in response to the sentiments and interests behind Honda's article, a news entrepreneur with a background in Japanese journalism in Hawai'i, Sheba Sometarō, was brought onto the management of the *Japan Times*. Sheba began his tenure at the *Japan Times* publishing a controversial open letter to the Home Minister in which he condemned the 'absolutism' of the government, declaring 'Japan is cursed the world over for its bureaucratic policy. A policy, domestic as well as international, not frank, truthful and straightforward, will fail. A Government which treats its own people as an ignorant mass will never stand. No nation that lies to the world will ever rise.'

In December 1921 Kennedy was again asked to resign from the *Japan Times* and was removed from the day-to-day management of *Kokusai*. Kennedy kept his office and his salary at *Kokusai* until 1923, when he was in effect kicked upstairs, for he soon became busier than ever as a consultant for the Foreign Ministry Information Bureau. In January 1922 Kennedy's successor as Managing Editor, President and titular owner of the *Japan Times* holding company (*Jyapan Taimuzu Kabushiki-gaisha*) was the controversial 'new broom', Sheba Sometarō. Sheba's appointment as a 'representative' President was part of an attempt by the newspaper to cover its financial links with the Foreign Ministry network by becoming an 'anonymous association'.

Kennedy's team at *Kokusai* had included colleagues from his time at the Associated Press in Tokyo. The two most important were Furuno Inosuke, who came to *Kokusai* from Kennedy's AP office, and the journalist Iwanaga Yūkichi (1883–1939). Their professional partnership would have profound implications for the future of news management in Japan. In 1923 Kennedy's successor as Director of *Kokusai* was Iwanaga, with Furuno just below in the chain of command. One of Iwanaga's first actions on becoming *Kokusai*'s new manager was to remove another eight high-ranking foreigners from the *Kokusai* administration.[92]

Kennedy died in January 1928. His funeral, at Holy Trinity Church, Tokyo, was attended by many of the great and good. Hugh Byas wrote a generous obituary with barely a hint of the rancour that had passed between them over the years, even praising Kennedy's achievements in smoothing the relationship between Japan and the West.[93] Privately, Byas's estimate was less diplomatic:

> A fact which has influenced my judgement on this matter as much as anything is that though Kennedy has lived in Japan for 16 years he has never, so far as I know, written an article showing personal inquiry into, or even personal interest in, any aspect of Japanese life. He has always been a mouthpiece, and as representative of the Associated Press of America and later of Reuters, he has been an effective exponent when one was needed.[94]

FROM *KOKUSAI* TO *RENGŌ* TO *DŌMEI*

Retrospectively, the temptation is to see the hand of Japan's political elites in drawing up a blueprint for domestic press control and international propaganda. But before 1931, even with the *Shin-Tōhō* agency making such inroads on the China news market, and with *Rengō* up and running after 1926, the Foreign Ministry network remained an essentially reactive force, a means of correcting what many saw as the unfair impressions meted out to Japan by its foreign press and by Western correspondents.

Kokusai was most obviously the creation of the Foreign Ministry. In most respects, *Kokusai*'s successor, *Nihon Shinbun Rengōsha* (*Rengō*) was no more than *Kokusai* minus Kennedy. However, with Kennedy's former subordinates, Furuno Inosuke and Iwanaga Yūkichi, moving on from *Kokusai* to take up the helm at *Rengō*, the new agency soon developed a focus that it had lacked under Kennedy. The biggest item on Iwanaga and Furuno's agenda at *Rengō* was the establishment of a single news agency to present Japanese news in East Asia and the West. This was realized in 1936 with the creation of *Shadanhōjin Dōmei Tsūshinsha* (*Dōmei*), and from then on, the Foreign Ministry network moved from a defensive to a proactive posture towards the news it handled, reporting and even making news as opposed to correcting it.

In January 1924 Iwanaga arranged a meeting in Tokyo with Roderick Jones of Reuters where he renegotiated the unequal treaty with Reuters, first acquiring (for £20,000) the right for *Kokusai* to use its own name on news items distributed within Japan, i.e. 'From Kokusai-Reuters' (Hatsu Kokusai Roitaa). His next move was to appoint Furuno as *Kokusai*'s agent in London, there to choose news items to be sent from London to Japan, a task previously performed by Reuters.[95] In a coordinated effort to end the wasteful duplication of effort by *Kokusai* and *Shin-Tōhō*, Iwanaga and Furuno lobbied government, newspaper owners and the business community and corralled Japan's major city newspapers into a cooperative to present a united front to the 'Ring' of European news agencies formed by Reuters, *Havas* and *Wolff*. In May 1926 they established *Nihon*

Shinbun Rengōsha (*Rengō*), a non-profit newpaper cooperative which merged the *Kokusai* and *Shin-Tōhō* agencies, and included members from eight major Tokyo and Ōsaka dailies. Merging with *Shin-Tōhō* enabled *Rengō* to evade a clause in the Reuters contract forbidding *Kokusai* from distributing its news in China. Now *Rengō* news could be carried under the *Shin-Tōhō* name in China.

Reuters foresaw difficulties in competing with Japan's new international news networks in East Asia and appealed to the Foreign Office to subsidize the cable costs from its UK transmitter at Rugby. From 1921 to 1931, the Hong Kong government allocated Reuters an annual subsidy of £2,400.[96] Notwithstanding William Turner's concerns about Japanese competition, Reuters expanded rapidly under his management in East Asia, with combined revenue for Reuters commercial services more than quadrupling in the decade 1918–28, (from £16,200 to £66,400), and reaching £73,000 in 1930. In 1936 less than 5% of the foreign news published by *Rengō*'s successor, *Dōmei*, was supplied by Reuters.[97] However, by 1937 Reuters' profits were down to £49,140 on the year.[98]

In the late 1920s, *Rengō* and AP combined forces to loosen the grip of the Reuters, *Havas* and *Wolff* 'Ring' on global news. In May 1932 Iwanaga gave Reuters formal notice of *Rengō*'s intention not to renew the 1928 agreement after its expiration in July 1933. In May 1933 Kent Cooper of AP and Iwanaga drafted an AP-*Rengō* agreement in Tokyo. Jones was furious and held out for compensation. *Rengō* was vulnerable to Jones's wrath because although AP would be able to replace Reuters as a source of world news, *Rengō*'s highly profitable financial news service, founded by Kennedy as the *Kokusai Keizai Shuppō*, was in turn dependent on financial news from Reuters. However, Reuters could not afford to cut *Rengō* off either, and Jones finally agreed that *Rengō* should be free to choose its affiliates. In 1934 in parallel negotiations, a new contract was agreed between AP and the European agencies which ended the 'Ring' that had dominated world news flows for over half a century. Cooper later described his friendship with Iwanaga as being based on 'our mutual adherence to the principle of a free press and freedom of international news exchange without government control'.[99] Just as the victory gave Iwanaga and Furuno the freedom to move ahead with their cherished national news agency, it also freed AP, a powerful news cooperative with a wealthy home subscriber base serving a population of 100 million, to offer East Asia not only American news from an American angle but world news in general, with all the advantages for American trade and influence attendant on its consumption.

Rather than celebrate the victory in terms of freedoms won for the fourth estate, Iwanaga and Furuno saw it as the overdue termination of Western domination of Asian news. In any case, *Rengō* was still only one among a number of powerful media organizations in East Asia: in Japan, it faced increasing competition from *Dentsū* in the battle for provincial press subscribers and, in China, from *Dentsū* and its American ally, UP.

In 1933, following two years of increasingly negative portrayal in the world's press as a result of the Manchurian Incident and Japan's withdrawal from the League of Nations, Furuno and Iwanaga lobbied hard for a merger of the two agencies' news gathering operations and an end to *Rengō*'s wasteful competition with *Dentsū*. Ultimately, the exigencies of Manchuria forced *Dentsū* and *Rengō* to cooperate with the Army and the Foreign Ministry in the creation of the *Kokutsū Tsūshinsha* devoted to news management in Manchukuo.[100] Although its Information Bureau ultimately took charge of *Kokutsū*, the involvement of the Army Ministry in setting up the new agency challenged the centrality of the Foreign Ministry in the management of Japanese news. This precedent established, the Navy, Army, Foreign and Communication Ministries all took a hand in setting up the *Dōmei* news agency.[101]

With the inauguration of *Dōmei*, the Foreign Ministry network came of age. The first President was Tanaka Tōkichi but in June 1936 conflicts of interest caused him to step down. His replacement in October 1936, following the amalgamation with *Dentsū*, was Iwanaga Yūkichi. When Iwanaga died in September 1939 Furuno Inosuke became President, going on to become one of the most powerful figures in the Japanese press, and, as a member of Konoe Fumimaro's think-tank, the *Shōwa Kenkyū Kai* (Shōwa Research Group), a trusted intermediary between the government and the press.[102]

The appointments of Iwanaga and Furuno sustained Foreign Ministry influence in *Dōmei*. Even more germane to the role of *Dōmei* in the Foreign Ministry network was the establishment in July 1936 of the Cabinet Information Committee (*Naikaku Jōhōiinkai*), and, the following year, the Cabinet Information Bureau (*Naikaku Jōhōbu*). The new cabinet institutions could be seen as a loss of Foreign Ministry influence were it not for the fact that as propaganda oversight moved to them, so also did many ex-Foreign Ministry Information Bureau personnel. From the beginning, the Committee was closer to a full bureau than a committee, a fact recognized by its elevation to Cabinet Information Bureau (*Naikaku Jōhōbu*) status under the first Konoe cabinet the following year.

In December 1940 the Information Bureau was again reorganized as the Cabinet Information Board (*Naikaku Jōhōkyoku*). This final metamorphosis oversaw the work of the Foreign Ministry Information Bureau and the information bureaux of the Army, the Navy and the Home Ministry Police. It also replaced the Foreign Ministry Information Bureau press briefings which had been running twice daily since 1920. The Board's first Director, Itō Nobufumi, came from the Foreign Ministry, but most Board members represented the Army and Navy. With the creation of the Cabinet Information Board, military and naval influences diluted the Foreign Ministry's concentration of influence over the network it had built since 1913.

JAPAN'S PRESS WARS IN EAST ASIA

From the early 1920s until the formation of *Dōmei* in 1936, the Foreign Ministry network fought a 'cold war' with the networks of the English-language press over the idea of Japan. In 1921 William Turner, Far East Manager for Reuters, wrote of 'the Tokio F.O. Publicity Department [Bureau]', '... you would scarcely believe ... the genuine enthusiasm, singleness of purpose and almost appalling persistency with which they work'. Turner feared that the revitalized *Shin-Tōhō* news agency would eventually force Reuters out of China 'because the disparity between what such a subsidized concern could sell the news at and what we could sell it at would be so great that only a few newspapers would regard it as essential to take our service'. Headed by future *Japan Times* President Date Gen'ichirō and powered, according to Turner, by Information Bureau funding of around £50,000 per annum, *Shin-Tōhō* news undercut the competition at every turn: charging $15 a month to foreign papers, $10 a month to Chinese papers, and nothing to Japanese papers. Against these prices, foreign papers subscribing to Reuters paid $650–750 a month, and Japanese and Chinese papers between $100 and $50 a month. The dice were loaded: through privileged access to Japanese cables and naval wireless, *Shin-Tōhō* received important Tokyo news, such as the news of Hara Kei's assassination in November 1921, well ahead of Reuters and other agencies. By the end of 1921, both the *North-China Daily News* and Thomas Millard's old paper, the *China Press*, had signed up for *Shin-Tōhō* bulletins. William Turner observed at the end of 1921 that Japanese policy was 'concentrated less on propaganda proper than upon perfecting their news-distribution organization in China': market share came first.[103] In the early 1920s, Reuters was feeling the pinch, hardened critics like the *China Press* and *North-China Daily News* were buying their world news bulletins from Tokyo at bargain prices, and the Foreign Ministry network was just finding its range.

Part of the explanation for what the Reuters manager described as the 'appalling persistency' of the Information Bureau lay in its operational culture. For the two key architects of the mature Foreign Ministry network, Iwanaga Yūkichi and Furuno Inosuke, working under John Russell Kennedy at *Kokusai* from 1913 to 1923 was a formative experience. They learned early on that *Kokusai*'s power as a source of news rested on narrowing the channels by which news travelled. They saw how, by taking over the Reuters operation in Japan and its cable service to and from Japan, and by enlisting Kennedy, who was also the AP representative in Tokyo, as Manager, *Kokusai* could shape, source and even colour the outflow of news from Japan. They observed that limiting access to cables by prohibitive costs and other means narrowed the options for news organizations, especially for the only alternative source of outgoing news of Japan, the English-language press.

Thus when *Rengō* was set up in 1926, with Iwanaga as its Director and Furuno running the London branch, they applied *Kokusai*'s narrow-channel concept in reverse, supplying fourteen major Tokyo and Ōsaka papers with foreign news chosen and filtered by Furuno at *Rengō*'s London office, and supplying other Japanese papers with news through the Teikoku agency. By keeping *Rengō*'s fees at an affordable level and incoming cablegram charges excessively high, Furuno and Iwanaga encouraged as many papers as possible to sign up to their new service.[104]

By 1927, according to Putnam Weale, Japan was spending ¥2,000,000 a year on propaganda in China, of which $60,000 went to the *North China Standard*. For Britain to compete with Japan in China, Weale thought an annual £25,000 would suffice. In response, Arthur Willert reminded Miles Lampson that Foreign Office policy was never to directly subsidize any newspaper, book or writer.[105] Three years later, a Shanghai report to the Foreign Office put Japan's annual subsidy to George Bronson Rea's *Far Eastern Review* at Gold $100,000 a year,[106] but US official estimates put Rea's subsidy at around half that amount.[107]

Meanwhile, in Tokyo, the frequency of Foreign Ministry Information Bureau English-language press conferences had increased from once a week in 1921 to three times a week in 1937. As Hugh Byas observed:

> The *Johobu* since its formation has followed a definite line of development. At first the office was open to supply information to those who wanted it. It was, so to speak, in the retail business, supplying the dope by individual injections, whereas business has increased so much that the correspondents are now sprayed *en masse*, as it were.[108]

☐

This chapter has attempted to show how the English-language newspapers of East Asia appeared from an official Japanese perspective. It examined both hostile developments and compromises reached in the relationship between these newspapers and individual journalists and the Foreign Ministry of Japan. In doing so, it identified some of the factors leading to the formation of the independent English-language press networks that would also contribute to their eventual harassment and closure. This chapter also showed the Foreign Ministry and other authorities working through a succession of national news agencies and newspapers, and contracting Tokyo correspondents to burnish Japan's image in reports sent to leading Western newspapers.

In the 1920s, the foreign-owned English-language press of China and Japan and Japan's semi-official English-language newspapers and news agencies fought a 'cold war' over the West's idea of Japan. As we shall see in Chapters 7 and 8, Japan turned up the heat in the early thirties, with a campaign of attrition against the staff, supplies and ownership of the foreign-owned English-language press networks of East Asia that moved into its final stage in the mid-1930s, in an overtly aggressive 'endgame' aimed at their effective nationalization as part of the expansion of the Japanese world in East Asia. That even this nationalization had to rely on a continued use of the English language shows how extensively they had 'colonized' the region, as Amō's 1943 remark maintained.

NOTES

1   Korea's last independent English-language newspaper, the *Korea Daily News*, closed in 1908. Taken over from its English owner, J.W. Hodge, in 1905, the SP thenceforth spoke for the Governor General's office. Chong (1987) is the authoritative dissertation on these newspapers in this period.

2   The Bureau began operations in 1920. It was officially inaugurated in August 1921.

3   For the scope of the new Bureau's global activities and its operational principles see *Gaimushō no Hyakunen* Vol. 1: 1,030–1,031. For a more detailed account of the Bureau's activities see the same source and volume: '*Dai yonjūyon gikai shitsumon yosō jikō narabini tōben*' (Questions and answers on matters discussed in the 44th Imperial Diet). Both references cited in Matsumura 2003: 62, 65.

4   Amō Eiji on the Western domination of East Asian media: *Nippon Times*, 18 November 1943. Quoted more fully below, and n.22.

5   Rozanski 1974: 363.

6   Pardoe 1989: 220.

7   Ion 1996: 80.

8   'I was a Secret Agent for Japan': *Daily Worker*, 22 December 1937.

9   The JC had derided the Western enthusiasm for Bushido when Nitobe's most famous book came out in a new edition in 1905. The underlying trend ensured an indifferent reception in the West for Nitobe's *Japan: Some Phases of her Problems and Development* when it appeared in 1931. The JC was merely being consistent when it gave the book a savage review. JC: 24 November 1931.

10 Young 1937: 5. This issue of *Fact* is reprinted in Volume 9 of O'Connor (2008) with an introduction by Hamish Ion.

11 See Toshihiro Yamagoshi's introduction to *I Speak for the Chinese* in Volume 10 of O'Connor (2008).

12 Although both Ashton-Gwatkin and Nitobe had been recruited, as a contributor and a translator respectively, for the team John Robertson-Scott assembled for his journal the *New East* in 1916–18.

13 *Times Literary Supplement* review of *Kimono*, 7 June 1921.

14 The only account of Ashton-Gwatkin's literary and diplomatic career is Nish (1994).

15 There are three accounts of Tim Conroy's life and times: a first, unpublished manuscript by Malcolm Kennedy, who was keen to expose Conroy as a fake and a hindrance to Anglo-Japanese relations, in the Kennedy Papers at Sheffield University; enlargements on this article in relation to the life and work of the journalist Malcolm Kennedy, in Pardoe 1989: 214–220; and O'Connor (2002, 2008a, 2008b), which examine Conroy's life, Malcolm Kennedy's attitude to him, and the appeal his 1933 book held for the British public.

16 FO 371/16243 [F8373/40/23]: T. Conroy to R. Vansittart, 25 November 1932.

17 O'Conroy 1933: 11.

18 FO 371/16243 [F 4624/40/23], Douglas Crawford to Robert Vansittart, 27 May 1932: '... his knowledge of Japan is profound'.

19 *Tōkyō Asahi Shinbun*: 21 October 1933, 2.
20 *Evening Standard*: 19 October 1933, 1. *Sunday Despatch*: 26 November 1933, 13.
21 Ion 1996: 80.
22 Kakegawa 1973: 545.
23 Purdy 1987: 191–2.
24 *Nippon Times*, 18 November 1943.
25 'An Increasing Interest': JA, 16 April 1926. FO 371/27969 [F 2013/1222/23], Craigie to Eden, 14 January 1941. Total foreign correspondents (all languages): 1913 = 3; 1920 = 5; 1926 = 7 or 8; 1933 = 20; 1936 = 35; 1937 = 40; 1941 = 30: 10 Anglophone press, 10 Axis press, 10 various.
26 Wildes 1927: 374–5.
27 FO 398/573 [P 3059/39/150], Tokyo report, 31 October 1938.
28 The *Gaimushō* distributed about 2,000 copies of the JT to embassies and consuls daily. Established in 1938, A.R. Wills' JN-W was another successful independent English-language organ, with 3,200 subscribers and 1,200 newsstand sales in 1941 (Grew 1944: 364).
29 Oba 1994: 4.
30 Australian Archives: MP431, file 929/16/69. Cited in Sissons 1987: 2.
31 Keene 1994: 14.
32 Despite using spoken Japanese to deal with officials and other journalists, Kennedy hardly used any Japanese-language sources in his journalism, and cited none at all in his books (Pardoe 1989: 281–2)
33 FO 371/27969 [F 2013/1222/23], Craigie to Eden, 14 January 1941
34 The quality of information coming from Sorge's Japanese sources more than made up for this deficiency. Not for entirely altruistic motives, Sorge passed on some of his most cogent information regarding Japanese war plans to Joseph Newman, Wilfrid Fleisher's replacement from September 1940 as the *New York Herald Tribune* correspondent in Tokyo. Newman does discuss the Sorge case but does not name Sorge as his source for the 'impressive story about a possible war' that was run in the *Tribune* on the morning of 21 June 1941, the very day Hitler launched Operation Barbarossa (Newman 1942: 301–302).
35 Russell 1928: 103–104, 93.
36 *Osaka Mainichi & Tokyo Nichi-Nichi*, 18 May 1937.
37 Young 1998: 141, 154.
38 Bickers 2000: 172.
39 For example, on 11 October 1911, when cables indicative of the oncoming revolution arrived at the CP, Thomas Millard's long years as a China watcher told him to ignore them (Rozanski 1974: 122).
40 Williams 1922: 159–69; Goodman 2004: 57.
41 Thorne 1978: 80.
42 Tong 1948: 7.
43 Goodman 2004: 10–11, 55–88.
44 Thompson 1920s: 15. Why '1920s'? The article 'Japan and the Foreigner' by H.A. Thompson was found in the fifth of the eleven reels of microfilm that hold the Hugh Byas Papers, Stirling Memorial Library, Yale University. The article had been torn from its original bindings, either by Byas or the Library, and microfilmed at Yale: Reel 5. See note in Bibliography.

45 Some of the material on John Russell Kennedy in this chapter was published
    in O'Connor (2005) 'John Russell Kennedy, 1861–1928: Spokesman for Japan
    and Media Entrepreneur'. In Hugh Cortazzi (ed.) *Britain & Japan: Biographical
    Portraits*, Volume V, (Folkestone: Global Oriental), 383–98.
46 Farnsworth 1996: 179–80. *Peking Chronicle*: Edgar Snow letter to Betty Price,
    January 1935. This letter is not clearly cited in Farnsworth's notes (1996: 425,
    n.3): it may be in the Edgar Snow Papers at the University of Missouri-Kansas
    City.
47 *Gaimushō gaikō shiryōkan: Preparations for the Peace Conference*: 521 (1918):
    'chaina puresu' (China Press). *'Mirado Rebyū' nado Amerika shimbun zasshi ga
    sakan ni hainichi no kiji wo ageru wa chūi ni ataishi, migi wa jakkan soshiki keitō
    aru undō ni arazu ya to suisatsu seraruru fushi ari'* (English translation above).
48 In 1912, Wang Zhenting (Wang Chen-t'ing) was Vice-minister of the Ministry
    of Industry and Commerce under Premier Tang Shaoyi (Tang Shao-yi), and
    V.K. Wellington Koo (1887–1985) was Cabinet Secretary. Koo later married
    Tang Shao-yi's daughter, May: *Gaimushō gaikō shiryōkan* 1919: *jiko san: Paris
    kōwa kaigi ni okeru chūgoku mondai toku ni santō mondai kansuru ken* (Foreign
    Ministry records 1919: Issue no.3: The China problem with particular refer-
    ence to the Shandong (Shantung) problem), files 106 and 134.
49 *Gaimushō no hyakunen*, Vol. I: 1033.
50 I have corrected some of the newspaper titles given in *katakana* in Ugaki's
    original chart.
51 USDS 893.911/41, 5 June 1919: Carl Crow Report on the Shanghai press.
52 Chao 1931: 61.
53 Tong 1948: 25. R.I. Hope was a British subject but of Indian and Chinese
    parentage. When Hope was working on Hollington Tong's *Peking Daily News*
    he became the subject of a racial slur in the rival *Peking Gazette*, edited by
    Eugene Chen. Hope went to see Chen and was severely beaten by Chen's
    'coolies'. As Tong saw it, that Hope became 'the type whose talents are for sale
    to the highest bidder', may be partly explained by this incident (Tong 1948:
    25–6).
54 See for example, *Gaimushō gaikō shiryōkan* (Foreign Ministry records) 1/3/2/,
    46–1-4.
55 Cited in Purdy 1987: 359, n.77.
56 *Gaimushō gaikō shiryōkan: gaikoku shinbun, tsūshin kikan oyobi tsūshin-in kankei
    zakken, tsūshin-in no bu, Beikokujin no bu*: (Foreign Ministry records:
    Miscellaneous matters relating to foreign newspapers, communications agen-
    cies and correspondents, correspondents section: American correspondents) 1
    1/3/2/ 50–2-2, August 1921.
57 *Gaimushō gaikō shiryōkan: gaikoku shinbun, tsūshin kikan oyobi tsūshin-in kankei
    zakken, tsūshin-in no bu eikokujin no bu*: (Foreign Ministry records:
    Miscellaneous matters relating to foreign newspapers, communications agen-
    cies and correspondents, correspondents section: British correspondents) 1
    1/3/2 50–2-2, May 1921.
58 *Bungei Shunjū*, August 1933.
59 See O'Connor, Peter (2005), Volume 4: *Lytton Commission on China and
    Manchuria*, 409–34.
60 Otto D. Tolischus: NYT, July 23 1943.
61 Tolischus 1943: 339.

62 Ōfusa 1981: 21–24.
63 FO 371/3817 [F 90451], Japan Confidential, Beilby Alston Note to Curzon, 18 June 1919: '... and when his Excellency [Shidehara Kijūrō, Vice-Foreign Minister] alluded to the unfriendly feeling in Japan in connection with the attitude of Great Britain at the Peace Conference on the subject of racial equality, I asked him how he could expect the world to recognize Japan's claims in this direction when the world was so greatly shocked by the atrocities committed in Corea, where the Japanese soldiery appeared to be "outhunning the Huns".' Alston attached to this Note a letter dated 25 April 1919 from W.M. Royds, Consul-General in Seoul, expressing outrage at Japanese behaviour in Korea, quoting apologia issued in the SP of 12 April 1919, and enclosing critical clippings from the JC of 27 and 30 April 1919. However, these attempts to raise Korea at the top table came to nothing, as a summary of Minutes commenting on Alston's Note stated that Balfour felt that it would be 'undesirable' to raise the Korean issue with the Japanese delegates to the Conference, and that it would be better dealt with by joint representations by British, French and US representatives in Tokyo.
64 Shimazu 1998: 16.
65 According to Purdy (1987: 66) Saionji stayed at the Hotel Bristol. According to Patrick Gallagher (later of the *Far Eastern Review*), who attended the Conference, Saionji stayed at the Hotel Meurice but soon left to spend more time with his mistress in rented accommodation at 54 Rue Bassano (Gallagher 1920: 43).
66 FO 395/334 [F 1242/730/150]: Minutes: Frank Ashton-Gwatkin, Miles Lampson, 1920.
67 See Matsumura 2001: 53–55.
68 Op. cit.
69 *Gaimushō no Hyakunen* Vol. 1: 742; Matsumura 2001: 55–59.
70 *Gaimushō no Hyakunen* Vol. 1: 1,034–1,035; Matsumura 2001: 65.
71 FO 395/17 [F 133472], J. Robertson-Scott Memorandum, June 1916.
72 *Gaimushō kiroku: senden: shinbun zasshi sōjū kankei zassan 'Faa Iisuto' no bu*, (Foreign Ministry records: Propaganda: miscellaneous documents concerning the operation of newspapers and magazines, 'Far East' section) 1/3/1/1/50, March 1921.
73 Not that Penlington's efforts on behalf of the Foreign Ministry network won him any special dispensations outside the capital. On 22 July 1932, the Governor of Kanagawa, Yokoyama Sukenari submitted a report to Home Minister Yamamoto Tatsuo, Foreign Minister Uchida Yasuya and Superintendent-General of Police Fujinuma Shōhei, on Penlington's movements there in which Penlington was described as 'a blacklisted American' (Teruo Ariyama Introduction to Volume 9 of O'Connor (ed.) 2004, p.4).
74 Penlington 1932.
75 Reprinted in O'Connor, Peter (2004) *Japanese Propaganda: Selected Readings. Series 1: Books, 1873–1942*, Volume 9, with an introduction by Ariyama Teruo.
76 Kincaid 1938: 30; O'Connor 2005, Volume 8: 283–90.
77 For example in *Gaimushō gaikō shiryō kan: gaimushō kiroku: senden kankei zakken; shokutaku oyobi hojōkin shikyū sonota senden hi shikyū kankei gaikokujin no bu*, (Foreign Ministry records, miscellaneous matters relating to propaganda; concerning the payments of commissions, bonuses and other

propaganda expenses, foreigner section) no's 1–4. Also, *Gaimushō kiroku senden kankei: hoshokin shikyu sendenshya sonota senden hi shikyu kankei gaikokujin no bu* (Foreign Ministry records, miscellaneous matters relating to propaganda; concerning the payments of commissions, bonuses and other propaganda expenses, foreigner section): *beikokujin no bu* (Americans section) is the relevant subsection here. In other cases, American journalists working for American news agencies in China were paid by the Japanese Foreign Ministry to inform on their employers, as shown in *Gaimushō kiroku: taibei kei hatsu undō* (Foreign ministry records: re. enlightenment campaign No.2. foreign section) *dai 3-kan*, 2: 3/8/2/287, *Taishō 3-nen*, correspondence between Duke Parry of W.R. Hearst's International News Agency, San Francisco, and Erich von Salzmann, Shanghai, indicating the sort of stories Parry thought US readers wanted, which a disgruntled Salzmann sent on to the *Gaimushō* to illustrate the crass nature of US media interest in China. Many *Gaimushō* initiatives were managed by Lindsay Russell at the Japan Society of New York. Russell himself oversaw the *Oriental Review* project, recruiting opinion leaders and journalists on the East coast. His liaison at the *Gaimushō* was often Matsuoka Yōsuke, with whom he could correspond in English as in *Gaimushō kiroku: senden kankei zakken: shokutaku oyobi hojokin shikyū sendensha sonota senden hi shikyū kankei gakokukujin no bu* (Foreign Ministry records: Miscellaneous matters relating to propaganda; concerning the payments of commissions, bonuses and other propaganda expenses, foreigner section) 4 August 1922, 1–3-1–35, Russell to Matsuoka, 25 September 1920, on the inadvisability of opening *Kokusai* branches in New York, Washington and Chicago (he was ignored). On the West coast, similarly detailed consultations took place between Japanese officials in San Francisco and local agencies media satellites such as K.K. Kawakami's Pacific News Bureau.

78 *Gaimushō gaikō shiryō kan: gaimushō kiroku: senden kankei zakken; shokutaku oyobi hojōkin shikyū sonota senden hi shikyū kankei gaikokujin no bu* (Foreign Ministry records: Miscellaneous matters relating to propaganda; concerning the payments of commissions, bonuses and other propaganda expenses, foreigner section) 2: 1-3-1, 35-2-2: Takamine Jokichi to Makino Nobuaki, 26 March 1913; and Lindsay Russell, Japan Society of New York, to Shibusawa Eiichi on the organization of the *Oriental Review*, 8 January 1912. Cited here in Chapter 2.

79 Iwanaga [Yūkichi] 1941: 143–5. Cited in Purdy 1987: 95, and 118, n.70.

80 Where Zumoto distinguished himself in establishing the *Vladivo Nippō* during the Siberian Intervention.

81 Chao 1931: 34, 36.

82 I use the title 'Cabinet Information Bureau' for *Naikaku Jōhōbu*. This is consistent with rendering *Gaimushō Jōhōbu* as Foreign Ministry Information Bureau. For *Naikaku Jōhōkyoku* I use the title 'Cabinet Information Board' because that was the usage in contemporary English-language publications in Japan. However, Kakegawa (1973, 2001) uses 'Cabinet Information Division' for *Naikaku Jōhōbu* and 'Cabinet Information Department' for *Naikaku Jōhōkyoku*.

83 JA: 4 July 1914.

84 Commons debates, 12 July 1920. JC, 16 September 1920.

85 Hasegawa 1966: 179.

86 Hasegawa 1966: 179.

87 Okamura 1941: 36.
88 Wildes 1927: 177.
89 FO 395/170 [F 122541/-/23], Miles Lampson to Stephen Gasalee, May 1917.
90 Hasegawa 1966: 62.
91 *Nihon oyobi Nihonjin*, March 1918; JA: May 1918.
92 Purdy 1987: 95.
93 JA: 17 January 1928.
94 Hugh Byas Papers c.1924, Yale, Reel 5.
95 And one in which Furuno was assisted by Hugh Byas, who was back at *The Times* in London between 1922 and 1926: Byas speech at Restaurant New Grand: 10 May 1937, Hugh Byas Papers, Yale, Reel 5.
96 FO 371/536 [P 4087/5/150], Clive to Eden, 21 October 1936. FO 371/536 [P 4589/5/150], Bowyer to Ridsdale, 14 December 1936.
97 FO 371/536 [P 4087/5/150], Clive to Eden, 21 October 1936. FO 371/536 [P 4589/5/150], Bowyer to Ridsdale, 14 December 1936.
98 Read 1992: 169–71.
99 Cooper 1942: 149.
100 *Manshūkoku Tsūshinsha* 1942: 19.
101 *Tsūshinsha-shi Kankōkai* (ed.) 1958: 424.
102 *Tsūshinsha-shi Kankōkai* (ed.) 1958: 421, 453.
103 FO 371/8028 [F 647/647/10], W. Turner Memorandum and private letter to 'Ross', R.N., 5 December 1921.
104 Even so, by the mid-thirties, *Rengō* owed the Communications Ministry ¥400,000 in cable charges: *Teitō Nichi-Nichi Shinbun*: 30 June, 1 July 1935.
105 FO 395/419 [P 331/57/150], B. Lenox Simpson Memorandum, February 1927.
106 FO 371/445 [P 1870/260/150], Miles Lampson letter, August 1930.
107 US National Records and Archives, RG. 165, Military Intelligence Division, 1766–511 (55) 17 January 1923. Cited in Rozanski 1974: 356, n.109.
108 Hugh Byas speech at Restaurant New Grand: 10 May 1937, Hugh Byas Papers, Yale, Reel 5.

3

Britain in East Asia and the *Japan Chronicle* network, 1891–1936

B ritain's relations with Japan during the period under review were neither static nor was British foreign policy towards Japan confined to a monolithic view. Rather, the relationship was in a state of constant development as different groups sought to influence foreign policy-makers. In London in the early 1900s, the Foreign Office Far East Department took soundings on events in East Asia from pro-Japanese newspaper men like H.A. Gwynne of the *Morning Post* and Valentine Chirol of *The Times*, and organized subsidies for Reuters, long the leading British news agency in East Asia. But it also heard from the British Association of Japan and the China Association, and figures like G.E. Morrison and Lord Northcliffe, all of whom in their different ways were concerned about the Japanese threat to British interests in China and felt uneasy that the Anglo-Japanese Alliance appeared to sponsor that threat. Between the wars, at the Far East Department and the British embassies in Tokyo and Peking, Frank Ashton-Gwatkin, John Pratt, Sir John Jordan, Miles Lampson, George Sansom and others represented a group that was uneasy with the insistence of Foreign Secretaries Edward Grey and Arthur Balfour on the need to maintain the Anglo-Japanese Alliance, and clearly at odds with the Japanophile tendencies of F.S.G. Piggott, and with what appeared to be the placatory stance of Robert Craigie, Lindley and other envoys.

In 1918 those characteristics of Japan noted in Britain's Paris Peace Conference *Handbook* would not, if they had been seen by the Japanese, have induced much confidence in their ally. Here we see the beginnings of a fundamental contradiction in official British views of Japan, between a realistic assessment of the nation in terms of its capacity and strength and a partial, impressionistic, usually negative view of its character:

> The astonishing progress the country has made in the last fifty years, and the victories gained over China and Russia, have to some extent turned the heads of the Japanese, and made them think themselves superior to Western nations, and look down with contempt upon other peoples of the East.[1]

In contrast, the *Handbook* described the Chinese as:

... a sober and industrious race, highly endowed with judgement, good sense, and tenacity ... The ideals of their intellectual life are not inferior to those in the Western world ...[2]

On the ground in Japan and China, the English-language newspapers took their own soundings on the character and ability of their host nation, and their editorial policy was often at odds with the line taken in Whitehall or Washington. Among British-owned newspapers in East Asia, the *Japan Chronicle* was consistently more critical of Japan and Japanese foreign policy, and the *Peking & Tientsin Times*, the *North-China Daily News* and the *Central China Post* were often more critical of nationalist Chinese policy than the Foreign Office would have wished. But such forthrightness was to be expected, since they were 'on the spot' and their journalists' experience of the issues was often immediate and personal.

Peter Lowe has pointed out that 'Insufficient understanding of Japan was shown by British government and British society in the 1930s. The qualities of character impelling Japan forward, the underlying tenacity, self-confidence, and willingness to endure profound hardship developing in its armed services and exhibited by its people were not properly recognized except by a few astute observers.'[3] Anthony Best has built on this perception:

... from the time of the Great War onwards, British policy in East Asia was characterized by a profound ambivalence about Japan and especially its potential threat to British interests. This arose because the policy makers within Whitehall held a double-sided image of Japan. On the one hand it was portrayed as a nation bent on regional domination, but on the other was seen as a backward power that lacked the resources necessary to achieve its goals. This dual image had its foundations in the Foreign Office's day-to-day experience of Japanese diplomacy and the observations made by the embassy in Tokyo about the political, economic and social life of Japan. In addition, it was influenced by commonly held racial assumptions about the inability of non-white nations to confront the modern Western states. The effect of this dual image was that Britain did not seek Japan's friendship, but at the same time did not view it as an irreconcilable enemy. This in turn helps to explain why Britain was prepared to see the end of the alliance in 1921, why it prevaricated about appeasing Japan in the 1930s, and finally why it underestimated the Japanese threat in 1940–41.[4]

Best's overview is framed by a discussion of British intelligence in East Asia, but it is helpful to our understanding of the newspaper networks' influence on official perceptions of Japan.

Did the British-owned English-language newspapers seriously challenge this 'double-sided image' in official Western views of Japan? None of the networks discerned in this study did much to alter the duality that Best has identified because their editorial line was firmly, even inevitably, drawn within the geopolitical parameters of the day. Their editorials may even have reinforced Japan's 'double-sided image' in Whitehall.

THE FOREIGN OFFICE, THE BRITISH PRESS, AND THE ENGLISH-LANGUAGE NEWSPAPERS OF EAST ASIA

To many embassy personnel in China and Japan, local newspapermen like Sheldon Ridge, George Woodhead, O.M. Green and Morgan Young were seen as a hindrance to diplomacy and kept at arm's length. Until the late 1930s, lumping together the editors of East Asia's English-language newspapers as an awkward brigade was about the closest the Foreign Office came to discerning any sort of press network. As for enlisting their help in any effort at improving Anglo-Japanese or Anglo-Chinese relations, the bruising handed out to the *New East* by the English-language press in 1916–18 was probably a sufficient deterrent.

Until the early 1920s, a group of senior journalists at *The Times* led by the foreign editor, Valentine Chirol and including the then editor, Moberly Bell, felt that, above and beyond observing its traditions of accurate reporting, the duty of *The Times* in East Asia was to uphold the good name of Britain's ally, Japan. This position had not presented J.O.P. Bland, *The Times* Shanghai and then Peking correspondent (1897–1910), with any difficulties. Nor did it challenge correspondents for *The Times* in Japan, all of whom, from H.S. Palmer to Frank Brinkley and John Penlington, were subsidized advocates of the Japanese case until Penlington's replacement by Lewis Carton in 1923.[5]

Alongside *The Times* correspondent in Peking, G.E. Morrison, Chirol had been closely involved with building the Alliance in 1902, promoting its renewal in July 1905 and July 1911 and, with R.P. Porter, putting together a series of *Times* special editions promoting Japan.[6] Morrison not only helped build the Alliance but used his extensive personal network in Britain and among the English-language newspapers of East Asia to promote war between Japan and Russia in 1904–5, despite the best efforts of Chirol, as Foreign Editor of *The Times*, to dilute the martial tone of Morrison's reports from China.[7] After 1915, Morrison came to see Japan, not Germany, as the greatest threat to British interests in China, and he did his utmost to persuade Lord Northcliffe, owner of *The Times*, to share this view. In this, Morrison was initially unsuccessful, although Northcliffe privately assured him of his support and of his wish to wage war on the pro-Japanese 'Old Gang', especially Chirol, at *The Times*. However, although he did not live to see it, Morrison's efforts ultimately bore fruit in Northcliffe's 'Watch Japan' campaign of January 1922.

Besides *The Times*, the other major British institution in a position to shape perceptions of Japan in East Asia was Reuters, which for twenty years, 1913–33, was closely connected to the Foreign Ministry network by agreements with the *Kokusai* and *Rengō* news agencies. Reuters tried to ensure that these contracts were financially rewarding, but their existence raised concerns, often vented in the *Japan Chronicle*, about the integrity of the Reuters correspondents in Japan. One Reuters correspondent in Shanghai, A.H. Wearne, was also receiving a monthly salary of $250 from Nationalist sources.[8]

Even during the period of its contractual agreement with *Kokusai*, Reuters was keenly aware of Japanese competition in China. In 1921 its Far East manager, William Turner, anticipated a long term strategy by Japan to dominate the Chinese news market:

> I have said that Tokio's aim is ultimately to control the bulk of the news printed in China. But I am certain that is not their only aim ... I know, for example, that Tokio deeply resents the fact that the chief sources of news in China for abroad are not Japanese. What I mean is that in China and Siberia ... REUTERS, the Associated Press of America and the United Press of America are the chief exporters of news for abroad. Well, it might be said, Japan cannot alter that situation. But she hopes, by possessing a well-established up-to-date news organization in China, with really good and reliable (from the Japanese view point) correspondents all over the country – she hopes in that way ultimately to create a favourable pro-Japanese news atmosphere in the big towns, which atmosphere, she reckons, is bound sooner or later to be reflected in the export news.[9]

At the same time, Reuters tried to broaden its market appeal, cutting analytical pieces and aiming for more scoops and headline items. Less analysis and more froth may have suited the efforts of one ex-Reuters correspondent, John Russell Kennedy, to help the Foreign Ministry network present a positive image of Japan. However, as mentioned in Chapter 2, Malcolm Kennedy, who had served as the Reuters correspondent in Japan since 1925,[10] resigned in mid-1934 in protest over the repeated spiking of his analyses of Japanese foreign policy and the sensationalization of his reports.[11]

In Whitehall, officials at the Far East Department were in close touch with the management of both Reuters and *The Times*, a triangular relationship that had served as a model for the Foreign Ministry network in managing the *Japan Times* and *Kokusai*. In 1917 and 1919, the Far East Department recognized the potential of the English-language newspapers for carrying propaganda and improving Britain's trade with East Asia but hesitated to embark on a propaganda programme on the scale of their perceived rival, Germany.[12] Unlike Japan, China and Germany, Britain had no institutionalized propaganda effort in peacetime. The truculence of British-owned newspapers in East Asia certainly grated with some officials at the Far East Department, but they made no concerted attempt to bring their editors into line, (in part because they were never entirely sure what line they themselves should take).[13]

In May 1926, *Rengō* replaced the *Shin-Tōhō* and *Kokusai* news agencies in China and Japan. *Rengō* was even more heavily subsidized than *Kokusai*, by 1930 to the tune of ¥200,000 per annum.[14] Earlier in 1926 the *Manchester Guardian* reported that the British government had 'set aside £600,000 to be applied to propaganda in China for the purpose of counteracting anti-British Soviet propaganda', but this did not signal any change in attitudes to propaganda at the Far East Department, where officials eventually traced the report back to a decision taken at the Shanghai Club the previous December to consider using propaganda to counter 'Bolschevik activities'.[15] However, in Hong Kong, where Chinese nationalism showed its teeth convincingly in the same year, the Governor's office set aside about $150,000 for subsidies to local Chinese-language and English-language newspapers.[16]

The most important British voice in China's English-language media was, of course, the *North-China Daily News*, alongside its weekly edition, the *North China Herald*. From its beginnings in 1850, the *North-China Daily News* gave extensive coverage to political and commercial developments in Britain and China but its editorials on East Asia tended to follow the Foreign Office line. In 1901 the *North-China Daily News* moved from Park Lane to its final home at 17 the Bund, and the owner of the land, H.E. Morris, swapped it for a 47% stake in the newspaper, becoming Chairman of the newspaper board, a position that carried considerable editorial power. Under Morris, the *North-China Daily News* grew ever closer to local interests represented on the Shanghai Municipal Council, and the newspaper's administrative and editorial staff became local bigwigs. One chief reporter, Edward Selby Little, was elected three times to the board of directors of the Shanghai Municipal Council of the International Settlement. The *North-China Daily News* published all the Municipal Council bulletins and the notices issued by the British Consulate in Shanghai. As a result, many Chinese came to see the paper as the official mouthpiece of British policy, although Britain's diplomatic establishment held it, like most 'treaty port' newspapers in China, in low esteem. The function that the *North-China Daily News* performed most skilfully, framing China and the Chinese in a way that made them seem less threatening and more manageable and thus acting as a cultural agent in the socialization of newcomers to the foreign community, also served to make the newspaper less palatable to both the Chinese and Whitehall.[17]

In Hankou for most of 1927 the *Central China Post* was at the sharp end of Guomindang pressure for the return of the British concession, its foremen bound by threats of murder to obey a strike order.[18] The Chinese-owned *Hankow Herald* had been more judicious in its criticisms of the Guomindang and was not disturbed. In the wake of the visit of Chiang Kai-shek to Moscow, the anti-British boycotts of 1925–6 and the loss of British prestige involved in the Chen-O'Malley Agreement returning the British concession at Hankou (Hankow) to China, some British newspapers in China, most notably the *North-China Daily News* and the *Peking & Tientsin Times* ran reports stigmatizing the Guomindang as 'Reds'. The Foreign Office had done its best to get the press in Britain to observe the distinction between the Nationalist and

Communist wings of the Guomindang, but it was unable to exert much control over the major players in China's British-owned press.[19]

The American-owned *China Weekly Review*, flagship of the *Advertiser* network in China, distanced itself from the 'exaggerated and hysterical' line taken by China's British-owned press in 1926–27, although its editor, John B. Powell, thought the Communists deserved whatever they got in the Shanghai purges.[20] Anticipating the 'Red sweeps' that would take place in Japan in 1927–28, the Foreign Ministry network put its anti-Communist credentials on display in the *North China Standard* and the *Far Eastern Review*. In the process, it found itself making common cause with the *Chronicle*'s old allies, H.G.W. Woodhead's *Peking & Tientsin Times* and the *North-China Daily News*, a coincidence of views that would, in Woodhead's case, develop into a peripatetic accommodation with the Foreign Ministry network. The *Chronicle* itself was uncharacteristically muted in its reaction to the suppressions of Communists in China and Japan in the late 1920s but it still kept its distance from the Foreign Ministry network.

As the political landscape changed in China, the Far East Department at the Foreign Office discussed a series of proposals for propaganda campaigns designed to shore up Britain's position in China. In July 1926, one such proposal advocated appointing a British businessman to head a publicity organization to get the British community in China to follow a common line and 'keep a steady expression of opinion before the Chinese on every point that crops up'.[21] This came to nothing, but faced with similar requests for action, the Department slowly came to accept the need for a more proactive approach to propaganda in East Asia. In 1930 Hugh Byas's departure from the editor's chair at the *Japan Advertiser* in order to concentrate on his correspondence for *The Times* and *New York Times* was a mixed blessing. The loss of a British voice on the most important American paper in East Asia was balanced by Byas's carefully argued dispatches to a leading US national daily. Nevertheless, with Reuters losing ground in China, the time seemed ripe for a change of direction.

In 1927, Miles Lampson, John Pratt and other Foreign Office officials had begun a campaign against O.M. Green that would result in his replacement as *The Times* correspondent in Shanghai and, in 1930, his resignation as editor of the *North-China Daily News* after twenty years in office.[22] Green's replacement by Edwin Haward did not immediately narrow the gap between the *North-China Daily News* and British policy in East Asia, but Haward helped make the newspaper 'less rancidly inflammatory' to the National Government.[23] Nevertheless, when the Shanghai Municipal Council began informal meetings with Chinese nationalists and abandoned its strict line on admitting Chinese residents to the parks, there was less common ground between the *North-China Daily News* and the Council than was apparent to many Chinese.

Following Green's departure, most advocates of the 'die-hard' stance lost their rostrum on the Bund. Rodney Gilbert returned to the US in 1929, George Sokolsky in 1930.²⁴ Randall Gould moved from UP Peking and Manila to the *Shanghai Evening Post and Mercury* in the autumn of 1930, where he was soon joined by H.G.W. Woodhead, and was promoted to editor in 1931.

Under Haward's editorial direction, the *North-China Daily News* made a conscious effort to win over Chinese readers and to commission more contributions from Chinese journalists. During the Sino-Japanese fighting in Shanghai in 1932 and in Peking in 1937 the paper adopted a less admonitory line on Chinese nationalism. However, during the crisis years of 1931–33, as more foreign correspondents transferred to Shanghai, the newcomers' need for an 'angle', local colour and brisk background material, not to mention their ignorance of the Guomindang's tangled relationship with the Chinese Communist Party and the vagaries of Sino-Japanese relations led them to overlook or discard much of the detail so vital to the Gilberts, Goulds and Sokolskys of the English-language press. Like Reuters, the 'Thunderer of the Bund' (also known as the 'kept lady of the Bund') was obliged to adapt to the breezier outlook of these newcomers as much as to its growing constituency of Chinese readers and the random strictures of Nationalist press control, or risk returning to the bleating insignificance of its treaty port days.²⁵

ROBERT YOUNG, MORGAN YOUNG, AND THE *JAPAN CHRONICLE* OF KŌBE, 1891–1936

As a small newspaper with a local circulation running in the low thousands, the *Japan Chronicle* was another paper that might never have escaped the treaty port rut, had it not been for the ideas and principles of its editor and founder, Robert Young, who wrote with an immediacy that made the *Chronicle's* name but proved difficult to maintain. Robert Young (1858–1922) founded the *Japan Chronicle* in 1891 and over thirty-one years gained it its reputation for fierce but scrupulous engagement with the politics and society of contemporary Japan. During his fourteen years as editor, Arthur Morgan Young (1874–1942) built strongly on this foundation, and was banned from Japan for his pains. In the last five years of the *Chronicle*, Edwin Allington Kennard (1902–77), edited the *Chronicle* with the help of a Foreign Ministry subsidy and benefited from its sale to the *Japan Times*.

Douglas Young's term of office as Managing Director began in 1926. Until his general ineptitude began to show through in the early 1930s in terms of failing revenue, a general loss of morale, and a move to the political centre as a consequence of loss of financial independence, the *Japan Chronicle* was probably the most professional and certainly the most clearly political of Japan's pre-war English-language newspapers. Its news reports were precise and informative and its essays and opinion pieces represented the cream of Japanese and expatriate intellectual life and scholarship. *Chronicle* writers and editors demonstrated a sure grasp of contemporary events, and two of its three editors were, in their day, among the most perceptive writers on Japan anywhere.

The writings of Robert Young are easy to study in surviving issues of his newspaper but, as others have found, there is little biographical information on the man himself.[27] Young was born in Westminster, London, on 9 October 1858, one of four children. The Youngs were not wealthy, but they had sufficient means to see their son into the Westminster Training School, and then a printer's apprenticeship with the publishers Spottiswoode. Robert Young took to his work and became a compositor and then Reader on the *Saturday Review*. The work was arduous, but it suited Young's innate passion for accuracy.

Young's parents were regular churchgoers, but both Robert and his brother George became interested in Positivism, and began attending lectures and courses at the South Place Religious Society (renamed the Ethical Society in 1887) in Moorgate, EC. Dr Moncure Conway, the American anti-slavery campaigner and revolutionizer of religious thought, who presided over South Place from 1864 to 1897, became a huge inspiration to Young and his brother George, who would both name their future home, and Robert his first son, 'Conway', in his memory. At South Place, Robert Young also came to know the militant atheist Charles Bradlaugh (1833–91) whose portrait would dominate the *Chronicle* offices in Kōbe.

Through lectures and study groups at South Place, and the influence of Conway and Bradlaugh, Robert Young developed an aversion to worship that would only harden with the death of two of his children and would be observed in a clause of his Will directing that 'no Christian religious ceremony' be performed at his funeral.[28] Trained to respect the fact and to distrust unthinking ceremony, Young's make-up set him at odds with late Victorian England, let alone Japan as he found it and as it would develop.

Robert Young first came to Japan in 1888, following a successful interview for a post as manager of the *Hiogo News* (1868–98) of Kōbe. In October 1889 he married an American, Annie Crockett Miller. Born in Yokohama in 1872, Annie was fourteen years younger than Robert. Her father, George Walker Miller was a retired merchant captain from Savannah, Georgia.[29] In 1891, at the age of thirty-three, Young left the *Hiogo News* to establish the *Kobe Chronicle* with a starting capital of ¥1000. The first issue of the *Kobe Chronicle* appeared on 2 October 1891. On 3 July 1897 Young began a weekly edition. On 8 January 1902 the *Kobe Weekly Chronicle* became the *Japan Weekly Chronicle*. On 5 January 1905 the daily edition of the *Kobe Chronicle* was renamed the *Japan Chronicle* and the paper grew from four to eight pages. In 1905 the new title marked the *Chronicle*'s popularity as the best-selling English-language newspaper in Japan. It also reflected Young's wish to gain a wider constituency for his paper, which now 'took the world as its province'.

Thus, within a few years of his arrival in Japan, Robert Young had established himself as a newspaperman in Japan and had become, if not a pillar of the Kōbe community, an active participant. Here is Young as his erstwhile leader writer Lafcadio Hearn saw him in 1894:

> Young is hearty and juvenile in appearance – serious face – dark beard – used to be a proof-reader on the Saturday Review, for which some culture is necessary. Is a straight thorough English radical. We are in perfect sympathy on all questions.[30]

Hearn's last point goes some way towards explaining the ambivalence of Young's position in Kōbe and in Japan's expatriate community. By temperament and upbringing, as a matter of principle (or disbelief) and above all because he felt that his work required it of him, Young's outlook on labour relations, armaments and militarism, on the Russian Revolutions of 1905 and 1917, on censorship, on Japan's wartime plutocracy and on her political development was that of a radical socialist.

Young and his newspaper soon gained a feisty reputation in Japan, largely through a series of clashes with Captain Francis Brinkley (1841–1912) and his newspaper, the *Japan Mail*. Like its junior contemporary, the *Japan Times*, the *Japan Mail* was a semi-official organ, promoting and defending Japan to the English-speaking world and receiving subsidies and other benefits from the Japanese government.[31] Brinkley's *Mail* defended 'squeeze' among government officials and the sale of young girls into prostitution by their parents. Reports of Japanese atrocities in Korea were 'iniquitous falsehoods' drummed up by 'the hostile orchestra' of the *Japan Herald*, *Japan Gazette* and *Kobe Chronicle* (known to *Japan Mail* readers as the 'Kobe Quibbler').[32] As a contemporary sniped, 'It is impossible to conceive Captain Brinkley in a position antagonistic to the government. The training of long years will suffice to deliver him from that unenviable predicament.'[33]

The *Chronicle* decried Brinkley's indiscriminate promotion of Japanese causes. In 1922 Young's obituary maintained that 'none of Robert Young's opinions was stronger than this, that paid advocacy is not a proper function of the Press'.[34] Young's own campaign for the ending of extraterritoriality may have won him his unprecedented audience with the Meiji Emperor in 1903, an honour not granted to Frank Brinkley, although he too had campaigned against the unequal treaties.[35]

Having little Japanese may also have made Young a less mellow observer than he might have been. Frank Brinkley's excellent command of the language brought him close to Itō Hirobumi and the Meiji elite, and this intimacy helped him to appreciate the establishment perspective in Japan. Brinkley's comfortable Meath squirearchy, Dungannon School and Trinity College, Dublin, background helped set him at ease among the oligarchs.[36] Brinkley's successor as spokesman for Japan, John Russell Kennedy, had a similar background: Glenalmond School in Scotland followed by Trinity College, Dublin, and service in the Cameron Highlanders. Russell Kennedy's near-successor at Reuters in

1925, the journalist Malcolm Kennedy, was another Glenalmond boy who worked in semi-official journalism in Japan and tended to move in the same circles as his predecessors. Claude MacDonald, the British ambassador to Japan during Kennedy's early years in Tokyo, was an officer in the 2nd Battalion, the Highland Light Infantry, and shared with Russell Kennedy the distinction of having fought in the Sudan campaign at the battle of El Teb in February 1884.[37]

Connections which might not have bred lasting attachments at home mattered greatly in the small British community in Japan and may have helped bring the British elites closer to a satisfying reflection of their own status among important Japanese. Frank Brinkley and John Russell Kennedy hobnobbed with the Japanese oligarchs and advanced the cause of the Foreign Ministry network but they were far more welcome among the embassy crowd in Tokyo and Karuizawa than the editors of the *Japan Chronicle*. Coming from a less exalted background did not prevent Young from being on good terms with some politicians, among them Tokonami Takejirō and Hara Kei, but the Japanese in his inner circle were all radical journalists and intellectuals. Moving in such circles, he would have felt little pressure to toe the official line.

In 1910, during an extended visit to England, Young was interviewed by the *Daily News* about the High Treason Incident (*Taigyaku Jiken*) of 1910, in which several hundred socialists, anarchists and sympathizers were arrested in Japan and twenty-six, including Kōtoku Shūsui, charged with plotting to assassinate the Emperor. In a January 1911 letter to *The Times*, Young had already described the trial as 'unjust in the extreme'.[38] In his interview, Young criticized the press blackout in Japan and described the trial by the Court of Cassation as:

... both unconstitutional and unprecedented. I understand that the Court of Cassation will try the twenty-six men and women in camera, so they are to have no public trial, and no chance of appeal, and we shall never know the facts.[39]

Japan, possibly advised by Kennedy, engaged in some well-planned news management to prepare Western opinion for a severe decision in the High Treason trial, putting out notices through Reuters in September 1910 and giving advance notice that Chief Prosecutor Hiranuma Kiichirō would be reaching a decision without providing details to the *Jiji Shimpō*. An official press conference was held for foreign newsmen in Tokyo on 16 January 1911. Two days later, the Court of Cassation handed down death sentences to twenty-four of the twenty-six accused. The following day, 19 January 1911, twelve of these sentences were commuted to life imprisonment, retaining the death sentence for Kōtoku Shūsui and eleven others.[40]

Robert Young was one among a very few informed opponents of this process and these decisions. He acted as a radical gadfly, stinging not only the Japanese judiciary but also the conscience of the Japanese press, declaring in his letter to *The Times*, 'the mouths of the accused have been shut, and any newspaper which dared give publicity to their defence would have been prosecuted under the law'. Kōtoku himself had been a journalist on the once-radical *Yorozu Chōhō*, and the silence of the Japanese papers over his fate marked a watershed in Japanese press history.

The High Treason Incident was one of a number of issues of national significance on which Japan's independent English-language press ventured far sharper comment than the vernacular press. Writers like Robert Young, his successor (but not his relation) Morgan Young and Hugh Byas at the *Japan Advertiser* were not restrained by the same loyalties or governed by the same hierarchies as Japanese newspapermen. As nationalist sentiment increasingly modified independent comment in Japan, the gap widened between the English-language press and the vernacular press reporting of major issues. Under Robert Young's editorship, this divergence was most obvious in the two presses' coverage of the High Treason Incident, the wars with China and Russia, the 'White Rainbow' incident (*hakkō jiken*),[41] the allied intervention in Siberia, the Korean independence movement of 1919–20, and, in 1920–22, the question of the renewal of the Anglo-Japanese Alliance. Under Morgan Young, the gap widened even further, especially after 1931.

Young's beliefs kept him out of church, but as a lifelong Spencerian, he went out of his way 'to teach the Christians Christianity', notably the foreign missionaries protesting the harshness of Japan's administration in Korea. As Young wrote in an important late letter to Bertrand Russell:

> The missionaries have always been puzzled that I should so stoutly defend the right of Christian missionaries in Korea to preach their doctrines without let or hindrance, despite the fact that I am a notorious unbeliever and a keen critic of them and their beliefs. The idea that one can defend the right of others to teach what he does not himself believe permeates very slowly into their minds.[42]

All three of his sons served, and the eldest died, in the 1914–18 war, but Young detested militarism, in Japan as in Britain and America. The *Chronicle* was highly critical of Britain's policy in South Africa before and during the Boer War, and of international intervention in Peking in the Boxer crisis. During Japan's 1894–5 war with China, Young's network of contacts in East Asia enabled the *Chronicle* to enhance its reputation by the breadth and accuracy of its war news, and it gained a world scoop on the attack on Formosa. This report and forecasts of an overwhelming Japanese victory were taken as championing the Japanese cause, and during the war patriotic lantern processions would pause outside the *Chronicle* building in Sannomiya, Kōbe, to cheer Young and his staff. A decade later, when the *Chronicle* refused to support Japan's war with Russia, the lantern processions fell silent as they passed the *Chronicle* headquarters.[43]

Young's principles increasingly set him at odds with Japan's foreign policy. As one obituary put it: 'Subsequent developments – the adminis- tration and annexation of Korea, the securing of rights in Manchuria – were contrary to his political philosophy, and he viewed with dislike the whole drift of Japanese policy as inimical to the sound development of the country and the true happiness of the people.'[44]

The *Chronicle* often attracted the charge that it was anti-Japanese. Responding in 1921 to one such accusation, Young maintained that he criticized Japan for the good of the Japanese:

> ... it is the Japanese people who have obtained advantage by the criticism of individual cases of injustice. Again, it is the Japanese people who will gain most from a decline in the power of the militarists who have exerted so much influence on the country's foreign policy for the last thirty years ... It is the Japanese people who would benefit and to describe criticism along these lines as anti-Japanese evinces a strange lack of perception.[45]

Even his obituary notice admits of Young, 'Occasionally the amount of artillery, which he employed, gave the impression that his opponent was more formidable than was really the case.'[46] Young's close friend, the Kōbe businessman David James, also felt that Young went too far. 'After the First World War,' he wrote, 'I saw more and more of Robert Young. By then, he was more a destructive critic of Japan than a constructive one. I felt that his work ... and influence in Japanese progressive circles was being defeated by carping criticism.'[47]

The feeling that his friend was stuck in an anti-Japanese rut led James to cooperate in an attempt to remove the *Chronicle* from Young's control. The idea was first put to James in 1921, as the *Chronicle*'s campaign against the renewal of the Anglo-Japanese Alliance was just beginning to warm up and find sympathetic echoes among other English-language newspapers in the *Chronicle* and *Advertiser* networks in East Asia. Acting on Foreign Ministry instructions, Ariyoshi Chūichi, Governor of Hyōgo Prefecture, approached a Kōbe shipping magnate named Itani. Itani in turn approached David James and in a conversa- tion deploring the rottenness of Japanese political life suggested to James that he get hold of the *Japan Chronicle* and run it in order to clean up the system, offering to put up ¥450,000 to purchase the newspaper from Robert Young. Itani professed agreement with James's views and promised him absolute editorial control. James accordingly approached Robert Young who at first rejected the proposal out of hand but later expressed more interest, although Itani's readiness in difficult times to put up such a large sum seemed a little suspect. However, James went travelling in Borneo and on his return journey met Lord Northcliffe, who was not only against the renewal of the Alliance but was conscious of a tide of opinion against it and felt sure that the forthcoming Imperial Conference would oppose it, as indeed it did. As a result, James felt that Young's independent opposition to renewal was less ill-judged than it had seemed earlier, and his enthusiasm for taking over the *Chronicle* weakened. James then learned by chance that far from being open-handed, Itani was remarkably close-fisted, and as a result managed to trace the scheme backwards from Itani's involvement to the Governor of Hyōgo and thence to the Foreign Ministry. Thus ended the first attempt by the Foreign Ministry network to take control of the *Japan Chronicle*.[48]

Young and the *Chronicle* made few friends at the Foreign Office or at the Tokyo embassy. In December 1917 Sir Conyngham Greene, the British Ambassador, acknowledged that '… the editors of the *"Japan Chronicle"* are very capable and well-informed'. However, as Greene saw it, the *Chronicle* writers:

> … seem to suffer from an exaggerated critical faculty with regard to the actions and sayings of all their fellow men and especially those in official positions – an idiosyncrasy which, in the case of the various Japanese with whose words and deeds the 'Chronicle' is naturally called upon to deal most frequently, leads to a disposition to dwell unduly upon every fault and to overlook the arguments or excuses which might be cited in favour of the persons criticized … Such a disposition, whilst apt to obscure the otherwise brilliant gifts of these writers, might nevertheless do little harm, since the Japanese recognize only the apparent ill-will of the paper and have ceased almost entirely, to pay attention to the views expressed by it; but, unfortunately, the opinions held and voiced by the British communities not only in the chief ports of Japan but also in the small mining camps of Corea, and especially in Kobe itself, are to a very great extent inspired by this journal, which thus, on the whole, exercises a detrimental influence on the relations between Japan and the British Empire.[49]

Greene and Young were bound to see things differently. Greene's private view of Japanese ambitions in the Pacific was no less critical than Robert Young's, but his profession required that he treat Japan with all the care and respect due to an ally in wartime.[50] In Young's sense of the function of the press, Japan and the Japanese were subject to the same unfaltering scrutiny as the rest of the world. Pleasing impressions of Japan that oiled the workings of the Alliance were not the proper work of the *Chronicle*.

Young's principled editorials often conflicted with the positions held by his country's representative in Japan, but they were clearly appreciated by E.R. Dickover, the US Consul in Kōbe:

> He was a radical, against militarism and imperialism and for self-government, even if government by others should be better than self-government. He worked constantly for international harmony and fought against secret treaties, tariff barriers, unfair subsidies, and other devices which tend to create ill-feeling among nations … to those who knew him well, Robert Young was not anti-any country, but treated every country alike in his criticism of what he believed to be wrong … Mr Young was

particularly friendly to and interested in the United States, as the truest representative of liberty in the modern world.[51]

Thus, by the early 1920s, the *Japan Chronicle* had become that rare thing, a local newspaper with an international readership and influence. Whether or not it qualified for Bertrand Russell's description as 'the best weekly journal in the world',[52] the *Chronicle* was undeniably appreciated as an uncompromisingly truthful reporter of Japanese life to the foreign community and the world at large. It was also deprecated as an unforgivably anti-Japanese paper that pandered to expatriate prejudices and stained the image of Japan around the world. Both views attest to the paper's influence. As Young's obituary notices testify, in addition to a solid subscription list among English-speaking expatriates in East Asia, the *Chronicle* was eagerly read by newspaper men and opinion leaders in Great Britain, Europe and the United States.[53]

Robert Young died of a heart attack at his home in Kōbe on 7 November 1922. He left a wife and three children: Douglas George, Eric Andrew and Ethel Margaret, each of whom suffered personal difficulties: both Douglas and Ethel were problem drinkers and Eric appears to have suffered from depression – but this is to anticipate. Ethel had married Reginald Stewart-Scott in March 1921 and was living in Britain when her father died. Under Robert Young's Will, ownership of the *Chronicle* passed to a trust, of which Robert's youngest son Eric was the sole member.[54] Eric, who was already managing the *Chronicle* presses, now became managing director of the firm. Arthur Morgan Young, who had been assistant editor since 1911, became editor. Unlike Robert Young, whose writing was largely concentrated on the *Chronicle*, Morgan Young wrote for many other publications, including *Asia* and, from 1925, the *Manchester Guardian*, and published five books on Japan.[55]

The immediate difficulties were financial. In the summer of 1922, the new English edition of the *Ōsaka Mainichi Shinbun* had poached some of the *Chronicle*'s Japanese linotype print workers. These defections brought the paper to its knees, as new staff had to be found and trained up from the beginning. In the summer before his death, Robert Young had to buy two new printing machines and engage new operators from England, but while these were sailing east, the daily edition lost pages and the *Chronicle* lost readers.

Now, with his father gone, Eric Young had to meet the payroll of large advertising and printing departments, a team of translators, a new editor at ¥1000 a month and a sizeable editorial department, heavy cable and paper costs, and find his own salary. These problems must have been daunting to someone with no financial training or management experience. Eric struggled on, but in 1926, perhaps because he could see no way out of the financial problems besetting the *Chronicle*, he committed suicide by leaping from the deck of an ocean liner.[56]

After Robert's death, his widow, Annie, had gone to San Francisco. In 1925 she married a US citizen, Thomas Harloe.[57] In her absence and with

Eric's suicide, the *Chronicle* reached an important turning point marked by the installation of Eric's older brother, Douglas George Young, as publisher. Douglas was notoriously ill-tempered. Tokyo Embassy officials described him as 'a half-crazy misanthrope with a grudge against the Japanese and ourselves', and as being 'always against the government'.[58] The historian of expatriate Japan, Harold Williams, who knew him personally, wrote that Douglas Young '… was not a journalist, nor was he a person of any great ability nor business experience'.[59] The Foreign Ministry described him as inexperienced (*mukeiken*), arrogant (*gōman*) and bureaucratic (*kanryōteki*).[60]

Early in Douglas's tenure, a feud set in between him and Morgan Young, which did little to improve morale at the paper. In 1927, in a characteristically intemperate move, Douglas closed down the advertising department altogether. In 1929 he stopped publishing the *Japan Chronicle Year Book*, then closed the Japan Chronicle Press and fired its staff of forty-five. The *Chronicle*'s financial problems were not irreversible but by these sackings and closures, Douglas Young cut off useful revenue and made recovery far more dependent on the newspaper's circulation than before. However, as an editorial forum, as a source of news at a news-hungry time, the *Chronicle* was on its way out. Foreign news stopped coming in when cable bills went unpaid and the *Chronicle* began copying items from other papers and using translations of vernacular press reports as page-fillers. By the early 1930s, circulation was down from the approximate 3,000 of 1925 to between 1,500 and 2,000.

Meanwhile, as Reuters' William Turner had complained in the early 1920s, some China papers in the *Chronicle* network found the prices charged by *Rengō*'s sister organization there, the *Shin-Tōhō Tsūshinsha* (New Eastern News Agency) irresistible compared to Reuters' prices. The adoption of *Shin-Tōhō* bulletins may explain the relative mildness of the *Chronicle* network China papers' line on Japan compared to the line taken by the *Advertiser* network there, but even this muted criticism helped close the gap between the *Chronicle* and its China affiliates in the 1930s. These newspapers were also subdued by confrontations with the unstoppable forces of Chinese nationalism, and by its censors. In 1930 the *North-China Daily News* began an uneasy but long-overdue accommodation with Chinese nationalism by replacing its long-serving editor, O.M. Green with Edwin Haward, a personnel change largely engineered by the Foreign Office.

By this stage, Morgan Young's essays and opinion pieces were almost the only fresh items in the *Chronicle*, but even here Douglas caused problems. In the spring of 1930, Morgan Young found that his salary had been docked ¥65 for 'free advertisement' because he had reprinted in the *Chronicle* an interesting American review of his book *Japan in Recent Times*.[61]

When the *Chronicle*'s financial situation continued to deteriorate, Douglas Young stopped paying the salary of a Japanese employee of the advertising department and fired two other advertising staff. The level of service deteriorated further and once-loyal advertisers began migrating to the blander pastures of the *Japan Advertiser* and the *Osaka Mainichi*. Official hostility added to these problems. Conyngham Greene may have had his own reasons for maintaining that Robert Young's *Chronicle* was ignored by the Japanese, but Morgan, Douglas and Eric Young were under constant police observation, (Morgan Young liked to bamboozle the gendarmes by signing himself 'Douglas Young' in hotel registers), and the *Chronicle* was often marked for close inspection (*sasatsu yō-chūi shi*) by the Home Ministry (*Naimushō*).

Alongside this surveillance, there came a second effort by Japanese official bodies aimed at bringing the *Chronicle* into line. On 30 May 1934, while looking for work in Japan after his resignation from Reuters, Malcolm Kennedy received an approach from Yamada Kōzō, Chief Secretary to Araki Sadao, the War Minister. According to Yamada, Douglas Young wanted to sell the *Chronicle* as it was not paying its way. Araki and others in his circle were interested in buying the newspaper if Kennedy would agree to replace Morgan Young as its editor and take a more friendly editorial line on Japan. Kennedy politely declined the offer. At the same time, Yamada claimed to have evidence that 'Douglas Young received money from Nanking at the time of the Shanghai Operations and from Zhang Xueliang (Chang Hsueh-liang) during the Manchurian trouble', a revelation that Kennedy found 'hard to believe'.[62]

Douglas Young died in May 1938 in the International Hospital in Kōbe. In 1935, Thomas Harloe died in San Francisco and his widow, Annie Harloe, formerly Mrs Robert Young, who had been living on and off in San Francisco, returned to Kōbe for a stay that lasted until 1939. Her influence on the course of events between her return in 1935 and her final departure for San Francisco in 1939 is not known, but with the departure of Morgan Young as editor in 1936 and all three of Robert Young's sons dead and his daughter, Ethel, 'an inebriate and a rather notorious person', Annie may have exercised a decisive influence on decisions made in 1938.[63]

THE *JAPAN CHRONICLE* NETWORK, 1891–1936

The great strength of the *Chronicle* lay in the quality of its writing. The unremitting brilliance of Robert Young's essays and squibs and Morgan Young's polemical writings attracted regular contributions from well-known expatriate scholars: Basil Chamberlain, Lafcadio Hearn, Hector Munro, James Murdoch, Ponsonby-Fane and G.C. Allen. In addition, both Young and his successor Morgan Young undertook intense, argumentative exchanges of correspondence with the intellectuals Uchimura Kanzō, Ishibashi Tanzan, Kagawa Toyohiko, Yamamoto Sanehiko of the political journal *Kaizō*, and the Russian *émigré* Ivan Kozlov, and gave them all ample space for their views. In the spring of 1923, Morgan Young openly called on the Soviet ambassador to China, Adolphe Joffe when he was taking the waters in Atami, and the Japanese newspapers were full of stories of the huge subsidies Joffe was handing out to Japanese socialists.[64]

Until 1938, when the *Japan Chronicle* began receiving subsidies in exchange for their support, the *Chronicle* network was characterized by relatively balanced criticisms of Japanese policies in East Asia, although its attitude to the operations of the Foreign Ministry network, particularly the *Japan Times*, was consistently hostile. Like their intellectual mentors Moncure Conway, Charles Bradlaugh and Bertrand Russell, neither Robert Young nor his successor Morgan Young could accept that the national interest required the suspension of critical judgement. The *Chronicle* was quite alone in holding to this principle in wartime, unlike H.G.W. Woodhead at the *Peking & Tientsin Times*, who was awarded a C.B.E. for his attacks on China's German press.

However, although its network gained few new adherents in East Asia in the 1920s, in the 1930s the *Chronicle* and its affiliates began to reflect the increasingly hostile views of Japan that were being expressed in the Western press and, despite its liberal tradition, and perhaps because it was being subsidized by Nanjing, moved closer to the pro-Guomindang outlook of the *Japan Advertiser* network in China.

Morgan Young refused to respect national conventions in Japan, no matter how strong the consensus. The sentiments of Chamberlain's 1912 polemic, *The Invention of a New Religion*, published by the Rationalist Press Association at Conway Hall and by the Japan Chronicle Press, of Putnam Weale's *Shanghai Express* report and the *Ōsaka Asahi Shinbun* 'White Rainbow' crisis of 1918, which the *Chronicle* was alone in connecting to the wider implications for press freedom in Japan, all posed a challenge to the authorities and framed the *Chronicle* and some of its network in intellectual and political opposition to official descriptions of the Japanese state.[65] As these official descriptions grew more radical, emperor-centred and nationalistic, the *Chronicle's* opposition was bolstered by contributions from such home-grown radicals as Uchimura Kanzō, Yoshino Sakuzō and others whose essays scrutinized the very notions that least bore scrutiny.

In China until the early 1930s, the *Chronicle* was close to H.G.W. Woodhead's *Peking & Tientsin Times*, Sheldon Ridge's *Peking Chronicle*, Harry Archibald's *Central China Post* in Hankou and four important Shanghai newspapers: the *North-China Daily News*, the *Shanghai Gazette*, the *Shanghai Mercury*, and the short-lived *Gazette*, (published in Shanghai but not to be confused with the *Shanghai Gazette*), edited by the *Chronicle's* roving correspondent, Gordius Nielsen. Between the Twenty-One Demands of 1915 and the Washington Conference of 1921–22, the network was most specifically united on the need to abrogate the Anglo-Japanese Alliance, but less specifically united on how to replace it, and during the crisis years of 1931–33 it was particularly divided on the wisdom or otherwise of intervention in Manchuria by the League of Nations.

In their unified stance against the Alliance with Japan, the newspapers in the *Chronicle* network were at one with the key players in the *Advertiser* network: the *China Weekly Review*, the *China Press* and the *Japan Advertiser*, whose campaign against the Alliance was overt, efficient and generously financed. As we saw in Chapter 2, Ugaki Kazushige's July 1923 ruminations about an anti-Japanese newspaper network came in the wake of the abrogation of the Alliance at Washington and the 'Watch Japan!' campaign drummed up by Lord Northcliffe. Japan put up a far slicker presentation at Washington than it did at Paris, but it did not sign up to the Washington system in 1922 with quite the same sense of having arrived at the top table as at the Peace of Paris.[66]

It may be that a niggling sense of international victimization, even conspiracy, felt by some Japanese and epitomized in 1923 by Ugaki's diary speculations gained in intensity as Japan passed through the successive international conferences of the 1920s and 1930s. From Paris in 1919 to Washington in 1922, through the various meetings of the Institute of Pacific Relations, at all the League of Nations conferences of the 1920s, and at the Naval Conferences at Geneva (1927) and London (1930), even while Japan sent its delegates and signed up to the Kellogg-Briand Pact and played the game according to the norms and ideals agreed at Paris, a general distrust of internationalism seems to have been growing among its delegates and their chiefs. It may be that this sense that the world had it in for Japan whatever it did had something to do with the mismanagement and gesture politics that characterized the Foreign Ministry and its representatives in Geneva in 1932–33.

In its relationships with the other newspapers in its network, the *Chronicle* and its contemporaries quoted with approval each other's leading articles in a cosy exchange of bylines ('JC', 'P&T Times', 'NCDN'). These papers exchanged staff and local news. Their editors kept in close touch, met when they could, and reviewed each other's books. The China editors, H.G.W. Woodhead, O.M. Green, Harry Archibald, Sheldon Ridge and Putnam Weale, and the Japan editors, Robert Young and Morgan Young were all active in the China Association and in the British Association in Japan Overseas in Japan, which had lobbied in Whitehall on behalf of mutual trade and political interests since 1907.

From about 1900 until his early death in 1921, O.M. Green, Woodhead and Robert Young were all in close touch with G.E. Morrison, *The Times* correspondent in Peking and, from August 1912, political adviser to Yuan Shikai. In these exchanges, Morrison's position was always that of a superior or mentor, closer both to the action, in China, and to power in Whitehall than they could ever be.[67] Morrison was such an institution in China, and so practised a networker in the diplomatic and media triangle of London, Peking and Tokyo, that it is hard to say whether Young, Woodhead and Green were in Morrison's network or he in theirs, but it is safe to say that, especially during his time as Yuan Shikai's publicist (1912–20), Morrison virtually managed the career and editorial line of some of those in his network.[68] Certainly, this group, combined with Morrison's impressive international diplomatic and media network, followed a common line on some important issues, most notably in their reactions to the Chinese Revolution of 1911 and the rise of Yuan Shikai, the Twenty-One Demands of 1915, the Nishihara Loans of 1917–18, Japan and China's competing interests and propaganda at the Paris Peace Conference (where Morrison was an adviser to the Chinese delegation), the Korean Independence movement in 1919, and the beginnings of their campaign against the renewal of the Anglo-Japanese Alliance. Young and Green agreed with Morrison on the need to check Japanese power in East Asia and, to official Japan, both Morrison and Young became associated with anti-Japanese sentiment, although their surviving correspondence is too scanty to find much indication of any concerted approach.[69] In an attempt to inculcate more friendly sentiments towards Japan, both men were introduced to the Meiji Emperor: Young in 1903, Morrison in 1909, a rare privilege that did nothing to soften their views.[70]

The *Chronicle* network had few consistent high-level contacts but some editors were well-placed: Putnam Weale as a paid consultant to the Chinese foreign ministry; O.M. Green as a China Association lobbyist and China correspondent for *The Times* and the *Daily Telegraph*; Morgan Young as the *Manchester Guardian* correspondent. Robert Young was admired by Bertrand Russell and Lord Northcliffe but this would hardly have helped his reputation in official Japan, even with the powers of his day such as Hara Kei and Tokonami Takejirō, both of whom were said to have liked Young personally and to have respected the work of the *Chronicle*.[71]

Unlike the *Japan Advertiser* network, the *Chronicle* network was short on American connections. None of the *Chronicle* network editors or staff wrote Japan correspondence for American newspapers, but Morgan Young, the *Chronicle*'s second editor, wrote the Japan correspondence of the *Manchester Guardian* from 1925 until 1936, and would have continued to do so if he had not been barred from returning to Japan. In December 1937 Young published *Japan's War on China*, an eighty-one page indictment of Japanese aggression in China, which Young described as 'Cæsarism', in a series of sixpenny monographs collectively entitled *Fact*.

Recovering his fortunes in London, Young came up with a ten-page journal, *The Far East Survey*, which may have been funded by the Guomindang.[72] Published in 1938, his *Imperial Japan* was critical, but not as bitter a book as it might have been. *Japan: The Pagan State*, an analysis of Emperor-worship and its consequences for China, appeared in 1939 to scant applause. The following year, Young gave a snappy summary of Japan's recent history ('So it is partly the fault of the rest of the world that the patriotism that sixty years ago seemed so quaint, picturesque and admirable in Japan is to-day something rather dreadful') in a lecture at London University that spring, that was published in a collection edited by Frederick Whyte, an ex-M.P. with Guomindang connections.[73] By 1941, Young had moved to Cowley, Oxford, where he persevered with the *Far East Survey* and with letters to *The Times* on events in East Asia but, as he might have been the first to admit, far from Japan and his chair at the *Chronicle*, he was a spent force. His death in January 1942 was little noticed in the British press.

☐

For all its freshness of approach, breadth of view and its closeness to the subject, the *Japan Chronicle* seems almost to typify the 'dual image' view of Japan summarized by Best.[74] Like the Whitehall policy chiefs whose perceptions they habitually ridiculed, the *Chronicle's* writers failed to reconcile their own dual images of the people they had made their special study. Over many years, the *Chronicle's* writers seemed incapable of discussing the challenge Japan posed to Western interests in East Asia without dwelling on the deficiencies of its army and navy and speculating on the follies of the military mind. In discussing Japan's education system, its politics, its press, its colonial policies, its medical knowledge, its sewage system, its telephone system, its railway and its postal services, the *Chronicle* and its sister newspapers in China dwelt on the backwardness of the Japanese as a people and on the small-mindedness of their administrations, while deploring the threat they posed to the security of East Asia. The *Chronicle* network's reporting of the growth of a nationalism based on unarguable, emperor-centred concepts merged frequently with these images of backwardness and weakness, but they did not always appreciate its power as a motivational force although they had never been slow to warn of similar dangers in their discussions of British imperialism.

Was there a flaw in the approach of the English-language newspapers of East Asia to Japan that prevented them conveying their concerns and interests in a way that would influence official policy? Christopher Thorne has written:

> The basic weakness of expatriate pressure groups in the Far East lay in their inability to appeal to a highly-placed societal value (unlike, say, those groups in the United States who had helped bring about the Kellogg-Briand pact) ... for all their Conservative connections, the means they advocated were too obviously at variance with one of the goals in questions, the preservation of good relations with potential Chinese customers. With their own extreme viewpoint expressly repudiated by those responsible for the formulation and execution of British policy, they were left stranded on the shores of the China sea by the retreating tide of British imperial will, as much as by the ebb of British military power.[75]

In making this point, one of the expatriate pressure groups Thorne had in mind was the China Association, rather than the English-language newspapers of East Asia, although in fact, the two were closely connected. But, first, did the English-language newspapers associated with the *Chronicle* appeal to 'highly-placed societal values' at home, particularly in the Foreign Office, or were their fortunes too attached to Britain's declining imperial power?

The *Chronicle* was not only an anti-Imperialist organ but, particularly in the 1920s, it was highly sympathetic to socialist thinking and far to the left of its English-language contemporaries in East Asia. In many ways the *Chronicle's* editorial line anticipated policy developments of the Foreign Office that would, as Thorne put it, leave the expatriate constituency 'stranded' in East Asia. In its critical attitude to Japanese policies in East Asia the *Chronicle* was out of step with the editorial line taken by conservative 'quality' broadsheets such as *The Times* and *Morning Post*, but not with the line pursued by popular British dailies such as Northcliffe's (but not Rothermere's) *Daily Mail* and Beaverbrook's *Daily Express*.

Thorne shows that the lobbyists of the China Association, on which both the *Peking & Tientsin Times* and the *North-China Daily News* were represented, failed 'to appeal to a highly-placed societal value' in Britain. However, their more conservative outlook did not inhibit the strong links the China Association maintained with the left-leaning *Chronicle* after 1907, when it amalgamated with the British Association of Japan, on whose Kōbe Committee, Robert Young and later Morgan Young maintained an influential presence until Morgan Young's departure in 1936.

These relationships were not consistent. Although these newspapers built enduring commercial and lobbying connections in East Asia and in Whitehall and Westminster, neither Robert Young nor Morgan Young were entirely at ease with the contempt in which some *North-China Daily News* and *Peking & Tientsin Times* writers seemed to hold the Chinese as a race, particularly when, as with Rodney Gilbert and H.G.W. Woodhead, such contempt was conflated with hints that Japan would sort out the chaos indigenous to all things Chinese and become the saviour of Western interests in China.

In 1923, reviewing Gilbert Collins's *Flower of Asia*, a novel set in Shanghai and Tokyo, the *Chronicle* was unwilling to accept its description of the settler communities in these cities:

> His Englishmen in the Far East are vulgarians of a literary convention such as do not really exist … Judging by his conventional descriptions of philistines and vulgarians, Mr Collins appears to be endowed with a full measure of the cheapest kind of snobbishness.[76]

However, four years later, when the 'Shanghai Mind' was identified and perhaps more skilfully diagnosed by Arthur Ransome (Ransome 1927) in a collection of *Manchester Guardian* articles published in Britain and the US, the *Chronicle*, now edited by the *Manchester Guardian*'s Japan correspondent, was at one with most British and American reviewers, though not yet with many among its China affiliates, in perceiving a distasteful narrowness in the 'Shanghailander' mentality.

The *Chronicle* network was far looser than the Foreign Ministry and *Japan Advertiser* networks, largely because its members were so independent minded. At times it was less a network than a group of like-minded mavericks. It also lacked the 'transnational' interweaving of purpose and mission with Japanese interests that characterized the *Advertiser* network in China. The dynamics were different. The *Chronicle* network never aimed, even after 1938, to 'speak for Japan' in quite the way the *Advertiser* network claimed to speak for Nationalist China. Nor did the *Chronicle* network reflect for British interests in Japan as clear an agenda as the *Advertiser* network projected for the US in China. These shortcomings may have helped the *Chronicle* survive as long as it did and by default deflected more hostile Japanese scrutiny towards the *Advertiser* in Japan, and towards its network in China.

Robert Young and Morgan Young and the China journalists O.M. Green, H.G.W. Woodhead and Harry Archibald, and Green and Woodhead's successors in 1930 and 1931 at the *North-China Daily News* and *Peking & Tientsin Times*, Edwin Haward and W.V. Pennell, may have seemed strange bedfellows, but their situation as editors of British-owned newspapers in the treaty ports of East Asia brought them to common perceptions and forced them to accommodate to similar dilemmas. From the early 1900s until their demise, incarceration or repatriation, each of these editors did his best to ride out and interpret his allotted view of huge shifts in the political landscape of East Asia. Inevitably, these newspapers had more in common on their way out on Thorne's 'retreating tide of British imperial will' than they had on their way up. And on their way out, for all their networks and connections, the combined influence of these newspapers did not constitute a force sufficient to hold them in place.

The *Japan Chronicle* network had at its centre two newspapers, the *Japan Chronicle* and the *North-China Daily News*, which shared a common editorial line on a number of issues, especially in relation to the broad church of the British world, but were separated by the editorial positions they adopted on the Empire and on Chinese nationalism. To the *Chronicle*, the rise of the Guomindang represented a long-overdue sign of Chinese unity in the face of European, American and, most of all, Japanese interests. As far as the *North-China Daily News*, the *Peking & Tientsin Times* and the *Central China Post* were concerned, the Nationalists posed a commercial, political and military threat to Britain in China whose most redeeming feature, when they saw it written in blood in the late 1920s, was not that they were not gangsters or opium dealers but that that they were not Communists.

However, over two decades, the position of the *Chronicle* and the British-owned China newspapers in its network came closer as the outspoken stance of the *Chronicle*'s founding proprietor and editor,

Robert Young, was adapted by necessity to the *Chronicle*'s reduced circumstances and financial and political changes brought about by new personnel. When Morgan Young became editor in November 1922 his outlook was no less radical than his predecessor's, but in 1926 his ability to express it was complicated by the appointment of Douglas G. Young as publisher following Eric Young's suicide.

Douglas Young's character has been discussed above. From late 1926, Morgan Young had to work round his new employer's mercurial changes of mood and strategy. In 1927 the recruitment from the *Peking & Tientsin Times* of Edwin Kennard as assistant editor may have brought the *Chronicle*'s editorial line even closer to that of the China papers in its network, although it continued to support Chinese nationalism and to criticize Japanese ambitions in China and the attitude of the Japanese press.[77]

Three years after E.A. Kennard joined the *Chronicle*, O.M. Green, the long-serving editor of the *North-China Daily News*, was finally winkled out of his forum on the Bund and the Shanghai correspondence of *The Times*. The brief followed by his replacement, the former Dominions journalist and India Office functionary, Edwin Haward, was not to resist but to contain and accommodate the march of Chinese nationalism. Rodney Gilbert returned to the US in 1929, George Sokolsky in 1931, following Green's departure. From 1931, what remained of the positions Green had represented were expressed on the *Shanghai Evening Post and Mercury* by its editor from 1931 to 1941, Randall Gould, and his star columnist, H.G.W. Woodhead, who had relocated from Tianjin.

One effect of these personnel changes in Kōbe, Shanghai and Tianjin was to bring the *Chronicle*, the *North-China Daily News* and the *Peking & Tientsin Times* away from their traditional positions. Under Douglas Young, the *Chronicle*'s liberal tradition became less axiomatic. Under pressure from both Whitehall and the Chinese Nationalists, the China papers in the *Chronicle* network learned to soften their attitude of resistance. In February 1932 another *Chronicle* affiliate, the *Central China Post* of Hankou, buckled under severe Nationalist pressure and trimmed its sails to the prevailing wind.

At the *Chronicle*, the departure of Morgan Young in 1936, his replacement by Kennard, and as will be seen in Chapter 7, a significant development in the relationship between the Chronicle and the Foreign Ministry in 1938 neutralized the *Chronicle* as a critical voice. The invasion of Shanghai by Japanese forces in 1932 and the occupation of 1937 served first to reduce to inconsequential protest and then to mute the old thunder of the *North-China Daily News* and to bring other outspoken voices, such as H.G.W. Woodhead's on the *Shanghai Evening Post and Mercury*, even more completely into a pro-Japanese, pro-Manchukuo line.

In commercial terms too, the *Japan Chronicle* demonstrated an inevitable accommodation to powerful interests, no matter how gradual. Under Robert Young, the *Chronicle* had been an early subscriber to the Imperial news system as represented by Reuters, which served the China ports and, at its tail-end, Japan, when the cable service became available in the early 1900s. Despite its disapproval of the contractual arrangements between Reuters and the Foreign Ministry network in 1913–14, the *Chronicle* maintained, with reservations, its Reuters subscription: it had little choice if it was to serve its readers with the world news and financial pages that were probably more of a sales point among its Kōbe readership, where mercantile interests were strongly represented, than its political outlook.

The *Chronicle*'s links to these larger global networks weakened in the late 1920s and early 1930s as Douglas Young's reckless management made them no longer affordable. The *North China Daily News* and the *Advertiser* network's *China Press* chose the *Shin-Tōhō* service over Reuters on grounds of sheer affordability. The *Chronicle* could not even afford *Rengō*'s charges and was reduced to filching news from other English-language newspapers. Under Douglas Young, Morgan Young's feisty polemics were all that remained of its liberal tradition. In other respects it became a cagey, spent force, more or less in line with its cowed contemporaries in China. Thus, notwithstanding Morgan Young's cheerful defiance, the overall editorial line of the *Chronicle* and its network, without actually adopting Japan's case in China, began to look less of an obstacle to their acceptance.

These shifts in outlook were too gradual to be overt, but they may help to explain why the Foreign Ministry network did not close the *Chronicle* or its network down or arrange a takeover of the *North-China Daily News* when Japan occupied Shanghai in 1937, or why the *Peking & Tientsin Times* survived the Tianjin Incident. No evidence has been found that any of the China papers in the *Chronicle* network accepted a Foreign Ministry subsidy, although one, Sheldon Ridge's *Peking Gazette*, was subsidized by Nanjing. Having driven the *Chronicle* into a financial corner, Douglas Young may have had no option but to take a subsidy from Zhang Xueliang during the Manchurian Incident and from Nanjing during the invasion of Shanghai.[78] Seen in this light, Douglas Young's financial arrangements with Chinese interests look almost like practice runs for the deal closed by his successor, Stanley Foley, and Morgan Young's, Edwin Kennard, in 1938.

NOTES

1   Paris Peace Conference *Handbook on Japan*, Foreign Office, March 1919, FO 373/4/15. Cited in Shimazu 1998: 104–5.
2   Paris Peace Conference *Handbook on Japan*, Foreign Office, March 1919, FO 373/4/15. Cited in Shimazu 1998: 213, n.74.
3   Lowe 1977: 284–5.
4   Best 2002: 3–4.
5   But note that there were often two or three stringers, usually in Kōbe, Yokohama and Tokyo, contributing reports to *The Times* (Hoare 1999: 104). Another, less direct, connection between *The Times* and the English-language

press lay in the person of Charles Hargrove, editor of the JA from 1912 to 1914, who was *The Times* Washington correspondent for some years both before and after his stint at the JA.

6   *The Times* published Japan supplements on 7 July 1910; 3 June, 15 July, 2 September, 14 October and 16 December 1916, and on 16 June 1921.

7   Woodhouse 2004: 13.

8   J.C. Huston, Confidential Memo to Julean Arnold, Commercial Attaché, Peking, 1 December 1923: Julean Arnold Papers, Hoover Institution, Stanford University, California. Cited in Rozanski 1974: 365, and 379, n.4.

9   FO 371/8028 [F 647/647/10], W. Turner Memorandum 'On Japanese propaganda in the Far East'. Secret dispatch to FO, via 'Ross', 5 December 1921.

10 Laxon Sweet briefly held the fort at Reuters between Russell Kennedy's replacement by Andrew Pooley and Malcolm Kennedy's arrival in March 1925.

11 Pardoe 1989: Pardoe 1989: 220. The final straw was Reuters' refusal to publish Kennedy's exposure of Tim Conroy (aka Taid O'Conroy).

12 FO 371/5361 [F 2495], V. Wellesley Memorandum on Commercial Policy, 11 August 1917.

13 FO 371/11679 [F 4349/307/10], *Propaganda in Hong Kong*, 14 October 1926. The FO may have been constrained by its unwillingness to break the terms of a secret Treaty Britain had signed with the Soviet Union to refrain from propaganda activities in Asia, as this might have given the Russians grounds for making propaganda against Britain in China

14 FO 371/536 [P4087/5/150], Clive to Eden, 21 October 1936. FO 371/536 [P 4589/5/150], Bowyer to Ridsdale, 14 December 1936.

15 FO 395/411 [P 73/73/150]. Minutes by R. Kenney, F. Ashton-Gwatkin, February 1926.

16 FO 371/11679 [F 4349/307/10], *Propaganda in Hong Kong*, 14 October 1926.

17 Bickers 1999: 28, 41, 59, 78.

18 FO 371/12498 [F2784/2784/10]: Commons discussion of the suppression of the Central China Post, 26 March 1927. Strike still on in October: FO 371/12948 [F7884/2784/10].

19 FO 371/11679 [F 4349/307/10], *Propaganda in Hong Kong*, 14 October 1926.

20 Powell 1945: 145. Powell's criticisms of the 'hysterical' anti-Communist line of the NCDN and other British papers should not be taken to indicate any Communist sympathies. Powell was indeed wary of the anti-Communist excesses of the British press, but like most journalists in the *Advertiser* network, his real sympathies lay with the 'genuine crusading spirit' of Chiang Kai-shek and the Chinese Nationalists (Abend 1943: 31). However, note that the FER and Foreign Ministry network's George Bronson Rea was keen to indicate that Powell had communist sympathies: 'I have just finished an article exposing Mr. J.B. Powell, who evidently is also on the pay roll of the Nationalists and the Soviet': *Gaikoku shinbun tsūshin kikan oyobi tsūshin-in kankei zakken, tsūshin-in no bu: beikokujin no bu* (Foreign Ministry Records: Miscellaneous matters relating to foreign newspapers, communications agencies and correspondents, communications section: American correspondents), 1–3-2, 50–2-2, George Bronson Rea, Shanghai, to Odagiri, Foreign Ministry, Tokyo, 9 September 1926.

21 FO 371/11697 [F 5530/5398/10], Archibald Rose to G.A. Mounsey, 13 December 1926.

22 FO 800/260, Chamberlain to Lampson, 11 April 1927. The official campaign to replace Green and to tone down the 'die hards' in China's English-language press is discussed in Bickers 1999: 151–2.

23 Bickers 1999: 152.

24 Initially to the NYT, where his 'realistic' acceptance of Japanese power in Manchuria and his scepticism regarding the League of Nations gained him a larger, more docile readership than he had in East Asia. See for example his NYT articles on 8, 15 and 29 November, 6 and 12 December 1931, and 3 January 1932.

25 Bickers 1999: 152.

26 Much of the material that appears on the *Japan Chronicle* in this section, in part of section 3 below, and in Chapter 7 was published in O'Connor, Peter (2002) 'The Japan Chronicle and its three editors: Robert Young, Morgan Young and Edwin Allington Kennard, 1891–1940', in Hugh Cortazzi (ed.) *Britain & Japan: Biographical Portraits, Volume IV* (Folkestone: Global Oriental), 334–47.

27 Notably Tomiko Kakegawa (2001), the most considered study of the JC by a Japanese historian. Ebihara Hachirō (1934) *Nihon ōji shinbun zasshi shi* (History of Western-Language Newspapers in Japan) (Tokyo: Taiseidō) and Itō Hitoshi (1956) *Nihon bundan-shi* (History of Japanese Literary Circles) (Tokyo: Kōdansha) also deal with the JC.

28 Family Division, High Court: Administration granted to George Young, 21 August 1924. Probate Index Effects ref.: 49.3.11.

29 My information on Annie Crockett Miller's background and other aspects of the Young family history comes from Susan Larkin, the Australia-born great-grand-daughter of Robert Young.

30 Lafcadio Hearn to B.H. Chamberlain, 23 October 1894. Hearn wrote *Kobe Chronicle* leaders daily from 11 October 1894 to 14 December 1894, but retired because of problems with his sight. MS6681/1/80: Harold S. Williams Collection, National Library of Australia, Canberra [hereafter HSW].

31 Brinkley received ¥10,000 a year from both the *Nippon Yūsen Kaisha* (NYK Line) and the Foreign Ministry in subventions for the *Japan Mail*.

32 *Japan Mail*: 23 December 1905.

33 NCH: 9 March 1894, 357.

34 JC: 16 November 1922, 632.

35 Young's presentation was kept under wraps (P&TT obit. November 1922; Pearl 1967: 194–6). In a separate article, 'M.Y.M.' recalled, 'a few years ago when Brinkley, Sir Valentine Chirol, and G.E. Morrison paid a visit to the Meiji Emperor, Brinkley was denied access but the others were granted an audience. The Imperial Household Agency explained that "no precedent existed for giving audience to resident journalists, either foreign or Japanese". This answer killed all criticism' ('M.Y.M.' 1915: 675). On this visit, see also 'Dr. Morrison in Japan': NCH, 12 June 1909, reporting Morrison's speech to the Yokohama Foreign Board of Trade.

36 *Nagasaki Press*: 1 November 1912.

37 Obituary of John Russell Kennedy: *The 79th News*: newsletter of the Association of the Cameron Highlanders, Inverness, July 1928, 193–4. The obituary is signed 'F.S.G.P', and was probably the work of another pro-Japanese member of Kennedy's circle, Francis Piggott. During the years that

both MacDonald and Kennedy were in Tokyo, they made a habit of dining together on the anniversary of the battle.

38 *Daily News:* 9 December 1910; NCH: 30 December 1910, 769. 'The Alleged Plot against the Emperor of Japan': *The Times*: 6 January 1911.

39 Robert Young edited the JC from 1891 to 1922, with breaks abroad, usually in Britain, in 1896, 1906, 1910, 1913–14 and 1919–20. During his 1913–14 visit, Young considered running for Parliament as a Liberal but business called him back to Kōbe. 'He had a comfortable house on Sydenham Hill and was to be seen every day in the National Liberal Club. The outbreak of the World War raised business questions which required his presence in Japan, and he returned and remained here until his death' (Hugh Byas 1937: 45).

40 Notehelfer, F.G. 1971, *Kōtoku Shūsui, Portrait of a Japanese Radical* (Cambridge U.P.), 197; *Jiji Shimpō*: 16 January 1911. See also NCH: 27 January 1911, datelined 16 January 1911.

41 For a full account of the JC's editorial line on the *Ōsaka Asahi Shinbun* incident, see Kakegawa in O'Connor (ed.) 2001: 31–5.

42 Young to Bertrand Russell, 27 October 1922, Russell Archive, Mills Memorial Library, McMaster University, Ontario, Canada: No. 710.048282.

43 'Robert Young: An Appreciation' (anonymous): JC, 16 November 1922, 644–5.

44 *The Times*: 9 November 1922.

45 JC: 10 February 1921, 172, in response to an article in *Chūō Kōron*, January 1921.

46 JC: 16 November 1922.

47 David James letter to Harold S. Williams, 12 March 1963. HSW Collection, Canberra: MS 6681/1/80

48 Op. cit., James to Williams.

49 FO 371/3235 (F 17504/-/23): 3 December 1917, Conyngham Greene to B. Munro Ferguson.

50 See FO 410/64 Confidential Print 11282, 410/64, Greene to Grey, 16 August 1915: 'The Japanese are, however, ambitious, conceited, and … arrogant. They are bent on making themselves masters of the Pacific.' Cited in Shimazu 1998: 104 and 213, n.73.

51 USDS 894.44 Young, Robert: E.R. Dickover, US Consul, Kōbe, to State Dept., 13 November 1922.

52 *Shanghai Gazette*: 9 November 1922.

53 Obituaries of Robert Young in the following organs attest to the diversity and breadth of the circulation of the JC in 1922: *The Times*, London, 9 November; *Japan Gazette*, c.10 November; *Nagasaki Press*, 10 November [republished without comment in the JT, 11 November]; JA, 11 November; SP, 11 November; *Ōsaka Mainichi* [English edition], 12 November; *Hōritsu Shimbun*, 12 November; *Herald Of Asia*, 14 November; *Chūgai Eigo*, 15 November; *Eigo Seinen*, 15 December; JC, 16 November; NCDN, 9 November; *Shanghai Gazette*, c.9 November; *Hongkong Daily Press*, c.12 November; P&TT, 14 November; *The New Russia* (Shanghai), December 1922. See also JC: 12 December 1922 for tribute first published in *Ostasiatische Rundschau*, Shanghai; 1 January 1923 for tribute by South Place Ethical Society; 7 January 1923 for Soyeshima Michimasa tribute to Young; 11 January 1923 for tribute by Mrs. Bradlaugh Bonner (daughter of Charles Bradlaugh).

54 NCH: 11 November 1922.
55 For the true authorship of *The Socialist and Labour Movement in Japan* (Kōbe, Chronicle Reprint, 1921), usually credited to Morgan Young, see Chapter 5, below.
56 *Gaimushō gaikō shiryōkan: zaihonpō gaiji shinbun kankei zakken: 'Japan Kuronikeru' shi no hainichi kiji kankei* (Foreign Ministry records: Miscellaneous matters concerning foreign-language newspapers in Japan: the 'Japan Chronicle', anti-Japanese articles in) A 350, 12–1, March 1928 – December 1933. December 1933, Hyōgo Governor Takesuke to Foreign Minister Hirota Kōki.
57 Personal communication from Susan Larkin. Thomas Harloe died in 1935.
58 'Misanthrope': FO 395/447 (P 2303/2303/150), T. Snow, Tokyo, to A. Willert, 18 November 1934; 'against the government': FO 371/18162 (F 392/392/23), Tokyo Chancery to Far East Department, 6 January 1934.
59 MS6681/1/80: HSW Collection, Canberrra.
60 *Gaimushō gaikō shiryōkan: zaihonpō gaiji shinbun kankei zakken: 'Japan Kuronikeru' shi no hainichi kiji kankei* (Foreign Ministry records: Miscellaneous matters concerning foreign-language newspapers in Japan: the 'Japan Chronicle', anti-Japanese articles in) A 350, 12–1: 20 December 1928, Hyōgo Governor Takesuke to Foreign Minister Tanaka Giichi.
61 Malcolm Kennedy Diary, 19 March 1930: Malcolm Kennedy papers, Sheffield University, UK. Kennedy's informant was Harry Griffiths, proprietor of the Kōbe bookshop, J. L. Thompson & Co.
62 Malcolm Kennedy Diary: 30 May 1934, Sheffield University. Cited in Pardoe 1989: 223, n.303.
63 Douglas Young's death and 'inebriate' Ethel (nee Young) Stewart-Scott: HSW Collection, National Library, Canberra: 'The children of Mr and Mrs Robert Young': MS6681/1/80. Death of Thomas Harloe and Annie Harloe's return to and departure from Kōbe: personal communications with Susan Larkin, March 2009.
64 Morgan Young to Bertrand Russell, 12 April 1923: letter 112600, Russell Papers, Russell Archive, McMaster University, Canada.
65 Kakegawa 2001: 33.
66 'Slicker campaign': Iwanaga 1934: 23–5; Iwanaga 1941, part 3: 143–5. Cited in Purdy 1987: 66–7 and 114, n.13, 94–5 and 118, n.70, respectively. See also Matsumura 2002: 74–6.
67 Morrison and J.W. Robertson Scott exchanged thirty-eight letters, many of them in 1916–18, when Scott was running the *New East* in Tokyo. G.E. Morrison Papers, State Library of New South Wales, Sydney, Australia.
68 Notably H.G.W. Woodhead, then on the P&TT, to whom Morrison wrote in 1912, 'The Legation is so well satisfied with your leaders that I think the time has come when you come to Peking for you to speak to Sir John Jordan about a subsidy. The time is opportune.' Morrison to Woodhead, 10 June 1912. Morrison subsequently recommended that Putnam Weale's 'sensational' messages to the *Daily Telegraph* and other British papers on the aftermath of the 1911 revolution should be 'pilloried': Morrison to Woodhead, 5 December 1912. Morrison Papers, State University of New South Wales, Sydney, Box ML MSS. 312/35–108, Correspondence 1850–1932.
69 Morrison exchanged only four letters with Young, compared to O.M. Green,

to whom he wrote fifty-four letters between 1911 and his death in 1920. Op.
cit., Morrison Papers, Sydney.

70 Apart from Robert Young and Morrison, the only other instance that I can
find of an English-language press journalist meeting the Japanese Emperor
was that of Malcolm Kennedy, who met the Taishō Emperor (and was not
impressed). In 1933, Miles Vaughn of UP and Joseph Grew arranged for Roy
Howard of Scripps-Howard to meet the Shōwa Emperor. In 1948 Vaughn
himself met the Showa Emperor in the course of preparing a book showcasing
the ordinariness and mortality of the Imperial house (Vaughn 1948).

71 JC: 7 January 1923, tribute to Robert Young by Soyeshima Michimasa.

72 Williams 1996, Vol.2: 193. Interestingly, a young Dorothy Borg worked on
the US equivalent of this publication, the *Far Eastern Survey* (Rand 1995: 319).

73 Young 1939: 67. Harold Parlett, now retired from the Foreign Office, was
invited to chair Young's University of London lecture on 'Imperial Japan' but
declined, on Foreign Office advice, for fear of seeming to give official
approval to Young's statements because, 'if the old leaven still works in him it
is unlikely that he will hand out any bouquets to the rulers of that country'.
FO 371/22181 [F 13489/71/23] Parlett to Stephen Gasalee, 17 December 1938.

74 Best 2002: 3–4. Cited above n.4.

75 Thorne 1972: 47.

76 JC: 26 July 1923. For a discussion of efforts in Shanghai and Whitehall to
change the 'die-hard' 'Shanghai Mind' image in 1928–31, see Bickers 1992.

77 Kakegawa 2001: 36–8.

78 See n.61 above, citing Malcolm Kennedy's *Diary*.

4

The United States in East Asia and the *Japan Advertiser* network, 1911–1936

B.W. (Benjamin Wilfrid) Fleisher (1870–1946), owner and publisher of the *Japan Advertiser* from 1908 to 1940, came to East Asia 'only by chance, and stayed because it offered him relief from the pressures and failures that had overwhelmed him at home'.[1] Fleisher was the son of Simon B. Fleisher, founder of the Fleisher Yarn Co. of Philadelphia. The Fleishers were Jews with origins in Germany, a fact frequently noted at the British Foreign Office[2] and at the Foreign Ministry of Japan, as well as by Ugaki Kazushige in 1923. The Fleishers' ancestry would also be raised in the mid-1930s when Nazis at the German embassy in Tokyo began winkling out potential impediments to cooperation between Germany and Japan.[3]

After graduating from the University of Pennsylvania in the 1880s, Fleisher joined the family business. In 1907, aged thirty-seven, following parental fury over losses of around $1 million on the stock market, he suffered a nervous breakdown. To help his recovery, Fleisher went on a world cruise. When Fleisher arrived in Yokohama in the autumn of 1907, there were five English-language newspapers in business but none of them struck Fleisher as real carriers of news. He abandoned his cruise and stayed on in the port in the hope of developing such a newspaper. There, he crossed paths with John Russell Kennedy, who became an early mentor. In 1908 Kennedy got Fleisher a job at $25 a month, selling advertising space and reporting for the *Japan Advertiser*, then owned by a journalist named Arthur May Knapp.[4] Instead of picking up gossip and contacts at the club bar, Fleisher surprised his colleagues by going out in search of news and advertisers. At the end of his first month, Fleisher's advertising commissions were so high that Knapp promoted him to advertising manager and shortly thereafter business manager, at a salary of $175 but removed his commission.[5]

However, Fleisher's ambitions were not satisfied. In 1908 he mounted a takeover bid for the *Advertiser* and with the help of Kennedy, who owned shares himself and knew the other shareholders, gained a controlling stake, for either $15,000 or $30,000.[6] Thus began Fleisher's proprietorship of the treaty port rag he would turn into one of the best edited and best connected American newspapers in East Asia.

In 1911 Fleisher took on further responsibilities, becoming business manager for a new publication in Shanghai, the veteran US journalist

Thomas Millard's *China Press* (see below). In 1913 Fleisher moved the *Advertiser* business to Tokyo. In 1914 after struggling with a high editorial staff turnover, he reached an arrangement with Walter Williams, Dean of the School of Journalism at the University of Missouri, whereby Williams would recommend Missouri graduates to join the *Advertiser* in Tokyo.

In 1914 Fleisher hired Hugh Byas as editor of the *Advertiser*. Born in Scotland in 1875, Hugh Byas had worked in the Dominions press, on the *Rand Daily Mail* in Johannesburg for seven years from 1902. In 1909 he had joined the staff of *The Times* in London.[7] Byas proved a capable editor; hard working, fair-minded, a gifted observer, a fastidious researcher, and an assiduous and discreet accumulator of Japanese contacts. Not only did he attract a supportive Japanese network for the *Advertiser*, but he consistently sought out and published original pieces by Japanese journalists writing in English. As editor, 1914–16, 1918–22 and 1926–30, when he left to concentrate on the Tokyo correspondence of *The Times* and *New York Times*, in which capacity he succeeded Fleisher's son, Wilfrid,[8] Byas brought editorial flair and consistency to the *Advertiser*, while in the long term his proprietor's cautious attitude to the reporting of East Asian affairs in Japan won the paper the authority and balance of the middle ground.[9]

By now, the *Advertiser* had begun to share in Japan's wartime prosperity. The daily edition went from three or four pages to eighteen and thirty-two pages on Sunday, packed with advertisements. Now fully settled with his wife and children in Tokyo in a house near the US embassy, Fleisher invested in production and editorial staff, both Japanese and American, built up a pool of translators to bring the *Advertiser* the best of the vernacular press, and sent correspondents to Washington, London, Peking, Shanghai and Manila. In 1911 the *Advertiser* became the first foreign newspaper in Japan to receive cabled news reports from abroad: swelling from about twenty words daily to include wires from all the main American and European news agencies, while its rivals, including the *Chronicle*, still relied on Reuters telegrams. Fleisher imported the most up-to-date printing plant in post-war Tokyo, took the *New York Times* as his typographic model, and set up the Advertiser Press to utilize spare capacity.[10]

Besides his managerial oversight in Japan, Fleisher worked hard at an official and commercial level to build the *Advertiser's* international reputation. Fleisher developed a flair for organizing special issues of the *Advertiser*, such as the Panama-Pacific Exposition number marking the opening of the Panama Canal in 1915, for which he garnered endorsements from Woodrow Wilson, Ōkuma Shigenobu, and Katō Takaaki, numerous motoring supplements, and the 1928 Enthronement issue (see below). Over the years, Fleisher founded or participated in numerous goodwill missions between Japan and the United States. In November 1916 Fleisher began soliciting interest for a new monthly magazine, *America-Japan*. He addressed the Secretary of State in

Washington, assuring him that the magazine would promote 'the better understanding and where possible co-operation of the business interests of Japan, China and the United States'. The magazine would 'avoid politics'. The 'fault of most of the journalistic work in the Far East has been that it was critical. It is now time for constructive work to be inaugurated.' The Premier of Japan, Minister of Foreign Affairs, and other dignitaries all assured the *Advertiser* of their support for the new venture.[11] This project reached fruition in 1919, when Fleisher launched the America-Japan Society (*Nichibei kyōkai*) and its periodical *America-Japan*, with Kaneko Kentarō as its first President. Many of those who helped get *America-Japan* off the ground had invested in the *Japan Times* and *Kokusai* in 1897 and 1914. It is tempting to assume that Fleisher's intermediary with officialdom in 1916–19 was his first mentor in Yokohama, John Russell Kennedy, but Fleisher, Byas and Kennedy had fallen out so badly over *Kokusai*, the *Outlook* affair and other wartime controversies that Fleisher probably went through other channels.[12]

In the same spirit, Fleisher helped organize goodwill gestures such as the gift in 1917 of a specially inscribed mallet from Kaneko Kentarō, President of the America-Japan Society, and in the autumn of 1926, a stone lantern from the Society's President, Tokugawa Iesato, to the School of Journalism at the University of Missouri, both presented in Missouri by the Japanese ambassador, Matsudaira Tsuneo.[13]

In 1919, Fleisher renamed the *Advertiser*'s weekend edition the *Trans-Pacific* both to publicize the activities of the Society and provide the sort of goodwill media that attracted official advertising and officially-connected advertisers.[14] When Fleisher was planning the relaunch of the *Advertiser*'s weekly edition, his network associate and financier since 1911, and the American Minister to China in 1920–21, Charles R. Crane (1858–1939) put his US commercial and official network at Fleisher's disposal.[15] As a result, J.P. Morgan, Jacob H. Schiff, Judge Elbert Gary, N.F. Grady and Crane himself all undertook to subscribe 'to many hundreds of copies of the magazine so that they may be distributed to reach Chambers of Commerce'.[16]

When Fleisher finally launched the *Trans-Pacific*, he hired the Dean of the School of Journalism at Missouri University, Walter Williams, as its editor. Having secured testimonials from US Secretary Lansing and others, Williams wrote to Woodrow Wilson asking for a letter of support for the new magazine, which he saw as being 'the means of real world-service', but was turned down on the grounds of propriety.[17] With two Missourians, Williams and his successor in 1920 Henry Kinyon, having edited the *Trans-Pacific*, Fleisher endowed a Japan Society of Missouri University Journalism prize in 1921. In July 1926 he arranged with *Dentsū*'s Mitsunaga Hoshiro for five of his best journalists to visit the Missouri School of Journalism.[18]

Thus the *Advertiser* solicited support and goodwill among business people and bureaucrats from the early stages of its development. Fleisher laid the groundwork for the *Advertiser* network with these institutional and commercial relationships as well as with other newspapers. Many of the Japanese and American contacts from these early years endured and would chip in when the paper nearly folded due to earthquake damage and a disastrous fire in 1923 and 1931.

Fleisher was in poor health from the late 1920s onward, and would lose the use of both legs in 1930, but in the 1920s he travelled a great deal and was a familiar face at the banquets and lectures of the Japan Society of New York and its offshoot, the Japan Peace Society, in Tokyo and New York. In August 1921 as a prelude to the Washington Conference, Fleisher lectured the Young Men's Association of Karuizawa (*Karuizawa Seinenkai*) on 'The Pacific Ocean Conference as Seen by Americans'. In his speech, Fleisher maintained that much of the hostility between America and Japan was due to misunderstanding; that ordinary people in both countries disliked the naval competition, that America had 'no definite policy' in East Asia, and that if only Japan and America could advance their mutual understanding, both countries would enjoy greater happiness.

This bland assessment was noted by local officials and reported to the Foreign Ministry, the Ministry of Home Affairs (*Naimushō*) and the police in Tokyo.[19] However, even in these cordial years, Fleisher's activities and movements were under close surveillance, especially his visits to the US embassy, which was an easy walk from his home. As one report put it, 'He often goes to the American Embassy and provides negative information about our country, which he repeats in newspaper articles.'[20] It was not difficult for Fleisher to visit the US embassy, as he lived next door.

Fleisher was keen to further American interests in East Asia through the young Missouri alumni who joined the *Advertiser* and its affiliates and most joined the American Association of Tokyo as a matter of course. In October 1920 Fleisher was pleased to report that the President, R.J. Moss, the Vice-President (and Post Commander for Japan of the American Legion), Glenn Babb and the Treasurer, Alvin Acola, were all Missouri alumni and all on the *Advertiser* team. Fleisher enthused:

> Just think what it will mean in ten years more or less when these young men develop into their stride and with their combined and individual knowledge of conditions in the Far East. Surely it will develop a force which will become a determining factor in the international relationship of the US and the countries of the Pacific.

Such was B.W. Fleisher's hope, expressed to a trusted associate 'late at night, with a bad head from too many dinners': to develop among the young Americans who came to the *Advertiser* a network of journalists whose combined experience and local knowledge would not only influence US policy on East Asia but become 'a determining factor' in its formulation.[21]

How did British officials in Tokyo view the *Advertiser* in these years? A few weeks after the May 1918 *Outlook* interview with Prime Minister Terauchi, Conyngham Greene, the British ambassador, tried to connect the dots between the *Outlook* interview and the sympathies of Mason's employer, B.W. Fleisher:

> Quite lately too the 'Advertiser' has been publishing a series of leading articles strongly deprecating Allied intervention in Siberia and contesting the strategic and political desirability of an advance to the Urals. This point of view, which is that up to now held by the State Department, is of course quite permissible in an American-owned newspaper, but I mention it only as a further evidence of want of complete sympathy with Allied convictions. However that may be, I have succeeded in getting Mr Mason replaced as Editor of the 'Advertiser' by Mr Hugh Byas, a British Subject ...[22]

In September 1923, the *Advertiser*'s links to Washington were strengthened when the *Advertiser* building and plant were destroyed in the earthquake and subsequent fires that struck Tokyo and Yokohama. Fleisher's circle in the US rallied round. Thomas Lamont of J.P. Morgan & Co., head of the American Group in the Four-Power China Consortium, got together with the Fleisher's old associate, Charles R. Crane, who set up loans totalling $50,000, topped up with another $50,000 from John D. Rockefeller III that was specifically hypothecated to Lamont. Moreover, a second mortgage on the *Advertiser* business was acquired by Japanese interests, and with the sums thus raised the plant was rebuilt and the *Advertiser* returned to business. In a September 1934 background note, a Far East Division, Department of State official explained that Fleisher had been helped in 1923:

> ... for the reason that it has been and still is the publisher's policy to reflect in his newspaper the attitude and policies of the United States. It was the feeling of all the Americans interested in the newspaper that something definitely beneficial to relations between the United States and Japan could be accomplished by a paper independent of any official patronage, that would be informative in its press columns and honest in its editorial column.[23]

In East Asia, B.W. Fleisher, Thomas Millard, John B. Powell, George Sokolsky and other American journalists agreed with their American sponsors, Walter Williams and Charles R. Crane, that what was good for American commerce in East Asia was good for America. There is no evidence that the *Advertiser*'s British editor, Hugh Byas, or his successor from 1930 to 1940, Wilfrid Fleisher, had any reservations about the role of the newspaper in promoting American interests.

The *Advertiser* lost favour in Japanese eyes as a result of the 1924 Exclusion Act, so that while Fleisher was struggling to recover from the effects of the earthquake, he also had to cope with the loss of advertising revenue from companies such as Mitsui and Mitsubishi. A costly printing plant that he had imported began to look like a white elephant until 1928 when Fleisher put together a sumptuous special edition of the *Advertiser* for the enthronement ceremony of the Shōwa Emperor. Fleisher's dedication to the 180-page *Enthronement Edition* could have been written by John Russell Kennedy:

> To the many who are interested in the promotion of international peace through the interpretation and advancement of a more correct under-standing of the aims, aspirations and ideals of the people of one nation to the peoples of other nations this book is dedicated.

Although the publication date was November 1928, the book claimed to provide 'a complete account' of the enthronement ceremonies for the Shōwa Emperor from his father's death on 25 December 1926 to the final investiture on 13 December 1928. Besides contributions from *Advertiser* staff, including Hugh Byas and Frank Hedges, there were twelve essays by Japanese authors, three by American and British authors, and illustrations. Towards the end of the book, Prime Minister Tanaka Giichi wrote an appreciation 'for the fruitful effort of *The Japan Advertiser* in the production of this *Imperial Enthronement Edition* to inter-pret the spirit of Japan as revealed in these ceremonies'.[24] This was followed by three pages of messages from other Royalty and Heads of State, and then by forty-four pages of advertising. The *Enthronement Edition* gained the approval of the palace, which rewarded Fleisher with a seal of recognition. Furthermore, printing contracts started to come in from the South Manchurian Railway headquarters in Dalian (Dairen), where the ex-*Advertiser* journalist Henry Kinney was now a well-paid consultant, described by J.B. Powell as 'one of the most effective propa-gandists for Japan'.[25]

On 4 November 1930, disaster struck the *Advertiser* again. The entire plant and premises were destroyed by fire, with losses estimated at ¥1,200,000.[26] Coming at a time of global economic hardship, the fire tested the goodwill of Fleisher's American connections to the utmost. Soon after the fire, Cameron Forbes, the US ambassador to Tokyo, cabled Martin Egan at J.P. Morgan, urging him and, by extension, Thomas Lamont, to 'give encouragement' to Fleisher in his hour of need.[27] On 11 November, Secretary of State Henry Stimson cabled the Tokyo embassy asking that a message be passed to Fleisher expressing his 'deep regret' that 'this loss has come to a friend'.[28] However, Rockefeller was inclined to call in the loan he had advanced in 1923.

Interest in the *Advertiser* was not confined to the US. As Cameron Forbes was aware, 'important Japanese interests' held a second mortgage on the *Advertiser*.[29] In December 1930 Dan Takuma of Mitsui, the serving Minister of Finance, Inoue Junnosuke, and other influential Japanese offered Fleisher funds on condition their aid was matched by American capital. Fleisher politely turned them down, but the Japanese group kept the door open.[30]

The possibility of Japanese interests gaining a stake in the *Advertiser* seems to have encouraged Forbes, Phillips and Undersecretary of State W.E. Castle, to lobby even more energetically for help from Fleisher's previous champions. In January 1931, Thomas Lamont at J.P. Morgan and Charles R. Crane agreed to an extension of the $50,000 loan they had provided in 1923. However, Rockefeller could not be persuaded to join them, and called in the $50,000 he had hypothecated to Lamont in 1923.

Fleisher's family, represented by William Wasserman, a business associate from Philadelphia, then came up with $75,000 and a plan of rescue that depended on help from Inoue, Dan Takuma and others, who came to terms with Wasserman and Lamont and agreed to match their $50,000 loans.[31] Thus, in March 1931, the *Advertiser* was able to make a fresh start as a new corporation with funding of $150,000 from a combination of American and Japanese interests. B.W. Fleisher continued as head, with a 45% shareholding in his name, but effective control of the new company's finances passed to an advisory committee composed of local businessmen and headed by a manager sent over from Philadelphia by Wasserman and Fleisher's family.[32]

Three points arise from the financial rescues of 1923 and 1930. The first two are in the context of the *Advertiser*'s official American connections. The third concerns the *Advertiser*'s official connections in Japan. First, the rescues of 1923 and 1930 show that the *Advertiser* had real friends in high places, in Washington and on Wall Street, with direct lines of credit to the close elite concerned with US policy in East Asia: Thomas Lamont, Stimson, and his Under Secretary, William Castle.[33] The second point raises a question: in agreeing to a joint US-Japan financial rescue on the basis of maintaining the *Advertiser* as a promoter of harmonious relations or a forum for constructive discussions on the relationship, did those on the US side realize the extent of the *Advertiser*'s involvement, through its network, in activities inimical to Japanese ambitions? If they knew, did they choose to look the other way? The evidence suggests that they were well aware of Fleisher's activities in China: Undersecretary William Castle was close to Carl Crow, had acted as an intermediary between Crow's 'China Compub.'[34] and the State Department in wartime, and must have known of Fleisher's consistent involvement in pro-nationalist, anti-Japanese media such as the *China Press*, *Millard's Review* and the *China Weekly Review*, and yet he and Thomas Lamont agreed to join Charles Crane in matching the financial commitment of Dan Takuma and Inoue Junnosuke.

Thirdly, the rescue attempts illustrate the strength of the *Advertiser*'s appeal to internationalist tendencies in Japan. In a January 1931 telegram, Cameron Forbes described Inoue Junnosuke as 'very definite in his belief in real necessity for continuance' of the *Advertiser*. It seems that Inoue and the group who helped rescue the *Advertiser* believed in its power to improve US-Japan relations. In the mid-1890s, Inoue had helped Shibusawa Eiichi get financial backing for the *Japan Times* and he had done the same for *Kokusai* in 1913–14. As financiers, Inoue and Dan went along with the 'economic diplomacy' associated with Shidehara Kijūrō for most of the 1920s. Both men had signed up to the ideals of Fleisher's Japan-America society and had attended the banquets and speeches of similar goodwill projects in the 1920s. Why else make their aid to the *Advertiser* conditional on it being matched by US interests?

At the same time, Inoue and others pursued their own agenda in the Japanese arena and, as with the *Japan Times*, their interest in the *Advertiser* may have been secured in pursuit of that agenda. There may also have been an element of *quid pro quo* in the rescue of the *Advertiser*, since Thomas Lamont had worked hard to finance Japan's growth in the 1920s and would champion Japanese incursions in Manchuria in the early 1930s. To Lamont, Inoue Junnosuke and Dan Takuma were men with whom he could do business, and their aid to the *Advertiser* in 1930 can be seen as a return of this goodwill.[35]

Finally, as we shall see in Chapter 7, Dan and Inoue's assistance to the *Advertiser* in 1930 can also be interpreted as a forewarning of its acquisition in October 1940 by the *Japan Times*. Like Inoue and Dan's 1930 rescue, the 1940 buyout by a circle close to Matsuoka Yōsuke and the South Manchurian Railway Company, may have been an attempt to create an internationalist forum as a foil to military influence.[36]

THE *JAPAN ADVERTISER* NETWORK IN CHINA

Unlike the *Chronicle*, the *Japan Advertiser* trod the middle ground in Japan, but whence this caution? We know that the *Advertiser* owed its survival, in part, to Japanese money, and to American money that came, again in part, from a pro-Japanese source, Thomas Lamont. However, besides these potential obligations and B.W. Fleisher's innate caution, the *Advertiser* was also inhibited by its situation in Japan. In an article written after the *Advertiser*'s amalgamation with the *Japan Times* in October 1940, Toshi Gō, the *Japan Times* editor, wrote of Fleisher:

> His leaders lacked the truculence of the *Japan Chronicle*, the strong personal opinions of Mr George Woodhead in the old *Peking and Tientsin Times*, or the several strong-minded editors of the *North-China Daily News*. Had Mr Fleisher been in Shanghai or Peking in the first place, I haven't the slightest hesitation in saying that he would have been in the forefront of the powerful opinion there … But remember again, he had a different public …[37]

In China, under extraterritoriality, newspapers published in the International Settlements were subject to the laws pertaining in their publishers' homeland (or their country of registration) rather than to the laws of China. Gō felt that had the *Advertiser* been as exempt from Japanese control as some of his contemporaries were from Chinese control, the *Advertiser* might have been more outspoken.

What Gō seems not to have realized was that through the *Advertiser* network of newspapers, journalists and news agencies in China, Fleisher was very much 'in the forefront of the powerful opinion' in China and closely connected to the expression of far more critical views of Japan than were ever published in the *Advertiser*. The Foreign Ministry official who noted in 1921 that 'Fleisher hides two faces under the same hood and is playing a double game' was right on the money.[38] By then, the *Japan Advertiser* network was well on its way to becoming the main grouping of English-language newspapers in China promoting American and Chinese interests (in that order) and opposing Japanese ambitions in China. Although such a position was not the natural concomitant of pro-American views, the network became aligned with the nationalist movement in China and with Chinese-language newspaper networks promoting the Guomindang as the Chinese solution to China's problems.

The *Advertiser* network was well-financed and well-connected. We have seen how, in 1911 and 1918, Crane put his Republican political and business network at Fleisher's disposal.[39] Crane and the *Advertiser* network backed likely winners among Chinese nationalists and Crane supported politicians, journalists and media entrepreneurs who shared these objectives, chief among them Paul Reinsch (1869–1923), US Minister to China 1913–19, and an adviser to the Chinese government from 1919 until his death, his long-standing associates Thomas Millard and B.W. Fleisher, and the journalists George Marvin, Putnam Weale, Carl Crow and, intermittently, George Sokolsky.

With little to go on save the knowledge that the Japanese thought along similar lines, the media projects of Crane, Fleisher, Millard and their Chinese associates were predicated on their belief in the power of the press to influence US foreign policy by effecting changes in public opinion. As the backer and publisher of an important American newspaper in China, Crane and Millard were convinced that the US could only benefit from their amplification of its voice in Chinese affairs. Their motivation in establishing both the *China Press* and *Millard's Review of the Far East*, and, with John B. Powell, the *China Weekly Review*, was thus a combination of the personal and the ideological.

The *Advertiser* network in China was, initially, supportive of Yuan Shikai and the Republic, but after Yuan's death it aligned itself with Sun Yatsen (Sun Yat-sen) and the early Guomindang and during and after the May Fourth Movement its media were consistently critical of Japanese activities in China. The political complexion of the network was heavily influenced by Crane, Millard's and Crow's Republicanism, as well as by the distaste Crane, Millard and others in their circle shared for the Japanese as a people. Crane and Millard also shared a horror of Bolshevism. Crane had been profoundly shocked by the Bolshevik seizure of power during a visit to Russia with the Root Commission in 1918. To Crane, part of the appeal of Millard's publishing schemes lay in his ability to frame them in terms of rescuing China from the Bolshevik abyss.[40] The Foreign Ministry network also consistently highlighted Japan's mission to eradicate the Communist menace in East Asia, but this did nothing to raise the Japanese in Crane and Millard's esteem.

In 1917 and 1918, Crane voiced his concerns about Bolshevism and the Japanese threat to China in personal meetings with Woodrow Wilson, whose electoral success he had largely financed. Wilson designated Crane as his personal representative on a mission to China, and in the spring of 1918, Crane sailed for Peking with Millard and Paul Reinsch. There he met with G.E. Morrison, Putnam Weale and other journalists to discuss press projects and to plan for the coming Peace Conference. Crane subsequently travelled to Shenyang (Mukden) where he met Zhang Zuolin (Chang Tso-lin), and to Shanghai where he met H.H. Kung and several Guomindang leaders, possibly including Sun Yatsen. Crane complemented Carl Crow's espousal of Wilsonian ideals by assuring the Chinese he met of continuing American friendship contingent on the embrace of Wilsonian ideals at the Conference and in the Covenant of the League of Nations. In return, Crane won a commitment to improve news communications between the two nations that would result in the Zhong-Mei (Chun Mei; Chinese-American) News Agency. Crane then returned to Washington and, in a meeting with President Wilson, recommended a strengthening of US support for China, especially on the Shandong issue, at the forthcoming Peace Conference, and urged him to commit the US to protect China and American interests there from the twin menaces of Japan and Bolshevism.[41]

His long association with Millard gave a transatlantic edge to Crane's ambitions for the US in China, for Millard had long argued that the Anglo-Japanese Alliance underwrote Japanese ambitions in China and was the great obstacle to American leadership there.[42] Although the newspaper, lecture and lobbying campaign backed by Crane and undertaken in 1920–22 by Millard in the US and by Putnam Weale at the Imperial Conference in London and (with Chinese funds) through Reuters, was not a deciding factor in the abrogation of the Anglo-Japanese Alliance, it was a model of its kind in the way it targeted opinion leaders and raised a media groundswell against renewal both in East Asia and in the West. Besides putting an end to the Alliance, Millard and Crane wanted to limit the power of the Japanese news agencies and their British ally, Reuters, in China, because, they believed, these agencies undermined America's 'national expansion and external relations'.[43]

It is important to note that despite Reinsch and Crane's position as American Ministers, these visits and campaigns were all private, unofficial initiatives bankrolled and mobilized by the closely linked interests of the *Advertiser* network: Crane was a shareholder in the *Advertiser*, Fleisher a shareholder in Crane and Millard's *China Press*, Millard by 1920 a paid consultant of the Chinese government busily campaigning for the abrogation of the Anglo-Japanese Alliance. The network promoted these unofficial interests but did so, quite sincerely, in the national interest of China and the United States (though not necessarily in that order).

At different stages in its development the *Advertiser* network in China comprised the daily newspapers *China Press, Shanghai Gazette,* the *Shanghai Evening Post and Mercury,* the weekly *Millard's Review of the Far East* and its successor the *China Weekly Review.* The *Advertiser* network was strongly represented on Crow's China Committee on Public Information and its newsletter, and on the Zhong-Mei news and translation agency, as well as on a series of Chinese-backed English-language newsletters directed at opinion leaders in the US.

This examination of the components and evolution of the *Advertiser* network in China has to begin with the founding of the *China Press,* and the history of *Millard's Review of the Far East* and its reincarnation as the *China Weekly Review,* for these were the foundations of the network. In 1911, B.W. Fleisher joined Thomas Millard, Carl Crow, and an ex-*Chicago Herald* writer, C. Herbert Webb, in setting up a new English-language daily, the *China Press,* in Shanghai. Fleisher would serve as Business Manager and Treasurer and sit on the Board of Directors alongside Hollington Tong and Millard.

Millard had assembled a raft of interests behind the *China Press*: the two largest American concerns in China, Standard Oil and British American Tobacco; several American-educated Chinese businessmen; the diplomat, financier and journalist Willard Straight (1880–1918); the future Minister to China (1920–21), US financier Charles R. Crane, and the Chinese government, which subscribed forty to sixty thousand dollars of the capital stock.[44]

The publishing group assembled by Millard and incorporated in the US, the China National Press Inc., also planned to launch new English-language dailies in Peking, Shanghai and Tokyo, two weeklies, one in Chinese, one in English, two monthly magazines, one in English, one in Chinese, and an annual China yearbook. Of these, the English-language daily, the *China Press,* was taken over by Chinese interests much earlier than its founders had planned. The first English-language weekly, *Millard's Review of the Far East,* ran for only five years. Its successor, the *China Weekly Review,* kept going until 1941, a bulwark of the *Advertiser* network. In the 1930s, true to its prospectus, the company began publishing the voluminous *Who's Who in China* under the name of the *China Weekly Review.*

Was there to be a common editorial approach? In February 1911, the prospectus for the National China Press Inc. stated that its policy would be 'fairly and reasonably to support the interests and rights of China, when these are assailed or encroached upon from any quarter whatsoever, but in so doing to REFRAIN FROM NATIONAL ACERBITIES'.[45] However, a few months earlier, one official American observer reported that 'Owing to Mr. Millard's attitude and reputation regarding Far Eastern questions, I am of the opinion that a venture of this nature will very likely be disappointing to Japanese interests.'[46]

Soon enough, Millard's opposition to the Anglo-Japanese Alliance and the unwelcome publicity he and others brought to the Twenty-One Demands won him the enmity of the Foreign Ministry network.

However, this was not the first time he had encountered its opposition. Before the *China Press* had even started in business, the Foreign Ministry network persuaded T'ang Yüan-chan, owner of the *National Review*, an English-language periodical published in Shanghai, whom Millard had named as the first President of his news syndicate, to try to take over the newspaper. Fortunately for Millard, the other directors held firm and T'ang resigned, to be replaced by Chung Mun-yew.[47]

Soon after its foundation in 1911, the *China Press* had a healthy circulation but $3,000 of its total $4,500 monthly income came from advertising, and $750 of the remaining $1,500 came from subscriptions held by British interests in China. This dependence made the *China Press* highly susceptible to attack from British interests. Concerned about the commercial threat represented by the newcomer, interests behind the *North-China Daily News* also put pressure on *China Press* shareholders and advertisers to withdraw their support.

By late 1914, the *China Press* was again in difficulties and Fleisher with all his contacts and business acumen could not get past British opposition and win sufficient advertising revenues. That October C. Herbert Webb, editing the *China Press* in Millard's absence, showed in a letter to Millard that he had traced the paper's problems back to an official source:

> Sir Everard Fraser, the British Consul-General here, had again taken a hand in the game. He was calling in the British advertisers and warning them to take their advertisements out of The China Press. The British here are pretty well under the thumb of the Consulate. Fraser was saying to them, 'I am not making this an official order. It is merely an unofficial request …'[48]

As Millard declared, 'the policy of an American newspaper in China is now *dictated from the British Consulate at Shanghai*'.[49] Millard's outrage was genuine enough, but it is clear that he was more upset by the infringement of American editorial policy by British interests than by the infringement of 'the interests and rights of China', that his 1911 prospectus vowed to defend. In August 1915 Millard was forced to resign and sell his majority shareholding in the *China Press* to a local American estate agent, who in 1918 sold it on for $300,000[50] to a syndicate headed by Edward Ezra, leader of Shanghai's Jewish community.[51] Thirteen years later, Millard still smarted from the role of the *North-China Daily News* in the failure of the *China Press* and, as an adviser on publicity to the Nanjing government, may have exacted some revenge.

In 1921, the *China Press* was again sold, this time to Sun Yatsen, but in 1922 he returned control to Ezra's heirs, under whom it thrived, enjoying by 1923 (according to its letterhead) 'the largest circulation of any foreign daily published in the Far East', although it was still 2,000 or so less than the *North-China Daily News* (and the *Japan Advertiser* on its front page 'ears' advertisements, either side of the masthead, carried exactly the same claim).[52] J.B. Powell, who had briefly taken over from

Webb as editor, now gave way to Charles Laval, previously of the *San Francisco Chronicle*.

Even after Millard's departure, the Foreign Ministry network kept the *China Press* in its sights. In October 1924, George Bronson Rea, writing in the Foreign Ministry network's flagship English-language journal in China, the *Far Eastern Review*, showed that although the *China Press* was legally an American commercial entity incorporated under the laws of Delaware, the Imperial Chinese government was one of the original shareholders. As Rea saw it, 'From its start therefore, the China Press was a Chinese-American enterprise in which the Chinese official stock holdings were concealed under its American registry.' The *China Press* was really a 'Chinese chameleon', which 'posed before the public as the exponent of American ideals and the organ of American interests'.[53]

In 1930, a Chinese syndicate acquired the *China Press* from the Ezra family. The new chairman of the board and legal adviser to the paper was Major Chauncey P. Holcomb, an influential American attorney in Shanghai. Besides Hollington Tong, as editor-in-chief and managing director, there were three Chinese businessmen on the board as well as the legendary Australian journalist W.H. Donald (1875–1946), working closely with Tong in developing the editorial line.[54]

In September 1931, the army of Zhang Xueliang passed out of Manchuria through the Great Wall, marking the cession of Chang's authority to Japan. While the Chinese Communist Party (CCP) bided its time, the Guomindang came to dominate the ideological landscape and newspapers like the *China Press* became ever more closely associated with Guomindang priorities, aided by intensive liaison between W.H. Donald, Hollington Tong and the Nanjing regime.

However, there were disagreements. In 1931, Harold Isaacs and Tillman Durdin resigned from the *Shanghai Evening Post and Mercury* over the recruitment of H.G.W. Woodhead by its editor Ted Thackrey. They migrated to the *China Press* where Isaacs then fell out with Durdin. Reports of the consequences of these disagreements differ. The editor of the *China Press*, Hollington Tong, then either asked Isaacs to leave or gave him 'leave of absence' to go to western China on condition he not return because Tong 'realized Isaacs was more interested in revolution than in reading copy, for he openly espoused the Marxian principles of revolution held by Leon Trotsky'.[55]

In October 1935, Hollington Tong was appointed chief censor of outgoing foreign news despatches and transferred to Nanjing. His replacement as editor-in-chief of the *China Press* was Kuangson Young, but Tong's influence was preserved by his simultaneous promotion to Managing Director of the *China Press*, and Donald stayed on the board. By 1937, the *China Press* had become the largest Chinese-owned English-language daily in China, with the highest Chinese readership in Shanghai, and sales of around 5,000 on weekdays.[56]

The continued success of the *China Press* outside his management may have been a motivating factor in Thomas Millard's next venture.

Certainly, the role of the *North-China Daily News* in undermining the *China Press* as an advertising medium made him keen to show that he could come up with a viable alternative to British media influence in China. In June 1917, B.W. Fleisher, Charles R. Crane and the interests that had combined to start the *China Press* in 1911 reassembled to found a new weekly, *Millard's Review of the Far East*, to be supervised by Millard but with John B. Powell, a Missouri alumnus as editor, and Hollington Tong as associate editor.

Like the *China Press*, the new journal would support nationalist China, but its support was not without strings. Writing to the American consul Julean Arnold in 1916, Millard described the new journal as 'a necessary adjunct to keeping the door open in China and sustaining American interests there'.[57] At the State Department, Robert Lansing also favoured the idea of a publication that would be 'distinctively American in character and give all proper support to American enterprise in the Far East.' He believed that 'such a journal will be of value to American interests' and advised Paul Reinsch to give Millard 'such assistance in the matter as propriety will permit.'[58] Around the same time, China's new Minister to Washington, V.K. Wellington Koo, convinced that the new review could help gain US backing for China, provided Millard with his entrée to the Chinese government with 'important letters to officials in Peking'.[59]

Charles Crane was right behind Millard's new project. Notwithstanding Millard's many endorsements from Chinese and American interests, Crane was crucial in persuading Millard to continue his efforts in China journalism. Crane provided not only most of the start-up capital, but also influence and contacts with the Wilson administration, whose idealism worried Millard.[60] Crane's backing lent Millard's project the legitimacy which accrued to Crane's position at the centre of an élite Republican group concerned with the direction of events in East Asia, among them Paul Reinsch, Stanley Hornbeck, Julean Arnold and Woodrow Wilson himself. This legitimacy was vital if Millard's reports and books were to be granted any credibility by the American reading public.

Nevertheless, in 1922 Millard took a decision that in some ways did compromise the independence of his outlook as a commentator on East Asian affairs, and would lead in 1929 to critical comments in British-owned papers in the *Chronicle* network regarding not just his independence but the credibility of other organs in the *Advertiser* network.[61] Since 1920, in addition to editing *Millard's Review of the Far East*, Thomas Millard had been putting a great deal of time and effort into the campaign to abrogate the Anglo-Japanese Alliance sponsored by Charles R. Crane and the Chinese government. In 1922 Millard accepted an invitation to become a full-time publicity adviser to the Chinese government. The post was incompatible with newspaper ownership or correspondence, so it was decided to wind down *Millard's Review of the Far East*, and then create a fresh incarnation under John B. Powell,

Millard's first and only editor. To accomplish this change, it was necessary to buy back the Millard Publishing Company stock from the original shareholders: Millard himself, Thomas R. Jernigan, and Stirling Fessenden, who would later become a leading American voice on the Shanghai Municipal Council.[62] Charles Crane duly reached for his cheque book and bought the stock, which Powell then bought from Crane. Powell then renamed the journal, first, the *Weekly Review of the Far East* (retaining, true to a Chinese superstition, the original Chinese-language title on the masthead). In 1923 Powell finally changed the English title to the *China Weekly Review*. Nevertheless, Millard's exit and Powell's promotion, acquisition and renaming of the journal may have been more cosmetic than real exercises in the independence of the fourth estate. A private note to the US commercial attaché showed that while Millard was receiving a monthly salary from the Guomindang at the end of 1923, so was Powell.[63]

Whether or not he knew about these payments, Crane's support for the new review eased off once Powell had it up and running. Meanwhile, Millard's Shanghai correspondence for the *New York Herald Tribune* went to Edgar Snow. At the same time, Powell asked Snow to be Associate Editor on the *China Weekly Review*. Snow had reservations about taking these posts but kept them for several years, staying on at the *China Weekly Review* until November 1929.[64]

The *China Weekly Review* inherited its predecessor's circulation of around 4,000 to 5,000 weekly, not including a growing subscription base in the US and Britain.[65] The Anglophone population of Shanghai in the early 1920s was between 8,000–10,000, but the *Review* also had readers in the outports, and was read and studied by Chinese in Shanghai and elsewhere. In a 1930 interview, Powell described the *Review*'s editorial policy as follows:

> The *Review* has consistently supported the program of an independent China that would be able to look after her own affairs and not become a colonial appendage of other European or Asiatic nations. This policy has generally conformed to American policy in respect to China. It has supported the Open Door Policy, Chinese autonomy in respect to tariff, as well as the abolition of extraterritoriality. In reference to China, it has consistently advocated a policy of political, economic and industrial reconstruction that would place the nation on an equal footing with other nations of the world. Only in this way will the so-called Far Eastern questions be solved, because a weak China constantly excited the covetous ambitions of other nations, while a strong China will have a stabilizing effect on world affairs.[66]

Few representatives of the Western powers could object to any of this – an orderly China, a China with whom they could do business, even an independent China – were all more or less on the cards but 'a strong China' was not overtly part of the consensus, although Britain's policy was now to accommodate (if only to contain) Chinese nationalism. Sharing his mentor, Millard, and their backer, Crane's distrust of the Japanese and of Communism, Powell gave the *Review*'s support to the nationalist faction that seemed most likely to withstand and even repel both invaders. However, Powell's abiding association with Millard, who was after all a paid adviser of Nanjing, led the *Chronicle* network's two biggest allies, the *Peking & Tientsin Times* and the *North-China Daily News* and, naturally, just about every organ in Japan's Foreign Ministry network, to question the purity of his motives.

These attacks on Powell came after the imposition of postal bans on both papers in the late 1920s. The *North-China Daily News* had already been banned from the use of the postal system for two months in 1927 on the orders of a local Guomindang general irritated by criticism in the paper.[67] In March 1929 the *North-China Daily News* published a leader headed 'The Pity of It!' This scathing but obviously well-informed attack on Guomindang infighting at the Third National Congress ended with this lofty denunciation:

> But who cares? The insensate squabbles of the politicians and militarists as to which shall be greatest among them, blinds them to all considerations of humanity. And Nationalist patriotism displays itself in fine speeches, in five-thousand-word manifestoes, in posturing for the deception of foreign powers, in anything but hard work and practical thought for their country.[68]

On 10 April telegrams from Nanjing appeared in the *Xinwenbao* and the *China Times* warning the foreign press against publishing 'insulting articles'. The *North-China Daily News* acknowledged this warning but asserted:

> Since the Nationalists broke with Communism, we have been specially on the watch for any improvement that might be welcomed, any sign of solid work that could be praised, and we have made every possible allowance for shortcomings … But we are certainly not going to pretend that all is for the best in the best of all possible worlds, nor refrain from censure in matters which go to fundamental principles such as the total failure of law in China to protect the individual.[69]

On 18 April, Nanjing announced that the *North-China Daily News* would be banned from the use of the postal system and pushed for the expulsion of George Sokolsky, author of 'The Pity of It!' Two days later, the *Peking & Tientsin Times* published an account of its contemporary's troubles amid a spirited defence of press freedom.[70] On 1 May the *Shanghai Evening Post and Mercury* ran an article reporting but not condemning the Nanjing Government's campaign to have Sokolsky, Dailey and Abend deported.[71] On 3 May the postal ban on the *North-China Daily News* was put in place and on the following day the Post Office refused to accept or undertake delivery of the paper. The newspaper published a condemnation of the action on 11 April[72] and on 6 May wondered whether it would not harm China's cause in the US, 'as people contrast the summary methods used to shut this paper's mouth with the Chinese Foreign Minister's glowing assertions of the satisfaction foreigners may expect from Chinese law'.[73] On the same day, the *Peking & Tientsin Times* condemned the postal bans on the *North-China Daily News* and the *North China Star* and the deportation campaign, which:

> ... follows closely upon the appointment of Mr Thomas F. Millard as Publicity Adviser to the Nanking Government; and the attack upon our Shanghai contemporary is, it is significant to note, enthusiastically applauded by Mr J.B. Powell in the 'China Weekly Review'. Mr Millard was himself at one time special correspondent in China of the New York 'Times', and distinguished himself – not for the first time – by his violently anti-British attitude. Mr J.B. Powell's paper has for some time past been virtually a Nationalist organ, and he has exploited every item of information detrimental of British and other foreign interests in China ... There are, unfortunately, some foreign journalists who, in return for a subsidy or even to gratify their spite against their fellow countrymen, will circulate any lying propaganda with which the Nationalist Government likes to furnish them.[74]

The ban on the *North-China Daily News* had been removed by mid-August 1929, and the replacement of O.M. Green as editor by Edwin Haward in 1930 may have helped maintain a relatively benign attitude to the paper in Nanjing in the early 1930s, when, in any case, Japanese actions in Manchuria and Shanghai gave it bigger fish to fry.[75]

Before then, some significant cards had been laid upon the table between the different press interests in Shanghai, as the *Advertiser* network responded tangentially to the *Peking & Tientsin Times* attack quoted above, justifying the decision to deport Sokolsky on the grounds that *he* was the propagandist, and a blackmailer to boot. On 19 April, in a piece in the *New York Herald Tribune*, Millard went into Sokolsky's links with Foreign Ministry network organs like the *Far Eastern Review*, and assailed the editorial policy of the *North-China Daily News*. On 25 April, the *China Critic* referred to Sokolsky as 'our Jewish friend' in an attempt, probably well-judged, to reduce his support in the Foreign Settlement. On 27 April, in an article that was probably coordinated with Millard, the *China Weekly Review* acknowledged Sokolsky's early support for the May Fourth movement but maintained that he deserved to be deported because 'in recent years he has lent himself to foreign propagandas which have had the effect of neutralizing his previous sympathetic attitude toward the Chinese'.[76] Privately, in a letter to the American consul, Powell denied the charge that Nanjing was subsidizing the *China Weekly Review* and dished out the dirt on Sokolsky: he referred to Sokolsky's own statements that he received a salary from the US legation for his reports on Chinese affairs. He also described payments made to Sokolsky by Chinese officials, British American Tobacco, the Japanese Mill

Owners Association and others who feared exposure in the *North-China Daily News*: the Guomindang deportation order had been made solely because of 'Mr Sokolsky's blackmailing activities with Chinese officialdom'.[77]

The *Review* carried on regardless, writing up Nanjing and keeping open its lines to power. Besides Powell and Snow, the most significant continuation from *Millard's Review* was Hollington Tong, who served as associate editor on the *China Weekly Review* until the mid-1920s, and eventually ran Nanjing's Ministry of Information. In 1931, apart from Powell and three American writers, the other editorial staff were all Chinese. By 1933 the editorial staff had shrunk to six, of whom four were Chinese.[78]

After about 1922, the *Review* took the view that since a Chinese administration of Shanghai was inevitable, it would be wiser to make a beginning by admitting Chinese members to the Council. In 1927, when there was considerable agitation for British or American military intervention in China, consistent with its 'strong China' policy, the *China Weekly Review* was the only foreign-owned paper to oppose such a move. This caused differences with the Shanghai Municipal Council and with the ex-*Millard's Review* shareholder, the American Stirling Fessenden, Secretary-General, then Chairman, of the International Settlement from the early 1920s until 1939.[79] However, early in 1927 the *Review* gave its unqualified support to the deal between Fessenden, the authorities in the French zone, the Guomindang, and the Green Gang leaders that led to the massacres of communists in April of that year and cut short the leftist takeover of Shanghai.[80]

At an earlier stage of these developments in the *Advertiser* network, a separate set of publications was launched by a more evidently transnational grouping in the *Advertiser* network. The American at the centre of this group, which included two foreign-educated Chinese, was George Sokolsky (1893–1962). The English-language newspaper he helped to found and wrote for was the *Shanghai Gazette*, which we have encountered in the context of the *Kobe Herald* affair.

In 1918, a circle around Sun Yatsen founded the *Shanghai Gazette*, an organ 'dedicated to the revolutionary and republican cause'.[81] Sun asked Eugene Chen (Chen Youren, 1878–1944), a Trinidad-born Chinese member of the Central Committee of the Guomindang to edit the *Shanghai Gazette*, and George Sokolsky to write for it. Both Sun and Chen were Cantonese, educated abroad: Sun in Hawai'i, Chen in Jamaica and London. Sokolsky was a Jew married to a Jamaican-born Chinese from Eugene Chen's own social circle. Both Chen and Sun were fluent English speakers (Chen did not speak Chinese), democratically inclined and strongly opposed to Japanese ambitions in China.

Chen had edited (with H.G.W. Woodhead) the *Peking Daily News* for a year from 1914, then founded the *Peking Gazette*, in which he opposed China's entry into the First World War and in mid-1915 attacked Yuan Shikai's acceptance of the revised Twenty-One Demands. In 1916, the

Gazette mocked Yuan's imperial pretensions and Chen had to leave Peking for his own safety.[82] In May 1918, with Yuan in his grave, Chen was imprisoned and nearly executed for an *exposé* of the corruption of Yuan's successor, the warlord Tuan Ch'i-jui.[83]

The *Shanghai Gazette* adopted an uncompromisingly anti-Japanese line from its first issue. In September 1918, Chen ran Putnam Weale's controversial 'Revolt in Japan' article. As noted above, a week or so later, at the height of the Rice Riots, the *Kobe Herald* caused an uproar by reprinting the article. In November 1919, possibly as a follow-up to official displeasure over the article, the *Japan Times* claimed that American interests were organizing 'anti-Japanese' newspaper campaigns in China. The *Shanghai Gazette* reacted with an article headlined: 'Another Japanese Canard killed: US Govt. Not Establishing Newspapers in China'.[84]

George Sokolsky was the personification of the Open Door in China. He managed and wrote most of the newsletters of the Bureau of Public Information. He wrote for newspapers in Japan, China and the United States. He was in with the Peking government through W.H. Donald, and deep in the confidence of Sun Yatsen and Eugene Chen. Even on Shanghai's Good Roads Committee, Sokolsky rubbed shoulders with Tang Jiezhi of the *Shangbao* and Powell of the *China Weekly Review*.[85] In 1922, Sokolsky married Rosalind Phang, gaining an *entrée* to influential political and business circles in Chinese society and to the core of the Guomindang through Rosalind's close friend Song Meiling, wife of Chiang Kai-shek and sister-in-law to Sun Yatsen.[86]

The *Gazette* employed Sokolsky from its launch late in 1918 until he fell out with Eugene Chen in the early 1920s. Sokolsky doubled as a *Gazette* journalist and an enthusiastic Guomindang publicist, disseminating the views of Sun Yatsen and the Guangzhou (Canton) group of the Guomindang among Westerners and Chinese radicals.[87] Sokolsky had come to Shanghai from Tianjin (Tientsin), where he got on friendly terms with the US Consul General in Shanghai and served as his informant on Chinese radicalism and the inner workings of the Guomindang. Under his own name and various pseudonyms ('G. Gramada', 'George Soks') Sokolsky contributed to a wide range of newspapers in China, the US and Japan including the *North-China Daily News*, the *China Weekly Review*, the *North China Star,* the *New York Times*, *New York Post*, the *Philadelphia Public Ledger* and the *Japan Advertiser*.[88]

However, in Japan, Sokolsky kept closer to the middle of the road. In August 1920 'G. Gramada' assured *Advertiser* readers that the May Fourth movement was metamorphosing into a 'middle-class democracy' tempered by conservative elements in the Chinese Chambers of Commerce.[89] The following spring, he felt sure that the leadership of the 'erratic and wild' Sun Yatsen would soon be replaced by more stable elements.[90] However, in Shanghai, Sokolsky attended meetings of the May Fourth student movement, acted as a conduit for sensitive information and funds from Sun Yatsen, and composed letters to

English-language newspapers in China on behalf of the Shanghai Students' Union. In the early 1920s, he set up and managed the Chinese Bureau of Public Information, with responsibility for an English-language newsletter which was mailed to US Congressmen, American newspapers and US government departments.[91] He was also involved in establishing the *Shangbao*, destined to become Shanghai's third largest Chinese-language daily. Sokolsky held *Shangbao* shares, acted as Treasurer, and wrote articles for the paper on foreign affairs under another pseudonym. Throughout the 1920s, the *Shangbao* was carefully surveyed by Japanese representatives in Shanghai, but Sokolsky's involvement escaped their notice.[92]

Working through W.H. Donald, the Peking Government invested in the *Shangbao* and the Chinese Bureau of Public Information. Sokolsky's part in these projects advanced his 'insider' reputation and led to his cultivation by official parties on all sides of the China equation: the US State Department, the Japanese embassy, and the British embassy. The British Foreign Office was less appreciative: 'Sokolsky is an American Jew with a flair for picking up the gossip and scandal current among Chinese politicians. His articles have a certain value but are long winded and inaccurate.'[93] Sokolsky was more highly rated by US officials in Shanghai, but his attacks on Guomindang infighting (above) in 1929 and the enmity this won him from Millard, Powell and the authorities in Nanjing complicated his relationship with US officials.

Perhaps the most ambitious endeavours of the *Advertiser* network in China were those aimed both at bringing bring news of the American world further into the mainstream of Chinese life and performing an equivalent service by bringing China to the attention of American readers. Between 1918 and 1925, B.W. Fleisher was closely involved in two initiatives along these lines financed by Charles R. Crane and engineered by the serving American Minister Paul Reinsch (1913–19), Millard, Powell, Carl Crow, V.S. McClatchy, editor of the *San Francisco Bee* and a ringmaster of anti-Japanese sentiment in California, the Zhong-Mei News Agency, established in 1918, and the less successful Trans-Pacific News Service, inaugurated in 1919. These international media projects supported the *Advertiser* network's short-term campaign to prevent the renewal of the Anglo-Japanese Alliance and were intended to check Japan's growing strength in the news agency business in China but their association with McClatchy lent substance to the suspicions of an anti-Japanese news network noted by Ugaki Kazushige in 1923.

As we have seen, in Japan B.W. Fleisher and his longest-serving editor Hugh Byas helped build a supportive professional network around the *Advertiser* by consistently commissioning and publishing original pieces by Japanese journalists writing in English. In China, newspapers associated with the *Advertiser* and Fleisher held to the principle of employing American-educated, near-bilingual Chinese journalists on their papers such as Hollington Tong on the *China Weekly Review* and *China Press*,

Jabin Hsu on the *China Press,* Eugene Chen on the *Shanghai Gazette* and Hsiao Fung-soh, with his column 'As a Chinese sees it' on the *Shanghai Evening Post* and commissioning articles from bilingual freelancers.

At the same time, these papers were highly conscious of the appetite for reading in English among young Chinese people, and John B. Powell credited himself 'with being the first foreign editor in China to discover the young English-reading Chinese subscriber' and of catering to the appetite for readable English news.[94] Allied to these trends and practices was an emphasis, in the *Advertiser* network, on organizing the provision of translated news. In the autumn of 1918, the first such initiative got underway with the establishment of the Zhong-Mei News Agency, organized to translate and distribute American news to the Chinese press.

The Zhong-Mei service was a runaway success. In the US, Walter Rogers of the Committee on Public Information organized a direct service of daily despatches which were translated by Zhong-Mei and distributed to the 300 Chinese papers on its books. In China, the agency established an effective grass roots network with hundreds of volunteer agents including teachers and employees of Standard Oil and British-American Tobacco, and a mailing list of 25,000 individual Chinese.[95]

The American Minister Paul Reinsch and Carl Crow, as the Far Eastern representative of the US Committee on Public Information, used the Zhong-Mei service to distribute the heady essence of Wilsonian idealism to Chinese newspapers and the English-language newspapers of East Asia.[96] Jabin Hsu had complained at the 1921 World's Press Congress that Western journalists raised Chinese expectations, only to have them dashed by the decisions of the Peace Conference. As Crow himself admitted, 'The official American War propaganda that I circulated so industriously in China was partly to blame for this hopefulness.'[97] Nevertheless, by 1928, one estimate was that eighty to ninety per cent of the main news in Chinese-language newspapers was being translated from foreign newspapers, much of it by Zhong-Mei.[98]

The Zhong-Mei agency was not entirely without credibility problems. In June 1925, the agency was accused in the *Peking & Tientsin Times* of inserting 'with conscious malice' an anti-British tone into its translation of a *Shenbao* article that did not exist in the Chinese original. The same accuser suspected that the Zhong-Mei agency had 'similarly touched up' anti-British reports attributed to the *Yishibao* of Tianjin.[99] The effort to distribute news from China in the US was far less effective, largely due to a lack of interest among the American public.

Before the Paris Conference, Zhong-Mei was the agency that communicated Wilson's Fourteen Points to China's budding nationalists. Towards the end of the Conference, it was the channel by which the decision of the Conference to allow the lease on the Shandong Peninsula to revert to Japan became known in China, igniting the May Fourth Movement and giving a huge impetus to Chinese nationalism.

For the second news distribution project, Paul Reinsch organized a meeting in Peking in early 1919 attended by B.W. Fleisher, V.S. McClatchy of the virulently anti-Japanese *San Francisco Bee*, Joseph Sharkey of AP Tokyo, Crow, and Powell of the *China Weekly Review*. The meeting resulted in the establishment of a fast, low-priced news agency, the Trans-Pacific News Service. In 1923 the group tried and failed to get Congressional approval for cheap access to naval radio facilities. The Trans-Pacific News Service had some success during the Washington Conference but it fizzled out thereafter.[100]

The *Advertiser* network had a more successful record with less ambitious ventures confined to the English-language news market in China. In a fight for control of the *Shanghai Mercury*, the *Advertiser* network came up against the financial muscle and determination of the Foreign Ministry network in Shanghai. In May 1919 Carl Crow noted with dismay that the *Shanghai Mercury* had a Japanese editor and manager and was controlled by Japanese interests, with circulation running at around 1,000 daily.[101] Two years later, in the autumn of 1921, Crow was deeply involved in a tussle with Japanese interests for control of the paper.[102] In May 1921 British Military Intelligence observed, 'Knowing that the "*Mercury*" has pro-Japanese tendencies, the Americans want to make sure that not a single paper in Shanghai writes a word in favour of the Japanese.'[103] In January 1923 the Japanese consulate in Shanghai acquired a controlling interest in the *Shanghai Mercury* and sacked its editor, J.W. Fraser.[104] However, in 1929 Crow was back in the picture as editor of C.V. Starr's newly acquired *Shanghai Evening Post*, the other half of the amalgam that would become the *Shanghai Evening Post and Mercury*.

In 1923, the *Shanghai Gazette* company took over the *Shanghai Evening Star*, but the resulting amalgamation then passed out of the control of Chen and the circle around Sun Yatsen and became part of a newspaper chain being built up by Edward Ezra, alongside the *China Press*. Ezra's group then changed the name to the *Shanghai Evening News*. In April 1928 the *Shanghai Evening News* was sold on by Ezra to Cornelius V. Starr's American Newspaper Company, registered in the US as 'an independent journal, with no especial purpose of propaganda or policy to serve except that of giving correct, unbiased information…', and renamed the *Shanghai Evening Post*.[105] Carl Crow became editor of this new organ but in 1929 the *Post* clashed with the National government over alleged libels, and criminal charges were brought against him. As a result, the *Shanghai Evening Post* was barred from the postal system from November 1929 to February 1930. On 6 August 1930, with the ban lifted, the *Evening Post* bought the *Shanghai Mercury* and the amalgamation became the *Shanghai Evening Post and Mercury*. As the only evening daily in Shanghai, the *Shanghai Evening Post and Mercury* became the second largest English-language newspaper in China (behind the *North-China Daily News*), its circulation shooting up from 4,800 in 1931 to over 7,000 in 1938: at its height in the late 1930s it took over 23% of the total English-language newspaper sales in Shanghai and 10% of the national total.

Although the *Shanghai Evening Post and Mercury* had strong American connections, before 1931, its support for Chinese aspirations and its opposition to Japanese incursions in China were not as overtly expressed as in most newspapers in the *Advertiser* network. The writings of two *Evening Post & Mercury* journalists, H.G.W. Woodhead and C. Yates McDaniel reinforced this impression of ambivalence (rather than balance) while those of a third, Randall Gould, who joined the *Shanghai Evening Post and Mercury* in 1931 and succeeded Thackrey as managing editor in 1934, were as forthright as ever. The turning point was the Manchurian Incident. As Gould recalled, proprietor Cornelius V. Starr's reaction was clear and immediate:

> 'Up to now I've never tried to lay down specific policy for the *Post*, but on this Manchuria thing – I must. We are against it!' Ted was completely of this view. Arriving a few days later to write the paper's editorials, I too saw the matter in that light ... In our paper we dealt with Japan and her policies realistically and without pulling punches. No other Shanghai newspaper hit the Japanese so hard.[106]

In January 1933, the *Shanghai Evening Post and Mercury* began publishing a Chinese edition, *Da Mei Wan Bao*. In December 1937 the Japanese military authorities in Shanghai tried to suppress this paper but the attempt failed as Starr had registered the *Post & Mercury* in the US. In 1939, the Guomindang authorities banned the *Da Mei Wan Bao* for publishing a speech by Chiang Kai-shek, but it was soon restored. By December 1941, when Japan occupied the International Settlement, the Chinese edition had a circulation of 40,000.

In 1930, H.G.W. Woodhead had left the *Peking & Tientsin Times* and Tientsin for Shanghai and a regular column on the newly merged *Shanghai Evening Post and Mercury* 'One Man's Comment For To-Day'.[107] Woodhead welcomed deeper Japanese incursions in China and argued the case among British and American interests for frankly exploiting the benefits of Japan's China policy. Although Woodhead appears to have backed Japan's ambitions in China from about 1926, no-one at the Foreign Office seems to have smelt a rat.[108] Woodhead was not a publicist in the Russell Kennedy or George Rea mould. Nor was he an indiscriminate supporter of Japan: he campaigned strongly against the renewal of the Anglo-Japanese Alliance, and his First World War journalism had won him a C.B.E. For many years, he had his own publications in Tientsin and seldom contributed articles to newspapers in the Foreign Ministry network.[109] Nevertheless, as the 'dean of the British die-hards', Woodhead was unpopular in Guomindang circles, and Chinese firms hesitated to advertise in the *Shanghai Evening Post and Mercury* for fear of appearing to be 'anti-Nanking'.[110]

THE *JAPAN ADVERTISER* NETWORK AND THE 'MISSOURI MAFIA'
In the thirty-five years that he ran the *Japan Advertiser*, B.W. Fleisher collected numerous long-term correspondences for US papers. For much of 1921–41, Fleisher, his son Wilfrid (1897–1976) and *Advertiser* staff wrote the Japan correspondence for the *New York World*, *Philadelphia Public Ledger*, *Chicago Daily News*, *New York Times*, *Elizabeth Daily Journal* (New Jersey), *St. Louis Post-Dispatch*, *New York Evening Graphic*, *New York Herald Tribune*, the news agencies International News Service (Hearst) and United Press, and a raft of trade journals. Usually, *Advertiser* staff members wrote the Tokyo dispatches but the work stayed in B.W. Fleisher's gift. The exception was Hugh Byas, who edited the *Advertiser*, with breaks, from 1914 to 1930, when he left to concentrate on his foreign correspondence, finally leaving for the US in 1941. Besides the Tokyo correspondence, the *Advertiser*'s close connections to three key American papers in China – the *China Weekly Review*, the *China Press* and *Millard's Review of the Far East* – meant that these too were part of its network in East Asia.

Alongside these correspondences and connections, the *Advertiser* network's influence in East Asia and in the US can be traced to its nurturing of the 'Missouri Mafia', a group composed of about sixty alumni of the School of Journalism at the University of Missouri who chose careers in English-language journalism in East Asia. From 1915 to 1930, by an arrangement made between B.W. Fleisher, Frederick Millard of the *China Press*, Carl Crow, John B. Powell of the *China Weekly Review* and Walter Williams (1864–1935), Dean of the School of Journalism, sixty Missouri alumni came to work in Japan and China: thirty to the *Advertiser* and from there to its associated China papers, thirty directly to associated newspapers and agencies in China.[111]

Of these sixty, thirty-five were American, twenty-one were Chinese, four were Japanese, including Robert Y. Horiguchi, whose mother was Belgian. None of the Chinese alumni went to work for the *Advertiser*: most joined Chinese-language newspapers in China.[112] Similarly, with the important exception of Horiguchi, who first worked for Hearst's International News Service in Chicago and in the late 1930s headed *Dōmei*'s operations in Hong Kong and worked for *Dōmei* in Shanghai, only a few Japanese alumni of Missouri worked in China. Five of the alumni were women: three Americans, two Chinese. Of the other well-known American women journalists in China in this period, one of the best known, Agnes Smedley, was a native Missourian though not a Missouri graduate while another, Helen Foster, better known in China by her pseudonym 'Nym Wales', married the best known Missouri alumnus, Edgar Snow.

With Walter Williams's active participation, the *Advertiser* became for young American journalists the best route to interesting, well-paid English-language journalism in East Asia. In the autumn of 1920, B.W. Fleisher predicted that, 'The Japan Advertiser will someday be an adjunct training school for the School of Journalism [at the University of Missouri].'[113] In November 1926 Fleisher's public estimate of the influence of Missouri alumni in East Asia on the reporting and 'interpretation' of Japan in the United States was not exaggerated:

> These men are reporting not only the West to the East, particularly the United States to Japan, but at the same time they are also interpreting Japan to the United States. For while they are on the staff of the Japan Advertiser, they are at the same time the Japan correspondents for many of the leading American dailies, such as the New York Times, New York World, New York Herald-Tribune, Christian Science Monitor, and scores of other American newspapers and periodicals, and also of English [British] daily publications. At different periods, practically every large news dissemination agency, such as the Associated Press, United Press, International News Service, Consolidated Press, etc., has been represented in Japan by University of Missouri graduates. Practically all of these men have spent at least three years in Japan and many of them after leaving Japan have become members of the staffs of leading newspapers and news dissemination organizations in the United States ... These are all young men, and from these men I am hopeful and confident that the great interpreters of the East to West and the West to the East will be developed.[114]

Between the wars, close cooperative relationships developed between American journalist-proprietors and regional managers like Millard, Fleisher, his sometime business manager and UP correspondent Carl Crow, John B. Powell, the International News Agency's 'Duke' Parry and around thirty-five American journalists who either graduated from Missouri or worked in the *Advertiser* network and were all at some point employed by or closely associated with newspapers and news agencies in the *Japan Advertiser* network. While some journalists, notably Miles Vaughn, UP's Manager for East Asia, George Bronson Rea, Denarius Dean, Newton Edgers, Frank Hedges and Relman Morin, made their East Asian reputation at or networked closely with the *Japan Advertiser* but in their despatches promoted the interests of the Foreign Ministry network.

B.W. Fleisher's connection with Walter Williams was close and enduring, and Williams's approval helped Fleisher make useful contacts in US journalism. In turn, the *Advertiser* connection brought Williams to Washington. In June 1918, when he was planning his journey to Tokyo to edit Fleisher's new magazine, the *Trans-Pacific*, Williams was approached by 'two high officials at Washington, confidentially', who asked 'that when I go to the Orient I do some national service in investigation of news services and other journalistic conditions with a view to American conditions in the Far East'. The service would be '... in the interest of winning the war and winning the world after the war'.[115] Williams's 'pull', as Fleisher described it, helped Fleisher secure letters of endorsement from Washington for special issues of the *Advertiser* and the *Trans-Pacific*.[116]

Williams's friendship also enabled Fleisher to showcase his journalistic enterprises, and his associated work in the America-Japan Society, in the American tradition of a liberal, campaigning press. Williams was a celebrated idealist on journalistic matters, and still known today as the author of the Journalist's Creed, which decorates the wall of the National Press Club in Washington. Whenever Williams visited Japan (November 1918-November 1919, and in August of 1922, 1925, and 1927) he would deliver speeches proclaiming the importance of social democratic values in the press and in society at large. A typical speech spoke of the press as a 'lighthouse which leads men to the sea of society', and of 'strict principles which all men and women engaged in this fascinating profession should live up to unfailingly', which he called 'the Seven Lanterns of Journalism'.[117] After each speech, he would urge that Japan, alongside the United States, be represented at the forthcoming Pan-Pacific Press Congress or the less frequent World Press Congress and this call was usually answered by the formation of a delegation of Japanese journalists.

Williams's exalted statements and official connections assured him of a distinguished reception in Japan from Zumoto Motosada, Shibusawa Eiichi, Hugh Byas, Mitsunaga Hoshiro, Soyeda Juichi, and Sugimura Kōtarō of the *Tōkyō Asahi Shinbun*. Fleisher's Japanese staff interpreted Williams's speeches and his English speaking staff reported them verbatim in the *Advertiser*. In 1922 Williams's lectures were hosted by Zumoto Motosada at the Tokyo Club and by Mitsunaga Hoshiro at *Dentsū* headquarters, in 1925 by Prince Tokugawa Iesato at his official residence, and in 1927 by the newly opened *Nippon Shinbun Kyokai* (Japan School of Journalism). In August 1927 Williams met Tanaka Giichi at his official residence.

At these official banquets, the person on Williams's right-hand side was always a significant dignitary like Shibusawa or Tokugawa Iesato, leader of the House of Peers (*Kizoku-in*) and President of the Pan-Pacific Association, whose gift to Missouri University of a stone lantern for whose gift to Missouri Williams had given in return a scroll, but on his left hand there was always either B.W. Fleisher or, as Fleisher's health declined, Hugh Byas. Speaking at these banquets and ceremonials and during visits to newspaper offices in Tokyo and Ōsaka and in newspaper interviews, Williams invariably promoted the American agenda of a liberal press as if such ideals were the natural concomitant of modernization. At least some of his listeners may have connected Williams's ideas with the *Advertiser*'s larger purpose in East Asia.

THE DECLINE OF THE *JAPAN ADVERTISER* NETWORK IN CHINA

The 30 May 1925 Incident coincided with the beginnings of a polarization among, mostly, American journalists in China. Most American journalists and correspondents in Shanghai came under Powell's wing at the *China Weekly Review* or joined Hollington Tong at the *China Press*, there to report the Nationalist revolution with respect and admiration, but after 1926–27 a younger group of journalists began to take an interest in the doings of the Chinese Communist Party.

In 1927, press restrictions and bans on the use of the postal service issued by the Nanjing regime brought to the surface festering resentments between established British newspapers in the *Chronicle* network and some pillars of the *Advertiser* network in China. In the autumn of 1926 and the spring of 1927, reports in the *North-China Daily News* and *Peking & Tientsin Times* of attacks on missions and of anti-foreign agitation and mistreatment at Hankou and Nanjing offended the Nationalists and these papers were denied the use of the postal system. In 1929, the *North-China Daily News* again offended Nanjing and the paper again received a postal ban.

The *China Weekly Review* and *China Press* were conspicuously untouched by such restrictions. In May 1929 the *Peking & Tientsin Times*, in attacking the postal bans and Nanjing's campaign to have Hallett Abend, George Sokolsky, Charles Dailey and Rodney Gilbert deported, saw the hand of Thomas Millard, since 1922 a full-time adviser on publicity to the Nationalists, in these decisions, as well as that of his old protégé, J.B. Powell.

These suppressions ran counter to the ideals of many American journalists at the time and marked the decline of the *Advertiser* network as an idealistic force in Chinese politics. Hollington Tong, Millard and Powell exerted an avuncular, even legendary attraction for some young American newcomers, but other journalists were uncomfortable with the involvement of the first two in the systematic tightening of Guomindang press controls, and found distasteful and maybe un-American the acceptance by all three of the unctuousness surrounding Chiang Kai-shek, his wife and their 'court' in Nanjing.

At the same time, the more guarded, less reflexively pro-Guomindang approach of Hallet Abend, Charles Dailey of the *Chicago Tribune,* and John Goette of Hearst's International News Service, suited the American Minister in Peking, J.V.A. MacMurray, who differed from his predecessors, Reinsch and Crane, in being generally indifferent to the activities of foreign journalists in China, and hostile to the circle around Millard and Powell.[118] Nevertheless, we need to see that, although Abend, Dailey and Goette might differ with local editors like J.B. Powell, Randall Gould and Sheldon Ridge, not to mention H.G.W. Woodhead and O.M. Green, on methods and allegiances, they were still fundamentally agreed that the 'China story' was the story of Chiang Kai-shek and the Guomindang and its struggle to unite China.

However, for another group of American journalists in China who had initially worked within the mainstream *Advertiser* network, the real story was increasingly about the Communist Party of China. Between the late 1920s and early 1930s a division opened between the older, established grouping of Powell, Millard, Tong and others who saw, and were paid to see, the Guomindang as China's best hope of achieving united, independent, national power, and a loosely associated circle of journalists around Edgar Snow and Harold Isaacs. On the whole, the pro-Guomindang group had closer and more durable connections with local English-language newspapers and were correspondents on the side, whereas the younger group tended to be or to see themselves as international correspondents first, local English-language journalists second.

Snow and his circle were particularly frustrated by the continuing civil war between the Guomindang and the forces of the Communist Party of China. For Snow, the China story was unfolding as much (or more) in Yan'an with Mao Zedong (Mao Tse-tung) and the Chinese Communist Party (CCP) as it was in Nanjing and Shanghai, Xinjing (Hsinking) and Tokyo.

Politically, Snow's circle had much more in common with the view of Robert Young in the post-First World War years and those of the current *Chronicle* editor, Morgan Young, than with the mainstream of the *Advertiser* network. The *Chronicle* had championed the socialist and labour movement in Japan and lamented the growth of radical nationalism in the 1920s and early 1930s, just as Snow, and especially Isaacs, were beginning to do in China in the late 1920s and early 1930s.[119] In the 1930s, after he had left the *China Weekly Review*, Snow in particular began asking how it was that the Red Army kept going and seemed to thrive despite Nanjing's superior forces and equipment, numerous foreign advisers and the uncritical support of their cheerleaders on the English-language press. Snow asked of the Communist armies, 'What held them up?' and decided:

> Here was *the* story of China, as newspaper correspondents admitted between despatches sent out on trivial side issues. Yet we were all woefully ignorant about it.[120]

If 'the real story of China' was not centred on the Guomindang, one implication was that Chiang Kai-shek and his charismatic wife did not have an automatic claim to ownership of the China brand and that the English-language journalists promoting Chiang Kai-shek did not necessarily 'speak for the Chinese'. This despite the almost proprietorial devotion of Thomas Millard, J.B. Powell, Randall Gould and Carl Crow (who in 1938 would publish a memoir whose title claimed that he did just that), to that pursuit.

By March 1935 J.B. Powell was clearly irritated by signs of American support for the CCP. Writing in the *China Weekly Review*, Powell launched an attack on *The Nation* and *The New Republic*, the very periodicals which had been the models for *Millard's Review of the Far East*, and 'the liberal and radical press in America' for publishing 'misguided' articles by Israel Epstein (writing as 'Crispian Corcoran') on the Communist movement in China.[121] Edgar Snow wrote to both US periodicals:

> The editor, who attacked you so heartily, is that rare creature, an idealistic American Don Quixote gone out to make the world safe for democracy. Like

the missionaries, he has staked his fortune upon General Chiang and cannot fail him now, even though he should violate all that Mr Powell once held dear. He hates Reds with a childlike naivete, and hasn't the faintest idea what Communism is.[122]

Snow always insisted that he was not a Communist, but he was clearly more sympathetic to the CCP than he was to the Guomindang, and his writings probably did more to gain international recognition for the CCP than the work of any other foreign writer of the day except Pearl Buck and, in the late 1920s, Harold Isaacs (although he turned apostate in 1937).

The polarization among US journalists in China irritated those charged with China policy in the State Department such as Nelson Johnson and Stanley Hornbeck and increased the disdain in which they held press reports from China.[123] In a relatively quiet period for China news, reporting these divisions made the China story even more of a 'puzzle' for newspaper readers in the US. Unsurprisingly, Mordechai Rozanski has shown that from 1927 to 1931, coverage of China news in US dailies dropped from a dominant position in foreign news to five percent of all foreign reports and a ranking of seventh among nations.[124]

This in turn affected the attitude of Guomindang officialdom to the press. Gone were the days of special treatment and unhindered access to the top echelons. We have seen the unsuccessful attempts to deport Dailey, Sokolsky, Abend and Rodney Gilbert. From 1929, the Central Executive of the Guomindang became even less tolerant of unfavourable publicity or unauthorized advocacy and frequently denied the use of the postal system to newspapers in disfavour. At such times, according to Hallett Abend, all copies of offending organs circulating outside the foreign concession would be seized and burned.[125] In the Nanjing era, with Hollington Tong and Eugene Chen running nationalist propaganda for Chiang Kai-shek, both the Shanghai Chinese-language press and the English-language press affiliated with the Guomindang were brought under greater control, their transnational background untangled and their nationalist line more tightly focused. Millard fell out of favour: resigning as an adviser in 1935, Millard complained that his salary had gone unpaid by Nanjing for three years and that he felt 'shunned' by 'the younger crowd of secretaries to the big shots'.[126]

Severe press management by the Guomindang was maintained after the retreat from Nanjing in 1937, in Hankou (Hankow), and from 1938 in Chongqing. Hollington Tong had been chief censor of outgoing foreign news despatches in 1935–37. In October 1937 he was promoted to Vice-Minister of the Fifth Board (Information) of the Guomindang Executive. It was in this capacity that, in 1938, he opened the International Press Hostel in Chongqing. What remained of the 'old guard' of the *Advertiser* network – W.H. Donald, Hollington Tong and, for a while, Eugene Chen – promoted this more focused nationalism from within the nationalist propaganda machine.[127]

In a survey of the role of China's English-language and Chinese-language media during the most overt period of Sino-Japanese hostilities that broke out in 1937, Yu Maochun has shown how the Guomindang lost ground to the Communist Party of China in the vital areas of radio and press propaganda. This was partly because the Guomindang's tightly controlled propaganda machine was infiltrated by the Communists, who took over radio stations, for example, but also, according to Yu, because many foreign journalists, resentful of the Guomindang's increasingly severe censorship and other restrictions, became closer to the Communists.[128] Among those who transferred allegiances in this way were not only radical journalists such as Israel Epstein, Agnes Smedley, Harold Isaacs, Edgar Snow and Anna Louise Strong, but newly-disenchanted figures such as Ilona Ralf Sues,[129] Tilman Durdin, Harrison Foreman, James Young, Brooks Atkinson and Maurice Votaw, Hollington Tong's former right-hand man. Others such as Hallett Abend and John B. Powell were critical of Guomindang restrictions, having suffered from attempted deportations and mailing restrictions, but these experiences did not soften their hostility towards the Communists.[130]

As we saw in Chapter 2, Jabin Hsu and Hollington Tong had complained at the 1921 World's Press Congress about the low quality of US reporting on China. In 1935 the commentator and novelist Lin Yutang noted the continuing influence of treaty-port die-hards whose reporting did little to redeem the situation:

> The plea here is essentially for a better understanding on a higher level of intelligence. Yet it is difficult to deny the Old China Hand the right to write books and articles on China, simply because he cannot read the Chinese newspapers. Nevertheless, such books and articles must necessarily remain on the level of the gossip along the world's longest bar.
>
> There are exceptions of course – a Sir Robert Hart or a Bertrand Russell – who are able to see the meaning in a type of life so different from one's own, but for one Sir Robert Hart there are ten thousand Rodney Gilberts, and for one Bertrand Russell there are ten thousand H.G.W. Woodheads.[131]

□

B.W. Fleisher tried to manage the *Advertiser* in Japan in a way least likely to offend the official world. He cooperated with Japanese officialdom and seldom openly challenged the newspapers of the Foreign Ministry network even when, as occurred over the Twenty-One Demands or the Manchurian Incident, he was probably in possession of a more controversial version of the facts. And yet, Fleisher was not trusted in Japan, and the *Advertiser* never enjoyed official confidence, despite Fleisher's best efforts. In Japan the *Advertiser* enjoyed better sales and a far better income and probably exerted far more influence on public opinion than its rivals, but the picture is less clear in the United States, where the

Japan Times, for all its faults and all the evidence of its official links, gradually became, alongside *Dōmei*, the default source of information for Japan watchers in the US and US correspondents in East Asia.

In China, the *Advertiser* network was more organized, more discreet and better financed and with a far clearer and stronger sense of mission than the *Chronicle* network. In Japan, the *Advertiser*'s voice was more measured than the *Chronicle*'s and yet its official contacts in the United States were intensely cultivated: the *Advertiser* was far more America's paper in East Asia than the *Chronicle* could ever be Britain's.

It is worth stressing here that among the three networks of the English-language newspapers of East Asia, the most direct and dynamic opposition lay between the *Japan Advertiser* network and Japan's Foreign Ministry network. As we saw in Chapter 2, the *Advertiser* network's initiatives against the Twenty-One Demands and the Anglo-Japanese Alliance were too private, being largely funded by Charles R. Crane, to be credited to America's or Nationalist China's network, yet the *Advertiser* network's official connections in China and in the United States were too enduring and consistent for them not to be. Therefore, because the priorities of the Foreign Ministry network were to increase Japanese prestige and to undermine Western influence and 'interference', particularly in China, the sheer energy and reach of the *Advertiser* network, its newspapers and its journalists, made it the main target of the Foreign Ministry network. Hence, for all his friendliness and discretion, the distrust that B.W. Fleisher, his staff, and (insofar as they were known) his associates in China were held in by Japanese officials was more intense and enduring than that reserved for the *Chronicle* and its network in China.

NOTES

1   Rozanski 1974: 20.

2   FO 371/23574 [F 10795/10796/23]: John Pratt, Ministry of Information, to Ashley Clarke, 3 October 1939, described Fleisher as follows: 'Mr Fleischer [*sic*] père is an American Jew & his wife is a French Jewess. It would be a little surprising if he sold out to the Nazis ...' Pratt's Anglo-Indian descent may have made him more sensitive to racial origins than of his colleagues, but his remarks were fairly typical. Fleisher's associate in the *Advertiser* network, George Sokolsky, was portrayed in a 1929 FO Minute as 'an American Jew with a flair for picking up the gossip and scandal current among Chinese politicians'. See note 93, below.

3   Fleisher himself appears to have shown a partiality for bringing young men of Jewish origin out to work on newspapers in East Asia.

4   Knapp reported the Russo-Japanese War for *Collier's Magazine*. In 1906, he published *Feudal and Modern Japan* (Yokohama: Japan Advertiser Press), and *Japanese Commercial Honor* (1911). On Knapp's death, Robert Young described him as a '*flaneur*'.

5   Rozanski 1974: 21.

6   Rozanski 1974: 21; Wildes 1927: 306.

7   Hugh Fulton Byas obituary: NYT, 7 March 1945. Byas probably came into Fleisher's view in 1911, when he was taken on as London correspondent of the *China Press*.
8   Wilfrid Fleisher replaced Byas at the *Advertiser* and wrote the *New York Herald Tribune* correspondence.
9   Byas left the *Advertiser* in 1922 to work for *The Times* in London (and as the *Advertiser*'s London correspondent), returning in 1926 to edit the *Advertiser* upon his appointment as *The Times* correspondent in Tokyo.
10 Bess 1943: 63–4.
11 USDS 894/917: B.W. Fleisher to Dept. of State, 25 November 1916.
12 See O'Connor March 2001 on wartime English-language journalism in Japan.
13 'Lantern for Journalism School': JA, 2 April 1926.
14 Fleisher to Walter Williams, 8 May 1915, Walter and Sarah Lockwood Williams Papers, University of Missouri at Columbia.
15 As Chair of the committee financing Woodrow Wilson's election in 1913, and a major contributor to Republican campaign funds, Crane was appointed as American Minister to China in 1913 but indiscretions to the press meant that Paul Reinsch was appointed instead. Crane finally took up his post in 1920, only to have it revoked in 1921 when Harding and the Democrats won the election, and Jacob Schurman was appointed to Peking.
16 B.W. Fleisher to Walter Williams, 27 July 1918, Walter and Sarah Lockwood Williams Papers, University of Missouri at Columbia.
17 USDS 894.917/1: Walter Williams, University of Missouri, Columbia, Missouri, to Woodrow Wilson, White House, 22 August 1918.
18 Mitsunaga Hoshiro to Walter Williams, 7 July 1926. Walter and Sarah Lockwood Williams Papers, University of Missouri at Columbia.
19 Okada, Governor of Nagano-ken, to *Gaimushō, Naimushō* and police authorities, 19 August 1921. *Gaimushō gaikō shiryōkan: gaikoku shinbun, tsūshin kikan oyobi tsūshin-in kankei zakken, tsūshin-in no bu, beikokujin no bu* (Foreign Ministry records: Miscellaneous matters relating to foreign newspapers, communications agencies and correspondents, correspondents section: American correspondents) A-F, 1 1/3/2 50–2-2, August 1921.
20 *Gaimushō gaikō shiryōkan: gaikoku shinbun, tsūshin kikan oyobi tsūshin-in kankei zakken, tsūshin-in no bu, beikokujin no bu* (Foreign Ministry records: Miscellaneous matters relating to foreign newspapers, communications agencies and correspondents, correspondents section: American correspondents) *dai-2 kan* 1/3/2 50–2, September 1921.
21 Fleisher to Williams, 29 October 1920: Walter and Sarah Lockwood Williams Papers, University of Missouri at Columbia.
22 FO 371/3238 [F 103353]: Conyngham Greene to A. Balfour, 10 April 1918.
23 USDS 894.918/17: Phillips, Far East Division USDS, note to Secretary of State, 25 September 1934.
24 Fleisher, B.W. (ed.) 1928: 123.
25 On Kinney's remuneration, see Abend 1943: 184. For Kinney as a propagandist, see Powell 1945: 309.
26 USDS 894.911/41: Cameron Forbes, Tokyo embassy, to USDS, 20 December 1930.
27 USDS 894.911/32, Forbes, Tokyo, to Martin Egan, J.P. Morgan Co., 7 November 1930.

28 USDS 894.911/31: Henry Stimson telegram to US Embassy Tokyo, 11 November 1930.
29 USDS 894.911/32, Forbes to Egan, 7 November 1930.
30 USDS 894.918/17: Phillips of the State Department maintained that Fleisher declined the Japanese offer for fear that it might oblige his paper to take a more pro-Japanese editorial line. Phillips, Far East Division USDS, to Secretary of State, 25 September 1934.
31 USDS 894.911/47 William Stix Wasserman, Philadelphia, to Castle, 24 January 1931; Castle to Egan, 27 January 1931.
32 Other relevant USDS documents on the financial rescue of the *Advertiser* are: 894.911/37 W. Castle to M. Egan, 28 November 1930; 894.911/39 Castle to Egan, 4 December 1930; 894.911/40 Forbes to Castle, 12 December 1930; 894.911/44 Forbes to Castle, 31 December 1930; 894.911/46 Wasserman to Egan, 16 January 1931, and to Castle, 17 January 1931.
33 Although he ended it in 1930, Rockefeller's loan to the *Advertiser* was significant as one among a series of Japan-related ventures undertaken by his family. In the early 1900s, Rockefeller had been cultivated by Takamine Jōkichi (1854–1922), Japan's key informal representative on the US East Coast, at lavish occasions held in Takamine's New York brownstone on West 173rd Street and at his estate at Merriewold Park in Sullivan County. Rockefeller's first press secretary, Joseph I.C. Clarke, may have been recommended by Takamine. Clarke went on to write *Japan at first hand* (1918) (O'Connor 2004, Volume 5). John D. Rockefeller III picked up his Japan-related interests after the Second World War, financing major extensions and improvements for the Japan Society of New York, at whose functions he had been a frequent guest and speaker since its foundation in 1906 (Angel et al. 1994).
34 China Committee on Public Information.
35 Cohen 1978: 278–9.
36 USDS 894.911/84: Stanley Hornbeck, USDS, to Under Secretary of State Sumner Welles, 5 June 1941, regarding Thomas Millard, Manila, to USDS, 21 May 1941.
37 JT: 13 October 1940.
38 *Gaimushō gaikō shiryōkan: gaikoku shinbun, tsūshin kikan oyobi tsūshin-in kankei zakken, tsūshin-in no bu, beikokujin no bu* (Miscellaneous matters relating to foreign newspapers, communications agencies and correspondents, correspondents section: American correspondents) 1 1/3/2/ 50–2-2, August 1921.
39 B.W. Fleisher to Walter Williams, 27 July 1918: Walter and Sarah Lockwood Williams Papers, University of Missouri at Columbia.
40 Root Commission experiences: Crane to Wilson, 28 March 1917; Crane to family, 8 July 1917. Overall reaction to the Russian Revolution: Crane to F.D. Roosevelt, 13 November 1937. All in the Charles R. Crane Papers, Institute of Current World Affairs, New York and cited in Rozanski, 350, n.51.
41 Rozanski 1974: 301–305.
42 Millard 1906: 9, 245.
43 USDS 893.00/2121: Millard to Wilson, 3 April 1914.
44 'Prostituting Extraterritoriality: Legalizing the Sale of Protection to Chinese Citizens' by George Bronson Rea: FER, October 1924: 461–63.
45 USDS 893.911/1: Consul-General A. Wilder, Shanghai, to Sec. of State, Washington, 25 February 1911.

46 USDS 893.911/110: Consul-General T. Simmons, Yokohama, to Sec. of State, Washington, 13 December 1910.

47 Millard to Crane, 3 July 1911, Crane Papers, Washington. Not long after this incident, the Yokohama Specie Bank made up for its failure to suborn the *China Press* by acquiring a controlling interest in the *Shanghai Times* for Japanese interests. See Chapter 2.

48 USDS 893.911/9: T. Millard, New York, to Robert Lansing, Secretary of State, Washington, 16 October 1915, quoting c.1914 letter from Webb, Shanghai.

49 Millard's emphasis, op. cit.

50 USDS 893.911/133: US Consul-General Edwin S. Cunningham to A.B. Ruddock, US Legation, Peking, 19 December 1921.

51 Powell 1945: 10.

52 Wildes 1927:374.

53 FER, October 1924: 461–3. Cited in Goodman 2004: 67.

54 Chao 1931: 70.

55 Asked to leave: Tong 1948: 10; given leave of absence: Rosholt 1994: 12, 14.

56 Ch'en 1937: 12.

57 Miller to Arnold, 22 September 1916, Arnold papers, Hoover Institution, Stanford University, California. Cited in Rozanski 1974: 282.

58 USDS 893.911/16: Lansing to Paul Reinsch, Peking, 12 October 1916. Cited in Rozanski 1974: 282, and 346, n.3.

59 Millard to Arnold, 4 November 1916, Julean Arnold Papers, Hoover Institution. Cited in Rozanski 1974: 282, and 346, n.4.

60 Between 1914 and 1921, Crane paid Millard about $70,000 on top of an annual personal subsidy of $5,000 which renewed from 1929 to 1935, when Millard was taken on for a second term as an adviser to the Chinese foreign ministry. 'Financial Records' file in Lawrason Riggs file, Charles R. Crane Papers, Washington. Cited in Rozanski 1974: 286, and 346, n.10.

61 See P&TT comments quoted below and note 73.

62 USDS 893.911/133: US Consul-General Edwin. S. Cunningham to A.B. Ruddock, US Legation, Peking, 19 December 1921.

63 J.C. Huston, Confidential Memo to Julean Arnold, Commercial Attaché, Peking, 1 December 1923: Julean Arnold Papers, Hoover Institution, Stanford University, California. The Memo records monthly payments to Millard ($500), Powell ($250), Putnam Weale ($300), A.H. Wearne of Reuters ($250), Grover Clark of the *Peking Leader* ($200), and similar sums to some French newspapers and journalists. Cited in Rozanski 1974: 365, and 379, n.4.

64 Farnsworth 1996: 32–3, 49.

65 Chao 1931: 76.

66 Op. cit.

67 FO 371/13950 [F 4094/2016/10]: Ingram, Peking, to FO, 27 June 1929. This holds a copy of a pamphlet, 'Muzzling the Foreign Press', published by the NCDN, which gives an account of the 1927 ban on page 21.

68 'The Pity of It!': 29 March 1929, NCDN.

69 'Freedom of the Press': NCDN, 11 April 1929.

70 'Freedom of the Press': P&TT, 20 April 1929.

71 'Deportation of Foreign Correspondents': SEPM, 1 May 1929.

72 'Freedom of the Press': NCDN, 11 April 1929.

73 'Nanking and the "NCDN"': NCDN, 6 May 1929.

74 'Aereopagitica': P&TT, 6 May 1929.
75 FO 371/13950 [F 4094/2016/10]: Ingram, Peking, to FO, 27 June 1929, Minute by Frank Ashton-Gwatkin, 13 August 1929.
76 'KMT Action Against Mr. Sokolsky and the NCDN': CWR, 27 April 1929.
77 Powell to J.V.A. MacMurray, 17 May 1929: MacMurray Papers. Cited in Cohen 1978: 169.
78 On 1 Dec. 1945, John B. Powell's son John William revived the CWR in Shanghai. See Chapter 8.
79 Powell 1945: 326.
80 Powell 1945: 160.
81 Chen 1979: 44–5.
82 Lin 1936: 117.
83 'Selling out China': *Peking Gazette*, 18 May 1918.
84 Discussed in USDS 893.911/88: 4 October 1920.
85 NCDN, 4 May 1921. Cited in Goodman 2004: 72.
86 Cohen 1978: 75–9; Goodman 2004: 70.
87 Cohen 1978: 74.
88 In Japan the *Philadelphia Ledger* correspondent was chosen by B.W. Fleisher. Fleisher may also have been asked to recruit the Peking correspondent if a 1921 Foreign Ministry report, in which B.W. Fleisher visited Peking in order 'to set up a correspondence of the *Public Ledger*' is reliable. In which case, Fleisher may have recruited Sokolsky (whose *Ledger* articles were unsigned). *Gaimushō gaikō shiryōkan: gaikoku shinbun, tsūshin kikan oyobi tsūshin-in kankei zakken, tsūshin-in no bu, beikokujin no bu*: (Foreign Ministry records: Miscellaneous matters relating to foreign newspapers, communications agencies and correspondents, correspondents section: American correspondents) 1 1/3/2/ 50–2-2, August 1921. Rozanski rounds out this possibility and illustrates the workings of the *Japan Advertiser* network by outlining Sokolsky's importance to Charles R. Crane and Stanley Hornbeck in undermining Japan's position in China and the Anglo-Japanese Alliance. 'His importance to Crane and Sokolsky was as the part-time correspondent of the Philadelphia *Public Ledger* Syndicate'. Reference in Rozanski 1974: 341, and 358, n.2, citing Sokolsky to Hornbeck 3 June 1921, and Hornbeck to Sokolsky 16 June 1921: Hornbeck Papers, Hoover Institution, Stanford University.
89 'G. Gramada' in JA: 28 August 1920.
90 'G. Gramada' in JA: 13 April 1921. Cited in Cohen 1978: 77.
91 USDS 893.912/6: 8 August 1919.
92 *Gaimushō Gaikō Shiryōkan*: 1–3-2, 46–1-4, January 1922 Report on the *Shangbao*. Cited in Goodman 2004: 66, and 84, n.44.
93 FO 371/13950 [F 2016/2016/10]: Kuomintang's attitude towards NCDN, 23 April 1929.
94 Powell 1945: 13.
95 USDS 811.91293/5: Carl Crow to Nelson T. Johnson and others, 20 December 1918: 'American Propaganda in China'. USDS 893.912/1: Reinsch to Consular Officers in China, 6 December 1918.
96 Yamagoshi Toshihiro online paper (1999). Full reference in Bibliography.
97 Crow 1938: 53.
98 Goodman 2004: 64.
99 'Wanted, An Explanation': P&TT, 25 June 1925.

100 Most of the details of this campaign from 1919 to 1923 are in USDS
811.74/233, 236A; 811.912/161; 811.91293/0, 2, 5–9, 11, 12, 14; 893.911/69.

101 USDS 893.911/41: Carl Crow report on foreign newspapers in China, Carl
Crow to Paul Reinsch, 5 June 1919, p3.

102 USDS 893.911/133: Carl Crow's supplementary report on foreign newspapers in China, 9 September 1921.

103 FO 371/6686 [F 3053/298/23]: Straits Settlement Secret Abstract, note 467.
Director of Military Intelligence to FO, 18 August 1921.

104 'Japanese Papers in China': JC, 1 January 1923.

105 Chao 1931: 65; Ch'en 1937: 9.

106 Gould 1946: 148–9. Nevertheless, following Japan's withdrawal from the
League of Nations, SEPM gave qualified support to international recognition
of Manchukuo (see Chapter 6).

107 Woodhead 1935: 221.

108 Woodhead's arrest, imprisonment, Japanese court martial and repatriation
in 1942 are described in Chapter 7, below.

109 Of Woodhead's eleven books and pamphlets in English, at least seven
supported Japan's position in Manchuria and its China policy generally.
These were: *Leaves from an Editor's Scrapbook* (Tientsin Press Ltd, 1923); *The
Truth About the Chinese Republic* (London: Hurst & Blackett, 1925); *A Selection
of Leading Articles* (Tientsin Press, 1927); *Current Comment on Events in China*
(Shanghai Evening Post and Mercury, 1930); *The Yangtze and its Problems*
(Shanghai Evening Post and Mercury, 1931); *Presenting Japan's side of the Case*
(alongside articles by George Bronson Rea, Shanghai: Japan Association of
China, December 1931) and *A Visit to Manchukuo* (Shanghai Evening Post
and Mercury, 1932). The last, *My Experiences in the Japanese Occupation of
Shanghai*, was published in England in 1943, largely echoes an account given
in a Chatham House lecture in 1942, held in PRO: WO 208/378a, and cited
in Chapter 7, below. Both the 1943 pamphlet and WO 208/378a are cited,
respectively, in Bickers 1999: 267 and Bickers 2004: 386, n.65.

110 Chao 1931: 67.

111 For a list of Missouri School of Journalism alumni in journalism in East Asia
and other members of the 'Missouri Mafia', see Appendix 1, below.

112 One curiosity of *American University Men in China* (AUCS), compiled and
published for the Chinese and foreign membership of the American
University Club of Shanghai in 1936, is that the only Missouri alumnus
listed was John B. Powell, editor of the CWR. Another university with a
strong journalistic tradition, Columbia, had fifty-three alumnae listed.
Other universities with members in the Club were: California (29); Chicago
(25); Cornell (27); Harvard (41); Michigan (27); New York (26); Pennsylvania
(36); Wisconsin (16) and Yale (23) (AUCS 1936: 216–27).

113 Fleisher to Williams, 29 October 1920: Walter Williams Papers, Walter and
Sarah Lockwood Williams Papers, University of Missouri at Columbia.

114 'Presentation of a Japanese Stone Lantern': University of Missouri Bulletin,
21 November 1926, B.W. Fleisher message, 25–6.

115 Walter Williams to B.W. Fleisher, 17 June 1918. Walter and Sarah Lockwood
Williams Papers, University of Missouri at Columbia.

116 B.W. Fleisher to Walter Williams, 27 July 1918. Walter and Sarah Lockwood
Williams Papers, University of Missouri at Columbia.

117 '"Press is Lighthouse Which Leads Men to Sea of Society" Declares Dean Williams at Tokyo Kaikan': JA, 5 August 1927.
118 For MacMurray's low opinion of the foreign press in China, see Rozanski 1974: 376.
119 Although Morgan Young's socialism would not prevent him from writing propaganda for the Guomindang before and after he left Japan in 1936, in the course of which he acknowledged the 'loyalty' of the CCP in joining the united front against Japan, he otherwise did them no favours (Young 1937: 74).
120 Snow 1944 [1937]: 21.
121 CWR, 16 March 1935. Cited in Farnsworth 1996: 181.
122 Edgar Snow to the editors of the *New Republic* and the *Nation*, 1 April 1935, Nym Wales Collection, Hoover Institute, Palo Alto, California. Cited in Farnsworth 1996: 182.
123 On Stanley Hornbeck's views on press and public opinion see his letter to the New Jersey *Call* of 7 March 1930, and his Memorandum, 11 December 1943, Hornbeck Papers, Hoover Institution. Cited in Rozanski 1974: 377, and 381, n.26.
124 Rozanski 1974: 376.
125 Abend 1943: 116.
126 Millard to Stanley Hornbeck, 28 October 1935: Hornbeck Papers, Hoover Institution. Cited in Rozanski 1974: 371-2 and 380, n.14.
127 Goodman 2004: 80.
128 Yu 1999: 201-13.
129 See Sues (1944). Ilona Ralf Sues, a once-trusted aide and confidante of both Tong and W.H. Donald, savages Hollington Tong's publicity machine from the inside, exposes Madame Chiang's vanity and impetuousness and dwells on Donald's reluctant acceptance of such faults for the greater good.
130 See 'Chinese censorship': CWR, 8 June 1935, p.41 and 'How censorship damaged China's cause abroad': CWR 22 June 1935, 113.
131 Lin 1935: 11.

5

Reporting Japan, 1918–1930

This chapter shows the networks of the English-language newspapers of East Asia in action: reporting, debating and campaigning on the key issues of the day, largely in Japan, during the years 1918–30. Although these were busy times for its network in China, for most of the 1920s the *Advertiser* consistently sat on the fence in its reporting of domestic issues in Japan. Therefore the focus is on the debates between the *Japan Chronicle* network and the Foreign Ministry network, largely as demonstrated in the pages of the *Japan Times*.

These alignments changed after 1931, when the *Japan Advertiser* network in China became the Foreign Ministry network's most overt media adversary in East Asia. From 1931 until its sale in October 1940 the *Advertiser* was itself more consistently challenged at home than was the *Chronicle*, as Japanese officialdom put increasing pressure on its journalists and other staff through a variety of agencies: sudden arrest of journalists and translators by the special 'higher' police, the constant presence of police spies, the censor, sudden withdrawal of telephones and uncertainties in the supply of newsprint. At the same time, the *Advertiser* business was threatened by a series of accidents that nearly put it out of business and, in contrast to the domestic pressures outlined above, a group of well-meaning Japanese helped to ensure its survival.

However, compared to the *Chronicle* network in China, the position of the *Advertiser* network there was greatly enhanced from the late 1920s by the advance of Chiang Kai-shek and the promotion of longstanding network figures such as Hollington Tong and Thomas Millard within the Guomindang publicity machine in Nanjing. In Japan, the *Chronicle*, perhaps because it appeared less influential on American perceptions, perhaps because the linchpins of its China network – the *North-China Daily News* and the *Peking & Tientsin Times* – were given such a hard time by the Nanjing regime in terms of postal bans, censorship and staff deportation threats, certainly suffered its share of police spies and censorship. However, the *Chronicle*'s frosty relationship with the British embassy and its location in Kōbe and its eventual accommodation with the Foreign Ministry Information Bureau in 1938 may have made it appear less of a threat to the authorities and therefore helped protect it from the degree of domestic assault suffered by the *Advertiser*.

THE NETWORKS AND THE ISSUES IN THE EARLY 1920S

What sort of coverage of Japan did the English-language newspapers of East Asia provide to their readers in the 1920s? The most consistently debated topics in the period under review were: Japanese militarism, expansion in China, the administration of Korea and the Korean independence movement, Japan's population problem and emigration, naval disarmament, and Japan's political development. In the early 1920s, the networks of the English-language press coalesced and divided around a series of controversies: the Korean Independence risings of 1919–21; the Shaw affair of 1921–22; the campaigns for and against the abrogation of the Anglo-Japanese Alliance in 1919–22; Lord Northcliffe's tour of East Asia and his subsequent 'Watch Japan!' campaign over the winter of 1922; and the Foreign Ministry network's campaign to prevent the 1924 US Immigration Act.

Bubbling under these issues was a range of contentions which impinged on the nature, needs and intentions of Japan and of the Japanese as a nation. From these, we can isolate a group of contemporary notions which the *Japan Times* and most Foreign Ministry network publications treated as truisms, but which the *Advertiser* and the *Chronicle* and their networks treated as contentious. Among these were: that Japan had special interests and natural rights in China and Korea; that Japan and Great Britain were natural allies; that Japan was overpopulated with a concomitant need for overseas expansion or emigration; that in East Asia Japan constituted an oasis of stability and developing democracy and was therefore the natural repository of Western confidence; that Japan was a victim of racial discrimination; and finally that Japan's special traditions and culture made it difficult for her to adopt wholesale various international agreements.

In the spring of 1919, with Matsuoka Yōsuke and John Russell Kennedy managing Japan's publicity at the Paris Conference, Japan's campaign for the insertion of a racial equality clause in the Covenant of the League of Nations was given huge coverage in the Japanese press. In the Foreign Ministry's network, banner headlines in the *Japan Times* and *Seoul Press* detailed Japan's determination to push through this vital change, implying that the racial equality proposal was intended as a universal principle, whereas the aim was to redress an anticipated imbalance in the treatment of Japanese compared to Europeans and Americans in and by the League of Nations, not the betterment of other races than the Japanese.[1]

However, Japan's failure to make this distinction clear and the coincidence of the racial equality proposal with Japan's stern handling of the spring 1919 independence demonstrations in Korea may have backfired on its image among Anglophone readers in East Asia, and among some officials in Whitehall and Washington, although it had no proven influence on the outcome of the racial equality campaign in Paris.

The *Japan Chronicle* dwelt on Japan's severity in quelling the Korean disturbances, flagging its readers with punchy headlines:

LIFE IN A JAPANESE PRISON IN KOREA
SERIOUS CHARGES OF BRUTALITY
STATEMENTS OF RELEASED GIRL STUDENTS
*
GENDARMERIE METHODS IN KOREA
WHAT HAPPENS TO KOREANS WHO TELL TALES

and editorials that drove home the point that while Japan pleaded for racial equality in Paris, Japanese soldiers and 'gendarmes' were firing villages and churches in Korea.[2] The *Japan Times* and the *Seoul Press* countered as best they could, sometimes by claiming to respect the Korean heritage: hence, 'Flogging is an old Korean punishment.'[3]

However, the significance of the *Chronicle* campaign can be partly assessed by the fact that, when the racial equality proposal failed to get a unanimous vote in Paris, the Japanese press ignored the *Chronicle* and said nothing about Japanese activities during the Korean independence movement but directed its fury against Japan's own advocates, Saionji and Makino. A typical broadside read, 'The anger of the nation for this glaring failure of theirs will be as fierce as the onset of a bloodthirsty animal pouncing upon its prey.'[4] From the viewpoint of the *Chronicle*, the *Kokumin Shinbun* may have seemed ill-qualified to voice such opinions as its owner, Tokutomi Sohō, had already been drafted in to manage the official viewpoint in Seoul, but obviously Seoul and Korea were not part of the issue when it came to popular judgements of Japan's effectiveness in Paris.

From 1919 to 1927, Governor General Saitō Makoto took a softer line on the Korean independence movement and the *Seoul Press* began to relax its position of admitting no possible wrong in Japan's rule. One sign of this change came in the pamphlet *The other side of the Korean question: fresh light on some important factors*, which did its best to put a positive interpretation on the destruction of church buildings by Japanese soldiers and police and the infamous massacre at Suwon where twenty-seven men and two women were 'shot down in cold blood' and openly discussed the floggings and torture inflicted on 'agitators'.[5] Fresh consultants, such as H.J. Mullett-Merrick, a sometime adviser to the South Manchuria Railway, and seasoned spokesmen such as Zumoto Motosada were brought in to back up the Japanese line.[6]

In the early 1920s, a war of words erupted between Governor-General Saitō's administration and a group of American missionaries over a group of linked issues: the 'kidnapping' of Prince Yi, the expropriation of Korean land, the 'Tokyo Hotel murder' of Bin Genshoku, the punitive expedition against Koreans sheltering in Jiandao (Chientao) in Manchuria, which would be repeated in 1936, and the continuing severity of the Japanese security forces. These debates and issues were reported and discussed in detail in the *Japan Chronicle*, the *North-China Daily News*, the *Peking & Tientsin Times* and other China papers. The presence of a number of articulate American missionaries keen to make known the excesses of the Japanese 'gendarmes' in Korea led to the *Advertiser* joining the debate as a cautious but persistent participant.[7]

The *Chronicle* and its affiliates did not question the ideological purity of the Korean independence movement. The *Chronicle* gave particular attention to the reports of one American missionary, Dr Frank W. Schofield, on the Japanese encouragement of prostitution in Korea ('Syphilizing the Koreans'),[8] conditions at the West Gate Prison in Seoul, and police-administered floggings.

Initially, the *Japan Times* and *Seoul Press* followed the line taken by most Japanese vernacular papers that the shouters of 'Mansei!' were simply trouble-makers encouraged by foreign missionaries and agitators, and that their cause did not deserve scrutiny. As one vernacular paper declared in June, 'We are fully prepared to keep silent where the national interests are concerned.'[9] The *Japan Times* and *Seoul Press*, which had been set up to meet broader criteria, nevertheless seldom printed the word "independence" without double quotation marks, just as few newspapers in China would print the name "Manchukuo" without quotes in the 1930s. In December 1919, badly stung, the *Seoul Press* referred to a 'Plot by unearthed Christians' to undermine the Japanese administration in Korea.[10] However, six months later the *Seoul Press* changed tack and began blaming the lower bureaucracy for exacerbating Korean grievances: '… it is not difficult to imagine the annoyance and irritation caused to many Koreans by arrogant petty officials. This sort of thing must be stopped by all means, if the Government really wants to win the hearts of the Korean people.'[11]

On 11 July 1920, G.L. Shaw, a British businessman based in Andon (Antung), Manchuria, was arrested by Japanese police for sedition and travelling without a passport. *Kokusai* sat on the news for over a month, finally cabling London in early August that, 'It is not too much to suppose … he was insidiously connected with the conspiracy of Korean agitators.'[12]

The *Chronicle* soon got wind of the story and led a campaign for Shaw's release.[13] Soon a small army of papers joined the fray. The Foreign Ministry network's *Japan Times*, *Herald of Asia*, *China Observer*, *North China Standard*, *Asian Review*, *Far Eastern Review*, *Seoul Press* and *Chicago Daily News* all cried fair. The *Chronicle* network's *Peking & Tientsin Times*, *North-China Daily News*, and Japan's *bête noire*, Putnam Weale, reporting for the *Chronicle* from Andon, and the *North China Star*, and *Peking Leader* all cried foul.[14]

The breadth and passion of the debate heightened international interest in Shaw and the Korean troubles in general. In August *The Times* ran a forthright dispatch from its Peking correspondent: 'Much resentment has been aroused in foreign circles in the Far East at the treatment of Mr Shaw, a British merchant, at Antung …'[15] In the US that autumn, the *Chicago Daily News* had run a story from its Tokyo correspondent, Junius B. Wood (described by the *Chronicle* as 'the *Chicago Daily News-cum Kokusai* correspondent')[16] doubting Shaw's innocence.[17] In

December, *The Times*, *Daily Telegraph* and *Daily Express* all carried reports of Japanese atrocities against Koreans in Jiandao.[18] When the *Japan Advertiser* ventured a criticism of Japanese military tactics against Koreans in Jiandao,[19] the Peking correspondent of *The Times* quoted the *Advertiser* [which] '… in condemning the conduct of the [Jiandao] expedition asks:- "What opinion can be formed by other countries except that this is a campaign of frightfulness, in which murder and massacre are deliberately employed?"'[20]

In April 1920, in the House of Commons Arthur Hayday M.P. urged the government to help Korea bring its case to the League of Nations. In May T.W. Grundy M.P. raised the question of the 'Korean outrages'.[21] Further urgent questions were faced by Cecil Harmsworth in July. In December a 'Friends of Korea' group, composed mostly of Welsh Labour MPs, was formed in the Commons, and on 21 July 1922, two such Friends, Sir R. Newman M.P. and F. Green M.P. questioned Harmsworth about the Jiandao incursions.[22]

In August 1920, a large party of US Congressmen visited Seoul where one of their number, Hugh Hersman, was an appalled witness of police beatings administered to unarmed Koreans. Following this incident, an independence movement memorial was presented to the Congressional party, which the *Chronicle* printed in full.[23] On 25 August Hersman addressed Korean students at the YMCA in Chongno, but the police broke up the meeting, administered beatings and arrested students. Backed up by the US Consul-General, Hersman refused to leave the hall until the students were released.[24] In September a cable from New York reported that 'An unfavourable sentiment has been created by the report of the clash between Mr Hersman and the Police at Seoul. It is expected that the Korean question will be again raised and the position criticized.'[25]

In August 1920, the Foreign Ministry network fought back with 'Asiatic Sinn Fein', an attack on Shaw by Patrick Gallagher in the *Far Eastern Review*. When the *Seoul Press* reprinted the article, Shaw took out a libel action against Gallagher and the *Review*. In loading Shaw's reputation with the pejorative associations of 'Fenian', the *Far Eastern Review* was at one with *Kokusai* and the *China Advertiser* of Tianjin, both of which in August imputed 'Fenian' motives to Shaw in his dealings with Korean 'malcontents'. As the *Chronicle* remarked, such mudslinging was all the odder for the fact that *Kokusai's* manager, John Russell Kennedy, and Patrick Gallagher, were both Irishmen.[26]

Back in Whitehall, on 22 September, C.H. Bentinck minuted that Shaw's prolonged detention was 'creating a very bad impression on British public opinion which may create an unfavourable reaction in the friendly relations existing between the two countries which H.M.G. are most anxious to avoid'.[27] In October the *New Statesman* warned, 'This country is not entitled to demand that Japan shall set Korea free … But we are entitled to say that her administration of one of her provinces is of such a kind, in our opinion, as to make it impossible for us to remain her ally.' [28] A Foreign Office minute described the article as, 'A very fair statement of the actual state of affairs' and urged its circulation to the Anglo-Japanese Alliance committee.[29] In an editorial headlined 'The End of a Chapter', the *Chronicle* pointed to the failure of the Anglo-Japanese Alliance to restrain Japan's hand in the Far East.[30]

On 8 December 1920, the accumulation of the Shaw case, Japan's administration in Korea and other incidents surfaced in a Memorandum by Frank Ashton-Gwatkin of the Far East Department, Foreign Office. Ashton-Gwatkin surveyed the recent history of Korea, citing accounts in the *Chronicle* and other local English-language newspapers of Japanese cruelty in East Asia and the South Seas, and concluded:

> In commenting on the ruthless record of Japanese colonization, it is unfair to draw too strict a parallel with the supposed canons of occidental nations. In the first place, as already pointed out, the idea of justice is simply non-existent; and so to a considerable extent is the idea of individual responsibility. For a whole village to be burned as punishment for the crime of one of its inhabitants is to the Oriental a natural vindication of outraged authority; for it is the community and not the individual which is the responsible unit. But it is these very excuses for the Japanese which call attention to the wide discrepancy between their ideals and our own, and to the doubtful wisdom of our lending the prestige of our good name to an ally whose way of thinking and acting is so essentially different from ours. Already, history regards Great Britain and the Anglo-Japanese Alliance as largely responsible for the handing over of Korea to Japan. Is our support, consciously or unconsciously, going to permit Japanese rule and its stern consequences to encroach further upon China and Siberia? The 'Bushido' propaganda has done much to convince us that ... the warrior's ideal is courtesy, gentleness and consideration. This impression has been supported by certain aspects of the Russo-Japanese war ... but it is contradicted by all expert experience of the ways of Japanese bureaucracy at home, and still more by the record of Japanese military government abroad.[31]

The *Chronicle* had derided the West's fascination with bushido since 1906. Now Ashton-Gwatkin contrasted 'Bushido propaganda' with a *Chronicle* report that 'old men, women and children, were beaten, cut down with swords, and run through with bayonets' at Pyengyang [Heijo]'.[32] Following Shaw's release in the summer of 1921, the *Chronicle* wondered aloud:

> We are not aware whether the liberation of Mr Shaw owed anything to the negotiations which were in progress for the renewal of the Anglo-Japanese Alliance, but we could well understand that if a case so discreditable to the Japanese authorities received due publicity in England, it would make an alliance impossible.[33]

In June *The Times* appeared to be toning down its Korean coverage in line with the more palatable images of Japan featured in its seventh

Japan Supplement. However, the controversy did not fade. In September *The Times* felt bound to comment on the fall out from the Shaw affair: 'Japanese Detention of Mr Shaw. British diplomacy criticized', but during this period of uncertainty for the future of the Alliance, despite the evident disapproval of some of its correspondents in East Asia for Japan's conduct in Korea and Japan's treatment of Shaw, the paper soon returned to its generally supportive attitude towards Britain's ally in East Asia.[34]

THE ANGLO-JAPANESE ALLIANCE RENEWAL ISSUE, 1920–22

While the *Chronicle* network ran adverse reports on Japan's administration of Korea and elsewhere and called for Shaw's release, it campaigned against the renewal of the Anglo-Japanese Alliance alongside its rival, the *Japan Advertiser* and its network. One major plank in the campaign against renewal was the claim that the Alliance obliged Britain to go to war against America if America were to attack Japan. In 1919–20 the *Advertiser* broadcast this danger in numerous articles, but early in 1921 the paper followed *The Times* and printed in full the terms of the Peace Commission Treaty which appeared to exempt Britain from fighting alongside Japan against America. Having dismissed this danger, some *Advertiser* articles in early 1921 even 'implied a certain support' for Alliance renewal, but the paper soon swung back into opposition.[35]

The *Japan Times* called for renewal of the Alliance and blackened Shaw's reputation in an effort both to justify his treatment and separate the issues. As for the Shanghai press and Millard:

> The average Shanghai dispatch dealing with anything that has anything to do with either Sino-Japanese or American-Japanese relations is usually so maliciously far from the facts that it is invariably disregarded by those who know, but, unfortunately, the average newspaper reader abroad has not been made familiar with the 'Shanghai liar' who appeared during the Russo-Japanese War and has been on the job ever since.[36]

Just as the *Chronicle* commonly referred to Zumoto Motosada's press office during the Siberian Intervention as the 'Vladivostok lie factory', so Millard became the 'Shanghai Liar' in the newspaper Zumoto had helped found twenty-four years earlier.

Millard had long seen the Alliance as the main threat to the Open Door policy and American interests in China. His most radical argument against renewal was that the Alliance risked bringing Britain, the Dominions and America into open warfare, to the benefit of Japan and Bolshevik Russia. Millard's patron, Charles R. Crane, conveyed this concern to Woodrow Wilson in the spring of 1920 and again in March 1921.[37] Learning through private contacts that Lloyd George was looking for a pretext to annul the Alliance, Crane and Millard lined up the campaign against renewal. The *Chronicle* led the campaign against renewal in Japan, while in China, all the English-language newspapers and journals in the *Chronicle* and *Advertiser* networks, spoke against renewal. In the Foreign Ministry network, the sole exception in supporting the abrogation of the Alliance was Zumoto Motosada's *Herald of Asia*, which maintained that Japan could manage perfectly well without it.

When Lloyd George announced in December 1920 that the question would be discussed the following June in London at a Conference of the Dominions, Crane saw his chance and sent Putnam Weale on an international lobbying drive. With introductions from Crane and the Chinese government, Weale lobbied Prime Minister Meighen of Canada, Senator Borah, Medill McCormick of the Senate Foreign Relations Committee, Secretary of State Hughes and the leaders of Australia and New Zealand at the Dominion Conference in London. The entire campaign was predicated on the need to contain Japanese power in East Asia. In early May 1921 the *China Weekly Review* ran a series of attacks on the Alliance. In June and July, while Putnam Weale held the front in London, Millard barnstormed America warning in speeches and articles of outright war between Britain and America if the Alliance continued.[38]

The Foreign Ministry followed the *Advertiser* network's campaign closely and did what it could to counter-attack. In April 1921, the *Japan Times* reported Weale's being sent abroad by the Chinese government (Crane's help was not mentioned), to present the case for having Japan 'thrown out of' Shandong, and quoted H.G.W. Woodhead in the *Peking & Tientsin Times*, which was also campaigning for the termination of the Alliance, to the effect that China was not yet ready to resume control of the areas administered by foreign powers.[39]

In May, the *Japan Times* published without comment a *Kokusai*-AP dispatch from New York, 'That China is seeking the support of public opinion in the United States to prevent the renewal of the Anglo-Japanese Treaty has been declared by Bertram Lenox Simpson (Putnam Weale) … in a public statement.'[40] During the Dominion Conference, the 'Lenox Simpson' byline headed numerous *Daily Telegraph* articles blaming the Alliance for the 'turmoil and intrigue which exists in China' and contending that it should be allowed to lapse.[41]

In Britain that summer, the case for renewal and for trusting Japan to maintain the integrity of China was argued in *The Observer* and *The Times* by J.O.P. Bland. Bland (1863–1945), an erstwhile *Times* correspondent in China, had been an adviser to the Foreign Ministry during the war with Russia and would be taken on by Japan again at the Washington Conference of 1921–22.[42] In three China books (1912, 1921, 1932), and in his *Times* reports, Bland helped lay the groundwork for the case that the Foreign Ministry network would prosecute throughout the 1930s: the inherent venality of the Chinese as a race; the hopelessness of attempting a Chinese political solution to China's problems; and the need for a strong, modernizing power to sort out China's chaos. In June Bland asked in a letter to *The Times*:

> Are the activities of the military party in Japan likely to be diminished if the Anglo-Japanese Alliance is now denounced? Are the growing forces of intelligent Liberalism in that country likely to be discouraged if Britain and America combine to condemn this proud and sensitive nation to isolation and a policy of coercion?

Discussing Bland's letter, the *Chronicle* argued that treating Japan as if its foreign policy was the product of a group of over-sensitive children was insulting to liberals and militarists alike, and suggested that 'any self-respecting Japanese would tell Mr Bland to take his Anglo-Japanese Alliance to a warmer place than Kobe is at the present time'. In its refusal to accept the argument that non-renewal would endanger the liberal tendency, the *Chronicle* was at one with many in the Foreign Office.[43]

In Shanghai, where the *Far Eastern Review* shared an office with the local branch of *Kokusai*, George Bronson Rea and Patrick Gallagher argued strongly for renewal. Miles Lampson noted that 'One must bear in mind that the writer is the servant of Japan' but he liked one of Rea's articles enough to have it typeset for the China Print.[44]

Meanwhile, Millard's activities continued to raise hackles at the *Japan Times*.

> Tommy Millard, the discoverer recently of the Anglo-French-Italian plot to dismember China, is continuing to have nightmares, and this time he is spending money on telegrams to President Harding which disclose a wicked Anglo-Japanese plot against the United States underlying the Anglo-Japanese Alliance. Of course, it is not Millard's own money that he is spending, but in these hard times it seems rather a pity to waste any coin in such hopelessly foolish propaganda as Millard persists in.[45]

Coming not long after Lord Curzon had given Japan formal notice that renewal could not be taken to be automatic, such banter failed to conceal the alarm felt in Tokyo. In the spring and summer of 1921, Britain approached Japan with a view to adapting the Alliance to a wider range of Pacific issues at a Conference to be held in Washington that winter. The writing was on the wall.

The prospect of a decisive meeting that winter galvanized the debate in the public sphere. Among the most worried souls in Tokyo was John Russell Kennedy, whose career depended on his capacity to keep at bay just those notions and images of Japan that had been highlighted in Ashton-Gwatkin's Memorandum. To the *Chronicle* and the *Advertiser*, Kennedy's position in the Foreign Ministry campaign for renewal had been compromised by his role in the virulent anti-British and anti-Alliance campaigns of 1915–16 which had followed British protests over the Twenty-One Demands. These had been followed by a secret agreement between Britain and Japan supporting Japan's claim to Shandong and the Pacific Islands in return for the withdrawal of Japan's opposition to China entering the war on the side of the Allies. Thereafter, *Japan Times* editorials had consistently supported the Alliance but the *Chronicle* frequently reminded its readers of its rival's 'curious change of tone'. On 16 August 1921, *The Times* correspondent in Tokyo, J.N. Penlington, raked over these embers in an almost acid assessment of Japanese opportunism:

> Japan has ardently desired to renew the Anglo-Japanese Alliance, because during the war that pact did not seriously restrict her efforts to obtain special and exclusive privileges in China. The virtual occupation of Shantung [Shandong] and many of the demands presented to China in 1915 apparently were not interpreted by the British Government as being incompatible with the terms of the Alliance. The Japanese are therefore anxious to renew an agreement which has proved so elastic.

Penlington's mysterious loss of commitment to Japan's cause in China reduced the *Chronicle* to actually defending British policy: as it pointed out, the British Government *had* objected to Japan's pursuit of these objects, and Britain had suffered for this protest in the Japanese press in a campaign supported by the *Japan Times*.[46]

The Anglo-Japanese Alliance came to an end at the Washington Conference that winter. Japan became party to a multinational treaty and agreed, in common with the other powers, to limitations on her naval power. However, the sincerity of Japan's agreement was questioned the following April, when a *Times* leader commented on revisions to Japanese naval policy made because 'supersession of the Anglo-Japanese Alliance compels Japan to meet future international crises single-handed'.[47] Soon the Foreign Office News Department had organized representations to 'the representative of the "Times", who calls here every day'.[48] Inside a week, a dithyrambic headlined *The Mystery of Japan* appeared, beginning, 'Today, in the midst of the spring in the Far Eastern Islands, when the cherry trees are in full blossom …'[49] Whatever calm had been restored by these effusions was undone within a week by an article published in the *Daily Mail* on 18 April 1922.

WATCH JAPAN!
SOME SIMPLE WORDS OF WARNING.

"OFFICIAL DENIALS"

By VISCOUNT NORTHCLIFFE

FOR what purpose are the great Japanese home and over-seas army and the great Japanese fleet being maintained?

Why are the Japanese people being taxed more severely than any other nation for the support of armaments?

The Washington Conference does not change the situation as much as we have been trying to think.

... We can hardly suppose that the Japanese have changed their plan for mastering China as the result of the Washington Conference. I venture to prophesy that they will merely alter their tactics and adapt them to the new circumstances.

... A close study of Japanese diplomacy indicates that the war party of Japan is as indifferent in its policy to the keeping of treaties as are many private Japanese traders in the regard of other people's patents and trademarks.

*   *   *   *   *

When calling attention to any matter that affects Japan we have always to remember that hourly, daily, weekly – morning, noon and night – Japanese propaganda is at work in the form of bribed newspapers, propaganda news agencies, propaganda plays, and propaganda films ...[50]

In 1910, Northcliffe had discussed with G.E. Morrison, *The Times* correspondent in Peking, the need to check Japanese power in East Asia.[51] Now Northcliffe finally made good on his earlier assurances in an article that synthesized the worst aspects of Japan's international relations in the previous decade: ambivalence during the Great War, perfidy over the Twenty-One Demands ('Fortunately, journalistic enterprise placed these demands before the world and they were frustrated, but they revealed the mind of Japan'), and a cynical indifference to international agreements. As proudly stated over the author's byline, the article ran simultaneously, in the *New York World*, *Sydney Sun*, *Melbourne Herald*, and the Calcutta *Englishman*, and 'such parts of it as are allowed to appear' in the *Osaka Mainichi Shinbun* and the *Tokyo Nichi-Nichi Shinbun*. On 19 April, Northcliffe's article appeared in *The Times* under a slightly different headline:

WATCH JAPAN!
PLAN TO CONTROL CHINA.

"OFFICIAL DENIALS"

In the *Contemporary Review*, H.A. Thompson put much of the blame for the 'Watch Japan!' campaign on Robert Young. During his November 1921 tour of Japan, just before the Washington Conference, Northcliffe had visited Young in Kōbe,

... and unquestionably took away a good many of his ideas ... Lord Northcliffe came home and wrote a series of inflammatory articles ... It was a triumph for Young, who probably managed to do more harm to Japan in his few hours with Northcliffe than has ever been done before. The obscure editor of a local journal ... when he got the ear of Lord Northcliffe, with his prodigious control over the British Press, it enabled Robert Young in one act to place his ideas before the whole English world.[52]

In May 1922, the *Asahi Shinbun* referred to Northcliffe's article as 'a nasty anti-Japanese composition that might have been written by Young of the *Japan Chronicle*' and the *Jiji* referred obliquely to the scaremongering anti-Japanese influence of 'a certain Scotchman resident in the Far East for many years'.[53]

Robert Young was only one of the local experts Northcliffe consulted during his tour of East Asia. In Shimonoseki, Northcliffe also engaged in discussions with the ferociously anti-Japanese Tim Conroy, otherwise known as Taid O'Conroy. In Tokyo he briefly met (and resolved to replace) *The Times* Tokyo correspondent, J.N. Penlington. In China, Northcliffe met *The Times* correspondent in Peking, David Fraser, 'who, when reproached with not keeping that paper informed regarding British sentiments towards Japanese policy in the Far East, produced a cable from the foreign editor's office instructing him to cease criticizing our Japanese allies'[54] and talked to the *Morning Post* correspondent and editor of the *Peking & Tientsin Times*, H.G.W. Woodhead, on the train between Peking and Tientsin.[55] In Shanghai, Northcliffe consulted O.M. Green, *The Times* correspondent and editor of the *North-China Daily News*, the *New York Times* correspondent and Foreign Ministry consultant, Frederick Moore, and William Turner, Reuters Manager for East Asia. Throughout his tour of Korea, the press baron's guide, thoughtfully supplied by the Foreign Ministry, was Honda Masujiroh.

Thus, Lord Northcliffe was exposed to a variety of opinions on Japanese military and naval ambitions and the future of the Anglo-Japanese Alliance, hearing from advisers to the Foreign Ministry and its network, and from working journalists associated with the *Japan Chronicle* network. But on 16 July, even before these discussions, Northcliffe had given an interview to the Reuters correspondent in Hong Kong, in which he explained that over the last two years he had come to the conclusion that the Anglo-Japanese Alliance had 'outrun its usefulness'. In a variation on the Twenty-One Demands controversy six years earlier, John Russell Kennedy and *Kokusai* did their ill-judged best to deny the accuracy of Northcliffe's statement but the truth came out and *Kokusai*'s reputation and Japan's credibility took another beating. As Northcliffe wrote in his 'Watch Japan' article: 'And as for official and ambassadorial "official denials", let the public study them in detail ... The result of that study supplies convincing evidence of their insincerity and worthlessness.'

REPORTING THE LABOUR AND SOCIALIST MOVEMENTS IN JAPAN

Was there a 'purposive and collective attempt by a number of people to change individuals or societal institutions and structures' in post-war Japan?[56] This definition of a social movement was not one that the English-language newspapers could employ too openly in its columns, given the fate of the *Kobe Herald* in 1918, but nevertheless they did their best to account for the unusual variety and vigour of extra-parliamentary activity in these post-war years. How did the

English-language papers define these movements? How did they rate their prospects for acceptance and influence?

Reporting the labour movement

In 1918, the *Japan Chronicle* reported a wave of strikes in collieries, mills, the docks, factories, steelworks and shipyards, in post offices, and on the railways. These were usually described in lengthy round-ups under such headings as *Labour Troubles in Japan* or *Industrial Unrest in Japan*. While the reports from other cities and far-flung areas were usually translations from the vernacular press, reports of industrial action in Kōbe and Tokyo came from *Chronicle* eyewitnesses and freelance writers. The *Chronicle* worked hard to do justice to the variety and volume of industrial protest in 1919. Headings were often perfunctory: *Today's Strikes* was a favourite. Strikes, lockouts, protests, negotiations, fresh claims, demands, management resignations, instances of sabotage, go-slows and dismissals were all surveyed in detail. The *Chronicle* seemed to delight in intricate, blow-by-blow accounts of local strikes, particularly the Mitsubishi Dockyard strike of 1920–21 and the even longer Kawasaki Shipyard strike involving Kōbe's 'Christian labourite', Kagawa Toyohiko. In July 1921 the Fukiai, Kōbe branch of the *Nihon Rōdō Sōdōmei* (Japan Federation of Labour), came under the spotlight when Bertrand Russell, then visiting Robert Young in Kōbe, attended a meeting and was cheered wildly for a short speech of encouragement in English.[57]

The *Chronicle* knew where it stood, but the *Japan Times* seemed to be searching for an appropriate line to take on these disputes. It often adopted a patrician conceit in its coverage of labour disputes, writing as if it too was to the manor born. The paper could hardly fail to notice the strikes of 1919, but in one whole-page survey only managed to ascribe the protests to 'the rapid advance of prices'.[58] A year later, the paper urged enlightened self-interest: 'A full dinner pail and a contented mind is a poor field for the so-called dangerous thought. The capitalists will find it to their interests to aid in the work.'[59]

The *Chronicle* was more sympathetic to the strikers' cause, but by the summer of 1919 the task of reporting them may have become wearisome. A strike by male operatives at the Hinode Spinning Company in the summer of 1919 was reported thus, 'Strikes have become such a fashion among the Japanese workers that they are ready to start one on the least provocation ... They did not forget to demand, at the same time, an increase of wages, thus following the "general trend of affairs".'[60]

In 1919–20, the *Chronicle* began publishing a series of reports headed *The Socialist and Labour Movement in Japan* under the byline 'An American Sociologist', or simply 'Sociologist', the pseudonym of a Russian activist, Ivan Kozlov.[61] The articles would be published unchanged in book form the following April.[62] In an advertisement for the compilation, the *Chronicle* emphasized its topicality:

While the ordinary reader of newspapers is aware that there is a militant Socialist movement in Japan ... few realize that the labour movement has reached the point of organization shown in this pamphlet or that political views and ideas which are so widespread in Europe and America have obtained such a footing in Japan.[63]

Kozlov's articles surveyed socialist doctrine, as well as 'the co-operative conception in general, which may be moderate Socialism, Communism, Syndicalism, or Anarchism' and its popularity in Japan, and surveyed the extent and efficiency of labour organization in Japan. Kozlov certainly thought in terms of a movement, and he was optimistic, without getting too specific, about systemic change:

> ... the socialist movement – in one form or another – will continue its growth more rapidly and more irresistibly, and it would seem probable that the day is approaching when it will occupy the same part in the councils of the Japanese people as it already occupies among the nations of Europe.[64]

However, in the same article the author noted that because of increasing attacks on socialists and striking workers by the membership of patriotic societies 'the immediate prospect is not a very pleasing one'.[65]

The articles show how close the *Chronicle* was to radical thinkers in Japan. The *Chronicle* published Kozlov's articles, translated and published Kagawa's novel and reported labour activism and organization in detail. Robert Young knew when Ōsugi was in Kōbe, the *Chronicle* covered the development of labour unions and the activities of the union organizers Suzuki Bunji and activists like Kagawa, as well as the efforts of industry to contain the protests, particularly Shibusawa Eiichi's *Kyōchōkai* (Harmonization Society). The labour unions received a better press from the *Chronicle* than did the *Kyōchōkai*, although when Tokonami Takejirō first mooted the *Kyōchōkai* in 1919 the *Chronicle* was amused but not hostile.[66] However, when Suzuki Bunji resisted its overtures, the *Chronicle* dismissed the *Kyōchōkai* on the grounds that it was Japanese exceptionalism and paternalism dressed up as social concern:

> The theory – manufactured strictly for foreign consumption – is that Japan is so close to the feudal system that its great traditions of responsibility still survive to create a family warmth in every employment unknown elsewhere. How far this is from the truth it needs no profound knowledge of modern Japan to understand.[67]

However, the *Japan Times* quoted with approval the *Keizai zasshi* view,

> It is clear then, that it is not fair to apply in this country a verbatim translation of labour legislation obtaining in Europe and America to factory workers only and that this by no means tends to solidify the foundation of the national existence.[68]

There was no mistaking the *Chronicle's* partiality. Reporting the growth of the railway workers' union, the paper declared, 'This despotic attitude of the railway authorities has had the effect of cowing the weak-kneed into secession from the Union, but on the whole the official action has affected the organization little.'[69] The *Chronicle* described the history, current organization, public meetings and internal politics of the *Yūaikai*, and applauded its involvement in the movement for universal suffrage. The paper welcomed Suzuki Bunji's return from a largely cere- monious role at the Peace of Paris. In the spring of 1921, Suzuki assured the *Chronicle's* Tokyo correspondent, 'I do not hate capitalists personally or individually, but I curse the system.' The labour movement was '... the forerunner or central army for the emancipation of humanity and the amelioration of the present unjust system'.[70]

The *Japan Times* adopted a dignified stance. It did not interview Suzuki or criticize him overtly, other than to refer to him as 'the Samuel Gompers of Japan', but his return from Paris was recorded with a photo- graph, an accolade of sorts, since the paper published so few. However, by the summer of 1921, the *Japan Times* was warming to Suzuki's 'moderate' approach.[71]

The *Chronicle* carried six interviews with Suzuki in 1921.[72] His home in 'a pleasant suburb' of Tokyo and his appearance were given sympathetic treatment. 'One thinks ordinarily, I believe, that foreign clothes on a Japanese make an apparently large man look smaller, but in Mr Suzuki's case there seems to be no minimizing of his stature and avoirdupois ...'[73] At the same time, the *Chronicle* acted as a defender of the faith: any will- ingness to compromise with paternalism met with sharp criticism. However, the *Chronicle* accepted Suzuki's pragmatic surrender over one strike: 'The explanation is, of course, that Mr Suzuki ... did not fancy the prospect of a useless martyrdom and found that Japan is different from France or England.'[74]

The *Chronicle* was also enthusiastic about the Christian labour activist and writer, Kagawa Toyohiko, who made his home in the slums of Kōbe. The *Chronicle* veteran, Thomas Satchell, translated and the *Chronicle* published Kagawa's novel *Across the Death-Line* (*Shisen o koete*) in 1921. The *Chronicle* publicized Kagawa's activities and his periodical, and railed against his February 1920 prosecution for an article in the journal *Kaihō*. To the *Chronicle*, Kagawa was more than a local hero:

> It is men of the type of Mr Kagawa who help towards a realization of the needs and to an understanding of how to remedy them. They are social physicians ... The authorities should rather sit at their feet and listen to what they have to say than shadow them and suspect them and worry about their dangerous thoughts.[75]

Kagawa gave three extensive interviews to the *Chronicle* in the summer of 1921.[76] In the first of these, his credentials were listed as, 'labour unionist, socialist, democrat, Christian and social worker'. In the third interview Kagawa vented his frustration over the treatment of the Kawasaki shipyard workers, declaring. 'We are the vanguard of the army of democracy, whose triumph means the end of unjust privilege both industrial and political … And this struggle will not end until democracy is achieved.'

In July's *Japan Times* coverage of the dockyard strikes, Kagawa was more prosaically 'a Socialist leader'. In August his role as publisher of *Rōdō Shinbun* and his arrest elicited two paragraphs in seventeen pages on the Kōbe situation. To the *Japan Times* the Kōbe strikers exhibited 'a lack of appreciation of actual economic conditions … that permission to them to regulate any part of the ship-building industry would be suicidal on the part of the employers'.[77] The paper urged the Minister of Home Affairs, Tokonami Takejirō, to crack down on the 'instigators of troubles',[78] an attitude which squared with statements by Tokonami that working men who took industrial action were the dupes of political activists.

In its reports and features, the *Chronicle* came as close to accepting socialist truisms as the *Japan Times* came to accepting Japan's conservative traditions. A *Chronicle* account of unionization among post office workers began, 'It is admitted on all hands that the best way for ensuring the betterment of labourers is for these labourers to organize labour unions through which to assert their rights', as if such a strategy was beyond dispute. Announcing the inauguration of a 'Japanese Labour Party' the *Chronicle* summarized its policies as, '… the enforcement of the universal suffrage system and the destruction of the capitalistic political parties'.[79]

Although the average *Chronicle* reader was probably closer to 'the capitalistic classes' than those bent on their destruction, they seem to have borne these assumptions without protest, even though foreign interests suffered considerable disruption in Kōbe and Ōsaka. Reporting industrial action at Lever Brothers and Dunlop Rubber in Kōbe, the *Chronicle* told its readers that the strikers saw these factories as 'very useful for experimenting upon, as it will only be foreigners who will suffer'.[80]

In the 1920s, the *Chronicle* seemed to lose heart, as 'the growing economic depression seems to have almost broken the spirit of Labour, which rose so high last year'. The *Chronicle* sympathized with the government's position between the rock of subsidizing capitalism to stave off unemployment and the hard place of holding up prices.[81] Later in the 1920s, the *Chronicle* bewailed the lack of progress in the labour movement.

Reporting the socialist movement
Newspapers need personalities, and one who attracted the attention of most until his murder in 1923 was the radical Ōsugi Sakae, whose unconventional private life and fiery speeches always provided good copy. A typical *Chronicle* report would have Ōsugi being led away by two or three policemen as soon as he rose to speak at a meeting. This story

would be leavened with references to Ōsugi's tangled love life: 'In one corner of the hall a fight arose between Mr Osugi Sakaye, the Socialist who gained much notoriety in connection with the 'Free Love' affair, and a workman, and this soon developed into a contest between the Socialist and a dozen guardians of law, culminating in the eviction of Osugi, protesting and fulminating.'[82] The most tenuous link that could be made with the newsworthy socialist was brought into the picture: 'Mr Osugi Sakaye [whose] name has acquired greater notoriety since Miss Kamachika, his sweetheart, made an unsuccessful attempt to murder him last year.'[83]

The *Japan Times* affected an amused tolerance for Ōsugi's 'antics' and frequently attributed his behaviour to drink.[84] Whether or not such accusations were justified, the reference 'apparently intoxicated' appeared quite frequently in descriptions of political events in the paper in these years. Rowdy Diet members in general and the *Kigensetsu* marchers involved in violent clashes with the police were tarred with the brush of intemperance.[85] The paper hesitated to accuse the police of suppressive behaviour: 'His speech was so violent the police authorities ordered the dissolution of the meeting.'[86] The *Chronicle* was quick to point to the heavy-handedness of the 'defenders of capital' but it sympathized with the policeman's lot when they struck for higher wages.

The *Chronicle* does not seem to have been much inhibited by a fear of the censor in its discussions of the socialist movement. In late 1921, 'Sociologist' provided *Chronicle* readers with a breezy comparison of Christianity and Communism.[87] An analysis of a philosopher detected 'Socialism under the guise of Buddhism'.[88] The *Chronicle* urged participation. Socialists should take part in mainstream politics: 'men to whom democracy and freedom are not mere political catchwords, men whose opposition to militarism and bureaucracy is genuine, will give a new interest to Japanese political affairs, and perhaps even galvanize into life some of the old political parties'.[89]

Clearly, socialism was far more than a newsworthy topic at the *Chronicle* in these years. The paper covered the full range of socialist politics: meetings, splits, arrests, scares and plots were reported frequently and in detail. In 1921 the *Chronicle's* Tokyo correspondent interviewed Sakai Toshihiko on a range of issues including the Siberian intervention, proletarian culture, the married state and the situation of tenant farmers.[90] The *Chronicle* also followed the fortunes of female socialists, especially big names like Itō Noe and Yamakawa Kikue, and the 'Red Waves' (*Sekirankai*) grouping, providing *Chronicle* readers in these years with an unusually rounded picture of the women's movement.

The *Chronicle* demonstrated a well-informed sense of the links between the different movements it reported: for example, the radicalization and change of name of the *Yūaikai* to the *Nihon Rōdō Sōdōmei* in 1919.[91] The *Chronicle* acknowledged that the government might well

Above: Key figures in the Foreign Ministry network, from left: Shibusawa Eiichi, Amō Eiji, Shiratori Toshio, Iwanaga Yūkichi, Furuno Inosuke. **Below:** Key presidents of the *Japan Times*: Zumoto Motosada, John Russell Kennedy, Tanaka Tōkichi, Ashida Hitoshi and Toshi Gō.

Left: November 1940, the *Japan Times* moves into the Japan Advertiser building in Kojima-ku. **Right:** The Yokohama Specie Bank Building, 24 The Bund, Shanghai, home to the *Far Eastern Review*, editor George Bronson Rea (left). Right: Captain Francis Brinkley, editor of the *Japan Mail*.

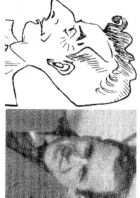

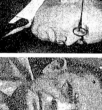
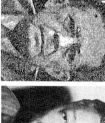

Key players in the
Advertiser **network in China
(from left):** Thomas F. Millard,
Charles R. Crane, Carl Crow,
John B. Powell, Hollington Tong.

Middle row from left:
Clarence Kuangson Young, C.V.
Starr, and the *Shanghai Evening
Post and Mercury* editors
Theodore O.T. 'T.O.T.' Thackery
and Randall Gould.

Bottom row from left:
George Sokolsky, Hallett Abend,
H.J. Timperley
and Harold Isaacs.

Ten Missouri University School of Journalism alumni and their mentors, Tokyo, 13 November 1921. Front from left: Morris Harris, unknown, Hugh Byas, Walter Williams, B.W. Fleisher, Henry Kinyon, Vaughn Bryant, two unknowns. Back from left: John Morris, Rheinhardt Egger, unknown, James McClain, Glen Babb, Mrs Alfonso Johnson, Alfonso Johnson, unknown, John Casey, Duke N. Parry. Courtesy University Archives, University of Missouri-Columbia, USA.

Above: The *Japan Chronicle's* three editors: Robert Young (1891–1922), Arthur Morgan Young (1922–36), and Edwin Allington Kennard (1936–40).

Right: The Japan Chronicle Building in Sannomiya, Kōbe, early 1930s. Layout: presses, ground floor; accounts, advertising, editor, newsroom, first and second floors; library, third floor. Courtesy H.S. Williams Collection, at the National Library, ACT, Australia.

Below, from left: Ernest T. Bethell of the *Korea Daily News*, championed in the *Chronicle*, H.G.W. Woodhead of the *Peking & Tientsin Times* and *Shanghai Evening Post and Mercury*, Lord Northcliffe (Alfred Harmsworth) and Taid O'Conroy (Tim Conroy). Northcliffe's April 1922 'Watch Japan' campaign may have been influenced by Robert Young, whom he visited in Kōbe in 1921, although Northcliffe also talked to Conroy (far right) as well as Woodhead and O.M. Green when he visited China.

Left: Banzais at the Greater East Asia Newspaper Conference, Tokyo, 17–19 November 1943.

The *Nippon Times* leads the press of Greater East Asia: anti-clockwise, *Nippon Times*, 23 December 1943; *Malai Sinpo*, Kuala Lumpur, 18 June 1944; the *Tribune*, Manila, 15 April 1942; the *Syonan Times*, Singapore, 21 February 1942, and the *Hongkong News*, 12 February 1942.

The pack… (right): April 1934, Amō Eiji delivers the Amō doctrine to the Tokyo press corps **… and the inside track:** centre right, Wilfrid Fleisher, *Japan Advertiser* and *New York Herald Tribune*, interviews Matsuoka Yōsuke, July 1940. Below right, Randall Gould, *Shanghai Evening Post and Mercury* and *Christian Science Monitor*, with Chiang Kai-shek, 1940.

Above right: Miles Vaughn, United Press, meets Shidehara Kiijūrō, c.1926, and (**left**) a contemporary postcard warns of the dangers of openhandedness in international relations.

The Japan Times & Advertiser news room, 1941. The two staff identified here were the Eurasians Jimmy Young and Trevor Gauntlett. Young is at the main table, eyes down, facing the camera. To his left, Gauntlett holds a cigarette. Young later served in China with the Japanese army. Gauntlett worked for the *Chronicle* in Kōbe as a translator.

SHORTSIGHTEDNESS

PREJUDICE

CREATE A WRONG VISION

AND HAUGHTINESS

RELIEF FUND

OF OTHERWISE TERRIBLE DISASTER

Above: With the departure of O.M. Green and the installation of Edwin Haward as editor, the *North-China Daily News* begins a belated accommodation with Chinese nationalism and the Guomindang: Sapajou cartoon reprinted (with not a little satisfaction) in the *China Weekly Review*, 17 August 1931.

Right: *The Japan Chronicle* runs a coded reference to the plagiarizing habits of the *China Press* in the early 1920s. To decipher, read every seventh word starting with the last, 'tomorrow'.

He is going to give his exclusive attention to study of foreign markets, it was disclosed in a brief announcement, calling on his Far Eastern agencies. A report circulated to-day and given to him this evening charging that he intends to steal a march in Michigan presidential primaries will be answered, he said, in the press.

"My eyes," he added, "are on China. It is the big country of to-morrow."

'keep the old order intact' but warned that if 'Japanese labour is kept in leading-strings, and its rights of combination and independent action circumscribed, Japan will come to be regarded in foreign countries as a hopelessly reactionary country, and any development of the principle of racial equality will be impossible'.[92] This conflation of the issues and clear appeal to pressure from abroad (*gaiatsu*) was a gambit the *Chronicle* used frequently during Japan's attempt to insert a Racial Equality clause in the Covenant of the League of Nations.

The spirit of opposition is evident in the *Chronicle's* reporting of the police treatment of socialists and those who appeared to harbour 'dangerous thoughts'. 'The Suppression of Socialism' was a common lead in the 1920s. The *Chronicle* derided the heavy hand of officialdom: 'Sunday Politics in Tokyo. Police make themselves Unpopular'; 'Police and Public Meetings. The Stupidity of Officialdom'[93] and flaunted its intimate knowledge of the advances made by socialism:

> Few people abroad are aware of the extent to which Socialism has obtained a foothold in Japan, for the organs of communication are very largely in semi-official hands, while independent correspondents experience a great difficulty in getting at the facts. As to the gentlemen who come from time to time to make a survey of Japan and go home and write books and articles on the subject, they are seldom brought into contact with the workers or their leaders ...[94]

The *Chronicle* condemned socialist violence, especially the murders of Suzuki Benzō in 1919 and Yasuda Zenjirō in 1921, an attack on a Foreign Ministry official late in 1920, various (usually bungled) bomb 'outrages' and any sign of rowdyism at meetings. However, it reserved its strongest contempt for official arrogance and for the bands of *sōshi* who 'like the pusillanimous exponents of violence in every country, pose as great patriots and defenders of law and order'.[95]

The *Japan Times* treated reports of attacks on labour activists by 'gambling associations' and 'rough fellows' as of no account, but bombings and other acts of violence were taken more seriously. The *Japan Times* showed a strong tendency to blame violent acts on Korean and Chinese dissidents.[96] The police often briefed *Japan Times* reporters with confidential details of a political case, as well as their own suspicions regarding the perpetrator, and reporters seldom questioned what the *Chronicle* would call the 'persecution' of socialists.[97]

REPORTING THE GROWTH OF NATIONALISM AND PATRIOTIC MOVEMENTS IN JAPAN

The *Chronicle's* enthusiasm for developments in the socialist and labour movement did not result in any diminution of the paper's traditional distaste for the growth in expression of nationalist sentiment. In these years, Japanese nationalism was expressed within Japan in a variety of official, group and individual activities ranging from the official encouragement of youth groups and the building of imperial shrines to the growth in the quantity and membership of patriotic societies and seemingly disorganized groups of *sōshi*, to the shrill pronouncements of those whom the *Chronicle* described as 'jingo professors'.

The way a newspaper reported such events as army manoeuvres, an Imperial indisposition, Japan's 'mytho-history', or something as obviously newsworthy as a spy story, said a lot about where it stood in relation to Japan's ideas of itself as a nation. In reporting events which had a national dimension, both the *Japan Times* and the *Japan Chronicle* began the post-war years expressing distaste for mindless patriotism, but the *Chronicle* maintained this stance until the late 1930s. Questions which interested foreign readers and Japan watchers such as, 'Is Japan militaristic?' and 'Is Japan democratic?' were often discussed in the context of Japanese nationalism.

The journalists who wrote for the English papers seldom used such catch-alls as 'fascism' to describe their rough equivalents in Japan, although 'Prussianism' had been used of some Japanese groups in 1914–18. In describing the *sōshi*, terms such as 'hired thugs', 'political bullies' and 'gambling associations' were used. The *Chronicle* favoured comparison to 'the Russian Black Hundreds' or referred to 'political ronin'. The latter term was used both for Tōyama Mitsuru's *Rōninkai* group and for similar associations of 'non-parliamentary politicians'. The term *kyokaku* (often translated as 'Dare to Dies') was another popular usage.

When Hara Kei was assassinated in November 1921 the English newspapers, the *Daily Mail* in particular, responded with blithe references to '*ronin*', and potted histories which linked the 'killers' of Hara to the killers of the Queen of Korea. The *Chronicle* admitted, 'all this must have impressed the readers of the *Daily Mail* as showing the extensive information of that journal', but it mocked these 'purveyors of fiction' and did its best to put them right. However, in doing so, the *Chronicle* sometimes lost its way, for example defining the *Genyōsha* as 'a body of soshi who make the political field its hunting ground'.[98]

The *Japan Times* was noticeably silent on the subject of patriotic societies in the slump years immediately following the First World War, although it hardly fought shy of issues relating to nationalism. The paper stuck to the use of the word *sōshi*, or 'gambling association'. Patriotic societies either went unmentioned or were described by the catch-all term *sōshi*, not by their title. This silence is not easy to explain. It may have stemmed from a reluctance to grasp the nationalist nettle or the *Japan Times* may have worried that reporting the patriotic societies in detail might mean treading on some important toes.

Certainly, the activities of well-connected patriotic societies did not sit easily with the overall picture presented by the paper to the outside world. The Japan of the *Japan Times* was moving towards democracy, was committed to internationalism and Shidehara diplomacy, and had signed up to the League of Nations, disarmament, and a mutually considered future for China. Such a Japan could be trusted by the great powers as an island of stability in the choppy waters of the Orient. Japan's patriotic groups' resentment of the *status quo*, of industrialization, of bourgeois politics, and of the increasingly moderate court centred on the Crown Prince, had no place in this tableau and yet it was a growing phenomenon and had to be reported somehow. The *Japan Times* tried to look on the bright side. Reporting Tokonami Takejirō's plans to 'promote national strength' through education, a more piecemeal selection of imported ideas, attention to the relations of workmen and capitalists and other strategies, the *Japan Times* commented, 'visible effects on social betterment throughout the country may be expected before long'.[99] The *Chronicle* was constitutionally incapable of such straight-faced optimism. For the *Japan Times*, supporting Tokonami Takejirō's drive for a calmer, less troubled nation came more easily. Similarly, reporting the platform of the newly formed breakaway 'Pure National Party', the paper was able to report without comment such aims as, 'To do away with the evils of formal education and make education more closely related with the actual state of affairs of national life' without comment.[100] As with the patriotic societies, the *Japan Times* allotted far less space and interest than did the *Chronicle* to Tokonami's huge programme fostering the national, rather than the local, spirit through Young Men's Associations.[101]

The *Chronicle* devoted considerable attention to what it called the 'official direction and promotion of national ideas' in Japan, in particular to Tokonami Takejirō's work with Young Men's Associations. In early 1918, the *Chronicle's* occasional contributor 'Japanglo' put the number of these associations at 23,000.[102] 'Japanglo' was caustic on the subject of Gotō Shinpei's role in the 'unification' of the Associations. Other organizations operating on a national scale such as village headmen and Patriotic Women were given a frosty reception by *Chronicle* writers, who seemed discomfited by the scale and ambition of Tokonami's programme.[103] In a retrospective discussion of the movement, the *Chronicle* regretted that what could have been socially useful mutual help and village protection associations were now being misdirected into a vast patriotic league. The paper was dubious of the 'forced subscriptions' raised by the members for building a 'Young Men's Hall' (*seinenkan*) near the Meiji Shrine.[104] It believed that the 'revolt' among the members against this aspect of their Associations should be taken by 'Mr Tokonami' and others as a warning of the membership's impatience with 'a multiplication of patriotic societies'.

Between February and April 1921, the *Chronicle* publicized and implicitly defended a sharp critic of the basis of ancestor worship, the 'Emperor cult' and the logic of the notion of the family state in Japan. The first occasion came in reporting and discussing the views of Kikuchi Kenjirō, former principal of the Mito middle school. Kikuchi questioned the wisdom of worshipping the ancestors of the sovereign, since many worshippers, especially those in Japanese colonies, could not possibly be related to the souls in question. As for the Japanese people, 'it is not a historically established view that they and their Emperor are derived from the same stock'. Clearly, filial piety and loyalty could only apply to immediate ancestors. As for the family system, 'people prefer independence to subjection'. As the nation was such a tenuous basis of morality, Kikuchi favoured an individual basis.

The *Chronicle* followed up this report with a series of critical discussions, the most trenchant coming in April, showing the relevance of Kikuchi's views to orthodox ideas of the national polity: 'His view of ancestor-worship strikes at the foundation of the cult which the statesmen of the Restoration era have so sedulously inculcated in the schools and throughout the whole administration.' Kikuchi's views struck at the notions of filial piety and loyalty, showing that 'much of the instruction about filial piety that is found in Japanese school books … is merely so much antiquated rubbish'. The *Chronicle* did not find it surprising that Kikuchi's views should be:

> … heatedly opposed by the champions of the old order, and especially by those who have sought to find in the family system and the doctrine of filial piety warrant and support for the Imperial cult they have formulated for the people … They evidently dimly perceive that Mr KIKUCHI's innovations are dangerous.

Among the 'champions' and formulators opposing Kikuchi's ideas, the *Chronicle* counted 'Dr Inouye' and 'Dr Hozumi' (Yatsuka, 1860–1912).[105]

The *Chronicle* followed this with a piece on the discovery by the Tokyo police that a large number of houses there were without ancestral shrines (*butsudan*), an omission which the police believed was 'the cause of the unrest in the minds of the people'. The *Chronicle* commented:

> To the Western reader, the thought of what would happen if the police went round and instructed householders that they should go to church more regularly so as to keep the Union Jack flying and hold Bolshevism at bay, invests a statement like the above with the unreality of a willow-pattern version of a Gilbertian joke … As for whether the setting up of shrines will have the desired effect on a generation nourished on a compost of Tolstoy, Kropotkin, Wilde, Herbert Spencer, Maeterlinck, Bertrand Russell, and other writers full of un-Japanese ideas, it is rather doubtful.[106]

In similar vein, the *Chronicle* criticized bushido and its Western champions such as General Sir Ian Hamilton (who wrote to the paper to protest).[107] The *Japan Times* reported official concerns about a similar lapse among middle school students by quoting an official spokesman, 'It is regrettable that the higher the education students receive in this country the more indifferent is their faith in ancestral spirits.'[108]

In September, reviewing Hara Katsuo's *Introduction to the History of Japan*, the *Chronicle* maintained that Hara's account was 'profoundly misleading', especially in its account of the Empress Jingo and the invasion of Korea. In any case,

Mr HARA does not inform his readers that no Japanese professor dare write the truth about the early history of Japan, or treat its mythological period as he would treat the mythological era of any other country.[109]

Similarly, reporting the discovery of ancient tombs in Kyūshū, the *Chronicle* doubted whether they could be properly excavated, for:

> [Japanese] archeologists are not permitted to give expression to the logical and scientific deductions they make from their studies, so we shall probably get nothing of value from this discovery unless some foreign archeologist is able to make an investigation.[110]

The *Japan Times* appeared to contradict this view when in August 1921 it reported a series of lectures given by the historian Miwa Yoshiteru. Miwa suggested that Emperor Jimmu's ascent to the throne had been from Mount Fuji, not Mount Takachiho in Kyūshū, a change of location that showed that 'a general revision in the Ancient history of the Empire may take place'.[111]

Some of those courting Japan's favour tended to over-egg the pudding. In 1920 the German ambassador complimented Japan on its two thousand year history and on never having been conquered. Reporting his speech, the *Chronicle* recalled the German academic who had calculated the very hour of Jimmu's accession to the throne in 660 BC, a feat which Chamberlain had compared to computing in cubic inches the size of the pumpkin which Cinderella's fairy godmother turned into a coach and six.[112]

To the *Chronicle*, the extraordinary loyalty and obedience of the Japanese people to the 'Emperor cult' were unnecessary and unhealthy. The paper decried the zeal of school teachers who risked their life in order to save the Imperial portrait ('the folly of dying for an enlarged photograph') from fire. In 1918 the *Chronicle* regretted that the habit had spread to Japan's colonies when the principal of a primary school in Yongsan, Korea, plunged into his burning school to save the portrait and perished (the photograph had already been rescued).[113]

The *Chronicle* consistently denigrated the general willingness to die for the Emperor. On the seventh anniversary of General Nogi's suicide following the death of the Meiji Emperor in 1912, the *Japan Times* applauded the spirit of the act but the *Chronicle* wondered 'how much of this honour General Nogi would have received had he left behind him merely his reputation for high character, inflexible rectitude and military genius'.[114]

The *Japan Times* was in no position to agree with the *Chronicle*. In the 1920s, the paper was increasingly used as a bulletin board for announcements of government policy, usually beginning 'The *Japan Times & Mail* through the *Kokusai* news agency is authorized to state …,' a formula introducing announcements on the likelihood of intervention in Siberia, and public campaigns including a 'Be kind to animals' movement, a celebration of time and punctuality in Tokyo, and a Safety First campaign, also in Tokyo, the success of which was marred by the death of two children: one, a five year old boy struck by one of the vehicles delivering road safety leaflets, the other, a boy cyclist in Hongō who received a signal from a policeman to stop and, in his keenness to obey, leapt from his machine and fell beneath the wheels of a moving car.[115]

Alongside its criticisms of patriotic suicide, the *Chronicle* found plentiful opportunities for mockery of the forgery of Imperial scrolls, the publication of indifferent Imperial poetry, the distribution of Imperial cigarettes at *geisha* parties, and other wrong turnings in the national drive. Introducing an item on the increase in the potato cultivation, the *Chronicle* suggested that, 'If the official fiat went forth that potatoes were good and that it was patriotic to eat them, there would probably result a greater variety in the national diet and a means of defying the rice corner manipulator.'[116]

The remark is interesting for more than its wit. Here and elsewhere, the *Chronicle's* highly critical view of Japanese nationalism may have prevented it from noting the fundamentally pragmatic outlook of many ordinary Japanese. It may not have suited the paper's outlook, or it may have challenged its investigative capabilities, to look more closely at the success of the government in inculcating popular acceptance of the synergy of Emperor, religion and nation. The *Chronicle* sometimes put its readers' entertainment ahead of its ability to report what was 'really going on' in Japan. In doing so, it sometimes propagated the very myths that it denigrated.

THE US IMMIGRATION ACT, 1924

In the years between the abrogation of the alliance and the 1924 US Immigration (Exclusion) Act, the Foreign Ministry network made intense efforts to overcome American hostility to Japanese immigration, with special issues of the *Japan Times* issued to consulates overseas, and a flood of pamphlets and goodwill speeches coordinated by the Japanese consulates in San Francisco and Los Angeles. Neither the *Chronicle* nor the *Advertiser* ever fully accepted that Japan's population problem forced her to send people to California, but the *Chronicle* was more vocal than the *Advertiser* in its criticisms of the speeches of the racist editorials of the newsman, V.S. McClatchy, with whom B.W. Fleisher cooperated in the Trans-Pacific News Service. In 1918, Terauchi Masatake had taken a qualified view of Japanese emigration:

> Japan is increasing her population at the rate of about half a million a year ... but it is not likely that we shall be pressed for the lack of land to live in during ten or fifteen years to come. For there is still much room in Chosen and also in Hokkaido which can be used for our colonization.[117]

In the English-language press, the tone of the debate over Californian Exclusionism swung between sweet reasonableness and high irritation, with the *Advertiser* attempting to play honest broker, the *Chronicle* critical of both sides, and the *Japan Times* on a hair-trigger. Both the *Chronicle* and the *Advertiser* trod carefully in the sensitive context of race, downplaying the views of S.S. McClure and hailing the conciliatory approach of ambassadors Morris and Shidehara. To the *Chronicle*, the Exclusionists' V.S. McClatchy was 'no doubt animated by the feeling that unless he is eternally vigilant the Japanese will get the better of the deal'.[118] B.W. Fleisher had business dealings with McClatchy in the early 1920s but kept them out of the public eye. Fleisher's business partner in Shanghai, Thomas Millard, showed less compunction about giving space in *Millard's Review of the Far East* to the views of McClatchy, whose *Sacramento Bee* had spearheaded the Exclusionist campaign:

> In forty years from 1923, Japanese population of the United States under operation of the Gulick plan will be in round figures 2,000,000; in eighty years, 10,000,000; in 140 years, 100,000,000. Long before then the white race will have succumbed in the economic competition, and the world's glorious republic will have become a province of Japan.[119]

Writing to *The Times* in 1921, J.O.P. Bland acknowledged the popularity of 'Mr McLure's vision of the Yellow Peril', and pointed to its roots in books like Lothrop Stoddard's *The Rising Tide of Color* (a screed very much on Lord Northcliffe's mind in 1921). Bland felt, 'the remarkable thing about it is that it should emanate from the same intellectual centres as the ideal of a world-wide League of Nations'. Although Asian emigration to the United States and Europe should be discouraged, Japanese emigration to China was natural and should be seen in a positive light.[120]

There was another aspect to the Act of 1924: the extent to which it was a response, albeit visceral, to the American public's concerns about Japanese expansion.[121] In this, as in so many other ways, the emigration issue was replete with opportunities for linkage. The Exclusion Act could be conflated with Japanese expansion, military and naval, colonization and repression in Korea, in short, with almost any action by the Japanese as a nation or as a race which might seem to threaten the United States at home or abroad.

In the spring of 1921, a Foreign Language Newspaper Bill came before the Hawai'ian legislature, which would have limited newspapers there to using either English or Hawai'ian. Reporting this development, the *Japan Times* resisted the temptation to goad its English-language press rivals.[122] However, in June, the reluctance of most parents of pupils at the Yokohama foreign school to agree to the admission of Eurasian children, alongside the recent enactment of strict US laws governing Japanese-language schools in California and Hawai'i, prompted the *Japan Times* to ask, 'DO WE WANT TIT FOR TAT?' because, 'The Japanese authorities would also be within their rights if they enacted a corresponding regulation to cover the foreign language schools in Japan.'[123]

On this and related issues, B.W. Fleisher's association with V.S.

McClatchy, whose campaign did so much to promote Exclusion, cannot have done the *Advertiser* much good as far as the Foreign Ministry was concerned, although Fleisher did his personal best to keep up friendly relations with Japanese officialdom. Outside Japan, however, the Foreign Ministry network tried hard to bring ordinary Americans round to the merits of the Japanese in their midst. From about 1915, when Kiyoshi Karl Kawakami set up his Pacific News Bureau, San Francisco became the West coast hub of Japanese propaganda, with a busy consulate and a thriving Japanese-language press.

Washington gave little moral leadership on the issue, and failed to anticipate the diplomatic fallout from its indifference to Japanese sentiment. In the end, the US Immigration Act of 1924 slowed Japanese immigration down to a token few, but the Act disappointed many pro-Western Japanese. Tsurumi Yūsuke warned that 'an explosive force has been lodged in the Japanese mind – an explosive force that those who seek ways of international peace and progressive democracy in Japan will have to reckon with for decades to come'.[124] Seven years after the Act, Hugh Byas thought that:

> There is an older generation of Japanese, many of them educated in the United States, who received a moral shock by exclusion and who would welcome revision simply to rehabilitate American idealism in the eyes of their countrymen.[125]

Writing just after the passing of the Act, B.W. Fleisher had mixed feelings:

> ... the Immigration Law has not helped the American cause in this part of the world. I do not consider that the Japanese are any worse off today than they were under the Gentleman's Agreement ... We did go about the matter like butchers with an axe while we could have done it in a courteous manner and not have offended these people.[126]

Whatever goodwill Fleisher had earned from all those years of glad-handing, after-dinner speechifying, special issues and stone lanterns, was called into question by the passing of the Act, as were many subscribers to the conciliatory view of international relations. Tsurumi Yūsuke's long journey from meeting Woodrow Wilson and touring the US with Nitobe to his elevated status as a public propagandist for the imperial drive in East Asia may not have been caused by the Act but it certainly gave him a good excuse.[127] Kaneko Kentarō felt compromised by the Act and resigned from the America-Japan Society. However, even though after 1924 Japanese-American goodwill became a quality more to be regained than celebrated, when the 1923 earthquake and the disastrous 1930 fire brought the *Advertiser* to its knees, those Japanese who saw its potential for improving Japan's international position were still ready to step in.

THE LONDON NAVAL TREATY, 1930

It is significant that the second of these rescue attempts also occurred at a bad time for US-Japan relations, following the signing of the London Naval Treaty in April 1930 and coming very close to the assassination attempt on Premier Hamaguchi Osachi that November. The Hamaguchi Cabinet's ratification of the Treaty may not have been the last gasp of parliamentary politics and of conciliatory diplomacy by Japan, but the bitter controversies that it aroused among the armed forces and patriotic groups, one of whose members fired the shots that would eventually end Hamaguchi's life, constituted important markers in that decline.

In the run-up to the London Naval Conference (*Rondon kaigun gunshuku kaigi*) of January-April 1930 the *Advertiser* gave considerable publicity to rumours that Britain was encouraging US naval expansion. The Foreign Office felt that Hugh Byas's articles on the subject had been written 'with some inspiration from the American Embassy' in Tokyo but chose not to attach any special importance to them.[128] On 15 November the *Advertiser* ran an article which seemed to show mischievous anti-British sentiment in emphasizing Ramsay MacDonald's outright rejection of the preliminary proposals of Japan's chief delegate to the Conference, Wakatsuki Reijirō. Britain's ambassador, Sir John Tilley, expressed the hope that 'this is not a typical attempt to make anti-British propaganda'.[129] The *Japan Chronicle* took the line that whatever agreement was reached, it would soon be disregarded by Japan as 'the last feeble effort of the movement for naval disarmament'.[130] The London Conference, like the Geneva Conference of the League of Nations, was interesting in media-historical terms in that it marked the first radio broadcast from London to Japan, with Wakatsuki reporting optimistically on the progress of the talks in mid-April as part of an attempt to soften the opposition to the Treaty expected in Japan. The *Japan Times* gave considerable publicity to Wakatsuki's return to Japan on 17 April, perhaps also to weaken the opposition to the agreement, but reported the Hamaguchi cabinet's approval of the Treaty on 23 April in carefully neutral terms, a sign of the intensity of opposition to the agreement, and perhaps of some pressure exerted on the *Japan Times* itself.[131] Morgan Young later described the Agreement of the Cabinet as 'Liberalism's last effort'.[132] Unsurprisingly, the composite effect of these reports and comments in the London and Tokyo press was not reassuring regarding Japan's future intentions.

□

The contribution of the English-language press of East Asia to the international image of Japan prevailing in the 1920s was indirect and is not easily measured. Nothing was simple. Discussion of the nature of Japanese settlers ran on irresistibly into the debates about Japanese militarism, Japan's treatment of her own immigrants and the people of her 'provinces', and naval disarmament. The *Chronicle*, by taking a critical line on so many issues, as opposed to the *Advertiser*'s more moderate coverage, may have speeded the hardening of attitudes towards Japan on the racial equality question, the independence movement in Korea, the question of the renewal of the Anglo-Japanese Alliance, the position of Japanese settlers in California and the Exclusion Act of 1924. This hardening of attitudes may in turn have caused a contraction of the middle ground in which the exchanges of Robert Young, H.G.W. Woodhead, Owen Green, Hugh Byas and Robert Young's successor, A. Morgan Young could be aired.[133]

NOTES

1   Shimazu 1998: 114–15.
2   JC: 5, 26 June 1919.
3   SP: 24 July 1919.
4   *Kokumin Shinbun*: 10 April 1919.
5   Herron Smith 1920: 7; O'Connor 2005, Volume 3: 581–620.
6   Mullett-Merrick, H.J., 'Japan's Record in Korea', *Asiatic Review*, April 1921, argued against comparing Korea to Ireland, for 'One is a Western nation and the other is an Eastern nation. One has moved for centuries in the forefront of the world's civilization; the other only ten years ago did not know what the world's civilization meant' (first page). Microfilmed in Byas Papers, Yale, Reel 6, but original destroyed. Mullet-Merrick also contributed an article along similar lines, 'What Japan is really Doing in Korea' to the journal *Japan and Korea* (1921: 7–15), also in Byas Papers, Reel 6, original destroyed. In the *Herald of Asia*, the Governor-General's adviser on the Korean press, Zumoto Motosada published much of Mizuno Rentarō, the 'Administrative Superintendent' of Korea's appeal to foreign missionaries to understand Japanese policies: 'We simply want to serve the people in all sincerity for the sake of their real happiness and prosperity' (*Herald of Asia*: 30 July 1921, 453–4).
7   JA: 'The Moral Failure in Korea', 28 May 1918; 'Missionaries Warned By Japanese About Activities in Korea', and 'Japanese Rule in Korea Past and Present': all by the Rev. Albertus Pieters, 5 October 1921.
8   P&TT: 4 December 1919.
9   *Yamato*: 15 June 1919.
10 SP: 12 December 1919.
11 SP: 1 June 1920.
12 Wildes 1927: 189.
13 JC: 8 August 1920.
14 P&TT: 17 August 1920; Peking Leader: 13, 20 August 1920.
15 *The Times*: 9 August 1920.
16 JC: 3 February 1921.
17 JC: 18 November 1920. This view was challenged in an article in the *San Francisco News Letter* of March 1921 and in several West Coast newspapers: JC: 3 February 1921.
18 'Japanese Punitive Methods': *The Times*, 7 December 1920; 'Japanese and Korea': *Daily Telegraph*, 7 December 1920; 'Japanese Disclaimer': *Daily Express*, 14 December 1920; 'The Charges Against Japanese Troops': *The Times*, 15

December 1920; 'Japanese Action on Korean Border': *The Times*, 16 December 1920; 'Korean "War" on Japan': *The Times*, 20 December 1920.

19 JA: 7 December 1920.
20 *The Times*: 15 December 1920.
21 JC: 6, 13 May 1920.
22 JC: 3 March 1921.
23 JC: 23 September 1920.
24 JC: 2 September 1920.
25 Mainichi-Chronicle cable to JC: 2 September 1920.
26 'The Arrest of Mr G. L. Shaw': JC, 26 August 1920.
27 FO 371/5353 [F 2206/56/23]: Bentinck Minute, 22 September 1920.
28 *New Statesman*: 23 October 1920.
29 FO 371/5353 [F 2608/56/23]: October 1921.
30 JC: 6 August 1920.
31 FO 371/5354 [F 3189/56/23]: 8 December 8 1920, Japanese atrocities in Korea and elsewhere, Far East Dept. Memorandum by Frank Ashton-Gwatkin.
32 JC: 29 March 1920.
33 JC: 30 June 1921.
34 *The Times*: 20 September 1921.
35 JC: 3, 10 March 1921.
36 JT: 15 January 1921.
37 For Crane's dealings with Woodrow Wilson, see Hornbeck, Stanley K. Papers, Hoover Institution, Stanford University, 'Crane MS'; and Crane, Charles R. Papers, Institute of Current World Affairs, New York. Cited in Rozanski 1974: 357, n.118.
38 Rozanski 1974: 342–5.
39 'The Chinese and Extraterritoriality': JT, 2 April 1921.
40 'China and Korea Appeal to America': JT, May 21 1921.
41 *Daily Telegraph*: 20 June 1921.
42 By his own admission, Bland had been hired by Japan during the war with Russia. In September 1921, Hara Kei, speaking in the Diet on his Cabinet's China policy, quoted with approval an article by Bland in *The Times*, 'in which the English writer explains the position and difficulties of Japan from an ultra-Japanese point of view' (JC: 29 September 1921, 447).
43 *The Times*: 24 June 1921, J.O.P. Bland letter. JC discussion: 18 August 1921. For F.O. on this argument see FO 371/5361 [F 2641/199/23]: 30 October 1920, and O.M. Green in NCDN: 23 November 1921.
44 'The Origin of China's Modern Troubles': FER, January 1921. Discussed in FO 371/6647 [F 965/965/10].
45 'And China Pays The Bill': JT, 9 July 1921.
46 'The Shantung Question': JC, 29 September 1921.
47 *The Times*: 4, 6 April 1922.
48 FO 371/8044 [F 1396/25/23].
49 *The Times*: 12 April 1922.
50 *Daily Mail*: 18 April 1922.
51 Woodhouse 2004: 40–1.
52 Thompson 1920s: 17. See Byas Paper, Bibliography, for the provenance of this citation.
53 *Asahi Shinbun*: 5 May 1922; JC: 11 May 1922.

54 Woodhead 1935: 71.

55 Turner's Memorandum 'On Japanese propaganda in the Far East', which found its way to the Foreign Office (FO 371/8028 [F 647/647/10]) in February 1922 was originally written in response to a request made by Northcliffe when they met in China. Turner did not trust Northcliffe or 'the Northcliffe people' not to publish it as it might have had consequences for his position at Reuters, so he passed the Memo on to the Foreign Office.

56 From Maya Zald and Roberta Ash, 'Social Movement Organizations: Growth, Decay, and Change'. In Joseph Gusfield (ed.) *Protest, Reform, and Revolution* (New York, 1970), 518. Quoted in Large 1981: 1.

57 'The Labour Troubles. Hon. Bertrand Russell attends meeting': JC, 28 July 1921.

58 'Japan in Ferment of Labor Troubles': JT, 26 July 1919, 983.

59 'His brother's helper': JT, 9 April 1920, 1367.

60 JC: 21 August 1919, 281.

61 On Ivan Kozlov: the pseudonym 'American Sociologist' was ascribed to Morgan Young in the endpapers of the Japanese edition of the articles published in the JC in 1918–21 and brought out in the 'Chronicle Reprint' series in the volume, *The Socialist and Labour Movement in Japan* (April 1921). Other articles in the newspaper were published after this collection came out under the 'American Sociologist' pseudonym, and bylined 'Ellis Whitman', in the English edition of the *Ōsaka Mainichi*. However, the author was not Morgan Young but Ivan Kozlov (1893/1902–1957), a Russian political writer who had studied sociology at the University of Minnesota. Kozlov's JC articles caught the attention of the Kōbe police but he had been under surveillance since at least 1918, when Robert Young persuaded Tokonami Takejirō, Minister of Home Affairs, not to deport him. Late in 1921 Kozlov was interviewed by Kōbe police and manuscripts and papers were removed from his home by the authorities. Kozlov took their disappearance up with Tokonami but to no avail. In July 1922, Tokonami's successor, Mizuno Rentarō, signed a fresh deportation order and on 26 July 1922, Kozlov sailed for Shanghai on the N.Y.K. *Haruna-maru*, seen off by ten policemen and by Robert and Mrs Young. What seems to have marked Kozlov's card was his membership of the Industrial Workers of the World, information received, apparently in good faith, from Kozlov's friend, Kagawa Toyohiko. After the deportation order was made public, Ōsugi Sakae came to Kōbe but the police kept him from Kozlov. Robert Young wrote to Bertrand Russell that autumn, 'Kagawa, however, never looked near, made no protest and when K. left, Mrs Young and I were the only people to see him off'. See 'The Deportation of Mr Kozlov', JC, 27 July 1922, and Young to Bertrand Russell, 27 October 1922: Russell Papers, McMaster University, Canada, No.710.048282. For a full discussion of Kozlov see Peter O'Connor's Introduction to the reprint of *The Socialist and Labour Movement in Japan* in Volume 7 of O'Connor (ed.) 2008.

62 JC: 11, 18, 25 November; 16, 30 December 1920; 3, 6, 10 January 1921; 3, 10, 24 February 1921.

63 JC: 21 April 1921, 532.

64 'The Socialist and Labour Movement in Japan. XI – Conclusion': JC, 24 February 1921, 263–4.

65 Kozlov 1921: 263.

66 'Baron Shibusawa Advocates Trade-Unionism': JC, 7 November 1918.
67 'Relations of Capital and Labour in Japan': JC, 28 August 1919, 314–15.
68 'A Japanese view of the eight hour day': JT, 22 November 1919, 1480.
69 'Trade Unionism in Japan': JC, 25 November 1920, 740.
70 'The Ideals of Japanese Labour': JC, 10 March 1921, 338–9.
71 'Labour's Status Today in Japan. Radicalism Appears To Have Seized Control from the Yuaikai': JT, 27 August 1921, 1309.
72 JC: 10, 31 March; 21 April; 19 May; 30 June; 11 August 1921.
73 JC: 30 June 1921.
74 JC: 7 August 1919.
75 JC: 5 February 1920, 144.
76 JC: 26 May, 16 June and 28 July 1921.
77 'Victims of a foolish policy': JT, 8 August 1921, 1172.
78 'The Parasites upon Labour': JT, 9 September 1921, 1383.
79 'Japanese Labour Party. War on Capitalistic Politics': JC, 1 January 1920, 7.
80 'The Labour Struggle': JC, 28 July 1921, 114.
81 'The Problem of Labour in Japan': JC, 6 May 1920, 506–507.
82 'Labour Meeting in Tokyo': JC, 29 May 1919, 815.
83 'Socialists and Social Unrest': JC, 19 September 1918, 396.
84 'Osugi in trouble again': JT, 6 March 1918, 2.
85 'Police clash with political agitators': JT, 12 February 1918, 1. 'Red Flags flew in Tokyo Wednesday': JT, 14 February 1920, 196.
86 'Socialists run afoul of police': JT, 27 November 1920, 1833.
87 'Communism as a Religion': JC, 27 October, 3 November 1921.
88 'The Abbot of the Daitoku-ji': JC, 6 January 1921, 16–17.
89 'Socialism in Japan': JC, 5 August 1920, 194.
90 'Socialism in Japan. An Interview with Mr Sakai': JC, 23 June 1921, 880; 'Marriage in the Socialist State. Mr Sakai's Views': JC, 4 August 1921, 163.
91 'Labour Movements in Japan': JC, 6 December 1919, 878.
92 'Japan's Labour Movement': JC, 13 November 1919, 726.
93 JC: 8, 24 July 1920.
94 'The Socialist Movement in Japan': JC, 12 September 1920, 789. The JC gave Sidney Webb and Kiyoshi Karl Kawakami as examples of 'gentlemen who come from time to time' to Japan.
95 'Politics in Tokyo': JC, 24 March 1921, 406.
96 'Chinese authors of bomb outrage': JT, 27 March 1920, 410.
97 'Open Season for Socialists Begins': JT, 17 September 1921, p1427; 'Bolshevist Plot in Japan Uncovered': 23 September 1921, p1110; 'Red Flag Flies at Socialist Meeting': 14 May 1921, 716.
98 JC: 29 December 1921, 920.
99 'Home Minister's Plan to Promote National Strength': JT, 31 May 1919, 725.
100 'Pure National Party Makes Good Resolutions': JT, 5 April 1919, 504.
101 The JT was connected with the magazine *Eigo Seinen*, founded around this time. Whether *Eigo Seinen* was connected with the *Seinenkai* or the self-improvement of young men is not known. *Eigo Seinen* is now a magazine for Japanese scholars of English literature, with the English title 'The Rising Generation' under the masthead.
102 'Keeping the Nation in Hand': JC, 24 January 1918, 124–5.
103 'The Young Men of Japan': JC, 15 September 1921, 375.

104 JC: 25 February 1921, 264; 22 September 1921, 427.

105 JC: 10 February, 165; 10, 24 March; 7 April, 439. All 1921.

106 JC: 7 April 1921, 456.

107 'The Nemesis of Bushido': JC, 28 July 1921, 115; 'Sir Ian Hamilton and Bushido': in Correspondence: JC, 3 November 1921, 621–2, 644.

108 'Students Fail In Ancestor Worship': JT, 28 May 1921, 787.

109 'Japanese and Veracity in History': JC, 1 September 1921, 302–303; 'Historical Accuracy': 22 September 1921, 408.

110 JC: 1 December 1921, 769.

111 'May Revise Early History of Japan': JT, 6 August 1921, 1180.

112 JC: 7 October 1920, 475.

113 'Fire at a School. Unfortunate Mistake': JC, 12 December 1918, 813.

114 JT: 20 September 1919, 1215; JC: 27 September 1919.

115 JT: July 9 1921, 1029; June 16 1921, 916; 24 December 1921, 1947; 29 December 1921.

116 JC: 12 December 1918, 807.

117 The *Outlook*: 1 May 1918; JA c.15 May 1918.

118 JC: 3 February 1921.

119 *Millard's Review of the Far East*: 13 September 1919.

120 'East and West: The Right Outlet for Japan': *The Times*, 18 January 1921.

121 Storry 1979: 92; Iriye 1972: 133.

122 JT: 26 March, 23 April 1921.

123 JT: 25 June 1921.

124 Tsurumi 1924: 104–5.

125 *The Changing Fabric of Japan* by Malcolm Kennedy, reviewed by Hugh Byas: JA, 15 May 1931.

126 B.W. Fleisher to Walter Williams, 13 August 1924: Walter Williams Papers.

127 Kushner 2006: 35–8.

128 FO 371/13519 [A 1942/30/45: Tilley to Chancery, 20 February 1929. 'Britain Responsible for American Naval Expansion Program': JA, 9 February 1929, by Hugh Byas.

129 FO 371/13526 [A 7662/30/45]. JA: 15 November 1929.

130 JC: 22 April 1930.

131 JT: 18 April 1930, 24 April 1930.

132 Young 1938: 53.

133 JA: 31 March 1931.

6

Reporting Japan in China, 1927–1937

For many Japanese, events in China raised the issues that most stirred the nation from early Shōwa until the conflict broadened in 1941. Chinese exigencies hastened the rise of military influence, the retreat of party politics and the concomitant inhibition of critical comment in the public sphere. And just as China dominated the public sphere in Japan, Japan's presence in China came to dominate perceptions of Japan received in the West.

An important early feature of the press controls operating in Japan in the 1930s is what appears to have been an official effort to keep newspaper readers, Japanese and foreign, from gaining knowledge of the extent of Japan's involvement in the government of Manchukuo. More specifically, gags imposed between September 1931 and March 1932 seem to have been designed to avoid allowing the Japanese public to gain the least hint that the establishment of Manchukuo was anything but the expression of the spontaneous will of the people of Manchuria.[1] Bans were likewise issued on reporting the establishment of a permanent Japanese army in Manchuria.[2] The intention may have been to forestall any adverse reaction among liberal elements in Japan, and in the armed forces themselves. Bans on reporting civil and other disturbances at home were intended to diminish news of discontent but may not have prevented rumours from spreading.

In July 1932, Joseph Grew was informed that most of the bans applied to the press published in Japan, which included the English-language newspapers, but not to despatches sent abroad. This meant that Hugh Byas could send to the *New York Times* information that Wilfrid Fleisher could not print in the *Japan Advertiser* but could despatch to the *New York Herald Tribune*. However, information restrictions in Tokyo meant that neither Byas nor Fleisher had that much to report. Byas's Tokyo despatches to the *New York Times* often contradicted Hallett Abend's despatches to the same newspaper from China, while Fleisher told *Tribune* readers no more than he could tell *Advertiser* readers (who included many Japanese) in Japan.[3]

Between the Manchurian Incident and late June 1932 all Japanese newspapers, including those in the Foreign Ministry network, operated under strict Metropolitan Police Board restrictions. Most journalists in Tokyo had to work their way round delays and gaps on the story in China. Most journalists patched together their reports and despatches from Foreign Ministry Information Bureau briefings, facts and commentary translated by *Rengō* and, after 1936, by *Dōmei*, and from what they could pick up from the local English-language newspapers, which were just as much in the dark. As a result, even seasoned observers like Wilfrid Fleisher, Hugh Byas and James R. Young tended to reflect the official view of events in China in their local and international reports. At the same time, correspondents in China often wired their stories direct to the US. As a result, there were often contradictions between reports wired from Tokyo and reports sent from in China.

After 1931, the *Advertiser* network should have been the predominant influence on news coming out of Tokyo, or at least the most significant corrective to dispatches emanating from the Foreign Ministry network. However, as the surveys of news of East Asia in US and British papers given in the concluding chapter of this study show, during the Manchurian Crisis references to the reports of the *Japan Times* in particular began steadily gaining on those of other English-language papers in the US and British press. Not only the *Japan Times* but also its leading vernacular contemporaries and Japan's national news agencies of the day, *Rengō* and *Dōmei*, built on this lead steadily throughout the 1930s. During the Pacific War it became unassailable.[4]

On the face of it, the *Advertiser* network certainly held the strongest cards in the US. Wilfrid Fleisher was managing editor of the *Advertiser* and the *New York Herald Tribune* correspondent. Hugh Byas was a past editor of the *Advertiser* and would become the longest-serving *New York Times* and London *Times* correspondent between the wars. James R. Young was an *Advertiser* journalist and INS correspondent. R.O. Matheson was an ex-*Advertiser* journalist and the *Chicago Tribune* correspondent. Frank Hedges was an ex-*Advertiser* editor who wrote the *Christian Science Monitor, Washington Post* (and *Daily Telegraph* Tokyo) correspondence. John B. Powell was a long-serving *Chicago Tribune* correspondent and a regular contributor to the *New York Herald Tribune* and the Associated Press.[5] For all of B.W. Fleisher's connections, for all the commitment and dedication of the 'Missouri Mafia' and distinguished mentors like Fleisher himself, Powell and Thomas Millard, the Foreign Ministry network took the lead on news of East Asia in the early 1930s and held on to it all the way to 1945.

A significant problem for Tokyo correspondents was that they were reporting from a city that was suffering a virtual news blackout, but despatches from *Advertiser* network reporters on the ground in China also had problems getting through to the outside world. Although he did not utilize it in 1932, in the middle 1930s Hallett Abend found that he could get round Guomindang censorship in China by utilizing a Japanese cable that ran from Hongqu in Shanghai to Nagasaki. Abend's friendly Japanese contacts let him use this line to send reports to Hugh Byas in Tokyo, who would then send them on to the *New York Times* office.[6]

Having an *Advertiser* or Missouri connection was no guarantee that a journalist would follow the *Advertiser*'s editorial line or enlist in its network. Frank Hedges (1895–1940) was a Missouri graduate, the

Advertiser's correspondent in Peking, and its editor from 1923 to 1927. In the 1930s he lent his support and his US correspondence to the Foreign Ministry network and from 1935 until his early death at the age of forty-four, he was a contributing editor of the *Japan Times*.

Miles Vaughn, United Press Far East manager and senior correspondent for China and Japan from 1924 to 1933, was another significant exception to the influence of the *Advertiser* network. Vaughn never worked on the *Advertiser* but he moved in the same circles and belonged to the same clubs as most *Advertiser* journalists and shared lodgings with Hedges in the mid-1920s. Vaughn's 'realistic' view of Japanese rights and ambitions in China was shared with Hedges, with the *Japan Times*' R.O. Matheson, with Bland, Woodhead, Penlington, Henry Kinney, Rodney Gilbert, and a significant group at the State Department in Washington. All were agreed that endemic venality and chaos doomed any Chinese solution to China's problems, and some went along with the concomitant view that a Japanese takeover in Manchuria and elsewhere in China would be no bad thing. As Vaughan put it in 1936, 'The more I studied the Manchurian question, the more I came to appreciate the Japanese viewpoint.'[7]

Such perceptions were common in Tokyo and Shanghai, but Vaughn and his circle were in the business of propagating them. In Japan, Vaughn's 'realist' circle came to enjoy considerable access to senior Japanese sources, military and civilian: early briefings, field passes in militarized areas and invitations to gatherings where they would hear the Japanese point of view unfiltered by official briefings. For sound journalistic reasons, for want of other information in a closely controlled information environment, and as a result of his closeness to the Foreign Ministry network, Vaughn's reports and the reports he approved for dispatch to UP in New York tended to echo the Foreign Ministry version when he was Far East Manager of UP in 1924–33. From 1933 to 1946, as a general manager at UP headquarters in New York, Vaughn was an important 'gatekeeper', exerting considerable influence on the final content of dispatches from East Asia. During these years, he gained a reputation among UP correspondents in China for inserting the gist, if not the entirety, of *Dōmei* dispatches into UP reports before sending them on to UP's member newspapers.[8]

China saw a considerable influx of new correspondents after 1931, but few had the contacts or had absorbed sufficient background to seek out and present a full picture and most were swept into the Guomindang's publicity operations. Older hands did well to update their readers on a fast-moving story with despatches that often contradicted those from Tokyo. Experienced journalists on China's English-language newspapers had their work cut out juggling prestigious Western newspaper dead-lines with the day job, but some had the contacts, the local knowledge, the persistence and sufficient language ability to get close to events. However, when it came to publishing their work, all foreign journalists ran the gauntlet of Guomindang press controls on outgoing cables and the local press. In short, the China story more or less got out in China and from China, but it was under-reported in the English-language newspapers of Japan and in despatches from Tokyo.

Both Morgan Young at the *Japan Chronicle* and Wilfrid Fleisher at the *Advertiser* suffered the same restrictions and information lags as other organs and their hard news items on the situation in China suffered in quality and accuracy, although both made up for these faults by translating and interpreting the cables that got through to the vernacular press. As we know, the *Chronicle*'s situation was complicated by the possibility that Douglas Young may have been receiving subsidies from Zhang Xueliang during the Manchurian Incident, as well as from Nanjing at the time of the Japanese attack on Shanghai in January–March 1932.[9] If Douglas Young did accept such subsidies, he would have had to enlist his editor, Morgan Young, for any such scheme to be effective. The advantage for the *Chronicle* would have been that accepting such subsidies would not inhibit its usual line on Japan.

In October 1930, the *Chronicle* was in even worse odour than usual with the British embassy for having reported the appearance in a London court of the son of Sir John Tilley, the British ambassador, for issuing a bounced cheque,[10] a story the *Advertiser* declined to publish.[11] Thus while Hugh Byas had the ear of Tilley's successor, Francis Lindley, who described him as 'a most trustworthy and well-informed journalist', Morgan Young was kept at arm's length by the Tokyo embassy.[12] In the early 1930s, when most embassies employed translators to keep them in touch with the vernacular newspapers and events in general, losing embassy contacts left a journalist at a disadvantage. By 1936, when the special police began arresting Japanese who worked as embassy translators, some Western diplomats in Tokyo may have been as much in the dark as the journalists.[13]

However, both the *Chronicle* and the *Advertiser* managed to report the other big story behind events in China: the Foreign Ministry's loss of control over the Kwantung Army in 1931–33. The *Chronicle* did its best to keep up with events at the Foreign Ministry until Morgan Young left Japan in 1936, but the *Advertiser* seems to have maintained a more specific focus on official confusion over Japan's strategy in China from September 1931 until its shotgun marriage with the *Japan Times* in October 1940.

THE MANCHURIAN INCIDENT

In the summer of 1931, tension was building in Manchuria between Japanese troops along the South Manchuria Railway line and the forces of Zhang Xueliang, although the 'Young Marshall' went out of his way to avoid provoking the Japanese. In late June the execution of Captain Nakamura Shintarō by Chinese troops was one source of tension. In August a Japanese ban on publishing details of the incident was lifted, and both the *Manchuria Daily News* and the *Japan Times* ran articles demanding compensation and apologies by the 'Mukden [Shenyang] authorities'.[14] A mass meeting of Japanese settlers was held in Dalian.[15]

In late August and early September there was increasing evidence of a build-up of Japanese troops in the area.[16]

Some correspondents were plain unlucky. On 3 August, the *New York Times* correspondent assigned to Manchuria, Hallett Abend, had received a dramatic tip from an official at the Japanese Consulate in Shanghai: 'We are going to take Manchuria before snow flies.' Primed for action, Abend immediately wired the *New York Times* and sailed for Dalian, where Japanese officials assured him that Japan's 'patience was at an end' and that 'the Empire would "endure no more affronts"'. Abend met similar frankness from Japanese sources at Shenyang, Xinjing, Harbyin (Harbin) and Andong (Antung) and witnessed overt preparations for a military operation to drive Zhang Xueliang's armies out of Manchuria. Day after day in the run-up to the Incident, Abend cabled detailed reports to New York from points along the South Manchurian Railway which the Japanese censors left intact, but they were either spiked or 'shunted into the deep inside pages' of the *New York Times*.[17] On 4 September, determined to put his knowledge to some practical use, Abend told the American Minister to China, Nelson Johnson, what he had heard but found him 'incredulous and not really interested' (an attitude Johnson conveyed to Washington, describing rumours of a plan to occupy Manchuria as 'highly improbable').[18] In early September W.H. Donald secured Abend a bedside meeting with Zhang Xueliang, whom Abend found 'sickly, emaciated, drug-blurred',[19] although Zhang recovered sufficiently to dine with Miles Lampson in Peking on the evening of 18 September.[20] Still in early September, bursting with the knowledge that the biggest story of his career was about to break, Abend received a cable from the *New York Times* instructing him to go to Nanjing to report the arrival of Mr and Mrs Charles Lindbergh on their round-the-world air trip. In Nanjing, Abend gave copies of his cables to Guomindang sources, but was told that Chiang Kai-shek was preoccupied. Abend fumed and waited for the Lindberghs in Nanjing. When the story broke on September 18, Abend begged the *New York Times* for permission to report events in Manchuria but was ordered to 'Stick with Lindbergh'.[21]

As Abend's experience shows, the *New York Times* made a slow start in reporting events in Manchuria. The paper did not use Abend's early cables because they contradicted the story they were getting from Hugh Byas in Tokyo. But they soon reached a compromise: from about 20 September through January 1932 the *New York Times* ran Abend's Shanghai and Nanjing cables and Byas's Tokyo cables in parallel columns and left their readers to sort out the contradictions for themselves.[22] Overall, the *New York Times*' coverage of both the Manchurian and the Shanghai Incidents was impressive: printing 1,707 columns of news between 1 September 1931 and 28 February 1933.[23]

One factor in this increased coverage was George Sokolsky, now back in the US and much in demand on the lecture circuit. Sokolsky wrote ten *New York Times* articles in November and thirteen in December 1931, and contributed frequently to the magazine section.[24] Sokolsky's approach was entirely pragmatic: he pointed to the limits of intervention by the League and predicted a Manchurian future based on mutually beneficial relationships between Chinese business interests and those formulating Japan's imperial agenda.[25] According to Edgar Snow, Sokolsky had received $60,000 from the Chinese government 'to conduct certain propaganda' but despite this largesse 'the Japanese appear to have got to him in New York'.[26] Harold Isaacs also drew attention to Sokolsky's work for 'Japanese-sponsored publications'.[27] Notwithstanding these allegations, the *New York Times* and other top publications continued to run Sokolsky's analyses of the situation in East Asia.

During the fast-moving military campaign that succeeded the events of 18 September, the English-language newspapers of East Asia struggled to keep up and develop a clear editorial line. The outlines of the incident seemed obvious enough to journalists visiting Mukden close to the 18th, but contradictions arose in the days and weeks that followed, as lines became crossed between military representatives, consular officials and reporters in Mukden and Tokyo.

In the Foreign Ministry network, the Manchurian Incident exposed inconsistencies and rivalries between the *Dentsū* and *Rengō* agencies in China. These were exacerbated in the 1930s by the duplication of propaganda functions among different government agencies.[28] In September 1931 it looked as if not only the Foreign Ministry itself but also its network had been kept outside the loop by the Kwantung Army. On 19 September the *Rengō* and *Dentsū* correspondents in Mukden both sent 'off-message' despatches to vernacular papers in Japan that supported Chinese claims that the occupation of Mukden had met little resistance from their forces, since only two Japanese soldiers were wounded.[29]

On 22 September, Hugh Byas's despatch to the *New York Times* prevaricated: '… the Japanese military plans were executed with a precision which plainly suggests long preparation for the event, but this does not in itself prove any aggressive or sinister designs'. That day's *Peking & Tientsin Times* was less accommodating:

> Kirin, September 22. – It was on Saturday evening that we first heard from Chinese sources of the coup carried out in Mukden and Changchun by the Japanese troops … The Chinese authorities, realizing the futility and danger of any resistance, rather than risk any untoward collision that would either give the Japanese excuse for more drastic action or put them wrong in the eyes of the world, are acting with the greatest possible caution and restraint.

Also on 22 September, the *Japan Advertiser* published without comment a version of events provided in Tokyo by the War Minister, Minami Jirō:

> At 10:30 o'clock Friday night, 18 September, about two companies of Chinese troops blasted a section of South Manchuria Railway lines at a point southwest of Peitayang … Upon receipt of a report to this effect, the

[Japanese] garrison company at Hushihtai rushed southward along the railway line to reinforce the contingent... For some time the garrison company was endangered and Lieutenant Noda was wounded seriously ...

The *Japan Times* accepted the Kwantung Army's version of events from the start. In its first leader on the incident, published on 20 September, the paper assured its readers of Japan's peaceful intentions and asked China to reciprocate Japanese 'moderation' and show less 'arrogance'.[30] On 22 September the day of Minami's statement, the *Japan Times* brought the 'Asian Monroe Doctrine' into the discussion, arguing that Japan had as much right to protect Japanese interests in Manchuria as the US had to protect American interests in Central America.[31] On 25 September a Tokyo despatch from Hugh Byas to the *New York Times* again seemed prepared to accept Japanese disclaimers of territorial ambitions in Manchuria at face value. That day's *Japan Times* emphasized that the occupation of Manchuria was predicated on the need to protect the Japanese living there.[32]

On 24 September, an English-language translation of 'The Tanaka Memorandum' was published in the *China Critic* of Shanghai. Henry Kinney, the South Manchurian Railway's spokesman in Manchuria, immediately pronounced it a forgery.[33] This was the second time in 1931 that the *Memorandum* had been published. It would reappear in mid-November in the *Journal de Genève*, eliciting protests from the Japanese Bureau at the League of Nations.[34]

In the 26 September *Peking Leader*, Harry Paxton Howard, an American stringer for UP, gave a blow-by-blow account of the Japanese attack on the Mukden Arsenal in the small hours of 19 September, describing Japanese grenades being thrown into the sleeping quarters of the workmen and the plundering of the arsenal's trench mortars.[35] Also on 26 September, a Reuters interview with a witness in the Mukden Arsenal corroborated Howard's account.[36] On 30 September the *Japan Times* published a detailed account of the events of the night of 18 September according to which 'several squads of the enemy resisted obstinately', which helped account for 'about 40 [Chinese soldiers] killed'. As for the lightness of Japanese casualties, 'It is also believed that the Japanese troops were enabled to occupy the enemy's barracks without sustaining a heavy loss because the enemy kept their barracks lighted while putting up their resistance'.

Despite disclaimers by Japanese officials quoted in the *Japan Times* and the *New York Times* in the weeks following 18 September a consensus developed among English-language journalists in China that the Incident and the succeeding occupation had been contrived by Japan.[37] This scepticism spread to most foreign correspondents in East Asia and, by 1932, to their colleagues in the US and Britain. The recollections of Miles Vaughn, who would not visit Manchuria until the enthronement of Puyi (Pu Yi) as the Kangde Emperor of Manchukuo in 1934, were at odds with this trend:[38]

> The Japanese version of the affair – and it generally agreed with that of our correspondents in Mukden – was that, on the night of the 18th, at about 10.30 o'clock, two or three companies of Chang Hsueh-liang's [Zhang Xueliang'] troops ... deliberately destroyed a section of the South Manchurian Railway ...[39]

This was disingenuous. In the autumn of 1931 the Japanese version of events was far from being anything like 'generally agreed' among 'our' United Press correspondents. Harry Paxton Howard's *Peking Leader* report is one example. Vaughn was either out of touch with events on the ground or rewriting the versions of events that even his own colleagues had reported. In mid-December 1931, when Vaughn was sending UP despatches from Tokyo reporting Japan's new Prime Minister Inukai Tsuyoshi's resolute opposition to any annexation of territory, Frederick Kuh was filing UP reports from Mukden, labelled 'uncensored', which described Japan's systematic seizure of all political, financial and commercial organizations in Manchuria.[40] In their reports as well as in later memoirs, none of the UP correspondents who went to Shenyang or who were based there – neither Kuh in Shenyang or Demaree C. Bess in Peking, nor H.R. Ekins in Shanghai – lent credence to the Japanese version of the events of 18 September and after.[41] Writing in 1936, Vaughn seems to have retrospectively conflated the sympathy felt for Japan's situation among his fellow correspondents in the autumn of 1931 with the dispatches actually coming out of Manchuria, which were far less sympathetic to the Japanese version.

On 25 October, the *Japan Chronicle* published a pointed review of the willingness of the Japanese press to accept the official version of events and report the Manchurian Incident as a *fait accompli*. As the *Chronicle* saw it, from the moment of the explosion of 18 September:

> ... there was a practical unanimity. Not a single Japanese newspaper failed to lend moral support to the Army. This unanimity is one of the most dangerous features of the whole situation ... This unanimity of opinion among Japanese seems to exclude from their purview altogether any idea that there can possibly be a Chinese point of view.[42]

One month after the Incident the *Chronicle* again criticized what it called the 'Army's Initiative', stressing that 'The danger in all this is much greater to Japan than China.'[43] As it had done for forty years, the *Chronicle* acted as a gadfly, stinging the conscience of the fourth estate.[44]

In October, the air between Tokyo and Washington became thick with statements attributed to US Secretary of State Henry Stimson by the Associated Press and *Rengō*, and counter-accusations made by Shiratori Toshio at his Foreign Ministry Information Bureau briefings to foreign journalists. Stimson was alleged to have complained that the Japanese army was running amok and trying to take over the whole of Manchuria, to which Shiratori responded, 'Our army is not running amok. It is Stimson who is running amok.'[45] In the *Far Eastern Review* George Bronson Rea invoked lofty principle:

> In the same manner that the United States has interpreted the Monroe Doctrine to safeguard its future peace and security, so Japan has the equal and undisputed right to invoke the same principles for the protection of its vital interests in Manchuria.

but acknowledged ominously that:

> Japan's right to invoke and apply the law of self-defense may be somewhat impaired by her adhesion to the League of Nations and by other international commitments.[46]

In November the *China Weekly Review*'s J.B. Powell sent Edgar Snow, Victor Keen, Reginald Sweetland and Frank P. Oliver to Shenyang 'so as to get first hand reports of the situation in south Manchuria'.[47] There Snow attended a press conference where General Honjō Shigeru announced that 'Under present conditions any evacuation of Japanese troops is not practical.'[48] In Harbin, Snow and his colleagues linked up with Powell and two other journalists, Glen Babb of AP and Frederick Kuh of UP, for a trip to Tsitsihar, where General Ma Chan-shan had commanded the only Chinese force to offer any resistance to the Japanese. Snow's report for the *China Weekly Review* attempts to grasp the geopolitical dimensions of the crisis and prefigures the sympathetic curiosity about the 'Reds' that would lead him away from the *Review*'s uncritical support for the Guomindang:

> … three virile contestants are in the arena. Japan, leading the industrialized West, with her samurai heart underneath excited by a dream of conquest, and accelerated by an essential economic urge for expansion; Red Russia, militant but not imperialistic, armed with a wholly new economic and social doctrine; and against them both, China, ancient but still possessed of an enormously puissant resistance, and a cultural tradition that historically has conquered all conquerors, with the erosive aid of time.[49]

In December 1931, calming measures were taken by two senior foreign journalists in Tokyo, Miles Vaughn and an unexpected advocate for the official version of events, Hugh Byas, the *New York Times* and London *Times* correspondent. On 2 December 1931 Byas participated in a JOAK network radio broadcast to the US. As can be seen from the transcript of this talk, Byas gave his unqualified support to the Japanese version of the Manchurian Incident.[50]

Not long after Byas's talk, Miles Vaughn broadcast to the US for the National Broadcasting Corporation (NBC). Before going on the air, Vaughn asked Shidehara Kijūrō, then Foreign Minister, for a statement of Japanese policy. At the time, the 'Shidehara diplomacy' that had prevailed over hardline Japanese thinking at the London Naval Conference was one factor encouraging Western expectations that the Minseitō cabinet had the Manchurian situation in hand and would be able to rein in the army. During his broadcast, Vaughn read out Shidehara's statement, which sounded a pacific note without making overt concessions to those who felt Japan had no business in China.[51] On 13 December, the second Wakatsuki cabinet resigned and Shidehara ceased to be Foreign Minister, but the broadcast, along with Byas's, may have helped buy time for Japan at this stage in the Manchurian campaign.

With most of Tokyo's international press corps reporting the official version of the China story and Vaughn and Byas broadcasting their confidence in Japan's pacific intentions, the *Chronicle* sceptical but ill-informed, and the *Advertiser* publishing official statements without comment or amplification, English-language newspaper readers in East Asia and the West may have initially granted credibility to the Foreign Ministry and Kwantung Army versions of events.

On 22 September, the Council of the League of Nations had asked both parties to withdraw their troops from the area. On 25 September, Yoshizawa Kenkichi, Japan's representative to the League, had promised the assembly that Japan would leave as soon as order was restored, to the general relief of most representatives. On 30 September the Council passed a resolution taking cognizance of Japan's promises and asking both sides to return to normalcy. In October, Japan having failed to withdraw, the League passed a resolution calling for withdrawal within three weeks. Observing no change in Japan's military position in December, the League appointed a Commission of enquiry into the dispute, a decision to which eventually Japan agreed, though the cabinet was far from unanimous.

Japan's agreement indicated a degree of confidence that, when the time came, the League could be persuaded to accept the Japanese case in Manchuria and to reject that of China. This decision increased the stakes for the Foreign Ministry network: from now on it had not only to build on the case it had disseminated for years, but make it legally watertight and internationally palatable.

Japan's decision to agree to the appointment of the League's Commission of enquiry also increased the stakes for the *Japan Advertiser* and the *Japan Chronicle* networks, which sought to present Japan's actions not only in terms of Chinese grievances and suffering but also as an overt challenge to the Washington system and the sanctity of treaties, as the overturning of agreed principles. Since principles were the stuff on which the League was founded and Japan justified its presence in China by legal as well as moral arguments, the networks were unlikely to run out of material.

Relations between the Foreign Office and the *North-China Daily News* had mellowed since the replacement of O.M. Green by Edwin Haward in 1930. In January 1932 John Pratt at the Far East Department learned that Harry Morris, owner of the *North-China Daily News*, was of the opinion that the Japanese coup in Manchuria had been agreed upon beforehand with Eugene Chen and the Guanzhou (Canton) Government in order, as Pratt explained in a Minute, 'to drive out, with the aid of Japan, Chang Hsueh-liang and Chiang Kai-shek'.[52] Morris had decided that 'it would not be prudent to allow any word of this to be published in the North-China Daily News' although it was 'well known to a fairly wide circle in China'. Within the Department, there was general agreement with Pratt's comment:

> My own information is to the effect that among the common people in Manchuria there is no hostility to the Japanese because they find them a welcome change to their own rulers.[53]

Chinese protests about Manchukuo were to be taken with a pinch of salt, therefore, especially if they came from Eugene Chen. Pratt, formerly Britain's Consul-General in Shanghai, summarized these revelations in the tone of one who had seen it all before:

> It illustrates very vividly the kind of snare that awaits the feet of anyone who undertakes to support the cause of China however able and attractive may be the representative that the Chinese Government send to Geneva.[54]

THE SHANGHAI INCIDENT

The Japanese invasion of Shanghai was the international news story of 1932. In January 1933 Hitler's accession to the Chancellorship of Germany pushed East Asia from its front page lead in most Western dailies, but the following month Japan's withdrawal from the League put it back in the headlines, only to be knocked off again by the Reichstag Fire and the suspension of civil liberties in Germany three days later.

For the English-language newspapers of Shanghai, the invasion of late January 1932 was a mixed blessing. Most newspapers increased their circulation, but the interruption to the business of the port and the city meant drastic cuts in advertising revenues.[55] However, many local journalists boosted their reputation during the invasion.

On 9 January 1932, an editorial in the *Minguo ribao* (*Min-kuo Jih-pao*), a Guomindang newspaper based in Shanghai, reported that a recent Korean assassination attempt on the Shōwa Emperor had 'unfortunately' failed, and at many treaty ports the newspaper's offices were attacked by Japanese vigilantes and *yakuza* in reaction to this affront.[56] On 18 January just as Chiang Kai-shek was arranging his return to power in Nanjing, five Japanese monks of the Nichiren Buddhist sect were beaten up by Chinese in the International Settlement, setting off a train of events and intensifying a Chinese boycott of Japanese goods. The attacks had been staged by a group of Chinese paid and organized by Tanaka Ryūkichi, an Assistant Army Attaché of Japanese special services,

Army Intelligence, at the Japanese consulate.[57] On 28 January, Shiozawa Kōichi, the commander of Japanese naval forces moored in the river at Shanghai, received Hallett Abend for cocktails and told him that at 11:00 p.m. that evening he would land his marines to protect Shanghai's 26,000-odd Japanese community in 'Little Tokyo'.[58] At 11:05 p.m. Japanese marines were landed in the city and full-scale fighting broke out when Chinese troops of the Nineteenth Route Army disobeyed orders from the new coalition of Chiang Kai-shek and Wang Jingwei (Wang Ching-Wei) and resisted Japanese marines in the crowded Chapei district. At 7:00 a.m. the next morning Japanese planes bombed Chinese troops and civilians. This was the world's first air raid on such a large and unprotected, civilian target and it set a new marker in the conduct of war, especially since the fighting in Shanghai was so accessible to Western journalists and photographers.[59]

Given their political and economic preoccupations, Britain and the US had been prepared, in differing degrees, to accommodate Japanese ambitions in Manchuria, but the Shanghai Incident posed a far more direct threat to Western commercial interests. Both Japan and China, for different reasons, wished the League to consider the Manchurian and the Shanghai Incidents as separate issues, but the emotional charge that the fighting in Shanghai carried in the English-language newspapers in China and in the world's press inevitably blurred the lines of events and ensured that Japan's 1932 attack on Shanghai was seen either as a continuation of the Manchuria campaign and of similar events, such as the earlier bombing of Zhengzhou (Chengchow), or as a prelude to other actions, such as the assault on Tianjin.

In late January, Attaché Tanaka Ryūkichi seeded the *Dentsū* news service with disinformation on the threat posed to Japanese in Shanghai.[60] One conduit for Tanaka's disinformation campaign was probably the Shanghai Press Union, set up by the Foreign Ministry Information Bureau the previous autumn to present the Japanese case on Manchuria.[61] In early October the Press Union distributed a mimeographed letter introducing itself as 'a Japanese intelligence organ, sponsored by the local Japanese Residents' Corporation, the Japanese Chamber of Commerce and Industry, the Japanese Amalgamated Association of Street Unions, the Japanese Cotton Mill Owners' Association in China, the local Japanese pressmen' and other representative bodies'.[62] In late January the Press Union distributed numerous English-language press releases issued by the Japanese Consulate.[63] In Japan, such releases led to press coverage that framed the resistance of the Nineteenth Route Army in terms of a communist threat.[64]

On 29 January, the *North-China Daily News* described 'brisk fighting in progress' in the Chapei district, with Japanese troops meeting 'sterner resistance' along the Jukong Road. On 30 January the *Shanghai Evening Post and Mercury* reported '*ronin* rule' by plain-clothes Japanese and Marines in Hongqu (Hongkew) in the International Settlement, 'armed with blackjacks, axehandles, baseball bats, bamboo poles, Japanese swords and automatic pistols'. Next day's *Japan Times* maintained that the Shanghai operations were predicated on the need to maintain peace and public order.[65]

In international public opinion, Japan's bombing of Shanghai, although it was directed against military targets, signified unacceptable behaviour. Horrifying scenes on the ground would be reported and photographed in local English-language newspapers, only to be met by profuse apologies from local diplomatic staff or stilted corrections in the *Japan Times* and sister papers, as Foreign Ministry network journalists covered for Kwantung Army soldiers. At the same time, coverage of events on their home ground by the *North-China Daily News*, the *Shanghai Evening Post and Mercury* and the *China Weekly Review*, to name only the main newspapers, undercut these official explanations and undermined the credibility of the Foreign Ministry network. In Britain, the press turned against the Japanese despite official concerns over the threat to British investments posed by the fighting, and in a despatch to the *New York Times*, Hallett Abend claimed that Japan lost the sympathy of the American public 'overnight' as a result of the bombing of Shanghai civilians.[66] On 31 January the *North-China Daily News* compared Foreign Ministry assurances to Britain that 'everything possible would be done not to endanger British lives and property, and that the International Settlement would not be used as a base for attack' with the facts on the ground:

> The reality is that lives, property and ordinary rights of foreign residents have been endangered by the Japanese forces; more, there has been wanton destruction of foreign and Chinese property ... while the International Settlement has been used as a base of attack from the very beginning ...[67]

Those charged with presenting Japan's case for invasion found little comfort in Shanghai's English-language press. The sentiments of Edward Thackrey's *Shanghai Evening Post and Mercury* editorial headlined, 'To Those who have Abused a Trust – Get Out!' were echoed in most reports from China published in the West.[68] The bayoneting of unarmed Chinese; a machine gun attack on the installations of the Texas Oil Co.; the destruction of the National Eastern Library; the shooting down of women and children in Hongqu Park; the firing of property by Japanese Marines and 'ronins'; obstruction of the Municipal Fire Brigade and removal of arms from the Municipal Police by Japanese forces; the bombing of the Liu Ying Road refugee camp by Japanese airplanes; the Japanese assault on the American Vice-Consul, Arthur Ringwalt and other foreign officials; the destruction of schools; the use of 'dum-dum' bullets by Japanese Marines; summary executions: all were recorded in terse, unbending prose.[69] This *Shanghai Evening Post and Mercury* report is typically outraged:

> Nothing can replace these treasures; nothing can restore the innocent lives
> lost in barbarous aeroplane bombings; but at least the world is learning the
> realities concerning Japan's self-appointed guardianship of China.[70]

Besides conventional journalism, Shanghai saw an increase in propaganda productions by both sides. In March editors at the pro-Guomindang *China Weekly Herald* reprinted a selection of articles (including many of those cited above) from the *North-China Daily News* and the *Shanghai Evening Post and Mercury* in a pamphlet entitled *A Month of Reign of Terror in Shanghai: What the Foreigners See, Say And Think From January 28 To February 27, 1932*.

The Foreign Ministry network responded swiftly with three Bulletins published by the Press Union.[71] In a preface, the first of these claimed that:

> ... despite the strong efforts to put Japan in a certain light on the part of
> certain sections of the Foreign press of China there is still an important array
> of editorial influence not blind to the facts and realities behind the present
> situation of China *vis à vis* (*sic*) her quarrel with Japan.

This pamphlet reproduced articles from the *Shanghai Times* (4 March), the *Peking & Tientsin Times* (undated), the *China Digest* (13 February), the *Tsingtao Times* (5 February), and a long letter to the *North-China Daily News* from the sometime British Member of Parliament, Trebitsch Lincoln, now the Buddhist monk 'Chao Kung' (9 February). The second pamphlet reprinted articles from the *China Digest* (19 March) and *Shanghai Times* (17 March) and reproduced a *Shanghai Times* montage of headlines from regional and national American newspapers under the title 'Our Foolish Contemporaries' (5 March). The third pamphlet reproduced three *Far Eastern Review* articles by George Bronson Rea (all February 1932), a leader from the *North-China Daily News* (15 February), two articles by H.G.W. Woodhead from the *Shanghai Evening Post and Mercury* (18 and 8 February), an article by Harry Archibald from the *Central China Post* of Hankou (Hankow) (3 February), and a leader from the Hearst chain's *San Francisco Examiner* (4 February).

The choice of newspapers and articles in both the *China Weekly Herald* and Press Union pamphlets was bound to be selective, if not obviously partisan. The *China Weekly Herald* compilation provided this explanation of its choice of articles on its back cover:

> There are four dailies in English circulating in Shanghai. The Shanghai Times
> has consistently been the mouthpiece of the anti-Chinese; and the China
> Press, of the pro-Chinese. Therefore nothing has been reproduced from
> either of them. The Shanghai Evening Post [& Mercury] has been most
> uncompromising in its denunciation of the Chinese foreign policy. Its 'One
> Man's Comment' is a daily contribution by Mr H.G.W. Woodhead, an
> avowed champion of the Japanese cause in the present quarrel. From the

North-China Daily News it is only necessary to quote its editorial of January 30, last: 'No journal has more faithfully criticized Chinese shortcomings than this.' So, it will be seen that no partiality to the Chinese has been the reason for the choice of the two papers.[72]

In the Press Union compilation, the pro-Japanese bias in the *China Digest*, *Shanghai Times*, *Tsingtao Times* and *Far Eastern Review* articles was leavened with material from two *Chronicle* network papers, the *Central China Post* and the *North-China Daily News* and the *Advertiser* network's *Shanghai Evening Post and Mercury*. Not for the first time, both sides in the debate quoted the two latter newspapers, and both sides sought to advance their case with articles by H.G.W. Woodhead, who maintained that China had thrown away the right to rule its destiny and that, for want of a workable alternative (he poured scorn on the League of Nations), Japan's China policies deserved a fair hearing.[73]

Woodhead appears to have pinned his colours to Japan's mast around 1926–27. By September 1931 he advocated a general acceptance of the new reality of Japanese power in East Asia, and in 1934, of international diplomatic recognition of Manchukuo. Was he rewarded for his advocacy? Certainly, up to late 1938 Woodhead seems to have enjoyed privileged access to senior Japanese figures, as a frank interview with Konoe Fumimaro in December showed, but there again, he reported the substance of this talk to the British Embassy in Shanghai.[74] Woodhead's advocacy was often erratic and based on highly individual impressions, although his support of extraterritoriality and British interests in East Asia hardly changed in thirty years of writing on East Asia. Unlike his friend Robert Young, Woodhead seldom rejected unthinking patriotism but, like Young, he refused to see any of the peoples of East Asia through rose-coloured glasses, especially the Chinese.

Woodhead's reputation as a 'die-hard' had gone before him when he arrived at the *Shanghai Evening Post and Mercury* in 1930. His transfer from the 'P&TT', long a bastion of the *Chronicle* network supporting the British presence in China, to his new posting was far from smooth. Like many of his new colleagues on the *Post & Mercury*, Woodhead denounced Japanese actions that winter, but he made no secret of his belief that hostilities would not cease until Chinese forces withdrew from Shanghai. His refusal to subscribe to the view that Japan's intervention in Shanghai had been unprovoked made him the target not only of scathing attacks in the paper's correspondence columns but of 'almost daily' assassination threats.[75] Continuing under Wilfred Pennell, the *Peking & Tientsin Times* echoed Woodhead's line on most Japanese policies and was duly banned from the posts on several occasions.

In February 1932 the line adopted by another *Chronicle* affiliate, the *Central China Post* of Hankow, became equally controversial. On 4 February the *Post*'s leader column, which carried the British coat-of-arms on its masthead and presented itself as Britain's officially favoured organ in Hankou, published an editorial on the Shanghai hostilities which read in part:

> What the outcome will be no one can say, but one thing is certain. The time for political quibbling and verbal jugglery is past. It is an issue that has to be fought out to a finish in which either that amorphous giant known as China will be battered into servility or the rest of the world through the arrant folly of their politicians and fatuous idealists will become subservient to her. The quicker the idealists at Geneva, Washington and London realize this the better it will be for all concerned.

This ran counter to the line taken by most *Chronicle* network papers since the departure of Green and Gilbert in 1930. The phrase 'battered into servility' brought objections from many Chinese, including representatives of Nanjing, to the British Consulate, and the British coat-of-arms disappeared from the leader page of the *Central China Post*. On 5 February the paper published a defence of its use of the phrase, and its leader columns scrupulously avoided comment on the Sino-Japanese conflict. On 24 February the British coat-of-arms reappeared on the leader page but *Central China Post* leader writers took a noticeably milder view of the turmoil around them.

Meanwhile, Harold Isaacs provided a furious alternative to the emerging anti-Japanese consensus among Western commentators. The twenty-one year-old Isaacs had founded *China Forum* in January 1932 after being dismissed from Hollington Tong's *China Press*. The journal was registered in Isaacs' name in the US but financed by the Shanghai CCP and by Isaacs' own earnings from journalism and translations. In January 1932 Isaacs stated the magazine's position in a press release:

> The *China Forum* is primarily the organ of no party or group, but will appear as the vehicle for the publication of news and views now suppressed, ignored or distorted in the imperialist, bourgeois and Kuomintang press of China.[76]

Isaacs was kept informed by a network of Chinese and Western informants in the Comintern and CCP underground whose real names he never learned.[77] *China Forum*'s primary target was the Guomindang, but Isaacs also attacked the Shanghai Municipal Council (SMC), the Mayor of Shanghai and the police for collaborating with Chiang Kai-shek's secret police, the Bureau of Public Safety, in hunting down 'subversive' Chinese, and the torture and summary executions that followed. Isaacs managed to publish three issues before the Japanese invaded Shanghai in late January, but the International Settlement then proclaimed a state of emergency and banned *China Forum* for six weeks, during which time Japan became the dominant power in Shanghai. *China Forum* started printing again on 15 March, arguing that Shanghai was Japan's bargaining chip for recognition of Manchuria, slamming Chiang Kai-shek for discouraging resistance to the Japanese, and reporting on kangaroo justice dealt out to Guomindang 'subversives'.

At the end of February, the *Evening Post* editor Ted Thackrey's eye-witness account of executions at the Kiangwan racecourse brought an order from the Japanese Consulate rendering all journalists' military passes invalid, although 'There was no direct refutation attempted in regard to the specific charges of slaughter of civilians.'[78] Next day's *North-China Daily News* summarized Japan's reply to the League of Nations and its overall failure to present its case in convincing terms:

> Japan, indeed, seems to have turned into a Blunderland, from which it is to be hoped she will soon be able to extricate herself by the exercise of a clearer perception of the realities so blandly commended to the League's attention. There is little inclination in Shanghai to overlook them; they starkly glower in the complete stagnation and possible ruin of the trade of this great port; in the grave accentuation of political dangers of the first magnitude and in the peril of Japan victimized by overweening military ambition. 'Deeds are louder than words.' In the light of that Japanese retort to the League let judgement be passed.[79]

The implication in the word 'Blunderland' that the invasion of Shanghai was simply a mistake, albeit a cruel and destructive one, echoed the outrage, contrived or otherwise, of the Foreign Ministry network's veteran US spokesmen, K.K. Kawakami, who described 'Japan's single-handed intervention in the Shanghai area' as 'a blunder of the first magnitude',[80] and the term would be used again in a May 1942 'peace feeler' broadcast to the US by the editor of the *Japan Times & Advertiser* to put a new gloss on the outbreak of war the previous December. Whether or not they soothed their intended audience, such euphemisms may have provided the Foreign Ministry network with some comfort in its sometimes hopeless effort to bridge the contradictions between official statements and military actions on the ground in China.

There are numerous instances in contemporary accounts of journalists and diplomats being privately assured by Japanese sources that the activities of the army in Manchuria and the navy in Shanghai were the disastrous consequences of a rift between 'liberal' elements in the government and the armed forces. However, in October 1931 the *Japan Times* emphasized that the government was operating normally, inde-pendent of military control.[81] By December the paper was stressing the unity of Japanese opinion on the Manchurian issue.[82] On 11 December the *Japan Times* said the nation was right behind the army in its efforts to maintain order and the open door in Manchuria.[83] In the same month, the paper rejected foreign intimations of a split between the government and military authorities, and declared that the army's work was entrusted to it by the Imperial Government.[84] By February 1932 the *Japan Times* was stressing the leading role of the armed forces, justified in the absence of any other effective leadership.[85] Later in February a *Japan Times* leader declared that Japanese militarism was no better and no worse than Western militarism and that Western criticisms of Japan's actions were hypocritical.[86] Adapting the logic of the Stimson declaration, the paper pointed to the US annexation of the Philippines, and asked rhetorically whether the US was ready to return the islands to Spain, since they had been acquired by force.[87]

Other organs in the Foreign Ministry network tried to claim the moral high ground. In June the *Asahi*'s English-language supplement, *Present Day Japan*, ran an article by the new Prime Minister, Saitō Makoto, claiming that Chinese troops had provoked the attack and that 'The hideous consequences lie at their door.'[88] Chiang's Vice-President, T.V. Soong (Song Ziwen), sniped back 'For resourceful invention, the far-famed diplomats of Japan certainly hold the palm' but neither the government in Tokyo nor the National government in Nanjing emerged untarnished from the Shanghai Incident.[89]

Underlining continuing confusion in the Foreign Ministry network, *Rengō* in Tokyo, the Japanese Consulate in Shanghai and the Shanghai Press Union all issued wildly conflicting figures of Japanese casualties in Shanghai. However, poor coordination in the Foreign Ministry network no longer automatically translated into success for the Nanjing presentation of events. Chiang Kai-shek's 'purgation' movement, which made a bloody start in April 1927 with the summary execution of thousands of Shanghai Communists and not a few unlucky passers-by, entered its fifth year in 1932. Before the Shanghai Incident, with Chinese strongholds collapsing before the Japanese onslaught in Manchuria, the Nanjing government had thrown six divisions into the fight against the Communists in central and southern China, with negligible results and little popular support. In May, even as a truce was established and a treaty was being negotiated for the withdrawal of Japanese troops and an end to the Shanghai fighting, Chiang Kai-shek picked up the traces of the Guomindang command and announced yet another punitive expedition against the Communist forces.

As the truce took hold in Shanghai, old hands like Powell, Gould and Abend dusted themselves off and went back to reporting the 'China story'. But for a younger group of American journalists that included Edgar Snow, his wife Helen (Nym Wales), Harold Isaacs and Rayna Prohme, witnessing so much suffering and destruction from positions of privileged safety may have led to reflections that helped broaden a developing split in the *Advertiser* network.

These became most evident in May 1932, when Harold Isaacs commemorated the fifth anniversary of Chiang's Shanghai coup and the accompanying purges by combining three issues of *China Forum* in a special edition entitled 'Five Years of Kuomintang Reaction', with a sinister Chinese face under an S.S. style officer's cap on the cover. Written with Agnes Smedley and the Trotskyite Frank Glass, this special issue documented five years of Guomindang rape, summary arrest, torture, beheading and murder of the opponents of Nanjing, accompanied by gory photographs and detailed statistics.[90]

'Five Years of Kuomintang Reaction' also exposed the role of British and American interests in Chiang's suppression of the Shanghai workers in 1927. This came as a severe embarrassment to the Shanghai establishment. The Municipal Council tried to close down *China Forum* but it was protected by Isaacs' extraterritorial rights. Edwin Cunningham, the US Consul in Shanghai, tried to get the State Department to revoke this protection. On 29 July the *New York Times* reported that the State Department was considering withdrawing Isaacs' extraterritorial privileges 'For the first time in the history of Chino-American relations', leaving him open to trial in the Chinese courts.[91] Fiorello La Guardia, the congressman for New York, then made a noisy intervention and the State Department hastened to assure him that Isaacs' extraterritorial status and rights as an American citizen were not threatened.[92] In Shanghai, H.G.W. Woodhead, of all people, galloped to Isaacs' defence with an article in the *North-China Daily News* in which he declared that revoking his rights would undermine the entire structure of extraterritoriality.[93]

In 1934, Isaacs finally fell out with the CCP and with Agnes Smedley over his opposition to Stalin, especially Stalin's strategic error in directing the CCP to compromise with Chiang Kai-shek. Isaacs then learned that he and *China Forum* had been played for a mug and he suffered disillusionment not only with the CCP but with other fellow travellers, particularly Edgar Snow, of whom he wrote in 1941, 'He is probably one of the ablest propagandists for Stalinism who still commands a general hearing. He maintains this position by cannily assuming an attitude of 'independence' and 'realistic' objectivity.'[94]

China Forum had a tiny circulation, but its history was more than a mercurial sideshow. Alongside reports by Snow, Epstein, Prohme, Smedley and Nym Wales, it marked an important parting of the ways. Christopher Thorne has shown that both sides of this divide were attracted by the prospect of moral regeneration and what General Stilwell would call 'the Puritan spirit'. In an echo of the 'transfer of credibility' described in Chapter 2, Stillwell joined Snow, Isaacs and Smedley in locating the Puritan spirit not in the 'court' of Nanjing but with Mao in the caves of Yan'an. Meanwhile, J.B. Powell, Randall Gould, Edna Booker and the *Christian Science Monitor* continued to invest their faith in Nanjing and Chongqing.[95] Thus, Japanese incursions in China did them no good in Western eyes, but some of the biggest upsets of 1931–33 had more to do with changes in Western opinion towards China than towards Japan. By the early 1930s, whether you were based in Surrey or Shanghai, being a Western observer of East Asia no longer automatically meant signing up for the Guomindang.

THE DEBATE ON MANCHUKUO

In March 1932, Japan established the new state of Manchukuo (*Manshūkoku*), with its capital at Xinjing, and its own ruler, 'Henry' Puyi (Pu Yi), who would be crowned Emperor of Manchukuo two years later. In September 1932 Japan became the first nation to recognize the new state, followed by Italy in November 1937 and by Germany in February 1938. Between the appointment of the Lytton Commission in December 1931 and the publication of its report in October 1932, the Foreign Ministry network worked to bring international opinion round to a more favourable view of the Manchuria and Shanghai Incidents. Japanese representatives and the Foreign Ministry network gathered witnesses and testimonials, preparing the ground ahead of the Lytton Commission's fact-finding journeys from Tokyo to Kyoto and Shanghai to Manchukuo. At the same time, planners in Tokyo selected spokesmen and gathered material for Japan's case in the forthcoming denouement in Geneva.

This massive public relations effort meant using anything that might turn the tide: explanation, persuasion, detailed argument, image-laden rhetoric. The Foreign Ministry network had to give Japan's reasons for military action and win support for them as part of Japan's new agenda in Asia. At the same time, it had to transcend its own arguments. Rather than simply purveying a sense of Japan's overwhelming military authority, the Foreign Ministry network had to convey the more positive and perhaps more intellectually satisfying impression of Japan as a powerful modern state committed to reform and renewal, East Asia's natural leader with its showcase in Manchukuo.

Although novelty was central to its appeal, this 'Asian leader' image had a pedigree and a constituency stretching back to the decade after 1894 when the victories over China and Russia and the publication of Nitobe Inazō's *Bushido* provided a seamless connection between theoretical exaltation and the demonstration of right over might. As the spy and cinema manager Amleto Vespa put it in the late 1930s, 'British Tories helped create this myth of a heroic Japan; and behind the myth has matured a monster Frankenstein that threatens those who helped to create it.'[96] As Vespa saw it, after the wars with Russia and China, Japan's role as the Asian colonizer of Asia seemed only meet and right, and 'brave little Japan' greatly exercised the imagination of the reading public in the West. Vespa was a paid-up Italian Fascist and a self-confessed political assassin but twenty years later, when he penned these remarks, anti-Japanese sentiment in Britain was so strong that his publisher was Victor Gollancz's Left Book Club. In twenty years, Japan had gone from a Tory pin-up to a bipartisan demon and 'bushido' had become a term loaded with scorn.

To reverse this deterioration and reclaim Japan's turn of the century position as the natural head of the new modern Asia, a posse of Western journalists with a background in East Asian journalism became *de facto* spokesmen for Japan in China. Chief among them were Henry Kinney of the South Manchuria Railway, George Gorman, Peking correspondent of the *Daily Telegraph*, who became an adviser to the government of Manchukuo in 1930,[97] and George Bronson Rea, who had been writing for Japan since his conversion from the Chinese nationalist cause in 1919.

In 1932, the Japanese Association of Shanghai published Rea's pamphlet *The Highway to Hostilities in the Far East*. In the spring of 1933, Rea took a position with the government of Manchukuo at a salary of $30,000 a year and subsequently opened an office in Washington[98] where, the *Chronicle* commented, 'he will represent Manchukuo officially as far as Manchukuo is concerned but unofficially, or not at all, as far as the United States is concerned'.[99]

Two other important members of Japan's Manchukuo team were the journalist Frederick Moore, a Foreign Ministry consultant since the early 1920s, and the ex-Chinese Maritime Customs official, Arthur Edwardes, who in the autumn of 1932 was appointed an adviser and London agent to the government of Manchukuo at a salary of £5,000 per annum.[100] John N. Penlington, sometime Tokyo correspondent for *The Times* and author of *The Mukden Mandate* (1932) also joined the team.

Between the autumn of 1932 and the spring of 1933, at the height of the Manchukuo debate at the League of Nations, Kinney, Rea, Penlington, Moore and Edwardes travelled to Geneva to support Matsuoka Yōsuke and Matsudaira Tsuneo's publicity team.[101] These and other spokesmen and the newspapers and agencies in the Foreign Ministry network took a common position on five main points: that Manchuria's historical and cultural links with China were tenuous – Manchuria as a region was distinct from 'China proper'; that China was a failed state – the Chinese were incapable of ruling themselves and could not be described as an 'organized people' nor China as 'an organized state' within the meaning of the Covenant of the League of Nations; that Japan's reaction to the 'explosion' of 18 September 1931 was a normal act of self-defence; that the creation of Manchukuo was the result of a genuine, spontaneous, natural and popular independence movement by the people of Manchuria, and that Japan was the victim of anti-foreign feeling stirred up by the Guomindang and their propaganda.

The first of these points had been made in scholarly books and articles published in Japan. In Dalian the *Manchuria Daily News* had also been highlighting the special nature of Manchurian folklore, architecture, language and history for some years.[102] In a note to Japan's Foreign Minister, Shidehara Kijūrō, Eugene Chen, Foreign Minister of the 'Left Kuomintang' in Guanzhou, was quick to emphasize that Manchuria was an integral part of China. On 26 September the *Canton Gazette* carried the text of this note, in which Chen reminded Shidehara of positions he had expressed during Chen's recent visit to Tokyo:

You replied that nothing could be further from the thought of the Government of Japan than the annexation of Manchuria and, if and when it should become necessary, your Government would be prepared to declare categorically that Japan recognized Manchuria as an integral part of the Republic of China and had no wish or intention to infringe Chinese territorial sovereignty in the region.[103]

Chen went on to question the good faith of Shidehara, given recent events. Chen's message indicates his awareness of the importance of not letting Japan's claim that Manchuria was not integral to China gain any permanence in international opinion. However, on reading this article in London, one Foreign Office official merely commented, 'Eugene Chen seems now to be rather out of the picture.'[104]

The second point, that China was a failed state, was a staple of most Japanese and pro-Japanese discussions of China, and in common use among Western settlers in China and Western commentators on East Asia, to some of whom Japan seemed the best solution to Chinese chaos and incompetence. The journalists Miles Vaughn, Rodney Gilbert, George Bronson Rea, H.G.W. Woodhead and to some extent Hugh Byas all belonged to the latter camp, part of a small but significant body of opinion in East Asia. The existence of this group made point two one of the most workable planks in Japan's platform, as it would invariably strike a sympathetic chord among Western observers.

The third point, that the Manchurian Incident was an act of normal self-defence, was more problematic. As we have seen, Japan's spokesmen and publicists promoted this interpretation in inverse proportion to the likelihood of its being accepted. After all, self defence does not begin on enemy soil. What matters here is point four: that the creation of Manchukuo was the result of a spontaneous, popular independence movement. Any newspaper reader or commentator who was willing to believe that the military occupation of Manchuria was an act of 'normal' self-defence might accept that Manchukuo was the creation of the Manchurian people, as long as press restrictions kept the details of Japan's political, commercial and military investment from allowing other interpretations into the public sphere, as they did in Japan. For the Foreign Ministry network, putting over point four meant persuading the world that the Chinese people themselves not only approved but yearned for the transformation of poverty-stricken, bandit-ridden, misgoverned Manchuria into the safe, well-ordered, industrial powerhouse of Manchukuo. It seemed logical that they should, and many observers gave Japan the benefit of the doubt. After all, if Manchukuo really was being transformed, then who was to say that its inhabitants did not benefit, whether or not they approved the transformation, whether or not their wish to be part of that transformation was spontaneous? Had not Britain done the same for India and for Ireland?

The creation of Manchukuo effectively began on 20 September 1931, the day after the main cities of Manchuria had been occupied by the Kwantung Army. On 25 September, the *Manchuria Daily News* announced the establishment of a 'committee for restoring normal status and preserving order in and about Mukden [Shenyang]'. In the months that followed, the *Manchuria Daily News* reported the appointment of various Chinese officials serving what were described as 'independence regimes' and 'self-government committees'. The paper carried a statement by Honjō Shigeru, Commander of the Kwantung Army:

> The movement to set up a new government has been started everywhere in Manchuria and Mongolia. While the Chinese people are drawn to the Japanese Army because of its strict discipline, none of them has manifested a wish to have old heads back over on them. The accumulation of the long suppressed indignation must have burst at length against the old warlords.[105]

The *Japan Times* backed this up with a leader pointing out that far from being an army of oppression, Japanese forces were in Manchuria to manage a return to civilized ways.[106] On 17 October, the *China Digest*, edited in Shanghai by Carroll Lunt, previously of the *Far Eastern Review*, quoted a report by the Peitaho correspondent of the *North-China Daily News*: Chinese soldiers retreating from Japanese forces had mistreated villagers and seized their belongings, and the correspondent asked 'which they would prefer to come to their villages, the Japanese soldiers or their own Chinese troops. They answered at once and with very positive emphasis – the Japanese.' In the *Far Eastern Review* George Bronson Rea urged his readers to accept that Japan had replaced the cruel despotism of Zhang Xueliang with stable government.[107] On 29 October, a *Japan Chronicle* report published part of 'a Rengo telegram of doubtful authenticity' which claimed that foreign businessmen in Shenyang agreed that 'the economic conditions of Manchuria will be bettered if General Hsueh-liang [Zhang Xueliang] does not come back to Mukden'. The *Chronicle* asked if there was 'a Black Chamber in China' which knew of Zhang's resignation before he did, and dismissed the news as 'as vicious a piece of untrue propaganda as has come our way for a long time'. All of which indicates that if the *Chronicle* was being subsidized by Zhang, he was less willing to retreat before Japanese power than was generally thought.[108]

On 31 October, the *China Weekly Review* summarized the establishment of twelve such regional committees and showed the hand of the Kwantung Army and the South Manchurian Railway in their creation, for example, '"Yingkow-Newchang Self Government Committee" formed under Japanese auspices with usual Japanese advisers.' In mid-November, in a further contradiction of Miles Vaughn's recollections, a UP despatch from Demaree Bess reported that:

> The Japanese-made governor of Mukden, Yuan Chin-kai, today told me that he took his job only after he had been threatened with imprisonment if he refused. He added that he is not and never has been a free agent because his every action must be approved by the Japanese.[109]

The validity of Japanese descriptions of Manchukuo as the spontaneous creation of a popular independence movement remained a hot topic in the English-language newspapers for some years. The Foreign Ministry network consistently denied that Manchukuo was a puppet state of Japan. The *Chronicle* and *Advertiser* networks insisted that it was, referring to 'the so-called state of Manchukuo' and printing its name in quotation marks to indicate its spurious origins, just as, in the context of Korea in the 1920s, the *Japan Times* and *Seoul Press* had printed the word 'independence'.[110]

The fifth point, that Japan was the victim of anti-foreign feeling incited by Guomindang propaganda, was at once both the least important and the most contentious issue, partly because, under the circumstances, the notion of Japan as any sort of victim was bound to be hotly contested, but also because any discussion of propaganda involved the journalists themselves, making them and their background a part of the story. Late in 1931 George Bronson Rea criticized US rhetoric on the Open Door because, as he saw it, American commercial interests in Manchuria were not significant enough to justify intervention over Manchuria. Rea scorned 'the college professor, the dilettante in diplomacy and the idealist and sentimentalist who believe that slogans, phrases and dialectics will safeguard the future and usher in the millennium', but he failed to make a clearer case to bolster Japan's sense of national victimization.[111]

On 1 March, the delegates of the Lytton Commission arrived in Tokyo under heavy police protection, there to be received by the Emperor, meet the Japanese political, military and business establishment, and mix with international-minded Japanese. They would have met Nitobe Inazō had he not been hiding in fear of his life after a chance remark that had offended the Imperial Reservist Association (*Teikoku zaigō gunjinkai*). On 4 March, the delegates attended a luncheon at the Japan-British Society and had conversations with Makino Nobuaki and other leading personalities. They dined with the industrialist Dan Takuma, who was assassinated the following morning. On 9 March 1932, the Republic of Manchukuo was formally established and Puyi, ex-Emperor of China, installed as Chief Executive over a government staffed by Chinese officials, with Japanese advisers. On 11 March, the Commission left for Shanghai via Kyoto. As Francis Lindley reported:

> Speeches at the official functions defended the Japanese viewpoint at such length as sometimes to create the impression, when the text appeared in the newspapers, of having been designed with an eye to placing the patriotic orthodoxy of the speaker beyond question in the minds of the more reactionary members of the public.[112]

In other words, just as Nitobe had been, and Dan Takuma should have been, and the Commission members might have been, without their police protection, even the most powerful members of the Japanese establishment stood in such fear of assassination that, even at meetings intended to clarify Japan's foreign policies, they felt bound to trumpet their patriotic *bona fides*. Inoue Junnosuke had been assassinated the previous month, and, as P. Broad minuted Lindley's report, Nitobe's absence, Dan Takuma's assassination and the heavy police presence around them must have given the Commission members 'an unpleasant impression', perhaps not unintended, of the earnestness of some patriotic groups in Japan,[113] although in fact these groups were far from united on the issue that brought the Commission to Tokyo, Japan's overseas expansion.[114]

On the evening of 14 March 1932, Lytton's group arrived in Shanghai and was met by V.K. (Vi Kuin) Wellington Koo (Gu Weizhun), acting as Chinese Assessor to the Commission, and by representatives of the Municipal Council. The main thoroughfares of the city were bedecked with posters declaring (in English), 'We Demand Only Justice' and 'China Honours the Nine-Power Treaty'. The Chinese press published editorials welcoming the Commission and warning them not to be deluded by Japanese propaganda. A remark by Lytton that the situation must be considered impartially gave rise to accusations of partiality. A reminder that 'the League expects that its members shall have peace in their hearts and not only in their mouths' was construed as pro-Chinese. The statement by Lytton on 16 March that 'it is not possible for any nation to cultivate hatred and hostility towards another nation and then expect the League to step in and save them from the consequences of that attitude' was interpreted by the *China Times* as implying that China had caused the dispute by inculcating hatred of Japan. On 26 March the Commission left for Nanjing. 'Chinese and Japanese hospitality cancel out, leaving the Commission little time for serious work', noted J.D. Roberts at the Foreign Office.[115]

At the end of August 1932, during a break at his summer lodge at Lake Chūzenji, Francis Lindley wrote an assessment of Japan's place in world opinion which took into account the many provocations that he felt Japan had suffered at the hands of the Chinese. Lindley had little faith in the League and its ideals, and he doubted that Japan would allow Geneva to forbid its ambitions in China. At the same time, he felt that the Report could 'scarcely fail to bring out' that the Manchurian Incident did not in itself justify the subsequent military actions of Manchuria, and that the Manchukuo government did not 'represent the free choice of the Manchurian people'. Even before the Report was published, it was clear to Lindley that Japan had failed to persuade the world of the validity of two key points in its position on Manchukuo.[116]

On 15 September, Japan recognized Manchukuo and appointed its first ambassador to the new state. Later that autumn, H.G.W. Woodhead spent a month investigating the situation in Manchuria for the *Shanghai Evening Post and Mercury*. In mid-October he published two articles giving his impressions of the new state. The first of these carried an interview with the Chief Executive of Manchukuo, Puyi, who 'emphatically dissented' from the view 'that he had been coerced into his present position and that he was not a free agent'.[117] The Chief Executive explained that he had chosen to accept office in Manchukuo because he was disenchanted with the Guomindang, who had not only tyrannized the people of China, waged civil war and perpetuated disorder but also reneged on the terms of the Abdication Agreement with the Manchu Dynasty and failed to return imperial property. Woodhead's second article carried an interview with Cheng Hsiao-hsu, the Prime Minister of Manchukuo, who told him that two Japanese, one of them an interpreter, attended all meetings of the Manchukuo cabinet. Cheng 'stated emphatically that no settlement of Sino-Manchukuo differences would be acceptable that involved the recognition of Chinese sovereignty over the new state in any form'.[118] Sending the articles to London, a member of the British Legation staff commented, 'The articles have apparently not given much pleasure in Chinese circles, although Woodhead thinks that his forthcoming articles on banditry in Manchukuo and conditions in Harbin will give less pleasure in Japanese circles!' At the Far East Department in Whitehall, one official minuted the file containing Woodhead's articles, 'They are of interest in tending to show that Pu-Yi's departure for Manchuria was spontaneous.' [119] Looking back on the trip in his 1935 memoirs, Woodhead himself seemed keen to demonstrate his impartiality and to tread the middle ground:

> I was given every facility for prosecuting my inquiries by the Japanese authorities – military and civil – and though by no means convinced that Manchukuo was then, or was likely in the future, to be the 'paradise' which the Japanese proclaimed their intentions of making it, I returned convinced that nothing short of a crushing military defeat would cause Japan to abandon the attempt to create a new State under her protection.[120]

In June 1942, when he was being interrogated in Bridge House preparatory to a Japanese court-martial, Woodhead produced what he thought was his trump card ('I got in the last word'): the fact that Prime Minister Hayashi Senjūrō had personally acknowledged his journalistic 'impartiality' by presenting him with a bronze statuette of a Japanese soldier during his cabinet (2 February 1937 to 4 June 1937).[121]

THE CHALLENGE TO JAPANESE INTEGRITY

In October 1932, the League of Nations published the Report of the Lytton Commission. In its conclusions, the Report reflected a conscious effort by the Commission and leading opinion at the League to placate Japanese sentiment by blaming both Japan and China for the situation in China. However, despite its conciliatory language and the scope it seemed to offer Japan for manoeuvre, the Report directly challenged each of the five key points in Japan's case for its actions and presence in Manchuria. The Report maintained that Manchuria was an integral part of China; that China was not a failed state; that Japan's reaction to the explosion of 18 September 1931 was not a normal act of self-defence; that the founding of Manchukuo could not be considered the result of a genuine and spontaneous independence movement, and that Japan could not be properly described as a victim of anti-foreign feeling, whether incited by the Guomindang and their propaganda, or by other agencies or nations.

As Japan's representative, arguing against these conclusions, Matsuoka Yōsuke's 8 December speech to the League blurred the lines between those like himself whose task it was to present Japan's case in foreign policy term, and those whose task it was to create and present Japan's case as propaganda:

> Manchoukuo, when fully developed, will form the corner-stone of peace in the Far East – that is our faith. If, Gentlemen, you wish to know more about Manchoukuo, I can inform you that there are in Geneva three gentlemen connected with the Manchoukuo Government. One is General Tinge, personal representative of the Chief Executive of Manchoukuo; another is George Bronson Rea, Counsellor to the Ministry of Foreign Affairs, who is regarded as one of the greatest authorities on Far-Eastern affairs; and the third is Mr Arthur H. Edwardes, formerly Inspector-General of the Maritime Customs of China, who has accepted the position of Adviser to the Manchoukuo Government.[122]

Matsuoka has been described as 'Japan's first "media foreign minister"'.[123] Witness his publicity management at the 1919 Paris Conference, his mingling with and cultivation of Japanese and Western journalists during postings at the South Manchuria Railway, at the Foreign Ministry and at his home in Tokyo and in Geneva in 1932–33; his belief that acerbic, headline-grabbing statements could persuade the American media to take an anti-war posture and undermine Roosevelt's campaign for a third term in August 1940, and his 21 July 1940 interview with Wilfrid Fleisher and 4 October 1940 'exclusive' with Lawrence Smith of International News to this end.[124] Ultimately, Matsuoka could be said to have thoroughly misjudged the American public by such endeavours, but that does not weaken the evidence of his faith in the power of the media.

Yet despite Matsuoka's awareness of the power of the media, and his obvious ability to distinguish between foreign policy pronouncements and propaganda, between diplomacy and 'public diplomacy', his sense of what would play well with the media seems to have deserted him at times during his exhausting tryst at Geneva. In late November 1932 Matsuoka had asked Eamonn de Valera, the new President of the League Council, to allow 'General Tinge' (Ding Shiyuan), Manchukuo's First Minister, and Rea to appear before the Council to present Japan's case for Manchukuo, and been turned down.[125] Now he was all for bringing them back.

Like most of the early Manchukuo Chinese officials, Ding was a discredited stooge. George Bronson Rea was a classic poacher turned gamekeeper, China's chief representative in Washington during the Twenty-One Demands crisis, then Japan's most durable foreign publicist following his conversion at the Paris Peace Conference. Like Rea, Arthur Edwardes had been personally frustrated by Chinese Nationalists, in his case the Guomindang, who had dismissed him as Inspector General of the Chinese Maritime Customs after less than a year in post. His responsibilities boiled down to propagandizing for Manchukuo and getting British companies to invest there.[126]

For all his sensitivity to international opinion, Matsuoka's willingness to have these three speak for Japan on Manchukuo seems naïve at best and points to a blind spot in his understanding of Western perceptions. Japanese propaganda had conspicuously failed to convey the validity of Japan's case on Manchuria but Matsuoka encouraged those who 'wish to know more about Manchoukuo' to consult its propagandists. His offer was consistent with Japan's presentation of Manchukuo as a valid, independent state, but in the context of a discussion centred on that very validity, it confused the issue and highlighted the gulf between Japanese convictions and Western perceptions.

Perhaps Matsuoka felt bound to cast doubt on the credibility of China, whose government he referred to as a 'fiction'. His 8 December speech questioned the neutrality of the League and pointed to a pro-China bias in the Lytton Report's acceptance of Chinese opinion:

> The Commission, declining to accept the solemn declarations of the Japanese government and attaching too little value to the detailed documents presented by them have ... apparently listened to the opinion of unidentified persons and given credence to letters and communications of doubtful or unknown origin.[127]

Here was 'anti-Japanese propaganda' again. Matsuoka and the other Japanese delegates clearly resented the Commission's refusal to grant 'credence' to pro-Japanese public opinion and to the Japanese version of events. It seemed there was no ducking the issue but instead Japan recommended that the League consult with its authorized storytellers.

On 24 February 1933, after extensive efforts to find a way out for Japan, forty-two of the forty-four member nations in the League voted to accept the findings of the Lytton Report. Acceptance posed a huge challenge to Japan. All the main points in Japan's case for being in China and for creating Manchukuo had been broadcast in years of propaganda. Now, directly contradicting Japan's entire propaganda effort on China, the League's acceptance of the Report presented Japan not only with the impossibility of gaining diplomatic recognition for Manchukuo, but the virtually unanimous international rejection of Japan's integrity as a nation. On 24 February 1933 Matsuoka Yōsuke began the process of withdrawal with a dramatic walkout from the Council chamber.

MANCHUKUO BECOMES A *FAIT ACCOMPLI*

In the January 1934 issue of his new monthly review, *Oriental Affairs*, H.G.W. Woodhead maintained his support for Manchukuo, urging international recognition on the basis that non-recognition only served to increase Japan's economic and political influence in the new state.[128] *Oriental Affairs* was promptly denied the use of the postal service, a ban still in place in November, although the Foreign Office felt that 'if no fuss was made' the Chinese would probably lift it.[129] In June *The Times* reported that the ban, together with other censorship of the foreign press, was regarded in Shanghai 'as calculated to arouse the suspicion that the Government wishes to conceal disagreeable truths'.[130] Nanjing's ambassador to London was unrepentant and described *Oriental Affairs* as a 'pro-"Manchukuo" mouthpiece'.[131] On 27 June a question on the ban was tabled in the House of Commons. In November Wang Jingwei, now Foreign Minister of the National government, said that he would support ending the ban and expressed interest in publishing Woodhead's *China Year Book* 'in collaboration' with Nanjing.[132]

Early in 1934, *The Times* and AP correspondents were granted interviews with Puyi but, unlike Woodhead, they were not allowed to ask direct questions.[133] In an interview with the *Sunday Express* in February the 'frail-looking bespectacled man in European morning clothes' was more forthcoming, with fond recollections of a youthful visit to Brighton where Gypsy Rose Lee had read his palm and predicted his ascension to 'the Dragon Throne at Changchun in 1934'. However, Puyi regretted that 'Unfortunately, public opinion in your country has been sadly misled during the past two years and the friendly and constructive attitude of the Japanese government towards Manchuria has been made the pivot of racial hatreds.'[134] The enthronement ceremony on 1 March was attended by Edgar Snow. Miles Vaughn and Frank Hedges came over from Tokyo. George Gorman put together a special Enthronement Edition of the *Manchuria Daily News*, penning a fourteen-page fictional dialogue entitled 'Monarch from the Gods' as a 'Souvenir' in a colour-printed 'Enthronement Supplement'.[135]

After Japan's withdrawal from the League of Nations in February 1933, Manchukuo gained acceptance in some unexpected quarters. In April 1933 Edgar Snow privately acknowledged that the creation of Manchukuo had redrawn the political map of East Asia as conceived at the Washington Conference. One could no longer 'think of Japan as an island power, but as a continental power, the strongest in Eastern Asia. Think of the center of Japan no longer as Tokyo, but Mukden or Hsinking [Shenyang or Xinjing].'[136] In 1934, Snow expanded on this view in the *Saturday Evening Post*.[137]

In May 1933, the *China Weekly Review* ran a series of articles on Manchukuo in the context of Sino-Japanese relations. In one such, Wang Jingwei, currently President of the Executive Yuan, explained why the Guomindang would neither resist Japan militarily nor make overtures of peace, but would seek a diplomatic solution:

... although Japan seems to have lost the sympathy of the world in general, her military and economic position has been secured. On the other hand, while China has obtained the moral support of the world, militarily she is in an isolated position and economically she is helpless.[138]

On 11 May 1933, the *Shanghai Evening Post and Mercury* began a series of articles by its news editor, C. Yates McDaniel, giving qualified support to Japan's position in Manchukuo:

If peace and security are maintained and the economic stabilization of the country assured, the great majority of the people will come to take less and less active interest in supporting or opposing whoever happens to be holding the reigns of power in Hsinking.

Later that year, Japan's 'accredited propagandist' Henry Kinney, quoted this article with approval in an unsolicited 'Memorandum on Manchukuo' sent to the Foreign Office in London. One official seems to have been persuaded, reasoning that, 'it is difficult to dissent from its main conclusion, which is that Manchukuo is settling down to regular development under Japanese tutelage, and that any reversal of this development is impossible'.[139]

In February 1934, the British Residents Association in Shanghai voted in favour of recognition, citing Woodhead's January *Oriental Affairs* article as a factor in their decision.[140] In August the *Manchuria Daily News* hailed the forthcoming visit of a British industrial commission to Manchukuo as an indication that 'the old country still retains its practical outlook'.[141] In September fourteen journalists from American provincial newspapers visited Japan and Manchukuo at the invitation of the Japan Press Association.[142] In 1934 "Manchukuo" was still being printed in Nanjing in double quotation marks but the new state was well on its way, if not to formal international recognition, then to international acceptance as a *fait accompli*.

THE AMŌ STATEMENT

These minor victories for the Foreign Ministry network came despite international alarm over what came to be known as the Amō Statement of April 1934. Morgan Young and Wilfrid Fleisher were both in Japan in mid-April when Amō Eiji delivered the statement in his capacity as Director of the Foreign Ministry Information Bureau.

According to Young, Amō made the statement in early April at an Information Bureau briefing attended by foreign journalists, most of whom took it for 'one of the essays in abstract principles in which Japanese Government Departments frequently indulge' and took little notice. On 17 April, the *Asahi Shinbun* published 'an inspired statement emphasizing Japan's attitude in a way that could not be ignored'.[143]

According to Fleisher, Amō made the statement 'unconsciously and accidentally' at a press conference for Japanese journalists on the evening of 17 April. From a bundle of papers on his desk, Amō picked up a telegram from Vice-Minister of Foreign Affairs Shigemitsu Mamoru to the Japanese minister to China, Ariyoshi Akira. This contained the gist of the 'Amō statement'. Presumably, an *Advertiser* representative took notes as Amō, 'Little realizing the importance his words might have', read out the telegram, because a translation appeared in the *Advertiser* the following morning, 18 April. The Foreign Ministry took this version and issued it in mimeograph form to a small number of foreign journalists.[144]

According to Dorothy Borg, Amō first gave a press conference for foreign, not Japanese, journalists on 17 April. At this first conference Amō was asked to explain Japan's position on foreign (i.e. non-Japanese) aid to China. Amō then produced a message on this subject which had recently been sent to Ariyoshi Akira, which he translated into English on the spot, explaining that his translation was unofficial but that the document was approved by Hirota Kōki. Later on 17 April Amō issued a statement labelled 'unofficial' to a second, *mixed* audience of Japanese and foreign journalists, but told some American journalists that it could be taken as official, and promised to provide an English translation. This he did on 19 April, probably using the mimeographs of the *Advertiser's* text that Fleisher mentions above. When the US State Department sought to file an authoritative text of the Amō's Statement it found that none existed. However, all the versions circulating agreed on the main points.[145] The version that found its way to Joseph Grew read, in part:

> This country considers it only natural that to keep peace and order in East Asia, it must act singlehanded and upon its own responsibility. In order to be able to fulfil this obligation, Japan must expect its neighbour countries to share the responsibility of maintaining peace in East Asia, but Japan does not consider any other country, except China, to be in a position to share that responsibility with Japan.[146]

Japan, according to Amō, assumed full responsibility for 'the preservation of peace in the Far East', and would oppose any attempt by China 'to avail herself of the influence of some other country with the idea of repelling Japan'.[147] Supplying China with military assistance or loans 'for political use' was also out of bounds as it 'would obviously tend to separate Japan and other countries from China and ultimately prove prejudicial to the peace of the East Asia'.[148]

The Amō Statement challenged the spirit and the letter of the Open Door policy enshrined in the Nine Power Treaty signed at Washington, and it effectively served notice of Japan's repudiation of the Washington system. In fact, the gist of the Amō Statement was hardly unfamiliar from *Japan Times*, *Far Eastern Review* and other Foreign Ministry network references to the 'Asian Monroe Doctrine'. In essence, Amō expanded the Asian Monroe Doctrine from Manchuria to the whole of China. Moreover, he reinforced this enlargement with the threat of force. In

March 1933 Japan had served notice on the League that 'the general principles of international law which govern the ordinary relations between nations' had to be 'considerably modified in their operation as far as China is concerned'.[149] Amō lifted the veils from this warning by explicitly opposing aid provided to China by states other than Japan on the grounds that this might open the way to international control.

Grew noted the unanimity of Japanese vernacular press support for Amō's statement but wondered whether he was seen as 'an enfant terrible or a hero'; in other words, to what extent he really spoke for Japan.[150] The Foreign Ministry eventually repudiated the Statement as unauthorized but in London the Foreign Office knew that the text as published in the *Asahi* represented Japanese policy, as it closely echoed sentiments expressed by the Foreign Minister, Hirota Kōki, in a 13 April telegram intercepted by British intelligence.[151] Whether Whitehall shared this knowledge with Washington is not known.

THE OUTBREAK OF FULL-SCALE WAR IN CHINA

Small scale clashes had occurred between Japanese and Chinese troops in China since 1935, partly as a result of an extension of overt control on the ground. At the end of 1936, the Xian (Sian) Incident forcibly persuaded Chiang Kai-shek to suspend his campaign against the Chinese Communists, now holed up in Yan'an in the north-west after their dramatic Long March, and face Japan. This reorientation of Chinese forces may have ensured that the next clash would be more enduring.

On 7 July 1937, Japanese troops conducting night manoeuvres at the Marco Polo Bridge near Peking clashed with the local Chinese garrison in what became known as the Marco Polo Bridge Incident (*Rokōkyō jiken*). Both sides moved reinforcements to the area and on 11 July Japan approved mobilization of troops from Japan. Fighting resumed on 27 July and the 'special undeclared war' continued, with breaks, until 1945. At the end of 1937, Chiang Kai-shek was driven out of eastern China and his base in Nanjing and into refuge in Chongqing. In 1938 the left Guomindang leader Wang Jingwei defected from Chongqing and began talking to the Japanese about setting up the puppet government that was eventually established in Nanjing in March 1940.

The Xian Incident did not turn the Nationalists into the only force defending China from Japan. As recent scholarship, building on revisionist views that surfaced in China in the 1980s, has made clear, Chiang was not on his own against Japan, but it is a simplification to say that the Guomindang dominated the Chinese front while the Communists held the rear.[152] Nevertheless, after Xian, Chiang Kai-shek's publicists found it easier to gather US support by focusing on the Nationalist element in China's defence. Thus began a large-scale campaign in Europe and the USA for financial and military aid, discreetly underlined by the possibility that Chiang might himself do a Wang and come to an accommodation with Japan. In the US, the

Nationalist campaign was backed by the moralizing fervour of its publisher Henry Luce, who subscribed to Stanley Hornbeck's view that China's 'disposition of good will' towards the US represented 'both a moral and a business asset': Chiang Kai-shek made the cover of *Time* magazine twice in 1936.[153] By the spring of 1939, most Americans favoured an embargo on any supplies to Japan which might help Japanese aggression in China, but were nevertheless firmly opposed to intervention in foreign wars.[154]

On 9 October 1937, Matsuoka Yōsuke released an uncompromising message to the American public through the Associated Press which was reprinted the following month in the SMR pamphlet *China Incident and Japan*:

SPEAKING FOR NIPPON

At last Nippon is in for the final, for a knock-out decision; a once-for-all cleaning of all tortuous tangles in the Sino-Nippon relations which have been plaguing the East for ages ... she is dealing with a festering sore deep down within the bosom of Eastern Asia threatening her very life as well as those of all Asian races with sure and inescapable death. It is calling for heroic surgery: She has taken up her scalpel. She will permit no foreign interference whatsoever here.[155]

In August 1937, during a break in London, Morgan Young had written to *The Times* predicting the takeover of Shanghai as the base of Japanese power in China and portraying Japan's failure to declare war against China as a deceitful means of observing the Kellogg Pact.[156] Early in 1938 Young sent *The Times* a blunt correction of a 20 January despatch from his old friend Hugh Byas in Tokyo because it 'so well sets forth the Japanese point of view that there is some danger of less-informed readers accepting it as proper'. Young agreed with Byas's statement that 'When the Japanese papers declare with pathetic daily insistence that what Japan seeks is China's friendship they are not being hypocritical.'[157] However, Young maintained that for Japan, '"friendship" today, like "sincerity" yesterday, means unquestioning submission' and concluded that 'Japan has always been ruled by soldiers' and that 'So long as soldiers rule there must be war.'[158]

Young's trenchant opinions may have been borne out, even before their composition, by the best known in a series of military atrocities by Japanese troops in China, the 'Rape of Nanking', which occurred over a six week period beginning in December 1937. Although the Guomindang government and bureaucracy and, less efficiently, its military rank and file, had already withdrawn from the city, Japanese forces ran amok and in over ten weeks of murder, mass rape and looting caused the death of approximately 200,000 civilians and prisoners of war in and around the city, seemingly unrestrained by their superior commander, General Matsui Iwane.[159]

During the killing spree that followed the triumphant entry of the

Japanese army into what had been a relative stronghold of Guomindang resistance, many incidents of cruelty committed by Japanese troops on unarmed Chinese were recorded on film, in photographs (some taken as souvenirs by the Japanese troops), and in the statements of surviving witnesses. The evidence as recorded by non-Chinese, non-Japanese diplomatic, medical, educational and religious mission staff, including German diplomatic personnel who had been instructed to play down the activities of their future ally, was given wide distribution in Western media.

Keen to counter these disturbing impressions, the Foreign Ministry network adopted a scatter-gun approach with numerous books and pamphlets, coordinating production with the SMR publicity department and with the San Francisco and Los Angeles consulates and three American authors in particular, Frederick Vincent Williams, Ralph Townsend and David Warren Ryder.[160]

For the purposes of this study it is interesting that between November 1937 and January 1938 reporters covering the activities of Japan's Central China Area Army (*Naka Shina hōmengun*) in Nanjing for the *Ōsaka Mainichi Shinbun* and the *Tōkyō Nichi-Nichi Shinbun* (but not for *Dōmei* or the *Yomiuri Shinbun*) seem to have felt no compunction in providing news reports and updates on a 'killing competition' between 2nd Lieutenants Mukai Toshiaki and Noda Takeshi of the Katagiri Detachment, based at Jurong on the outskirts of Nanjing. According to these reports, Mukai and Noda were encouraged by their superiors to engage in a 'competition' whereby the officer who could kill a full 100 people before the invasion and occupation of Nanjing was completed would win a prize awarded by his superiors. In the event, Mukai was reported as having killed eighty-nine people and Noda seventy-eight by 11 December. Apparently encouraged and rewarded by their senior officers, Mukai and Noda were reported to have extended the competition from a goal of 100 dead to 150 dead, an achievement both reached sometime in December, although reports of the numbers and dates vary considerably.[161]

The *Manchester Guardian*'s Harold Timperley, the *New York Times*' Hugh Byas and the *Japan Advertiser* all reported the assault on Nanjing and cited the *Ōsaka Mainichi* and *Tōkyō Nichi-Nichi* in sending their reports of Mukai and Noda's 'killing competition'. The first report on the 'competition' came from Byas: it was uncritical but telling. Under a breezy headline, Byas reported the race between Mukai and Noda competition in the language of a sports report:

TWO JAPANESE NEAR GOAL IN RACE TO KILL 100 OF FOE

A dispatch from the Shanghai front gives details of a race between two Japanese officers to see who will be the first to slay 100 Chinese with the Japanese sword. Mukai and Noda had laid a wager on this accomplishment and have since been trying hard to win the bet. At last accounts they were approaching the end of the contest, for as the result of the fighting for the capture of Kuyung, in the advance on Changchow, Mukai claimed eighty-nine victims and Noda seventy-eight. Mukai's best day was set down as fifty-five slain in a raid between Wusih and Changchow. A condition of the match is that no victims shall be counted unless they were resisting when killed.[162]

The following day's *Japan Advertiser* ran the only report in Japan's English-language press, in equally jaunty terms:

SUB-LIEUTENANTS IN RACE TO FELL 100 CHINESE RUNNING CLOSE CONTEST
Sub-lieutenant Toshiaki Mukai and Sub-lieutenant Takeshi Noda, both of the Katagiri unit at Kuyung, in a friendly contest to see 'which of them will first fell 100 Chinese in individual sword combat before the Japanese forces completely occupy Nanking' are well in the final phase of their race, running almost neck to neck.

On Sunday when their unit was fighting outside Kuyung, the 'score', according to the Asahi, was: Sub-lieutenant Mukai, 89, and Sub-lieutenant Noda, 78.[163]

A week later, the *Advertiser* ran a chirpy update:

CONTEST TO KILL FIRST 100 CHINESE WITH SWORD EXTENDED WHEN BOTH FIGHTERS EXCEED MARK
The winner of the competition between Sub-Lieutenant Toshiaki Mukai and Sub-Lieutenant Iwao [Takeshi] Noda to see who would be the first to kill 100 Chinese with his Yamato sword has not been decided, the Nichi Nichi reports from the slopes of Purple Mountain, outside Nanking.

Mukai has a score of 106 and his rival has dispatched 105 men, but the two contestants have found it impossible to determine which passed the 100 mark first. Instead of settling it with a discussion, they are going to extend the goal by 50.[164]

In July 1938, *The Manchester Guardian*'s Harold Timperley carried both articles in an appendix to a book on the resumption of full-scale war in China.[165] Timperley may well have been the *Advertiser*'s source for the 'killing competition' reports they ran in December. Clearly, the *Advertiser* and Timperley were in close touch. In another appendix Timperley quotes *Dōmei* press releases sent to the *Advertiser* giving the names of Japanese military units involved in what he calls the 'capture' of Nanjing and other cities during the October-December 1937 campaign.[166] Timperley contradicts himself by reporting that 'little or no mention was made in Japanese papers of conditions in Nanking following the occupation by Japanese forces' and that 'A survey of English-language papers published in Japan revealed no reference to the accounts widespread in Shanghai and the world over reporting Japanese atrocities in Nanking or elsewhere.'[167] Nevertheless, neither the *Japan Chronicle*, in the year that it lost the feisty leadership of Morgan Young and not long before it began accepting a Foreign Ministry subsidy, nor the *Japan Times* provided more than perfunctory reports of events in Nanking. Neither paper reported the 'killing competition'.

☐

In the post-war critique of Japan's modern history, the events in the years covered in this chapter have been referred to as the 'dark valley' (*kurai tani*) period, not only because of their sombre associations but also, on occasion, because such a description inhibits further discussion. A debate over whether these years represented an exception or a continuation of previous trends has made the 'dark valley' epithet itself the subject of controversy, but in terms of the news and information available *at the time* it seems perfectly apt. After 1931, Japanese and foreign journalists, news agencies and their readers were often kept in the dark about campaigns and activities carried out under the Japanese flag. Much of the correspondence from Japan that seemed bland and mendacious to better informed readers in the West was the result of attempts, often mangled by the censor, to get out what little information foreign journalists were able to glean from the guarded sources available to them, further inhibited by their professional reluctance to provide information whose accuracy they could not guarantee.

For most of the 1930s, Japan's attitude towards the West appeared increasingly menacing and arrogant. This impression was conveyed by the Manchurian Incident and the invasion of Shanghai, by Japan's withdrawal from the League, the Amō statement, by Japan's withdrawal from the 1936 London Naval Conference and the following November by its signature of the Anti-Comintern Pact with Nazi Germany, which Italy joined in 1937. The Pact was largely directed at confronting Soviet Russia, and Japan's General Staff representative, Ōshima Hiroshi, went to great lengths to insert riders that would not tie Japan into a confrontation with other Western powers. However, the Pact heralded a period of more overt hostility to Western interests in East Asia, and this hostility may have played its part in the thoroughness with which Japanese atrocities were recorded in Nanjing and reported in the West, though it does not explain why they were reported in Japan.

NOTES

1   On 26 September and 13 November 1931, and 19 February and 13 March 1932.
2   On 13 March, 27 May and 30 May 1932.
3   USDS 894.918/7: Grew to State Dept., 9 July 1932.
4   See Chapter 9.
5   For most of his twenty-six years in Shanghai, Powell also wrote the Shanghai correspondence for *The Manchester Guardian* and *The Daily Herald*, the British Labour Party organ.
6   Abend 1943: 140.

7   Vaughn 1937: 119.
8   Mackinnon and Friesen 1987: 137
9   Malcolm Kennedy Diary: 30 May 1934, Sheffield University. Cited in Pardoe 1989: 223, n.303.
10 'A Young Man in Trouble': JC, 28 October 1930.
11 FO 395/447 [P 2303/2303/150]: Report of Roger Tilley Case in 'Japan Chronicle'; Thomas Snow, Tokyo, to Arthur Willert, FO, 18 November 1930.
12 FO 371/17073 [F 122/33/10]: Lindley, Tokyo, to FO, 10 December 1932.
13 USDS 894.918/21: 'Increased control of news in Japan'; Grew to State Dept., 13 April 1936.
14 MDN: 17, 18 August, 8 September 1931; JT, 18 August, 13 September 1931. The MDN was based in Dalian but it seems to have observed press restrictions current in Japan.
15 Bing-Shuey Lee 1933: 31.
16 In 1933, the JC found retrospective evidence of a compact between 'certain southern Chinese leaders' to obtain Japanese support for a rebellion against Nanking. The CWR speculated that 'this intrigue may have had considerable to do in precipitating the Japanese intervention'. See 'A southern Chinese': JC, 6 May 1933; also 'Nanking-Canton Politics and the Japanese Menace': CWR, 13 May 1933, 405–406.
17 Abend 1943: 173.
18 *Foreign Relations of the United States*: 1931, III, 1–3, 95–6. Cited in Thorne 1972: 152.
19 Abend 1943: 153.
20 Thorne 1972: 141.
21 Abend 1943: 148–54.
22 May 1973: 517.
23 *Current History*, Vol. XXXVIII, No.1, 11.
24 Cohen 1978: 177.
25 NYT: 27 September 1931.
26 Farnsworth 1996: 135.
27 Isaacs 1951: 371.
28 Kushner 2006: 32.
29 Bing-Shuey Lee 1933: 39.
30 'Can Peace be Preserved in Manchuria?': JT, 20 September 1931.
31 'Critical Situation in Manchuria': JT, 22 September 1931.
32 'Repercussions on Manchuria': JT, 25 September 1931.
33 FO 371/15506 [F 7649/1391/10]: G. Badham-Thornhill, Military Attaché, Peking, to Miles Lampson Peking, 28 October 1931. According to Badham-Thornhill, Zhang Xueliang's 'Publicity Department' first published the Memorandum in English in June 1931, Zhang having paid Shidehara Kiijūrō $14,000 for a copy. However a Minute to this document states that the Memorandum first circulated at the Pacific Conference in 1929. Henry Kinney believed the author of the Memorandum was Baron Taube, the sometime Reuters correspondent at Mukden.
34 'Comment les Japonais se represent le respect des traits' (What the Japanese mean by respect for treaties): *Journal de Genève* c.12 November 1931.
35 *Peking Leader*: 26 September 1931, 'Heroism and Devotion to Duty Revealed in Massacres in Mukden'.

36 Reuters despatch datelined Tientsin, 26 September 1931.
37 Most notably the missionary Sherwood Eddy and the journalist Upton Close (Josef Washington Hall).
38 Vaughn's book was first published in 1936 as *Covering the Far East* (New York: Covici Friede). This account cites the 1937 British edition, *Under the Japanese Mask*.
39 Vaughn 1937: 247.
40 May 1973: 517.
41 Besides Vaughn and the four UP correspondents mentioned above, the UP pool of correspondents in China included Earl Leaf, Edwin P. Hoyt, F. McCracken Fisher, Israel 'Eppy' Epstein, Jack Belden, John Morris, Martin Sommers, Ray Marshall, Robert Clurman, Stanley Rich, Walter Logan, Walter Rundle, Weldon James and William McDougal. A trawl through available reports and memoirs by these and other UP correspondents in China from c.1925 to 1946 turns up none who saw China as the instigator of the events of 18 September
42 This was unfair to two of the JC's oldest Japanese allies, *Chūō kōron* and *Kaizō*, both of which questioned the need for the Manchurian invasion. In November 1932, *Chūō kōron* published a complete translation of the Lytton Report, surely evidence of a willingness to offer another 'point of view'. Cited in Kasza 1988: 48–50.
43 JC: 25, 31 October 1931.
44 The JC celebrated its 40th anniversary on 2 October 1931.
45 One indication of the confusion of the times is that J.B. Powell attributed the 'run amok' remark to President Hoover himself: Powell 1945: 187.
46 'Japan's Right to Defend Herself!': FER, October 1931, 4.
47 CWR: 14 November 1931.
48 Farnsworth 1996: 123.
49 CWR: 14 November 1931.
50 Zumoto 1932; reprinted in O'Connor 2005, Vol.4: 435–83.
51 Vaughn 1937: 294.
52 FO 371/16142 [F 542/1/10]: 'Manchuria' Minute by John Pratt, 19 January 1932, summarizing information received from Harry Morris and Mr Marker, Shanghai agent of Arnhold Brothers Ltd., via Sir H. Goffe.
53 Op. cit.
54 Op. cit.
55 For example, the SEPM doubled its circulation during the crisis, but all the additional copies were printed at a loss (Woodhead 1935: 227).
56 Jordan 2001: 11.
57 Jordan 2001: 11, 7. Jordan adds that the Japanese representative on the Shanghai Municipal Council was apparently unaware of the role of Japanese provocateurs in organizing the attacks on the monks and that his demands for apology and compensation were repeated by Japan's delegate to the Conference at the League of Nations (Jordan 2001: 7, and 247, n.6).
58 Fenby 2004: 209. The Japanese community in Shanghai numbered between 26,000 and 32,000 and was Japan's largest expatriate grouping according to Jordan (2001: 7).
59 The conflict also allowed British intelligence plentiful opportunities to assess the quality of Japan's forces (Best 2002: 100–101).

60 Jordan 2001: 20.
61 Jordan 2001: 36.
62 USDS 894.91293/4: E. Cunningham, Shanghai, to USDS and US Legation, Peking, 23 November 1931.
63 USDS 893.911/287: E. Cunningham, Shanghai, to USDS and US Legation, Peking, 8 March 1932.
64 Jordan 2001: 37.
65 'Japan's Navy Acts in Shanghai': JT, 31 January 1932.
66 Jordan 2001: 64, and 256, n.21, citing NYT of 29 January 1932.
67 'Dangerous Misrepresentations': NCDN, 2 February 1932.
68 Including the *Manchester Guardian*, for whom Thackrey reported until the end of 1932, when he was replaced by H.J. Timperly.
69 Bayoneting: 'Volunteer Stabs Chinese prisoner': SEPM, 30 January 1932; Machine-gunning: 'Gunboat Fires on Texas Oil': NCDN, 2 February 1932; Library: 'Cultural Loss to the Nation': NCDN, 3 February 1932; Shooting: 'Tales of Horror are Told by Residents Trapped in Hongkew': SEPM, 3 February 1932; Firing of property: 'Newsmen Lose Credulity as reports Belie Chapei Scene': SEPM, 9 February 1932; Obstruction: 'Fire Brigade's Part': NCDN, 11 February 1932; Liu Ying Road Refugees: 'Refugee Camp Bombed': NCDN, 12 and 15 February 1932; Ringwalt: 'U.S. Vice-Consul Ringwalt Roughly Handled by Ronins': SEPM, 15 February 1932; Schools: 'Seven Schools Destroyed': NCDN, 17 February 1932; Dum-dums: 'German Doctor Relates Case of Dum-Dum Bullets': SEPM, 18 February 1932; Executions: 'Gruesome Sights Mark Race Track': SEPM, 22 February 1932.
70 SEPM: 31 January 1932.
71 The Press Union, Shanghai: *The Sino-Japanese Conflict: The Situation Reviewed by American and British Editors in China*; *The Shanghai Incident Misrepresented: Shanghai Editors Draw Attention to Incorrect Reports in American Newspapers*, and *The Shanghai Incident*.
72 *China Weekly Herald* 1932: 24.
73 Woodhead's arguments in favour of exploiting Japan's commitment to China first appeared in his column, 'One Man's Comment For To-Day', in the SEPM, before being published, alongside similar contributions by George Bronson Rea from the FER, in the collection *Presenting Japan's Side of the Case* (1931), reprinted in O'Connor (ed.) 2004, Vol.8.
74 FO 371/22181 [F 13307/71/23]: Sir A. Clark Kerr, Shanghai, 31 October 1938.
75 Woodhead 1935: 222.
76 Far Eastern Press Correspondence, File 9, 1/3/32: Harold Isaacs Papers, Massachusetts Institute of Technology. Cited in Rand 1995.
77 Rand 1995: 108–9.
78 'Eye-Witness Stories of War Pass from Shanghai Horizon': SEPM, 25 February 1932.
79 'In Blunderland': NCDN, 26 February 1932.
80 Kawakami 1932: 26.
81 'A Japanese Reaction': JT, 25 October 1931.
82 'Echoes on Manchuria': JT, 8 December 1931.
83 'A Reply to Newton D. Baker': JT, 11 December 1931.
84 'H.I.H. Prince Kanin': JT, 22 December 1931.
85 'Naval Ministry's Instructions': JT, 11 February 1932. Cited in Fält 1985: 33.

86   'Japan's Militarism': JT, 19 February 1932.
87   'Recognition of Manchuria': JT, 21 February 1932. Cited in Fält 1985: 30.
88   'The Shanghai Affair'; 'The March of Events at Home and Abroad': *Present Day Japan*, June 1932.
89   Bing-Shuey Lee 1933: 253.
90   For more on *China Forum* and Isaacs, see Shanghai Municipal Police files, Special Branch reports, report no's 2527/34 and 2713 (Special Box No.26), Reel 6.
91   'American Warned of Trial by China': NYT, 29 July 1932.
92   Rand 1995: 115–6.
93   Rand 1995: 116. Rand does not give the date of this article.
94   'An Apologist for Chinese Stalinism': *Fourth International*, Vol.2, No.6, July 1941, 190–1.
95   Thorne 1978: 22–23. Here Thorne also quotes the *Christian Science Monitor* 25 July 1942 as an example of a type of preciousness that clouded the American view of China: 'How many have considered what a different balance the world might have today were not the Generalissimo a Christian and his wife American-educated?'
96   Vespa 1938: 284.
97   Gorman had been writing for the Foreign Ministry network since a brief stint on the *Japan Times* in 1926. In that year he moved to edit the *North China Standard* in Peking. When the *Standard*, established in 1919, closed in March 1930, he became an adviser to the government in Xinjing. In March 1933 he became editor of the *Manchuria Daily News*, a post he occupied until 1937.
98   Hoyt 1978: 68.
99   JC: 29 July 1933.
100 Best 1999: 227, 229.
101 The publicist's lot was not easy. Early in their journey to Switzerland, a train carrying Kinney and Penlington was held up in Manchuria by bandits who went off with the manuscript of their refutation of the Lytton Report and most of their clothing, forcing the premier advocates of Japan's case in East Asia to walk back to Harbin in their underwear (Young [A.M.] 1938: 156; Young [James R.] 1943: 141).
102 For example, see 'Side Lights on Archeological Relics in Manchuria' by S. Umemoto: January-September 1930, in the MDN Monthly Supplement.
103 'Full Text of Foreign Minister Eugene Chen's communication to Baron Shidehara in connexion with Manchuria Incident': *Canton Gazette*, 26 September 1931.
104 FO 371/15496 [F 6320/1391/10]: Manchurian Situation; Canton Consul Herbert Philips to FO, 29 September 1931.
105 MDN: 5 October 1931.
106 'American-Japanese Relations': JT, 7 October 1931.
107 'Fundamentals': FER, Vol.28, 1932.
108 A reference to Herbert O. Yardley's indiscreet account of Washington's 1920s espionage programme, *The American Black Chamber* (Indianapolis: Bobbs Merrill, 1931), which was even more surprisingly published in Japanese in the same year by Ōsaka Mainichi Shimbunsha.
109 United Press, Mukden: 14 November 1931.

110 And much as in the early 1940s some Londoners referred to 'that so-called Mr Hitler'.
111 'Stay Out of It!': FER, Vol.27, 1931.
112 FO 371/16163 [F 3373/1/10]: Ambassador Francis Lindley, Tokyo, to FO, 12 March 1932.
113 Op. cit. P. Broad Minute.
114 For divisions on overseas expansion among patriotic groups involved in the February, March and May Incidents of 1932 see Wilson 2002: 117–19.
115 FO 371/16165 [F 3645/1/10]: Memorandum, G.V. Kitson, Shanghai to FO, 30 March 1932.
116 FO 371/16178 [F 7165/1/10]: Francis Lindley, Tokyo, to FO, 30 August 1932.
117 SEPM: 13 October 1932. However, Colonel Itagaki Seishirō had begun attempts to 'coax' Puyi into heading the new state in Port Arthur in late January (Jordan 2001: 19, and 248, n.25).
118 SEPM: 14 October 1932.
119 FO 371/16183 [F 845/1/10]: Adrian Holmes, Peking, to FO, 24 October 1932.
120 Woodhead 1935: 229.
121 Pro: WO 208/378a, Chatham House Lecture, 12 November 1942, 7. Cited in Bickers 2004 (2003): 386, n.65.
122 Japan, Delegation to the League of Nations, 1933: 159.
123 Lu 2002: 214.
124 Op. cit: 214–15.
125 Matsuoka Yōsuke dispatch to Foreign Ministry, no.38–1, received 23 November 1932.
126 Best 1999: 228–9.
127 Japan, Delegation to the League of Nations, 1933: 95.
128 'The Status of Manchukuo: The Question of Recognition': *Oriental Affairs*, January 1934, 8–10.
129 FO 371/18151 [F 6676/3927/10]: Harcourt-Smith note, 6 November 1934.
130 'Chinese Censorship': *The Times*, 23 June 1934.
131 FO 371/18151 [F 3927/3927/10]: Chinese ambassador to C.W. Orde, FO, 27 June 1934.
132 FO 371/18151 [F 7450/3927/10]: Report of meeting with Wang Jingwei, 3 November 1934; H. Cadogan, Nanking to H.G.W. Woodhead, 9 November 1934. Woodhead's asking price for the series he had nurtured since 1912 was $40,000. These negotiations appear to have collapsed but Woodhead seems later to have transferred the series to Guomindang interests, for in 1940–41, 1943, and 1944–45 the Council of International Affairs in Chungking published a series of editions under the imprint of, respectively, the Commercial Press, Shanghai, Thacker & Co., Bombay, and the China Daily Tribune Publishing Co., Shanghai.
133 FO 371/18139 [F 1041/1041/10]: A.G. Major, Mukden, to FO, 5 February 1934.
134 'Mr Pu Yi. The Man Who Re-ascends A Throne This Week Talks Exclusively To The "Sunday Express"': *Sunday Express*, 25 February 1934.
135 *Manchuria Daily News*, 'Souvenir', *Enthronement Supplement*, 1 March 1934.
136 Farnsworth 1996: 184.
137 'Japan Builds a Colony': *Saturday Evening Post*, No.206, 1934, 12–13.
138 'Why We Resist': CWR, 13 May 1933, 420–1.

139 FO 371/17104 [F4106/283/10]: A.W.G. Randall Minute of 26 June 1933 regarding Henry Kinney's 'Memorandum on Manchukuo', dated 22 May 1933.
140 FO 371/18103 [F 2185/126/10]: J.F. Brenan, Shanghai, to Peking Legation, 10 February 1934.
141 'Great Britain': MDN, 11 August 1934.
142 FO 371/18169 [F 6384/57/23]: R. Clive, Tokyo, to FO, 27 September 1934.
143 Young 1938: 203–204.
144 Fleisher 1941: 259–62.
145 Borg 1964: 75–6.
146 Grew 1944: 129.
147 Grew: op. cit.
148 Grew: op. cit.
149 Nish 1977: 299–300.
150 Grew 1944: 128.
151 Best 1999: 9–10; Brooks 2000: 175.
152 See van den Ven, Hans 2003: 209–11; 219, discussing Chiang's operational strategy in December 1937 for the crucial battle of Xuzhou, with Guomindang, not Communist, forces fighting guerrilla warfare in the Japanese rear; 221, on Chiang's need for a military success to bolster Guomindang propaganda drive in Europe.
153 Thomson 1973: 89.
154 Cohen 1971: 146.
155 SMR 1937: 1–2.
156 'British interests in China: Shanghai as Japanese base', letter from Morgan Y oung: *The Times*, 18 August 1937.
157 This statement appears to contradict Byas's more forthright 4 August 1937 NYT article.
158 'A Great Eastern Empire: Reply to Japanese Aims': letter from Morgan Young to *The Times*, 26 January 1938, replying to a Hugh Byas Tokyo report of 20 January 1938.
159 Hunter 1984: 174.
160 O'Connor 2004 (ed.), Vol. 9; 2005 Vol.9: 77–166; 193–328; Vol. 10: 1–229; Kushner 2006: 40–4.
161 The *Ōsaka Mainichi Shinbun* of 9 February 1938 reported that Mukai Toshiaki achieved 250 deaths which put him ahead of Noda Takeshi, whereupon Mukai invited Noda to extend the competition to 1,000 deaths. Discussion of the eventual tally and outcome of the 'competition' continues today on the Internet. In late 2005, the Tokyo District Court found for the *Asahi Shinbun* and the *Mainichi Shinbun* and the journalist Honda Katsuichi against the descendants of 2nd Lieutenants Mukai and Noda in a libel action the descendants had brought against them for reporting the 'killing competition' in books and articles on Japan's wartime record in China (*Asahi Shinbun*: 23 August 2005). Note that an earlier report in the *Tōkyō Nichi-nichi Shinbun* (30 November 1937), indicates that the 'killing competition' actually began *before* the Japanese army entered Nanking and that the target was set higher, at 150 deaths, once both men had reached 100 killings during the Nanking Incident, on 11 December. See also *Tōkyō Nichi-nichi Shinbun*, 13 December 1937. For a close examination of the circumstances and actuality

of the 'killing competition' issue and its post-war critique, particularly in the 1970s, see Wakabayashi, Bob T., 2000, 2007. In both his 2000 paper and in his own contribution to his edited compilation of 2007, Wakabayashi convincingly demonstrates that the 'killing competition' itself was a fabrication lent credibility by Japanese news reports and by the horrific background of events in Nanking. For Timperley, Byas, other foreign correspondents and many commentators since, if the Japanese themselves were reporting these events, that was sufficient verification, but the story is more complicated.

162 NYT: 6 December 1937.
163 JA: 7 December 1937.
164 JA: 14 December 1937.
165 Timperley 1938: 284, 285.
166 Timperley 1938: 282.
167 Timperley 1938: 286.

7

Endgame, 1936–1941

In the spring of 1933, following its adoption of the Lytton Report, Japan withdrew from the League of Nations. Withdrawal did not constitute a wholesale rejection of the larger internationalist interests of the League, but as this account has tried to demonstrate, the League's adoption of the Report implied an unacceptable challenge to the highly-developed sense of national integrity held by important groups in Japan. Adoption of the Report constituted not only a rebuke by the international community, but also raised and seemed to answer fundamental questions about Japan's commitment to the ideals of the League. There is certainly an argument that because the larger interests of the League clearly no longer coincided with those of Japan, Japan's withdrawal put an end to the formal commitment to internationalism that membership had represented. However, as Burkman (2008) has shown, Japan's engagement with the ideals of the international community did not abruptly cease in February 1933. Compared with the pained defiance to come in the late 1930s, even the Foreign Ministry network's continued efforts to persuade the wider world of the correctness of Japan's case in Manchuria were part of this continuing engagement.

At home in Japan, there was considerable support for Matsuoka Yōsuke's decision to lead his delegates out of the Council chamber, and for the views he expressed on a 1934 speaking tour in which he gave a series of 180 speeches to a total audience estimated at 690,000.[1] In these speeches, Matsuoka advocated the abandonment of political parties, without specifically attacking his old party, the *Seiyūkai*, and hinted at a Mussolini-style 'march on Rome', telling his followers to be in a state of readiness.[2] Whether Matsuoka was riding the tiger of Japanism or leading the nation into an even stronger version is hard to judge. The popular appetite for the opinions he expressed between February 1933 and August 1935, when he was suddenly made Director of the South Manchurian Railway, was undeniable.[3]

Besides a small number of independent-minded intellectuals at Japanese universities, the most significant individual challenges to the patriotic or nationalistic consensus in early Shōwa were posed by the constitutional lawyer Minobe Tatsukichi (1873–1948) and the *Minseitō* politician Saitō Takao, if measured by the furore they aroused. Minobe's 'emperor-organ' theory certainly challenged constitutional theory and set the positions taken by *Seiyūkai* on their head, but the Minobe crisis of 1935–36 had less to do with constitutional niceties than with silencing the questioning, rational voice of the middle ground on the validity of *kokutai*, the national polity. Similarly, the solution to the crisis brought on by Saitō Takao's 1940 Diet speech questioning the overt consensus that Japan was fighting a 'Holy War' in China required not only that Saitō be expelled from the Diet but also the dissolution of political parties and the establishment in October 1940 of the Imperial Rule Assistance Association (*Taisei Yokusankai*).

In the late 1930s, with the vernacular press for the most part cheer-leading Japan's cause in East Asia, the foreign-owned English-language newspapers of Japan presented minor but irritating exceptions to the national consensus. In 1938 the *Japan Chronicle* began receiving a monthly subsidy from the Cabinet Information Bureau. The *Japan Advertiser* of Tokyo had rejected a similar arrangement in 1934 but was forced into selling out to the *Japan Times* in October 1940. In December 1940 the *Japan Chronicle* joined the *Advertiser* in the Foreign Ministry network. However, the American-owned *Japan News-Week*, which had only started publication in November 1938, continued to run outspoken criticisms of Japanese and Axis policies until the day after Pearl Harbor.

In the closing years of this endgame, the tone of many Japanese prop-aganda statements swung even more firmly towards a sense of betrayal, of national victimhood, unrecognized sacrifice and outrage over 'anti-Japanese' machinations by China and the Western powers, as well as outright rejection of the right of the Western powers even to think of helping China economically or militarily, or to negotiate with Japan.[4] This was between Japan and China and the Red menace, and all other options were closed. In August 1937 Hugh Byas diagnosed what he described as a 'blind spot' in Japanese perceptions of Chinese resistance. The Japanese seemed out of touch with events:

> Incredible as it may seem, the Japanese are permeated with a belief that they have received nothing but rebuffs and insults from the Chinese ... Japan's view is that she wants to be a friend to lead, develop and defend China, and so Japan is humiliated by China's hostile refusal. The Chinese masses' deep fear of and animosity towards Japan are treated as if they were noxious prod-ucts of the Kuomintang propaganda. Not a single Japanese statesman, publicist or newspaper has ever suggested that the Manchurian affair, the Shanghai bombardment, the Jehol campaign, the creation of the East Hopei regime, the orgy of smuggling associated with that regime and other events may have been responsible for Chinese fears.[5]

Such blind spots were not so much 'incredible' as the predictable conse-quences of a tightly rationed information supply. Those Japanese who sought a deeper understanding of Japan's case beyond the ubiquity of rhetorical accounts found hard news in short supply. Either they consumed Japan-engendered exhortations which had little coherence outside the national context, or they retreated into the private integrity of secret diaries. As one American scholar defined it, the choice lay between 'the martyrdom of enforced silence and a complete conversion to army-dominated visions of their country's future'.[6] The middle ground, the narrow public space held by the journals and discussion groups that had mushroomed in and since Taishō and by the independent English-language newspapers of East Asia was shrinking fast.

ENDGAME IN JAPAN

With the establishment of the *Dōmei* agency in January 1936, competition between the Foreign Ministry network and the foreign press networks entered a bitter endgame. At foreign press offices, telephones were impounded and cables were delayed, not sent or simply not delivered. The censor became even less predictable. Journalists came under closer scrutiny and became liable to sudden arrest and equally sudden release.

Japan and Germany grew closer after the accession to the German Chancellorship of Adolf Hitler in January 1933. By the mid-1930s, the *Japan Times* had become something of a showcase for Japan-German amity, running pictorial features on Axis events in Europe, advertising and reviewing German films and granting the pronouncements of leading Nazis officials the same typographical and editorial prominence as those of home-grown bigwigs.[7] In Tokyo, German officials and their agents became interested in the networks of the foreign press in East Asia and reacted swiftly to any aspersions of the Nazi regime they detected there.

At the *Japan Advertiser*, the Fleishers' Jewish ancestry may have made them more visible targets for Nazi aggression. Many of the young men whom the *Advertiser* recruited from the University of Missouri and elsewhere were of Jewish extraction, and, like Ugaki Kazushige in 1923, Tokyo's Nazis may have read some significance into this.[8] In February 1934, the German Commercial Counselor warned B.W. Fleisher that if the *Advertiser* did not moderate its tone towards Germany, he would be 'reported to Berlin'.[9] On 4 August 1934, when the *Advertiser* ran an article by Vere Redman disparaging the Hitler regime, and referring to the German government as 'the dominant gang', the *Advertiser* received a joint letter of protest from most of the German colony in Tokyo and eighty-six cancelled subscriptions, 1% of the readership.

US ambassador Cameron Forbes once described B.W. Fleisher as a 'quivering aspen', although whether this referred to a willingness to bow before authority or a nervous disposition, given the nervous breakdown Fleisher suffered in his youth, is unclear. In 1935 Forbes' successor Joseph Grew maintained that the *Advertiser* had always followed 'a very cautious and conservative policy'.[10] Under the motto, 'Independent and Constructive', the leader column of the *Japan Advertiser* had followed a flexible line towards Japanese expansionism and the Fleishers had always tried to meet officialdom halfway, especially since Inoue and Dan's timely aid following the fire of November 1930. In 1933 Fleisher allowed Japanese anti-British propaganda on the Indian cotton trade to appear in an *Advertiser* textiles supplement circulated in the US.[11] In January 1938 the *Advertiser's* weekly magazine, the *Trans-Pacific*, ran virulent anti-British articles translated from the magazine *Hinode* and was banned by the government of Burma.[12]

As time went by, such accommodations no longer seemed enough to maintain official favour for the *Advertiser*. In August 1934, in the wake of the Amō Statement, the *Advertiser* was heavily criticized by Amō Eiji, who now seemed to view the paper as overtly anti-Japanese, either by policy or design. A debate on the paper's future seemed to be in progress between representatives of the Foreign Ministry network, the South Manchurian Railway and the Army, but the signs were that it was unresolved. That autumn, Wilfrid Fleisher was tentatively offered, and rejected, a subsidy by the Foreign Ministry.[13] Early in 1935 Yoshida Shigeru asked Wilfrid Fleisher if it would not be a good idea to combine the *Advertiser* with the *Japan Times*. Fleisher replied that since the *Advertiser* was a morning paper and the *Japan Times* was an evening paper, both were needed by the community. Yoshida then suggested that the *Advertiser* view Japan's position more sympathetically. In the late 1920s, around the time of the *Enthronement Issue*, the *Advertiser* press had been printing books by Fleisher's former protégé Henry Kinney and others promoting the South Manchurian Railway and the transformation of Manchuria into an East Asian super-state (e.g. Kinney 1928). However, in 1935 the South Manchurian Railway abandoned the Advertiser Press in favour of Zumoto Motosada's Herald Press, with which it produced numerous South Manchurian Railway pamphlets and booklets setting out the Japanese case in North China. In the same year, the Railway joined Mitsui in warning Fleisher that it might not be able to maintain its current level of advertising in his publications.[14]

In the late 1930s, when 60% of its 4,000-odd subscribers were Japanese, the authorities were keeping a close watch on the *Advertiser*. In February 1938 the *Advertiser's* Frank Hedges conducted an unusually frank interview with General Araki which, when published, drew a number of anonymous threats from patriotic groups, and caused an increase in police surveillance and interference.[15] In the summer of 1939, the *Advertiser's* well-tried technique of using Japanese authors for the expression of controversial views ran into trouble. On 4 July a polemic by Ozaki Yukio in favour of Japan taking a neutral position in the next war might have escaped censure had not Ozaki gone on to question the benefits for Japan of supporting the military adventures of Germany and Italy. The 4 July issue had already been printed when the police suppressed it and confiscated the copies still remaining in the *Advertiser* premises (while no attempt was made to call in those already on the street).[16] Later that month, when the *Advertiser* published a reader's letter claiming that the current anti-British agitation in Japan was government-inspired, Fleisher was summoned to the Ministry of Home Affairs and warned against printing anything connecting the government with the agitation (but assured that he was free to publish anti-British material).[17]

One year later, in July 1940, the *Advertiser* headlined a report of an anti-British, pro-Axis meeting at the Hibiya Hall 'Meeting Fawns on Axis'. The police sent for the *Advertiser*'s chief translator and demanded an apology. Moved by protests from the German ambassador, the Foreign Ministry warned the editor, Wilfrid Fleisher, that unless he modified his tone he would be starved of newsprint.[18] At a time when a great many vernacular newspapers were being closed or amalgamated, this was a threat to be taken seriously.

In the same month, Wilfrid Fleisher met the newly appointed Foreign Minister, Matsuoka Yōsuke at his home to conduct an interview that, although intended 'for background only', showed Matsuoka in unequivocal pro-Axis mode, predicting that 'In the battle between democracy and totalitarianism, the latter adversary will without question win and will control the world. The era of democracy is finished and the democratic system bankrupt.'[19] This exchange soon found its way to the *New York Herald Tribune*, for whom Fleisher was Tokyo correspondent.

In the mid-thirties, as part of the war of attrition against the foreign press, an outbreak of what the foreign press called 'spionitis' broke out in Japan and in those parts of China under Japanese control. Holidaymakers who took photographs in controlled areas or asked questions about their surroundings were detained incommunicado. The newspapers worked these incidents into major scares. As Hugh Byas put it: 'The Police find a Molehill and the Press Makes a Mountain Out of It.'[20]

In January 1940, the Japanese arrested Vincent Peters in Kōbe on an espionage charge. The case against Peters was strong and the British were keen to recover him. They therefore decided to arrest a prominent Japanese in London to use as a bargaining chip. On 14 July 1940 the London correspondent for the *Asahi Shinbun* and other Japanese papers, Takayuki Eguchi, was arrested in London on an undisclosed charge. He would remain in a series of prisons and camps in Britain and India without charge or a trial for nearly six years.[21] The German-born wife of a Japanese painter, Mrs Millie Yoshi, was also arrested.[22]

On 27 July 1940, in the month that Matsuoka gave his fiery *Japan Advertiser* interview, security forces in Tokyo detained sixteen British business people and journalists on espionage charges. Among those arrested were Melville James Cox (1884–1940), the Reuters correspondent in Tokyo.[23] Cox died two days after his arrest, either before or after jumping or being thrown from his cell window at *Kempei-tai* headquarters.[24] In his eight years in Tokyo, Cox had gained a reputation for asking awkward questions at Information Bureau conferences that may have won him some unwelcome attention. However, Kenneth Selby-Walker, Reuters Manager in Tokyo, felt that as far as the police were concerned, Cox's professional status alone was enough to justify his arrest.[25] Following the arrests of July 1940, outrage in London was

echoed in Tokyo by Craigie, who insisted on reprisals against Japanese
in Britain, India and the South-east Asian colonies, leading directly to a
War Office decision on 1 August to arrest ten Japanese suspected of espionage.[26] Foreign Office notes regarding the arrests show that they were a
direct reprisal for the arrests in Japan. The first four arrests were of
Japanese businessmen in London 'who have a certain standing, even if
there is not evidence in every case of espionage activities. It is essential
also to take in the chief representative of the Japanese News Agency as a
quid pro quo for Mr Cox.'[27] On 4 August five more arrests of Japanese
took place: three in Rangoon plus Kobayashi Ichirō, the head of *Dōmei*
in Singapore, and a Japanese merchant in Hong Kong.[28] Not long afterwards two Japanese journalists in London and the Japanese press attaché
in Singapore, Shinozaki Mamoru, were arrested. On 16 September two
more Britons were arrested in Tokyo, and Craigie was reported to be
pressing the authorities for their release.[29] The Japanese then proved
unwilling to exchange Peters for Eguchi, sentencing him to eight years
penal servitude in September 1940. In August Hugh Byas had reported a
lessening of tensions between Britain and Japan, and the release by
Japan of some of those arrested.[30] But Byas's old employer was about to
feel the heat.

A little under a year earlier, in October 1939, B.W. Fleisher had authorized one of his British staff, the ex-M.P. Ernest Pickering[31], to offer the
Japan Advertiser to the Ministry of Information in London for £80,000,
but the price was too high.[32] Not long afterwards, Toshi Gō, the editor of
the *Japan Times*, made an offer for the *Advertiser* that B.W. Fleisher
rejected. According to a wartime account by the ex-*Advertiser* writer
Demaree Bess, Gō then 'called on [Wilfrid] Fleisher to warn him that he
would not be permitted to sell the *Advertiser* to any foreign interests,
Axis or otherwise'.

'Do you mean that I cannot sell my newspaper even to a group of
Americans?' asked Fleisher.
'You possess only one buyer,' replied Goh, [sic] 'and that is the Japanese
Imperial Government.'[33]

Thereafter, the official campaign of intimidation intensified. Translators
and office boys were arrested and held for days on trumped up charges,
journalists were threatened, telephones impounded, paper supplies
withdrawn, and Gō warned Fleisher that 'Japanese fanatics might do
something rash'. In August 1940 Wilfrid Fleisher returned from a break
in Karuizawa to find the *Advertiser* office crawling with detectives and
half his staff in custody. Finally, the Fleishers saw the writing on the
wall. In September Wilfrid Fleisher called the *New York Herald Tribune*,
first, to explain that it was impossible for him to send them much
beyond summaries of official communiqués, and secondly, to ask the
Tribune not to send any more payments to his Tokyo account beyond
the end of September.[34] Fleisher then visited Gō and told him that he

was ready to negotiate a sale. As Fleisher recalled, 'From the very moment I approached Mr Gō until the *Advertiser* was transferred to him two months later, all police interference with the paper ceased.'[35]

In 1908, with the help of John Russell Kennedy, B.W. Fleisher had paid between $15,000 and $30,000 for the *Advertiser*, the cost to be paid in instalments over several years. In a deal agreed on 10 October 1940, Kennedy's successor on the *Japan Times* paid Fleisher US$100,000 (approximately ¥416,000) for what had become in thirty-two years the foremost American newspaper in East Asia: 50% down, the rest to be paid in instalments. Since early September Wilfrid Fleisher had been holding out for a further ¥50,000 to pay for employee bonuses and passages home, but now he caved in to what his father would later describe as 'a blackmail price'. On the day agreement was reached, Grew reported that although both sides had agreed to report the transaction as 'a friendly sale' in their respective newspapers, negotiations had been 'extremely unpleasant and in the end they came to virtual confiscation accompanied by the threat that unless Mr Fleisher signed the agreement today, no further opportunity for a sale would be offered and "swift measures" would be taken to render the continuance of the newspaper impossible'. Indeed, Gō told Fleisher that 'a strong faction' in the Foreign Ministry wished to confiscate the *Advertiser* without any payment.[36]

Gō then moved the entire *Japan Times* staff and equipment into the *Japan Advertiser* premises. On Monday, 14 October 1940, the *Japan Times* and the *Japan Advertiser* were combined under a new masthead, the *Japan Times & Advertiser*, with publication scheduled for an eight-page morning and a four-page evening edition, thus maintaining each newspaper's schedule prior to amalgamation.[37] The *Advertiser*'s weekly edition, the *Trans-Pacific*, was relaunched as the *Japan Times Weekly and Trans-Pacific*. Of the thirteen editorial staff then writing for the *Advertiser* – managing editor Wilfrid Fleisher, Don Brown, Newton Edgers, Richard Fujii, Al Downs, Richard Tennelly, James Tew, Thelma Hecht, George Gorman, Jasper Bellinger, Ernest Pickering, Ray Cromley and Joseph Newman – only four stayed on at the *Advertiser* after the sale. These included two recent British arrivals, ex-M.P. Ernest Pickering and Gorman who had arrived just before the sale to be taken on as news editor in place of Don Brown, who returned to the US.[38] The other two were the Americans Bellinger and Tennelly, both of whom were later interned.[39] Tennelly also became Tokyo correspondent for NBC and Reuters. Downs stayed on for Hearst's International News Service, Ray Cromley for the *Wall Street Journal*, Newman for the *Herald Tribune*, taking over from Wilfrid Fleisher until 15 October 1941, when he returned to the US.[40] On 30 November 1940, the Fleishers, father and son, and their families sailed from Yokohama on the *Yawata Maru*, bound for California, almost thirty-three years to the day since B.W. Fleisher first set foot on Japanese soil.

Two months later the *Japan Chronicle* came into the semi-official fold.

The sale of the *Chronicle* reflected both the financial deterioration of the newspaper under Douglas Young and his successor, Stanley Foley's management and the difficulties of reporting in an increasingly restrictive climate, but it was also an extension of previous agreements.[41]

The reporting problems were real enough. On 15 September 1936, the Kōbe police ordered that day's *Chronicle* suppressed because of a leader suggesting Japan compensate the families of Chinese killed in the recent Chengdu and Pakhoi incidents. In the summer of 1936, Morgan Young left for a holiday in England, acknowledging official pressures in a letter to Hugh Byas, 'Mr Amau [Amō Eiji] flatters me by being interested in my departure.'[42] In October 1936 the British ex-Shanghai journalist Edwin Allington Kennard became editor. In August 1937 the *Chronicle* published another article that gave offence and in October Kennard was summoned and briefly detained by the Kōbe district court. Meanwhile, Morgan Young's application for a visa to return to Japan as the correspondent for the *Manchester Guardian* was rejected by the Japanese embassy in London. Amō was indeed 'interested in his departure'.

Fearing that it might sell up, the British embassy offered financial assistance to the *Chronicle* in June and November 1940. When he accepted the second offer, Stanley Foley, the *Chronicle's* business manager, assured the embassy that a sale was not being considered. However, on 17 December 1940 the British ambassador, Robert Craigie, learned that the *Japan Chronicle* was about to be sold to the *Japan Times & Advertiser*. The transfer took place on 23 December 1940.[43] On 1 January the following year the *Chronicle* officially changed hands, although its staff remained in the Kōbe premises. In Kōbe, Terao Isao, chief translator, became editor-in-chief of the *Chronicle*.[44] A British citizen, J.R. ('Reggie') Price was brought in as Editorial Writer. Other editorial staff members who stayed on after the sale were Leslie Nishigori, S.V. dos Remedios (chief proof-reader), G.T.W. Gauntlett, a rewrite man recently transferred from Tokyo, two translators, Nishikawa Tadao and Takahashi Kazuo and a nineteen-year-old newcomer to journalism, Theodore Van Doorn, as the main news reporter.[45] This group stayed on at the *Chronicle* building in Sannomiya, Kōbe, and liaised with their new employer, the *Japan Times & Advertiser* in Tokyo.[46]

In March 1941, on the eve of his departure from Japan, Stanley Foley confessed to Robert Craigie that the Cabinet Information Bureau (*Naikaku Jōhōbu*) and its successor the Cabinet Information Board (*Naikaku Jōhōkyoku*) had been subsidizing the *Chronicle* since 1938. On condition that the *Chronicle* not pursue an anti-Japanese policy and that the arrangement be kept secret, the Bureau had paid the *Chronicle* ¥3,000 a month, distributed as follows:

Mrs Harloe (chief beneficiary of the Young Estate, proprietors of the paper)	¥1,000
Mrs Harloe's daughter [Ethel]	200
Mr Kennard (editor)	230

Mr Foley (business manager)	200
Other Expenses	1,370
	¥3,000

'Substantial retiring allowances', as Craigie put it, were also paid to Stanley Foley and Edwin Kennard. As 'chief beneficiary of the Young Estate', Robert Young's widow, again a widow since 1935 with the death of her second husband, Thomas Harloe, Annie Harloe would also have received the lion's share of the sum 'considerably in excess of ¥300,000', most of it paid in foreign currency, for her first husband's creation.[47] Joseph Grew's information was that the purchase price was half that – 'about ¥150,000'. Grew also learned from other sources that the deal was done without any application of 'objectionable pressure' on the *Chronicle*.[48] Craigie felt that Kennard 'had had no part in the actual transaction and had probably interpreted his loyalty to his employers as precluding him from bringing this matter to my attention'.

Technically, the December 1940 sale did not mean the end of the *Chronicle* until the paper ceased publication at the end of January 1942, at which time all but a skeleton staff transferred to the *Japan Times & Advertiser* in Tokyo. It could be said that the *Chronicle* informally and secretly lost its independence when Foley brokered the deal with the Cabinet Information Bureau in 1938. On 4 January 1942 even before the *Chronicle* was formally wound up, its name entered the masthead of the *Japan Times & Advertiser* in Tokyo, as *The Japan Times & Advertiser Incorporating The Japan Chronicle and The Japan Mail (JT&AJCJM)*.[49] Formally, the *Chronicle* ended its corporate life on 31 January 1942, the last copy number being 15529. On 1 January 1943 the portmanteau masthead was simplified to the *Nippon Times*, printing of the incorporated edition ended in Kōbe and all the remaining staff moved to Tokyo, where Leslie Nishigori became an editor alongside Trevor Gauntlett and other *Nippon Times* staff.[50]

In April 1941, Craigie reported that since the sale, the *Chronicle* (by which he meant the skeleton Kōbe edition), now receiving a subsidy of ¥4,000 a month, had become 'gradually more pro-Axis until at present there is nothing to distinguish it from the *Japan Times & Advertiser*'.[51] In Kōbe, a police censor stood by the press and read through each issue before it was put to bed. The *Japan Times* did not send any supervisory staff to Kōbe or take any special measures to ensure that the remnants of the *Chronicle* staff followed an official line, but Theodore van Doorn, another member of the *Chronicle* staff remembers Reginald Price, the British journalist who succeeded Kennard as editor in Kōbe, having 'to watch his P's and Q's regarding Japanese politics'.[52]

Robert Craigie does not mention the sale of the *Chronicle* in his memoirs, but seems to retrospectively discount its editorial integrity in remarking that, '...after the sale of the *Japan Advertiser* to Japanese interests in 1940, the only independent and reliable source of news in Japan was the British Embassy bulletin' (edited by Vere Redman).[53] The

Chronicle was sold to the *Japan Times* two months after the *Advertiser*, but, as Craigie implied, it had been neither 'reliable' nor 'independent' since it began taking a Foreign Ministry subsidy in 1938.

Reacting to the sale of the *Chronicle* at the Foreign Office, T.E. Bromley minuted, 'This is very regrettable and a sad decline from the standard set when Mr Morgan Young was in Japan.' But these were crocodile tears. When Morgan Young was in Japan, he was seen by the Foreign Office as 'one of the greatest thorns in the side of the [Tokyo] Embassy'.[54] Nor had the Foreign Office seen any need to protest in May 1937 when the Japanese embassy in London turned down Young's application for a visa to return to Tokyo. Both in London and his final home in Oxford, Young continued to be cold-shouldered by the Far East Department at the Foreign Office until his death in 1942. The services of Hugh Byas, on the other hand, were much sought-after in Whitehall and at the BBC, but by April 1941 he had left Tokyo for the US and a short, final career as a Japan specialist at Yale.

JAPAN NEWS-WEEK

With the *Chronicle* and the *Advertiser* now wrapped in the coils of the *Japan Times & Advertiser*, Craigie was not quite correct in claiming that the last independent voice of British journalism in Japan had been silenced: one organ of the foreign-owned foreign press was still being published: the magazine *Japan News-Week*, edited by an American, but staffed by British and American reporters.

The first weekly edition of *Japan News-Week* came out on 12 November 1938. It was edited by Newton Edgers, an American with experience on the *Advertiser*, and published by another American, Ward R. 'Bud' Wills. Edgers assured Joseph Grew that his journal would be free of official Japanese support or subsidy and that it was to be 'a sheet published by Americans for Americans'.[55] However, the first issue also acknowledged that 'we are probably pro-Japanese in the sense that, having lived here for some time, we have got to know the people and consequently rather to like them'.

Japan News-Week did publish a good many forthright, critical articles on developments in Japan. The weekly editorials did not mince their words and were especially critical of Matsuoka's foreign policy pronouncements.[56] In early 1941, Grew complained to Wills regarding criticisms of US foreign policy on Japan in the 25 January 1941 issue of the magazine, but his protest was tempered by the fact that, with the sale of the *Chronicle*, *Japan News-Week* was the last foreign-owned English-language publication left in Japan.[57] After the sale of the *Advertiser*, the subscription list of *Japan News-Week* showed a considerable increase, a mixed blessing given, first, the difficulty of obtaining paper and printer's ink and secondly, the fact that profits did not come from sales but from advertising. Newsstand sales were also on the up, an increase Wills put down to the reluctance of many Japanese readers to appear on the subscription list.

By February 1941, the magazine had received numerous encounters with the censor, several sharp warnings from the police, and repeated protests from the German embassy over the consistently anti-Axis tone of the magazine. In August 1940 the local, German, D.N.B. news agency offered Wills 'a relatively large sum' for *Japan News-Week*. Wills turned them down, less on patriotic grounds than because he learned that it was no longer possible to transfer payments abroad. *Japan News-Week* remained strongly pro-American and anti-Axis but consistently opposed the application of embargoes and sanctions by Washington. However, in the absence of other sources, *Japan News-Week* became so reliant on the *Dōmei* agency that the British embassy tried to redress the balance by having one of their staff, Vere Redman, appointed to the editorial team. After the *Advertiser* was sold, the optimistic Wills nourished hopes of *Japan News-Week* replacing it as the organ of choice for the American community. To this end, and keenly aware of the importance of having at least one 'American' voice publishing in Japan, Grew encouraged local US businesses to buy advertising space in *Japan News-Week*.

However, in March 1941, Wills received an offer from the Cabinet Information Board to purchase the paper. When he refused, fearing that it would then become a propaganda sheet (and upon learning, again, that he would not be able to take the money out of Japan), Mitsui, Mitsubishi and other Japanese firms failed to renew their advertising contracts. The British Information Bureau, run by Wills' new colleague Vere Redman at the British embassy, then offered to defray Wills's advertising losses but he turned down this offer for fear of losing his independence.[58]

In the same month, *Japan News-Week* published some outspoken editorials. The first of these drew a comparison between the aims and ideals of Britain and the United States and other 'Democracies' and the 'Totalitarian Powers', drawing on recent speeches by President Roosevelt and Chancellor Hitler and referring retrospectively to Matsuoka Yōsuke's July 1940 interview to point to the irreconcilability of the two systems. *Japan News-Week* maintained that the US could not object to any nation adopting any system of government, even a totalitarian one, but that the US would surely oppose any power that imposed its will on others. Therefore 'so long as Japan chooses to conduct peaceful negotiations with other countries' Japan might find cause for comfort in US policy.

The second March 1941 editorial took the form of a reply to criticisms of the first received from a Japanese reader who wanted *Japan News-Week* to acknowledge that 'in attacking one of the Triple Allied Nations' they were attacking the other two as well. This reader took the earlier editorial to task for including the regime of Chiang Kai-shek among the Democracies. In replying to the first point, *Japan News-Week* noted that the terms of the Tripartite Alliance did not provide for the subordination of the will and destiny of the signatories of the Alliance to the direction and dictates of a single entity. It was 'incredible' that Japan should relinquish its own autonomy and national personality for the sake of two distant countries, or 'depart so far from its traditional course as to acquire the complete membership in that type of superstate under Nazi domination which Germany now envisages', particularly since 'the Japanese statesmen have frequently emphasized that the changes and reforms they contemplate are not to be based on Nazi or Fascist models'.[59]

Similar distinctions between the national polities of Japan and Germany and Italy had been aired in the English-language and vernacular press since becoming official writ in July 1937 in the pages of the *Kokutai no hongi* and other semi-sacred official texts, so *Japan News-Week* may have felt that it was on safe ground. However, after Japan, Italy and Germany signed the Tripartite Pact in Berlin on 27 September 1940 it seemed unlikely to most staff members that *Japan News-Week* would be tolerated much longer. Indeed, for about two months after the Pact, 'the customary greeting of Tokyo foreign residents to the staff of *Japan New-Week* was: 'What! Not in jail yet?' and the journal's continued existence led to rumours that it was receiving Japanese support.[60]

In mid-April 1941, W.R. Wills was summoned to the Cabinet Information Board and dressed down for publishing anti-German material, to which he replied that his paper was not so much anti-German as pro-Japan-American friendship. The Board spokesman then told Wills that the Japanese Navy regarded *Japan News-Week* as 'an important channel for Japanese-American relations' and that both the Information Bureau and the Navy wanted it to continue. With this in mind, the Information Bureau told Wills that it could offer the paper ¥10,000 to help meet its financial difficulties. Rather than turn down this offer outright, Wills said that it would be more useful if Japanese companies that had previously withdrawn their advertising contracts would renew them. Within a few weeks Mitsui and Mitsubishi had taken him at his word.[61]

In late April, *Japan News-Week* published another controversial editorial disputing current Japanese thinking regarding US assistance to Britain in the war against Germany. *Japan News-Week* clearly supported the spirit of US assistance and rejected any possibility of Britain's 'surrender to Nazi domination'. However hopeless Britain's position might appear to some in Japan, US aid was not predicated on opportunism but on upholding fundamental principles and ideals against the 'Nazifascist conquerors of Europe'. This editorial was the final contribution of its associate editor, Charles N. Spinks, a tenured member of faculty at Tokyo University of Commerce, who returned to the US at the end of April, leaving Wills, Phyllis Argall and a few others to hold the fort.[62] On 9 August 1941 Spinks' byline appeared below the fourth in a series of five articles depicting 'the stranglehold the Nazis have obtained on Japan'. According to Spinks, since the sale of the *Japan Advertiser* to the *Japan Times* 'controlled by the Japanese Foreign Office', the former American daily has been fully geared to the Nazi Fifth Column, despite the efforts of its able publisher, Toshi Go, to keep it a first-rate newspaper.'[63]

In early September, an editorial challenging Hitler's infallibility and scorning his plans for world conquest was pre-released to foreign correspondents in Tokyo and summarized in reports in the US. Upon its publication in *Japan News-Week*, Wills was summoned to the Cabinet Information Board and informed that in addition to showing an unfriendly attitude towards Japan for the last three months, his latest article represented 'an attack on Japan's fundamental policy' (*Kokutai*) and that if he persisted in such attacks the authorities 'would have to let the law take its course'. The Board warned Wills that if a Japanese newspaper had published such material its editor would have been jailed. Wills learned that Board officials had been flooded with enquiries from Japanese missions abroad asking if the fact that the editorial had been published represented a change in Japanese foreign policy. Brushing aside his assertion of the rights of an American newspaper to express impartial opinion, the Board told Wills that he would have to conform to Japan's policy. The optimistic Wills interpreted this relative transparency as a veiled hint that the Board wished to avoid the permanent suppression of *Japan News-Week*.[64]

FORCES BEHIND THE AMALGAMATION OF
THE ENGLISH-LANGUAGE PRESS IN JAPAN

In 1931–33 and again in 1936–7, a curious phenomenon could be observed at the Japan Times Building in Uchisaiwaichō: the *Japan Times* criticized Japanese foreign policy. In midsummer 1931, the Foreign Ministry had for the first time since 1897 withdrawn its subsidy from the *Japan Times* as an expression of its dissatisfaction with the management of the paper under the ownership of Sheba Sometarō. The paper had recently adopted an unusually independent tone and was in financial difficulties but Sheba, who had joined the *Japan Times* in 1921 in controversial fashion by publishing an open letter addressed to the Home Minister in which he condemned the 'absolutism' of the government, and had gained control as a 'representative' President in January 1922, was holding out for a higher price for the paper than the Foreign Ministry was willing to pay.[65] The withdrawal of the Foreign Ministry subsidy in 1931 forced Sheba to sell up in late 1932, when the caretaker president Date Gen'ichirō resigned after less than a year in office. The Foreign Ministry network regained effective control of the newspaper in January 1933, appointing Ashida Hitoshi, a *Seiyūkai* diet member and ex-Foreign Ministry Information Bureau Director, as President.

Ashida was on cordial terms with Shiratori Toshio, one of his successors at the Information Bureau, but in 1933 Ashida professed sympathy with the majority viewpoint at the League of Nations on the Manchurian issue. This may have prompted the War Office to refuse financial assistance to the *Japan Times* even after the Foreign Ministry resumed its subsidy. Perhaps the War Ministry found too many 'weak-kneed' elements at the paper, not the least of them Nitobe Yoshio, son of Inazō, who became the registered editor in January 1933, Frederick Moore, Hugh Byas and Malcolm Kennedy all having rejected the editorship in late 1932.[66]

The second display of independence was the paper's lukewarm reaction to the Anti-Comintern Pact of 25 November 1936. The *Japan Times* observed that the Pact certainly heralded an important new direction for Japan and a departure from international isolation, but it was not sure where that direction might lead the nation.[67] A month later, the newspaper felt that the Hirota cabinet had misjudged the public reception of the Pact and voiced concern for the effect of the Pact on Japan's relations with Britain and the US.[68]

Early in 1937 the *Japan Times* embarked on a series of leaders criticizing Japanese foreign policy, recommending that it be made on more 'trustworthy' criteria and maintaining that the Japanese people were by no means unanimous in approving of the policies adopted in the last five years.[69] In March the paper went further, asserting that the Japanese people felt that errors made in foreign policy were the cause of many of their current difficulties. In the same month, the *Japan Times* singled out Japan's China policy as particularly unsuccessful. The paper claimed that the policy towards Russia was mistaken, because relations with Moscow had deteriorated since Japan signed the Anti-Comintern Pact. In June the *Japan Times* felt that the public had been misinformed when the Anti-Comintern Pact was signed, being given the impression that it was a military alliance.[70]

What are we to make of this rebellion? The line taken on the Anti-Comintern Pact points to inspiration from its opponents at the Foreign Ministry. This may have been a general protest against military influence on Foreign Ministry decisions, or it may have been aimed specifically at the Pact, whose drafting had been largely the work of a General Staff appointee. The Pact had only been reluctantly agreed by some in the Foreign Ministry, who feared that it might nudge Japan closer to fascism. In December 1936 the *Japan Times* stressed that Japan enjoyed democracy under the Emperor, that the parliamentary system suited Japan well, and that the public had a democratic duty to support the Diet.[71] This was the basis of the *Japan Times* opposition to the Pact, but there may have been an element of turf warfare in it as well, following the creation in July 1936 of the Cabinet Information Committee (*Naikaku Jōhōiinkai*). This body did not remove the propaganda brief from the Foreign Ministry, but it made the Foreign Ministry Information Bureau more vulnerable to the concentration of military influence that was then most pronounced at Cabinet level. The inauguration of the Cabinet Information Committee did not mark the end of the Foreign Ministry network, but it signalled a hardening of tone and purpose in the global presentation of Japan.

In September 1937, following the appointment of the first Konoe cabinet, the Cabinet Information Committee was upgraded to a Bureau.

246 English-Language Press Networks of East Asia, 1918–1945

Despite his paper's independent stance, Ashida Hitoshi was chosen to serve in the new organization alongside Amō Eiji and Iwanaga Yūkichi. However, on 10 January 1940[72] an article appeared in the *Japan Times* announcing Ashida's resignation after a full seven years at the helm. Ashida was Chairman of the 'Political Affairs Investigation Committee of the Seiyukai Party and' as the article explained 'it is largely in view of the growing amount of time and attention that his party duty will claim that he has found it necessary to withdraw from his duties on The Japan Times'.[73] Toshi Gō succeeded Ashida as President and editor of the *Japan Times*, although Ashida stayed on as a Director.

In December 1940 Ashida's tenure at the Cabinet Information Bureau (*Naikaku Jōhōbu*) was not extended to membership of its successor, the Cabinet Information Board (*Naikaku Jōhōkyoku*). Neither was Gō appointed to the Board. This was an institutional setback. The Cabinet Information Board had a preponderance of service personnel on its executive committee, reflecting the steady diminution of Foreign Ministry influence on propaganda and news management. Without representation at this level, the *Japan Times & Advertiser* fell outside the relatively benign purview of the Foreign Ministry and became subject to the control of a cabinet increasingly dominated by military and naval representatives. At the same time, two prominent members of the Board, Amō Eiji and Furuno Inosuke, President of *Dōmei* since the death of his close colleague Iwanaga Yūkichi, served as the bridge between the government and the press. With these two on the Board, matters had come full circle for the *Japan Times & Advertiser*. In 1913–23 Japan's first national news agency, *Kokusai* and the *Japan Times & Mail* had been different parts of the *Jyapan Taimuzu Kabushiki-gaisha*. Now the *Japan Times & Advertiser* looked up to *Kokusai*'s confident young heir, whose Chairman had once been their President's office boy.

Gō's 'activities in the field of international affairs' and his 'wide circles of friends in many foreign countries' were puffed in the *Japan Times* article announcing Gō's appointment. On 22 January Gō and Joseph Grew were photographed together at a tea party for 'prominent Japanese' sponsored by Grew at the Tokyo Club.[74] Gō was an able and experienced publicist. In 1919 he had worked on Japan's publicity team at the Paris Conference under Matsuoka Yōsuke and alongside John Russell Kennedy. In 1934–36 he had run the Shanghai and then the New York offices of the South Manchurian Railway, and he had overseen the production of the *Manchuria Year Book* for three or four years from 1932. For eight months in 1939 he had served as Japanese Commissioner to the New York World's Fair.[75]

Once installed, Gō's priority was to increase the *Japan Times* appeal for American readers in East Asia. Two new journalists from Salt Lake City and Chicago were taken on at starting salaries of $100 (¥400–450) a month, more than double the usual starting rate. Gō believed that some previous administrators at the *Japan Times* had been misusing the Foreign Ministry's ¥7,000 a month subsidy to pay low salaries to foreign journalists and pocket the difference, but he announced that he was determined to 'clean house'.[76]

Gō negotiated the acquisition of the *Japan Advertiser* that October and the *Japan Chronicle* in December and ran the three newspapers as an amalgamated concern until August 1945. Was the decision to buy the *Advertiser* his alone? If not, whose was it? And why not simply shut down the *Advertiser* and *Chronicle* after buying them out? Was there a plan or a man with a plan to create the *Japan Times & Advertiser*?

In May 1941 the septuagenarian Thomas Millard, writing from Manila, offered some answers to these questions.[77] As Millard saw it, 'The Japan Advertiser was bought at the instance of Matsuoka backed by a powerful group of Japanese financial interests, the idea being to have an organ close to the Foreign Office in which their opposition to the Military Party could be expressed.'

Millard was in semi-retirement but he was not outside the loop. He had been operating at the centre of East Asia's media wars for thirty-five years or more and he knew all the players in the *Advertiser* story, Matsuoka not least. When B.W. Fleisher and his family finally left Japan in November 1940, he stopped off in Manila on his way home, and it seems unlikely that he would not have discussed the sale of the *Advertiser* with his oldest and closest business associate.

At the State Department, in June 1941, Stanley Hornbeck found Millard's argument 'plausible and probably accurate'. As he pointed out, Gō had kept close to Matsuoka since they had worked together in 1919. Hornbeck also found it significant that Gō had been promoted to Shanghai manager of the South Manchurian Railway during Matsuoka's Vice-Presidency in 1927–29, and later to manager of the New York office. As Hornbeck saw it, Gō was 'a Matsuoka man'.[78]

The most immediate evidence of Matsuoka's personal involvement in the acquisition of the *Advertiser* came just after Wilfrid Fleisher and Gō had reached an agreement. Gō had threatened to confiscate the paper without compensation if Fleisher attempted to change the terms agreed, but Fleisher went over his head and persuaded Matsuoka to arrange for the whole $100,000 purchase price to be paid immediately rather than in instalments.[79]

The appointment at the *Advertiser* that autumn of the erstwhile Peking correspondent of the *Daily Telegraph*, George Gorman, also leads back to Matsuoka. Gorman's eventful career in the Foreign Ministry's China network included stints at the *North China Standard*, as an adviser to the government of Manchukuo in 1932 and on the *Manchuria Daily News*, and a key role in bringing the *Peking Chronicle* under Japanese control. In March 1933 Gorman became editor of a revamped *Manchuria Daily News* but was replaced in October 1935 when new staff members joined from *Rengō*, the *Japan Times* and the Foreign Ministry of Manchukuo.[80] Gorman moved to the *Peking Chronicle*, which was then sold for $20,000 by the British journalist, Sheldon Ridge to front men for the Japanese embassy. This transfer was negotiated by Gorman, whom the Far East

Department of the Foreign Office in London inaccurately described as 'an Irish-Canadian adventurer-journalist', for he was born in Liverpool – there was more substance in their claim that he was 'hand-in-glove with the Japanese'.[81] Gorman replaced Ridge until mid-September 1939, when the German embassy installed its own candidate. According to an Australian report, Gorman was then appointed to the post of 'chief editorial adviser to the "Japan Times"', a post he held until 8 December 1941.[82] According to a US report, Gorman met with his old acquaintance from South Manchuria Railway days, Matsuoka Yōsuke, at the Foreign Ministry in 1940 and in October 1940, just before the sale of the *Advertiser*, Gorman joined the *Advertiser* newsroom, replacing Don Brown as news editor.[83] Having served the Foreign Ministry network as a cuckoo in Sheldon Ridge's nest at the *Peking Chronicle*, Gorman was probably installed at the *Advertiser* either to help nudge out the Fleishers or simply to hold the fort when they left.

We saw the beginnings of Matsuoka Yōsuke's association with the circle around the *Japan Times* in Chapter 2 of this account, when he and John Russell Kennedy managed Japan's press relations at the Paris Conference in 1919. Chapter 4 saw the Japanese grant semi-official assistance to the *Japan Advertiser* in 1923 and in 1930. In the second instance, the *Advertiser* received financial help from Inoue Junnosuke and Dan Takuma, and from commercial interests associated with the China Consortium and J.P. Morgan, encouraged by the State Department. Both Inoue and Dan belonged to the internationalist tendency in Japan that supported the *Advertiser*'s 'hands across the ocean' reputation. The assassination of both men in February and March 1932 in the Blood League Incident (*Ketsumeidan Jiken*) was accompanied by threats to other well-known internationalists, most notably Shidehara Kijūrō.

On the morning of 8 March 1932, *Nihon oyobi Nihonjin* ran an attack on the *Advertiser* for publishing photographs of arms captured from Japanese forces in China. On 9 March B.W. Fleisher was visited by six policemen who warned him that a group of 'patriotic fanatics' were 'on their way to mob the *Advertiser*'. Fleisher went to the Foreign Ministry where he was received by Shiratori Toshio and treated to 'a diatribe against all things American, declaring that Japan was the only nation that had any sanity and that the United States had gone mad with anti-Japanese feeling'. Ambassador Forbes arranged for the Fleishers and their families to be given police protection, and made representations to the Army regarding the disadvantages of encouraging any attack on the 'very moderate' *Advertiser*.[84]

In considering the forces and factors behind the sale and amalgamation of Japan's main three English-language newspapers, we should take into account two other institutions. The first of these was the army, and more specifically the General Staff (*Sanbō Honbu*). In 1934, in the wake of the Amō Statement, the Army Ministry Press Office published 'The Essence of National Defence and Proposals to Strengthen It' (*Kokubō no hongi to sono kyōka no teishō*), a pamphlet stressing the importance of manipulating public opinion at home and abroad. This pamphlet distinguished communication, information and propaganda as vital components of national power and called for the creation of a government ministry charged with their management and reinforcement.

In September 1934, William Turner, the General Manager of Reuters in East Asia and a frequent memorandist to both the Foreign Office in London and the US State Department, had described the Army Press Office as 'the most active propaganda factory in Japan'.[85] Following the establishment of *Dōmei* in January 1936 the inauguration of the Cabinet Information Committee in July provided military interests with a strong voice in what would evolve as the central mechanism for media control in Japan and its growing empire. When the *Advertiser* was sold in October 1940 the Cabinet Information Bureau was pressing ahead with the nationwide 'unification' of the Japanese press.

In November 1930, just after the fire at the *Advertiser* premises and two weeks before the assassination attempt on Hamaguchi Osachi, the Far East Department of the Foreign Office ignored the advice of the *Daily Telegraph*'s Lord Camrose that now might be a good time to acquire a controlling interest in the *Advertiser*. Nearly ten years later, Fleisher's representative, Ernest Pickering, failed to sell the *Advertiser* to the Ministry of Information, a failure that Robert Craigie at the British embassy capped with a low bid for a 49% stake not long after, which was also rejected. Rumour had it that the *Asahi Shinbun* made overtures to the *Advertiser* as well.[86] Fleisher also put out feelers in the US but his asking price of $200,000 was too high.[87] His best offer from America came from a consortium fronting for the German embassy in Tokyo. This group offered $500,000 cash, to be paid in New York, an inducement that must have made the Fleishers stop and think, but which they also rejected, 'on patriotic grounds'.[88]

Neither party to the final, October 1940 sale respected their agreement to describe it as a purely businesslike arrangement. In interviews given in Manila in November 1940 and in the US in 1943, B.W. Fleisher claimed that negotiations had been conducted under duress, and described the $100,000 he had been paid as a 'blackmail price'.[89] In January 1941 Gō disputed these claims from his rostrum at the *Japan Times & Advertiser*, cast doubt on Fleisher's managerial ability and held that it was he, not Gō, who had initiated the sale and that the decision to sell had been made peaceably. To scotch persistent rumours of German involvement, Gō denied that any 'foreign money' had gone into the acquisition.[90]

All in all, Thomas Millard's May 1941 contention that Matsuoka Yōsuke's role in acquiring the *Advertiser* 'to have an organ close to the Foreign Office in which their opposition to the Military Party could be expressed' seems plausible. Millard's interpretation certainly fits with Matsuoka's habit of using the media as a diplomatic weapon, if we look at his management of Japan's position at Geneva in 1932–33 and if we look forward to the *Japan Times & Advertiser's* treatment of the headline achievements of his Foreign Ministry in 1940–41.[91]

Few of those observing what David Lu has called 'the Matsuoka cyclone' of the late 1930s and early 1940s[92] would claim that Matsuoka was following a political course that was in any way set or planned, but Matsuoka's political thinking was not without its own internal coherence and he possessed a talent for getting the core of an issue across not only to his followers but to the public at large. It would be difficult to describe him as an opponent of 'the Military Party' (*Gunbatsu*), but he was not their most reliable ally nor, despite championing partnerships with the most aggressive powers of the day, was he an unwavering supporter of military solutions. Matsuoka's 21 July 1940 *Advertiser* interview with Wilfrid Fleisher trumpeting 'several centuries' of totalitarianism indicates that he then favoured a 'positive' foreign policy, but this may have also part of his desire to motivate Foreign Ministry bureaucrats towards a less cautious, more proactive diplomacy.

When the sales of the *Advertiser* and *Chronicle* took place at the end of 1940, Matsuoka seems to have been moving into the more accommodating 'international' persona that was most familiar to his American friends. However contradictory, both positions seem to have been sincere, and Matsuoka's contacts with members of both the 'international' and the 'military' circles do not appear to have damaged his position in either camp at the time.

THE LOUDEST VOICE IN THE ROOM

Between 1936 and 1942, the institutional successors of the Foreign Ministry Information Bureau and their representatives in the field conducted an increasingly uncompromising clampdown on the press of East Asia. While in Japan between 1938 and 1942, a press cull overseen by Iwanaga and Furuno of *Dōmei* saw the vernacular fourth estate reduced from seven hundred and thirty-nine daily newspapers to fifty-four,[93] Japanese-language papers in China were reduced to a single publication, *Tōa Shinpō* (East Asia Report) and Chinese-language papers in areas under Japanese control were managed by the Propaganda Section of the North China Army (*Hokushigun Hōdōbu*) and by *Dōmei*, the main organ reshaping the Chinese news industry to Japanese requirements.

Even before the signing of the Tripartite Pact in September 1940, German embassy representatives had involved themselves in press control in China as in Japan, adding further occupational hazards to writers on the foreign-owned English-language press. In March 1938 the German Consul-General in Shanghai took offence at an article in the *China Weekly Review* published the previous month which seemed 'a deliberate insult to the Head of the German Reich' and lodged a protest with the US Consul, as the *Review* was registered in the US.[94] After the signing of the Pact these pressures intensified with the backing of the Japanese authorities, as thousands of European Jews sought safe haven in the International Settlement. The head of the German Transocean News Service, F. Cordt, liaised extensively with officials of the Wang Jingwei (Wang Ching-wei) regime and J.B. Powell's *China Weekly Review* summarized anti-American reports put out by the agency in its 4 October 1941 issue, with frequent references to 'Jewish influence' and Roosevelt as 'the paid servant of Jewry'.[95]

In July 1941, H.J. Archibald's *Central China Post* was under threat from militant strikers at its press in Hankou, probably backed by Japanese forces, who were now in control of the city. Archibald's home was trashed by a Chinese gang.[96] The Reuters office in Hankou was also in danger. The *Central China Post* closed down on 25 July while its plight was being considered in Whitehall.[97] On the same day Reuters employees were called out. Negotiations dragged on into October, but neither the *Post* nor the Reuters office resumed business.

The experiences of Emily Hahn in Shanghai and Hong Kong, the stalwart defiance of Carroll Alcott with his radio broadcasts, bullet-proof vest and police escort, and the close shaves with bombs and bullets that Hallett Abend, Hollington Tong, J.B. Powell and Randall Gould experienced have all been recorded in memoirs. Even before the occupation of Shanghai, both Chinese and Western newspaper premises were under considerable pressure from gangsters cooperating with Japanese interests, particularly during the 1940–44 Wang Jingwei regime in Nanjing. J.B. Powell records coming across the detached head of a *Shunbao* assistant editor one evening in early 1940 in the French Concession, with a message attached to it holding a 'warning to editors' who criticized the Japanese or Wang Jingwei. Other journalists were taken to No 76 Jessfield Road in the 'badlands'. One such was Jabin Hsu, who was held prisoner for over a month until he handed over his family fortune. Powell recalled a bomb thrown into the offices of *Hua Mei Wan Pao*, next door to the building shared by the *China Weekly Review* and the *China Press*. Hand grenades were thrown at the windows of the *Shun Pao*. Bombs exploded on the front steps of the *Shanghai Evening Post and Mercury*, and Samuel H. Chang, editor of the *Post's* Chinese edition, was shot in the back and killed by an assassin in a German restaurant on Nanking Road in the International Settlement. One night six armed gangsters attempted to enter the *China Press* printing plant but were detected by a night watchman and then by the police. In the ensuing fracas a Chinese pedestrian was killed and several more wounded. The *Chinese Year Book* for 1943 described the 'terrorist activities perpetuated against newspapermen in Shanghai who were loyal to the National Government' and provided a tally of attacks on journalists that had occurred under the Wang Jingwei regime: six murders, three attacks, four deaths from bombing attacks on newspaper offices, six such bombing incidents, thirteen kidnappings and twenty threatening letters.[98]

In July 1941, Wang Jingwei's newspaper, the *Central China Daily News*, published a 'blacklist' of local newspapermen scheduled for early 'deportation': seven foreigners including Powell himself, C.V. Starr, publisher of the *Post*, Randall Gould, its editor, Carroll Alcott of the *China Press* and the American radio station XMHA, Norwood Allman, lawyer and registered owner of the *Shen Bao*, and some eighty Chinese journalists. Following this publication, the Shanghai municipal police stationed guards at all newspaper offices in the International Settlement. Powell was lucky to escape a grenade attack. A few days later an intermediary with Japanese and Wang Jingwei contacts suggested that Powell sell the *China Weekly Review*, an offer he rejected. When the Japanese occupied the Hongqu section of the International Settlement they seized the Chinese post office and banned the transmission of offending newspapers by mail. Anti-Japanese staff at the post office succeeded in smuggling issues of some newspapers out of Japanese-controlled Shanghai and into what Powell called 'Free China', including the 6 December 1941 issue of the *China Weekly Review*, J.B. Powell's final edition. C.V. Starr, Randall Gould, Powell's son William, Carroll Alcott and Hallett Abend had all left on some of the last American ships before the Japanese occupation. Powell elected to stay on both in order to maintain the operations of a secret radio station and out of what he called 'loyalty to the community', although he noted that several American and British newspapermen 'went over' to the Japanese, denounced former colleagues as spies and stayed in position on the two newspapers that the Japanese wished to continue publication, the *Shanghai Evening Post and Mercury* and the *Shanghai Times*.[99]

Those journalists who had resisted bribery, threats and bullets before the occupation and stayed on were imprisoned after it. Although they could not be called the primary targets of the Japanese authorities, particularly rough tactics were applied to the networks of the American and British-owned English-language press in China, where the assault was both more overt and aggressive than it had been in Japan in the run-up to Pearl Harbor. Just as in Japan the degree of intimidation of Western newspapers and journalists in the early 1930s and in 1937–8 had coincided with the heightening of Sino-Japanese hostilities and Japan's deteriorating relations with Britain, the United States, France and the Netherlands, so in China, after Pearl Harbor the treatment of both Western and critical Chinese newspapers and their staff became overtly aggressive. Both vernacular and English-language newspapers in China were starved of paper, telephones and other equipment, suffered the withdrawal of postal services, and were bought out, shut down or merged with other papers. In Chongqing, the Guomindang stronghold since 1938, journalists quartered at 'Holly' Tong's Ministry of Information Press Hostel operated under cheerfully administered but drastic censorship.

Meanwhile, in Tokyo, Hugh Byas, William Turner, Wilfrid Fleisher, Relman Morin, Glenn Babb and James Young and other experienced correspondents had left or were preparing to leave Japan, and were being replaced by newsmen like Otto Tolischus, Richard Tennelly,

Joseph Newman, Al Downs and others. Like most of the 1940–41 intake of correspondents for Western English-language newspapers, Tolischus and Newman had extensive experience elsewhere but were relative newcomers to the Japanese scene and ill-prepared to surmount the usual barriers of language, seek out and cultivate sources, evade the intensive and systematic police surveillance now in place between them and such information as they might gather, and get round the censorship governing cable and telephone transmissions between Japan and the US.

At the same time, international uncertainties meant that Western demand for news of Japan was greater than ever. There were at least ten full-time Tokyo foreign correspondents for Western English-language newspapers and news agencies in January 1941, where there had only been five in 1920 and three in 1913. Meanwhile, the tone of the vernacular press in Japan became increasingly vociferous, with little restraint from official bodies. This marked a change from even the heady days of January 1934, when popular feeling certainly ran high, but politicians did not hesitate to denounce inflammatory publications and drum-beating journalism.[100]

What was the thinking behind the amalgamations of 1940–41 and how did they influence the ability of the Foreign Ministry network to shape perceptions of Japan within and outside Japan?

During a period when the coverage of Japan and East Asia in general raised their profile considerably in Western newspapers, and that increase was reflected in the population of accredited correspondents, the culls, subsidies and amalgamations of 1936–42 encouraged by Amō Eiji, Furuno Inosuke, Iwanaga Yūkichi and others in the Foreign Ministry network did not so much remove as attempt to transfer what Furuno saw as the 'overpowering' influence of the English-language newspapers of East Asia on the world's idea of Japan. Toshi Gō's amalgamated organ might not be to the taste of local ex-*Chronicle* and ex-*Advertiser* readers, but it more than made up for local indifference by its gains in international authority.

By December 1940, the *Japan Times & Advertiser* had become Japan's most-read English-language daily, followed by the *Osaka Mainichi*, which had very little international circulation or audience, and *Japan News-Week*. The day after Pearl Harbor, with the closure of *Japan News-Week*, the *Japan Times & Advertiser* became Japan's most significant English-language publication: one newspaper speaking with one voice where four discrete and controversial organs had once spoken with many. And it spoke from Tokyo, the new centre of East Asian news.

Consider the realities of the amalgamation from the standpoint of the English-language newspaper market within Japan. The increased demand for Japan news had never done much to help the sales of Japan's independent English-language press or lessen their dependence on advertising, as their combined circulations between the early thirties and 1938 dropped from about 13,000 to 6–7,000 copies (from the

Advertiser's 9,000 added to the *Chronicle*'s 4,000 down to the *Advertiser*'s 4,000 added to the *Chronicle*'s approximate 2,600).[101] Benefiting from a subsidy of around ¥7,000 a month for most of the period under study, the *Japan Times* printed a steady 4,000 copies daily from 1918 to October 1940, but that figure roughly tripled after the incorporation of its rivals in October and December of that year. A.R. Wills' *Japan News-Week* had 3,200 subscribers and 1,200 newsstand sales in January 1941.[102] Following *Japan News-Week*'s closure after Pearl Harbor, the *Japan Times & Advertiser* probably chalked up an increase in its local circulation. At the same time, it seems probable that many readers of the English-language newspapers of Japan duplicated their newspaper buying and reading habits as international tensions increased, and that those who did not buy all local available English-language newspapers probably borrowed copies from those who did, so that the local repeat readership of all available English-language news sources vacillated considerably, whatever the numbers came to in terms of subscriptions and newsstand sales.[103] Like gold in a crisis, hard news was at a premium and its provenance did not greatly much matter.

Until the amalgamations, where newspaper readers lived affected their choice of newspaper. All the English-language newspapers in Japan claimed a national readership but they were all printed on presses within or near to the newspaper office. If we take the *Chronicle* as an example, this Kōbe paper had its own readership in the southern half of Japan. In many outlying areas, missionaries and other isolated foreigners depended on the *Chronicle* for domestic and outside news. For geographical reasons, the *Chronicle*'s main competition was not the *Advertiser* but the *Osaka Mainichi* English edition (witheringly described by the *Chronicle* editor E.A. Kennard as 'our near-English contemporary'). From the *Chronicle*'s point of view, the *Advertiser* and *Japan Times* were competitors in Kantō and northern Japan. The *Advertiser*, the *Japan Times* and the *Chronicle* were all morning papers. Before the amalgamations, a reader wanting the *Advertiser* in Kōbe would not find it at a newsstand until late morning, as the midnight express from Tokyo reached Ōsaka at the end of a nine-hour journey, and the *Advertiser* then had to be distributed through local agencies to Kōbe and environs. Only the most dedicated *Advertiser* readers in Ōsaka and Kōbe bothered to wait, so most took the *Chronicle* until January 1942 then switched to a short-lived Kōbe edition of the *JT&AJCJM* until January 1943 when all production moved to Tokyo under the masthead of the *Nippon Times*.

There was method in the amalgamation. There were many foreigners in Kantō who depended on the *Chronicle* for their news. Not all Allied nationals in Japan were interned after Pearl Harbor: only US, British and Dutch men between eighteen and sixty years were rounded up on the morning of 8 December. Their wives and children remained at home, and they could still buy the paper. Besides Allied nationals, there were some thousands of French, German, Italian, Spanish, Swiss, Swedish, White Russian, Indian, Jewish and other nationals (many of them refugees from Europe) in Kantō and southern and northern Japan who took the *Chronicle* both as a matter of choice and availability.[104]

By late 1941, Japan's news network ruled the roost in Japan and Korea and stood on the brink of the media leadership of much of China and of Greater East Asia. Now, surely, at last, Japan's side of the story could be told without fear of 'correction' by the domestic or vernacular press of East Asia. How did the Japanese media use this opportunity?

Following the amalgamation with the *Japan Advertiser* in October 1940, the editorial line of the *Japan Times & Advertiser* did not immediately exhibit conspicuous changes. Under Toshi Gō the paper continued to support Japan's position in the growing international crisis. The tone was not noticeably aggressive, although it sometimes caused offence. On 10 December 1940 some irritation was caused at the State Department by an 'Eturo' (Katō Etsurō) cartoon showing Matsuoka Yōsuke, Ribbentrop and Ciano marching arm-in-arm and leading a child, who appeared to represent General Franco. US President Roosevelt was pictured standing to one side of this line, slyly proffering a bag of money to the 'child' Franco as if to lure him away from such company. The caption was 'At it again'. Reviewing this cartoon, Joseph Grew saw little gain in protesting the 'obnoxious effigy' of Roosevelt as a child molester but felt it might be worth saving as 'ammunition' in the event of any future Japanese protest about US press cartoons of the Emperor.[105] In January 1941 Grew submitted further cartoons caricaturing Roosevelt that appeared in the 20, 23 and 28 January editions of the *Japan Times & Advertiser* and another caricaturing the Secretary of State on 18 January.[106]

According to Millard's May 1941 letter to Stanley Hornbeck, the acquisition of the *Japan Advertiser* and the establishment of the *Japan Times & Advertiser* were followed by a series of publicity build-ups to test the strength of the 'internationalist' circle around the new amalgamation and to see how far Matsuoka's 'internationalism' would be tolerated by the 'Military Party' at the Foreign Ministry.

The first of these *ballons d'essai* floated the suggestion that 'Matsy', as Millard called him, visit the US at the invitation of the US Government. When it became apparent that Washington was not receptive to this idea, the *Japan Times & Advertiser* spun this 'fizzle' into a suggestion that the invitation had emanated from Washington and that Matsuoka had turned it down. The Tokyo paper next advanced a plan couched in vague terms for the US and Japan to cooperate in restoring peace in China, but according to Millard 'the Military Party' promptly sat on that idea. The *Japan Times & Advertiser* then ran leaders campaigning for a compromise with Chiang Kai-shek in China but, within twenty-four hours, Matsuoka received a request through channels between Tokyo and Chongqing to issue a denial of all possibility of compromise. This he duly issued and the *Japan Times & Advertiser* argued for the legitimate expansion of Japan's hegemony and a fight to the finish in China.

Since that climb-down, Millard concluded in May 1941 that 'the Times-Advertiser has done nothing except to raise rumours and raise a dust.' The 'net result of it all', Millard concluded, was that 'the Military Party still is in complete control of the Tokyo Government and its Foreign Policy. Well, we have known that for several years.'[107] As Millard saw it, Matsuoka's conclusion of the Alliance with Germany and Italy and the neutrality pact with Russia in April 1941 did not constitute a challenge to this 'control', nor was Matsuoka under specifically military pressure in advancing and concluding these arrangements. Nevertheless, Matsuoka's stock began to fall in military circles following the outbreak of hostilities between Russia and Germany in June 1941, an event which surprised all but the Sorge circle at the time. Matsuoka's sudden change of tack in favour of abandoning the Pact and his outspoken advocacy of war against Russia confused both his military and his internationalist allies. On 18 July 1941 the second Konoe Cabinet resigned *en masse* in order to form a third Cabinet without Matsuoka and he made his final return to the political wilderness.

At the end of June 1941, in the wake of Germany's surprise offensive on the Soviet Union, the *Japan Times* under Toshi Gō had been a model of circumspection, stressing in a 29 June editorial that 'Particular obligation rests upon the press and on those who have influence with the people, to preserve perfect equanimity, to refrain from committing the country to any undue expressions of opinion during the present formative period.'

Three weeks later, finding himself without the support of his mentor and obliged to adapt to new political circumstances at home and seismic international developments, Gō began to distance himself from Matsuoka's plans to develop the *Japan Times & Advertiser* as an internationalist foil to aggressive tendencies at the Gaimushō. Gō's change of stance was not immediately apparent. On 21 September 1941 Otto Tolischus cabled the *New York Times* that the *Japan Times*, 'the organ of the foreign office' believed that Japan was too committed in China to consider war on another front. Nevertheless, on 12 October 1941 the *Japan Times & Advertiser* signalled its acceptance of the Pact with Germany by publishing a feature headlined 'Youth Today Wiser Than 10 Years Ago; Education Ministry Survey Finds Thinking More Wholesome, Constructive' in which a survey revealed that '58.6 per cent [of the students surveyed] expressed their friendship for Germany, 30 per cent for Italy' adding that 'among those who said they liked Germany were those in the intellectual class'.

The failure of Konoe's third cabinet and the appointment of Tōjō Hideki as Prime Minister meant further adaptation to circumstances and Gō's editorials of 18 and 19 October emphasized that it was quite natural for the premier to be a soldier since Japan was on the defensive and all other important leaders – Hitler, Mussolini, Roosevelt, Stalin and Churchill – had a military background. On 21 October the paper described Tōjō as a symbol of Japanese unity and enthused, 'It would be impossible to find anywhere else in the world any greater power and authority held, with the fullest approval of the people, in one man.' Where once Gō had pursued a proactive internationalist agenda, proposing that Matsuoka visit Washington, and promoting US-Japanese cooperation and a compromise on China, now he adapted to circumstances and called for unquestioning loyalty to a nationalist agenda.

Gō's most obvious retreat from his paper's internationalist mission came just when the delicate negotiations between Japanese Ambassador to the US Nomura Kichisaburō and Secretary of State Cordell Hull in Washington stood in great need of concrete evidence of Japan's peaceful intentions. At this juncture, on 31 October and 5 November 1941, Gō wrote and the morning edition of the *Japan Times & Advertiser* published belligerent editorials rejecting American terms and hardening those of Japan.

Gō's 31 October editorial, 'Mortgage on China', described a recent US offer of 'lend-lease' to the Guomindang in Chongqing as 'a mortgage on the Republic' in which the US effectively bought future control, including naval bases and the removal of trade restrictions, of China from a government which did not represent China. Chiang Kai-shek's hands were tied by the agreement, which, whatever the short-term benefits in munitions and financial aid, blocked any lasting peace with Japan. The editorial referred to these 'demands' as having been obtained by force, and contrasted them with the 'cooperative' and 'reciprocal' approach of Japan. However, the editorial hinted that Japanese restraint was being tested to the limit: 'Japan has had more reasons to resort to war and has given more evidence of its readiness for peace by refusing to meet direct challenge.'

When Tokyo's dwindling foreign press corps read 'Mortgage on China' they immediately cabled it to their foreign desks. In the US, with only two other Japan-based English-language sources, the limited-circulation *Japan News-Week* and the *Osaka Mainichi* to check the story against, US foreign editors took the article as coming straight from the Gaimushō. Fearful of the effects of Gō's editorial on popular feeling in both countries, US Ambassador to Japan Joseph Grew protested to Foreign Minister Togo Shigenori, who said he was unaware of the article in question but called Gō over when all three were present at a Soviet embassy reception on 7 November. Grew himself saw the *Japan Times* as 'the mouthpiece of the Foreign Office' but could not be sure that the editorial was dictated by the *Gaimushō*. As Grew recorded it, in their exchange at the Soviet Embassy, Gō told Grew that he was solely responsible for the editorial and had 'written it himself as indicating Japan's maximum demands which would undoubtedly be far beyond what the Government would ask for in the conversations. I told him that he could have no conception of the harm that he had done.'[108]

At midnight on 4 November 1941, the next day's *Japan Times & Advertiser* was passed out to Tokyo correspondents, and Gō's second editorial, headlined 'American Peace Terms', began, 'This is not the time, when Pacific States are teetering on the brink of war, for Japan to make known its terms but rather for the United States specifically to say what terms of settlement that country intends to take towards its acts of aggression.' Throughout the editorial, the US was described as the aggressive party, Japan as the determined but misunderstood peace-maker. America had 'unloosed blows at this country, and has instituted direct and indirect pressure, all designed to weaken this country, with the ultimate intention of forcing Japan to conform to American policies'. Returning to the 1931–33 crisis, Gō asserted that 'the United States condemned the establishment of the independent state of Manchukuo, and in doing so intimidated other states which would have accepted the Xinjing Government in the community of nations'.

The substance of the editorial lay in Gō's presentation of seven 'points of restitution' required of the US: an end to economic and military aid to Chongqing; a request to 'leave China completely free to deal with Japan'; ceasure of all economic encirclement of Japan; US acknowledgement of the leadership of Japan's Co-Prosperity Sphere in the Western Pacific; US recognition of Manchukuo; the unfreezing of Japanese and Chinese assets in the US, Great Britain and elsewhere; and the restoration of all trade treaties and shipping and commerce restrictions placed on Japan. As Gō concluded, American destructiveness was countered by Japanese constructiveness, 'Therefore there can be no retreat by Japan from any such admirable, wholesome course.'

Having read the 31 October editorial on the night of 4 November, Joseph Grew sent a letter of protest to the *Japan Times & Advertiser*, which was published in the 5 November issue three columns away from the controversial 5 November editorial.

However, Gō's message had already gone out to the world. On Wednesday 5 November, an Associated Press news agency report published in the *Washington Post* summarized the spirit and content of 'the foreign office-controlled Japan Times and Advertiser' leader under the headline 'Japan Lists Steps for US To Ease Crisis'. On 6 November the *Washington Post* ran an indignant leader headlined 'Warmongering' which interpreted Gō's leader thus: 'Japan is putting a gun up to Uncle Sam's head in the form of a seven-point program: the United States must agree – or else!' The seven-point proposal was:

> … the coolest piece of impertinence with which any self-respecting nation could be confronted. It is painful evidence of the contempt which our Janus-faced foreign policy has aroused in little Japan. But in the form of a gun this seven-point program becomes a challenge to our national unity. The program, of course, is not official. It appears in the *Japan Times-Advertiser*, but, since this paper has become an official organ, we are justified in regarding the program as official.

The *Post* used the article to beat US isolationists over the head and to recommend the nation to abandon a neutral position:

> … the American isolationists levelled the charge of warmongering at those Americans who wish only to take off our false face and our shackles and put

our country in a posture of positive defense. The charge should be returned to the accusers … The firmness of the State Department can gather reality only from the national Will … The strain between Japan and America has never been more severe. It is severe enough to call for a vote for the comprehensive revision of the Neutrality Act so decisive as to leave the Japanese under no illusion as to American unity.

On 5 and 6 November the *New York Times* also reported Gō's 5 November leader and responded in outraged tones. Headlined to appeal strongly to the patriotism of *New York Times* readers, 'Japanese Ask Us To Reverse Stand Or Face Conflict' Otto Tolischus's 5 November despatch from Tokyo summarized the *Japan Times & Advertiser* leader and predicted that in a forthcoming Diet speech Premier Tōjō Hideki would repeat the gist of 'what the Japan Times Advertiser calls Japan's "standpat aims" – namely, the successful conclusion of the China "incident" and the establishment of the "East Asia co-prosperity sphere" … But a "standpat" attitude on the part of the United States is denounced as "outrageous".' Attitudes were clearly hardening: in the bellicose argot of the day, 'standpat' or 'stand pat' was the equivalent of today's 'red lines' – negotiating positions that cannot be fudged.

On 6 November, under the headline 'Japan's Seven Points', a *New York Times* leader announced 'The Japanese outline of what the United States must do or "face the alternatives" should not be dismissed as one more phase of an anti-American press campaign. Its publication by the Japan Times Advertiser [*sic*] indicates that it has the sanction, if not the inspiration, of Tokyo's Foreign Office.' As the *New York Times*, until now a leading voice of US isolationism saw it, 'The sum of these demands … is that the United States get out of Asia, but the implication goes even deeper than that. They suggest that the United States abandon all its recognized obligations under international agreements and substitute surrender to Tokyo for freedom of action under the law. They propose that we repudiate all our professions of good faith and abjure all the practices of international good behaviour that we have painstakingly sought to build up over 150 years.'

Again on 6 November, another editorial in the *Japan Times & Advertiser* described the flight of Kurusu Saburō to join the negotiations in Washington as 'a last opportunity [for the United States] to make amends for aggression and restore the occasion for an amicable settlement'. The editorial warned that 'there is always the possibility, even the probability, of a direct march on the Burma Road', which the British were using to transport war supplies to Guomindang forces resisting Japan in China. The *Christian Science Monitor* immediately reported the editorial under the headline 'Kurusu's Trip: 'Last Chance for US.' The 7 November *New York Times* duly reported this editorial under the headline 'Japan Threatens To Hit Burma Road', quoting its claim that Japan's patience 'has reached the point of exhaustion'.

On 18 November an editorial in the morning edition of the *Japan*

Times & Advertiser declared that 'The formidable cordon of naval and air bases which America has developed round Japan in concert with Britain, the Netherlands East Indies, Australia, and Chungking, constitutes a direct threat against the Japanese Empire.' Grew commented despairingly, 'Typical of the viewpoint here. It is always we who threaten; it is always us who are the potential aggressor, never Japan. Thus does the United States wholly "misunderstand" Japan's peaceful intentions in developing the New order and the Co-Prosperity Sphere, and thus do we render an adjustment of relations impossible by "encircling" (a word so loved by the Nazis) innocent and unoffending Nippon.'[109]

In his diary for 5 November, Grew reflected, 'If anything could render utterly hopeless the prospect of our coming to an understanding with Japan, this editorial, from a newspaper known to be the organ of the Japanese Foreign Office, would appear to do it, and my guess is that the American people will not be sympathetic to further efforts towards reconciliation.' His comment was particularly relevant to the 5 November editorials, but it could have applied to most *Japan Times & Advertiser* editorials during the last months of peace. On the day Grew set down this despairing note, the *Japan Times* ran a translation of an article from *Kaizō* in which Ishihara Kōichirō advocated an early attack on the Dutch East Indies, repeating a theme which had been urged on the government, with variations, in the *Kokumin Shinbun* of 24 and 29 April, 30 June and 18 August 1940, and in the *Asahi Shinbun* of 14 July 1940. Nevertheless, one of Grew's most persistent concerns was that indignant US media reactions to Gō's *Japan Times & Advertiser* leaders were reducing his government's room for manoeuvre in the Washington talks.[110]

Grew's disappointment in the *Japan Times & Advertiser* was bound to be influenced by his inner circle at the US embassy in Tokyo. The first in this circle was Eugene Dooman, Grew's Counsellor at the embassy from 1937 to 1941. Dooman, who was born in Ōsaka, had worked in US diplomacy in Japan since 1912, when he was a student interpreter, until 1942, when he returned to Washington. The second and third members were Grew's neighbours, B.W. Fleisher and his son Wilfrid, both of whom left Tokyo at the end of November 1940. The fourth figure was Hugh Byas, who left in April 1941. An important adjunct of this circle was the relationship between Grew, Byas and Robert Craigie, the British ambassador.

Unusually well-qualified to understand the Japanese point of view, Dooman accepted the notion of spheres of influence and accepted that Japan must be expected to have hers. Fleisher senior was a veteran initiator of US-Japan friendship gestures but he was more ambivalent about Japanese ambitions in China than any of the others, including his son Wilfrid, who in the months before Pearl Harbor was one of the few US media correspondents capable of providing American readers with an understanding of the dilemma faced by the Japanese government.

To this end, Wilfrid Fleisher was the first to start avoiding the censor by telephoning to read his story directly to a copytaker in New York. After July 1941, writing from his new base at the *New York Herald Tribune*, Fleisher tried to show American readers how economic sanctions limited Japan's options and to bring home to them the multiplicity of factions, actors and policy divisions faced by politicians there.[111]

Byas left for the US in April 1941, so he was outside the Tokyo loop in the months before Pearl Harbor, but the length of his association with Grew and the others means that he cannot be discounted as an influence. Like Dooman and Wilfrid Fleisher, Byas viewed Japanese ambitions, especially in China, with some sympathy. Byas's career path had taken him out of Britain to the Dominions, then back to Fleet Street, thence to Tokyo and the *Advertiser* network and, remaining in Tokyo, to a position where he reported Japan and East Asia events to the British world and to the US with perhaps a greater degree of detachment than colleagues who knew only Tokyo and their motherland. Although he became increasingly critical of Japanese policies in China in the 1930s and sympathized with the Chinese as a people, Byas's London *Times* and *New York Times* reports consistently questioned the validity of China as a sovereign state. This portrayal of China as a failed state or 'sick man' of Asia was not unusual at the time, and Byas's professional integrity and independence are unquestionable, yet he shared this view of China with a number of writers on East Asia whose task it was to present the case for Japanese leadership of East Asia. Byas's biographer, Peter Oblas, has pointed out that Byas's publisher at the *New York Times*, Adolph Ochs (who was also in charge of editorial policy), and his editor at *The Times* of London, Geoffrey Dawson shared a conservative outlook, Ochs favouring isolationism, Dawson favouring appeasement in East Asia, neither advocating intervention against Japan in China. Despatched from the virtual news blackout imposed on Tokyo by official press controls, Byas's sometimes anodyne readings of Japan's forward policy in China suited the editorial line held by his masters in New York and London, while more alarming and controversial despatches from correspondents and stringers on the spot were initially buried in inconspicuous columns, but eventually run alongside reports from the experienced and more detached but occasionally under-informed Byas.[112]

Thus, Grew's circle in Tokyo was more sympathetic to Japanese ambitions in East Asia than were his colleagues at the State Department, most notably Henry Stimson, Stanley Hornbeck and Cordell Hull. Following a loss of face during the Manchurian Incident, Stimson was determined not to be outmanoeuvred by Japan. Hornbeck was taking bets from his colleagues on Japan's unwillingness to face conflict with the US. Hull was inflexible, presenting Japan with sweeping general principles that made a *modus vivendi* difficult to achieve.

Both Grew and Craigie were convinced that the fall of Matsuoka and the subsequent September 1941 proposal from Konoe for a summit with

Roosevelt showed that the 'moderates' in Tokyo were once again exercising influence and that there was all the more reason for Britain and the US to respond positively to their overtures. They were partly encouraged in this belief by meetings with Japanese politicians: Grew with Matsuoka's successors, Toyoda Teijirō and, from November 1941, Tōgō Shigenori, Craigie with Shigemitsu Mamoru, who was close to Matsuoka and had been optimistic about the prospects for Japan's relations with Britain and the US consequent on his appointment.[113] This led Grew and Craigie to believe that a 'carrot and stick' approach to Japan was the best way to reach an understanding, but Washington's 'Four principles' counter-proposal to Konoe was too conditional to help him present the Army with the *fait accompli* he had hoped for.

Grew's fears regarding the dangers of bombastic editorials in the *Japan Times & Advertiser* were confirmed in the months before Pearl Harbor. Short of experience, time and language ability, newly-appointed Western journalists were heavily dependent on official briefings and the *Japan Times*. Relying on narrow channels of information, Western journalists seized on Gō's editorials and such scraps of information as they could find to provide a superficial, fragmentary and insensitive impression of the situation. With the departure of Wilfrid Fleisher and Hugh Byas, few in the US press corps in Tokyo in the summer and autumn of 1941 showed that they even began to understand the fateful political struggle going on in Tokyo.[114] After so many months – or years – of simplistic, uninformed reporting by their own countrymen, Grew read the *Japan Times & Advertiser* editorials of 31 October and 5 November with dismay and anticipated the furious reaction of the foreign press in Tokyo and at home in the US and Britain. Grew's view that war could have been avoided seems intuitively correct: even at this late stage the road to Pearl Harbor was not inevitable. However, events on the ground made it increasingly difficult for either side to find a diplomatic way out of the *impasse*.

On 13 November 1941, the American journalist Randall Gould, himself an ex-*Japan Times* reporter and in 1941 an important player in US propaganda efforts on behalf of the Guomindang in Chongqing writing for the *Christian Science Monitor*, Gould wrote of the 5 November editorial:

> ... the Japan Times Advertiser [is] often but inaccurately described as a Foreign Office organ. Actually this English-language daily ... is under Foreign Office control but employed as a launcher of trial balloons. Its utterances have no official support and relatively few Japanese know anything about what it says. Toshi Go, its Publisher-Editor, is an acute individual ... He has a sound idea of what will arouse talk among Americans, and he deserves great credit for obtaining much publicity for his paper through the kindness of the Tokyo foreign correspondents who find themselves starved for information they can safely telegraph home, and who seize eagerly upon Times Advertiser editorials as 'safe and insane' – that is, something that will

not get them into trouble with the censor yet at the same time spectacular enough to be printed by the American newspapers. The worst feature of this situation is the fact that thousands of careless readers in the Unites States tend to believe that Times Advertiser impudence is an official belief or expression.

Like Thomas Millard in May 1941, Gould believed that all the *Japan Times & Advertiser* had done was 'raise a dust' – cause a brouhaha, but to no great purpose. Furthermore, the US public was more equivocal on the question of war than the newspapers they read. On 16 November the *Washington Post* reported a Gallup poll in which the question was asked 'Should the United States take steps now to prevent Japan from becoming more powerful, even if this means risking war with Japan?' In September 1941, after Japan occupied southern Indochina, 70% of respondents answered yes to the question. When Gallup asked the same question in a poll published in the *Post* on 14 November 1941, after the *Japan Times & Advertiser's* 5 November editorials had been splashed across the US and the *Post* had published its indignant 6 November leader, the number answering Yes had gone down to 64%. Interpreting the fall, the *Post* of 16 November described the American people as 'less belligerent, but far from conciliatory'. The Gallup poll can be seen as one measure of the influence of the *Japan Times & Advertiser* editorials of October-November 1941, but it is hardly decisive.

Toshi Gō survived to direct the *Japan Times & Advertiser*, the *Japan Times & Advertiser Incorporating The Japan Chronicle and The Japan Mail* and the *Nippon Times* until the spring of 1945, when his name disappeared from the top of the leader column. Clearly, he needed no lessons in which direction to take the erstwhile 'internationalist forum' that Matsuoka had envisaged in late 1940. That autumn, in complex and delicate negotiations between Admiral Nomura and Cordell Hull in Washington (complicated by the well-meaning but confusing involvement of the 'John Doe' associates), the United States had become increasingly insistent on concrete evidence of good intentions from Japan. Some basis for a *modus vivendi* between Japan, the United States and Great Britain was sorely needed, but the *Japan Times & Advertiser* chose to meet one of the most serious challenges of its publishing life by joining the lusty chorus of its vernacular contemporaries.

On whose behalf did the *Japan Times & Advertiser* act in publishing the provocative articles of October and November 1941? Matsuoka was out of the picture and Tōgō Shigenori was in command, but the Cabinet Information Board was up and running, with a number of familiar figures from the Foreign Ministry network on board. If these were the agencies behind Gō's aggressive leaders, what did they hope to gain? Was a tough line intended to make Japan's impending negotiating position look unexpectedly generous? Or in the hiatus created by Matsuoka's departure and the new uncertainties caused by the outbreak of hostilities between Russia and Germany, was Gō simply out of the loop and unaware of the third Konoe cabinet's readiness, however reluctant, to compromise on China in its negotiations with the US?

Could matters have turned out differently if Matsuoka Yōsuke had retained his grip on power and maintained his backing for the internationalist principles of the *Japan Times*? It is ironic that although the circle around Grew and Craigie saw Matsuoka's fall as a victory for the 'moderates', Matsuoka had been almost alone in opposing Japan's move into southern Indochina on the grounds that it would provoke a hostile Anglo-American reaction. By the time the move was made in late July, Matsuoka had been removed from office.[115] But with or without Matsuoka's support, given the tightening encirclement of Japan and the changing political landscape in Tokyo, could Toshi Gō have presented a rational, internationalist alternative to the rumblings from the *Gaimushō*? And if he had done so, would the US press corps in Tokyo have been capable of presenting US readers with a more nuanced picture of the situation?

In the autumn of 1941, US-Japan communications turned on far more than the pronouncements to the *Japan Times & Advertiser*. The foreign press corps could also turn to *Japan News-Week*, the *Osaka Mainichi*, *Dōmei* English-language press releases and NHK Radio Tokyo. More considered but less newsy perspectives were available to Anglophone readers in Ishibashi Tanzan's *Oriental Economist* and the Foreign Affairs Association periodical *Contemporary Japan*.

Furthermore, both sides used other channels in intensive and serious efforts to find a solution to the *impasse* of November 1941, one of the most hopeful avenues being the offer of a Japanese withdrawal from South Indochina. In a belated nod to Matsuoka's earlier opposition to Japanese incursions there, Tokyo first put this compromise on the table in Washington on 18 November 1941, nearly a fortnight after reports of Gō's 5 November editorials reached the US. The mood in Washington was just as Grew, Craigie and their circle feared. On Tuesday 25 November Henry Stimson famously noted in his diary Roosevelt's remark 'that we were likely to be attacked, perhaps by next Monday … The question was how we should manoeuvre them into the position of firing the first shot without allowing too much danger too ourselves.' On 26 November, when Cordell Hull rejected compromise on southern Indochina, Washington effectively challenged Japan, in the words of Dirty Harry, to 'Go ahead, make my day'.

In January 1941, convinced that Japan was not prepared to fight the US, Stanley Hornbeck had urged the US State Department not to 'accept at face value, as examples of Japanese national intention, the noises made by the Japanese press and Mr Matsuoka'. However, the continuing pervasiveness of propaganda messages from the Japan network in East Asia and the US and the persistent feistiness of most *Japan Times & Advertiser* editorials during this period may have clouded Washington's view of Japan's negotiating position and prevented Japan's more conciliatory and workable diplomatic positions from being taken more seriously in Washington. Therefore, it is possible to describe Gō's *Japan Times & Advertiser* editorials as a contributory factor to the outbreak of war. But whether a continuation of Matsuoka's plans for the *Japan Times* and his later departure from power, or a more independent line from Gō could have helped prevent war is hard to judge, not only because this is purely speculative and because Matsuoka's character and principles were so extraordinarily inconsistent, but because so many other, larger, factors were at play.

The understanding of the situation in Tokyo displayed by State Department officials in Washington and by Grew and his circle, was often all too similar to the perspective of US reporters in Tokyo, most of whom subscribed to the description of forces in Tokyo as being divided between the 'militarists' and the 'moderates'. Usui Katsumi has questioned the dichotomy between 'the evil jingoistic, adventuresome military and the good, peace-oriented moderate Foreign Ministry'. He has shown that some of the strongest resistance to the 'Renovationist' group in the *Gaimushō* and diplomats (and *Gaimushō* spokesmen) such as Kawai Tatsuo and Shiratori Toshio came from two foreign ministers with a military background, Ugaki Kazushige and Nomura Kichisaburō.[116] Hull, Stimson, Hornbeck and Roosevelt were all receiving a great deal of intelligence from their department and in correspondence from US officials on current thinking in Tokyo but, to quote Ernest May, 'the opinions of individuals are not necessarily direct functions of the information they receive'.[117] We cannot know whether or not less bellicose editorials by the *Japan Times & Advertiser* would have led to less superficial and insensitive reportage by US correspondents in Tokyo, and that this in turn could have checked the deterioration in US-Japan relations. However, as May observed in his assessment of US press coverage of Japan, 'one cannot discard entirely the hypothesis that better reportage on Japan might have altered the course of events ... If writers for readers of American newspapers had perceived more accurately the ordeal of Japanese statesmen in 1941, they might not have so zestfully urged on the administration an uncompromising attitude toward Konoe ... Probably war would have come when and as it did. But one cannot be sure.'[118]

Looking back in February 1943, Robert Craigie's explosive 'Final Report' condemned US diplomatic inflexibility in general and in particular its failure to seize the chance Japan offered of a compromise over southern Indochina in November 1941. Craigie maintained that a less rigid US response to Japan in October-November 1941 could have enabled a postponement of war 'until a time of our own choosing – our time, that is, not Hitler's'.[119] In many respects, Craigie's views chimed with those of Joseph Grew. Although the Report was suppressed by the British Foreign Office and was not available in East Asia, it was also in line with the emphasis on US inflexibility taken in retrospectives published in the *Nippon Times* and sister publications.

Nevertheless, some perspective is called for here. The US-Japan crisis was only the latest in a series of confrontations that Japan had faced in the twentieth century, first with the Soviet Union, then with Nationalist China, and finally with the US, Britain and the Netherlands. Despite the crucial importance of the US-Japan relationship in 1940–41, it was not the only story, and it had been relatively insignificant for most of the inter-war period.

Even if the US-Japan relationship had been the only axis on which events turned, it would still be simplistic to narrow US-Japan communications to the *Japan Times & Advertiser* and claim that Japan offered Western opinion little more than Gō's windy leaders in the autumn of 1941. Both sides used other channels in intensive and serious efforts to find a solution to the *impasse* of November 1941. However, the continuing pervasiveness of propaganda messages from the Foreign Ministry network in East Asia and the US and the persistent feistiness of most *Japan Times & Advertiser* leaders during this period may have clouded Washington's view of Japan's negotiating position and prevented Japan's more conciliatory and workable diplomatic positions from being taken more seriously in Washington.

For seeding such clouds, the *Japan Times & Advertiser* and its editor must bear some share of responsibility for what followed. However, both Gō's position and habits of discourse and the newspaper's unique authority as Japan's best known and most closely attended public channel to the US in late 1941 were only developing characteristics in an official network that had been accumulating since at least 1921, when Hara Kei and Ijūin Hikokichi primed the propaganda weapon with the establishment of the Information Bureau in the Foreign Ministry. Toshi Gō no more fell into the editorial chair at the *Japan Times & Advertiser* in 1940 than Japan and the United States fell into a state of intense mutual distrust in the autumn of 1941: it all took time and effort.

NOTES

1 Lu 2002: 110, and 136, n.12.
2 Lu 2002: 112–13.
3 Before leaving for Manchuria, Matsuoka had hoped that his popularity would propel him to the leadership of Japan or at least the Foreign Ministry, but although that was not yet to be, his appointment to the SMR presidency may have constituted a recognition of the threat his growing political base posed to the *Seiyūkai* (Lu 2002: 115–18).
4 Young 1998: 141, 154.
5 'Japan Feels Aggrieved: Cannot Understand View That She is Not Entitled to Lead China' by Hugh Byas: NYT, 4 August 1937. Byas Papers, Yale, Reel 11. Cited in O'Connor 2001: 3.
6 Wheeler 1972: 70. Cited in Storry 1979: 143.
7 See for example Hermann Goering, Reichsminister for Air in JT: 13 January 1935.
8 See Chapter 2. See also plates: 1921 photograph of Fleisher, Williams and Missouri graduates.

9   FO 371/17762 [C 1147/1147/18]: F. Lindley to John Simon, 22 January 1934.
10 USDS 894.918/17: Grew, Tokyo, quoting Forbes on Fleisher and giving his own assessment to State Dept., 29 January 1935.
11 Sanji Muto, *Textiles and Tariffs* supplement, JA, July 1933.
12 'Britain Considered China's Accomplice': *Trans-Pacific*, 13 January 1938. Discussed in FO 371/22177 [F 4471/9/23]: Burma Office, 27 April 1938.
13 USDS 894.918/17: W.T. Turner (Reuters) 'Memorandum of Statement by Mr Wilfrid Fleisher', September 1934.
14 USDS 894.918/17: Grew, Tokyo, to Secretary of State, Washington, 29 January 1935.
15 USDS 894.911/60: Grew to State Dept., 2 March 1938, regarding Araki interview in 3 February 1938 JA.
16 'Riches, Power seen for Japan if Neutral in Next World War – Participation Opposed as Profiting Nothing and Certain to Pull Nation Down in Common Ruin' by Ozaki Yukio: JA, 4 July 1939. Discussed in USDS 894.918/31, Grew to State Dept., 6 July 1939.
17 JA, 18 July 1939: reader's letter. Discussed in FO 371/23556 [F 7673/176/23]: Craigie telegram, 21 July 1939.
18 FO 371/24730 [F 3609/66/23]: Robert Craigie telegram, 14 July 1940.
19 JA: 21 July 1940.
20 'Nervous Japan Gripped by Spyphobia' by Hugh Byas: NYT *Magazine*, 10 February 1935.
21 Neal, Edna R. in Cortazzi (ed.) 1999: Eguchi Takayuki was detained under Article 12 (6c) and (5a) of the 1920 Aliens Act.
22 'Five more Japanese seized by British': NYT, 5 August 1940.
23 William H. Honan, *Visions of Infamy* (1991) also speculatively attributes the 17 August 1940 death of Cox's associate, Hector C. Bywater, to Japanese agents in the US. Selby-Walker himself withdrew before the Japanese in advance reached Java, but along with three other journalists he was killed in a torpedo raid off Sumatra in March 1942 (Read 1992: 229–30).
24 Most journalists doubted the suicide verdict, viz., 'Torture Story Told By Writer's Widow': *New York Sun*, 12 September 1940. Foreign Office files support it, as does Hughes (Hughes 1972: 51–5). Peter Elphick doubts the suicide verdict but surmises that Cox was an agent of the British Special Intelligence Service (Elphick 1997: 248–51). Phyllis Argall airs the possibility that Cox's interrogators were hanging him outside his cell window to make him talk when he fell, but is less conclusive on his connection with espionage (Argall 1945: 175).
25 FO 371/24738 [F 3669/653/23]: K. Selby-Walker letter to Reuters, London, 14 August 1940, p.6.
26 FO371/24738 F3680/653/23 Craigie to Halifax 31 July 1940. Cited in Best 1995: 124.
27 FO 371/24738, Ashley Clarke, 31 July 1940. Cited in Read 1999: 248.
28 'Five more Japanese seized by British': NYT, 5 August 1940.
29 'Protests Tokyo arrests': NYT 23 October 1940.
30 'London-Tokyo rift now diminishing': NYT 7 August 1940.
31 Pickering first came to Japan by following up an acquaintance with Nagai Ryūtarō and taught English at Tokyo University from 1927 to 1931. Returning to Britain, he became a Liberal M.P., providing one of the few unqualified defences of Japan's position in Manchuria given in the Commons debate of

27 February 1933. Pickering then returned to Japan to write *Japan's Place in the Modern World* (London 1936). For more on Pickering see my introduction to his book in O'Connor (2004).

32 FO 371/23574 [F 10795/10795/23]: Pratt (Ministry of Information) to Clarke, F.E. Dept., 3 October 1939.

33 Bess 1943: 66.

34 USDS 894.918/37: Hornbeck, Dept. of State, reporting message from G.F. Eliot of *New York Herald Tribune* regarding Wilfrid Fleisher telephone call from Tokyo, 17 September 1940.

35 Bess 1943: 66; Fleisher 1941: 317–18. Note that in FO 371/24728 [F 5516/53/23], Craigie to FO, 7 November 1940, Craigie maintains that B.W. Fleisher had the option of retiring to California and leaving the management of the paper to Don Brown, the news editor, and Davies, the business manager. However, Craigie believed that the Japanese would sooner or later have 'eliminated American control'. Thus in retrospect Fleisher's decision to get out while he could be compensated was sensible, as was Britain's decision not to buy the JA in the summer of 1939, when Pickering tried to broker a deal, as the newspaper would very probably have been removed from their control upon the outbreak of war, if not sooner.

36 USDS 948.918/34: Grew to Secretary of State, October 10, Section One and Two, 10 October 1940.

37 Okamura (ed.) 1941: 54.

38 FO 371/21001 [F11610/1043/10]: Howe to A. Eden, 11 April 1937. FO 371/23487 [F12419/372/10], S.H. Lamb to Halifax, 16 October 1939. See Appendix 4 for a fuller account of Gorman's career.

39 FO 371/24728 [F 5516/53/23]: Craigie to Halifax, 7 November 1940. Gorman would also be interned briefly in a hotel in Yokohama before being repatriated on the *Gripsholm*.

40 Newman 1942: 257–62. Newman provides a close and reliable account of the last hours of the *Advertiser*, down to the description of 'our heavily littered and abused news room on the third floor of the *Advertiser* building, which was near the Imperial Hotel and faced elevated railroad tracks'. Because the *Japan Times & Advertiser* then took over the building, these were the premises that a young Donald Richie entered when he joined the *Nippon Times* after the war, as recollected in the March 1997 centenary edition of the *Japan Times*.

41 Given the financial problems of the JC, it is worth noting that in 1936 Douglas Young also owned and was running the *Kobe Herald and Osaka Gazette*. It is possible that he acquired it from its owner-editor Alfred Curtis in 1926 following Eric Young's suicide. When or how Young acquired and/or amalgamated the *Osaka Gazette* with the *Kobe Herald* is unclear.

42 Morgan Young to Hugh Byas: 18 September 1939, Byas Papers, Yale University.

43 FO 371/24728 [F 5646/53/23]: Craigie telegram, 17 December 1940.

44 His official title was 'editorial representative'.

45 Personal communication with Theodore Van Doorn, October 2005. See note in Bibliography.

46 The Sannomiya building was destroyed during the B-29 bombing attacks on Kōbe in 1944–45.

47 FO 371/27902 [F 4760/27/23]: Craigie to Eden, 18 April 1941.

48 USDS 894.911: Grew, Tokyo, to Dept. of State, 20 December 1940.

49 See Caren (1999) on JC, 88, 89; on JT and JA, 94, 96, 96.

50 In today's JT, the *Advertiser, Chronicle* and other 'incorporated' titles and the date of their acquisition are reproduced below the small masthead above the daily leader and the 'Readers in Council' letters column, usually around page 14.

51 FO 371/27902 [F 4760/27/23]: Craigie to Eden, 18 April 1941.

52 Personal communication with Theodore Van Doorn, October 2005.

53 Craigie 1946: 160.

54 FO 371/19367 [F 4888/4888/23]: Minute, July 1935.

55 USDS 893.911/359: Grew to State Dept., 16 November 1938.

56 The following JN-W editorials were considered inflammatory at the time: 'Inconsistency', 21 December 1940; 'Looking Forward', 4 January 1941; 'Fish and Fowl', 25 January 1941; and 'Japan's Obligation', 15 February 1941.

57 USDS 894.911: Grew to W.R. Wills, 21 January 1941. The English-language *Osaka Mainichi & Tokyo Nichi Nichi* continued to be published under that title until January 1943 when it became known as the *Mainichi*, and then as the *Mainichi Daily News*, but it had been under Japanese ownership since it foundation in 1922 as the *Osaka Mainichi*. The contents were largely translations from the vernacular edition. For this reason, I have not discussed the *Osaka Mainichi* or its subsequent incarnations in any systematic way in this study.

58 USDS 894.911/74: Grew to State Dept., 17 March 1941.

59 'Grim Contrast': JN-W, 22 March 1941; 'Autonomous Japan': JN-W, 29 March 1941. Discussed in USDS 894.911/75: Grew to State Dept., 8 April 1941.

60 Argall 1945: 187–90.

61 USDS 894.911/76: Grew to State Dept. 30 April 1941.

62 'No Compromise': JN-W 26 April 1941. Discussed in USDS 894.911 (document number not stated therein): Grew to State Dept., 7 May 1941.

63 'Hitler Rules Japan. Non-German Stooges Assist Nazi Fifth Column' WP, 9 August 1941.

64 'Two Year Plan', JN-W, 6 September 1941. Discussed in USDS 894.911/85: Grew to State Dept., 11 September 1941.

65 Controversy seems to have dogged Sheba's tenure at the JT. In 1927, Malcolm Kennedy received a visit from a journalist named Russell who asked for advice. Russell had been approached by a disgruntled ex-JT writer named Pearson who had 'an old score, which he wants to pay off on Sheba, editor of the "Japan Times"'. Pearson wanted Russell to 'blow up the office of the "Japan Times"' and, if possible, do in Sheba at the same time, for £100 and a passage out of Japan. Obviously, nothing came of this conspiracy but it seems worth noting here. Malcolm Kennedy Diary, or 29 September 1927, Kennedy Papers, Sheffield University, UK.

66 Although Kennedy did agree to act as a contributing editor from time to time.

67 'Suspended Judgement': JT, 28 November 1936.

68 'Fascism Unwanted': JT, 6 December 1936.

69 'As the Year Dawns': JT, 5 January 1937; 'Government and Diet': JT 23 January 1937; 'Ugaki a Moses?' JT, 26 January 1937; 'Newer and Bigger Navies': JT, 21 February 1937.

70 'No Easy Task': JT, 5 March 1937; 'Sato Diplomacy': JT, 10 March 1937; 'Sino-Japanese Cooperation': JT, 18 March 1937; 'Tokyo and Moscow': JT, 25 March 1937. Cited in Fält 1985: 88–9.

71 'Budget Criticism': JT, 2 December 1936; 'Reform of Diet System': JT, 24 December 1936; 'Parliamentary Government': JT, 26 December 1936.

72 According to Okamura (ed.) (1941), Ashida resigned as President in late December 1939 but the 10 January 1940 article seems to contradict him.

73 'Ashida Resigns as President, Editor of Times – Toshi Go Named Successor – Retiring Chief to devote More Time to Party Duties': JT, 10 January 1940.

74 The photograph later appeared in Okamura (1941: 51) captioned 'Japanese-American relations don't seem so strained in this informal scene taken at the Tokyo Club on January 22 when Ambassador Grew sponsored a tea party for prominent Japanese. The smiles represent Mr Toshi Go, president of The Japan Times, Limited.'

75 USDS 894.911/66: Grew, Tokyo, to State Dept., 13 March 1940; Tokyo News Service (ed.) (1948: 30) shows Gō resident in Shibuya-ku and a member of both the Tokyo and the American Clubs.

76 USDS, op cit.

77 USDS 894.911/84: Stanley Hornbeck, USDS, to Under Secretary of State Sumner Welles, 5 June 1941, regarding Thomas Millard, Manila, 21 May 1941. This file holds a one-and-a-half page excerpt from Millard's letter, probably typed up within the State Dept., and a covering note by Hornbeck. The first page of Millard's letter is not included so there is no indication of the recipient although it was probably Hornbeck. Millard died in Seattle in September 1942.

78 Op. cit. Hornbeck covering note and speculations.

79 USDS 948.918/34: Grew to State Dept., October 10, Section Two, 10 October 1940.

80 USDS 893.911 Manchuria/8: Stuart Grummon, US Consul, Dairen, to Edwin Neville, US Embassy, Tokyo, 3 September 1935.

81 FO 395/458 [P 1113/2/150]: M.E. Dening to Chancery, 2 April 1932; Miles Lampson to Arthur Willert, 15 April 1932. FO 371/21001 [F 8927/1043/10]: Young telegram to FO, 1 November 1937.

82 Commonwealth of Australia Security Service. Ref. G.2978/43/DD, Director-General of Security for Queensland, report on Aileen Brown Gorman and George William Gorman received from War Department, Washington through C.I.C., 15 May 1944. The same report states that Gorman wrote a number of 'maliciously anti-American and anti-British' articles in the Japan Times & Advertiser under the pen name 'McGinty' during this period. I am indebted to Deborah Takahashi for sharing this document with me.

83 FO 371/21001 [F 11610/1043/10]: Howe to A. Eden, 11 April 1937. FO 371/23487 [F 12419/372/10], S. H. Lamb to Halifax, 16 October 1939.

84 USDS 894.911/51: Cameron Forbes, Tokyo, to State Dept., 9 March 1932.

85 USDS 894.918/17: W.T. Turner (Reuters) 'Memorandum of Statement by Mr Wilfrid Fleisher', September 1934.

86 USDS 894.911: unsigned Far East Division note; copied to Coville, EAS, 16 April 1940.

87 FO 371/23574 [F 10795/10795/23], J. Pratt (Ministry of Information) to Ashley Clarke, Far East Dept., 3 October 1939. Pickering left 'in a rather disgruntled frame of mind' after the Ministry balked at his price, although they did seriously consider setting up a similar arrangement to that governing the New East in 1916–18, and with some of the same personnel.

88 The sale to the *Japan Times* was surely no more 'patriotic', albeit far less rewarding. USDS 918.794/34 (Part Two): Grew to State Dept., 10 October 1934, and USDS 894.911/66, Grew to State Dept., 13 March 1940.

89 'Tokyo's Captive Yankee Newspaper' by Demaree Bess: *Saturday Evening Post*, 6 February 1943, is a useful complement to Wilfrid Fleisher's own memoir (Fleisher 1941).

90 'Business Deal Only': *Japan Times & Advertiser Incorporating the Japan Chronicle and the Japan Mail*, 8 January 1941.

91 On becoming Foreign Minister in July 1940, Matsuoka engaged Hasegawa Shinichi, a journalist with long experience in the hinterland between politics and the fourth estate, beginning with Hara Kei, as his personal secretary with responsibility for relations with the press. Hasegawa's home was near Matsuoka's in Sendagaya and the two frequently discussed tactics as they rode in Matsuoka's official car (Lu 2002: 148, 149). Hasegawa also had a long association with the JT and would become one of its post-war editors as well as the editor of its 1966 official history.

92 Lu 2002: 148–52.

93 Kakegawa 1973: 545, citing Uchikawa and Kōuchi 1961: 27.

94 USDS 893.911/345: M. Fischer, German Consul, to C.E. Gauss, US Consul Shanghai, 3 March 1938, regarding 'Hitler and Mussolini's Failure in the Far East', CWR, 26 February 1938.

95 Powell 1945: 352–3.

96 FO 371/27701 [F6980/858/10]: Ashley Clarke FO to M. de la Vallette, Min. of Inf., 30 July 1941.

97 FO 371/27701 [F6952/858/10]: Charles Watney, London corresp. *Central China Post* to R.K. Law, FO, 25 July 1941.

98 Council of International Affairs, Chungking 1943: 'Newspapermen and martyrs', 674–76.

99 Powell 1945: 334–42.

100 Diet for 24 January and 2 February 1934 discussed in USDS 894.918/16: Grew, Tokyo, to State Dept., 21 February 1934.

101 FO 398/573 [P 3059/39/150], Tokyo report, 31 October 1938.

102 Grew 1944: 364.

103 The Foreign Ministry distributed about 2,000 copies of the JT to foreign embassies and consulates and friendly cultural institutions.

104 Personal communication from Theodore Van Doorn, November 2005.

105 USDS 894.911/4: Grew to State Dept., 11 December 1940.

106 USDS 894.911/6: Grew to State Dept., 1 February 1941.

107 USDS 894.911/84: Hornbeck to Sumner Welles, 5 June 1941, Millard to Hornbeck, 21 May 1941.

108 Grew added, 'Somebody else told me that Go had published the editorial as a protest against the secrecy under which the conversations [in Washington] were being held' (Grew 1944: 474–5).

109 Grew 1944: 481; diary entry for 18 November 1941.

110 Grew 1944: 471–6; Purdy 1987: 360, n.79.

111 See e.g. 'Japan must move quickly to consummate her conquests in Asia or face economic ruin and defeat.' NYHT 27 July 1941.

112 See Oblas 2003: 42, n.64. and May (1973), also Oblas's (2009) 'biographical history' of Hugh Byas, esp. Chapters 4 and 7 for Byas's influence on the US and European discourse on China.

113 FO 371/24667 F3590/43/10 Shigemitsu/Butler conversation 19 July 1940, cited in Best 1995: 122.
114 See May in Borg (ed.) 1973 for a fuller account of the deficiencies of US correspondents in Tokyo in 1941, esp.525–30.
115 Sims 2001: 223.
116 Usui in Borg (ed.) 1973: 127, 127–48.
117 May in Borg (ed.) 1973: 530.
118 May, op. cit.
119 Papers of the Prime Minister's Office, 3/158/4, Craigie Report to Eden, 4 February 1943. Cited in Lowe 1982: 119.

8

Publicity warriors: the Japan network, 1941–1945

In his alternate history novel, *The Man in the High Castle* (1962), Philip K. Dick's inverted prescience has the *Nippon Times* emerging from the Pacific War as top media dog in Japan's most coveted Anglophone conquest and a prestigious media outlet for the undisputed ruler of the Pacific, the 'China District' and more. In a defeated America, divided between the Reich and Japan, the natural location for Tagomi, a senior trade official representing Japan in the 'Co-prosperity Pacific Alliance', is a suite of offices on the twentieth floor of the Nippon Times Building on Taylor Street overlooking San Francisco Bay.[1] Adapting Philip Dick's projection to the conventional truth, how did Japan's fortunes in the Pacific War and its aftermath affect the Foreign Ministry network and its flagship?

On 7 December 1941, Japan's pre-emptive attack on the US Pacific Fleet in Pearl Harbor launched an astonishing series of military and naval upsets that would cut down the institutions and standard bearers of Western influence in Asia. Within six months of Pearl Harbor, Japanese forces had overrun American, British and Dutch forces throughout South-east Asia and occupied the Philippines, Borneo, the Celebes, the Malayan peninsula, Singapore, Indonesia and Rangoon – cutting supplies to China along the Burma Road. On 10 December, Henry Ching, editor of the *South China Morning Post*, noted in his 'Bird's-Eye View' column, 'Trouble about fighting the Japanese is that the blighters don't seem to have tiffin.'[2] Hongkong surrendered on Christmas Day.

The Foreign Ministry network had run English-language and vernacular media in Japan and East Asia until its gradual supersession by military-dominated Cabinet propaganda bureaux and the Information Board of 1940. In the wake of Pearl Harbor what should be more accurately described as the Japan network neutralized all pro-British and most US-backed challenges to its media programmes in East Asia and dramatically advanced its remit and purpose in Greater East Asia.

The end came for *Japan News-Week* on the morning of 8 December 1941, when 'the entire editorial staff' including journalist Phyllis Argall and her editor W.R. Wills was arrested[3] alongside forty-three other Americans and a number of Britons. Among those rounded up were Vere Redman, who was also an ex-*Japan News-Week* staff writer, now running the British Information Bureau at the British embassy, Redman's second-in-command Frank Hawley of *The Times*, J.R. 'Reggie' Price of the *JT & AJCJM*, Robert Bellaire, Jasper Bellinger and Richard Tennelly of the *Advertiser*, Reuters and NBC, Relman Morin, Max Hill and Joseph Dynan of AP, Ray Cromley of the *Wall Street Journal*, and Otto Tolischus of the *New York Times*. As a citizen of a defeated nation, Robert Guillain of Havas was treated as a neutral and remained at large.

Even such veterans of semi-official journalism as Russell Kennedy's old *Kokusai* protégé Percy Whiteing, who had succeeded James Young at the International News Service following Young's arrest in January 1940, and George Gorman, one of the Foreign Ministry network's most faithful operatives, were incarcerated. Vere Redman was also vulnerable, for all his credentials in semi-official journalism (*Japan Times*, *Contemporary Japan*, and contributions to a well-circulated propaganda pamphlet in 1938).[4] On 8 December, Japanese police dragged him from the hall of the British embassy despite Robert Craigie's attempt to stand in their way.

Over the winter of 1940–41, Redman had used the Tokyo embassy's diplomatic pouch to get Phyllis Argall's *Time* magazine reports on Japan to the Shanghai legation, which then posted them on to the US. By the same means, Argall had supplied H.G.W. Woodhead's *Oriental Affairs* with weekly reports on Japan.[5] In such arrangements, which came out during Argall's interrogation at Sugamo prison, the lines of some species of network, whether of espionage or professional affiliation was never entirely clear, probably emerged in the eyes of her questioners.

The links between journalism and espionage were very much in the official mind at the time. On 18 October 1941, the Japanese police had picked up the Soviet spy and journalist (*Frankfurter Zeitung, Börsen Zeitung, Tägliche Rundschau*) Richard Sorge in Tokyo. Sorge's connections with Agnes Smedley, the *Frankfurter Zeitung* correspondent in Shanghai, and with Ozaki Hotsumi of the *Asahi Shinbun*[6] were noted and extensively investigated. Other connections would be drawn from the interrogation of J.B. Powell in Shanghai over that winter. The following summer even Toshi Gō would be arrested and held briefly on an unspecified charge. In 1944, Sheba Kimpei was arrested when he was on the editorial staff of the *Nippon Times*.[7] In New York, Randall Gould speculated that any Japanese newspaperman consorting with foreigners was in danger.[8] As one of Otto Tolischus's police interrogators put it, 'All newspaper men are spies because they try to find out the truth. Japanese correspondents abroad are spies; so are Japanese newspaper men at home. We could arrest all of them.'[9]

Eighteen months earlier the arrests of July 1940 had caused outrage in Tokyo and in London and led in August to the retaliatory arrest of ten Japanese in Britain, India and the South-east Asian colonies. In September 1941, two Britons, J.G. Martyr and one Mason, had been arrested in Tokyo, and in early November Britain had responded by arresting two Japanese, Suzuki and Matsunaga, in Karachi and Rangoon.

Compared with this tit-for-tat frenzy, Britain's reaction to the 8 December round-ups seems muted: a low-key sweep of Japanese in Singapore, and at home the internment of 114 Japanese businessmen, professionals and seamen at the Taplow Hotel on the Isle of Man.[10]

On 7 December, the FBI picked up Karl Kiyoshi Kawakami (1873–1949), Washington correspondent of the *Hōchi Shinbun*, at his Washington D.C. home and interrogated him for some months as a 'dangerous foreigner', ending a forty-year career of Japan-US bridge-building and propaganda (in Kawakami's case the two activities were sometimes hard to separate).[11] On the same day, Kawakami's son, Clark, an American citizen, resigned as the *Dōmei* correspondent in Washington and in a farewell letter described the attack on Pearl Harbor as 'the blackest and most shameful page in Japanese history'.[12] On 23 December, the State Department announced to its legation in Berne, Switzerland, that only Japanese journalists 'suspected of activities inimical to this Government' had been arrested and were being held in 'a comfortable hotel' and asked that the Swiss government, now the US-Japan intermediary, request 'reciprocal good treatment' for US correspondents in Japan and Japanese-occupied territories.[13]

CLOSING DOWN CHINA

The Japanese occupation of the International Settlements in Shanghai took place on 8 December. The business of journalism ended at the *China Weekly Review*, *China Press* and *North China Daily News*. The offices of the first two were sealed, but not long afterwards a Japanese newspaper, the *Tairiku Shimpō* moved into the North China Daily News Building on the Bund. The *Shanghai Times* continued under the nominal editorship of E.A. Nottingham, whom H.G.W. Woodhead later described as a classic representative of 'quislingdom'.[14] When the Japanese occupied the International Settlement, C.V. Starr's *Shanghai Evening Post and Mercury* was a thriving concern and the Chinese edition, *Da Mei Wan Bao*, had a circulation of 40,000. The *Shanghai Evening Post and Mercury* continued under the editorship of its business manager, George Bruce, under Japanese military supervision. Bruce was interned in mid-1942 and died a few months later. According to J.B. Powell, another C.V. Starr title, the *Shanghai Evening Post*, was kept going during the occupation by American journalists who 'went over'.[15] Whether the *Shanghai Evening Post and Mercury* was able to continue after Bruce's death is unknown.[16] When Charles Miner returned to the *Shanghai Evening Post and Mercury* premises in September 1945, Japanese sentries were still on guard but the plant was not up and running.

The occupiers were in a bind. Their instinct was to cleanse their new territories of Western influence but few of those under their control had any command of Japanese, which did not become the official language of the Shanghai Municipal Council until early 1943. Adapting current Western publications to their needs was the next best way of conveying the Japanese ideal, not only to the British, who were still needed to run the Shanghai Municipal Council, but to the Axis personnel who were taking it over.[17] Hence the continuation of the *Shanghai Evening Post and Mercury*. The occupation made little difference to the *Shanghai Times*, which continued the role it had played since at least 1921.

As a doughty opponent of Japanese incursions in China, the *China Weekly Review*'s John B. Powell was a natural trophy for the new masters of Shanghai. On 20 December 1941, Powell was arrested by the Japanese authorities. He was held and interrogated in the converted Bridge House Apartments in Hongqu for most of 1941–42, where his health deteriorated rapidly. After his repatriation in 1943 and prolonged hospitalization (partly financed by Chiang Kai-shek), Powell participated in the Allied war effort as a conspicuous symbol of Japanese brutality, frequently denouncing the Japanese in print and lectures in the US.[18] He died in February 1947, just after giving a lecture to Missouri School of Journalism students.[19] Two fellow-inmates of the Bridge House were Victor Keen of the *New York Tribune* and one unfortunate, W.R. Davies, an engineer employed by the Shanghai Power Company whom the Japanese had mistaken for R.W. Davis, managing director of the *North China Daily News*, then in Hongkong.[20]

As with James Young early in 1940, and Phyllis Argall, Otto Tolischus and others in the wake of Pearl Harbor, the interrogation of J.B. Powell was characterized by a search for official links to Washington. Powell's interlocutors worked hard to connect him and the *Review* to the US naval attaché in Shanghai, and through papers seized from the attaché's office to H.G.W. Woodhead and Frederick Opper, also arrested, of the *Shanghai Evening Post and Mercury*, as well as the Missouri alumnus (1921) and ex-*Advertiser* writer Morris Harris, in the late 1930s a correspondent for AP Shanghai.[21] His interrogators repeatedly confronted Powell with a *New York Herald Tribune* article by Wilfrid Fleisher that had also appeared in *Asia* magazine and the *Nation* and that Powell had reprinted in the *China Weekly Review*. The article referred to 'a plot to overthrow the Emperor and establish a fascist state'. Powell's decision to run the article was taken as evidence of his lack of respect for the Emperor. Another article Powell had run in the *Review* in 1932 referring to Puyi as 'a puppet of a puppet' – that is, as a puppet of the Japanese Emperor who was himself a puppet of the Japanese army – did not help Powell's case either.[22]

Notwithstanding his generally accommodating posture towards the Foreign Ministry network, H.G.W. Woodhead was initially treated no less severely than the uncompromising Powell. Woodhead was arrested by Japanese police on 5 March 1942 and held in Bridge House for three months.[23] In June Woodhead, Powell and Victor Keen all went before a Japanese court-martial on charges of espionage and conducting subversive propaganda against Japan. Their trial and treatment were reported in glowing terms in the *Shanghai Times* and with solemn brevity in *The Times*.[24] Close to the trial, a Mr Morley, former adviser to the Press Attaché at the British embassy in Shanghai, told Woodhead's captors that he could 'guarantee' Woodhead's conduct on condition he say nothing about his treatment.[25] In early September 1942 Woodhead was repatriated on the exchange ship *Kamakura Maru* to Lourenço Marques, where in an interview he described Shanghai as resembling 'a large internment camp'.[26] He arrived in the UK in October. He was later appointed head of the Far Eastern Reference Section of the Ministry of Information.[27]

Among the last journalists to be picked up were the Britons Sheldon Ridge[28] and R.T. Peyton-Griffin. Ridge, who was thirty when his career in China began at the *Shanghai Mercury* in 1905, had owned and edited the *Peking Chronicle* in the 1930s, taking subsidies from both the Guomindang and the German Transocean news agency. In 1937, on the advice of a British intermediary, the journalist George Gorman, Ridge sold the paper to Japanese interests but stayed on under Gorman until 1939. Ridge may still have been working, under Japanese direction, on the *Peking Chronicle* or the *Shanghai Evening Post* when he was arrested in 1943.[29] By then he was in his late sixties and his age and his cooperative past may have helped delay his incarceration. Ridge's death in 1945 probably came during internment.[30] Peyton-Griffin had edited the *North-China Daily News* since 1938. He was interned from 1943 until September 1945.[31]

By the end of 1941, all the independent English-language newspapers in Japanese-controlled areas of China had been silenced or become Japanese mouthpieces, but there was some foreign resistance in 'Free China'. Right after Pearl Harbor, the Office of Strategic Services (OSS) had put together the 'Dragon Plan' in China, a major intelligence initiative utilizing C.V. Starr's *Shanghai Evening Post and Mercury* staff and insurance interests in Shanghai as agents and cover, but this stalled due to political and military rivalries in Washington and Chongqing. Back in New York, Starr revived the Plan under the heading 'the Counter Japanese Division of the COI' (Coordinator of Information) and in December 1942 he again offered his paper to the OSS as a cover for intelligence and 'Morale Operations' against the Japanese. The OSS took up Starr's offer and in January 1943 launched a New York edition of the *Shanghai Evening Post and Mercury* as a propaganda and intelligence-gathering operation. On 31 October 1943 Starr sent Randall Gould, Charles Miner and the newspaper's repatriated ex-editor Frederick B. Opper to Chongqing to start an edition of the paper there and to collect information for the OSS, despite some opposition from General Stilwell and the War and State Departments. The Chongqing edition of the *Shanghai Evening Post and Mercury* continued as an OSS intelligence project until June 1945, when publication was suspended because of Guomindang 'wartime censorship restrictions which go far beyond considerations of military security'.[32] The New York edition continued until Japan's surrender. By July 1944 the OSS had spent $350,000 on these two publications.[33]

What was at stake for Japan? In closing down or taking over these English-language newspapers, Japan sought to negate the challenge to its agenda and co-opt the authority and credibility that American-British- and Chinese-owned English-language organs had built up among their readerships. Japan sought to roll back the West's 'news colonies' in East Asia and to impose its own Tokyo-centred media framework, with regional hubs in Singapore, Shanghai and Xinjing.

Even at the height of hostilities between Japan and the West, Japan never abandoned its effort to promote a 'proper understanding' of Japan's mission in Asia. Amō Eiji, Furuno Inosuke and Iwanaga Yūkichi put their life into strengthening Japan's ability to make its nature and its activities understood on Japan's terms through a national news service for this very purpose. What was at stake was the Western world's idea of Japan, especially the West's view of Japan's place in China.

Japan's purpose in gaining control of the competing networks of the English-language press of East Asia seems clearer than that of the United States in attempting to shore them up. Certainly, the situation that would arise in 1943–44, with the New York and Chongqing editions of the *Shanghai Evening Post and Mercury* pitted against two or possibly three Japanese-run papers in Shanghai, the *Shanghai Evening Post*, the *Shanghai Evening Post and Mercury* and the *Shanghai Times*, seems a triumph of gallantry over strategy on both sides. But setting up Randall Gould and the Chongqing edition probably looked like an unbeatable investment to the OSS in 1943, as it neatly combined support for the Guomindang with opposition to Japan. And of course in supporting 'Free China' in 1942 the US was also cannily positioning itself for post-war amity – or so it must have seemed at the time. In doing so, US policy finally came to occupy ground that the *Advertiser* network had been salting since 1911. In this sense, the priorities of the *Advertiser* network lived on after the demise of most of its constituent parts.

'PUBLICITY WARRIORS': REORIENTING
THE PRESS IN GREATER EAST ASIA

Scurrying to keep up with the conquering forces of Japan, the reporters, photographers and newsreel cameramen of *Dōmei*, the *Asahi* and *Yomiuri* and lesser media wrote up and recorded the headline moments of these epochal advances. Behind the front lines *Dōmei* staff ran mopping-up operations recruiting and reorienting the news industries in newly conquered East and South-east Asia. New branches of *Dōmei* were set up or previously suppressed branches revived. Shanghai and Xinjing became news hubs for China and Manchukuo and Singapore for all of South-east Asia.

For *Dōmei*, the drive into the new territories was not only a matter of media business reorganization but also of uniting news institutions and personnel to proclaim Japanese policies and ideals and to manage local news and opinion in the Greater East Asia Co-Prosperity Sphere (*Daitōa Kyōeiken*). In 1942–44, Japan's hopes for the coordinated development of the Co-prosperity Sphere depended heavily on the ability of *Dōmei* and other media institutions to unite and motivate journalists and newspapers throughout the conquered territories behind the ideology of their new masters. In October 1942 the Army Information department assigned specific areas to different media organizations. In China, *Dōmei* had served as the main organ shaping the news industry to Japanese requirements. However, the Army Information department's Outline Policy for South-east Asia Newspapers (*Nanpō Shinbun Seisaku Yōryō*) divided supervision and reorientation of the local press between *Dōmei* and Japan's three leading metropolitan newspapers, the *Asahi*, *Yomiuri* and *Mainichi*, each paper being respectively assigned to Java, Burma and the Philippines.[34] Thus *Dōmei* ran China in partnership with the military, and shared South-east Asia with Japan's three major metropolitan newspapers.

In Japan, the Foreign Ministry network had become the loudest and most far-reaching 'voice in the room' by suppressing or suborning the competition. Now the Japan network was forced to confront a large and stubborn elephant in that room, that of language. Since its establishment in 1936 *Dōmei* had contracted with Western news agencies and set up its own network to gather world news. By 1940 *Dōmei* was broadcasting extensively to Europe and the Americas in English and French and its English-Language News Department, headed by Ian (Yonosuke) Mutsu, who had been recruited from the *Japan Times*, had been considerably enlarged. In South-east as in East Asia the intention in the 1920s and 1930s had been less to suppress the English-language competition than to flood the market with pro-Japanese news to influence Anglophone readers (and if that meant pushing old enemies like Reuters to the wall, so much the better).[35] Following the establishment of media control over English-language and local vernacular media, the plan was to replace English, the language of Western imperialism, with Japanese, the language of pan-Asian liberation. In this, however, *Dōmei* and its sister organizations met with mixed success.

In December 1942,[36] on the anniversary of the attack on Pearl Harbor, the editor of the *Japan Times*, Toshi Gō, announced and on 1 January 1943 effected a change of title to the *Nippon Times*, with the *Japan Times Weekly* edition becoming the *Nippon Times Weekly*. The new titles reflected the ongoing effort to reinforce national identity by disseminating the Japanese language abroad, although to rename Japan 'Nippon' and Japanese things and ideas 'Nipponese' was also to acknowledge the power, if not specifically of English, the language of the foremost enemy, then of Roman letters, the alphabet of Western thought.

Two years into a war that may still have looked like a good idea, despite the continuing psychological and strategic consequences of Midway, Gō reminded his readers that the *Japan Times* had been founded in 1897 'to reveal Japan as she really is to the world and to make known the Japanese point of view truthfully to the peoples abroad', and he reset this mission in the frame of the present hostilities:

It was in line with this object that prior to the outbreak of the War of Greater East Asia, the Japan Times, Limited, purchased the 'Japan Advertiser', published in Tokyo, and the 'Japan Chronicle' published in Kobe, the former of which represented American interests and the latter British interests. Through this bold and effective step the Japan Times, Limited, corrected the anomalous situation in which Japan was represented to the outside world by alien interests which naturally could but do so inadequately and unsatisfactorily. Not only did this move thus frustrate the possibility of foreign subversion of the media through which Japan was being made known to the world; it also made the 'Japan Times' without question the most influential and representative foreign language paper published within the Greater East Asia Co-Prosperity Sphere – a paper written, edited, and managed exclusively by Japanese and thus reflecting most accurately and completely the real Japan.[37]

In the autumn of 1943, the *Nippon Times* became Japan's chosen forum for the ideological conversion of Asian media to the virtues and benefits of the Greater East Asia Co-Prosperity Sphere. The showcase for this new prominence came during the three-day Greater East Asia Newspaper Conference (*Daitōa Kyōeiken Shinbun Kai*) held in Tokyo, 17–19 November 1943, held just after the 5–6 November Greater East Asian Conference (*Daitōa Kaigi*). These two conferences brought together all the key bodies involved in the massive reorganizations of the media that had been taking place in Japan since 1939: the Cabinet Information Bureau, the press sections of the Army and Navy, and the main administrative body for Japan's newly conquered territories, the Greater East Asia Ministry (*Daitōashō*).

The Newspaper Conference was officially sponsored by the Japan Press Association, whose newspaper *Nihon Shinbun Kaihō* carried the Conference reports.[38] Although all major Japanese news organizations were represented at the Conference, the publication most closely involved was the *Nippon Times* under its President and editor, Toshi Gō.[39]

In effectively hosting the Greater East Asia Newspaper Conference the *Nippon Times* built on its reputation and history to stand at the head of 'Greater East Asian' media as, in Gō's words, 'without question the most influential and representative foreign language paper published within the Greater East Asia Co-Prosperity Sphere'. This was not an idle puff. For the eighty-odd journalists invited to the Newspaper Conference and the numerous representatives of Japan's new territories in South-East and East Asia who had gathered in Tokyo to attend both conferences, the *Nippon Times* was an obvious forum not only for the Newspaper Conference but also for the drive for ideological unity that it was set up to spearhead.

Proselytizing the Greater East Asia Co-Prosperity Sphere was not a minor departure from the internationalist '*raison d'être*' the *Japan Times* had proclaimed in 1897. However, the *Nippon Times* seems to have found a new sense of purpose in the Conference and to have made a final shift from 'weak-kneed' Shidehara-style internationalism to serve as the cutting edge of the national cause. Echoing Zumoto Motosada's defunct title of 1916–23, in November 1943 the *Nippon Times* became the herald of the new Asia, even if the heralding had to be done in English.

In mid-October, a month before the Newspaper Conference, Toshi Gō had presided over a Round Table gathering sponsored by the *Nippon Times* and held at the Imperial Hotel. Participants had included Lieutenant-General Homma Masaharu,[40] Kimura Izawa from the Information Board, the novelist Kimura Ki, *Nippon Times* managing editor Togasaki Kiyoshi and editorial executive, Hasegawa Shinichi. Gō set the tone with a speech celebrating the sweeping away of American and British power and heralding Philippine independence. Homma and Kimura talked up the roles of General Aguinaldo and Jose Laurel in the independence movement.[41] Under its youthful, articulate President, the *Nippon Times* set out its pan-Asian stall.[42]

From 17 to 19 November, under 'earpieces' declaring 'For Common Prosperity and Well-Being' and 'For Independence and Fraternity', the *Nippon Times* ran front page leads on the 'resolute determination to do their utmost in publicity activities for the successful prosecution of the War of Greater East Asia' displayed by delegates from Burma, Hongkong, Borneo, Malai (Malaya), Java, the Celebes, Ceram, Manchukuo and Borneo assembled at the *Daitōa Kaikan* in Marunouchi. The 18 November issue ran an article by Amō Eiji, now head of the Cabinet Information Board, aligning the Conference with the pan-Asianist mission of the Greater East Asia Co-Prosperity Sphere: 'The Anglo-Americans not only encroached upon East Asia politically and exploited East Asia economically, but also converted East Asia into their "news colony" ... they misused the right of communication ... Thus, though we all lived in East Asia, our eyes looking at East Asia were kept covered.'[43]

On the same day Prime Minister Tōjō Hideki, who had just hosted the previous Conference and was facing mounting opposition from his own cabinet and the military for his conduct of the war, hosted a luncheon for the delegates. Carried in full under the front page headline 'Prime Minister Exhorts Delegates to Press Meet – Urges Publicity Warriors to Widely Disseminate Principles of War Prosecution and E. Asia Construction at Lunch Given Them', Tōjō's speech stressed the delegates' new role in the drive for ideological unity, although the rest of his address could have been lifted from the late 1930s: 'the crucial and primordial factors, above all else, are how well the Press of Greater East Asia leads and guides the popular opinion in their respective countries so that every single member of the one billion peoples of Greater East Asia will come to feel a burning desire and deep urge to march forward towards the attainment of our common ideal ...'.[44] Following this peroration Takaishi Shingorō, Chairman of the *Mainichi Shinbun*, Kitano

Kichinai, managing editor of the *Asahi*, Shōriki Matsutarō of the *Yomiuri*, Hori Yoshitaka of *Dōmei*, and Matsukata Jisaburō of the Manchukuo Press Association and other leading Japanese newspapermen jointly proposed the establishment of a Greater East Asia Press Association.[45]

The Conference finally adopted a 'Resolution Thanking Officers and men on the Front Lines'. The front page of the 19 November evening edition of the *Nippon Times* ran a Declaration celebrating the idea that 'Asia has returned to our own Asia and its organs of ideological warfare have also recovered their natural structure' and concluding, 'We, who stand in the vanguard of ideological warfare by virtue of our profession, do hereby resolve to devote ourselves to the great mission of developing Asia and establishing world peace by smashing Anglo-American trickery and intrigues through mutual collaboration and wholehearted endeavour among ourselves.'[46]

At the final banquet, congratulatory cablegrams were read out from the Union of European Newspapers and from Dr Otto Dietrich of the Reich Ministry for Public Enlightenment and Propaganda (*Reichsministerium für Volksaufklärung und Propaganda*) which declared that 'The journalists of Greater East Asia in a spirit of true journalism have torn the network of lies and false news of the Anglo-Saxon countries.' The Conference resolved to establish the Greater Eastern Newspaper Union (*Daitōa Shinbun Renmei*), replacing the Japan Newspaper Association, to be headed by Tanaka Tōkichi, past President of the *Japan Times*. Furuno Inosuke then led banzais for the Emperor, followed by the chief Chinese delegate who led banzais for Greater East Asia.

For this study, the significance of the Conference lies in its consequences for the Japan media network in general and the *Nippon Times* and allied English-language media in particular. The commitment of the *Nippon Times* to Greater East Asia and the Co-Prosperity Sphere did not begin and end with the November Conference but the tenets of Japan-led Pan-Asianism became far more overt than hitherto. Henceforth the paper would serve up a heavy diet of commentary, news and cartoons pushing a simplistic but coherent editorial line on Greater East Asia.

The leader page of the *Nippon Times* displayed a range of new, recaptured and revived titles. A prominent new double-column page-deep section, *East-Asia's Editorial Forum*, featured a headline graphic showing a collage of mastheads. Sheldon Reid's *Peking Chronicle*, acquired by Japan with the intervention of George Gorman in 1937, was there. The *Shanghai Times* masthead featured in the collage. So did that of the *Shanghai Evening Post*, presumably continuing with American staff under Japanese control.

The *Nippon Times* graphic also displayed the masthead of the English-language *Hongkong News*, founded in September 1941 and moved to the premises of the *South China Morning Post* shortly after the surrender of Hongkong on 25 December. The Japanese-language *Shanghai Nippō* had also moved into the *Post's* Wyndham Road premises in 1942, whence this and a stream of other Japanese-run English- Japanese- and Chinese-language organs were turned out on the *Post's* printing presses.[47] The graphic featured other English-language papers newly established or taken over in South-east Asia – the Manila *Tribune*, *Syonan Shinbun*, *Malai Sinbun*[48] – whose editorials were summarized in the columns below. There the *Kita Sumatra Sinbun* (North Sumatra News) listed improvements in school provision made since the overthrow of the 'former despotic Dutch rulers', while Singapore's *Syonan Sinbun* lauded Japan's treatment of the peoples of the 'cooperative sphere':

> In treating the peoples of the occupied territories, Japan has given full weight to their racial histories and cultural backgrounds so as to give each and every race or nation its rightful place in the family of cooperative and harmonious community. Japan expects every race or nation in the cooperative sphere to contribute each in its own way the very best that it has to offer towards the construction of a harmonious and cooperative Greater East Asia.[49]

By late 1943, Japan was running a successful, dynamic international network leading Asian opinion through 'publicity warriors' operating from media hubs in Tokyo, Shanghai, Xinjing and Singapore. The *Nippon Times* was distributed to 'Nippai' offices in Hanoi, Saigon, Bangkok, Rangoon, Shōnan (Singapore), Medan, Padang, Palembang, Kuching, Jakarta, Macassar and Bukit-Tingi at ¥0.15 for the morning edition, ¥0.08 for the evening edition. But there were clouds on the horizon.

On 4 December 1943, the *Nippon Times* ran a cartoon by 'Eturo' (Katō Etsurō) headlined 'Defeated at Every Hour of Battle' that mocked the long 'island-hopping' campaign by the United States to reassert its hold on the Pacific and denied US success in turning the tide of war since Midway eighteen months earlier. The cartoon showed an exhausted Roosevelt trying to pull the hands of a large clock back, while its face marked five successive defeats at Bougainville and four in the Gilbert Islands.[50] But even before the Newspaper Conference three weeks earlier, US Marines had invaded Bougainville in the Solomons. And a few days after the Conference the Marines took the Gilbert Islands.

On 11 December, in another dig at the Pacific campaign, an 'Eturo' cartoon showing marine life making themselves at home in the holed and darkened hulls of enemy warships carrying the sign 'Pacific Apartments'. A few weeks later US troops invaded the Marshalls, launching further assaults and establishing significant beachheads there and in the Caroline Islands and in the Marianas in February. By the autumn of 1944, the Pacific War had turned even more decisively against Japan and the nation responded with suicide attacks on Allied warships. In November American and Japanese forces began the desperate struggle for Iwo Jima. Between July and January 1944 the US resumed B-29 raids on Japan from Chinese airfields. City dwellers took hell from the air, with massive damage to the nation's buildings and incalculable effects on civilian morale.

Throughout, largely dependent on *Dōmei* and Army press releases, the Japan media network talked up Japanese successes and recognized only Allied defeats. The steadily increasing ferocity of Allied assaults in the South Pacific, in China and on the Japanese mainland was consistently underreported in the *Nippon Times* and sister papers. However, where bad news could not be concealed, the chosen messenger was invariably a 'Dōmei military analyst' rather than an Army or Navy spokesman.[51]

Backing up this overall tendency, the *Nippon Times* and sister organs highlighted moral and material weaknesses in the Allied cause. In December 1943, a *Nippon Times* leader reported Foreign Minister Shigemitsu Mamoru's observations in a radio broadcast on the 'hypocrisy of the United States and Britain's war aims' and 'the voracious British and American desire to dominate the world that lurks ill-concealed behind their empty propaganda phrases, and in their unrealizable dream of satisfying their unholy ambitions by overthrowing Japan'.[52] Three days later the *Nippon Times* reported US planes' 'dastardly action' in bombing the hospital ship *Buenos Aires Maru* in the South Pacific and machine-gunning survivors in their lifeboats, ran a *Dōmei* release citing an article in the British magazine, *The Economist*, emphasizing the high morale and military invincibility of Germany under the headline 'Warning Given British Public of German Might', and reported plans for an exhibition at Mitsukoshi designed 'to bare in all its naked ugliness the insidious ideological trickery of Jewish manipulated American motion pictures'.[53]

SETTING THE RECORD STRAIGHT

Not too long into the war, possibly as an indication of second thoughts, detailed accounts of the events that had led to the opening of hostilities began to appear in editorials and in books published by the Japan network, in particular the *Japan Year Book*. These brought swift responses in news media, but in East Asia both the Japan network and the Guomindang network ran conspicuously detailed retrospectives of their position and experience in their English-language year books.[54] For Chiang and publicity advisers such as Hollington Tong, the audience for these retrospectives would have included not only the residents of Tong's International Press Hostel in Chongqing and waverers such as Theodore 'Teddy' H. White, but also White's sometime mentor, Henry Luce, who had given the Guomindang top billing in such media as *Time*, *Fortune* and *Life* magazines – the Chiangs would appear on the cover of *Time* no fewer than eleven times between 1927 and 1955 – and raised funds through the body United Service to China, Inc.

On 26 May 1942, Toshi Gō made a short-wave radio broadcast from Tokyo on NHK's International station. Speaking in fluent English, Gō maintained that:

... when matters approached a crisis in November [1941] the Japanese Government, through speeches of responsible officials, through the

convening of an extraordinary session of the Imperial Diet and through
various other acts made it very evident that Japan regarded the situation
with utmost gravity ... There was no attempt to lull the Americans into a
sense of security. On the contrary, Japan made every effort to warn the
Americans of the seriousness of the crisis. Because of the seriousness of the
crisis the Japanese took the unprecedented step of sending a special envoy
on a special mission to make a last-minute appeal to the United States to
show some sign of conciliation ... [If the United States had responded] in
even the slightest friendly fashion [Japan would have been] more than cooperative in working for peace ... The opening of the war, therefore, far from
being an act of treachery on the part of Japan, came only as a last resort as
Japan had made every peaceful effort and had given warning after warning.
It was only the mistaken complacence of American leaders which brought
on the war. If American leaders had been as well-informed about Japan as
Japanese leaders were about America the blunder would not have
happened.[55]

Gō's use of the euphemism 'blunder' in his final sentence ('... the
blunder would not have happened') reads like a coded concession remi-
niscent of the apologies both of Foreign Ministry network organs and
the delicate protests voiced by the *North-China Daily News* during the
naval invasion of Shanghai in early 1932. However, any semantic
nuances that Gō may have intended fell on deaf ears at the *New York
Times*:

It is important that a prompt answer be made to Mr Go's attempt to feel us
out, not because there is any danger of our forgetting Pearl Harbor. Mr Go
will have to live much longer than Methuselah to see that happen – but
because there is a third nation that is bound to be deeply interested in the
fate of this first tentative Japanese 'peace' feeler. That nation is China. We
may be sure that the significance of Mr Go's broadcast at this particular
moment has not escaped the Chinese people. It is important, therefore, that
Mr Go be told at once that we are not remotely interested in peace with the
present rulers of Japan. We are interested in making war. And we shall
continue to make war, at whatever cost to us and however long it takes, until
the military and naval power of Japan is destroyed.[56]

In July, in *The Chinese Year Book 1943*, the Guomindang published a
retrospective on the progress of 'the war of resistance'. As with most official Guomindang publications, great attention was paid to the
organization of the administration, with extensive charts all leading
upwards to the *Zongcai* or General Director, Chiang Kai-shek, a title only
previously held by Sun Yat-sen. But the *Chinese Year Book* also published
a detailed survey of 'the loyal, progressive and fearless wartime press of
China': wall sheets, army newspapers, the Central News Agency, the
official vernacular paper, the *Central Daily News* (*Da Gong Bao*). 'Free
China' was now served by only two English dailies, the *National Herald*,

formerly the American-owned *Hankow Herald*, and the *Chengtu News Bulletin*, published by the Canadian mission in the former Sichuan (Szechuen) capital. Fifty-six representatives of the foreign press had registered with the Nationalist authorities in Chongqing in 1942, most of them residents of Hollington Tong's International Press Hostel.[57] Besides these, John B. Powell's son, John William, who had joined the Office of War Information (OWI) in November 1942, was stationed as a news editor in Chongqing, sending on to Chinese newspapers stories received from the OWI New York office.[58] Upon Japan's defeat, the younger Powell would return to Shanghai to revive his father's weekly.

In November 1943, *The Japan Year Book* for 1943–44 countered with a 'Nipponese' perspective the issues covered by the July 1943 *Chinese Year Book*. maintaining that inflexibility on the part of the US had been an important contributory factor to the current hostilities, citing US Secretary of State Cordell Hull's rejection of the Japanese proposals that included the November offer to withdraw from 'French Indo-China' (South Indochina) and Hull's unwillingness to end US aid to 'the Chungking Regime'. 'In reply Japan pointed out the unreasonableness of certain of these proposals, but Cordell Hull however failed to show any signs of concession ... As no sincerity was shown on the Part of America to continue negotiations, Japan decided to close the negotiations and on 7 December (8, Japan time) issued the memorandum ... toward America and the negotiations were broken off.'[59]

Chapter VIII took a longer view and compared the clash of Japan and the United States to the inevitable clash of Britain and Germany in the First World War. The *Year Book* maintained that 'The American advance westward in recent years, however, seems to be far less justifiable as compared with the Nipponese request for supremacy in East Asia ... Providence therefore urged Nippon to do what Nippon should have done in and for this realm with its usual silent, yet irresistible power, and Nippon could not help to declare war against the United States and the British Empire.'[60]

Running through the key markers in the history of US-Japan relations, Chapter VIII stayed well within the lines of Toshi Gō's *Nippon Times* editorials and his radio broadcast: US inflexibility, Japan's lack of choice, the freeing of Asia.[61] On 10 September 1944, Toshi Gō and the *Nippon Times* published a pamphlet by Kakehi Mitsuaki defiantly repeating the case Gō had made for Japan in happier days. The following January, the seventh edition of *The Chinese Year Book* for 1944–45 gave its account of the 'war of resistance' in Chapter XXI, 'Japanese Aggression and the Pacific Theatre of War', and of the importance of Japan's unconditional surrender.[62]

In December 2007, in a speech to the Tokyo Rotary Club, Ogasawara Toshiaki, President of the *Japan Times* since 1983, offered a positive retrospective of his newspaper's 110-year history of internationalism, citing the 'Japonicus' editorials, written by a Foreign Ministry bureaucrat Takayanagi Kenzō, Kiyosawa Kyōshi and Ueda Shinnosuke and published in six issues of the *Nippon Times* from March 1944 until shortly before the end of the war.[63] The 'Japonicus' peace feelers were also broadcast on short-wave radio directed towards the US and Great Britain.[64]

An examination of four leading US national dailies during this period demonstrates either an ignorance of the significance of the 'Japonicus' messages or a determination to keep them secret, for they are not mentioned.[65] In any case, at the Pentagon, the priority had become the unconditional surrender of Japan, just as the Guomindang insisted. US media reports of other peace feelers from Tokyo typically included highly dismissive reactions from figures such as Admiral William F. 'Bull' Halsey, Commander of the US Third Fleet from late-May 1945 until Japan's formal surrender on the deck of his flagship, USS *Missouri*, on 2 September 1945.[66] However, the exchanges known as the 'Zacharias broadcasts' were picked up by *Dōmei* Radio, which became the conduit for negotiations that might have led to peace but faltered for reasons that range from a tragic mistranslation about Japan's willingness to accept the Potsdam Declaration[67] to sheer intransigence and unresponsiveness on the part of Japan. The Zacharias broadcasts probably helped persuade those elites who were open to peace negotiations that unconditional surrender would not be so dire an experience as they feared and therefore probably played some part in internal discussions and the acceptance of surrender after 6–9 August.

PEACE, 'HISASHIBURI!'

True to form, the Japanese surrender offer of 10 August 1945 was made on the radio by *Dōmei*, not by a military spokesman. With peace came the removal, often temporary, of many familiar, even notorious faces and the return of some old ones. The impulse to revive pre-war titles that occurred in Shanghai following the withdrawal of Japanese forces in September 1945 was not mirrored in Japan by a revival of the *Advertiser* or the *Chronicle*. With the *Nippon Times* docile and largely functioning as an occupation bulletin – supplied even to the class 'A' war criminals in Sugamo prison[68] – it seems unlikely that SCAP would have supported such ventures and, after all, the owners of both papers had been paid real money for their titles. SCAP did not have its sights set on any return to the pre-war balance of the fourth estate – English-language or vernacular.

Dōmei was another matter entirely. On 14 September 1945, SCAP effectively neutered the agency by establishing strict controls over its content and, by abolishing its overseas broadcasting rights, choking off its access to international news networks. At a stroke SCAP reduced *Dōmei*'s news power to that wielded by *Kokusai* under the one-sided agreement that John Russell Kennedy had brokered with Reuters thirty-two years earlier. Ten days later SCAP removed *Dōmei*'s government subsidies and Furuno decided to dissolve the agency, publicly announcing his decision on 27 September.[69] He went on to beat off a plan for a new agency put together by a combination of *Yomiuri*, *Asahi* and *Dentsū* interests (working with his sometime ally Kent Cooper) and to lay the groundwork for the creation of the *Jiji* and *Kyōdō* news agencies. On 2 December 1945, just as he seemed about to make a comeback, Furuno was indicted as a class A war criminal alongside Tokutomi Sohō, NHK President Shimomura Hiroshi, and *Yomiuri* President Shōriki Matsutarō. Furuno was held in Sugamo prison from 12 December until 31 August 1946, then released and purged until August 1951.

Perhaps because SCAP had bigger fish to fry, Toshi Gō was never indicted. His name disappeared from its usual position below the *Nippon Times* masthead early in 1945 but he appears to have continued to edit the paper until the end of the war. Others seemed to benefit from their accommodation with the pre-war order. When Miles Vaughn returned in 1945 to reestablish the United Press he was welcomed with open arms despite his rumoured collaboration with *Dōmei* when he was managing UP in New York after 1933. In 1948 Vaughn put together a pictorial book, intended to highlight the ordinariness of the Emperor in the spirit of the new constitution, which must have required close liaison with SCAP and the *Kunaichō*. In early December 1948 Vaughn flew to China to interview Chiang Kai-shek for the *Washington Post*. On 30 January 1949, Vaughn, Ueda Teizō (Sekizō), managing director of *Dōmei* and a pre-war President of *Dentsū*, and three others drowned on a duck-hunting expedition in Tokyo Bay.[70] The following year, 'Japan's Pulitzer', the Vaughn-Ueda Prize, dedicated to honouring 'excellence in international reporting', was set up to honour both men, effectively closing the book on Vaughn's mixed record.

In 1946, with its readership greatly increased by recent additions to the English-speaking population, managing editor Togasaki Kiyoshi became President of the *Nippon Times*, a position he held until 1956.[71] Togasaki steered the *Nippon Times* through the complicated and awkward realignment of editorial lines and values that would have come with any occupation by a foreign power, but were exacerbated by SCAP's inherently hostile attitude to the press.[72] In 1956 Togasaki was succeeded by a Foreign Ministry official, Fukushima Shintarō, who returned the paper to its original title on 1 July of that year.

Published by the Foreign Affairs Association in December 1948, *The Japan Year Book 1946–48* provided a recantation of a decade of Japanese foreign policy. Chapter VI revised most of the perspectives of the previous decade under such subheads as 'Nanking – Reign of Terror', 'The Trend Toward Political Dictatorship in Japan', 'Military Alliance Against the U.S.', 'American Advance in the Central Pacific', 'Alternative – First Atomic Bomb', 'Second Atomic Bomb', 'The Japanese Surrender Offer' and 'Reconquest of the Philippines' culminating in 'The Japanese Acceptance of the Potsdam Terms'.

REVIVALS IN SHANGHAI AND THE 'LOSS' OF CHINA

Guomindang control of the English-language press and Western correspondents in China was not as menacing as the Japanese version, but the end result was not so different: essentially a gag on critical commentary in the Chinese press and in despatches by foreign correspondents. In June 1944, Charles Miner and Randall Gould had decided to close down the Chongqing edition of the *Shanghai Evening Post and Mercury* because of the difficulties of both Guomindang and US military censorship there. In the spring of 1945 both T.V. Soong, acting President of the Executive Yuan and Minister of Information Wang Shih-chieh assured US Ambassador Patrick Hurley that censorship would soon ease, but within a few weeks Daniel Berrigan and Harold Isaacs were refused permits to return to China as correspondents for the *New York Post* and *Newsweek*.[73]

In 1943 both Britain and the US had renounced the unequal treaties. Around 4,000 Americans returned to Shanghai following Japan's surrender, but they were no longer welcome and no longer protected by extraterritoriality. Journalists were no exception. Following the withdrawal of Japanese troops from China in September 1945, those English-language newspapers that tried to start up again had to contend with both Guomindang pressures and the rising power of the Communist Party of China.[74]

On 1 December 1945, almost four years to the day since its closure, J.B. Powell's son, John William (1919–2008), born in Shanghai and like his father an alumnus of the School of Journalism at Missouri, resurrected the *China Weekly Review* and kept it going, despite considerable interference from both Guomindang and Communist officialdom and the intense disapproval of the US State Department, until July 1953, providing some of the most cogent assessments of the Cold War in East Asia available to contemporary readers and suffering the consequences.[75]

In September 1945, Charles Miner returned to Shanghai to reclaim the *Shanghai Evening Post and Mercury*. He found the premises still under Japanese military guard, despite Japan's surrender, and was obliged to sneak in through a window. Most of the plant had been looted but on 25 September Miner managed to bring out a four-page tabloid edition with a front-page headline announcing 'Victory Brings Rebirth!' In 1946 Randall Gould took over as editor and began a long battle to keep his newspaper going. On 15 June 1949, at the end of a series of bruising disputes with labour unions, trade leagues, Guomindang censors and, in May-June 1949, incoming Communist authorities who 'insisted that we should bear responsibility for the paper but that a workers committee should have authority to censor what was published', Gould and Miner closed down the *Shanghai Evening Post and Mercury* for good. But their troubles were not over. In late July 1949 both men were held in their offices in a lock-in by their employees that lasted over fifty hours until C.V. Starr, the owner, agreed to remit funds for severance pay for the employees.[76]

The *China Press* had been up and running since October 1945, although who revived it is not clear. In 1948 the lawyer and sometime

Shen Bao editor Norwood Allman returned to Shanghai following intern-
ment in Stanley camp and service with the US Office of Strategic
Services (OSS). Allman took over and kept the paper going until the
Communists gained control of Shanghai in late May 1949.[77]

In October 1945, R. T. Peyton-Griffin, editor from 1938 to 1941 and
newly released from two years of internment, had started publishing the
North-China Daily News again. Over the next five years, Peyton-Griffin
carefully stepped around hostile labour unions, drastic cuts in
newsprint, considerable interference from Guomindang censors and a
noticeable intensification of anti-British sentiment in Shanghai. In June
1949 the last English-language daily in China (the Guomindang-backed
China Press and *China Daily Tribune* having been suspended in late May)
caused an uproar by reporting the mining of the Yangtze by Nationalists
at Woosung and was obliged to prepare an apology for presentation to
the Communist Military Control Bureau.

Commenting on this incident, a *Christian Science Monitor* staff writer,
Ronald Stead, compared Randall Gould's refusal to accept Communist
controls with Peyton-Griffin's more flexible approach:

> But this is the point: Mr Gould would be in far greater danger if he
> continued to produce the paper with any qualification attached to his edito-
> rial authority. ... He is fortunate to have had a legitimate reason for ceasing
> to be an editor under the system where all editors who retain their jobs are
> almost certain to be stooges ... The British editor of the North China Daily
> News, a Shanghai English-language morning newspaper, is less fortunate.
> When I was last in Shanghai I asked him whether he thought his paper
> would be preferentially treated if the Communists ever captured the city. My
> thought was that the British might expect something in the nature of special
> consideration because they had not figured in an anti-Communist role,
> while the Americans had done so to the extent that they had equipped and
> trained Nationalist forces fighting in China's civil war. The British editor
> seemed to think I might have something there. But today he probably
> doesn't. Neither do I. The Communists have forced him to run an uncondi-
> tional apology ... Obviously the editor had nothing to apologize for ... But
> he has apologized – unreservedly. He has undertaken not to give offense in
> the future. So as an editor, within the democratic meaning of the phrase, he
> has had it.[78]

Peyton-Griffin probably had had it. He soldiered on, managing to keep
his newspaper going past its centenary in 1950. The *North-China Daily
News* finally closed down in March 1950 and Peyton-Griffin died the
following December. The righteous tone of the *Christian Science Monitor*
was becoming increasingly common in 1949. Between 1945 and 1949
most despatches from China swung wildly between burying Chiang Kai-
shek and announcing his resurrection and a mixture of defiance,
bewilderment and feverish anticipation as Communist forces closed in
on Shanghai.

What is more interesting is the distinction drawn between the investment of the US and that of Britain in the fortunes of the Guomindang. In the long game of mutual commercial and national interest played since the founding of Thomas Millard's *China Press* in 1911, the China newspapers of the *Chronicle* network had accommodated without really embracing the Guomindang, while the *Advertiser* network in China had grown ever closer to Nanjing and then Chongqing. At the same time, although their editorial line often ran ahead of the sympathies of the US State Department, the *Advertiser* increasingly reflected current thinking in Washington, particularly with regard to the growth of Communism in China. Edgar Snow, Agnes Smedley, Harold Isaacs and Anna Strong were notable exceptions, but exceptions nonetheless.

As the most consistent apologists for Guomindang corruption and what often looked like military ineptitude in the English-language press of East Asia, the *Advertiser* network clearly backed the losing side although it hardly figured in the 'we lost China' recriminations that began with the 26 January 1945 issue of *Amerasia* magazine. The success, after Pearl Harbor, of the *Advertiser* network's long campaign to bring US involvement firmly behind the Guomindang did not translate into ignomy for its newspapers and journalists when the Nationalists lost the nation. Rather, growing contempt, suspicion and in some cases legal action were reserved for those who favoured the winning side[79] or, in the case of the Truman administration, were seen as having been insufficiently supportive of the Guomindang.

Compared to the *Advertiser* network, or those remnants of it that kept up some semblance of activity in 1941–45 and returned to revive their publications in post-1945 Shanghai, the Foreign Ministry or Japan network could be said to have had a good war, despite losing it. Even without his main fictional premise, the conquest of the United States, Philip Dick's contention that the *Nippon Times* would achieve even greater prominence as the voice of Japan now reads like a fair projection of events on the ground in the early 1940s. The further point is that the *Nippon Times* lost none of its prominence in the immediate post-war era as it made a swift about-turn from cheering on the Japanese conquest of Asia to cheering on, in Henry Luce's shiny new coinage, the American Century.

NOTES

1 Dick 2001 [1962]: 26, 62. He located the less prestigious *Tokyo Herald* on Market Street.
2 Hutcheon 1983: 88.
3 Argall 1945: 205.
4 'North China As Seen By Foreigners' (1938) (Tokyo: *Bunka Jōhōkyōku*). Introduced and reprinted in O'Connor (ed.) 2005, Vol.8, 255–342.
5 Argall 1945: 204–209.
6 Ozaki was also an occasional contributor to *Contemporary Japan*, run by the Foreign Affairs Association of Japan.

7   Sheba 1952: 203.
8   'Public Opinion in Japan Stopped Before It Starts': CSM 17 August 1942.
9   'Writer tells of tortures Japanese used on captives': NYT 27 July 1942.
10 See Itoh (2001), *Epilogue*. As camp leader, the general manager of Mitsui Bussan maintained morale despite a reading diet confined to the *Daily Mail*, *Express* and *Sunday Pictorial*.
11 USDS (RG 59); FBI (File 65–1678); Military Intelligence Division (RG 165).
12 USDS 894.91211/7: State Dept. confidential press release no.632, 13 December 1941.
13 USDS 894.912/7A: State Dept. to US Legation, Berne, 23 December 1941.
14 In Woodhead's 1942 Chatham House lecture held in WO 208/378a, lecture: page 6. Hallet Abend confirms that the *Shanghai Times* was subsidized by Japan and continued publication 'unmolested' after 8 December (Abend 1943: 39). See also Obituary, H.G.W. Woodhead, *The Times*, 1 October 1959.
15 Powell 1945: 342.
16 The *Shanghai Evening Post*, sold to C.V. Starr in 1929, featured in the *Nippon Times* column *East Asia's Editorial Forum* in 1943. It seems that the occupation powers continued to publish this *Shanghai Evening Post* as well as the *Shanghai Evening Post and Mercury* and the *Shanghai Times*. How long the *Shanghai Evening Post and Mercury* continued after George Bruce's internment is unknown. Charles Miner found the SEPM plant unused and damaged when he returned to Shanghai in September 1945 (but not so damaged that he was unable to print a revived edition that month).
17 Bickers in Henriot and Wen-hsin Yeh (eds.) 2004: 249.
18 'J.B. Powell, newspaper man, dies; survivor of Japanese brutalities': NYT, 1 Mar. 1947. Chiang Kai-shek sent $10,000 to help with Powell's hospital bills. The Chinese National Press Association raised another $11,000.
19 Powell 1945: 364–91. See Wilkinson 2000: 238, and 237–9 for the experiences of those Americans who stayed on in Shanghai after Pearl Harbor.
20 Powell 1945: 378.
21 Fred Opper was also known by the nickname Fritz. Opper was arrested in Shanghai and repatriated on an exchange ship. In 1943 he returned to China to work on the Chonqing edition of the SEPM with Randall Gould (n.74 below) with whom he had worked on the SEPM in Shanghai and on the JT in Tokyo. Opper stayed on to become ABC's Far East correspondent in 1946, then moved to head ABC's London Bureau. From 1953 to 1972 he broadcast from West Germany for Radio Free Europe (NYT Obituary 19 April 1994, cited in Yu 1996: 300, n.14).
22 Powell 1945: 373–6; and Powell 1946: 52.
23 Woodhead speech to Chatham House: 'The Japanese Occupation of Shanghai: Some Personal Experiences', 12 November 1942, in PRO: WO 208/378a; cited in Bickers 2004: 386, n.65, but dated as 21 November. This version of Woodhead's lecture was not published but in 1943 he brought out a pamphlet, 'My Experiences in the Japanese Occupation of Shanghai' that is cited in Bickers 1999: 267.
24 'Shanghai Court Martial', dateline Melbourne 15 June 1942: *The Times* 16 June 1942.
25 In Woodhead's 1942 Chatham House lecture held in WO 208/378a, page 7.
26 *The Times*: 8 September 1942.

27 Vere Redman is reported to have held the same post from November 1942: *The Times*, 5 November 1942.
28 William Sheldon Ridge (1875–1945) was known by his middle name. Career details: *Shanghai Mercury* 1905–6; *National Review* (Shanghai) 1907–16; *Peking Daily News* 1917–21; *Far Eastern Times* 1922–26; *Peking Chronicle* (owner) 1930–39. The Ridge Family Papers are held at SOAS, University of London.
29 FO 371/21001 [F8927/1043/10], Young telegram to Foreign Office, 1 November 1937.
30 The Ridge family papers held at SOAS, University of London, do not hold any details of the circumstances of Ridge's death.
31 R.T. Peyton-Griffin, obituary: *The Times*, 30 December 1950.
32 Gould 1946: 337. In the final June 1945 edition under the front page headline 'Deleted by Censor'.
33 Yu 1996: 60–7, 105–106. Yu's judgement is that in their eighteen months as an OSS project, the New York/Chonqing SEPM edition won scant support for the Guomindang, partly because of frequent publication of Nationalist intelligence leaks.
34 *Tsūshinshashi*, p.616, cited in Purdy 1987, 375.
35 *Gaimushō gaikō shiryōkan: Zai Pekin Dōmei Tsūshinsha Eibun-bu Kakushō joseikai shishutsu hō rensei ni kansuru ken*, 20 January 1940.
36 JT: 8 December 1942.
37 *Nippon Times Weekly*, Vol. XIV, No.1, 1 January 1943.
38 Purdy 1987: 377–8.
39 The name of the company remained the Japan Times Limited (*Jyapan Taimuzu Kabushigaisha*).
40 Later indicted for his role in the Bataan Death March and executed in April 1946.
41 'Days of P.I. Revolution Recalled at Gathering on Eve of Independence': *Nippon Times* (NT), 15 October 1943.
42 In the same issue of NT, the *Nippon Eigashya* (Japan Film Co.) advertised 'Two masterpieces in Filmdom': 'Daitōa News' (Greater East Asia News) and 'American Tragedy – The Philippines Became Independent' alongside a series of documentary films 'presented to the People in Greater East Asia' including *Shōidan Bakugeki* (Incendiary bombing) alongside a quarter-page advertisement for seven similar productions from the *Riken Kagaku Eiga Kabushiki-gaisha* (Scientific Film Production Company).
43 NT: 18 November 1943, also cited in Chapter 2.
44 NT: 19 November 1943.
45 'East Asia Journalists Pledged to Winning War – 8 More Delegates Speaking at Session Concur on Unprecedented Role Newspapers Occupy Today – All Report Courageous Fight of Southern People for Creation of New Order': NT: 19 November 1943.
46 'Declaration adopted by General Assembly of Greater East Asiatic Newspapers': NT: 19 November 1943 (evening edition).
47 Hutcheon 1983: 92.
48 The *Shanghai Evening Post* masthead used in the graphic was the version used before the 1930 amalgamation with the *Shanghai Mercury*.
49 NT: 1 December 1943.
50 NT: 4 December 1943.

51 Purdy 1987: 397.

52 'The Keynote of Japan's Diplomatic Policy': NT (leader), 13 December 1943.

53 NT: 13 December 1943.

54 The *Japan Times* and then the *Foreign Affairs Association of Japan* had been producing the *Japan Year Book* since about 1918. In Tokyo the *Tōa-Keizai Chōsakyoku* (East-Asiatic Economic Investigation Bureau) began publishing a *Manchuria Year Book* in 1931. H.G.W. Woodhead and a series of publishers beginning with the *Peking & Tientsin Times* and continuing with the *North China Daily News* had been compiling the annual *China Year Book* since 1911. The Nanjing and now Chonqing Ministry of Information under Hollington Tong had produced a *China Handbook* in 1934 and again in 1945 (for 1937–45). In 1940, Chongqing either took over or bought the *China Year Book* title, changed it to the *Chinese Year Book* and produced volumes every few years.

55 'Tokyo Insists Peace Was Kurusu's Goal – War Came Because We Failed to Understand Japan, Editor Says': NYT, 27 May 1942. Bracketed sections summarized from NYT report of the broadcast.

56 'Feeler from Japan': NYT leader, p.22, 27 May 1942. This response has something of George Sokolsky's righteous abrasiveness to it, although by 1942 Sokolsky had moved on from the NYT with his column 'These Times' syndicated by King Features in 300 US dailies. Not one to get bogged down in problems of consistency, Sokolsky had praised Roosevelt throughout the autumn of 1941 for trying to avoid war with Japan, but in 1942 had jettisoned the conviction that Japanese hegemony in East Asia mattered little to US interests (Cohen 1978: 244–7).

57 Council of International Affairs, Chungking 1943: 664–89. The full list is given here in Appendix 5.

58 O'Brien 2003: 4.

59 Interdepartmental Committee for the Acquisition of Foreign Publications 1943: 207–208. Possibly this Committee lived in Washington, where this edition of the 1943–44 *Japan Year Book* may have been republished. The 'Restricted' block on the front board is unique to this edition of the *Japan Year Book*.

60 Op. cit.: 259.

61 These markers were: the Perry Expedition; the 'Gentleman's Agreement'; 1915 Sino-Japanese Treaty (Twenty-one Demands); 1917 Ishii-Lansing; 1919 Peace of Paris; 1921–22 Washington Conference ('To Arrest Nippon's Expansion'); 1924 US Immigration Act; 1931 Manchurian Incident; 1933 Japan's withdrawal from the League; 1934 Amō Statement; 1937 'China Affair' and USS Panay Incident; November 1938 New Order statement; July 1938 Arita-Craigie accord; Second World War in Europe; September 1940 Tripartite Pact; 1939–41 US 'Two-Ocean' plans for naval expansion; November–December 1941 breakdown in US-Japan negotiations in Washington; Pearl Harbor, and Japan's victorious progress in 1941–42.

62 Council of International Affairs 1946: 350–5, 356–70.

63 Kiyosawa 1998: 158: diary entry for 15 March 1944.

64 Ogasawara also cited the lone stance taken by the *Japan Times* in supporting renewal of the contentious ANPO (contraction of *anzenhoshō*) Security Treaty with the US in February-May 1960 during the second Kishi Nobusuke cabinet. Both instances tend to qualify the claim to independent internationalism as

well as demonstrate the willingness of the newspaper to bow to official requirements: publishing veiled appeals for peace with at least partial Foreign Ministry approval; adapting to the realities of the Cold War and supporting the semi-legal renewal of a Treaty against which millions of ordinary citizens and probably quite a few of its own readers had demonstrated. Part of the problem for the post-war *Japan Times* is that a realistic assessment of its role in Japan's pre-war international relations would require a thorough examination of the durability and intimacy of its relationship to the Japanese government. In an article in the *Japan Times* 100th anniversary edition of 22 March 1997, the veteran *Japan Times* film critic and novelist Donald Richie referred to 'the *canard* that the paper was a creature of the Gaimusho – not true because things are never that simple in Japan'. This neatly demonstrates the newspaper's approach to a problem that undermined its credibility for most of its first half century: neither completely admitting its official connections nor completely denying them. Now retired from the Presidency of the Japan Times, Ogasawara Toshiaki's December 2007 speech can be found at http://www.tokyo-rc.gr.jp/jts/0707_22.htm – viewed October 2009.

65 *Wall Street Journal*, *New York Times*, *Christian Science Monitor* and the *Washington Post*: 1944–45. Search conducted on the ProQuest Historical Newspapers database.

66 'Says Allies Must Accept Nothing But All-Out Surrender', UP to WP, 20 February 1945. For other 'peace feeler' news and reactions, see 'Japanese Feelers on Peace Spurned', NYT: 18 May 1945; 'Tokyo Denies Talk Of Bid For Peace', NYT: 20 May 1945, and 'Grew Denies Any Tokyo Bid; Sees Tale as Divisive Tactic', NYT, 11 July 1945.

67 Purdy 1987: 404, citing *Dōmei English Language News*, 28, 31 July 1945.

68 'MacArthur closes Asahi, Tokyo paper': NYT, 19 September 1945.

69 Purdy 1987: 425.

70 'Japan's Pulitzer', the Vaughn-Ueda Prize for International Reporting was set up in 1950, honouring the memory of both men but overlooking Vaughn's mixed record of editorial transparency.

71 Togasaki was an American citizen, born in San Francisco and educated at the University of California at Berkeley. A committed Christian, he became Grand Master of the Tokyo Masonic Lodge in 1960–61.

72 Gayn (1948) and Coughlin (1952) provide two of the best accounts of the Japanese press and foreign correspondents during the Occupation.

73 Gould 1946: 335–7. *Newsweek's* choice of Harold Isaacs seems a little cheeky, given the allegations against the Guomindang he had made in *China Forum* in the early 1930s (see Chapter 6).

74 Recent scholarship has provided some of the history of the Western journalists who returned to China after the defeat of Japan in 1945 but contemporary accounts are still essential, e.g. Hahn (in Hongkong) (1946 [1944]: 259–341) and Alcott (1943: 309–44). Abend (1943: 286–96) describes Shanghai under Japanese occupation in 1938–39, and (332–53) describes life in 1940–41. Gould (1941) provides a partisan account of events in Chonqing in that year. Gould (1946: 317–27) covers life and bomb threats to the SEPM and his colleagues Woodhead and others in 1937-early 1941, and (327–40) discusses working with Hollington Tong and Fritz 'Opperts' (Frederick Opper) on a Chonqing edition of the SEPM in late 1943 and 1944. Wilkinson (2000:

296 English-Language Press Networks of East Asia, 1918–1945

231–49) has more on Gould in Shanghai 1937–49. French (2009) provides the most recent overview of the experiences of Western journalists in China.

75 Powell, his wife and another journalist faced but were not convicted of charges of sedition in an unsuccessful prosecution by the Dwight Eisenhower administration in 1956 for Powell's revelations in the *China Monthly Review* regarding US conduct of germ warfare in Korea and China. Although the main charges were dismissed in 1959, Powell was unable to find work in journalism in the US and it took him until 1985 to clear his name. O'Brien (2003) provides the authoritative account of Powell and his work with the *Review* in 1945–53. See Powell's own (1980) account of the controversy that destroyed his career. Wilkinson (2000: 243–4) compares Gould and the SEPM's intransigence towards a changed Shanghai with Bill Powell and the revived CWR's openness to critical Chinese opinions of US support of the Guomindang.

76 'Shanghai editor describes Lock-In – Changsha captured. Two Days and Nights of Terror': Randall Gould, CSM 5 August 1949.

77 French (2009: 224, 249) says that Allman revived the paper in 1948. Waseda University library holds a microfilm run of a title called the *China Press* started 29 August 1911, published by China National Press, suspended 8 December 1941, resumed 9 October 1945, that I have not seen but the starting date is the same as Millard's 1911 organ (see 'Starts a paper in Shanghai', NYT 30 Aug. 1911).

78 'This World … Chinese Communism bares two faces': CSM, 2 July 1949.

79 Notably staff at the office of Naval Intelligence, the State Department China expert John S. Service and the journalists Philip Jaffe, Kate Mitchell and Mark Gayn.

9

Conclusions

First, a caveat: journalism was not the only source of information shaping international perceptions of Japan and East Asia in general. Many English-language press journalists wrote topical books on Japan and China, and other writers of books on Japan sourced their accounts in back-numbers of the English-language press. Therefore, although this study presents a case for considering the English-language press networks of East Asia as factors in shaping events in East Asia and the way they were seen in the West, it is important to acknowledge that these networks constituted only three – or four, with the Guomindang network – groups of voices among many competing for attention.

As far as many Japanese were concerned, the English-language newspapers and their journalists in East Asia, even some of those who wrote for the Foreign Ministry network, had it coming to them. For perhaps the greatest threat the English-language press networks of East Asia networks seemed to pose to Japanese interests lay in the 'news colonies' Amō Eiji and his circle at the Foreign Ministry felt they imposed on East Asia through their links to wider global press networks, and the threat of political and cultural colonization implicit in these media hegemonies. The ferocity of the Foreign Ministry network's response in the endgames played out in Japan and China attests to the strength of these perceptions. Between 1936 and December 1941 those newspapers in the *Japan Chronicle* and *Japan Advertiser* networks that had not come to accommodate the Foreign Ministry point of view and which remained uncooperative were targeted for takeover or closure. Before Pearl Harbor, these targets were met in Japan. After Pearl Harbor, the Foreign Ministry network morphed into the Japan network, which mopped up what remained of the English-language press in Japan and closed down or turned the English-language press in China and in 'Greater' East Asia.

A major theme of this book has been Japan's reliance on foreign, usually British or American, journalists, writers, agents and spokesmen to write, organize and present the Japanese position to the Western world. In the period under review, close to one hundred of these hired publicists came to Japan's semi-official journalism from a variety of backgrounds. The writings and the positions held by these non-Japanese publicists challenge established binaries like semi-official/independent and government/opposition and raise difficult questions which this book has tried to address, sometimes by looking beyond the East Asian context. To what extent did the work of the journalists on the foreign-owned English-language newspapers promote an imperialist master narrative? Were outspoken English-language papers like the *Japan Chronicle* and Eugene Chen's *Shanghai Gazette* engaged in a pre-war struggle for press freedom in East Asia or did they represent the advance guard of Western intellectual hegemony, at a time when Japan and China were struggling to present themselves on their own terms? And were Japan's terms just a means of camouflaging information control at home and propaganda abroad, or was there more to them than met the Western eye? Similarly, was the struggle between Reuters and the 'Ring' news agencies and Japan's succession of national news agencies a struggle for press freedom, as AP's Kent Cooper saw it when he combined with Japan to break the 'Ring' and Reuters' hold on East Asian news, or an escape from Western cultural and political hegemony in Japan, as his erstwhile allies Iwanaga Yūkichi and Furuno Inosuke saw it?

Working in the Foreign Ministry network, Irishmen, Englishmen, Australians, Americans and Asian Americans wrote and sometimes ran Japan's informal diplomacy in East Asia. Some were little more than mercenary hacks, but others were wholeheartedly committed to presenting the Japanese case. However, their compatriots on the independent English-language newspapers of East Asia and those serving as consultants to the Chinese government often resented these recruits to the Foreign Ministry network. These resentments led to rivalries between foreign journalists and media entrepreneurs in East Asia that developed alongside the more overt competition between the Western powers and Japan, and between Japan and competing groups in China, which were reflected in the history of the English-language press networks of East Asia given here. Another complication came from vocal, expatriate, Anglophone readers settled in China and Japan, of whom a significant element anticipated Japan's incursions in China in the early 1930s with some eagerness, constituting a sympathetic readership for Foreign Ministry network publications. At the same time, the pro-Guomindang consensus in the *Japan Advertiser* network helped create what amounted to a fourth network, as newspapers like the *China Press* and the *China Weekly Review* followed the Nanjing line, although some notable American journalists turned away and looked north-east to Yan'an.

THE ARGUMENT

Although the English-language press networks of East Asia were all, including the Foreign Ministry network, linked to press networks operating in the Empire by institutional and individual commonalities, their spheres and modes of operation were often too transnational and too distant from the beaten paths of Empire to lend significant support to the Imperial press system and its press networks or elicit the sympathy of and benefit from the support of the British world. The English-language press networks of East Asia bear comparison with the networks of information and communication serving the British Empire and with the Imperial press system serving the British world in the Dominions and closer to home, for example in Ireland, as discussed by Bayly (1996), Kaul (2003 and 2006, ed.) and Potter (2003 and 2004), sharing career paths into and out of Fleet Street and its outposts in South Africa and Canada and other Dominions. However, as affiliations based in the inland cities and outports of East Asia, the networks studied here operated on the furthest edges of the British world.

The most 'British' of the networks, the *Japan Chronicle* network was far from united. The *Japan Chronicle*, the *North-China Daily News*, the *Peking & Tientsin Times* and, following lengthy confrontations in 1927 and 1932, the *Central China Post*, took a common editorial line on a number of issues, for example as outpost lobbyists in the British world, expressed since the early 1900s through their membership of the China Association and the British Association in Tokyo and Kōbe, which had been affiliated since 1907. However, the *Chronicle*'s line on the subject of Empire, and in the 1920s on Chinese nationalism set it at odds with its affiliates in China. Again, for all its socialist credentials and for all the bloodletting of 1927–29, the *Chronicle* welcomed the rise of the Guomindang, while to the *North-China Daily News*, the *Peking & Tientsin Times* and the *Central China Post* they posed an obvious and significant threat.

As editor of the *Chronicle* from 1922 to 1936, Morgan Young's outlook was no less radical than his predecessor's, but he needed to find a compromise between the *Chronicle*'s principled past and the viewpoints, after 1926, of a new employer operating in reduced circumstances at a time of seismic political change. Under Morgan Young the *Chronicle* supported the Guomindang, questioned Japanese activities in China and challenged the supine attitude of the Japanese press towards them, but by the late 1920s, it had become a more cautious newspaper.[1]

In the late 1920s and early 1930s, prompted by personnel changes pressed on it by Whitehall, the leader of the *Chronicle*'s China network, the *North-China Daily News*, experienced the strictures of Nanjing censorship and began an accommodation with Chinese nationalism. The *Peking & Tientsin Times* and, especially after a confrontation in early 1932, the *Central China Post*, did likewise. Besides Chinese Nationalist power, they were in part persuaded by the Japanese might demonstrated by the Manchurian Incident and the naval invasion of Shanghai in early 1932. Thus, under Morgan Young and Douglas Young, the *Chronicle* supported Chinese nationalism over Chinese Communism, but kept a beady eye on what it could learn (given the scarcity of unfiltered China news bulletins in Tokyo) of Japanese policies in China. At the same time, under pressure from Whitehall and the Nanjing Guomindang, the China-based English-language papers in the *Chronicle* network took the path of least resistance and became less openly pro-Japanese.

The acceptance by Morgan Young's successor, E.A. Kennard, and by new management, of a Foreign Ministry subsidy in 1938 further muted the *Chronicle*'s line on Japanese policies. When the *Japan Times* finally bought the *Chronicle* in December 1940 there was little change in the *Chronicle*'s outlook that had not already been achieved by the monthly Foreign Ministry subsidies. The growing acceptance of Manchukuo as a *fait accompli*, Nationalist censorship, the Japanese occupation of Shanghai in 1937, and possibly some anticipation of their position in a post-war settlement placed further restraints on the editorial line of British-owned newspapers in the *Chronicle* network in China even as it slackened restraints on other commentators, notably the *Shanghai Evening Post and Mercury*'s star columnist, H.G.W. Woodhead, who moved even closer to the *Chronicle's* limited scrutiny of Japanese incursions.

Although the English-language press networks of East Asia in some instances served the interests of the British world in East Asia, they did so from different positions and operated in very different modes and degrees of transnationalism to, for example, English-language papers in the Dominions. The *Japan Advertiser* network, like the *Chronicle* network, certainly had its share of schisms. This network both promoted American interests and worked the seams of transnationalism to such an extent as to serve almost as the press division of Chinese nationalism. As a result, the *Advertiser* network became fragmented: most were ardent supporters of the Nanjing Guomindang line; others became wary supporters; still others became disenchanted and began to exhibit in their writing a passionate interest in the fortunes of the Chinese Communist Party.

In the view of the managers of the Foreign Ministry's English-language press network, Britain moved from the supportive ally that in 1907–10 colluded in its suppression of E.T. Bethell's critical voice in Korea and whose media provided sympathetic coverage of Japanese aims, to motivating Reuters as Japan's competitor in China, and finally to an enabler of 'news colonization' to be fought in price-wars and takeovers and, after Pearl Harbor, with all the means at Japan's disposal. In 1913–14 the early Foreign Ministry network itself was in danger of becoming an unwilling recruit to the Imperial press system as a result of its one-sided agreement with Reuters, but its efforts to circumvent the terms of this agreement and undercut Reuters' position in the China news market were making headway even before the Anglo-Japanese Alliance had run its course.

Meanwhile, national interest required that the operations of the Foreign Ministry network be run on extended transnational lines both in Japan, largely among cooperative Anglophone journalists, and in China, where cooperation between Japanese, Anglophone and Chinese media professionals became essential to the smooth operation of its English-language media, just as it did to the media the Foreign Ministry Information Bureau ran with other nationals in other languages and in other countries. None of this may seem to have mattered after 1937, still less after 8 December 1941, when most Anglophone journalists in China and Japan were rounded up and interrogated. However, the different experiences of Woodhead and John B. Powell at the Bridge House prison in Shanghai, like those of George Gorman and Percy Whiteing compared to Otto Tolischus, James R. Young and, most notoriously, Melville James Cox, in Tokyo, indicate that in China as in Japan the treatment meted out to journalists was heavily contingent on their published record of news and reportage on Japan and its policies in China.

The foreign-owned English-language press networks of East Asia also related to other press networks representing other global interests. The *Japan Advertiser* network was closely tied to the US State Department, to financial linkmen between the US and Japan such as Thomas Lamont, and, most immediately, to the North American press and its news agencies: hence its importance not only to the Foreign Ministry network but to the Guomindang and the Chinese Communist Party.

In these broader contexts of the Imperial news system, the US media networks and the British and American worlds they served and which subscribed to them clearly mattered most in Fleet Street and Whitehall and in New York and Washington, but they commanded closer attention in Tokyo than did the two foreign-owned press networks of East Asia, whose real importance for Japan lay in direct proportion to the strength of their relationship with these wider global interests.

The scope of the Foreign Ministry network, as enlarged by its institutional hub, the Foreign Ministry Information Bureau (*Gaimushō Jōhōbu*), proactively reflected both these criteria in its US media network, with news hubs in New York and San Francisco consulting directly with Tokyo and liaising with local consulates and the embassy in Washington, and in the breadth of the network in the British Dominions built by the Anglo-Irish John Russell Kennedy and other expatriate newsmen in the 1920s. In 1936, in another demonstration of the importance it attached to global connections, the Foreign Ministry network ended *Dentsū*'s news exchange agreement with the United Press by the amalgamation of *Dentsū*'s news agency division and *Rengō* to form the *Dōmei* agency. That the UP agreement was cancelled, despite the fact that, with the help of sympathetic gatekeepers at UP such as Miles Vaughn, the Foreign Ministry had succeeded in bringing the editorial line of UP's Tokyo bureau close enough to the official for the two to be almost indistinguishable during the crisis of 1931–33 and later, illustrates the importance the Foreign Ministry network attached to international media connections, especially those between the English-language press networks of East Asia and the US.

The commonalities and continuities between the English-language press networks of East Asia and the powerful, mass-circulation global networks discussed in the Introduction ensured that the failure of some of the English-language press networks discussed here, in East Asia between December 1941 and 1943, then in China between 1945 and the early 1950s, and finally during the disintegration of readerships and commercial power accelerated by the post-war national independence movements, and the general collapse in the *cachet* and currency of the British world and the proportionate surge in American prestige, were not unrelated. This point is worth stressing, if only to demonstrate that the English-language press networks of East Asia are both a concept and a historical reality, and that just as both aspects could be situated in the burgeoning contexts of Empire and the British world in their heyday, they could fit the same contexts in their years of disintegration.

CORRECTIVES AND EXCEPTIONS

As discussed here and in Chapter 2, the editorial lines adopted by the English-language press networks of East Asia were not cast in stone. Over time, their personnel frequently took new jobs and subscribed to new editorial outlooks, did side jobs for newspapers associated with rival networks, covered for colleagues on rival networks, and often defied the overall patterns and roles discerned here.

The most significant instances of newspapers not fitting the circumstances or following the allegiances that might have been expected from their membership of a particular network have been covered here: the *Japan Times* rebellions under Ashida Hitoshi in the late 1930s; the history of American and Japanese cooperation at the *Japan Advertiser* between Russell Kennedy, Inoue Junnosuke, Dan Takuma, Thomas Lamont, and the representatives of J.P. Morgan, Rockefeller and Charles Crane; the possibility of subsidies received by the *Japan Chronicle* from both Zhang Xueliang and the Nanjing regime in the early 1930s, and by Morgan Young from the Guomindang after 1936; the monthly subsidies the *Japan Chronicle* received from the Foreign Ministry from 1938; Edgar Snow and others' allegations of George Sokolsky's role as a paid advocate of Japan in East Asia, China and the US; and finally the possibility that Matsuoka Yōsuke was following an internationalist, anti-militarist agenda in amalgamating the *Japan Chronicle* and the *Japan Advertiser* with the *Japan Times* late in 1940.

Of the three main press networks described here, the Foreign Ministry network proved to be the most durable and the least given to self-doubt and the most committed employer of foreign journalistic talent, even under the increase in military influence that took place in the 1930s. Even as the Foreign Ministry network took over and in effect nationalized the flagship enterprises of its rival networks, the preponderance of military influence on Japanese media in 1940–41 weakened its ability, through the *Japan Times & Advertiser*, to help Japan's case even after it had gained almost complete control of the channels of public communication between Japan and the West. After 1933 the Foreign Ministry network succeeded in gaining informal international acceptance for Manchukuo as a *fait accompli* but there were few takers for its larger effort, as the dominant voice among the English-language newspapers of East Asia, to sell Japan's late bid for imperial power.

The *Japan Advertiser* network had an ambitious, well-funded agenda for the promotion of American interests in China at the expense of not only Japanese but British ambitions. Despite numerous publicly celebrated attempts at promoting US-Japanese friendship and consistently accommodating Japanese officialdom, the *Japan Advertiser* itself was usually seen in an adversarial light by the Foreign Ministry. Meanwhile, in China, the fragmentation of the *Advertiser* network and the mixed reports coming out of China may have been responsible for a loss of interest among the American public. This in turn may have made some members of the network more dependent on Chinese support and therefore more representative of Chinese interests. In Japan, the *Advertiser* was harassed and isolated and was bought by the Foreign Ministry network in October 1940.

The *Japan Chronicle* network proved the least cohesive of the three networks, having a membership too independent and opinionated to represent a unified force or influence. These divisions may have undermined the collective authority of its most important members, the *Chronicle*, the *North-China Daily News* and the *Peking & Tientsin Times*. Under Douglas Young, the impoverished *Chronicle* itself may have begun taking Guomindang subsidies in the early 1930s. Presumably these would have ceased in 1938 when its executives agreed to accept financial support from the Foreign Ministry network in return for modifying their line on Japanese incursions in China. In December 1940 the *Chronicle* had joined the *Japan Advertiser* in the *Japan Times* stable, presided over by the Foreign Ministry network.

INFLUENCE AND ACCESS

How did the English-language press networks of East Asia influence the shaping of perceptions of East Asia in the Western press? This study has leaned towards the approach adopted by the American scholar Warren Cohen in qualifying his assessment of the role of press, business and diplomatic groups in the formulation of US policy on China, namely: 'My aim is not to measure the elusive quality of *influence* but rather to chart lines of access to decision-makers and to the public.'[2]

Rather than attempt to measure influence, what follows aims to quantify the access that the English-language press networks of East Asia gained to the Western press and their readerships. In the four US and two British newspapers used for this survey, these lines of access were predominantly those drawn by their correspondents and stringers in East Asia, who cited the local press in their reports, although in wartime, particularly 1941–45, citations to the English-language press of East Asia were invariably made by journalists on the domestic staff of the newspapers concerned.

The survey that follows searched the online databases of a select group of American and British national dailies for references to the titles in the English-language press networks of East Asia: in the US, the *Christian Science Monitor*, *New York Times*, *Wall Street Journal* and *Washington Post*; in the UK, the *Manchester Guardian* and *The Times*. References were counted which quoted or cited any of the titles in the networks, whether in a positive or negative or a qualified context. This narrowed the search to only ten of the thirty-six English language titles that have been identified as belonging to the three networks researched here: the other twenty-six titles did not register on the databases used in this search.[3] That access to US and British readerships is also compared with the access gained by select Japanese vernacular newspapers.

The English-language papers and periodicals whose access to US and British newspapers and their readerships is surveyed here are, in the Foreign Ministry network, the *Japan Times* (and *Nippon Times*), the *Far Eastern Review* and the *Seoul Press*. The *Japan Advertiser* (and Guomindang) network newspapers surveyed are the *Japan Advertiser*, *Shanghai Evening Post and Mercury*, *China Press* and *China Weekly Review*. The *Japan Chronicle* network has been represented in this survey by the *Japan Chronicle*, *Peking & Tientsin Times* and *North China Daily News*. The publications that appear below do so simply because they were cited in the US and British newspapers surveyed. The Japanese vernacular newspapers surveyed for their appearance in the Western press were the *Asahi*, *Yomiuri* and *Mainichi Shinbun*. The period surveyed was 1913–49, five years before and four years beyond the focus of this study, 1918–45. The purpose of this longer perspective was to begin the survey with the formation of the *Kokusai* News Agency in Japan and to extend it to the retreat to Taiwan of the Guomindang and Mao's declaration of the People's Republic of China in October 1949.

The search for access in the US and British papers databases listed above was for clear citations to or references to articles – leaders, commentary, op-eds, features – published or opinions expressed in or news reported in the English-language press of East Asia, as represented by the select group listed above. There were four surveys. The first, shown in Figure 4, below, compared the access of the English-language press networks of East Asia to US and British readerships by comparing the combined references in US and British newspapers of one network's titles with the combined references to each of the others. The second survey, shown in Figure 5, measured the access of eight English-language press titles (omitting the *Seoul Press*, which had only eight references and the *Peking & Tientsin Times*, with only twenty-seven) in terms of references to their writings in the four US and two British newspapers. The third survey, shown in Figure 6, compared the Japan and China English-language press results with those of the three vernacular newspapers in Japan. The fourth survey, shown in Figure 7, compared the figures for US and British references to the English-language press of Japan with the figures for references to the English-language press of China.

A glance at the numbers in Figure 3, below, should give some perspective to this survey and to the relative strength of the three networks shown in Figure 4. For the period 1913–49, the figures for Western newspaper references to or reports using material from the individual newspapers shown here are given in Figure 3:

Foreign Ministry network	Japan Times	640
	Far Eastern Review	58
	Seoul Press	8
Japan Chronicle network	Japan Chronicle	256
	North-China Daily News	286
	Peking & Tientsin Times	27
Japan Advertiser network	Japan Advertiser	94
	China Press	238
	China Weekly Review	109
	Shanghai Evening Post and Mercury	193

Figure 3. The English-language press networks of East Asia:
citations in US and British press, 1913–49.[4]

What these numbers tell us is that as far as the Western press was concerned the default source for news of East Asia, although usually qualified by the description 'semi-official' or 'organ of the Japanese Foreign Ministry', was the *Japan Times*. The other titles in the Foreign Ministry network that registered in the consciousness of Western editors and their readers were barely noticeable. In the *Japan Chronicle* network the two lead papers, the *Chronicle* itself and the *North-China Daily News*, enjoyed steady and consistent access to US and British newspaper readerships. In the *Japan Advertiser* network, the discrepancy between the most-cited title, the *China Press*, and the title that led and inspired the network from Tokyo, the *Japan Advertiser*, is an indication of the growing power of the Guomindang within the network, and of the status of a title run by US-educated Chinese who answered to Nanjing yet commanded the sympathy and used the work of a large corps of Western newsmen. The *China Weekly Review* nurtured and in turn was itself increasingly sustained by the Guomindang's growing dependence on US support in the struggle with the Japanese. That J.B. Powell's weekly gained greater access to Western readerships than B.W. Fleisher's daily points to the shift from the *Advertiser* network's original mission to promote US interests in East Asia to the Guomindang's need for US support in promoting its own interests against all comers, not least the Chinese Communist Party.

In the first survey, shown in Figure 4, the Foreign Ministry network, the darkest-shaded of the three, shows the highest spikes. Its newspapers, or some of them, are clearly the most frequently mentioned in the Western press surveyed. The Foreign Ministry network spikes all occur around major events in Japan's relations with the West: the 21 Demands of 1915, the Manchurian Crisis of 1931–33, with a huge spike in the years 1940–42 in the run-up to Pearl Harbor and the outbreak of war and Japan's phenomenal run of military and naval victories and a lesser spike in 1944–45 as the war turned in the Allies' favour.

The second darkest gradation in Figure 4 shows that the Foreign

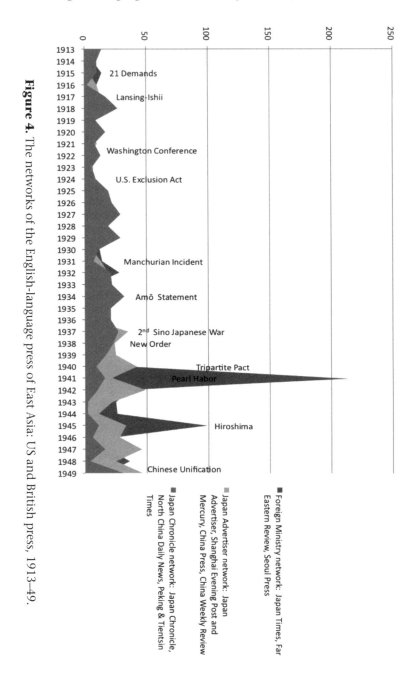

Figure 4. The networks of the English-language press of East Asia: US and British press, 1913–49.

Ministry network did not have it all its own way. The *Japan Chronicle* network posed a significant challenge to the Foreign Ministry network from the early years of the period surveyed until the early 1940s, when it was co-opted in Japan and closed down by Japan in China, for much of the time eclipsing the Foreign Ministry network in the newspapers surveyed. This picture is complicated by the knowledge that from 1938 the *Chronicle* itself was receiving a subsidy in return for muting its criticism of Japan, and that it was bought out and amalgamated with the *Japan Times* at the end of 1940, and that O.M. Green, the editor of the most cited China newspaper in the *Chronicle* network, the *North-China Daily News*, was also *The Times* correspondent for 1920–30. The *North-China Daily News* closed down in December 1941 and did not reopen until after the withdrawal of Japanese forces from Shanghai in September 1945. The *Peking & Tientsin Times* closed for good in 1941. Even so, references to these newspapers continued to appear in the Western press in 1941–45, often in relation to the fortunes of staff who had been interned.

The newspapers of the *Japan Advertiser* network are almost invisible in the earlier years of this survey, making their first visible appearance in Figure 4 at the meeting that sealed the major power shift of the first half of the twentieth century, from Britain to the US, and the rise of the US as a Pacific power: the Washington Conference. While the *Advertiser* network raises a relatively low profile at Washington, we can see it gaining in prominence with the Manchurian crisis and with the second Sino-Japanese War in 1937 as Western newspapers increasingly turned to the China papers in the *Advertiser* network for reports from the ground. The V-shaped dip in citations to *Advertiser* network reports that occurs in 1941 reflects the complexities of newspaper ownership in wartime East Asia: the closing down of most *Advertiser* network China papers at the end of that year, the co-option of the *Advertiser* and *Shanghai Evening Post and Mercury* titles by the Japan network with the occupation of the International Settlements, and a corresponding surge in references to the *Japan Times & Advertiser* – initially at just those points where the *Advertiser* network is out of contention. With the revival of the *Shanghai Evening Post and Mercury* in Chongqing and New York, references to this title pick up again.

Figure 5 illustrates the performance of eight of the ten titles factored into Figure 4. Here the *Seoul Press*, with eight citations, and the *Peking & Tientsin Times*, with twenty-seven, have been removed both because their numbers are so far below those of the other titles and because doing so makes the graph more readable. As an individual title, the consistent, sustained lead of the *Japan Times* and all its incarnations (*Japan Times & Advertiser*, *Nippon Times*) is demonstrated, without being dragged down by the weaker papers in its network. The competition for Western attention posed by the *North-China Daily News*, *Japan Chronicle* and *China Press* is most evident in the 1920s and 1930s, but falls away as these newspapers are amalgamated or closed down in the 1940s. This

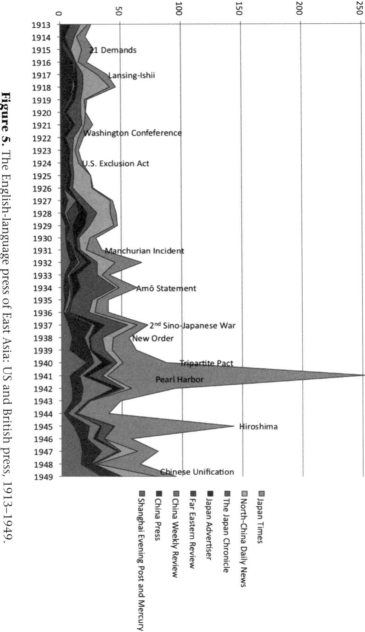

Figure 5. The English-language press of East Asia: US and British press, 1913–1949.

graph offers a closer picture of events shown in outline in Figure 4: here there is a clear trough in citations for all titles in 1942–44, with large spikes before and after those years, where in Figure 4 the trough is an amplification of the V-shaped dip in *Advertiser* network citations. In 1944 the figures pick up again. The quantity of citations to those newspapers that were still running or were revived increases after 1945, during an uneasy period for the English-language press in China and, after considerable realignments to the reality of the Occupation, what looks like boomtime for Japan's main remaining English-language newspaper, the *Nippon Times*, boosted by demand from the conquering forces and by Japanese readers keen to catch up with news of their country from what was at times seen as the mouthpiece of SCAP.

Figure 6 compares the attention paid to three groups of newspapers – the English-language press of Japan, the English-language press of China and the vernacular press of Japan – in the columns of the select group of US and British newspapers surveyed. In this survey, predictably, the English-language press of Japan as a group is the most cited of the three. However, Japan's vernacular press, represented here by the *Asahi*, *Yomiuri* and *Mainichi*, easily pushes the English-language press of China into third place.

The extent to which Western papers cited Japan's vernacular press appears to challenge my claim that, being unable to read or speak Japanese, correspondents in Tokyo were dependent on the English-language press and to Foreign Ministry briefings for their information. However, it does not mean that these correspondents were closet newspaper-level readers of Japanese, rather that they cited vernacular newspaper articles from compilations of translations provided by the English-language papers. Hugh Byas, Wilfrid Fleisher and the editors of the *Japan Chronicle* all enjoyed the services of interpreters and translators but for the average correspondent, these compiled articles in translation would have been the closest they came to reading 'Japanese'.

The other significant factor is the Western appetite for English-language news from China as opposed to English-language news of China. Overall the preferred source of news of China was not the English-language press of China but the English-language press of Japan, with a strong preference for the *Japan Times* and the *Chronicle*, as we know from Figure 5. However, as we also know from Figure 5, the China newspapers in both the *Chronicle* and *Advertiser* networks offered strong competition to and sometimes eclipsed the Japan-based newspapers, as the *China Press* did the *Japan Advertiser*.

Given these considerations, the inclusion of the vernacular press here tends to skew the picture in Figure 6. However, for American and British readerships, the relative significance of news of or from the two nations is confirmed in Figure 7, with citations to news from the English-language newspapers of Japan clearly ahead of citations to news from the English-language newspapers of China. Given that for most of this period Japan was the nation making and most focused on managing

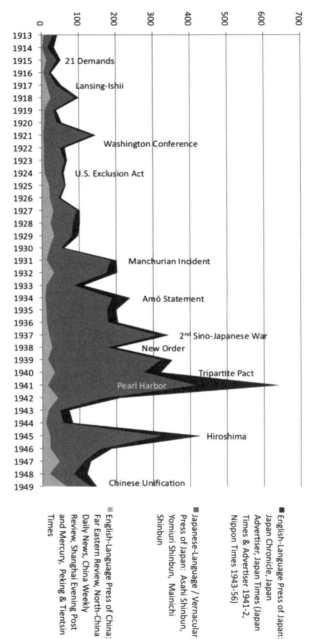

Figure 6. The English-language press of Japan compared to the English-language press of China and the vernacular press of Japan: US and British press, 1913–1949.

news in and of China, this difference is understandable, but it also indicates, very broadly, that US and British newspapers and their readers were more interested in Japan (and Japan's activities in China) than they were in China itself. Mordechai Rozanski's theory, discussed here in Chapter 4, that polarization between pro-Guomindang reporting and pro-CCP reporting by US journalists in China made the China story too complicated for US readers, seems intuitively correct here. Rozanski's survey of thirteen major US dailies from 1927 to 1931 showed that coverage of China news in US dailies dropped from a dominant position in foreign news to five percent of all foreign reports and a ranking of seventh among nations.[5] Figure 7 backs this up: it shows declining US (and British) citations of the English-language press of China in the years 1927–31. In 1927–28 citations to the English-language press of China fell away while citations to the English-language press of Japan rose. There was a noticeable spike in citations in 1931, with the Manchurian Incident, but the spike for the English-language papers of Japan was much higher than it is for those of China.

On most indicators, this survey demonstrates that the Foreign Ministry network was ahead of the *Advertiser* and *Chronicle* networks on points, though not without a keen struggle. Even without the many newspapers and periodicals that were not cited in the US and British press, Figure 4 shows the Foreign Ministry network surging ahead of the other two as a network, while Figure 5 shows that the *Japan Times* version of events was far more broadly and frequently distributed than that of the most-cited newspapers of the other two networks. In Figure 6 the English-language press of Japan was more often cited than both the vernacular press of Japan and the English language press of China. If we balance this overall success with the keen competition between the front-running *Japan Times*, *North-China Daily News*, *China Press* and *Japan Chronicle*, the *Japan Times* is still well ahead of the rest (when the power behind it allowed them to function).

Although the question of influence remains unresolved in the strict sense of the term, this survey clarifies the extent of the access that the English-language press networks of East Asia enjoyed to a select group of US and British newspapers and therefore their readerships. All in all, had historical databases been available to the managers of the Foreign Ministry network, they should have taken some comfort from the access gained to US and British readerships by their leading title, the *Japan Times*, although this reaction would have been tempered by the dismissive context – 'semi-official', 'Foreign Office organ' – in which this newspaper was discussed. Given the same information, the State Department officials and local consuls who observed Charles Crane's support for the *Advertiser* network with such distaste might have had second thoughts, while those who lobbied for financial aid for the *Advertiser* and argued for the continued support of the *Shanghai Evening Post and Mercury* should have been confirmed in their enthusiasm. Had the Far East Department in Whitehall enjoyed access to this data, they

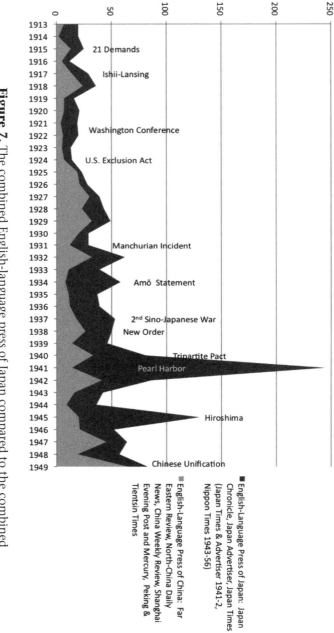

Figure 7. The combined English-language press of Japan compared to the combined English-language press of China: US and British press, 1913–1949.

might well have revised their opinion of the *Japan Chronicle* a long time before Robert Craigie's regretful report following its sale to the *Japan Times* in December 1940, and reconsidered their view of the *North-China Daily News*, the *Peking & Tientsin Times* and other titles.

This raises the question: why didn't they? Even without the tools of analysis available today, the Far East Department of the Foreign Office suffered no shortage of information about the competition between the English-language newspapers of East Asia and Japan's investment in them as tools of propaganda. Whitehall was not indifferent to the power of the English-language press of East Asia, but its attention too often translated into an attitude of irritation when more serious and sustained scrutiny might have led to more concrete support and a cannier utilization of their power. The very newspapers in the *Chronicle* network that the Foreign Office and its satellites saw as the greatest hindrance to their management of relations with Japan and China were those that were cited with the most respect by national dailies in the very nation that Britain would turn to for aid in East Asia, the United States.[6]

At the same time, any such speculations would have to be tempered by the fact that in China, where until 1937 the Communists rather than the Japanese were still perceived by Whitehall as the most ominous threat to British interests, access to these databases would not have provided a more informed picture of that threat. The rising political strength and growing appeal of the Communist Party of China went largely untraced in the English-language newspapers of East Asia, where the Guomindang monopolized the China brand and only an awkward but articulate minority among Western observers talked up the other claimant to power in China.

Given these qualifications, Barak Kushner's recent description of Japanese propaganda as a 'successful failure' could apply to all three of the English-language press networks of East Asia.[7] The three networks all gained access to readers of the *Washington Post, New York Times, Christian Science Monitor, Wall Street Journal, Manchester Guardian* and *The Times*. These readerships all had opportunities to consider the views of the leading newspapers in each network, but how many of them did so cannot be known. Although the *Japan Times* was the most frequently cited of all the newspapers in East Asia, this frequency does not appear to have translated into greater Western public sympathy for Japan's case in general and for Japan to be given a free hand in China in particular. However, until the late 1920s there was a growing consensus in favour of Japanese intervention among Anglophone settlers until the China papers in the *Chronicle* and *Advertiser* networks made a closer accommodation with Chinese nationalism. Japan was also gaining steady acceptance for the establishment of Manchukuo until the 1932 invasion of Shanghai. Japan's failure to persuade Western readerships of the justness of her cause in East Asia probably had less to do with Foreign Ministry network papers being more frequently cited than those of the other networks than it did with the contradiction between shocking but highly newsworthy events on the ground and the case Japan advanced to justify its agenda.

The *Japan Chronicle* network gained credibility at the expense of the Foreign Ministry network and the leaders and features of the *Chronicle* and *North-China Daily News* were often respectfully cited in articles published not only in the *Manchester Guardian* and *The Times*, both consistently friendly to these papers, but in the US papers as well. At the same time, for all the public indignation the *Chronicle* network may have inspired in these readerships about the brutal realities of Japanese power, it is hard to find an instance where a significant element of national policy changed as the result of a *Chronicle* network article. Although the network's papers successfully campaigned on some major issues, such as the abrogation of the Anglo-Japanese Alliance, they did so as part of a chorus of voices calling for change. The same point can be made of the *Advertiser* network: highly respected, ably edited, and likewise campaigning for the abrogation of the Alliance that was agreed at Washington, but unable to claim any substantial role in realigning US policy on East Asia until Pearl Harbor shoved the United States firmly behind the Guomindang. The *Advertiser* network had long argued for a greater commitment to China in US foreign policy. However, with the ultimate victory of the Chinese Communists, the commitment of American funds, airpower, materiel and advisers to Chongqing did not yield the sort of results for which any network would want to take credit.

What could these networks tell the West about East Asia? In December 1907, G.E. Morrison addressed the annual dinner of the China Association at the Whitehall Rooms in Shanghai. In his speech, which was attended by H.A. Gwynne of the *Morning Post*, William Keswick of Jardine Matheson and a mixed gathering of Shanghai's great and good, Morrison appealed to the humour and sympathy of the members of his audience but he certainly did not placate them:

Not long ago, an insurrection in the Southern part of China was suppressed by a well-known Viceroy with great severity. A native newspaper in Canton, hostile to the Viceroy, gave vent to its hostility by the publication of a story alleging that on the occasion of the execution of a well-known rebel, the Viceroy, of whose courage there had never been any question, had caused the heart of the rebel to be cut out and had drunk some of his blood. One of the foreign Ministers in Peking, shocked by this story, telegraphed to the foreign official who in geographical distance was stationed nearest to the native city where the alleged barbarity was committed, and asked if he could confirm the story. By return of telegram, he received the reply, 'Can confirm.' Some time later he himself met that foreign official and asked him how it was possible that, in so short a time, he could confirm the story, seeing that in point of postal distance he was as far removed from the scene of the alleged barbarity as London is from Siberia. He replied, 'I never had any hesitation in sending a confirmation, I did not even inquire. It was just the sort of thing that the brute would do.' (Laughter).

As Morrison continued:

> They were too apt to believe those stories. They too readily forgot their experiences during 1900, and the gruesome fictions that were then published about the fate of those who were besieged in Peking. At that time he [Morrison] had the honour of being pictorially represented as being boiled in oil in the same cauldron with his Excellency, the Russian Minister. (Laughter). There was much to condemn in China. We who knew how high were the administrative ideals, both in this country and in America, who remember how unscathed we emerged from those amazing enquiries into the expenditure in connexion with some of our recent wars, naturally condemned administrative methods which failed to live up to our standard. It was natural that we, who were the most superior of all God's people (laughter), whose mission it was to pry into the internal affairs of other less favoured countries, should condemn procedure in China that would never be tolerated here. It was natural, for example, that the system of the purchase of rank in China, still so common in that empire, should be condemned by those nondescript capitalists of alien origin whose entry into their ranks was adding so greatly to the dignity and prestige of our hereditary aristocracy. (Laughter).[8]

And so on. In 1907, the settler community in China seems to have allowed and even to have appreciated Morrison's scrutiny of its right to judge the Chinese by standards its members signally failed to live up to. The confidence of the local official made them laugh. The ridiculousness of Morrison's being portrayed as boiled in oil made them laugh. Mention of their God-given superiority made them laugh. And the notion of the dignity and prestige of Britain's landed aristocracy made them laugh again. It is hard to be certain whether their mirth was a laughing-off of offence or the result of shared insights or indeed the confident laughter of the arrogant, but it could indicate a willingness to scrutinize their own formation of images and prejudices regarding the Chinese and their nation.

No estimate of the combined significance of the English-language press networks of East Asia can ignore their contribution to the accumulation of images of East Asia conveyed to the Western press and its readers. But Morrison's speech and the reactions of his listeners raise the question: to what extent were the images and ideas of Japan transmitted by the English-language press networks of East Asia picked up by the Western press because they were 'just the sort of thing the brute would do'? Although the transmission of information and of actual photographic images improved vastly in terms of speed and clarity, and the sense of responsibility of reporters and journalists between 1918 and 1941 improved on that displayed by Morrison's local official 'not long' before 1907, the fundamentals do appear to have changed in the 1920s and 1930s, at least, and the ascription of brutality to the other, as examined in this study, does not always appear to have been as automatic as Morrison depicted it in 1907.

The question might be one of appetite: what sort of China and what sort of Japan and what sort of Korea did the Western press want from its correspondents? The Introduction to this study referred to the historiography of the image approach to East Asia. Writing in 1975, the late Richard Storry allocated four descriptive titles to stages in the Western image of Japan: the Lotus Land, the Gallant Ally, the Ghastly Menace and the Busy Beehive.[9] To this we might add a fifth, generalized, image transmitted by these newspapers – and even by this study – that of Japan the Propagandist, both in the 'bad', for example, Soviet sense and as a hangover from the days of the Yellow Peril. From A.M. Pooley's critical accounts (1915, 1917, 1920), those of Montaville Flowers (1917), Peter de Mendelssohn's critical wartime analysis (1944), Valliant (1974) and Kushner (2006), the notion of Japan as an inveterate manager of its international image has come to constitute an image in itself. The power of the Propagandist image has come and gone and seems now, alongside the Menace image, to be shifting to China, but these generalized images are still very much part of the discussion on modern East Asia. Their durability only adds to the mystery of the image approach: its typology is emotive and indeterminate, but everyone knows these images when they see them and they won't go away.

In the same vein, even the most austere analysis of the English-language press networks of East Asia has to acknowledge that these were accumulations of human enterprise, the work of people, and that of these people, more were settlers than were natives of the places that they wrote about.

At the beginning of this account, surveying recent scholarship on transnational networks in Shanghai and East Asia, I quoted the description by Robert Bickers and Christian Henriot that most clearly encapsulated the independence of the settler communities, as 'opportunistic groups [that] carved out new livelihoods and new roles' 'in the interstices of' 'a network of multiple overlapping imperialisms'.[10] Overall, the networks of the English-language press of East Asia united most effectively when a cause combined the individual prejudices of those who wrote for them with potential commercial advantage and political aggrandizement. Like many of the settlers they served, the primary loyalty of the newspapers discussed here was to their own interests, their staff and their community and to those officials, business people and journalists in China and Japan with whom they formed mutually beneficial relationships.

This self-interest was not a limitation. Because the English-language press networks of East Asia were so embedded in Bickers and Henriot's 'networks of multiple overlapping imperialisms', they served in larger wars and played their part in greater games than what sometimes looks too much like inter-port rivalry would seem to show. Above all, as Bayly (1996) showed in the context of the 'information orders' of 'native informants' and the press in eighteenth–nineteenth century India, the English-language press of East Asia provided Britain, Japan and the

United States with information networks that allowed them to domi-nate and then to compete for control in the Treaty Ports of Japan and the International Settlements of China when, respectively, the Japanese and the Chinese did not exert ownership. This was perhaps their most substantial achievement: providing layers of cultural hegemony, in the Gramscian sense, for Britain and the United States in East Asia and in many ways preparing Japan and Korea, if not China, for further adapta-tion to Western norms.[11]

But of course they did not have it all their own way. In the long view, the history of the English-language press networks of East Asia is one of a long cessation of control from Western-run networks to those of the host nation: first through the loss of extraterritoriality and its conse-quences in Japan; then in China, where after 1911 both Chinese nationalism and Japanese imperialism began to co-opt and build on those parts of the foreign networks that could be used to promote their ends; and finally in mopping-up operations in Tokyo and Shanghai in the first few weeks of the Pacific War.

This longer view presents recurring themes and a pressing sense of circularity. Near the beginning of this book we saw Uchida Yasuya, Matsuoka Yōsuke, Toshi Gō and John Russell Kennedy around the top table and Wellington Koo and Thomas Millard lobbying in the hall as unequal but competing interests at the creation of the League of Nations in Paris in 1919. We saw them again in 1933: Uchida in Tokyo, Matsuoka and Kennedy's protégé George Bronson Rea facing down Koo and his foreign publicists in Geneva, where the measured idealism of 1919 has come down to an impressive but ultimately toothless gesture of condemnation. Further along we saw the Matsuoka cyclone gusting through Berlin, Moscow and Washington leaving a trail of treaties, pacts and vivid rhetoric for Toshi Gō to dust off and represent to a nervy West. We saw the internationalist *Japan Times* of Itō and Zumoto reach out to the world in 1897 and yet morph into the feisty Foreign Ministry network of 1940, with Toshi Gō's *Japan Times & Advertiser* taking on all comers and biting off its own internationalist tail. We saw the *Advertiser* network progress from a bustling Treaty Port sales sheet to a raft of America-first organs that damned Japanese incursions yet looked the other way when gangsters and Guomindang thugs decapitated their rivals in the streets of Shanghai. And we saw the spiky polemics of the *Chronicle* and its sisters in Shanghai, Peking and Tianjin increasingly blunted and accommodated until even the gamy rant of China's last Englishman, H.G.W. Woodhead, smelled truer than the pasteurized fare served up further along the Bund and in Kōbe.

And yet, for all their failings, the English-language press networks of East Asia anticipated the transnational worlds that were so radically shaken and restructured there between September 1931 and October 1949. In these years of seismic political change, fresh combinations of interest and 'native talent' reshaped these networks. Since 1949, although few of the institutions have survived, the templates of the networks outlined in this study have continued to evolve and to shape our perceptions of East Asia. If there is a pithy maxim, somewhere between Marx's remarks on history as farce and tragedy and Blake's on good intentions on the road to hell, to wrap all this up and tell us that idealism always ends in tears then, all being well, it is still too soon to reach for it.

NOTES

1   Some of these are mentioned in Kakegawa 2001: 36–8.
2   See Cohen 1978: 4, and n.1 regarding the terms 'opinion leader' and opinion maker'.
3   *The Times* Digital Archive 1785–1985; *The Guardian* Archive (for *The Manchester Guardian*); ProQuest Historical Newspapers (for the US newspapers). See Bibliography for the full list of press network titles researched and details of their location. Because the accuracy of searches in any newspaper database is only as good as the quality of the OCR software utilized by the database owners and creators, the results were subjected to checks that were initially intended to be methodically random but perforce became even more thorough.
4   Data for Japan's three successive national news networks as well as Reuters reports from China and Japan was also mined for the same period, 1913–49. The results showed the *Dōmei* and *Rengō* agencies well ahead of Reuters, as follows: *Kokusai*: 16 citations; *Rengō* 765; *Dōmei* 3762; Reuters China 476; Reuters Japan 374. However, without being able to locate or discriminate precise data from the same selection of databases for the two powerful US agencies, UP and AP, for Japan's Shanghai-based *Shin-Tōhō* agency or for the *Advertiser* network's Trans-Pacific News Service, these results were too skewed to justify a graph.
5   Rozanski 1974: 376. The ranking among nations was: 1. Britain 2. France. 3. Germany 4. Switzerland (League of Nations). 5. Canada 6. Italy 7. China.
6   See for example USDS 894.44, No.21: E.R. Dickover, US Consul in Kōbe, to Secretary of State, Washington, 13 November 1922, 'I feel that through the death of Robert Young this Consulate has lost a valuable friend.' USDS.
7   Kushner 2006: 10.
8   'The China Association: Dr Morrison on Chinese Reforms': NCH, 6 December 1907, 594–5.
9   Storry, Richard (1975) 'Japan and Britain: Chance for both nations to create new images.' In *The Times*, 7 May 1975. The article prepared British readers for the State visit of Queen Elisabeth II and her consort to Japan in that year.
10 Bickers and Henriot 2000: 2.
11 Matsuda (2007: 5) describes the 'two-way street' envisioned by John D. Rockefeller for Japan-US cultural programmes and cites a 1951 'Tokyo Times' article that pointed out that Japan had already experienced 'the one-way imposition of culture by a foreign country'.

Bibliography

I UNPUBLISHED MATERIAL

Abbreviations
AUCS: American University Club of Shanghai.
FO: Foreign Office.
SMR: South Manchurian Railway Company.
USDS: United States Department of State

A OFFICIAL RECORDS

1 Public Record Office files at the National Archives, Kew, UK
FO 228 Foreign Office consular correspondence (China, excluding Shanghai).
FO 262 Foreign Office consular correspondence (Japan).
FO 371 Class list for Foreign Office (Political) correspondence between London and British Embassies in Tokyo and Peking from c.1906 to 1941.
FO 372 Class list for Foreign Office (Treaty Department) correspondence from c.1906 to 1941.
FO 395 Class list for Foreign Office, (News Department, code 'P' [Information, Policy and News]), correspondence from 1916 to 1939.
WO 208 Class list: War Office documents, notably files and correspondence of the Directorate of Military Intelligence relating to treatment of British residents of Shanghai in 1941–43.

2 Gaimushō gaikō shiryōkan (Gaimushō archives), Roppongi, Tokyo, Japan
Gaimushō Kiroku Senden kankei: hoshokin shikyu sendenshya sonota senden hi shikyu kankei Gaikokujin no bu (Foreign Ministry Records: propaganda, propagandists and other items paid with bonuses, Foreign Section).
Gaimushō Kiroku: Taibei Keihatsu Undō ni kansuru 2, Gaikokujin no bu (Foreign Ministry Records: Re. Enlightenment campaign No.2. Foreign section).
Gaikoku Shinbun Ronchō (Editorial tone of foreign newspapers].
Gaikoku Shinbun Kisha Shōhbun Kankei Zakken. (Punishment of foreign correspondents, and miscellaneous items).
Gaikoku Shinbun Tsūshin Kikan oyobi Tsūshin-in Kankei Zakken, Tsūshin-in no bu: Beikokujin no bu (Miscellaneous Matters relating to Foreign Newspapers, Communications Agencies and Correspondents: American correspondents).
Gaikoku Shinbun Tsūshin Kikan oyobi Tsūshin-in Kankei Zakken, Tsūshin-in no bu: Eikokujin no bu (Miscellaneous Matters relating to Foreign Newspapers, Communications Agencies and Correspondents: British correspondents).
Jiko san: Paris Kōwa Kaigi ni okeru Chugoku Mondai toku ni Santo Mondai kansuru

ken. (Issue no.3: The China problem with particular reference to the Shandong problem).
Kankoku Faru Easuto (Korea: *Far East*).
Kankoku Jyapan Veyū (Korea: *Japan View*).
Kankoku Jyapan Taimuzu (Korea: *Japan Times*).
Kankoku Seoru Pressu (Korea: *Seoul Press*).

3 National Archives and Records Administration, Washington DC

Record Group 59: Records of the Department of State relating to the internal affairs of China, 1910–29; 1930–39; decimal file 893.

Record Group 59: Records of the United States Department of State relating to internal affairs of Japan, 1910–29; 1930–39; 1940–44; decimal file 894.

Record Group 59: Records of the United States Department of State relating to political relations between China and other states, 1910–29.

Record Group 59: Records of the United States Department of State relating to political relations between China and Japan, 1930–44.

Record Group 165: Military Intelligence Division. [Cited from Rozanski (1974).].

Record Group 263: Shanghai Municipal Police files.

B PRIVATE COLLECTIONS

Julean Arnold, (1876–1946), Papers, Hoover Institution Stanford University, California, US Arnold was appointed US Consul-General at Hankou in 1914 and then US commercial attaché in China from 1914 to 1940. I have not personally researched the Arnold Papers at the Hoover Institution. In this book, all citations to the Julean Arnold Papers originate in Rozanski (1974).

Hugh Byas (1875–1945), Papers Manuscript group No121 (Hist Mss Film 95) Manuscripts and Archives, Yale University Library, New Haven, Connecticut, US This collection consists of scrapbooks, writings, notes, research files, photographs, and letters. The main collection runs from 1914 to 1941, with some earlier cuttings, covering the period of Byas's journalistic career in Japan as editor of the *Japan Advertiser* and correspondent for *The Times* and *New York Times*, but there is also material relating to lectures he gave at Yale University between 1942 and his death in 1945. Byas was also associated with the *New East*, the *Herald of Asia*, and numerous journals in Great Britain and the US. In February 1980, the entire Byas archive was microfilmed and the original material discarded to save space, and there are therefore no box numbers, but only microfilm reels arranged thematically and numbered 1–11. This book accordingly cites Reel 4 (Byas correspondence, Foreign Relations of Japan); Reel 5 (Journalism and the *Kokusai* and *Dōmei* News Agencies); Reel 6 (Korea, Manchukuo, Miscellaneous), Reel 7 (The *New East*, Press Regulations and Propaganda) and Reel 11 (Miscellaneous Notes).

China Association Papers, SOAS Library, University of London, UK The China Association was initially a social group that became a highly organized lobby for the interests of British business firms in Hong Kong and the China ports. The Association's papers reveal links between the Association and two China press journalists: Owen Mortimer Green, of the *North China Daily News,* a busy lobbyist on behalf of the Association, and H.G.W. Woodhead of the *Peking &*

Tientsin Times. The papers are also revealing on the organizational links between the China Association and branches of the British Association of Japan in Yokohama and Kobe.

Charles R Crane Papers, Institute of Current World Affairs, Hanover, New Hampshire, New York, US A key member of the *Japan Advertiser* network, Charles R. Crane was a multimillionaire with extensive connections in Washington who financed the establishment of publications in East Asia and bankrolled the careers and campaigns of journalists such as Thomas Millard, Carl Crow and Putnam Weale. He served briefly as US Minister to China. I have not personally visited or researched the Crane Papers. Most references given in this book to the Crane Papers come from Rozanski (1974).

Stanley K Hornbeck, Papers, Hoover Institution, Stanford University, California, US I have not personally visited or researched the Hornbeck Papers at the Hoover Institution. In this book, most citations to the Hornbeck Papers come from Rozanski (1974). Other citations to Hornbeck at the US Department of State are the result of searches made by the author in USDS RG. 59 (see note above).

Malcolm Kennedy Papers, Library, University of Sheffield, UK In 1917, Kennedy went to Japan as a language trainee then became a military Attaché. He worked for some years for the Rising Sun Petroleum Company, and in March 1925 became the Reuters correspondent in Tokyo for about five years. He then joined the Rengō news agency. Malcolm Kennedy's long connection with Japan makes his papers and diaries worth studying. He knew everyone who was anyone in Tokyo and the treaty ports between the wars, and his friendships with British and American journalists – Hugh Byas, John Russell Kennedy, the Fleisher family, J.W. Robertson Scott, Frank Ashton-Gwatkin, John N. Penlington, Laxon Sweet – and Japanese – Iwanaga Yūkichi, Baba Tsunego, Zumoto Motosada – make his diaries extremely useful. Unusually, all of Kennedy's diaries for the period 1917–30 are indexed for subjects and persons, making searches relatively easy.

GE Morrison, (1862–1920), Papers, State Library of New South Wales, Sydney, Australia Morrison was the Peking Correspondent of *The Times* for many years, before becoming a publicity advisor to the government of Yuan Shikai. Morrison enjoyed a busy correspondence with numerous figures associated with this book, notably: O.M. Green, H.G.W. Woodhead, J.W. Robertson Scott, Putnam Weale, Melville Stone and Robert Young, but because the bulk of this correspondence occurred before the period under study, it has not been frequently cited.

Ridge Family Papers, Library, School of Oriental and African Studies, University of London, UK PP Ms 30 Photographs and papers of William Sheldon Ridge (1875–1945) and his wife Frances. Ridge worked on a number of publications including the *Peking Daily News* and the *Far Eastern Times*. In the 1930s Ridge edited the *Peking Chronicle*, which he sold to Japanese interests in 1937, but stayed on at the paper until 1939. He was arrested and interned by the Japanese in 1943 and died in 1945. Other Ridge papers are held at the Hoover Institution at Stanford University, but I have not researched these.

The Bertrand Russell Archives, Mills Memorial Library, McMaster University, Hamilton, Ontario, Canada Before and after visiting Japan in July 1921, Bertrand Russell corresponded with Robert Young of the *Japan Chronicle*, with Young's successor Morgan Young, and with Yamamoto Sanehiko, editor of *Kaizō*, a radical magazine under whose auspices he had been invited to Japan. Russell contributed articles and letters to the *Japan Chronicle* and was commissioned by Yamamoto to write articles on contemporary political movements for *Kaizō*. Russell's correspondence with Yamamoto continued until the early 1950s, when Yamamoto asked Russell to help his campaign against the spread of nuclear armaments.

Nym Wales (Helen Foster Snow), Papers, Hoover Institution, Stanford University, California, US Helen Foster Snow, whose pen name was Nym Wales, worked as a journalist in China, for many years alongside Edgar Snow, whom she married and divorced, and, like her husband, travelled to Yan'an where she researched and wrote about the CCP. I have not personally researched in this archive. All citations to the Wales Papers come from Farnsworth (1996) and Rand (1995).

Western Historical Manuscripts Collection, University of Missouri at Columbia This Collection supplied the following: *University of Missouri Bulletin* material and the *Missouri Historical Review* (cited here in Appendices); the University of Missouri School of Journalism MA Theses listed in Bibliography; clippings of newspaper articles related to journalism in Japan including articles from trade journals such as *Editor & Publisher and The Fourth Estate*, *The Quill*, the *Japan Advertiser*, the *Trans-Pacific*, *Millard's Review of the Far East*, and special issues of the School of Journalism campus newspaper, *The Daily Missourian* prepared for visits by Japanese dignitaries, some organized by the America-Japan Society. Other relevant Papers in this collection (though not used in this book) are those of John B. Powell, mostly consisting of the manuscripts of his books and articles, Carl Crow and Duke Needham Parry. NB. The Edgar Snow Papers, also not cited here except where referred to in Farnsworth (1996) are held in the library collections of the University of Missouri-Kansas City.

Harold S Williams Papers, National Library of Australia, Canberra, Australia The Australian businessman Harold Williams lived and worked in Kōbe from 1919 to 1941, and again after the war until his death in the late 1980s. During that time he amassed a unique and largely unmined archive of books, photographs and original newspapers related to the history of foreigners in Japan. I have made particular use of materials relating to the *Japan Chronicle* in MS6681, notes on Newspapers in Japan: MS6681/1/80, MS6681/1/59, MS6681/3/7, and MS6681/2/57 and MS6681/3/27. There are also some notes on B.W. Fleisher in MS6681/3/17, as well as entries on the English-language newspapers in Japan before the period under study in this book, including the early history of the *Hiōgō News*, Robert Young's first employer in MS6681/1/87.

Walter and Sarah L (Lockwood) Williams Papers, Western Historical Manuscripts Collection, University of Missouri at Columbia Walter Williams founded the School of Journalism at the University of Missouri and was

Dean of the School for many years and President of the University from 1931 to 35. Williams had a long association with East Asia, and was especially close to B.W. Fleisher of the *Japan Advertiser*. Late in life he married one of his students at the University of Missouri, Sarah Lockwood. This archive contains his correspondence with Japanese officials in the US, with US officials in Japan, with B.W. Fleisher at the *Japan Advertiser* and with Mitsunaga Hoshiro, founder of *Dentsū*. It also holds numerous clippings of newspaper articles by Williams and others relating to his visits to Japan and China and to his work for the Pan-Pacific Conference of Journalists and the World Conference of Journalists. There are also numerous photographs of groups of American and other journalists taken during Dr Williams's visits to Japan and China.

C PERSONAL COMMUNICATIONS

Theodore Van Doorn, (1920–2009) In 1939, the nineteen-year old Theodore Van Doorn, born in Kōbe to a Japanese mother and a Dutch-American father and brought up and educated there, was taken on as a reporter at the *Japan Chronicle* in the early years of its existence under a Foreign Ministry subsidy, as negotiated since 1938 by the then Business Manager, Stanley Foley, and the editor, Edwin Kennard. When the *Chronicle* was sold to the Foreign Ministry in December 1940, Kennard and Foley left Japan, but Van Doorn stayed on with the skeleton staff maintained at the *Chronicle*'s Kōbe headquarters. Mr Van Doorn began an e-mail correspondence with me in October 2005 from his home in California where, aged eighty-five, he had begun to consider putting together an autobiographical account of his Japan years. A great many important details on the organization and staffing of the *Chronicle* in the years 1939–42 were checked with Mr Van Doorn.

Susan Larkin of Melbourne, Australia, is the great-granddaughter of Robert Young. Mrs Larkin is currently working on a biography of an ancestor who married into the Young family and whose life intersected with other descendants of Robert Young. She has proved an invaluable source of information and advice not only on Young but on the fortunes of his wife and children after his death in 1922.

Deborah Takahashi, of Sydney, Australia, is the paternal granddaughter of the journalist and publicist George Gorman (1888–1956). She is currently researching the life and career of her grandfather and has generously shared her research with me for this book. Her own enquiries into the activities and motivation of her grandfather and his family promise an extremely useful case study as well as the only dedicated source of information on Gorman.

II PUBLISHED MATERIAL

A DIARIES IN JAPANESE

Hara Kei (1950) *Nikki*. Edited by Hara Keiichiro in 9 volumes (Tokyo: Kangensha).
Ugaki Kazushige (1971) *Ugaki Issei Nikki* (Tokyo: Misuzu Shobō).

B NEWSPAPERS AND PERIODICALS

Runs and sometimes only a few issues of the following English-language newspapers and periodicals based in East Asia have been studied, depending on their availability. Details of articles in Japanese- Korean- and Chinese-language newspapers and periodicals are provided in notes.

Where runs exist, the following list of English-language newspapers gives details of their location and the extent of the run. However, many newspapers have not survived in proper runs in library holdings, but only in isolated copies in the diplomatic correspondence in which they or the issues they raise are discussed. Many newspapers have been preserved and are located in libraries and other collections as hard copies or microfilm, but in some cases, evidence of a newspaper's existence only survives in references made to it by other newspapers. The *Japan Chronicle*, *Japan Times*, *Japan Advertiser*, *China Weekly Review*, *Peking & Tientsin Times* and *North-China Daily News* all made frequent references to the situation and statements of their 'contemporaries' and offer a useful, if biased, source on the journalistic staff, ownership, editorial line and affiliations of other newspapers.

Further information on holdings of English-language newspapers in East Asia can be found in: Nunn, G. Raymond (1979) *Japanese periodicals and newspapers in Western languages: an international union list* (London: Mansell); King, Frank H.H. and Clarke, Prescott (1965) *A Research Guide to China-coast newspapers, 1822–1911* (Cambridge: Harvard University Press). Spaulding Robert M. (1962) *Bibliography of Western-language Dailies and Weeklies in Japan, 1861–1961* (University of Michigan) exists only in photocopy and is useful, but incomplete. For newspapers discussed in British diplomatic correspondence with China, Japan and Korea, the series: *Index to Foreign Office Correspondence*, volumes for the period under study, is essential. Unfortunately, many files recorded in the *Index* have not been preserved.

Key to Newspaper archives

Colindale: The British Library, Newspaper Library, Colindale, London, UK.

FO: Foreign Office correspondence held at the Public Record Office, National Archives, London.

SOAS: University of London, School of Oriental and African Studies, (SOAS) library.

Shakai Jōhō Kenkyūjo: (Institute of Socio-Information and Communication Studies), University of Tokyo, Japan.

USDS: the National Archives, United States Department of State, Record Groups 59, diplomatic correspondence, and 263, Shanghai Municipal Police files.

PQ: ProQuest Historical Newspapers (digital archive).

Central China Post: FO.

China Critic: FO.

China Forum: SMP files (on microfilm at Chūō University Library, Tama campus).

China Press: USDS, FO.

China Times: isolated references in Japan Chronicle.

China Weekly Review: SOAS has microfilm 1922–41 and the revived edition, 1945–49). Colindale: 1921–26, 1937; often discussed with clippings in USDS RG. 59.

Christian Science Monitor, 1913–49: PQ.

Contemporary Japan: SOAS: 1932–1940; incomplete.

Far East, The (ed. Penlington): SOAS, microfilm 1917–22.

Far Eastern Review, The: 1918–36 (monthly): FO, USDS and Colindale: 1919–41. Earlier copies are available from Datamics Inc., Washington.

Far Eastern Times: FO.

Hankow Herald: FO.

Harbin Herald: FO, USDS.

Harbin Observer: FO.

Herald of Asia, 1916–23: FO.

Japan Advertiser (daily), 1918–40: hard copies are held at *Shakai Jōhō Kenkyūjo,* (Institute of Socio-Information and Communication Studies), University of Tokyo. An incomplete run from 1918 to 1938 is available from the Washington-based microform publisher, Datamics Inc.

Japan Chronicle: SOAS 1919–41 (incomplete); Colindale: 1900–30; often discussed, with clippings, in FO.

Japan News-Week: copies preserved in USDS; some discussion in FO correspondence.

Japan Times: A short run of the Weekly edition, 1938–41, is held at SOAS, London University. Colindale holds the Weekly edition, 1897–1922. The entire daily edition, 1897-present, is held at *Shakai Jōhō Kenkyūjo.* Most of the *Weekly* edition from 1897-present is for sale in microfilm by the Japanese publisher, Yūshodo.

Kobe Herald, 1918–20: FO.

Manchester Guardian, 1913–49: *The Guardian* archive, at *The Guardian* website.

Manchuria Daily News: Colindale, 1912–40, FO, USDS.

Millard's Review of the Far East, 1917–23: USDS.

New East: SOAS 1916–18, incomplete; on microfilm.

New York Times, 1913–49: PQ.

North-China Daily News, 1918–41: SOAS hard copies; Colindale.

North China Herald and Supreme Court and Consular Gazette: SOAS 1850–1940, incomplete.

North China Standard: FO, frequent references in *Japan Chronicle.*

North China Star: USDS.

Oriental Affairs: SOAS: 1933–41 (incomplete).

Peking Chronicle: FO, USDS.

Peking Daily News: FO, USDS.

Peking Leader: FO, USDS.

Peking & Tientsin Times: Colindale, 1894–1902, FO.

Seoul Press: FO.

Shanghai Evening Post and Mercury: USDS, FO.

Shanghai Times: FO.

Shanghai Gazette: FO

Showdown: PRO, USDS, re. Bruce Lockhart.

The Times, (London), 1913–49: *The Times* Digital Archive, 1785–1985.

Trans-Pacific (published by the *Japan Advertiser*): FO, SOAS: 1933–38.

Wall Street Journal, 1913–49: PQ.

Washington Post, 1913–49: PQ.

C SECONDARY WORKS IN ENGLISH
1 Books, Pamphlets, Articles and Collections in English
Abend, Hallett (1930) *Tortured China* (New York: Ives Washburn).
—— (1940) *Chaos in Asia* (London: The Bodley Head).
—— (1943) *My Life in China, 1926–1941* (New York: Harcourt, Brace).
—— (1943) *Pacific Charter* (London: The Bodley Head).
—— (1944) *Treaty Ports* (New York: Doubleday, Doran).
—— (1946) *Reconquest: Its Results and Responsibilities* (New York: Doubleday, Doran).
Akimoto Shunkichi (1935) *The Lure of Japan* (Tokyo: Hokuseido Press).
Alcott, Carroll (1943) *My War with Japan* (New York: Henry Holt & Company).
Allman, Norwood F. (1943) *Shanghai Lawyer* (New York: McGraw-Hill).
'American Sociologist, An' [*pseud.* Kozlov, Ivan] (1921) *The Socialist and Labour Movement in Japan* (Kōbe: Chronicle Reprints, *The Japan Chronicle*). The author in the back section of this book is falsely stated as being Arthur Morgan Young.
American University Club of Shanghai (1936) *American University Men in China* (Shanghai: Comacrib Press).
Anderson, Benedict (1991 [1983]) *Imagined Communities: Reflections on the Origin and Spread of Nationalism* (London: Verso).
Argall, Phyllis (1945) *Prisoner in Japan* (London: Geoffrey Bles).
August, Thomas G. (1985) *The Selling of the Empire: British and French Imperialist Propaganda, 1890–1940* (Westport, Conn. and London: Greenwood Press).
Auslin, Michael R. (2004) *Negotiating with Imperialism: The Unequal Treaties and the Culture if Japanese Diplomacy* (Cambridge, Mass.: Harvard University Press).
Barr, Pat (1967) *The Coming of the Barbarians: A Story of Western Settlement in Japan 1853–1870* (London: Macmillan).
Bassett, R. (1952) *Democracy and Foreign Policy: A Case History. The Sino-Japanese Dispute 1931–33* (London: Longmans, Green).
Baty, Thomas (1959) *Alone in Japan* (Tokyo: Maruzen).
Bayly, C.A. (1996) *Empire and Information: Intelligence Gathering and Social Communication* (Cambridge: Cambridge University Press).
Beasley, W.G. (1987) *Japanese Imperialism, 1894–1945* (Oxford: Clarendon Press).
Belden, Jack (1949) *China Shakes the World* (New York: Harper).
Best, Anthony (1995) *Britain, Japan and Pearl Harbor: Avoiding War in East Asia, 1936–1941* (New York and London: Routledge).
—— (2002) *British Intelligence and the Japanese Challenge in Asia, 1914–1941* (London: Palgrave Macmillan).
Bickers, Robert (1999) *Britain in China: Community, Culture and Colonialism, 1900–1949* (Manchester: Manchester University Press).
Bickers, Robert (2004 [2003]) *Empire Made me: An Englishman Adrift in Shanghai* (London: Penguin).
Bickers, Robert and Henriot, Christian (eds.) (2000) *New Frontiers: Imperialism's new communities in East Asia, 1842–1953* (Manchester: Manchester University Press).
Bing-Shuey Lee, Edward (1933) *Two Years of the Japan-China Undeclared War And the Attitude of the Powers* (Shanghai: Mercury Press).
Bland, J.O.P. (1912) *Recent events and present policies in China* (London: Heinemann).

—— (1921) *China, Japan and Korea* (London: Heinemann)

—— (1932) *China, the pity of it* (London: Heinemann).

Borg, Dorothy (1964) *The United States and the Far Eastern Crisis of 1933–1938* (Cambridge, Mass.: Harvard University Press).

—— and Okamoto S. (eds.) (1973) *Pearl Harbor as History: Japanese-American Relations, 1931–1941* (New York: Columbia University Press).

Booker, Edna Lee (1941) *News is my Job: A Correspondent in War-Torn China* (New York: Macmillan).

Brooks, Barbara J. (2000) *Japan's Imperial Diplomacy: Consuls, Treaty Ports, and War in China, 1895–1938* (Honolulu: University of Hawai'i Press).

Burkman, Thomas W. (2008) *Japan and the League of Nations: Empire and World Order, 1914–1938* (Honolulu: University of Hawai'i Press).

Byas, Hugh (1943) *Government by Assassination* (London: Allen & Unwin).

—— (1945) *The Japanese Enemy: His Power and his vulnerability* (New York: Knopf).

Caren, Eric C. (1999) *World War II Extra: An Around-The World Newspaper History from the Treaty of Versailles to the Nuremberg Trials* (Edison, NJ: Castle Books).

Carr, E.H. (1995 [1939]) *The Twenty Years' Crisis 1919–1939* (London: Papermac).

Carr, Harry (1934) *Riding the Tiger: An American Newspaper Man in the Orient* (Boston and New York: Houghton Mifflin).

Cary, Otis (ed.) (1995) *Eyewitness to History: the First Americans in Postwar Asia* (Tokyo: Kodansha International).

Chang, Jung and Halliday, John (2005) *Mao: The Unknown Story* (London: Jonathan Cape).

Chamberlain, B.H. (1912) *The Invention of a New Religion* (London: Rationalist Press Association/Watts & Co; Kōbe: The Chronicle Press).

Chen, Percy (1979) *China Called Me* (Boston, MA: Little, Brown).

China Weekly Herald, The (1932) *A Month of Reign of Terror in Shanghai: What the Foreigners See, Say And Think From January 28 To February 27, 1932* (Shanghai: China Weekly Herald, Comacrib Press).

Ch'en, Tzu-Hsiang (November 1937) *The English-language Daily Press in China* (Yanjing: Collectanea Commiss Synodal), Vol.X, No.11.

—— (1925) *The Awakening of the Orient and Other Addresses*. (New Haven: Yale University Press).

Clarke, Joseph I.C. (1918) *Japan at first hand: her islands, their people, the picturesque, the real, with latest facts and figures on their war-time trade expansion and commercial outreach* (New York: Dodd, Mead and Co.) Reprinted and introduced in O'Connor, Peter (ed.) (2004), Volume 5.

Cohen, Warren I. (1971) *America's Response to China: An Interpretive History of Sino-American Relations* (New York: Columbia University Press).

—— (1978) *The Chinese Connection: Roger S. Greene, Thomas W. Lamont, George E. Sokolsky and American-East Asian Relations* (New York: Columbia University Press).

Collins, Gilbert (1923) *Flower of Asia: A novel of Nihon* (London: Duckworth).

Cooper, Kent (1942) *Barriers Down* (New York: Farrar and Rhinehart).

Cortazzi, Hugh and Daniels, Gordon (eds.) (1991) *Britain and Japan 1859–1991* (New York and London: Routledge).

Coughlin, William J. (1952) *Conquered Press: The MacArthur Era in Japanese Journalism* (Palo Alto, Calif.: Pacific Books).

Craft, Stephen G. (2004) *V.K. Wellington Koo and the Emergence of Modern China* (Lexington, Kentucky: University Press of Kentucky).

Crager, Kelly E. (2009) Review of Burkman, Thomas W., *Japan and the League of Nations: Empire and World Order, 1914–1938* in H-US-Japan, H-Net Reviews, March 2009. URL: http://www.h-net.org/reviews/showrev.php?id=23792.

Crosland, T.W.H. (1904) *The Truth About Japan* (London: G. Richards).

Craigie, Robert (1945) *Behind the Japanese Mask* (London: Hutchinson).

Crow, Carl (1938) *I Speak for the Chinese* (London: Hamish Hamilton).

Cryle, D. (1997) (ed.) *Disreputable Profession: Journalists and Journalism in Colonial Australia* (Rockhampton: Central Queensland University Press).

Deacon, Richard (1982) *A History of the Japanese Secret Service* (Taiwan bootleg: no publisher).

de Mendelsohn, Peter (1944) *Japan's Political Warfare* (London: George Allen & Unwin).

Dick, Philip K. (2001 [1962]) *The Man in the High Castle* (London: Penguin).

Doenecke, Justus D. (1984) *When the Wicked Rise: American Opinion-Makers and the Manchurian Crisis of 1931–33* (Lewisburg: Bucknell University Press).

Dower, John (1986) *War without Mercy: Race and Power in the Pacific War* (New York: Pantheon Books).

Farnsworth, Robert M. (1996) *From Vagabond to Journalist: Edgar Snow in Asia, 1928–1941* (Columbia: University of Missouri Press).

Farrar, Ronald T. (1998) *A Creed for My Profession: Walter Williams, Journalist to the World* (Columbia: University of Missouri Press).

Fenby, Jonathan (2004) *Chiang Kai-shek: China's Generalissimo and the Nation He Lost* (New York: Carroll & Graf).

Fleisher, Benjamin W. (ed.) (1928) *Enthronement of the One Hundred Twenty-fourth Emperor of Japan* (Tokyo: The Japan Advertiser).

Fleisher, Wilfrid (1941) *Volcanic Isle* (New York: Doubleday, Doran).

—— (1942) *Our Enemy Japan* (New York: Doubleday, Doran).

—— (1945) *What to do with Japan* (New York: Doubleday, Doran).

Flowers, Montaville (1917) *The Japanese Conquest of American Opinion* (New York: G.H. Doran).

Foreign Affairs Association of Japan (ed. unnamed) (November 1943) T*he Japan Year Book 1943–44* (Tokyo: The Foreign Affairs Association of Japan ['Republished by the Interdepartmental Committee for the Acquisition of Foreign Publications']).

Foreign Affairs Association of Japan (ed. unnamed) (1948) *The Japan Year Book 1946–48* (Tokyo: The Foreign Affairs Association of Japan).

Fox, Grace (1969) *Britain and Japan* (Oxford: Oxford University Press).

Fujisawa Rikitarō (1923) *The Recent Aims and Political Development of Japan* (Oxford: Oxford University Press).

Fält, Olavi K. (1985) *Fascism, Militarism or Japanism? The interpretation of the crisis years of 1930–1941 in the Japanese English-language press* (Oulu: Studia Historica Septentrionalia 8: Societas Historica Finlandiae).

—— (1990) *The Clash of Interests: The Transformation of Japan in 1861–1881 in the eyes of the local Anglo-Saxon press* (Oulu: Studia Historica Septentrionalia 18: Societas Historica Finlandiae).

Freeman, Laurie Anne (2000) *Closing the Shop: Information Cartels and Japan's Mass Media* (Princeton: Princeton University Press).

French, Paul (2007) *Carl Crow: A Tough Old China Hand: The Life, Times, and Adventures of an American in Shanghai* (Hong Kong University Press).
—— (2009) *Through the Looking Glass: Foreign Journalists in China, from the Opium Wars to Mao* (Hong Kong: Hong Kong University Press).
Frédéric, Louis (2002) *Japan Encyclopedia* (Cambridge, Mass: Belknap Press of Harvard University Press).
Gallagher, Patrick (1920) *America's Aims and Asia's Aspirations* (New York: The Century Co.).
Garon, Sheldon (1997) *Molding Japanese Minds: The State in Everyday Life* (Princeton: Princeton University Press).
Gayn, Mark (1941) *The Fight for the Pacific* (New York: William Morrow).
—— (1944) *Journey from the East* (New York: Alfred Knopf).
—— (1948) *Japan Diary* (New York: William Sloane Associates).
Gilbert, Rodney (1926) *What's Wrong with China* (London: John Murray).
—— (1929) *The Unequal Treaties* (London: John Murray).
Gilmore, Allison B. (1998) *You Can't Fight Tanks with Bayonets: Psychological Warfare against the Japanese Army in the Southwest Pacific* (Lincoln: University of Nebraska Press).
Gluck, Carol (1985) *Japan's Modern Myths: Ideology in the Late Meiji Period* (Princeton: Princeton University Press).
Gould, Randall (1941) *Chungking Today* (Shanghai: The Mercury Press).
—— (1946) *China in the Sun* (New York: Doubleday, Doran).
Grande, Julian (1934) *Japan's Place in the World* (London: Herbert Jenkins).
Green, O.M. (1941) *China's Struggle with the Dictators* (London: Hutchinson).
—— (1943) *The Foreigner in China* (London: Hutchinson).
Grew, Joseph C. (1944) *Ten Years in Japan: A contemporary record drawn from the diaries and private and official papers of Joseph C. Grew, United States Ambassador to Japan 1932–1942* (New York: Simon & Schuster).
Guillain, Robert (1981) *I Saw Tokyo Burning: An Eyewitness Narrative from Pearl Harbor to Hiroshima* (New York: Doubleday, Doran).
Gulick, Sidney Lewis (1905) *Evolution of the Japanese*.
—— (1905) *The White Peril in the Far East* (London: Fleming H. Revell).
—— (1914) *The American Japanese Problem: A Study of the Racial Relations of the East and West* (New York: Charles Scribner's Sons).
Hahn, Emily (1946 [1944: Philadelphia: Blakiston]) *China to Me: A Partial Autobiography* (New York: Garden City Publishing).
Hamilton, Ian (1905) *A Staff Officer's Scrapbook: The War in the Far East 1904–1905* (London: John Murray).
Hammond, Phil (ed.) (1997) *Cultural Difference, Media Memories: Anglo-American Images of Japan* (London: Cassell).
Hanazono Kanesada (1924) *The Development of Japanese Journalism* (Tokyo: Tokyo Nichi-Nichi Press).
—— (1926) *Journalism in Japan and its early Pioneers* (Ōsaka: Ōsaka Shuppansha).
Harmsworth, Alfred, Lord Northcliffe (1923) *My Journey Round the World (16 July 1921–26 Feb. 1922)* (London: The Bodley Head).
Hauser, Ernest O. (1940) *Shanghai: City for Sale*, Special Authorized Edition (Shanghai: The Chinese-American Publishing Co.; ['The American Bookshop']).

Haven, Violet Sweet (1944) *Gentlemen of Japan: A Study in Rapist Diplomacy* (Chicago: Ziff-Davis).

Hedges, Frank (1935) *In Far Japan* (Tokyo: Hokuseido Press).

Henning, Joseph (2000) *Outposts of civilization: race, religion, and the formative years of American-Japanese relations* (New York: New York University Press).

Henriot, Christian (1993) *Shanghai, 1927–1937: Municipal Power, Locality, and Modernization* (Berkeley: University of California Press).

Henriot, Christian and Yeh, Wen-hsin (eds.) (2004) *In the Shadow of the Rising Sun: Shanghai under Japanese Occupation* (Cambridge: Cambridge University Press).

Herron Smith, Frank (2005 [1920]) *The Other Side of the Korean Question* (Seoul: The Seoul Press). Reprinted in O'Connor, Peter (ed.) (2005) Volume 3, 581–620.

Herzstein, Robert Edwin (2005) *Henry R. Luce, Time, and the American Crusade in Asia* (Cambridge: Cambridge University Press).

Hoare, J. E. (1994) *Japan's Treaty Ports and Foreign Settlements: The Uninvited Guests, 1858–1899* (Folkestone: Japan Library).

Huffman, James L. (1980) *Politics of the Meiji Press: the Life of Fukuchi Gen'ichiro* (Honolulu: University of Hawai'i Press).

—— (1997) *Creating a Public: People and Press in Meiji Japan* (Honolulu: University of Hawai'i Press).

—— (2003) *A Yankee in Meiji Japan: The Crusading Journalist Edward H. House* (Lanham: Rowman & Littlefield).

Hughes, Richard (1972) *Foreign Devil: Thirty years of Reporting from the Far East* (London: Deutsch).

Hung, Chang-tai (1994) *War and Popular Culture: Resistance in Modern China, 1937–1945* (Berkeley: University of California Press).

Hunter, Janet (1984) *Concise Dictionary of Modern Japanese History* (Berkeley: University of California Press).

Hutcheon, Robin (1983) *SCMP: The First Eighty Years* (Hongkong: South China Morning Post).

Inahara K. (ed.) *The Japan Year Book 1936* (Tokyo: The Foreign Affairs Association of Japan / The Kenkyusha Press).

Iriye Akira (1965) *After Imperialism: The Search for a New Order in the Far East, 1921–1931* (Cambridge, Mass.: Harvard University Press).

—— (1972) *Pacific Estrangement: Japanese and American Expansion, 1897–1911* (Cambridge Mass.: Harvard University Press).

—— (ed.) (1975) *Mutual Images: Essays in American-Japanese Relations* (Cambridge: Harvard University Press).

—— (ed.) (1980) *The Chinese and the Japanese: Essays in Political and Cultural Interactions* (Princeton, NJ: Princeton University Press).

—— (ed.) (1990) *American, Chinese and Japanese Perspectives on Wartime Asia, 1931–1949* (Wilmington: SR Books).

Isaacs, Harold (1951 [1938]) *The Tragedy of the Chinese Revolution* (Stanford, Cal.: Stanford University Press).

Itoh Keiko (2001) *The Japanese Community in Pre-War Britain: From Integration to Disintegration* (Richmond, UK: Curzon).

Iwanaga Shinkichi (1980) *Story of Japanese News Agencies: A Historic Account, from Meiji Restoration (1868) to the End of World War II (1945)* (Tokyo: Tsūshin Chōsakai).

James, David H. (1951) *The Rise and Fall of the Japanese Empire* (London: Allen & Unwin).

Japan, Delegation to the League of Nations (January 1933): *The Manchurian Question: Japan's Case in the Sino-Japanese Dispute as Presented before the League of Nations* (Geneva: Imprimerie de La Tribune de Genève). Reprinted in O'Connor, Peter (ed.) (2005) Volume 6, 29–196.

Japan Times (1997) *The Japan Times front page, 1897–1997* (Tokyo: Japan Times).

Johnson, Sheila K. (1988) *The Japanese through American Eyes* (Stanford: Stanford University Press).

Jordan, Donald A. (1976) *The Northern Expedition: China's National Revolution of 1926–1928* (Honolulu: University of Hawai'i Press).

—— (2001) *China's Trial By Fire: The Shanghai War of 1932* (Ann Arbor: University of Michigan Press).

Kakehi Mitsuaki (September 1944) *Three Centuries of Wars of Aggression and Conquests* (Tokyo: Nippon Times).

Kawabe Kisaburo (1923) *The Press and Politics in Japan: A Study of the Relation between the Newspaper and the Political Development of Modern Japan* (Chicago: University of Chicago Press).

Kiyosawa Kiyoshi (1998 [1980], Soviak, Eugene (ed.) *A Diary of Darkness: The Wartime Diary of Kiyosawa Kiyoshi* (Princeton, NJ: Princeton University Press).

Kasza, Gregory J. (1988) *The State and the Mass Media in Japan, 1918–1945* (Berkeley: University of California Press).

Kato Masuo (1946) *The Lost War: A Japanese Reporter's Inside Story* (New York).

Kaul, Chandrika (2003) *Reporting the Raj: The British Press and India, 1880–1922* (Manchester: Manchester University Press).

Kaul, Chandrika (2006) (ed.) *Media and the British Empire* (London: Palgrave MacMillan).

Kawakami, Kiyoshi Karl (1921) *What Japan Thinks* (London: Macmillan).

—— (1932) *Japan Speaks on the Sino-Japanese Crisis* (London: Macmillan).

—— (1933) *Manchoukuo, Child of Conflict* (London and New York: Macmillan).

Keene, Donald (1994) *On Familiar Terms: A Journey Across Cultures* (London, New York: Kodansha International).

Kennedy, M.D. (1924) *The Military Side of Japanese Life* (London: Constable).

—— (1930) *The Changing Fabric of Japan* (London: Constable).

—— (1935) *The Problem of Japan* (London: Nisbet).

—— (1969) *The Estrangement of Great Britain and Japan 1917–35* (Manchester: Manchester University Press).

King, Frank H.H. and Clarke, Prescott (1965) *A Research Guide to China-coast Newspapers, 1822–1911* (Cambridge: Harvard University Press).

Klehr, Harvey and Radosh, Ronald (1996) *The Amerasia Spy Case: Prelude to McCarthyism* (Chapel Hill: University of North Carolina Press).

Kokusai Bunka Shinkokai (June 1936) [The Society for International Cultural Relations] *Catalogue of Periodicals Written in European Languages and Published in Japan* (Tokyo: K.B.S. Publication Series – B. No.27).

Kushner, Barak (2006) *The Thought War: Imperial Japanese Propaganda* (Honolulu: University of Hawai'i Press).

Large, Stephen S. (1972) *The Rise of Labor in Japan: the Yūaikai 1912–19* (Tokyo: Sophia University).

—— (1982) *Organized workers and socialist politics in interwar Japan* (Cambridge: Cambridge University Press).

—— (1992) *Emperor Hirohito and Shōwa Japan* (New York and London: Routledge).

Lasker, Bruno and Roman, Agnes (1938) *Propaganda from China and Japan*: *A Case Study in Propaganda Analysis* (New York: Institute of Pacific Relations).

Lasswell, Harold D. (1927) *Propaganda Technique in the World War* (Cambridge, Mass.: M.I.T. Press).

Lederer, Emil and Lederer-Seidler, Emy (1938) *Japan in Transition* (New Haven, Conn.: Yale University Press).

Lehmann, Jean-Pierre (1978) *The Image of Japan*: *From Feudal Isolation to World Power, 1850–1905* (London: Allen & Unwin).

Lent, John A. (1971) *The Asian Newspapers' Reluctant Revolution* (Ames, Iowa: Iowa State University Press).

Littlewood, Ian (1996) *The Idea of Japan*: *Western Images, Western Myths* (London: Secker & Warburg).

Lin, Yutang (1935) *My Country and My People* (New York: Reynal and Hitchcock).

—— (1936) *A History of the Press and Public Opinion in China* (Oxford: Oxford University Press).

Lo, Hui-min (1978) (ed.) *The Correspondence of G.E. Morrison*, Volume II: 1912–1920 (Cambridge: Cambridge University Press).

Lowe, Peter (1977) *Great Britain and the Origins of the Pacific War*: *A Study of British Policy in East Asia, 1937–1941* (Clarendon Press: Oxford).

—— (1981) *Britain in the Far East*: *A Survey from 1819 to the Present* (London: Longman).

—— (1997) *Containing the Cold War in East Asia*: *British policies towards Japan, China and Korea, 1948–53* (Manchester and New York: Manchester University Press).

Lu, David J. (2002) *Agony of Choice: Matsuoka Yōsuke and the Rise and Fall of the Japanese Empire, 1880–1946* (Lanham, Boulder, New York, Oxford: Lexington Books).

Lyons, Eugene (ed.) (1937) *We Cover the World: by Fifteen Foreign Correspondents* (New York: Harcourt, Brace and Company).

Mackinnon, Stephen R. and Friesen, Oris (eds.) (1987) *China Reporting*: *An Oral History of American Journalism in the 1930s and 1940s* (Berkeley: University of California Press).

Martin, Brian G. (1996) *The Shanghai Green Gang: Politics and Organized Crime, 1919–1937* (Berkeley: University of California Press).

Matsuda, Takeshi (2007) *Soft power and its Perils: U.S. Cultural Policy in early postwar Japan and permanent dependency* (Stanford: Stanford University Press).

Matsusaka Yoshihisa Tak (2001) *The Making of Japanese Manchuria, 1904–1932* (Cambridge, Mass.: Harvard University Press).

Maugham, W. Somerset (1926) *The Outstation*. In *The Casuarina Tree* (London: Heinemann).

May, Henry John (1937) *Little Yellow Gentlemen* (London: Cassell).

Millard, Thomas F. (1906) *The New Far East*: *an examination into the new position of Japan and her influence upon the solution of the far eastern question, with special reference to the interests of America and the future of the Chinese empire* (New York : C. Scribner's Sons).

—— (1919) *Democracy and the Eastern Question* (New York: The Century Co.).

—— (1924) *Conflict of Policies in Asia* (New York and London: The Century Co.).

—— (1928) *China, Where it is Today and Why* (London: Williams & Norgate).

—— (1931) *The End of Extraterritoriality in China* (New York: ABC).

Mitchell, Richard H. (1983) *Censorship in Imperial Japan* (Princeton, NJ: Princeton University Press).

Misselwitz, Henry Francis (1941) *The Dragon Stirs: An Intimate Sketch-Book of China's Kuomintang Revolution, 1927–29* (New York: Harbinger House).

—— (1943) *Shanghai Romance: A Story of the China that Was* (New York: Harbinger House).

—— (1945) *Japan Commits Hara-Kiri: Vignettes of America at War* (San Mateo: D. Melvin Paulson).

Mittler, Barbara (2004) *A Newspaper for China: Power, Identity and Change in Shanghai's News Media, 1872–1912* (Harvard MA: Harvard University Asia Center).

Moore, Frederick (1943) *With Japan's Leaders: An Intimate Record of Fourteen Years as Counsellor to the Japanese Government, Ending December 7, 1941* (London: Chapman and Hall).

Morris, John (1943) *Traveller from Tokyo* (London: Cresset Press).

Munday, Madeleine C. (1940) *Rice Bowl Broken* (London: Hutchinson).

Newman, Joseph (1942) *Goodbye Japan* (New York: L.B. Fischer).

Nish, Ian (1976) *The Anglo-Japanese alliance: the diplomacy of two island empires, 1894–1907* (Westport, Conn: Greenwood Press).

—— (1977) *Japanese Foreign Policy: 1869–1942, Kasumigaseki to Miyakezaka* (London, Boston: Routledge & Kegan Paul).

—— (ed.) (1988) *Contemporary European Writing on Japan: Scholarly Views from Eastern and Western Europe* (Woodchurch, Kent: Paul Norbury Publications).

—— (1993) *Japan's Struggle with Internationalism: Japan, China and the League of Nations, 1931–3* (London: Routledge & Kegan Paul).

—— (ed.) (1994) *Britain & Japan: Biographical Portraits* (Folkestone: Japan Library).

Nitobe Inazō (2002 [1900]) *Bushido: The Soul of Japan* (Tokyo: Kodansha International).

—— (1931) *Japan: Some Phases of her Problems and Development* (London: Ernest Benn).

Nunn, G. Raymond (1979) *Japanese periodicals and newspapers in Western languages: an international union list* (London: Mansell).

North-China Daily News & Herald Ltd. (1927) *The Soviet in China Unmasked: Documents Revealing Bolshevistic Plans and Methods, seized in the U.S.S.R. Embassy, Peking, April 6, 1927. Reprinted from the North-China Daily News, Shanghai, May 11, 1927* (Shanghai: North-China Daily News & Herald Limited).

Oakes, Vanya (1943) *White Man's Folly* (Boston: Houghton Mifflin).

Oba Sadao (1994) *The 'Japanese' War: London University's WWII Secret Teaching Programme and the Experts Sent to Help Beat Japan* (Surrey: Japan Library).

Oblas, Peter B. (2009) *Hugh Byas, a British editor who became a leading expert on Japan between the First and Second World Wars: A biographical history on newspaper journalism* (Lampeter: Edwin Mellen Press).

O'Brien, Neil L. (2003) *An American Editor in Early Revolutionary China: John William Powell and the China Weekly/Monthly Review* (New York and London: Routledge).

O'Connor, Peter (ed.) (2004) *Japanese Propaganda: Selected Readings. Series 1: Books, 1872–1943*, Volumes 1–10 (Folkestone, Kent: Global Oriental).

—— (ed.) (2005) *Japanese Propaganda*: *Selected Readings. Series 2*: *Pamphlets, 1891–1939*, Volumes 1–10 (Folkestone, Kent: Global Oriental).

—— (ed.) (2008) *Critical Readings on Japan, 1906–1948: Countering Japan's Agenda in East Asia. Series 1, Volumes 1–10: Books* (Folkestone, Kent: Global Oriental).

—— (ed.) (2010) *Critical Readings on Japan, 1906–1948: Countering Japan's Agenda in East Asia. Series 1, Volumes 1–10: Pamphlets*.

O'Conroy, Taid (1933) *The Menace of Japan* (London: Hurst & Blackett).

Ōfusa Junnōsuke (1981) *A Journalist's Memoir*: *50 Years' Experience in an Eventful Era* (Tokyo: privately printed).

Ōka Yoshitake (1986) *Five Political Leaders of Modern Japan. Itō Hirobumi, Ōkuma Shigenobu, Hara Takashi, Inukai Tsuyoshi, and Saionji Kinmochi* (Tokyo: University of Tokyo Press).

Okamura Shigenori (1941) *Jyapan Taimuzu Shōshi* (*A Short History of the Japan Times*) [bilingual] (Tokyo: Jyapan Taimuzu-sha).

Oliver, Frank (1939) *Special Undeclared War* (London: Jonathan Cape).

Osborne, Sidney (1918) *The Problem of Japan* (London: Allen & Unwin).

—— (1919) *The Isolation of Japan* (London: Allen & Unwin).

—— (1921) *The New Japanese Peril* (London: Allen & Unwin).

Pal, John (1963) *Shanghai Saga* (London: Jarrolds).

Paris, John (*pseud.* Frank Ashton-Gwatkin) (1921) *Kimono* (London: Collins).

—— (1924) *Sayonara* (Good-bye) (London: Collins).

—— (1925) *Banzai!* (Hurrah!) (London: Collins).

Pearl, Cyril (1967) *Morrison of Peking* (London: Angus and Robertson).

Penlington, J. N. (2004 [1932]) *The Mukden Mandate* (Tokyo: Kenkyūsha). Reprinted in O'Connor, Peter (ed.) (2004) Volume 9.

Pickering, E.H. (1936) *Japan's Place in the Modern World* (London: Harrap).

Pierson, John D. (1980) *Tokutomi Sohō, 1863–1957*: *A Journalist for Modern Japan* (Princeton: Princeton University Press).

Piggott, F.S.G. (1950) *Broken Thread*: *An Autobiography* (Aldershot: Gale & Polden).

Pooley, A.M. (1915) *Count Hayashi's Secret Memoirs* (London: Evelyn Nash).

—— (1917) *Japan at the Cross Roads* (London: Allen & Unwin).

—— (1920) *Japan's Foreign Policies* (London: Allen & Unwin).

Porter, R.P. (1918) *Japan, the Rise of a Modern Power* (London: The Times Ltd).

Potter, Simon J. (2003) *News and the British World: The Emergence of an Imperial Press System* (Oxford: Oxford Historical Monographs; Oxford University Press).

—— (2004) (ed.) *Newspapers and Empire in Ireland and Britain* (Dublin: Four Courts Press).

Powell, John B. (1945) *My Twenty-Five Years in China* (New York: Macmillan).

Press Union, The (1932) *The Sino-Japanese Conflict*: *The Situation Reviewed by American and British Editors in China* (Shanghai: The Press Union). Reprinted in O'Connor, Peter (ed.) (2005) Volume 4, 483–516.

—— (1932) *The Shanghai Incident Misrepresented*: *Shanghai Editors Draw Attention to Incorrect Reports in American Newspapers*, (Shanghai: The Press Union). Reprinted in O'Connor, Peter (ed.) (2005) Volume 4, 517–28.

—— (1932) *The Shanghai Incident* (1932) (Shanghai: The Press Union). Reprinted in O'Connor, Peter (ed.) (2005) Volume 4, 529–75.

Price, Willard (1938) *Japan's New Horizons* (Tokyo: Hokuseido Press).

Rand, Peter (1995) *China Hands*: *The Adventures and Ordeals of the American*

Journalists Who Joined Forces with the Great Chinese Revolution (New York: Simon & Schuster).

Ransome, Arthur (1927) *The Chinese Puzzle* (London: Allen & Unwin).

Read, Donald (1992) *The Power of News: The History of Reuters, 1849–1989* (Oxford: Oxford University Press).

Real, M (1989) *Super Media* (Newbury Park: Sage).

Redman, H. Vere (1935) *Japan in Crisis: An Englishman's Impressions* (London: Allen & Unwin).

Redman, H. Vere and Mogi Sobei (1935) *The Problem of the Far East* (London: Victor Gollancz).

Robbins, Jane (2001) *Tokyo Calling: Japanese Overseas Radio Broadcasting, 1937–1945* (Florence: European Press Academic Publishing).

Robertson Scott, J.W. (1916) *Japan, Great Britain and the World: a letter to my Japanese friends* (Tokyo: Japan Advertiser War Publications).

—— (1947) *Faith and Works in Fleet Street: An Editor's Convictions after Sixty-Five Years' Experience of Journalism with A Little Plain Speaking about Japan and about our Countryside on the basis of some acquaintance with both* (London: Hodder & Stoughton).

Russell, Bertrand (1968) *The Autobiography of Bertrand Russell. Volume II: 1914–1944.* (London: George Allen & Unwin).

Russell, Oland D. (1928) *Achi Kochi: Being the Rambling Observations of an American Newspaperman in Tokyo with Here and There Just a Little Satire* (Tokyo: The Japan Advertiser Press).

Rosholt, Malcolm (1994) *The Press Corps of Old Shanghai, 1920–1938* (Amherst: Palmer Publications).

Said, Edward W. (1991 [1978]) *Orientalism* (Harmondsworth: Penguin).

Sato, Barbara (2003) *The New Japanese Woman: Modernity, Media and Women in Interwar Japan* (Durham, NY: Duke University Press).

Satow, Ernest (1921) *A Diplomat in Japan* (London: Seeley, Service & Co.).

Scherer, James A.B. (1938) *Japan Defies the World* (New York: Bobbs-Merrill).

Schodt, Frederick L. (1994) *America and the Four Japans: Friend, Foe, Model, Mirror* (Berkeley: Stone Bridge Press).

Selle, Earl Albert (1948) *Donald of China* (New York: Harper).

Shimazu Naoko (1998) *Japan, Race and Equality: The Racial Equality Proposal of 1919* (New York and London: Routledge).

Sheba Kimpei (1952) *I Cover Japan* (Tokyo: Tokyo News Service).

Sheean, Vincent (1935) *In Search of History* (London: Hamish Hamilton).

Sherry, Norman (1990) *The Life of Graham Greene: Volume One 1904–1939* (Harmondsworth: Penguin).

Sims, R.L. (2001) *Japanese Political History since the Meiji Renovation, 1868–2000* (London: Hurst).

Smith, Adrian (1996) *The New Statesman: Portrait of a Political Weekly, 1913–1931* (London: Frank Cass).

Snow, Edgar (1944 [1937]) *Red Star Over China* (London: Victor Gollancz).

Soejima Michimasa and Kuo, P.W. (1925) *Oriental Interpretations of the Far Eastern Problem* (Chicago: University of Chicago Press).

Sokolsky, George E. (1932) *The Tinder Box of Asia* (New York: Doubleday, Doran).

Spaulding, Robert M. (1962) *Bibliography of Western-language Dailies and Weeklies in Japan, 1861–1961* (University of Michigan: privately mimeographed).

Steiner, Jesse F. (1944) *Behind the Japanese Mask* (New York: Macmillan).
Steiner, Zara (2005) *The Lights That Failed: European International History, 1919–1933*. (Oxford: Oxford University Press).
Stone, Melville E. (1921) *Fifty Years a Journalist* (Freeport, New York: Books for Libraries Press).
Storry, Richard (1957) *The Double Patriots: A Study in Japanese Nationalism* (Boston: Houghton Mifflin).
—— (1979) *Japan and the Decline of the West in Asia, 1894–1943* (London: Macmillan).
Strother, Edgar E. (1927) *A Bolshevized China – The World's Greatest Peril* (Shanghai: North-China Daily News and Herald Ltd.).
Sues, Ilona Ralf (1944) *Shark's Fins and Millet* (New York: Garden City Publishing).
Sugimoto, Etsu (Inagaki) (1966 [1926]) *A daughter of the Samurai: how a daughter of feudal Japan, living hundreds of years in one generation, became a modern American* (Rutland, VT.: Tuttle).
Thorne, Christopher (1972) *The Limits of Foreign Policy: the West, the League, and the Far Eastern Crisis of 1931–33* (London: Hamish Hamilton).
—— (1978) *Allies of a Kind: The United States, Britain and the war against Japan, 1941–1945* (New York: Oxford University Press).
—— (1985) *The Issue of War: States, Societies, and the Far Eastern Conflict of 1941–1945* (New York: Oxford University Press).
Tiltman, H. Hessell and Etherton, P.T. (1928) *The Pacific: A Forecast* (London: Ernest Benn).
—— (1932) *Manchuria: the cockpit of Asia* (London: Jarrolds).
—— (1934) *Japan: Mistress of the Pacific?* (London: Jarrolds).
Timperley, H.J. (1938) *What War Means: Japanese Terror in China. A Documentary Record* (London: Victor Gollancz).
Tokyo News Service (ed.) (1948) *The Japan Who's Who and Business Directory, 1948 Edition* (Uchisaiwaichō, Tokyo: Tokyo News Service Ltd [Nippon Times Building]).
Tokutomi Iichirō [Sohō] (1922) *Japanese-American Relations* (New York: Macmillan).
Tolischus, Otto D. (1943) *Tokyo Record* (New York: Reynal & Hitchcock).
—— (1945) *Through Japanese Eyes* (New York: Reynal & Hitchcock).
Tong, Hollington K. (ed.) (1944) *China After Seven Years of War* (New York: Macmillan) [copyright Chinese News Service, Inc.].
—— (ed.) (1946) *China Handbook, 1937–45* (Chungking [Chongqing]: Chinese Government Information Office).
—— (1948) *China and the World Press* (Nanking: no publisher named).
—— (1950) *Dateline China* (New York: Rockport Press).
Tsao Wen-yen (ed.) *Chinese Year Book, 1944–45* (Shanghai: China Daily Tribune Publishing Co.).
Tsurumi Yūsuke (1926) *Present Day Japan* (New York: Columbia University Press).
Turnbull, C.M. (1995) *Dateline Singapore: 150 Years of the Straits Times* (Singapore: Singapore Press Holdings).
Utley, Freda (1936) *Japan's Feet of Clay* (London: Faber & Faber).
van de Ven, Hans J. (2003) *War and Nationalism in China, 1925–1945* (London and New York: RoutledgeCurzon).

Vaughn, Miles W. (1937) *Under the Japanese Mask* (London: Lovat Dickson).
—— (1948) *The Emperor of Japan: My Impressions of the Emperor of Japan* (Tokyo: Toppan Insho Kabushiki-gaisha).
Vespa, Amleto (1938) *Secret Agent of Japan: A Handbook to Japanese Imperialism* (London: Victor Gollancz).
Wasserstein, Bernard (1998) *Secret War in Shanghai: Treachery, Subversion and Collaboration in the Second World War* (London: Profile Books).
White, Theodore and Annalee, Jacoby (1946) *Thunder Out of China* (New York: William Sloane Associates).
Wildes, Harry Emerson (1927) *Social Currents in Japan, With Special Reference to the Press* (Chicago: University of Chicago Press).
—— (1934) *Typhoon in Tokyo: The Occupation and its Aftermath* (New York: Macmillan).
Williams, Jean and Harold S. (1996) *West Meets East: the Foreign Experience of Japan* (Volume II) (New South Wales: Halstead Press).
Williams, Walter (ed.) (1922) *The Press Congress of the World in Hawaii* (Columbia, MO: E.W. Stephens).
Wilkinson, Endymion (1983) *Japan Versus the West: Image and Reality* (Harmondsworth: Penguin Books).
Wilson, Sandra (2002) *The Manchurian Crisis and Japanese Society, 1931–33* (New York and London: Routledge).
Woodhead, H.G.W, and Norton, Arnold (1926) *Occidental Interpretations of the Far Eastern Problem* (Norman Wait Harris Memorial Foundation, Chicago: University of Chicago Press).
Woodhead, H.G.W. (1927) *A Selection of Leading Articles* (Tientsin [Tianjin]: Tientsin Press).
—— (1929) *Extraterritoriality in China. The Case against Abolition* (Tientsin [Tianjin]: Tientsin Press).
—— (1920) *Leaves from an Editor's Scrapbook* (Tientsin [Tianjin]: Tientsin Press).
—— (1930) *Current Comment on Events in China* (Shanghai: Shanghai Evening Post and Mercury).
—— (1931) *The Yangtsze and its Problems* (Shanghai: Shanghai Evening Post and Mercury).
—— (1935) *Adventures in Far Eastern Journalism: A record of thirty-three years experience* (Tokyo: Hokuseido Press).
Woodhead, H.G.W., Rea, George B., et al. (December 1931) *Presenting Japan's side of the case* (Shanghai: Japan Association of China). Reprinted in O'Connor Peter (ed.) (2004), Vol. 8.
Woodhouse, Eiko (2004) *The Chinese Hsinhai Revolution: G.E. Morrison and Anglo-Japanese Relations, 1897–1920* (London: RoutledgeCurzon).
Yokoyama Toshio (1987) *Japan in the Victorian Mind: A Study of Stereotyped Images of a Nation 1850–80* (London: Macmillan).
Young, A. Morgan (1928) *Japan Under Taisho Tenno, 1912–1926* (New York: William Morrow).
—— (1938) *Imperial Japan: 1926–1938* (London: Allen & Unwin).
—— (1939) *The Rise of a Pagan State: Japan's Religious Background* (London: Allen & Unwin).
Young, Douglas M. (ed.) (1933) *Kobe – The Premier Port of Japan. Illustrated. Issued in Commemoration of the First Port Festival, November 1933* (Kōbe: Kobe and Osaka Press Ltd.).

Young, James R. (1943) *Behind the Rising Sun* (New York: Doubleday, Doran).

Young, Louise (1998) *Japan's Total Empire*: *Manchuria and the culture of wartime imperialism* (Berkeley: University of California Press).

Yu Maochun (1996) *OSS in China*: *Prelude to Cold War* (New Haven and London: Yale University Press).

Zumoto Motosada (2005 [1932]) *Sino-Japanese Entanglements 1931–32 (A military record)* (Tokyo: Herald Press). Reprinted in O'Connor, Peter (ed.) (2005) Volume 4, 435–82.

2 Articles and speeches in English

Abend, Hallett (1937) 'Ten Years in the Orient'. In Lyons, Eugene (ed.) (1937) *We Cover the World: by Fifteen Foreign Correspondents* (New York: Harcourt, Brace and Company), 153–82.

Angel, Robert, Hall, Ivan P. et al. (September 1994) 'The Mutual Understanding Industry: Three Views on the Shaping of American Perspectives on Japan'. JPRI Working Paper No.2: http://www.jpri.org/publications/workingpapers/wp2.html.

Ariyama Teruo (2004) Introduction to O'Connor, Peter (ed.) (2004), Volume 9.

Baty, Thomas (July 1929) 'Korea, Japan, and Freedom'. In *Asiatic Review*.

Beard, Miriam (August 1924) 'Japan's Lively Press': *New York Times*, 10 August 1924.

Bess, Demaree C. (February 1943): 'Tokyo's Captive Yankee Newspaper': *Saturday Evening Post*, 6 February 1943, 22, 66.

Best, Anthony (1999) '"That Loyal British Subject"?: Arthur Edwardes and Anglo-Japanese Relations, 1932–41'. In Hoare, J. (ed.) *Britain and Japan: Biographical Portraits*, Volume III (Folkestone: Japan Library), 227–39.

Bickers, Robert (1992) 'Changing Shanghai's "Mind": Publicity, Reform and the British in Shanghai, 1927–1931' (London: China Society Occasional Papers).

—— (2000) 'Who were the Shanghai Municipal Police?' In Bickers, Robert and Henriot, Christian (eds.) (2000) *New Frontiers: Imperialism's new communities in East Asia, 1842–1953* (Manchester: Manchester University Press), 170–91.

Byas, Hugh (December 1916) 'Journalism in Japan': *The Times, London*, 16 December 1916.

—— (June 1937) 'Twenty Years After'. In *Contemporary Japan*, 43–51.

—— (1939) 'Land of the Rising Sun'. In *We Saw it Happen: The News Behind the News That's Fit to Print* (New York: Simon and Schuster), 190–319.

Chomsky, Noam (1969) 'The Revolutionary Pacifism of A.J. Muste: On the Backgrounds of the Pacific War'. In Chomsky, Noam, *American Power and the New Mandarins: Historical and Political Essays* (New York: Pantheon Books) 159–220.

Dirlik, Arif (Spring 2004) 'Transnationalism, the Press and the National Imaginary'. In Goodman, Bryna (ed.) *Special Issue: Transnationalism and the China Press, China Review*, Volume 4, (1), 11–26.

Fält, Olavi K. (1988) 'Image of Japan in Foreign Newspapers Published in Japan Before the Meiji Restoration'. In Nish, Ian (ed.) *Contemporary European Writing on Japan: Scholarly Views from Eastern and Western Europe*. (Woodchurch, Kent: Paul Norbury Publications), 22–44.

Fujita Hiroshi (July-September 1991), 'English-Language Periodicals in Japan'. In *Japan Quarterly*, 298–306.

Goodman, Bryna (2004) 'Semi-Colonialism, Transnational Networks and News Flows in Early Republican China'. In Goodman, Bryna (ed.), *Special Issue: Networks of News: Power, Language and Transnational Dimensions of the Chinese Press, 1850–1949, The China Review*, Vol.4, No.1, Spring 2004, 55–88.

Gould, Randall (1937) 'China in Revolt'. In Lyons, Eugene (ed.) (1937) *We Cover the World: by Fifteen Foreign Correspondents* (New York: Harcourt, Brace and Company), 327–50.

Haruhara Akihiko (October-December 1994) 'English-Language Newspapers in Japan'. In *Japan Quarterly*, 474–84.

Hedges, Frank (1937) 'One Must Know Japan'. In Lyons, Eugene (ed.) (1937) *We Cover the World: by Fifteen Foreign Correspondents* (New York: Harcourt, Brace and Company), 303–26.

Hoare, James (1994) 'British Journalists in Meiji Japan'. In Nish, Ian (ed.), *Britain and Japan: Biographical Portraits*. (Folkestone: Japan Library), 21–32.

Hosoya Chihiro (1982) 'Britain and the United States in Japan's View of the International System, 1919–37'. In Nish, Ian (ed.) *Anglo-Japanese Alienation 1919–1952: Papers of the Anglo-Japanese Conference on the History of the Second World War* (Cambridge: Cambridge University Press), 3–26.

Huffman, James (1984) 'Freedom and the Press in Meiji-Taishō Japan'. In *Transactions*, The Asiatic Society of Japan, Third Series, Vol. 19, 137–67.

—— (2004) 'Selected Writings of E. H. House'. Introduction to House selection in O'Connor, Peter (ed.) (2004) Volume 1, 37–44.

Ikei Masaru (1980) 'Ugaki Kazushige's View of China and His China Policy, 1915–1930'. In Iriye, Akira (ed.) (1980) *The Chinese and the Japanese: Essays in Political and Cultural Interactions* (Princeton, NJ: Princeton University Press) 199–219.

Ion, A. Hamish (1996) 'Japan Watchers: 1903–31'. In Howes, John F. (ed.) (1996) *Nitobe Inazō: Japan's Bridge Across the Pacific* (Boulder, San Francisco, Oxford: Westview Press), 79–106.

Itō Takashi and Akita, George (1981) 'The Yamagata-Tokutomi Correspondence: Press and Politics in Meiji-Taisho Japan'. In *Monumenta Nipponica*, Vol. XXXVI, (4), 391–423.

Jonas, F.M. (1934–35) 'Foreign Influence on the early press of Japan'. *Transactions of the Japan Society of London,* 32.

Kakegawa Tomiko (1973) 'The Press and Public Opinion in Japan, 1931–1941'. In Borg, D. and Okamoto S. (eds.) *Pearl Harbor as History: Japanese-American Relations, 1931–41*, (New York: Columbia University Press), 533–49.

—— (March 2001) 'The *Japan Chronicle* and its editors: reflecting Japan to the press and the people, 1891–1940'. In O'Connor, Peter (ed.) (March 2001) *Special Issue: Informal Diplomacy and the Modern Idea of Japan, Japan Forum* 13 (1), 27–40.

Kawakami, K.K. (October 1927) 'The Japanese Press: Journalism in a Small Country with Newspapers of Startlingly Big Circulation'. In *Asia*, Volume XXVII, 795–801, 863.

Kincaid, Zoë (2005 [1938]) 'Women in North China'. In *North China As Seen by Foreigners* (Tokyo: Bunka Jōhō Kyoku) [Cultural Information Bureau]. Reprinted in O'Connor, Peter (ed.) (2005) Volume 8, 255–342.

Koito Chūgo (August 1997) 'A commitment to truth, a dedication to excellence'. JT: August 9, 4.

Lewis, Su Lin (2006) 'Echoes of Cosmopolitanism: Colonial Penang's "Indigenous" English press'. In Kaul, Chandrikar (2006) (ed.) *Media and the British Empire* (London: Palgrave Macmillan), 233–49.

Löwenthal, Rudolf (January 1937) 'Western Literature on Chinese Journalism: A Bibliography'. In *Nankai Social and Economic Quarterly*, Vol. IX, No.4, (Nankai Institute of Economics, Tientsin [Tianjin] China), 1007–66.

Martin, Frank Lee (1918) 'Journalism in Japan'. In *Bulletin, University of Missouri School of Journalism*, XIX, (10).

Matsumura Masayoshi (2001) 'Japan Calling: The origins and early days of the Ministry of Foreign Affairs Information Department in the early 1920s' (trans. Peter O'Connor and Matsumura Masayoshi). In *Transactions, The Asiatic Society of Japan*, series 4, vol. 16, 50–70.

May, Ernest R. (1973) 'U.S. Press Coverage of Japan, 1931–41'. In Borg, D. and Okamoto S. (eds.) *Pearl Harbor as History: Japanese-American Relations, 1931–41* (New York: Columbia University Press), 511–32.

Miwa Kimitada (1984) 'Nitobe Inazō and the Development of Colonial Theories and Practices in Prewar Japan'. In Institute of International Relations, IIR Research Paper A-50 (Tokyo: Sophia University).

Moore, Frederick: (April 1917) 'Why China enters the war: Her Strange Position on the Side of Japan and Her Hopes of Support from England and the United States'. In *Asia*, Vol. XVIII, No 2, 83–90.

Morrison, E (1997) 'Grub Street Inventor: James Harrison's Journalism, Old and New, In Geelong, Melbourne and London'. In Cryle, D. (1997) (ed.) *Disreputable Profession: Journalists and Journalism in Colonial Australia* (Rockhampton: Central Queensland University Press).

'M.Y.M.' (1915) 'Links with the old journalism'. In the *Far East*, 13 March 1915, 675–6.

Nagasaka Keiichi (July 1943) 'New Information Chief Amau'. In *Contemporary Japan*, 838–44.

Neal, Edna Read (1999) 'Takayuki Eguchi'. In Hoare, J.E. (ed.) *Britain & Japan: Biographical Portraits*, Volume III (Folkestone: Japan Library), 240–56.

Nish, Ian (1982) 'Japan in Britain's View of the International System, 1919–37'. In Nish, Ian (ed.), 1982, *Anglo-Japanese Alienation 1919–1952: Papers of the Anglo-Japanese Conference on the History of the Second World War* (Cambridge: CUP), 27–55.

Nish, Ian (1994) '"In One Day Have I lived Many Lives": Frank Ashton-Gwatkin, Novelist and Diplomat, 1889–1976'. In Nish, Ian (ed.), 1994, *Britain & Japan: Biographical Portraits* (Folkestone: Japan Library), 159–75.

Oblas, Peter B. (2003) "On Japan and the Sovereign Ghost-State: Hugh Byas, Journalist-Expert, and the Manchurian Incident". In Journalism History 29:1 (Spring 2003) 32–42.

O'Connor, Peter (March 2001) 'Japan's English-language press during the 1914–18 War: *The Skibbereen Eagle* bites back'. In *Bulletin* (2), March, Faculty of Contemporary Society, Musashino University, Tokyo, Japan, 23–37.

—— (April 2001) (ed.) 'Introduction'. In O'Connor, Peter (ed.) 'Special Issue: Informal Diplomacy and the Modern Idea of Japan'. In *Japan Forum* 13 (1), 1–10.

—— (April 2001) 'Endgame: the English-language Press networks of East Asia in the run-up to war, 1936–41'. In O'Connor, Peter (ed.) 'Special Issue: Informal Diplomacy and the Modern Idea of Japan'. In *Japan Forum* 13 (1), 64–76.

—— (2002) 'The Japan Chronicle and its three editors, 1891–1940. 1891–1940.' In Cortazzi, Hugh (ed.) *Britain & Japan: Biographical Portraits*, Volume IV (Folkestone: Japan Library), 334–47.

—— (2002) 'Timothy or Taid or Taig Conroy or O'Conroy (1883–1935): "The Best Authority, East and West" on anything concerning Japan'. In Cortazzi, Hugh (ed.) *Britain & Japan*: Biographical Portraits Volume IV, (Folkestone: Japan Library), 348–60.

—— (2005) 'John Russell Kennedy, 1861–1928: Spokesman for Japan and Media Entrepreneur'. In Cortazzi, Hugh (ed.) *Britain & Japan: Biographical Portraits*, Volume V, (Folkestone: Global Oriental), 383–98.

—— (June 2006) 'The Ministry's Man: Miles Vaughn Uncovered.' In *No.1 Shinbun* [Foreign Correspondents Club of Japan], Vol. 38, (6), 8–9.

Ogasawara Toshiaki (2007) 'The Japan Times 110 years of History Alongside the Modern History of Japan'. Speech to the Tokyo Rotary Club 5 December 2007 http://www.tokyo-rc.gr.jp/espeech/espeechm_old.htm (July 2009) gives a translation of this speech, which was originally given in Japanese.

Okamoto Shumpei (1980) 'Ishibashi Tanzan and the Twenty-One Demands'. In Iriye Akira (ed.) (1980) *The Chinese and the Japanese: Essays in Political and Cultural Interactions* (Princeton, NJ: Princeton University Press), 183–98.

Pardoe, Jon (1994) 'Malcolm Kennedy and Japan'. In Nish, Ian, (ed.), 1994, *Britain & Japan: Biographical Portraits* (Folkestone: Japan Library), 177–86.

Pardoe, Jon (2002) 'British Writing on Contemporary Japan, 1924–1941: Newspapers, Books, Reviews and Propaganda'. In Gordon Daniels and Chushichi Tsuzuki (eds.) *The History of Anglo-Japanese Relations, 1600–2000*, Volume 5, 281–304.

Potter, Simon J. (May 2003) 'Communication and integration: the press and the British world in Britain and the Dominions c.1876–1922'. In *Journal of Imperial and Commonwealth History*, vol. XXXI, (2) 190–206.

Powell, J.B. (1936) 'The journalistic field'. In American University Club of Shanghai [AUCS] *American University Men in China* (Shanghai: Comacrib Press), 122–148.

Powell, J.B. (October 1946) 'Missouri Authors and Journalists in the Orient'. In *Missouri Historical Review*, Vol. 41, 45–55.

Powell, John William (1980) 'Japan's Germ Warfare: The U.S. Cover-up of a War Crime'. In the *Bulletin of Concerned Asian Scholars*, October/December 1980.

Raper, G.A. (1893) 'Japan'. In *Sell's Dictionary of the World's Press* (London), 148–50.

Robinson, Michael, E. (1984) 'Colonial Publication Policy and the Korean Nationalist Movement'. In Myers, Ramon H., and Peattie, Mark E. (1984) *The Japanese Colonial Empire, 1895–1945* (Princeton, NJ: Princeton University Press), 312–43.

Sawada Setsuzō (1913) 'Newspapers in Japan'. In *Transactions, Japan Society of London* 11, 188–208.

Sissons, D.C.S. (1987) 'James Murdoch (1856–1921): Historian, Teacher and Much Else Besides'. In *Transactions, The Asiatic Society of Japan*, 4 (2): 1–57.

Stein, Guenther (June 1936) 'Through the Eyes of a Japanese Newspaper Reader'. In *Pacific Affairs*, Vol. IX, No.2, 177–90.

South Manchuria Railway: (2005 [1937]) 'China Incident and Japan' (Tokyo: October 1937). In O'Connor, Peter (ed.) (2005) Volume 8, 55–116.

Storry, Richard (1975) 'Japan and Britain: Chance for both nations to create new images'. In *The Times*, 7 May 1975.
—— (1979) 'The English-language presentation of Japan's case during the China Emergency of the late nineteen-thirties'. In Nish, Ian and Dunn, Charles (eds.) *European Studies on Japan* (Tenterden, Kent: Paul Norbury Publications), 47–65.
Thompson, H.A. (1920s) 'Japan and the Foreigner'. In Hugh Byas Papers, Yale University, Reel 5 [original destroyed].
Thomson, James C. Jr. (1973) 'The Role of the Department of State'. In Borg, D. and Okamoto S. (eds.) *Pearl Harbor as History*: *Japanese-American Relations, 1931–41* (New York: Columbia University Press), 81–106.
Valliant, Robert B. (1974) 'The Selling of Japan: Japanese Manipulation of Western Opinion, 1900–1905'. In *Monumenta Nipponica*, Vol. XXIX, (4), 415–38.
Wainright, S.H. (April 1921) 'Missourians in Japan'. In *Missouri Historical Review*, Vol. 15, (3), 468–86.
Wakabayashi, Bob Tadashi (Summer 2000) 'The Nanking 100-Man Killing Contest Debate: War Guilt Amid Fabricated Illusions, 1971–75'. In *Journal of Japanese Studies*, Volume 26 (2), 307–40.
Wakeman, Frederick and Yeh, Wen-hsin (1992) 'Introduction'. In Wakeman, Frederick and Yeh, Wen-hsin (eds.) *Shanghai Sojourners* (Berkeley, Institute of East Asian Studies: University of California Press), 1–14.
Wildes, Harry Emerson (January 1927) 'Press Freedom in Japan'. In *The American Journal of Sociology* 32, 601–14.
Wilkinson, Mark (2000) 'The Shanghai American Community, 1937–1949'. In Robert Bickers and Christian Henriot (eds.) *New Frontiers*: *Imperialism's new communities in East Asia, 1842–1953* (Manchester: Manchester University Press), 231–49.
Yamagoshi Toshihiro (1999) 'The Media Wars: Launching the May Fourth Movement: World War I and the American Propaganda Activities in China, Led by P. S. Reinsch and Carl Crow'. Cited in Goodman 2004: 66, 84n43 as: http://www.geocities.jp/crow1919jp/may_4th/english/may4th_e.html#sec7.
Yeh, Wen-hsin (1992) 'Progressive Journalism and Shanghai's Petty Urbanites: Zou Taofen and the Shenghuo Enterprise, 1926–1945'. In Wakeman, Frederick and Yeh, Wen-hsin (eds.) *Shanghai Sojourners* (Berkeley, Institute of East Asian Studies: University of California Press), 186–238.
Youm, K.H. (1992) 'Japanese Press Policy in Colonial Korea'. In *Journal of Asian History*, 26:2, 140–59.
Young, A. Morgan (August 1913) 'Japanese Press Censorship'. In *Asia* magazine.
—— (December 1937) 'Japan's War on China'. In *Fact*, No.9, (London: Fact), 7–81.
—— (1939) 'Imperial Japan'. In Whyte, Frederick A. (ed.) *World Outlook* (London: Nicholson & Watson), 45–67.
Young, Robert (July-December 1897) 'The Case of the Foreign Residents in Japan'. In *The Nineteenth Century*, Vol. XLII, (London: Sampson, Low, Marston & Stebbing), 305–16.
Yu, Maochun (1999) 'Chinese Codebreakers, 1927–45'. In *Intelligence and National Security* 14, (1) (Spring) 201–13.
Zumoto Motasada (1902) 'Journalism in Japan'. In *Transactions*, Japan Society of London, 6, 108–22.

3 DOCTORAL DISSERTATIONS AND MASTERS THESES IN ENGLISH

Bibber, Joyce Kathleen (1969) *The Chinese Communists as viewed by the American periodical press, 1920–1937*. Ph.D. dissertation: Stanford University.

Chen, Binggang (1984) *John William Powell and China*. M.A. thesis: University of Missouri.

Cheng, Jason [Ju-shien (Zhixing)] (1963) *Walter Williams and China, his influence on Chinese journalism*. M.A. thesis, University of Missouri.

Chong, C. S. (1987) *The Korean problem in Anglo-Japanese relations, 1904–10: Ernest Thomas Bethell and his newspapers, the Daiham Maeil Sinbo and the Korea Daily News*. Ph.D. dissertation: London School of Economics.

Daniels, Jerry (1967) *Journalist Hugh Byas' Views on Japan, 1937–1945: a study of Japanese foreign policy before Pearl Harbor and the role of Japan in the post-war period*. M.A. thesis: University of Tennessee.

Inwood, S. (1971) *The Role of the Press in English Politics during the First World War*. D.Phil. dissertation, Oxford University.

Kasza, Gregory J. (1984) *Political regimes and mass media policy in Imperial Japan, 1868–1945*. Ph.D. dissertation: Yale University.

Lau, Wei-San (1949) *The University of Missouri and journalism of China*. M.A. thesis: University of Missouri, Columbia.

Leong, William Wan Yee (1938) *The effects of censorship and Japanese pressure on the Chinese and foreign press in China*. M.A. thesis: University of Missouri, Columbia.

Pardoe, Jon (1989) *Captain Malcolm Kennedy and Japan, 1917–1945*. Ph.D. dissertation: Sheffield University.

Purdy, Roger W. (1987) *The Ears and Voice of the Nation: The Dōmei News Agency and Japan's News Network, 1936–1945*. Ph.D. dissertation: University of California at Santa Barbara.

Rozanski, Mordechai (1974) *The Role of American Journalists in Chinese-American Relations, 1900–1925*. Ph.D. dissertation: Pennsylvania University.

Shewmaker, Kenneth Earl (1966) *Persuading Encounter: American Reporters and Chinese Communists, 1927–1945*. Ph.D. dissertation: Northwestern University.

T'ang, The-Ch'en (1933) *The American press and the Manchurian question: a quantitative study*. M.A. thesis: University of Missouri, Columbia.

Yin, Sherman Kuang-jung (Yin, Xueman) (1962) *The China Weekly Review*. M.A. thesis: University of Missouri.

Note: A number of MA theses relevant to the study of the English-language press of East Asia were written by students of Yanjing (Yenching) University. These were rescued from Yanjing University Library when hostilities broke out between Japanese and Chinese forces in 1937, but subsequently lost. As they have neither been used in this book nor yet found, I have listed them in *Appendices* (3) below.

D SECONDARY WORKS IN JAPANESE

Books and pamphlets in Japanese

Ebihara Hachirō (1932) *Nihon ni okeru gaiji no shinbun zasshi* (History of Foreign Newspapers and Magazines in Japan) (Tōkyō: Hankyōdō).

Ebihara Hachirō (1934) *Nihon ōji shinbun zasshishi* (History of Western-Language Newspapers and Magazines in Japan) (Tokyo: Taiseidō).

Haruhara Akihiko (1985) *Nihon shinbun tsūshi, 1861-nen–1971-nen* (History of the Japanese press, 1861–1973) (Tokyo: Shinsensha).

Hasegawa Shinichi (1966) *Jyapan Taimuzu monogatari: bunkyū gan'nen kara gendai made / The Japan Times Story: from the first year until the present* [bilingual] (Tokyo: The Japan Times).

Hokushigun hōdōbu (December 1939) *Hokushigun hōdō senden gaiyō* (North China Army, Information Department: Guidelines on propaganda for the Information Department, North China Army).

Iwanaga Yūkichi Denki Henshū-kai (1941) (eds.) *Iwanaga Yūkichi-kun* (Iwanaga Yūkichi) (Tokyo: Toppan Insho Kabushiki-gaisha).

Manshūkoku Tsūshinsha (1942) *Kokotsū jū nen shi* (Kokotsū's Ten-year History) (Hsinking: Manshūkoku Tsūshinsha).

Mitarai Tatsuo (1952) *Shinbun taiheiki* (Newspaper chronicle) (Tokyo: Masu Shobō)

Nakashita Masaharu (1996) *Shinbun no miru Nit-Chū kankei shi: Chūgoku no Nihonjin keiei shi* (Looking at the history of Sino-Japanese relations through newspapers: Japanese-run newspapers in China) (Tokyo: Kyūban shuppan).

Okamura Shigenori (1941) *Jyapan Taimuzu shoshi / A Short History of the Japan Times* (Tokyo: Jyapan Taimuzu-sha) [bilingual].

Rikugunshō (October 1934) *Kokubō no hongi to sono kyōka no teishō* (The Essence of National Defence and Proposals to Strengthen It).

Tsūshinsha-shi Kankōkai (ed.) (1958) *Tsūshinsha-shi* (History of news agencies). (Tokyo: Taihei Insatsusha).

Uchimura Kanzō (1981–84) *Uchimura Kanzō Zenshū* (Collected writings of Uchimura Kanzō) (Tokyo: Iwanami).

Uchikawa Yoshimi (1967) *Shinbunshi wa* (On the history of newspapers) (Tokyo: Shakai Shisōsha).

2 Articles in Japanese

Ibuki Yoshitaka (1965) 'Shinbun' (Newspapers). In *Kōbe-shishi* (History of the City of Kōbe), Vol.3, 801–824 (Kōbe: Kōbeshi).

Iwamura Masashi '"Waga Tōsō' Nihongo ban no kenkyū – Hitura [Hitler] no "Dai nichi hen ken" mondai wo chūshin ni.' ['My struggle/Mein Kampf': Research on the Japanese version, with particular reference to Hitler's anti-Japanese prejudice]. In *Mediashi kenkyū* [Media History], 16, April 2004, 53–73.

Iwanaga Yūkichi (November 1934) 'Kaku kuni seifu yōrosha e no chūmon' (Cooperation is indispensable in the exchange of news). In *Shinbun oyobi shinbun kisha* (Newspapers and newspaper correspondents), Volume 15, no.197, 22–34. Special Japanese-English issue; English version 23–5.

Kakegawa Tomiko (1983) 'Japan Keronikeru to Robaato Yangu' (The Japan Chronicle and Robert Young). In *Uchimura Kanzō Zenshū: Geppō* (Collected writings of Uchimura Kanzō: Notes) 32: 6–9 (Tokyo: Iwanami).

Maruyama Tsurukichi (1922) 'Chōsen chian no genjō oyobi shōrai' (Public Peace and Order in Korea, Present and Future) (Keijō: Chōsen Sōtofuku, Jimukan, 1922), 4–5.

Matsumura Masayoshi (1971) 'Gaimushō Jōhōbu no sōsetsu to Ijūin shōdai buchō' (The foundation of the Foreign Office Information Bureau and its first head, Ijūin [Hikokichi]).' In *Kokusai hō gaikō zasshi*, vol.70, no.2, Tokyo.

—— (2002) 'Washington Kaigi to Nihon no kōhō gaikō' (The Washington Conference and Japan's public diplomacy'). In *Gaimushō Chōsa Geppō*, 2002, (1), 47–74.

O'Connor, Peter (March 2005) 'Mejia no rekishi ni okeru kuni ni imeji' (Media history and national images). In *Gendai Shakai no Ron Ten*, Gendai Shakai Gakubu, (Faculty of Contemporary Society), Spring, Musashino University, Tokyo, 126–41.

—— (October 2008) 'Katarare nakatta rekishi (1) aru eijishi no 111 shunen' (untold history (1) of an English-language [newspaper] in its 111th year). In *Issatsu no Hon*, Asahi Shinbunsha, Tokyo, 3–7.

—— (November 2008) 'Katarare nakatta rekishi (2) futatsu no shasetsu, okina eikyō' (untold history (2) two highly influential editorials). In *Issatsu no Hon*, Asahi Shinbunsha, Tokyo, 23–7.

Appendices

APPENDIX 1: THE 'MISSOURI MAFIA'

A. Graduates of the School of Journalism, University of Missouri, working in journalism or involved in the press in East Asia, with graduation year or period of study, 1910–42[1] (Total: 68)

1. Graduates in Japan and China (41: 20 Americans [inc.1 Japanese American]; 21 Chinese. Women: 3 US, 2 China)

John B. Powell 1910
Hollington K. Tong 1911
Hin Wong 1912
Margaret Powell Woods 1916
Maurice E. Votaw 1919
Irene Fisher 1919
Chen Chung 1920
Horace Felton 1920
Don D. Patterson 1920
Norman Ulbright 1920
Louise Wilson 1920
Morris James Harris 1921
Victor J. Keen 1922
Henry Misselwitz 1922
John Rippey Morris 1922
P.Y. Chien 1923
Kan Lee 1923
Y.P. Wang 1923
Chin-Jen Chen 1924
Mrs Liang S. Hsu (Eva C. Chang) 1924
Yen Chih Jao 1924

Thomas Ming-heng Chao 1925[2]
Edgar Snow 1925–26
Edgar C. Tang 1927
Robert Y. Horiguchi 1931[3]
David C.H. Lu 1932
James D. White 1932
Teh-ch'en, Tang 1933
Hsin-Yeh Ma 1934
Wei Ma 1934
Francis W. Gapp 1935
James Shen 1935
Kyatang Woo 1935
Mrs Kyatang Woo (Betty L. Hart) 1935
Nan-Wei Cheng 1937
Karl Espilund 1938
Heng-Yu Li 1938
John W. Powell 1940–42
Hugh Crumpler 1941
David Mun-Sen Leong 1942
Ju-tung Lee 1943

2. Graduates in Japan only (19: 15 Americans, 4 Japanese)

Vaughn Bryant 1911
Henry Kinyon 1912
Joseph Glenn Babb 1915
Ralph Turner 1916
Ben Kline 1916
Frank King 1917, JA, then *Japan* magazine
Edgar Rheinhardt Egger 1918

Frank H. Hedges 1919
John Casey 1920
Duke N. Parry 1920
James H. McClain 1921
Alfonso Johnson 1922
Erwin F. McEwen 1923
F.M. Flynn 1924
Tarawa Haruji 1926

Edgar A. McLaughlin 1931   Matsuda Marita 1936
Yamasaki Tōsuke 1934   Iwateki Ichiro 1937

3. Graduates in India (1: US)

Stewart Hensley 1934

4. Graduates in the Philippines (7: 1 US; 6 Filipino)
    Roy Coleman Bennett 1914
    Vincent Roseno Marfari 1921
    Eliseo Quirino 1921
    Richard O. Reyes 1924
    Jesus Zafra Vanelzuela 1925
    Resuvaecion (Rex) D. Drilon 1937
    Alexander Liosnoff 1942

B. Other Missourians in East Asia (Total: 12)

1. Missouri School of Journalism Faculty working and teaching in East Asia (2)

Frank L. Martin *Japan Advertiser*, *Trans-Pacific*, Yenching University, Peking
Vernon Nash, Yenching University, Peking

2. Missouri graduates in China (not School of Journalism) (3)

Thomas Franklin Fairfax Millard
Oscar E. Riley, BSc. 1911, BA 1912: *Japan Advertiser* then Sec. Japan Society of New York
Harry Ridings BSc. 1912: Business Manager, *Japan Advertiser*

3. Journalists from the State of Missouri who worked in Japan and China (3)

Carl Crow (b. Farmington, Missouri)
Emily Hahn (Mrs Charles Boxer)
Agnes Smedley (b. St. Joseph, Miss.)
Miles W. Vaughn (1891–1949), b. Nebraska, Missouri (grad. Univ. Kansas) United Press.

4. Missourians working in the law in China (4)

Judge Lebbius Wilfley, b. St. Louis, Miss., U.S. judge appointed to Congress of the United States Court for China, Shanghai (appointed 1908)
Arthur Basset, Missouri graduate, 1st US District Attorney at Shanghai, then businessman (British American Tobacco)
Nelson Lurton, US Court Commissioner in Shanghai
Stewart R. Price. b. Gallatin, Miss. (Interned, repatriated on S.S. Gripsholm)

C. American Associations and Clubs in China and Japan[4] (Total: 20)

1. In China (17)

American Association of China (1926)
American Association of North China (1915)
American Association of South China (1921)
American Association of Tientsin (1923)
American Club of Shanghai (1917)
American College Club of Harbin (1922)
American University Club of Shanghai (1917)
American University Club of Swatow (1922)
Anglo-American Association (1918)
Association of Chinese and American Engineers (1921)
Chinese Anglo-American Friendship Association (1913)
Chinese Ku Klux Klan (1924) (Organized by Chinese Americans)
Chinese Student Club of Foochow (1919) (Chinese students returned from US and Europe)
Chinese-American Association (1913); of Canton (1917)
Pacific Conference Association (1921)
Pan-Pacific Association (1920)
Union Club of Shanghai (1919) (Membership of US, British and Chinese businessmen)

2. In Japan (3)

American Club of Tokyo
Japan Alumni Association of the University of Missouri[5]
Missouri Society of Japan

APPENDIX 2

Unpublished and lost Yenching University Master's Theses on the foreign press in China, the reporting of China in Western newspapers, and Chinese propaganda[6]

Chao, En Yuan [趙恩源], 'Journalism in China' (Peking 1930)
Fisher, Francis McCracken, 'Instances of the effects of a controlled news policy in the *Peiping Chronicle* and an inquiry into its cause' (Peking 1933)
Li, Heng Yü [李横宇], 'Chinese news in *The Times*, London, 1933' (Peking 1935)
Li, Hsiu Shih [黎秀石], 'Chinese news in the *New York Times* during an abnormal period: as an illustration of the indispensability of international publicity for China' (Peking 1935)
Lu, Chi Hsin [盧棋新], 'Study of the types of new writing in the English and Chinese newspapers' (Peking 1929)
Shen, Chien Hung [沈劍虹], 'An international publicity programme for China' (Peking 1932)
Sung, Te Ho [宋德和], 'English language journals of opinion in China' (Peking 1934)
T'ang, Pei Chen [湯佩珍], 'The history of the foreign press in Peiping and Tientsin' (Peking 1933).

APPENDIX 3: THE YOUNGS OF KŌBE

This entry is an attempt to disentangle the identities of those who held the surname Young and were active in journalism and related fields in Kōbe during the period under review. Most of the information on Annie and Ethel came to me from Sue Larkin, Robert Young's great-granddaughter.

Robert Young (1858–1922), founder of the *Japan Chronicle*.

Annie Young (1872–1941), born Annie Crockett Miller, in Yokohama. Married Robert Young in 1889 in Kōbe, then moved to San Francisco after Robert Young's death and in 1926 married Thomas Harloe, who died in 1935. Annie lived in Kōbe and San Francisco between 1931 and August 1939, when she returned to San Francisco for good. She was therefore in Kōbe in 1938 when the *Chronicle* began taking a subsidy from the *Gaimushō*.

Robert and Annie Young had three sons and a daughter:

Arthur Conway Young, b. Kōbe 1891; died on the Somme, August 1917.

Douglas George Young, b. Kōbe August 1893, d. in May 1938 in the International Hospital, Kōbe. Douglas served in the Air Force in WW1. Managing Director of the *Japan Chronicle* from 1926 until his early death, aggravated by heavy drinking.

Eric Andrew Young, the youngest son, became Managing Director of the *Chronicle* on his father's death in 1922. In 1926, possibly to escape the weight of this responsibility, Eric committed suicide by leaping overboard from an ocean liner.

Ethel Margaret Young, b. Kōbe in 1903, married a merchant seaman, Reginald Stewart-Scott, on 12 March, 1921, in Sussex. They had two children, June, b.1922 and Reginald b.1924. In 1925 the family moved to Tianjin when Reginald was offered a job there. Ethel and Reginald were divorced by order of HM Supreme Court in Shanghai in 1934. Ethel was interned in the Santo Tomas internment camp in Manila from 1942 to 1945. After the war Ethel returned to Kōbe to sell her father's property. She was repatriated to the UK from Ōsaka in 1969 and died in Launceston, Cornwall in April 1977.

Douglas M. Young, not to be confused with Robert Young's second son, Douglas G. Young, was a cousin of Robert Young. He came to Japan in 1902 and joined the *Japan Chronicle*, and reported the Russo-Japanese War of 1904–5 for the *Chronicle* and the *Daily Express*, getting a world scoop for both papers on the fall of Port Arthur. In July 1906, he left the *Chronicle* to found the Far Eastern Advertising Agency (*Tōyō Kōkoku*), which specialized in 'import advertising': that is, advertising foreign goods and agencies, mostly in the English-language newspapers. Douglas married a Japanese woman and the couple adopted a Japanese girl whom they named Kathleen. All three left Japan for good in September 1941.

Arthur Morgan Young (1874–1942) was not related to Robert Young. In 1922, after serving c.1910–22 as deputy editor of the *Chronicle*, he succeeded Robert

Young as editor, 1922–36. In 1936 he was banned from re-entering Japan. He stayed on in London then moved to Hollow Way, Cowley, Oxford, where he died in January 1942. His wife May Louisa died in November 1970. A.M. and May Young had two children, Ernest Morgan and Lucy. Ernest Young stayed on in business in Kōbe then returned to the UK in the 1970s.

APPENDIX 4: FOREIGN CORRESPONDENTS IN CHONQING, 1942[7]

Date of Registration	Name	Newspaper or News Agency
January	George K. T. Wang	United Press
	Robert P. Martin	United Press
	W. MacDougal	United Press
	F.M. Fisher	United Press
	W. Burchett	London Daily Express
	Harrison Forman	London Times and New York Times
	I. Nomerotsky	Tass News Agency
	M.F. Yakshamin	Tass News Agency
	A.H. Monin	Tass News Agency
	Charles Fenn	Friday Magazine
	Jack Belden	International News Service
	James L. Stewart	Time
	Guenther Stein	Manchester Guardian
	Margit Stein	London News Chronicle
	Spencer Moosa	Associated Press
	G.M. MacDonald	London Times
	Roderick K. MacDonald	Sydney Morning Herald
	Peter Kiang	International News Service
	Thomas Chao	Reuters
	L.C. Smith	Reuters
	Betty Graham	London Daily Mail and International News Service
	Francis Lee	International News Service
February	Eve Curie	New York Herald Tribune
March	Andre Guibut	France Indépendent
	Raymond Clapper	American News Columnist
April	Douglas Wilkie	Sydney Sun
	A. Wagg	London Allied Newspapers
	Mark Tannian	Field Afar, New York
	Water Bosshard	Zurich Zeitung
	R. Barnett	Institute of Pacific Relations
	F. Karaka	Bombay Chronicle
May	Arthur Moore	Statesman, Calcutta

Date of Registration	Name	Newspaper or News Agency
June	Edgar Snow G. Waterfield Henry Bough W. McGaffin David An Chang Han-Fu	London Daily Mail Reuters Reuters Associated Press Korean National Herald Supress, Moscow
July	Norman Soong I. Epstein A.W. Tozer	Overseas News Agency Allied Labour News 20th Center Fox Movie Co.
September	Karl J. Eskelund J. Fischbacher J.R. O'Sullivan Theodore White M. Subhan	United Press France Indépendent Associated Press Time and Life Indian Journalist
October	E.O. Hauser N.E. Protsenko	American Reader's Digest Tass News Agency
November	A.T. Steele Martin Moore S. Tomara P. Grover H. Matthews	Chicago Daily News London Daily Telegraph New York Herald Tribune Associated Press New York Times
December	S. Speight Brooks Atkinson F. Cancellare H.S. 'Newsreel' Wang	Sydney Morning Herald New York Times A.C.M.E. United News

APPENDIX 5: EXCHANGE RATES

Yen-Dollar, 1874–1940[8]

Year	Dollars per 100 Yen
1874	101.58
1882	91.31
1891	78.01
1892	69.84
1893	62.12
1894	50.79
1897	49.31
1914	49.34

Year	Dollars per 100 Yen
1918	51.47
1920	49.78
1923	48.94
1924	42.10
1925	40.93
1926	46.08
1927	47.38
1929	46.13
1930	49.38
1931	48.37
1932	28.10
1933	25.23
1934	29.51
1938	28.50
1939	25.98
1940	23.44

Official Sterling – US Dollar – Chinese Dollar rates[9]

	£1.00	US$1.00
1926	Ch.$9.00	Ch.$2.00
1930	Ch.$17.20	Ch.$3.40
1935	Ch.$13.00	Ch.$2.70
1937	Ch.$16.40	Ch.$3.40
1940	Ch.$71.00	Ch.$18.00
1941	$1.00 = 4/3d[10]	

APPENDIX 6: JAPAN CORRESPONDENTS
OF *THE TIMES*, LONDON, 1868~2009[11]

Yokohama
Major-General Henry Spencer Palmer 1885–1892
N.P. Kingdon 1894–1895

Tokyo
Captain Frank Brinkley 1897–1912
Charles Rodolph Hargrove 1912–1914
John N. Penlington 1914–1923
Ronald Lewis Carton 1923–1924
Lt. Colonel T. Orde Lees, 1924–1926
Hugh Fulton Byas 1926–1941
Otto David Tolischus [also *New York Times*] 1941
Frank Hawley 1946–1952
Eric Valentine Blakeney Britter 1952–1954
Charles H. Hargrove 1954–1960
Ronald Douglas Hildebrand Preston 1960–1963
John Alexander White 1963–1964
Fred Albert Emery 1964–1967
Henry Johnstone Morland Scott Stokes 1967–1969
Michael Hornsby 1969–1972
Peter Bruce Hazelhurst 1972–1982
Richard Hanson [stringer] 1982–1984
David William Watts 1984–1992
Joanna Pitman 1992–1994
Gwen Robinson 1994–1996
Robert Whymant 1996–2002 [d.2002]
Richard Lloyd Parry [Asia Editor] 2002~
Leo Lewis [Business Editor] 2003~

APPENDIX 7: THE ENGLISH-LANGUAGE PRESS OF JAPAN, 1861–1956

The English-language press of Japan, 1861–1956: adapted from J.E. Hoare (1994: 181-8)						
Name	Place	Dates	Frequency	Owner, manager, publisher	Editor	Notes
1. *Nagasaki Shipping* List & Advertiser	Nag.	June-Oct., 1861	B	A.W. Hansard	Same	Hansard moved to Yokohama and started the *Japan Herald*.
2. *Japan Herald**	Yok.	1861–1914	1861–67 B, then D; S	1861-64 A. W. Hansard 1864-67 Hansard and J.R. Black 1867-70 A. T. Watkins and M.E. Hansard 1870–1902 J.H. Brooke 1902–1904 Brooke's sons 1905–1914 *Deutsche Japan Post*	Same 1870–88 Brooke 1888–93 J.F. Pinn 1893–1902 Brooke 1902 E. Harrison 1905–1912 T. Satchell	Pinn leased the *Herald* from Brooke. After 1902 it was run as an English-language version of the *Deutsche Japan Post*.
3. *Japan Express*	Yok.	1862	W	R. Schoyer	Same	Schoyer was an American.
4. *Japan Commercial News*	Yok.	1863–65		F. Da Roza	Same	Plant and goodwill sold to *Japan Times* consortium.

Name	Place	Dates	Frequency	Owner, manager, publisher	Editor	Notes
5. *Japan Times** (daily advertising sheet known as *Japan Daily Advertiser*)	Yok.	1885–70	D W M	Consortium. Known members: C. Rickerby, N.P. Kingdon, B. Seare	C. Rickerby	Plant and goodwill sold in 1870 to *Japan Mail* consortium.
6. *Japan Gazette*	Yok.	1867–1923		1867–74 J.R. Black; 1874–76 J.R. Anglin and C.D. Moss; 1877–86 J.R. Anglin and W.H. Talbot; 1886–91 'Yokohama Publishing Co.'; 1885 'Japan Gazette Publishing Co.'	Same; ? A.H. Cole; 1877(?)–79 W.H. Talbot; 1880–? Call; 1887–88 W.T. Watt; 1889 E.P. Nuttall; 1891 W. Dening; 1891–93 Mrs A. Vaughan Smith; 1884 H. Tennant; 1898? Norman; 1899 R. Hay; 1901 E.R. Thomas; 1901–08 L.D. Adam	Offices and plant were destroyed in the 1923 earthquake.

Table title: The English-language press of Japan, 1861–1956: adapted from J.E. Hoare (1994: 181–8)

The English-language press of Japan, 1861–1956; adapted from J.E. Hoare (1994: 181–8)

Name	Place	Dates	Frequency	Owner, manager, publisher	Editor	Notes
7. *Hiogo News** (Daily edition *Hiogo Shipping List* 1869–1880)	Kōbe	1868–98	W 1869 B 1880 D; S	1868 F. Braga 1869 J.E. Wainwright 1869–88 F. Walsh & Co. 1888 J. Creogh 1894 'Hyogo Pub. Co.'	1868 F. Mayer 1878 H. Liddell 1881 J. Creogh 1890 J. Saunders 1891 H. Tennant 1894–98 P. Skinner 1898 B.A. Hale	Plant destroyed by fire in 1898. Title and goodwill sold to *Kobe Chronicle* and most staff taken on by R. Young there.
8. *Hiogo and Osaka Herald*	Kōbe	1868–75	W	1868–69 A.T. Watkins 1869–75 F.M. Cruchley	1868–69 A.T. Watkins 1869–75 F.M. Cruchley	
9. *Nagasaki Times & Shipping List*	Nag.	1868–69	W	F. Walsh	F. Walsh	The *Shipping List* came out four times a week.
10. *Nagasaki Shipping List*	Nag.	1869–70	B	Nagasaki Printing Office (owned by C. Sutton)		

The English-language press of Japan, 1861–1956: adapted from J.E. Hoare (1994: 181–8)						
Name	**Place**	**Dates**	**Frequency**	**Owner, manager, publisher**	**Editor**	**Notes**
11. *Japan Mail*** Daily paper *Japan Daily Advertiser* until 1879; then *Japan Daily Mail* Title July 1878 and July 1879: *Japan Mail*, with which is incorporated the *Japan Times*.	Yok. From 1912 Tok.	1870–1917	D W 1869 B 1880 D; S	1870–71 H.N. Lay, W.G. Howell, and W. Cargill 1871–77 Howell 1877–1878 G.C. Pearson 1878 Fischer & Pitman 1878 Fischer 1881–1912 F. Brinkley 1912–14 Brinkley's estate; acquired by John Russell Kennedy 1914–17 Half share owned by *Kokusai Tsūshinsha* 1918 amalgamated with *Japan Times* as *Japan Times & Mail* until 1940	1870–77 W.G. Howell 1877 G.C. Pearson 1878 F.V. Dickens 1878 C. Rickerby 1879 J. Bulgin 1879–80 H. Gribble 1880? Cole 1880 J. Creogh 1881–1912 F. Brinkley 1912 T. Satchell 1913 J.M. Barnard	For much of its history the *Mail* was associated with the Japanese government. In 1918 the *Mail* was amalgamated with the *Japan Times*. **The entire *Japan Weekly Mail*, 1877–1917 is being reprinted (see below).
12. *Nagasaki Express**	Nag.	1870–74	W	1870–72 F. Braga and A.A. Foncea 1872–74 Braga		Bought by C. Sutton and John Clark and renamed *Rising Sun and Nagasaki Express* (q.v.).
13. *Nagasaki Gazette*	Nag.	1872(?)–73	W	A. Loueiro	T. Staiding	A *Shipping List* was issued four times a week.

Name	Place	Dates	Frequency	Owner, manager, publisher	Editor	Notes
14. *Tokei Journal***	Tok.	1874–75	W			
15. *Yokohama Daily Bulletin*	Yok.	May–Nov., 1874	D	1870–72 F. Braga and A.A. Foncea 1872–74 Braga		Probably owned by the same group as *Tokei Journal* above.
16. *Cosmopolitan Press*	Nag.	1876–8		T.F. Kenneally	T.F. Kenneally	
17. *Niphon Standard*	Kōbe	1876–77				
18. *Merkur*	Yok.	1876	B	Probably Suter	Suter	
19. *Rising Sun and Nagasaki Express* * *Daily Shipping List* to 1897 *Nagasaki Press from 1897*	Nag.	1873–74(?) to 1920s	W D	1873–74 C. Sutton and J. Clark 1874–92 C. Sutton 1892–96 C.A. Norman 1896–97 administered by British Consul, Nagasaki	1873–74 J. Clark 1874–96 C.A. Norman 1895 W. Fegan 1896 E. Morphy 1898–1902? Palmer 1904 E.R. Parson	1879 Clark left for Shanghai to found and edit *Shanghai Mercury*.

The English-language press of Japan, 1861–1956: adapted from J.E. Hoare (1994: 181–8)

The English-language press of Japan, 1861–1956: adapted from J.E. Hoare (1994: 181–8)						
Name	**Place**	**Dates**	**Frequency**	**Owner, manager, publisher**	**Editor**	**Notes**
20. *Tokio Times**	Tok.	1877–80	W	E.H. House	E.H. House	Subsidized by Japanese govt.
21. *Japan Times**	Yok.	Jan.–July, 1878	W	C. Rickerby	Same	Sold to the *Japan Mail*.
22. *Kiu Siu Times*	Nag.	Jan.–Feb, 1878				
23. *Kobe Advertiser*	Kōbe	1878–79		F. Cruchley	Same	
24. *Kobe Shipping List*	Kōbe	1882				
25. *Anglo-Japanese Review**	Tok.	1885–86	W	*Mainichi Shimbun*	F.W. Eastlake	
26. *Tokyo Independent**	Tok.	1886	W	F.W. Eastlake	Same	Carried items in *Romanji*, i.e. Japanese written with Roman letters.

The English-language press of Japan, 1861–1956: adapted from J.E. Hoare (1994: 181–8)						
Name	Place	Dates	Frequency	Owner, manager, publisher	Editor	Notes
27. *Kobe Herald* *Kobe Herald and Osaka Gazette*	Kōbe	1886–1939?	D (annual by 1930s)	1886–1926 Alfred W. Curtis 1926–1939(?) Douglas M. Young	1886–1917 Curtis 1917–19 A.J.S. Willes 1919–26 Curtis 1926–36 Morgan Young or Douglas M. Young 1936–39 Douglas M. Young	Willes charged with *lèse majesté* 1918, fled to *North China Standard*. Amalg. w. (unheard of) *Osaka Gazette* 1934; still going 1936.[12] By late 1930s one annual issue published to keep title rights.
28. *Japan Review and Daily Advertiser*	Kōbe	1889	D	A.W. Quinton	Same	
29. *Tokyo Mail*	Tok.	1889–90	Thrice weekly	Published by the *Japan Mail*		

The English-language press of Japan, 1861–1956: adapted from J.E. Hoare (1994: 181-8)						
Name	**Place**	**Dates**	**Frequency**	**Owner, manager, publisher**	**Editor**	**Notes**
30. *Japan Advertiser* 1908 *Japan Advertiser Weekly* became *Trans-Pacific 1919* *Japan Times Weekly & Trans-Pacific* Nov 1940-June 1942	Yok. 1908 Tok. 1913	1890–1940	D W	1890–1904 R. Meiklejohn 1904 A.M. Knapp 1904–8 consortium of Yokohama business people and J.R. Kennedy 1908-October 1940 B.W. Fleisher but note financial rescues of 1923 and 1931 and indebtedness to US-Japan interests. 1940 Nov.-1943 Jan. *Japan Times & Advertiser* (FM)	1890 1891 R. Hay 1898 G.A. Adam 1891–92 Knapp 1902–4, 1906 E. Hamilton B.W. Fleisher 1908–10 John N. Penlington 1910–12 Hugh Byas 1914–16 Gregory Mason 1916–18 Hugh Byas 1918–22, 1926–30 Frank Hedges 1923–26 Wilfrid Fleisher 1930–1940	1 Uchiyamashita-chō 1-chome, Kojimachi-ku. 1890–91 an advertising sheet; newspaper thereafter. Oct 1940 bought by *Japan Times* at behest of FM. **Walter Williams ed. *T-P* 1918–19. Henry Kinyon ed. 1920-?
31. *Japan Echo**	Tok.	1890–91	F	L. Salabelle	J. Murdoch	
32. *Tokyo Spectator**	Tok.	1891–92		F.W. Eastlake	Same	

				The English-language press of Japan, 1861–1956: adapted from J.E. Hoare (1994: 181–8)	
Name	**Place**	**Dates**	**Frequency**	**Owner, manager, publisher**	**Editor**	**Notes**
33. *Kobe Chronicle** 1902–1942 *Japan Chronicle*	Kōbe	1891–1942	D W	1891–1921 Robert Young 1922 Family trust headed by Robert Young's widow, Annie Young, (remarried 1925 - Annie Harloe); managed by Eric Young (suicide 1926) 1926–37 managed by Douglas Young 1937 managed by Samuel Foley 1940 December sold to *Japan Times & Advertiser*	1891–1921 R. Young (1894–95 Lafcadio Hearn co-editor) 1922–36 A.M. Young 1936–40 E.A. Kennard 1940–41 Reggie Price (ed. adviser) 1942 Feb. Toshi Gō (as part of *JT&A*)	Received Japanese government assistance in opposing unequal treaties. See Appendix 4 for notes on the Youngs of Kōbe. 1938-Dec 1940 subsidized by FM. Dec 1940 Bought by *Japan Times* at behest of FM.
34. *Eastern World**	Yok.	1892–1908	W	F. Schroeder	Same	Occasional articles in German.

The English-language press of Japan, 1861–1956: adapted from J.E. Hoare (1994: 181–8)						
Name	**Place**	**Dates**	**Frequency**	**Owner, manager, publisher**	**Editor**	**Notes**
35. *Japan Times** 36. *Japan Times and Mail 1918–40* *Japan Times & Advertiser Nov. 1940–Feb 1942* *Japan Times & Advertiser Incorporating The Japan Chronicle and the Japan Mail Jan 1942–Dec 30 1942* *Nippon Times Jan 1 1943–July 1956*	Tok.	1897 to date	D W	Presidents 1897–1911 Yamada Sueji 1911–14 Zumoto Motosada 1914 Japan Times Kabushikakaisha 1914–16 John Russell Kennedy 1916–18 Miyabara Jirō 1918–21 John Russell Kennedy 1921–24 Hattori Bunshiro 1919–33 Sheba Sometarō Vice-President/General Manager 1924–25 Tanaka Tōkichi 1925–31 Itō Yonejirō 1931–3 Date Genichirō 1933–40 Ashida Hitoshi 1940–4? Toshi Gō 1944–5 Matsumoto Tadao 1945–56 Togasaki Kiyoshi 1956 Fukushima Shintaro	1897–1911 Zumoto Motosada 1911–14 Takahashi Kazutomo 1914–18? Baba Tsunego 1918–21 John Russell Kennedy 1922–32 Sheba Sometarō 1933–40 Ashida Hitoshi (Nitobe Yoshio registered editor in 1933) 1940–45 Toshi Gō 1945–56 Togasaki Kiyoshi	Nov. 1924: 22 2-chome Uchisaiwai-chō. October 1941 moves into Japan Advertiser Bldg. at 1 Uchiyamashita-chō 1-chome, Kojimachi-ku. 1950: 1 Uchisaiwai-chō 1-chome, Chiyoda-ku. Japanese-owned and edited. Historically regarded as close to the Japanese government, particularly the FM

The English-language press of Japan, 1861–1956: adapted from J.E. Hoare (1994: 181–8)						
Name	**Place**	**Dates**	**Frequency**	**Owner, manager, publisher**	**Editor**	**Notes**
37. *Kobe Daily News*	Kobe	1899–1902	D	A. Rozario		
38. *The Far East*	Tok.	1912–23	F.	J.N. Penlington	J.N. Penlington	Penlington was also *The Times* (London) correspondent in Tokyo 1912–1923. *FE* subsidized by FM until Penlington lost *Times* corresp. in 1923. Plant destroyed in 1923 earthquake
39. *The New East*	Tok.	1916–18	F.	Fronted by John Robertson-Scott; financed John Sale, of Sale & Lazar Ltd., Yokohama and London / Hugh Byas was Business Manager 1916–17	John William Robertson Scott	Financed indirectly by British Foreign Office organizing a tax concession to John Sale

The English-language press of Japan, 1861–1956: adapted from J.E. Hoare (1994: 181–8)						
Name	**Place**	**Dates**	**Frequency**	**Owner, manager, publisher**	**Editor**	**Notes**
40. *Herald of Free Asia*	Tok.	1916–23 1937–38	F.	Zumoto Motosada Business manager Hugh Byas 1916–17	Zumoto Motosada (1862–1943) Hugh Byas an active contributor	Started with government assistance. Destroyed in 1923 earthquake; revived Sep 1937–Dec. 1938. Herald Press active publisher 1930–43.
41. *Osaka Mainichi* *Osaka Mainichi & Tokyo Nichi-Nichi Mar 1925–Jan 1943* *Mainichi 1943–present*	Ōsaka	1922–present	D.			English edition of *Ōsaka Mainichi Shinbun*. Chinese edition in China late-30s–1945
42. *Japan News-Week*	Tok.	1938 Nov. to Dec. 8 1941	W.	W.R. 'Bud' Wills	Newton Edgers Associate ed. Charles N. Spinks W.R. Wills	American: the last independent English-language publication in Japan after December 1940. Some 2,300 subscribers and 1,200 newsstand sales in Jan. 1941

The English-language press of Japan, 1861–1956: adapted from J.E. Hoare (1994: 181–8)

Name	Place	Dates	Frequency	Owner, manager, publisher	Editor	Notes

Key: Changes in title are shown in the first column. Frequency of publication: D = daily; B = twice weekly; W = weekly; F = fortnightly; M = monthly; FO = Foreign Office (London); FM = Foreign Ministry (Tokyo). An asterisk indicates that substantial runs of a title are available. Nunn, Godfrey R. *Japanese Periodicals and Newspapers: an international union list* (London: Mansell 1979) is useful but outdated. The British Library Newspaper Library at Colindale has a finding aid on its website at http://catalogue.bl.uk/ and all of its holdings are available in microfilm. The Washington microfilm publisher Datamics has extensive collections (but only takes postal enquiries). Yushodo Archives, a division of the Tokyo-based publisher Yushodo Press has some English-language press titles in microfilm, notably the *Japan Times*. The publisher Edition Synapse of Tokyo is reprinting a facsimile edition of the entire run of the *Japan Weekly Mail*, 1877–1917, from the Yokohama Kaikō Shiryōkan collection, in two series: the first covering 1877–99, will be completed in 2010; the second, covering 1900–17, was ongoing at the time of writing.

APPENDIX 8: THE ENGLISH-LANGUAGE PRESS OF CHINA

The English-language press of China: a selective chronology, 1845–1949

Name	Place	Dates	Frequency	Owner, manager, publisher	Editor	Notes
1. *China Mail*	Hong Kong	1845–1952	W D (1854)	James Kemp 1866 E. Andrews 1866 Nicholas Dennys 1872–1908 George Bain 1904–6 W.H. Donald Managing Director	1863–70, 1872–73? Nicholas Dennys 1873?-79 James Bulgin 1879–1908 George Bain 1904–6 W.H. Donald	Oldest extant paper in China in 1930. 1952 *bought by South China Morning Post.*
2. *North China Herald*	Shanghai	1850	W	Both owned by the North China Daily News & Herald Ltd. Main shareholders H.R. Morris and G. Morris	*NCH* 1856–61 C. Compton 1863–66 Robert Jamieson 1866–78 R. Gundry 1878–80 G. Haden 1881–85 F.H. Balfour	North-China Building, 17 The Bund. *NCDN* Circ. in 1931 7817: 6663 in Shanghai (Chao 1931). *NCH* a Wednesday paper.
North China Daily News		1864–1941 1945–1950	D	R.W. Davis managing director *NCDN* 1930–41	*NCDN* 1902–16 H.T. Montague Bell 1920–30 O.M. Green 1930–8 Edwin Haward 1938–41 R.T. Peyton-Griffin, 1945–50 R.T. Peyton-Griffin	Both closed 1941–45. Revived 1945–49 circulation 'a few hundred' (*The Times* 7 Apr. 1951). O.M. Green was also *The Times* Shanghai corresp. 1920-30.

The English-language press of China: a selective chronology, 1845–1949

Name	Place	Dates	Frequency	Owner, manager, publisher	Editor	Notes
3. *Shanghai Mercury*	Shanghai	1879–1930	D	1879–1911 Part-owner John D. Clark 1923 Japanese consulate gain control.	1879-1911 John D Clark 1919-21 J.W. Fraser 1923-25 R Peyton-Griffin	14 Foochow Rd., Shanghai. Sahara Tobushi bought controlling interest from British in 1905. 1929 sold to *Shanghai Evening Post.*
4. *Hong Kong Telegraph*	Hong Kong	1881–1916 1916	D	Robert Fraser-Smith 1916 bought by *South China Morning Post.* 1924–41 Ben Wylie MD (of HKT and South China Morning Post); Frederick Percy Franklin manager	1881–95 R. Fraser-Smith 1916-37 Alfred Hicks 1937-37 J.B. Shaw then N. Stockton 1937-41 S. Gray	Robert Fraser-Smith 'one of the most fearsome editors the Colony ever had'.[13]

The English-language press of China: a selective chronology, 1845–1949

Name	Place	Dates	Frequency	Owner, manager, publisher	Editor	Notes
5. *China Times*	Tianjin	1886–91	D	Tientsin Press Ltd.	Alexander Michie J.O.P. Bland and Sir John Jordan contributors	*CT* ceased publication in 1891 on death of Michie in 1891. The same company began the *P&TT* in 1894.
6. *Peking & Tientsin Times*	Tianjin	1894–41	D	A.W. Bellingham Same Co & plant that published Michie's *China Times* to 1891. 1911–? George Collingwood general manager	1894–95 A.W. Bellingham 1897–1907 Alice Vaughan-Smith (1901–3 co-ed. W. McLeish) 1907–11 H.E. Redmond 1911–14 David Fraser 1914–30 H.G.W. Woodhead 1930–41 Wilfred Pennell	18 Victoria Rd., Tianjin. In 1922–27 E.A. Kennard served as an assistant to Woodhead before leaving for Kōbe to become assistant editor of the *Japan Chronicle* under A.M. Young.

The English-language press of China: a selective chronology, 1845–1949

Name	Place	Dates	Frequency	Owner, manager, publisher	Editor	Notes
7. *South China Morning Post* *South China Weekly Post*	Hongkong	1903–41 1945~	D W	1903–1907 Alfred Cunningham Hongkong & Shanghai Bank major shareholder 1903–23 J. Scott Hartston director 1923–41 J. S. Harston Chairman 1945–50? R. A. Wadeson Chairman	1903–4 Douglas Story 1904–7 Alfred Cunningham 1907–11 G. T. Lloyd 1911 A. Hamilton 1911–24 Thomas Petrie 1924–57 Henry Ching 1949–62 Wilfred V. Pennell assoc. ed.	1916 bought *Hongkong Telegraph.* 1941–45 *SCMP* bldg taken over by Japanese *Hongkong News. Hongkong Nippō* and other Japanese-run papers printed there in 1942–45. *SCMP* revived 1 Sep. 1945. In 1952? *SCMP* bought *China Mail*
8. *Shanghai Times* *Shanghai Sunday Times*	Shanghai	1901–45	D W	1901 founder Frank B. Ball 1930–45 under Japanese control	1901–2 Thomas Cowen 1902–6 George Collingwood Alfred Morley, ex-*HK Telegraph & SCMP* 1930?–37 R.I. Hope 1937?–45 E.A. Nottingham	32 Avenue Edward VII. Publication contd. after 1941 Japanese occupation of Shanghai.

						The English-language press of China: a selective chronology, 1845–1949
Name	**Place**	**Dates**	**Frequency**	**Owner, manager, publisher**	**Editor**	**Notes**
9. *Central China Post*	Hankou	1904–41[14]	D	1904–20? 1920s–41 H.J. Archibald	1920s–41 H.J. Archibald	Corner of Peking and Hunan Rds., S.A.D. No.3 Hankou. 1927 long strike and clash with GMD. 25 July 1941 *CCP* & Reuters Hankou closed by Japanese authorities.
10. *Israel's Messenger*	Shanghai	1904–41	F M	The China-Palestine Co.	Editor NE Ezra	52 Avenue Road, Shanghai. Official journal of the Shanghai Zionist Association founded 1903. In July 1933 *IM* champions Japan as leader of Greater Asia and NE Ezra calls on J Minister Shigemitsu to say so.[15]

The English-language press of China: a selective chronology, 1845–1949						
Name	**Place**	**Dates**	**Frequency**	**Owner, manager, publisher**	**Editor**	**Notes**
11. *Far Eastern Review*; pro-C 1912–19, then pro-J	Manila; moved to Shanghai	1904–41	M	George Bronson Rea, but subsidized by Japan: in 1920s Japanese subsidy of Gold $100,000 year	Edited 1904–34 George Bronson Rea (1870–1936) Patrick Gallagher assoc. ed. W.H. Donald ed. staff before 1919 Ed. 1934–41 C.J. Laval	Yokohama Specie Bank Bldg., 24 The Bund, Shanghai. 1912–19 pro-Chinese; 1919–41 pro-Japanese. 6000 worldwide. Bronson died 1936. *FER* still going in August 1941.
12. *Manchuria Daily News* *Manchuria Month* (monthly supplement)	Dalian	1908–40	D M	1921–33 Hamamura Z. 1933–40 Consortium of Kantogun, SMR, FM and Manchukuo interests 1933 March Lt. Gen. Takayanagi Yasutarō President	1921–33 Hamamura Z. March 1933–Oct. 1935 George W. Gorman	Financed by Japanese official bodies in Tokyo and Xinjing.

The English-language press of China: a selective chronology, 1845–1949					
Name	**Place**	**Dates**	**Frequency**	**Owner, manager, publisher**	**Editor**	**Notes**

Name	**Place**	**Dates**	**Frequency**	**Owner, manager, publisher**	**Editor**	**Notes**
13. *China Press*	Shanghai	1911–41	D	Thomas F. Millard financed by Charles R Crane B.W. Fleisher shareholder and Business Manager 1917/18 control passed to Edward I Ezra 1921–22 Sun Yatsen buys and sells back to Ezra 1931 Feb. Chinese syndicate bought *CP* from Ezra estate for taels 260,000. Main owner H.H. Kung, Chiang Kai-shek's brother-in-law. Chauncey P. Holcomb; dirs. W.H. Donald, W. Findley Manager 1938 E.T. Tsu	1911–15 Millard 1915–23 Herbert T. Webb** J.B. Powell 1923–25 1925–30 Charles Laval 1930–35 Hollington Tong 1935–38 Kuangson Young 1938 James D. Hammond 1940–41 Wu Giadang (K.T. Woo) 1948–49 Norwood Allman	14 Kiukang Road, Shanghai. 1930s moves to 160 Avenue Edward VII. 1911 CP circulation soon passed NCDN, but NCDN fought back. Millard resigned 1915. **In Sep. 1924 Webb won judgment against *CP* for breach of 5-year contract.[16] Norwood Allman revived *CP* 1948

The English-language press of China: a selective chronology, 1845–1949

Name	Place	Dates	Frequency	Owner, manager, publisher	Editor	Notes
14. *Millard's Review of the Far East*	Shanghai	1917–22	W	1917–22 Thomas Millard (retired after 2 years). Charles R. Crane finances.	1917–20 Thomas Millard	113 Avenue Edward VII in 1920. *CWR* 1931 at 160 Ave. Edward VII;
The Weekly Review of the Far East		1922–23		1922–41 John B. Powell Holding co. throughout: Millard Publishing Co., inc. in Delaware, US.	1922–25 Hollington Tong assoc. ed. 1920/22–1941 J.B. Powell 1925–29 Edgar Snow assoc. ed.	1933 at 38 Avenue Edward VII. 4–5000 sales. Millard retired in 1922 to write Nanjing publicity. Powell edited *MRFE*
China Weekly Review		1923–41 1945–50 Sep 1950-July 1953	D M	1945–53 John William Powell	1945–53 John William Powell	then bought Millard out and changed the title. Revived 1945–53 by John B. Powell's son, John William Powell.
China Monthly Review						

The English-language press of China: a selective chronology, 1845–1949

Name	Place	Dates	Frequency	Owner, manager, publisher	Editor	Notes
15. *Shanghai Gazette* *Shanghai Evening News* *Shanghai Evening Post*	Shanghai	1918 1941–45	D	Sun Yatsen 1923 SG buys *Shanghai Evening Star*. Edward Ezra buys amalgamation as companion to *China Press*; changes name to *SEN* *SEN* sold to *Shanghai Evening Post* in April 1928. *SEP* owned by American Newspaper Co. President C.V. Starr.	1918 Eugene Chen (Chen Youren) 1929 Carl Crow ed. *SEP*.	*SG* started by Chen at behest of Sun Yatsen. In 1918 *SG* ran the B.L Simpson 'Revolt in Japan' article that led to the *Kobe Herald* affair. The Ezra chain changed name to *SEN* 1923. *SEP* barred from post 1929–30.
16. *North China Standard*	Peking	1919–31	D	Japanese, founded J. Russell Kennedy on behalf of FM	1919–20 Henry Satoh (Satō Kenri) John Willes 1920-? George W. Gorman 1928–31	Set up by J.R. Kennedy as a foil to *Peking Leader*. Willes ex-ed. *Kobe Herald*

The English-language press of China: a selective chronology, 1845–1949

Name	Place	Dates	Frequency	Owner, manager, publisher	Editor	Notes
17. *Peking Leader*	Tianjin Peking Nanjing 1928	1920	D	1920 Chinese interests in Peking 1924–28 Syndicate of US and Chinese business interests inc US Ch. of Commerce Peking 1929 bought by Nanjing govt. Dr Philip Tyau of Nanjing FO became Managing Director 1930 Shanxi authorities took over briefly during Feng Yu-hsiang rebellion vs central govt, but returned to Nanjing govt. with collapse of Northern revolt	1920–24 MTZ Tyau or Grover Clark** 1925 Grover Clark, editor and President 1926–27 Hallett Abend 1928–48 Edward Bing-Shuey Lee (born/educ Canada) from GMD Central Publicity Dept.	About 1,200. USDS sources say Clark edited 1920–24; Chao (1931) says Tyau. Abend 1943 shows Clark receiving subsidies from Zhang Zuolin and Feng Tuxiang (Feng Yu-hsiang). 1930 Tyau Director Intelligence & Publicity, dept Foreign Office of Nanjing govt.
18. *North China Star*	Tianjin	1920?–37?	D	US corp. registered US consulate-general, Tianjin. Capital stock G. Main owner Dr. Charles J. Fox, Tianjin lawyer	Charles J. Fox	1931 circ. 3,000.[17] 1918 Peking correspondent Sheldon Ridge.

The English-language press of China: a selective chronology, 1845–1949

Name	Place	Dates	Frequency	Owner, manager, publisher	Editor	Notes
19. *Far Eastern Times*	Peking	1923–28 (bilingual)		Bertram Lenox Simpson Manager Carroll Lunt	Bertram Lenox Simpson (Putnam Weale) Chinese ed. T.L. Sung (later executed for CP links)	Weale assassinated October 1930.
20. *China Digest*	Shanghai	1925–?	W	Carroll Lunt	Carroll Lunt founder editor	1930 24 The Bund, 3000 weekly. Started in Peking, moved to Tianjin then to Shanghai in 1926.
21. *Shanghai Evening Post and Mercury* *Shanghai Evening Post and Mercury* Ditto	Shanghai Shanghai New York Chonqing Shanghai	1930–41 1941–42 1943–44 1945–49	D (evening)	American Newspaper Company, Federal Inc. President CV Starr, American Asiatic Underwriters Inc. 1941–42 Japanese-controlled 1943–44 New York and Chonqing eds. Sep. 25 1945–June 15 1949 revived US-owned Shanghai edition	1930–35 Ted O. 'TOT' Thackrey; 1935–41 Randall Gould 1941–42 George Bruce Randall Gould, Charles Miner 1945–46 Charles S. Miner 1946–49 Randall Gould	1930 CV Starr buys *Shanghai Mercury* 1931 circ. over 4800; 90% readers in Shanghai. 1931 Chinese edition *SEPM Da Mei Wan Bao.* 3 editions in 1941–45: Shanghai (Japanese), New York (US) and Chonqing (US)

The English-language press of China: a selective chronology, 1845–1949

Name	Place	Dates	Frequency	Owner, manager, publisher	Editor	Notes
22. *Oriental Affairs*	Shanghai	1934–41	Monthly	H.G.W. Woodhead	H.G.W. Woodhead	Founded by Woodhead Jan. 1934
23. *Peking Chronicle*	Peking	1930–39	D	William Sheldon Ridge 1930–37 Wilfred Chao 1937–?	William Sheldon Ridge 1930–37 George Gorman 1937/8–39 A.V. Wedekind 1939–?	Wilfred Chao a straw man for Japanese embassy Revived 1945 according to Chinese Year Book 1944–45
24. *Finance & Commerce*	Shanghai	1920?–?	W	Chairman W. Turner of Reuters Dirs: F.R. Davey, V. Meyer, E. Kann, W.J. Hawkings 1930 Manager K. Begdon	O.T. Breakspear, ex-*Hongkong Daily Press*	4 Avenue Edward VII. Influential non-political business weekly giving Reuters trade & financial service.
25. *Hongkong News*	Hongkong	1941–45	D	Eto or Ogura backed by Japanese authorities Chishiki 1944–45	Eto or Ogura 1941–44 Fukuzawa 1944–45	Set up in Connaught Rd. in Sep. 1941. Took over *South China Morning Post* bldg. in Dec. 1941. *Hongkong Nippō* also moved in in 1942.

APPENDIX 9: THE ENGLISH-LANGUAGE PRESS OF KOREA

The English-language press of Korea c.1890–1937

Name	Place	Dates	Frequency	Owner/Manager	Editorial and Other Staff	Notes
1. *Seoul Press*	Seoul	1890?–1937	D	J.W. Hodge 1906 Korea Resident-General (*tōkan*) buys *SP* 1910 Korea Governor-General (*sōtoku*)	1890?-1906 J.W. Hodge 1906–8/9 Zumoto Motosada 1909–10 Honda Masujiroh 1917–25 Yamagata Isoh 1926?–37 Frank Y. Kim	From 1905 Hodge subsidized by FM. Daily except Mondays. Closed in 1937
2. *Korea Daily News* *Daihan Maeil Shinbo* (Korean)		1904 1905	D	1904–8 Yang Ki-Tak and Ernest T. Bethell (1872–1909)	1904–8 Ernest Bethell 1908–18 Bethell's ownership transferred to other staff member. 1918 closed down.	*KDN* bilingual then English after foundation of *Daihan Maeil Shinbo* in May 1905. In 1907 Bethell was arrested by Japanese with British help and briefly imprisoned. Bethell died two years later aged thirty-seven.

NOTES

1   Powell, John. B. (1946) 'Missouri Authors and Journalists in the Orient', *Missouri Historical Review*, Vol. 41, (October), 45–55; Wainright, S.H. (1921) 'Missourians in Japan'. In *Missouri Historical Review*, Vol. 15, No.3, (April), 468–86.

2   Author (1931) *The Foreign Press in China* (Shanghai: China Institute of Pacific Relations).

3   In Abend 1943: 78, 80, 85, 88.

4   The year given in brackets after the name of the institution is the date of surviving USDS (RG 59) documents referring to it and may not be the earliest year that it was active.

5   President H.H. Kinyon; Vice-President Edith Parker; Secretary Duke N. Parry; Treasurer: Ben. G. Kline; President Emeritus, R.F. Moss (Missouri grad. businessman). Sixteen charter members.

6   From Löwenthal, Rudolf, (January 1937) 'Western Literature on Chinese Journalism: A Bibliography'. In *Nankai Social and Economic Quarterly*, Vol. IX, No.4, (Nankai Institute of Economics, Tianjin), 1061–2. Enquiries to librarians at Beijing University and Harvard Yenching Libraries followed by a full search of Yenching holdings at both institutions failed to turn up these theses. Their inclusion here, with authors' names in Chinese, has been made in the hope that it may help lead to their discovery.

7   Council of International Affairs, Chungking (Chongqing) 1943: 664–89.

8   *Nihon Kindai-shi Jiten* (Tokyo: Tōyō Keizai Shimpōsha) 1958.

9   From Fenby (2003: xxii): rates given by the *North-China Herald* 1937-December 1940.

10 Hutcheon 1983: 83.

11 Compiled by archivists at *The Times* archive, London, 2008.

12 Kokusai Bunka Shinkokai (June 1936: 18) has *Kobe Herald and Osaka Gazette*, f°, pp.4, ed. D.M. Young, which is correct. The same source gives D.M. Young as editor of the *Japan Weekly Chronicle* in 1936, surely en erroneous reference to Douglas G. Young, who was then dealing with Morgan Young having been refused re-entry to Japan and had not yet appointed E.A. Kennard as his successor as editor.

13 Chao 1931: 59

14 King & Clarke (1965: 106) list a *Central China Post* in Hankou by this title that 'may have been a Chinese publication' and give two possible Chinese titles in Wade-Giles: Ch'u pao or Chung-yang yu-pao. It seems a reasonable assumption that the *Central China Post* that was in business in Hankou from at least 1927 until it was closed down in 1941 was the same publication.

15 'Jews & "Great Asia" – Shanghai Ezras as enthusiasts', JC: 5 July 1933. See also 'Confessions of Ezras': JC: 23 July 1933 on Ezra involvement in opium smuggling to US since 1920s. The twins Isaac Isaac and Judah Isaac Ezra were both sentenced to 'twelve' years imprisonment in the US and then deported.

16 'Editor wins $44,865 judgment in China': NYT 28 September 1924. The article reads: 'Herbert Webb, for thirteen years editor of the *China Press* until he was discharged last March, today received a judgment of $44,865, under a decision of the United States Court in China. Mr Webb sued his employers charging that they broke a five-year contract of employment that he held with them.' Webb did edit in Millard's absence in 1914.

17 Chao 1931: 73. Chao – who was there at the time - places the *North China Star* in Shanghai (in the French concession) but all other sources place it in Tianjin.

Index

Hope, R.I., ed. *Shanghai Times* (c.1930–1937), 70, 88n53
Hori Yoshitaka, *Dōmei*, 282
Horinouchi Kensuke, 74
Hornbeck, Stanley Kuhl (1883–1966), 134, 149, 155n88, 247, 255, 261, 264, 265, 270n77
House, Edward Howard (1877–80) *New York Tribune*, ed. *Tokio Times*, xiii, 9, 31
Howard, Harry Paxton, UP, 150, 195, 196
Howard, Roy (1883–1964), Scripps-Howard, 120n70
Hoyt, Edwin P., UP, China, 226n41
Hozumi Yatsuka (1860–1912), 178
Hua Mei Wan Pao, Shanghai, 251
Hughes, Charles Evans (1862–1948), US Secretary of State, 165
Hull, Cordell (1871–1955), US Secretary of State (1933–1944), 257, 261, 263, 264, 265, 286
Hurley, Patrick (1883–1963), US Ambassador to China, 289

Ienaga Toyokichi (Iyenaga Toyokichi), East and West News Bureau, New York, 38
Ijūin Hikokichi (1863/4–1924), 266
Imperial Press Conferences (1909–1946), 20
Imperial press system, 15, 18, 19, 21, 24, 47, 298, 299, 300
Imperial Reservist Association (*Teikoku zaigō gunjinkai*), 212
Industrial Workers of the World, 186n61
Inoue Junnosuke (1869–1932), 77, 126, 127, 128, 213, 234, 248, 302,
Inoue Katsunosuke (1860–1929), Japanese ambassador to London, 39
International Press Association (*Kokusai Shinbun Kyōkai*), 22, 37
Inukai Tsuyoshi (1855–1932), 196
Iriye Akira, 4
Isaacs, Harold Robert (1910–1976) *New York Times*, *Honolulu Advertiser*, *China Press*, Havas Shanghai, CBS, *Newsweek*, 4, 61, 133, 148, 149, 150, 194, 204, 206, 207, 228n90, 289, 291, 295n73, and *plates* ii

Ishibashi Tanzan (1884–1973) ed. *Oriental Economist*, Prime Minister of Japan (1956–1957), 107, 264
Ishihara Kōichirō (1890–1970), 260
Israel's Messenger (1904–1941), Shanghai, 371
Itagaki Seishirō (1885–1948), 229n117
Itō Hirobumi (1841–1909), as *Resident-General of Korea* (*Tōkan*), 33, 34, 37, 76, 100
Itō Nobufumi (1885–1960), Director, Cabinet Information Board, 83
Itō Noe (1895–1923), 174
Iwanaga Yūkichi (1883–1939), Director of *Rengō* and *Dōmei*, 83, 84, 85, 90n79, 246, 250, 253, 278, 298, and *plates* i
Iwo Jima, 283

Jabin Hsu, journalist, news manager, 141, 150, 251
Jaffe, Philip (1885–1980), *Amerasia*, 297n79
Jallianwallah Bagh (Amritsar) Massacre (13 April 1919), 17
Japan Advertiser (1890–1940) Yokohama, Tokyo: access to Western readerships, 304, 305, 306, 307, 308, 309, 310 and Figs. 3, 4, 5 and 6 and 'all-India information order', 15, and anti-Communism, 97, 129, anti-British, 19, 125, 235, as a Sino-American network, 67, neutrality of, 67, 69 (Fig.1), attack by *Nihon oyobi Nihonjin*, 248, Building, *plates* i, and campaign against renewal of Anglo-Japanese Alliance, 17, 18, 103, 109, Conyngham Greene and editorship, 49, correspondences for US papers, 41, 144, critical of Japanese foreign policy, 57, 162, early history, 121, 122, 123, earthquake damage and US rescue, 125, Enthronement Edition, 126, fire and US-Japan rescue, 126, 127, 128, Foreign Ministry distrust, 129, 303, and Guomindang, 25, 108, 116, 129, 298, sale to *Japan Times*, 233, 237, 238, 240, 247, 249, 280, and 'killing competition', 222, 223, and *Kokusai* service, 41, and Manchurian